W9-ARU-436

PREFACE

This Study Guide has been developed to accompany *Principles of Microeconomics* by Karl Case and Ray Fair. For students using Case and Fair's *Principles of Economics* (Chapters 1 – 38), the corresponding chapter numbers appear in parentheses. When referring to specific pages, the *Microeconomics* reference is given. I have devised this Guide to help you as you learn the concepts that are presented in the text; if used consistently throughout your course, this Guide can enable you to master the material in what is likely to be your first economics course. In addition, you'll be given opportunities to learn how to apply these concepts in a variety of situations. Most economists stress the need to develop competence in three major areas—the application of economic concepts to real-world situations, the interpretation of graphs, and the analysis of numerical problems. This Guide gives you practice in developing these important skills.

I believe that learning how to apply concepts creates a better and more long-lasting understanding of the material than mere memorization does. A reasonable goal for a non-economics major is to have absorbed enough insight to understand the economic content of an article in a publication like *The Wall Street Journal* or *Newsweek*.

STUDY GUIDE CONTENTS

The Study Guide contains one chapter for each chapter in the text. In general, each chapter has two large sections and an Answers and Solutions section.

The *Objectives: Point by Point* section tells you what you should be able to accomplish after you've studied the material. It gives a summary of the chapter's important ideas. Each point is followed by some multiple choice questions, so that you can monitor how well you're understanding the concepts. You'll find some applications and examples, along with specific learning tips, comments and "helpful hints". Concepts that may prove particularly troublesome are covered here. Many of these "tricks" and memory aids have been suggested to me by students.

The *Practice Test* section contains *Multiple Choice Questions* and *Application Questions*. These questions provide opportunities to practice the skills—graphing, numerical analysis, application of concepts—presented in the text. Go through this section thoroughly. These exercises give you an opportunity to try your hand at using economic principles and practices—often in fairly complex situations. Do the problem sets in the textbook, too. The *Multiple Choice Questions* are quite tough. Think of each multiple choice question as four true-false statements; don't just decide on the one "right" answer—determine why the other three options are wrong.

The *Answers and Solutions* feature numerical and graphical solutions. Be aware, though, that real-world analysis is much more difficult to condense into such a simple form.

The textbook is divided into several parts. I've provided a Comprehensive Review Test for each part of the textbook. If you have problems with any of the questions on

v

the review test, treat it as a red light—go back and review that material before proceeding.

STUDY RECOMMENDATIONS

I recommend the following procedure for using this Guide to improve your effective understanding and use of the key principles and practices from the text.

1. Read the textbook chapter. There is no substitute for this step! Ideally, you should do this before the material is presented in class; in any case, don't wait until the day before your prof has scheduled a test! Use the *Point by Point* section of the Guide to identify the key issues and to test your knowledge.

2. Attend class regularly. In study after study, researchers have shown that regularity of class attendance is the single best predictor of performance.

3. Now that you're acquainted with the material, use the *Learning Tips* to polish your understanding.

4. Complete the practice sections to test your ability to utilize key concepts. If you fail to complete an exercise correctly, even after having seen the answers, reread the text. If you're still stuck, ask your prof for clarification.

5. Before a scheduled examination, read the *Point By Point* sections for review.

6. Before a scheduled examination, do the relevant Review Test.

With a conscientious and consistent use of this Guide, you can improve your understanding of economics and your ability to use and apply the concepts contained in this field of study. Learning can be interesting, as well as enjoyable.

This Guide has been written with the hope that, after the final exam, it will have helped you to gain a better understanding of economic issues and analysis and of the exciting and challenging concerns that we must address in our contemporary world.

Best wishes to you with your study of economics. I hope that you will find it to be a rewarding and worthwhile experience, and that this Guide will stimulate you in your endeavors.

Please send any comments or suggestions about this study guide to me, care of Economics Editor, Prentice Hall, 1 Lake Street, Upper Saddle River, NJ 07458.

Thomas Beveridge
Hillsborough, North Carolina
July, 1998

STUDY GUIDE

PRINCIPLES OF
MICROECONOMICS

STUDY GUIDE
Thomas M. Beveridge
North Carolina State University

FIFTH EDITION

PRINCIPLES OF
MICROECONOMICS

CASE & FAIR

Prentice Hall, Upper Saddle River, NJ 07458

Acquisitions Editor: *Rod Banister*
Associate Editor: *Gladys Soto*
Production Editor: *Joseph F. Tomasso*
Formatter: *University Graphics, Inc.*
Manufacturer: *Quebecor Printing, Inc.*

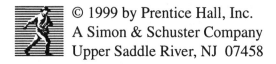 © 1999 by Prentice Hall, Inc.
A Simon & Schuster Company
Upper Saddle River, NJ 07458

Printed in the United States of America

10 9 8 7 6 5 4 3 2 1

ISBN 0-13-095729-1

Prentice-Hall International (UK) Limited, *London*
Prentice-Hall of Australia Pty. Limited, *Sydney*
Prentice-Hall Canada Inc., *Toronto*
Prentice-Hall Hispanoamericana, S.A., *Mexico*
Prentice-Hall of India Private Limited, *New Delhi*
Prentice-Hall of Japan, Inc., *Tokyo*
Simon & Schuster Asia Pte. Ltd., *Singapore*
Editora Prentice-Hall do Brasil, Ltda., *Rio de Janiero*

Contents

Part 4

Part 5 (9)

ACKNOWLEDGMENTS

I am grateful to the many students whose questions, through the years, have given me a better insight into the difficulties that arise when microeconomics is approached for the first time. The practice material included in this Guide springs largely from such "after class" discussions.

The beneficial influence of Steven Pitts (Houston Community College) continues to be felt in the Graphing Tutorial in Chapter 1 and throughout the text. The efforts of these reviewers and other correspondents have added much to the quality of the final product. Gladys Soto of Prentice-Hall deserves credit for keeping things moving smoothly. Needless to say, any remaining *lapsi calami* are my responsibility.

This Guide is dedicated to the memory of my father and to my mother, Pam, Andrew (our own "micro" economist, who did much to disrupt its production), and to Merlin and Rory, to whom all lunches are free.

THE SCOPE AND METHOD OF ECONOMICS

1

OBJECTIVES: POINT BY POINT

After completing this chapter, you should be able to accomplish the objectives listed below.

General Comment

Much of this chapter is devoted to setting out the framework of economics. Don't be overwhelmed and don't try to remember it all. Chapter 1 is simply a good place to gather together this information, which will be dealt with more fully as the chapters go by.

OBJECTIVE 1: Define economics.

Because of conditions imposed by nature and the choices previously made by society, resources are scarce. Economics studies how we choose to use these resources to best satisfy society's unlimited wants. In a sense, it is the "scientific study of choice." (page 1)

PRACTICE

1. Which one of the following best describes the study of economics? Economics studies
   A. how businesses can make profits.
   B. how the government controls the economy and how people earn a living.
   C. how society uses its scarce resources to satisfy its unlimited desires.
   D. the allocation of income among different sectors of the economy.
   Answer: C. All of the options represent aspects of the study of economics. However, the most general statement is given in C—economics is the study of choice.

OBJECTIVE 2: State four reasons for studying economics.

A study of economics helps us to learn a way of thinking, to understand society, to understand national and global affairs, and to be an informed voter. Essential to the economic way of thinking is the concept of "opportunity cost"—choices involve forgoing some options. Accordingly, the applicability of the economic way of thinking is very extensive. (page 2)

OBJECTIVE 3: Distinguish between the concepts of opportunity cost, marginal cost, and sunk costs.

"Marginal" is a frequently used term in economics and it's important to understand it right away. "Marginal" means "additional" or "extra." "Marginal cost," then, means "additional cost."

Suppose you've bought a non-returnable, non-transferable ticket to the zoo for $10. This is a *sunk cost*. You've paid whether or not you visit the zoo.

Let's change the example a little. Suppose you win a free admission to the zoo and decide to go this Saturday. The trip is not entirely free, however. You still have to bear some costs—travel, for example. There is certainly an additional cost (caused by the trip to the zoo). It is a *marginal cost*. Suppose you always buy lunch on Saturdays. The cost of lunch is not a marginal cost since you'd have had lunch whether or not you went to the zoo. In this sense, the cost of lunch is not contingent on the trip to the zoo—it's not an extra cost.

If wants exceed the resources to satisfy them, choices must be made and some alternatives must be forgone. You choose to visit the zoo this Saturday. The *opportunity cost* is the value of the activity you would have undertaken instead—that is, the next most-preferred activity. Perhaps it might be playing a round of golf or studying for a big economics test. The opportunity cost of the trip to the zoo is the value you attach to that *one* activity you would otherwise have chosen. (page 2)

> **Opportunity Cost and Marginalism:** The "big concept" in this chapter is *opportunity cost*, with *marginalism* and *efficiency* a close second and third. You'll see all three repeatedly throughout the textbook. For practice on the concept of opportunity cost, try Application questions 5 and 7 below. For practice on marginal thinking, look at Application question 8.

TIP: Any time you make a choice where one alternative is chosen over others, remember that an opportunity cost is involved.

PRACTICE

2. Your opportunity cost of attending college does not include
   A. the money you spend on meals while at college.
   B. your tuition.
   C. the money you spend on traveling between home and college.
   D. the income you could have earned if you'd been employed full-time.
   Answer: A. You would have bought food whether or not you were at college. All the other expenses occur solely because of attending college.

3. _____ may be defined as the extra cost associated with an action.
   A. Marginal cost.
   B. Sunk cost.
   C. Opportunity cost.
   D. Action cost.
   Answer: A. See p. 3.

4. Jean owns a French restaurant—La Crème. Simply to operate this week, he must pay rent, taxes, wages, food costs, and so on. This amounts to $1,000 per week. This evening, a diner arrives and orders some Château Neuf du Pape wine to go with her meal. Jean has none and sends out to Wine World for a bottle. It costs $20, and Jean charges his guest $30. Which of the following is true for Jean?
   A. The marginal cost of the wine is $20.
   B. The marginal cost of the wine is $30.
   C. The sunk cost of the meal is $1,020.
   D. The sunk cost of the meal is $1,030.
   Answer: A. The sunk cost is the up-front expense of $1,000. The extra cost that Jean bears for buying the wine is $20.

OBJECTIVE 4: Define market efficiency in terms of profit opportunities.

The rapid elimination of profit opportunities is a signal that a market is operating efficiently. The stock market is a good example. If a stock is priced "too low," there will be increased bidding and the price will be driven higher, eliminating the excess profits. At a farmers' market, Farmer Brown may charge 60¢ for a dozen eggs although the going rate is 50¢. She might make excess profits for a while, but this will not persist in an efficient market. (page 4)

OBJECTIVE 5: Make clear the difference between microeconomic and macroeconomic concerns.

Economics is split into two broad parts. *Microeconomics* focuses on the operation of individual markets and the choices of individual economic units (firms and households, for example). *Macroeconomics* deals with the broad economic variables such as national production, total consumer spending, and overall price movements. Economics also contains a number of subfields, such as international economics, labor economics, and industrial organization. (page 7)

PRACTICE

5. **Macroeconomics** approaches the study of economics from the viewpoint of
   A. individual consumers.
   B. the government.
   C. the entire economy.
   D. the operation of specific markets.
   Answer: C. Macroeconomics looks at the big picture—the entire economy.

6. **Microeconomics** approaches the study of economics from the viewpoint of
   A. the entire economy.
   B. the government.
   C. the operation of specific markets.
   D. the stock market.
   Answer: C. Microeconomics examines what is happening with individual economic units (households and firms) and how they interact in specific markets.

7. Which of the following is most appropriately a microeconomic issue?
   A. The study of the relationship between the unemployment rate and the inflation rate.
   B. The forces determining the price level in an individual market.
   C. The determination of total output in the economy.
   D. The aggregate behavior of all decision-making units in the economy.
   Answer: B. Microeconomics examines what is happening with individual economic units (households and firms) and how they interact in specific markets.

OBJECTIVE 6: Distinguish between positive and normative economics.

Economists classify issues as either positive or normative. Positive questions explore the behavior of the economy and its participants without judging whether the behavior is good or bad. *Positive economics* collects data that describe economic phenomena (descriptive economics) and constructs testable—cause-and-effect—theories to explain the phenomena (economic theory). *Normative economic questions* evaluate the results of behavior and explore whether the outcomes might be improved. (page 8)

PRACTICE

8. A difference between positive statements and normative statements is that
   A. positive statements are true by definition.
   B. only positive statements are subject to empirical verification.
   C. economists use positive statements and politicians use normative statements when discussing economic matters.
   D. positive statements require value judgments.
   Answer: B. A positive statement is not necessarily true by definition and can be disproved by empirical verification.

OBJECTIVE 7: Explain the value of the ceteris paribus assumption within the context of economic modeling.

Economists (and other scientists) construct models—formal statements of relationships between variables of interest—that simplify and abstract from reality. Graphs, words, or equations can be used to express a model. In testing the relationships between variables within a model it is convenient to assume *ceteris paribus*, that all other variables have been held constant. (page 11)

Scientists use models to focus on the most essential elements under examination. Distracting real-world detail is set aside. Many factors may have affected your decision to buy Case and Fair's textbook—theory attempts to isolate the key factors.

PRACTICE

9. "An increase in the price of shampoo will cause less shampoo to be demanded, *ceteris paribus*." *Ceteris* paribus means that
   A. there is a negative relationship between the price and quantity demanded of shampoo.
   B. the price of shampoo is the only factor that can affect the amount of shampoo demanded.
   C. other factors may affect the amount of shampoo demanded but that these are assumed not to change in this analysis.
   D. the price of shampoo is equal for all buyers.
   Answer: C. The price of shampoo is equal for all buyers and there may be a negative relationship between the price and quantity of shampoo demanded, but *ceteris paribus* means that any other factors that may affect the amount of shampoo demanded are assumed to be constant.

OBJECTIVE 8: State the fallacies discussed in the text, give examples, and explain why such statements are fallacious.

Beware of false logic! The *fallacy of composition* involves the claim that what is good for one individual remains good when it happens for many. The fact that one farmer gains by having a bumper harvest *doesn't* mean that all farmers will gain if each has a bumper crop. The *post hoc, ergo propter hoc fallacy* occurs when we assume that an event that happens after another is caused by it. (page 12)

Two examples of the fallacy of composition: One person who stands up to see a good play at a football game derives a benefit—therefore all will benefit similarly if the entire crowd stands up. Running to the exit when there is a fire in a theater will increase your chances of survival—therefore, in a fire, we should all run for the exit.

PRACTICE

10. Which of the following is not an example of the fallacy of composition?
    A. Jane leaves work at 4:00 each day and avoids the rush-hour traffic at 5:00. Therefore, if businesses regularly closed at 4:00, all commuters would avoid the rush-hour traffic.
    B. John stands up so that he can see an exciting football play. Therefore, if the entire crowd stands up when there is an exciting play, all spectators will get a better view.
    C. Since society benefits from the operation of efficient markets, IBM will benefit if markets become more efficient.
    D. Since Mary on her own can escape from a burning building by running outside, individuals in a crowded movie theater are advised to run outside when there is a fire.
    Answer: C. This example is arguing from the general to the specific. The fallacy of composition argues from the specific to the general.

OBJECTIVE 9: State and explain the four criteria used to assess the outcomes of economic policy.

Economists construct and test models as an aid to policy-making. Policy-makers generally judge proposals in terms of efficiency, equity (fairness), growth, and stability. (page 13)

PRACTICE

11. The nation of Arboc claims to have achieved an equitable distribution of income among its citizens. On visiting Arboc, we would expect to find that
    A. each citizen receives the same amount of income.
    B. Arbocali residents believe that the distribution of income is fair.
    C. Arbocali residents believe that the distribution of income is equal.
    D. each citizen receives the amount of income justified by the value of his or her contribution to production.
    Answer: B. Whether or not the distribution of income is equitable depends on what Arbocali citizens believe to be fair.

Use the following information to answer the next two questions.

Nicola and Alexander each have some dollars and some apples. Nicola values a pound of apples at $3 while Alexander values a pound of apples at $1.

12. In which of the following cases has an allocatively efficient trade taken place?
    A. The market price of apples is $3 per pound. Nicola sells apples to Alexander.
    B. The market price of apples is $1 per pound. Nicola sells apples to Alexander.
    C. The market price of apples is $2 per pound. Nicola sells apples to Alexander.
    D. The market price of apples is $2 per pound. Alexander sells apples to Nicola.
    Answer: D. When the market price of apples is $2 per pound and Alexander is the seller, he gains $1. Nicola also gains because she receives goods she values at $3 for a payment of only $2.

13. In which of the following cases has an allocatively efficient trade not taken place?
    A. The market price of apples is $3 per pound. Alexander sells apples to Nicola.
    B. The market price of apples is $1.50 per pound. Alexander sells apples to Nicola.
    C. The market price of apples is $1.50 per pound. Nicola sells apples to Alexander.
    D. The market price of apples is $2 per pound. Alexander sells apples to Nicola.
    Answer: C. An efficient trade can occur only when some participant is better off and no participant is worse off (or if the gainer can adequately compensate the loser). In Option A, Alexander gains $2 and Nicola does not lose. In Option B, Nicola and Alexander both gain. In Option D, Alexander and Nicola both gain. In Option C, Alexander gains 50¢ but Nicola loses $1.50.

OBJECTIVE 10: Construct and interpret graphs.

Economic graphs depict the relationship between variables. A curve with a "rising" (positive) slope indicates that as one variable increases, so does the other. A curve with a "falling" (negative) slope indicates that as one variable increases in value, the other decreases in value. Slope is easily measured by "rise over run"—the extent of vertical change divided by the extent of horizontal change. (page 19)

> **TIP:** Economists almost automatically begin to scribble diagrams when asked to explain ideas, and you'll need to learn how to use some of the tools of the trade. In economics, graphs often feature financial variables like "price," "the interest rate," or "income." Usually the dependent variable is placed on the vertical axis and the independent variable on the horizontal axis. In graphing economic variables, however, it's a pretty safe bet that the *financial* variable will go on the vertical axis every time. Application questions 9 and 10 and the Graphing Tutorial offer some graphing practice.

> **TIP:** Make a point of examining the graphs you see accompanying economics-based articles in the daily newspaper or news magazines. It's quite common to find examples of deceptive graphs, especially when variables are being compared over time. A graph comparing, say, the difference between government spending and tax revenues can be quite misleading if the vertical axis does not start at zero.

> **Graphing Pointer:** It is a natural tendency to shy away from graphs—they may seem threatening—but this is a mistake. To work with economic concepts, you must master all the tools in the economist's toolkit. Trying to avoid graphs is a unwise as trying to cut a piece of wood without a saw. See the Graphing Tutorial if you are uneasy.

PRACTICE

Use the diagram below to answer the next four questions.

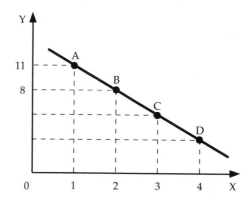

14. In the diagram above, the slope of the line is
    A. positive and variable
    B. positive and constant.
    C. negative and variable.
    D. negative and constant.

    Answer: D. The diagram shows a straight line—straight lines have a constant slope. Visually, or by using the "rise over run" formula, the relationship is negative because, as one variable increases in value, the other decreases in value.

15. The slope of line between Point A and Point B is
    A. 3
    B. ⅓.
    C. −3.
    D. −⅓.

    Answer: C. Use the "rise over run" formula. The rise is −3 (from 11 to 8) and the run is +1 (from 1 to 2).

16. At Point D, the value of Y is
    A. −3.
    B. 3.
    C. 5.
    D. 2.

    Answer: D. As X "steps up" in value by 1, Y "steps down" in value by 3. At Point B, X has a value of 2 and Y has a value of 8. Moving to Point D, X increases by 2 and Y decreases by 6, from 8 to 2.

17. In the diagram above, when the line reaches the vertical (Y) axis the value of Y will be
A. 3.
B. 8.
C. 11.
D. 14.
Answer: D. As X "steps down" in value by 1, Y "steps up" in value by 3. At Point A, X has a value of 1 and Y has a value of 11. X decreases by 1 and Y increases by 3, from 11 to 14.

PRACTICE TEST

I. MULTIPLE CHOICE QUESTIONS.

Select the option that provides the single best answer.

_____ 1. Local farmers reduce the price of their tomatoes at the farmers' market. The price of corn is 30¢ per ear. A passing economist notes that, *ceteris paribus*, buyers will purchase more tomatoes than before. Which of the following is TRUE? The economist is
A. implying that the price of tomatoes will fall even further.
B. assuming that the price of corn remains at 30¢ per ear.
C. assuming that tomatoes are of a better quality than before.
D. implying that corn is of a poorer quality than before.

_____ 2. Which of the following is not given in the textbook as a criterion for judging the results of economic policy?
A. Economic stability.
B. Employment
C. Efficiency.
D. Equity.

_____ 3. Economic growth may occur if
A. more machines become available.
B. more workers become available.
C. workers become more efficient.
D. all of the above.

_____ 4. Economics is the study of how
A. scarce resources are used to satisfy unlimited wants.
B. we choose to use unlimited resources.
C. limitless resources are used to satisfy scarce wants.
D. society has no choices.

_____ 5. The opportunity cost of Choice X can be defined as
A. the cheapest alternative to Choice X.
B. the most highly-valued alternative to Choice X.
C. the price paid to obtain X.
D. the most highly-priced alternative to Choice X.

_____ 6. In economics, efficiency means that
A. income is distributed equally among all citizens.
B. there is a low level of inflation and full unemployment of economic resources.
C. total productivity is increasing at a constant and equal rate within each sector of the economy.
D. the economy is producing those goods and services that citizens desire and is doing so at the least possible cost.

_____ 7. Which of the following statements is true?
 A. Microeconomics studies consumer behavior, while macroeconomics studies producer behavior.
 B. Microeconomics studies producer behavior, while macroeconomics studies consumer behavior.
 C. Microeconomics studies behavior of individual households and firms, while macroeconomics studies national aggregates.
 D. Microeconomics studies inflation and opportunity costs, while macroeconomics studies unemployment and sunk costs.

_____ 8. Which of the following statements is true?
 A. There is a positive relationship between the price of a product and the quantity demanded.
 B. There is a positive relationship between the number of umbrellas bought and the amount of rainfall.
 C. There is a negative relationship between height and weight.
 D. There is a negative relationship between sales of ice cream and noon temperature.

_____ 9. Oliver Sudden discovers that if he cuts the price of his tomatoes at the farmers' market, his sales revenue increases. Expecting similar results, all the other tomato sellers follow his example. They are guilty of committing
 A. the fallacy of composition.
 B. the fallacy of _post hoc, ergo propter hoc._
 C. the fallacy of correlation.
 D. _ceteris paribus._

_____ 10. The quantity of six-packs of Quite Lite beer demanded per week (Qd) in Hometown is described by the following equation:

$$Qd = 400 - 100P,$$

where P (in dollars) is the price of a six-pack. This equation predicts that
 A. 300 six-packs will be bought this week.
 B. a $1 rise in price will cause 100 more six-packs to be bought this week.
 C. 300 six-packs will be bought per $100 this week.
 D. a 50¢ rise in price will cause 50 fewer six-packs to be bought this week.

_____ 11. The _ceteris paribus_ assumption is used
 A. to make economic theory more realistic.
 B. to make economic analysis more realistic.
 C. to avoid the fallacy of composition.
 D. to focus the analysis on the effect of a single factor.

Use the following diagram below to answer the next four questions.

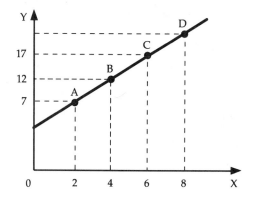

_____ 12. In the preceding diagram, the slope of the line is
   A. positive and variable.
   B. positive and constant.
   C. negative and variable.
   D. negative and constant.

_____ 13. In the preceding diagram, the slope of the line between Point A and Point B is
   A. ½.
   B. ⅖.
   C. −⅖.
   D. −½.

_____ 14. In the preceding diagram, at Point D, the value of Y is
   A. 5.
   B. 8.
   C. 19.5.
   D. 22.

_____ 15. In the preceding diagram, when the line reaches the vertical (Y) axis the value of Y will be
   A. 2.
   B. ½.
   C. 7.
   D. 12.

Use the following diagrams to answer the next four questions.

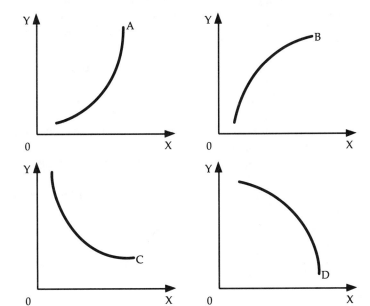

_____ 16. Of the four diagrams, which curve has a slope that is negative and decreasing?
   A. A.
   B. B.
   C. C.
   D. D.

_____ 17. Of the four diagrams, which curve has a slope that is positive and increasing?
   A. A.
   B. B.
   C. C.
   D. D.

_____ 18. Of the four diagrams, which curve has a slope that is positive and decreasing?
   A. A.
   B. B.
   C. C.
   D. D.

_____ 19. Of the four diagrams, which curve appears to be described by the equation $y = x^2$?
   A. A.
   B. B.
   C. C.
   D. D.

_____ 20. During the debate about balancing the federal government's budget, it was proposed that Medicaid benefits be reduced. This proposal was criticized because low-income families (who receive Medicaid) would spend a higher percentage of their income on medical services than high-income families would spend. This argument was based on concerns about
   A. economic growth.
   B. efficiency
   C. economic stability.
   D. equity.

Use the following information to answer the next two questions. The Channel Tunnel, linking the United Kingdom and France, was originally planned to cost $100 million. After work had begun and the two excavators were under the English Channel, with $70 million already spent, the estimate of the total bill was revised to $150 million.

_____ 21. To an economist, the $70 million that had already been spent is best thought of as a
   A. sunk cost that was important in determining whether to complete the project.
   B. sunk cost that was not important in determining whether to complete the project.
   C. marginal cost that was important in determining whether to complete the project.
   D. marginal cost that was not important in determining whether to complete the project.

_____ 22. At this point the marginal cost of completion was best estimated as
   A. $30 million.
   B. $50 million.
   C. $70 million.
   D. $80 million.

II. APPLICATION QUESTIONS.

1. The small nation of Smogland is unhappily situated in a valley surrounded by mountains. Smogland's Secretary of the Environment has determined that there are 4000 cars in operation, each of which pollutes the air. In fact, Smogland's air is so unhealthy that it is rated as "hazardous." If emission controls, costing $50 per car, are introduced, the air quality will improve to a rating of "fair." A survey has revealed that, of the 40,000 inhabitants, 10,000 would value the air quality improvement at $5 each, and the other 30,000 would value it at $7 each. The Secretary of the Environment has asked you to analyze the issue and make a recommendation.

2. Refer to the following diagram.

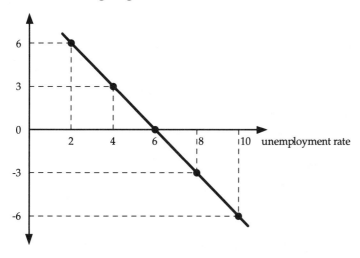

   a. Construct a table from the data presented in the diagram.
   b. Calculate the slope of the line.
   c. Calculate the inflation rate when the unemployment rate is 9%.
   d. Calculate the inflation rate when the unemployment rate is 5%.

3. What are some elements of the opportunity cost of "clean" air? In total, the "cost" of cleaner air increases as we remove more and more pollution. Do you think, however, that the extra (marginal) cost of cleaner air increases as we progressively remove pollution? Graph the behavior of "extra cost" (vertical axis) and "cleanness of air" (horizontal axis).

4. Suppose that the opportunity cost of attending today's economics class is study time for a math test. By not studying you will lose fifteen points on your test. Attending the econ. class will increase your future econ. test score by no more than three points. Was your choice—to attend the econ. class—rational?

5. Suppose you had a summer internship in a bank just before your senior year. You are "noticed" and are offered a full-time position in the bank, with a salary of $25,000 a year. A rival bank, also keen to attract you, offers you $27,000 for a similar position. After much thought, you decide to return to college to complete your economics degree. Based on the information given, what was the opportunity cost of your decision?

   If you had chosen one of the banking jobs instead of resuming your studies, how could you have explained your decision to your parents, who would have pointed out that you would have "wasted" three years of college? How might "sunk costs" figure into your explanation?

6. Choose a local natural resource with which you are familiar, e.g., an acre of farmland or a nearby lake.
   a. List three alternative uses for your chosen raw material.
   b. Choose one of the three uses. What is the opportunity cost of this use? Should you include the cost of clean-up (if this is appropriate) following use?
   c. Is the resource renewable or not? If not, should this be factored into your calculations?
   d. Describe how your community has chosen to use the resource so far, if at all. Who and what have determined that choice?

7. Suppose you're asked to choose one job out of three. Job A pays $30,000; Job B, $20,000; and Job C, $15,000. In all other respects they are identical. Which would you choose? What is the opportunity cost of your choice? Is it rational to choose Job C? What is the opportunity cost of Job C?

8. Suppose you're offered three deals, each of which will give you $11 in return for $8. Your profit will be $3 in each case. Deal A is a straight swap—$11 for $8.

   Deal B involves four steps and you can quit at any point.
   - Step 1. $5 in exchange for $2
   - Step 2. $3 for $2
   - Step 3. $2 for $2
   - Step 4. $1 for $2

   What would you do? Go all the way through the four steps and collect a total of $3 profit? A better solution, stopping after two steps, would yield $4.

   Deal C also involves four steps.
   - Step 1. $4 in exchange for $1
   - Step 2. $4 for $2
   - Step 3. $2 for $2
   - Step 4. $1 for $3

   Would you collect your $3 profit or stop after two steps and gain $5?

   Moral: If the effects of extra (marginal) steps are assessed, you can raise your profits above $3. Without examining each step, the chance of greater profits would have been missed.

9. Using your own intuition, graph each of the following relationships in the space on the following page.
   a. height and weight of males.
   b. (on the same graph) height and weight of females.

   c. Do these lines have a positive slope or negative slope?
   d. Have you drawn the relationships differently? If so, why? By referring to your own observations, you have constructed a model!
   e. Which factors have you "held constant"?
   f. i. Again using your own intuition, sketch in the space below the relationship between the price of California wine and the consumption of California wine.
      ii. According to your theory and your diagram, is there any point, even if wine is free, at which consumers will not wish to buy any more wine?
      iii. Will the total number of dollars spent on wine remain the same at every price level?

g.   i.   Using your own intuition, sketch in the space below the relationship between the interest rate and house purchases.

     ii.   According to your theory and your graph, is there any interest rate that will completely deter house purchases?

10. Suppose there is a relationship between two variables, X (on the horizontal axis) and Y (on the vertical axis), and that you have collected the following data.

X	2	4	6	8	10
Y	5	6	7	8	9

a. Do we have a positive or a negative relationship?
b. Describe (in words) what these data would look like graphically.
c. Calculate the slope (rise-over-run) of the line.
d. Graph the relationship below.

11. Suppose that you have a new brand of low alcohol, reduced-calorie beer, "Quite Lite," that you intend to market. What variables do you think will be important in determining the amount of Quite Lite that people will want to buy? You should be able to develop a fairly long list of variables. You have begun to construct an economic model of consumption behavior. Now prune down your list to include, say, the five most important variables.

Now work out in which way each variable will impact the consumption of Quite Lite. You should be able to work out a specific cause-and-effect pattern in each case. A higher price for Quite Lite should cause less to be bought. A price hike for competing beers should increase the demand for Quite Lite. Note that not all variables have been included in the model; an all-inclusive list would (1) be cumbersome and (2) distract from the major elements in the model. You have wielded Ockham's razor!

The variables that you have compiled in your list will be continually changing their values. To isolate the effect of any one on the consumption of Quite Lite you must invoke the ceteris paribus assumption. You might think of this as being the economic equivalent of the "standard temperature and pressure" conditions applied in the natural sciences.

Use the model that you developed for Quite Lite beer. Putting "quantity demanded" on the horizontal axis, graph each of the relationships in the model.

12. Which of the following statements are positive and which are normative?
    a. The moon is made of green cheese.
    b. States to the west of the Mississippi have lower state income tax rates than states to the east have.
    c. The federal government should be made to balance its budget.
    d. The most serious economic problem confronting the nation is unemployment.
    e. We should abolish the minimum wage.
    f. We should index-link the minimum wage to the rate of price inflation.
    g. If the federal budget deficit is reduced, then interest rates will decrease.

ANSWERS AND SOLUTIONS

PRACTICE TEST

I. SOLUTIONS TO MULTIPLE CHOICE QUESTIONS

1. B. If the price of corn fell, perhaps very sharply, buyers might buy more corn and fewer tomatoes. Therefore, the economist is assuming that the price of corn is not going to change. That's what *ceteris paribus* implies.

2. B. Unemployment is certainly an important economic variable, but it is not one of the criteria for evaluating the results of economic policy. See p. 14.

3. D. Growth will occur if resources become more plentiful or more productive.

4. A. Economics is about choice—how we ration scarce resources to meet limitless wants.

5. B. Price is not necessarily a reliable guide to value for a particular individual. Opportunity cost is the measure of the value placed on the next most-preferred item forgone as a result of Choice X.

6. D. Efficiency means that producers are using the least costly method of production to supply those goods that are desired by consumers.

7. C. To review the micro/macro distinction, see p. 7.

8. B. There is a *negative* relationship between price and quantity demanded, so A is incorrect. The greater the rainfall, the larger the number of umbrellas bought.

9. A. Just because an action done by one individual produces a given outcome, the same action done by many need not.

10. D. Put in numbers. If P = \$2, then Qd will equal 400 – 100(2), or 200. If the price rises by 50¢, then Qd will equal 400 – 100(2.5), or 150—a fall of 50.

11. D. The *ceteris paribus* assumption freezes the effect of all but one change so that the effects of that change may be examined.

12. B. The diagram shows a straight line—straight lines have a constant slope. Visually, or by using the "rise over run" formula, the relationship is positive because, as one variable increases in value, the other also increases in value.

13. A. Use the "rise over run" formula. The rise is +5 (Y goes from 7 to 12) and the run is +2 (X goes from 2 to 4).

14. D. As X "steps up" in value by 2, Y "steps up" in value by 5. At Point C, X has a value of 6 and Y has a value of 17. Moving to Point D, X rises by 2 and Y rises by 5, from 17 to 22.

15. A. As X "steps down" in value by 2, Y "steps down" in value by 5. At Point A, X has a value of 2 and Y has a value of 7. X decreases by 2 and Y decreases by 5, from 7 to 2.

16. C. The relationship shows that as the X variable increases in value, the Y variable decreases in value—a negative relationship. The slope is decreasing because, as X increases in value, the decrease in the value of Y becomes smaller and smaller.

17. A. The relationship shows that as the X variable increases in value, the Y variable also increases in value—a positive relationship. The slope is increasing because, as X increases in value, the increase in the value of Y becomes larger and larger.

18. B. The relationship shows that as the X variable increases in value, the Y variable also increases in value—a positive relationship. The slope is decreasing because, as X increases in value, the increase in the value of Y becomes smaller and smaller.

19. A. As x assumes higher values, the values of y will increase more rapidly.

20. D. For equity, read "fairness". Critics of the proposal argue that it is unfair to make poor families spend a larger part of their lower income on medical services.

21. B. The \$70 million had already been spent and was unrecoverable—a sunk cost. Sunk costs should have no impact on the decision to continue the project. See p. 3.

22. D. To complete the project would cost \$80 million more than had already been spent.

II. SOLUTIONS TO APPLICATION QUESTIONS

1. The (marginal) cost of the air quality improvement is valued at $50 × 4000, or $200,000. The benefit derived from the improvement is valued at ($5 × 10,000) + ($7 × 30,000), or $260,000. Smogland should proceed with the implementation of emission controls.

2. a.

UNEMPLOYMENT RATE (%)	INFLATION RATE (%)
2.0	6.0
4.0	3.0
6.0	0.0
8.0	-3.0
10.0	-6.0

   b. Slope is −1.5.
   c. −4.5%.
   d. 1.5%.

3. In order to have cleaner (if not clean) air, we might wish to reduce emissions of cars, homes, and factories. The next most preferred use of the resources used to achieve this would be included in the opportunity cost. An initial 5% improvement in the quality of the air might be accomplished quite simply—perhaps by requiring more frequent car tune-ups—but, progressively, the "cost" of achieving more stringent air cleanliness standards will rise. The marginal cost will increase. This will graph as an upward-sloping line that rises progressively more steeply.

4. The answer cannot be determined given the information. This choice may well have been rational. Perhaps the three extra points save you from flunking the course while, in the math class, you are confident of making an easy "A."

5. The opportunity cost is the salary forgone—$27,000 if you had chosen the first bank. Presumably, the offer of the job at the bank was based on your abilities—some of which would have been developed while at college. That time, then, was not wasted. You could have taken the bank job and explained that the three years of college got you the internship ands sufficient skills to be noticed in the first place. Also, the three college years cannot be relived—decisions should be based on the future, not the past.

6. This is an open question. The natural resource might be a river, a seam of coal, deer, a piece of waste land used as a dump, prime agricultural land, or downtown lots. The main point is that using the resource one way means that it is not available for other uses. The final part of the question may lead you into a consideration of private property rights, social pressure, and the role of the government.

7. Choose Job A! The opportunity cost is $20,000 (the value of the next best alternative forgone—Job B). The opportunity cost of both Job B and Job C is $30,000—the value of the surrendered Job A. Choosing either B or C is not rational since the reward is less than the cost.

9. a. and b. See the diagram below.

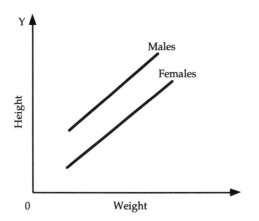

    c. Both positive—as height increases, so does weight.

    d. Probably the lines will be different. Perhaps, at any given height, males may weigh more than females, for example.

    e. Race, geographical location and age are factors that have been ignored.

    f.   i. See the diagram on the next page.

          ii. Even if wine is free, consumers are likely to reach a point of satiation. This is shown on the diagram as the quantity at which the line reaches the horizontal axis.

         iii. It depends on your demand for wine, of course, but probably not. We take up this issue in Chapter 5, when we consider elasticity of demand. In general, we'll find that total spending declines at high prices.

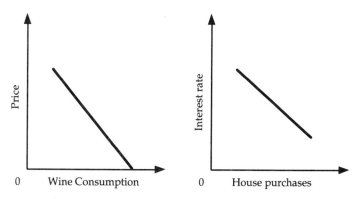

    g.   i. See the diagram above.

         ii. It depends on the demand for houses, of course, and is shown as the point at which the line reaches the vertical axis.

10. a. It's a positive relationship.

     b. The line would be "rising" to the right.

     c. Rise over run: Y rises by one unit every time X rises by two units, so the slope is $+\frac{1}{2}$.

     d. See the diagram below.

11. Your shortlist of variables probably will include the price of Quite Lite, the prices of its competitors, advertising, the time of year, health attitudes, the income of potential buyers (launching a new product during an economic downturn might be difficult, for instance), and so on.

     The negative relationship you will have modeled (if not, why not?) between price and quantity demanded is called the demand curve. A movement along this curve indicates that price has changed causing a change in the amount of beer demanded, with all other variables held constant *(ceteris paribus)*. (Keep this conclusion in mind when you read Chapter 4.)

12. Positive statements are testable; normative statements are opinions.

     a. Positive. A statement need not be correct to be positive.

     b. Positive. Data can be gathered and analysis undertaken.

     c. Normative, as signaled by the use of "should".

     d. Normative. This is an opinion, even during the Great Depression.

     e. Normative. This is an opinion, as signaled by the use of "should".

     f. Normative. This is an opinion, as signaled by the use of "should".

     g. Positive. This statement can be tested.

APPENDIX TO CHAPTER 1

1A

Introduction: Why a Special Section on Graphing?

You may be surprised by the amount of mathematics—geometry in particular—which you encounter in economics. The professor introduces a new concept and quickly draws a graph to illustrate the idea—economic theory and graphs are inseparable. This union of a social science course and mathematical techniques can baffle some students. You could struggle so much with the techniques that you miss the powerful insights which economics has to offer. This section is designed to help you gain a working understanding of graphing techniques and to help you apply this knowledge to economics.

Why Are Graphs Important?

Graphs are important for several reasons. First, graphs are a compact way of conveying a large amount of information. An old adage says that "one picture is worth one thousand words". This is particularly true in economics as the movement of an economic variable over time or the relationship between two economic variables can be quickly grasped through the use of graphs. Second, as Case and Fair mention in the appendix to Chapter 1, economics uses quantitative (mathematical) techniques more than any other social science. Every academic discipline possesses its own "tool kit" which must be mastered in order to truly appreciate the content of the course. In an economic principles class, the primary "tool" is graphs. Third, there is a clear relationship between student success in economics and skill with graphs. Research on student performance indicates that of the skills which lead to success (verbal, quantitative reasoning, graphing) graphing ability is vital. Fourth, an important component of a vibrant democratic society is *economic literacy*: a basic understanding of certain central economic concepts. Citizens who follow current events will constantly encounter graphs as print and television journalists use the visual medium to communicate with its audience.

Why Graphs Trouble Many Students

Several factors may cause you to have difficulty with graphs. Several years may have elapsed since you completed a high school geometry course. Consequently, many graphing skills which were developed have been forgotten. More fundamentally, you read every day; however, you do not practice math every day. Therefore, most students enter an economic principles class with a stronger reading ability than a mathematical ability. Because of this, you must remember that the graphs in your textbook are not photographs worthy of only a glance; *graphs must be studied.*

General Tips for Studying Graphs

Here are some general tips which should assist you in developing their graphing skills:

1. *Relax*! Remember that math is simply another language; therefore, graphs are just a specific form of communication.
2. When studying a graph, first identify the labels which are on the graph axes and curves. These labels are like road sings which inform the reader.
3. Once the labels are recognized, try to understand what economic intuition lies behind the curve (e.g. the demand curve indicates that as the product price falls, the amount which consumers wish to buy increases).
4. Get into the habit of tracing the graphs which are in the text and copying the graphs as reading notes are taken.
5. *Draw, draw, draw*!!! The process of learning economics must be an active process. Graphing skills can be enhanced only by repeated attempts to graph economic concepts.

What Are Graphs?

Graphs are a visual expression of quantitative information. Economic theory attempts to establish relationships between important concepts. If the value of a concept changes, the concept is considered a *variable*. Graphs illustrate the relationship between two variables. If two variables have a *direct* (positive) relationship the value of one variable increases as the value of the other variable increases. If two variables have an *inverse* (negative) relationship, the value of one variable decreases as the value of the other variable increases.

Example 1: As children get older, they grow taller. There exists a direct relationship between a child's age and its height.

AGE	6	7	8	9	10
HEIGHT	48″	50″	52″	54″	56″

This relationship can be graphed:

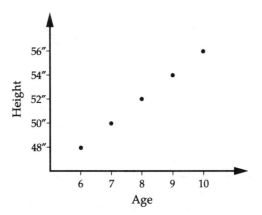

Example 2: After attending class, sleeping, eating, and working at a part-time job, a student has seven hours which can be used for studying or socializing. There exists an inverse relationship between time spent studying and time spent socializing.

STUDYING	7	5	3	1	0
SOCIALIZING	0	2	4	6	7

A graph of this relationship is shown below:

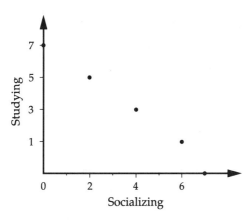

Types of Graphs

There are two types of graphs. *Descriptive* graphs relate the observed association of two variables. The graphs in Examples 1 and 2 are descriptive graphs. Newspapers often express monthly unemployment data in descriptive graphs. *Analytical* graphs convey the hypothetical relationship between two variables. The existence of association is derived from economic theory and its accuracy is the object of economic research.

Example 3: An understanding of a firm's goals and its constraints leads to the development of a hypothesis which states that as wages rises, a firm would hire fewer workers. Graphically, this relationship is expressed as:

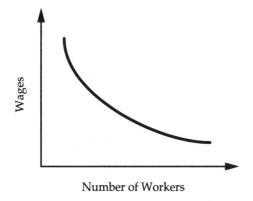

Often, the value of one of the variables determines the value of the other variable. In these cases, the former variable is called the *independent* variable; the latter variable is called the *dependent* variable. Normally (but not always), the independent variable is placed on the horizontal axis and the dependent variable is placed on the vertical axis.

Drawing Graphs

Earlier, we examined the direct relationship between a child's age and its height. One would expect another direct relationship between a child's age and its weight.
Example 4:

AGE	6	7	8	9	10
WEIGHT	70 lbs	75 lbs	80 lbs	85 lbs	90 lbs

Graph this relationship on the axes below.

Combining the two series of data yields the following table:

AGE	6	7	8	9	10
HEIGHT	48″	50″	52″	54″	56″
WEIGHT	70 lbs	75 lbs	80 lbs	85 lbs	90 lbs

Example 5: Graph the height-weight combination for each age on the axes below.

Is the relationship between height and weight direct or inverse? _____
Because the graph depicts the changes in two variables over time, it is called a *scatter diagram*.

Example 6: Graph the relationship between the annual U.S. unemployment rate (U%) and the years 1987–1997.

YEARS	1986	1987	1988	1989	1990	1991	1992	1993	1994	1995	1996	1997
U%	7.0	6.2	5.4	5.3	5.5	6.7	7.4	6.8	6.1	5.6	5.4	5.0

Year

Because this graph depicts the movement of one variable over time, it is called a *time-series* graph. Between what years is there a direct relationship? _____ Between what years is there an inverse relationship? _____

Reading Graphs

In addition to graphing economic relationships, students must develop the skill of reading graphs.

Example 7: Below are a time series graph of the movement of the poverty rates for U.S. families between 1986 and 1996 and a scatter diagram indicating the association between poverty rates and unemployment rates. Study both graphs and answer the following questions:

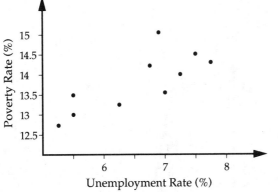

YEARS	1986	1987	1988	1989	1990	1991	1992	1993	1994	1995	1996
U%	7.0	6.2	5.5	5.3	5.5	6.7	7.4	6.8	6.1	5.6	5.4
Poverty Rate %	13.6	13.4	13.1	12.8	13.5	14.0	14.5	15.1	14.5	13.8	13.7

1. What are the poverty rates in:
   a. 1987 _____
   b. 1990 _____
   c. 1995 _____

2. What are the poverty rate/unemployment rate combinations in:
   a. 1988 _____ _____
   b. 1992 _____ _____
   c. 1996 _____ _____

3. When is there a direct relationship between poverty rates and time?

4. Is there ever an inverse relationship between poverty rates and unemployment rates?

Understanding and Calculating Slopes

The *slope* of a curve is one measure of the relationship between two variables. It indicates both the type of relationship (direct or inverse) and the rate of change of one variable as the other variable changes. For a straight line, the slope is constant. For a curve, the slope changes from one point along the curve to another. At any particular point, the slope of the curve is identical to the slope of the straight line which is tangent to that point. The slope of a line is calculated by identifying two points on the line and computing the ratio of the change in the variable on the vertical axis and the change in the variable on the horizontal axis. (In high school geometry, this was referred to as "the 'rise'; over the 'run'"; more formally, the slope was the "change in Y divided by the change in X".)

Example 8:

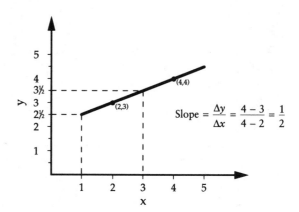

$$\text{Slope} = \frac{\Delta y}{\Delta x} = \frac{4-3}{4-2} = \frac{1}{2}$$

Example 9:

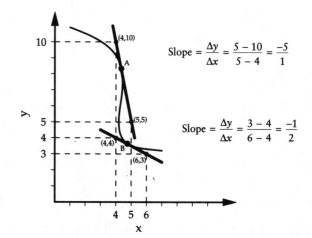

$$\text{Slope} = \frac{\Delta y}{\Delta x} = \frac{5-10}{5-4} = \frac{-5}{1}$$

$$\text{Slope} = \frac{\Delta y}{\Delta x} = \frac{3-4}{6-4} = \frac{-1}{2}$$

In Example 8, any two points alone that line will show a slope of 1/2. In Example 9, the slope varies: at point A, the slope is −1; at point B the slope is −(1/2). These slope numbers can be interpreted indicating the unit change in the value of Y in response to a one unit change in X. For Example 8, Y will increase by 1/2 in response to a one unit change in X. At point A in Example 9, Y decreases by 1 and, at point B, Y decreases by 1/2. The fact that the slope is positive in Example 8 means that there is a direct relationship between Y and X. The negative slope in Example 9 illustrates an inverse relationship between Y and X.

Solving Equations

Often, the economic relationship between two concepts can be expressed in algebra with an equation. The advantage of this approach is that we can calculate the specific impact that a change in one variable has upon another variable.

Example 10: It is a reasonable assumption that as the price of a good rises more of that good will be supplied. This positive relationship can be expressed with an equation. Let P represent price and Qs represent quantity supplied. For our purposes, let $Qs = -10 + 80P$. Thus, if $P = 1$, then $Qs = 70$. The table below captures this relationship:

Price	1	2	3	4	5
Quantity supplied	70	150	230	310	390

1. What is Qs if P = 7? _____
2. What is Qs if P = 10? _____

The table can be graphed. The line is a supply curve, as you will see in Chapter 4—it is usually labeled "S".

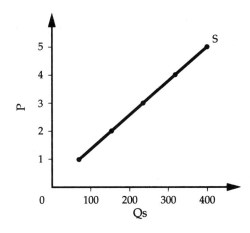

3. What is the slope of the line? _____

If the equation is $Qs = -10 + 50P$, the slope of the line will change. Below is the new table.

Price	1	2	3	4	5
Quantity supplied	40	90	140	190	240

4. Draw this new line on the graph below. Label it S1.

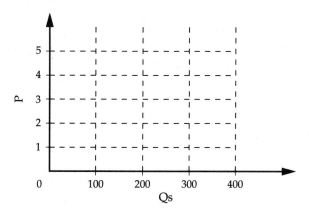

5. What is the slope of this line? _____

If the equation for the supply curve is Qs = −20 + 75P, answer the question below.

6. Complete the following table.

Price	1	2	3	4	5
Quantity supplied					

7. Graph the line shown in the table on the graph below. Label it S2.

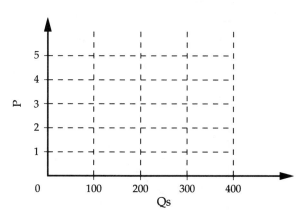

8. What is the slope of the line? _____
9. What is Qs if P = 8? _____
10. What is Qs if P = 20? _____

ANSWERS AND SOLUTIONS

SOLUTIONS TO PROBLEMS IN APPENDIX 1

Example 4:
See the following diagram.

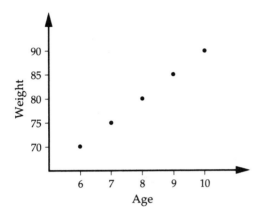

Example 5:
See the following diagram.

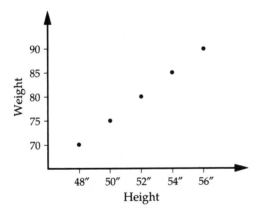

The relationship between height and weight is direct (positive).

Example 6:
See the following diagram.

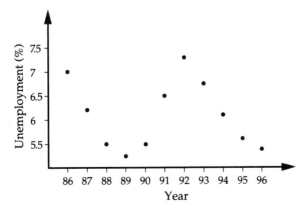

Between 1989 and 1992, there is a direct (positive) relationship.
Between 1986 and 1989, there is an inverse (negative) relationship. There is also an inverse relationship between 1992 and 1997.

Example 7:
1. a. 13.4%
    b. 13.5
    c. 13.8%
2. a. 1988   5.5%   13.1%
    b. 1992   7.4%   14.5%
    c. 1996   5.4%   13.7%

Example 10:
1. $Qs = -10 + 80P = -10 + 80(7) = 550$.
2. $Qs = -10 + 80P = -10 + 80(10) = 790$.
3. Slope = rise/run = 1/80. A 1 unit increase in P leads to an 80 unit increase in Qs.
4. See the diagram below.

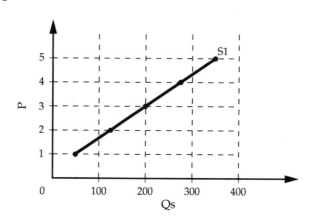

5. Slope = rise/run = 1/50. A 1 unit increase in P leads to a 50 unit increase in Qs.
6.

Price	1	2	3	4	5
Quantity supplied	55	130	205	280	355

7. See the diagram below.

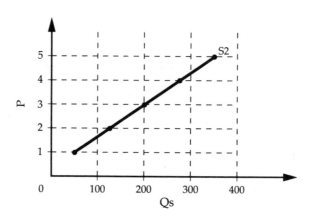

8. Slope = rise/run = 1/75. A 1 unit increase in P leads to a 75 unit increase in Qs.
9. $Qs = -20 + 75P = -20 + 75(8) = 580$.
10. $Qs = -20 + 75P = -20 + 75(20) = 1480$.

THE ECONOMIC PROBLEM: SCARCITY AND CHOICE

OBJECTIVES: POINT BY POINT

After completing this chapter, you should be able to accomplish the objectives listed below.

OBJECTIVE 1: Identify the three basic economic questions.

Economics studies the production and consumption choices that are made by society and the outcomes that occur. Solutions must be found to three "basic questions": *what* goods should be produced?; *how* should the goods be produced?; and *for whom* should the goods be produced? Every economy (consisting of firms, households, and the government sector) must transform its scarce natural, capital, and human resources into usable production. In a complex society the opportunity to cooperate and specialize offers great scope for increased production—but decisions must be made regarding the extent of cooperation, who specializes in what, and how goods are distributed. *(page 26)*

> **Opportunity Cost:** Economics has to do with making choices when constraints (scarcity) are present. Constrained choice occurs, for example, when you go to the grocery store with only a $5 bill in your pocket—you have to make choices based on this limitation. Unconstrained choice would be if you were allowed to take as many groceries home as you wanted, free of charge. Sadly, though, we know there's "no such thing as a free lunch."

> Practical examples of the consequences of choice and the costs of such choices include: present vs. future benefits (for example, do you study hard now so that, at exam time, reviewing is easier, or do you take it easy now and sweat it before the exam?), and capital vs. consumer production (for example, should we produce taxicabs or sports cars?).

> **LEARNING TIP:** Everyone has been confronted with some version of the following scene: A favorite grandmother gives you a free choice from two or more items (ice cream sundaes, for example). From your viewpoint, is your chosen ice cream sundae free? Or is there an opportunity cost? If you have a range of sundaes from which to choose, what is the cost? The dollar amount of the chosen sundae? All the other sundaes you could have had? The opportunity cost is the next most favorite sundae.

> **LEARNING TIP:** To calculate opportunity cost, use the "give up to get" approach. If you can determine what (next-best) choice was forgone to get your preferred selection, you have determined opportunity cost. This is most clearly seen as a movement along a production possibility frontier.

PRACTICE

1. Which of the following statements about the operation of an economy is false? Each economy has a mechanism to determine
   A. what is produced.
   B. how to satisfy all of the desires of its citizens.
   C. how much is produced.
   D. how goods and services are distributed among its citizens.
   Answer: B. Because resources are limited, the economy cannot satisfy all the desires of its citizens.

OBJECTIVE 2: Explain what is meant by "comparative advantage" and relate this concept to the theory that individuals can gain from specialization and exchange.

A producer has a *comparative advantage* in the production of Good A if, compared with another producer, she can produce Good A at a lower opportunity cost.

The *theory of comparative advantage* provides the rationale for free trade. Given a two-country, two-good world, Ricardo showed that trading partners can benefit from specialization in the production of the good in which they have the comparative advantage. The increased production could be traded. In terms of the *production possibility frontier* (ppf) diagram, trade will be advantageous if the ppfs have differing slopes because differing slopes indicate differing costs.   (page 28)

> **LEARNING TIP:** If you're like most individuals, you'll need several numerical examples to strengthen your grasp of comparative advantage. The Applications take you through all the steps included in the text.

> **Comparative advantage** hinges on the concept of opportunity cost. The producer (person, firm, or country) with the lowest opportunity cost will hold the comparative advantage in that product. Don't be misled—it is irrelevant whether or not the producer can produce *more* of the good. The issue revolves around the relative opportunity costs.

PRACTICE

Use the following information to answer the next five questions. Arboc and Arbez are two economies that produce computer chips and VCRs. In Arboc, a one-unit increase in computer chips requires a four-unit decrease in VCR production. In Arbez, a one-unit increase in computer chips requires a three-unit decrease in VCR production. In each economy, costs remain constant.

2. Which of the following statements is false?
   A. In Arboc, the opportunity cost of 1 computer chip is 4 VCRs forgone.
   B. In Arbez, the opportunity cost of 1 computer chip is 3 VCRs forgone.
   C. The opportunity cost of 1 computer chip is greater in Arboc than in Arbez.
   D. An increase in the Arbocali production of computer chips requires a decrease in the Arbezani production of VCRs.
   Answer: D. An increase in the Arbocali production of computer chips requires a decrease in the *Arbocali* production of VCRs. In fact, both independent economies might choose to increase computer chip production.

3. Which of the following statements is true?
   A. In Arboc, the opportunity cost of 1 VCR is 4 computer chips forgone.
   B. In Arbez, the opportunity cost of 1 VCR is 3 computer chips forgone.
   C. The opportunity cost of 1 VCR is greater in Arbez than in Arboc.
   D. Arbez can produce more VCRs than Arboc can produce.

Answer: C. We don't know whether Arbez has an absolute advantage in VCRs (Option D). The information tells us only about relative performance. Arbez, in fact, may be a very small country capable of producing only a few VCRs. In Arboc, the opportunity cost of a VCR is ¼ of a computer chip forgone, and in Arbez, the opportunity cost of a VCR is ⅓ of a computer chip forgone.

4. In _____ , the opportunity cost of 1 computer chip is _____ VCRs forgone, which is less than the opportunity cost of 1 computer chip in _____
   A. Arboc, ¼, Arbez.
   B. Arboc, 4, Arbez.
   C. Arbez, 3, Arboc.
   D. Arbez, ⅓, Arboc.
   Answer: C. In Arboc, each computer chip "costs" 4 VCRs forgone. In Arbez, each computer chip "costs" 3 VCRs forgone. VCRs cost less in Arbez.

5. In _____ , the opportunity cost of 1 VCR is _____ computer chips, which is less than the opportunity cost of 1 VCR in _____
   A. Arboc, ¼, Arbez.
   B. Arboc, 4, Arbez.
   C. Arbez, 3, Arboc.
   D. Arbez, ⅓, Arboc.
   Answer: A. In Arboc, each VCR "costs" ¼ of a computer chip forgone. In Arbez, each VCR "costs" ⅓ of a computer chip forgone. VCRs cost less in Arbez.

6. According to the information above,
   A. Arboc has a comparative advantage in the production of both goods.
   B. Arboc has a comparative advantage in producing computer chips, and Arbez has a comparative advantage in producing VCRs.
   C. Arboc has a comparative advantage in producing VCRs, and Arbez has a comparative advantage in producing computer chips.
   D. Arbez has a comparative advantage in the production of both goods.
   Answer: C. Arboc has a comparative advantage in the production of VCRs (1 VCR costs ¼ of a computer chip forgone), and Arbez has a comparative advantage in the production of computer chips (1 computer chip costs 3 VCRs forgone). Note: No country can be relatively better at producing both goods!

OBJECTIVE 3: Explain why a production possibility frontier has a negative slope and why the slope depicts the concept of opportunity cost.

A production possibility frontier depicts the boundary between possible and impossible (unattainable) levels of production. Choosing to employ resources for one use prevents them from being employed for other uses—there is an *opportunity cost* involved in the choice. The *production possibility frontier* portrays graphically the opportunity cost of transferring resources from one activity to another in a two-good environment. Assuming that all resources are fully employed, as more of Good A is produced, fewer resources are available to produce Good B.   (page 31)

> **Why Does the ppf Slope Downward?:** The production possibility frontier is the key piece of economic analysis in this chapter. It's always presented as having only two goods or bundles of goods. It slopes downward because "the more you get of one thing the less you get of the other." The more you study economics, the less time you have for other activities. The opportunity cost of an extra hour of studying economics is the value of an hour of other activities.

GRAPHING POINTER: When drawing a ppf, remember that the frontier extends from the vertical axis to the horizontal axis. It is a mistake to leave the frontier unconnected to the axes. If the frontier is not connected, it implies that an infinitely large quantity of either good could be produced, which is exactly the opposite message that the ppf is intended to give.

PRACTICE

7. Along the production possibility frontier, trade-offs exist because
   A. buyers will want to buy less when price goes up, but producers will want to sell more.
   B. even on the frontier itself, not all production levels are efficient.
   C. at some levels, unemployment or inefficiency exists.
   D. the economy has only a limited quantity of resources to allocate between competing uses.
   Answer: D. Along the ppf, resources are fully and efficiently employed. However, since resources are scarce, an increase in the production of Good A requires that resources be taken from the production of Good B.

OBJECTIVE 4: Interpret what is depicted by a production possibility frontier.

The ppf shows all the combinations of Good A and Good B that can be produced when all resources are employed efficiently. Points inside the ppf represent unemployment and/or inefficiency while points outside are currently unattainable. An outward movement of the ppf represents growth. Growth occurs if more resources become available or if existing resources become more productive (e.g., through better education, more efficient techniques of production, or technological innovations).
(page 32)

Production Efficiency and Economic Efficiency: The thought of a great volume of production, with all resources employed, is an attractive one. For this reason, it's often difficult to understand that, in serving the needs of consumers, producing the *right* goods is more important than mere quantity. This distinction lies at the heart of most confusion about production efficiency and what is called economic efficiency. Having the Eskimo economy fully employed and producing refrigerators may help you see the point. It would be "better" (more efficient) for the Eskimos to have some unemployment but be producing warm clothing. Turning out the refrigerators is productively efficient, while making the warm clothing is economically efficient. Ideally, you'd want to be on the ppf (being productively efficient) and producing the economically efficient mix of output.

LEARNING TIP: Think of the ppf as a way to depict opportunity cost and constrained choice. In general, you want to be somewhere on the curve because any production combination inside the curve means that you're losing production, which is inefficient. Production on the curve means that resources are being used to the maximum (no unemployment). The inefficiency of a mismatch between an "efficient" production mix and society's needs is easily explained—just because we're producing "on the line" doesn't mean we're meeting society's needs as effectively as possible. Employing all our resources to produce taxicabs, for example, is unlikely to be desirable!

LEARNING TIP: Suppose we are on the ppf and, at one point, can produce 16 cars and 5 pickups while, at another point, we can produce 12 cars and 7 pickups. Note that the opportunity cost is calculated by looking at the *change* in production levels—2 extra trucks cost 4 cars.

> **LEARNING TIP:** Reducing unemployment does not shift the ppf. Remember the underlying assumptions! The ppf is drawn *given* a set of resources (whether or not the resources are being used). Unemployment represents a situation where the resources are not fully utilized. If unemployment is reduced, the economy moves closer to the ppf.

PRACTICE

8. Which of the following is **not** an assumption underlying the ppf?
   A. Technological knowledge is fixed.
   B. Resources are fully employed.
   C. Resources are efficiently employed.
   D. The quantity of labor resources is variable.
   Answer: D. When drawing a ppf, the quantity of all resources is assumed to be fixed.

9. The production possibility frontier represents
   A. the maximum amount of goods and services that can be produced with a given quantity of resources and technology.
   B. those combinations of goods and services that will be demanded as price changes.
   C. the maximum amount of resources that are available as the wage level changes.
   D. those combinations of goods and services that will be produced as the price level changes.
   Answer: A. The production possibility frontier represents what it is "possible to produce" given the available resources and technology.

10. The Arbezani economy is operating at a point inside its ppf. This may be because
    A. the economy has very poor technological know-how.
    B. Arbez is a very small nation and can't produce much.
    C. poor management practices have led to an inefficient use of resources.
    D. Arbez has only a small resource base.
    Answer: C. Very poor technological know-how or a small resource base will result in a ppf that is close to the origin. Fully and efficiently employed resources would still be on the ppf.

OBJECTIVE 5: Explain why increasing opportunity costs occur and how this relates to the production possibility frontier diagram.

Increasing opportunity costs are present when the production possibility frontier bulges outwards from the origin. Increasing costs occur if resources are not equally well suited to the production of Good A and Good B.   (page 33)

> **LEARNING TIP:** Why is the ppf bowed-out? The geometry of the ppf flows from its economics. A bowed-out production possibility frontier indicates that the opportunity cost is increasing as resources become more heavily allocated to the production of one good. The ppf has that bowed-out shape because of the imperfect adaptability of resources to different uses. A farmer wishing to produce dairy products, for example, will select the most suited resources first, and production will increase sharply. Further increases will be less easy to achieve and more expensive in terms of lost production of other goods as resources more suited to other endeavors are pressed into dairy service. If resources were identical in their productive abilities, the opportunity cost of re-allocation would be constant and the ppf would be a straight line (a constant slope).

PRACTICE

11. There are increasing costs in the economy of Arbez. To portray this fact in a production possibility diagram we should
    A. move the ppf outwards (up and to the right).
    B. draw the ppf bulging outwards.
    C. shift the ppf's endpoint on the horizontal axis to the right.
    D. shift the ppf's endpoint on the vertical axis upwards.
    Answer: B. The slope of the ppf represents the behavior of opportunity cost as production level changes. A straight ppf represents constant costs. To show increasing costs the ppf is bowed outwards from the origin.

OBJECTIVE 6: Identify ways in which economic growth may occur.

Economic growth may occur if an economy increases the quantity or quality of its resources—the production possibility frontier shifts outward. Additionally, technological change and innovation can increase productivity. (page 34)

> **Investment and Capital:** "Investment" and "capital" are two terms that have very specific meanings in economics. Beware! Investing doesn't just mean buying something. To an economist, investing means only the creation of capital. What, then, is capital? Capital refers to man-made resources usable in production. A hammer is capital; a share of GM stock is not. A nail is capital; a dollar bill is not. Buying a hammer is capital investment; buying GM stock is not!
>
> If this capital/non-capital distinction is giving you problems, ask yourself if the purchase of the item in question increases the economy's ability to produce. If it does, it's an investment in capital.

OBJECTIVE 7: Identify and distinguish how economic systems differ in their solutions to the three basic questions. State the "mistakes" to which an unregulated market system is prone.

The two "pure" types of economic system are the command economy and the *laissez-faire* economy. A *command (planned) economy* has a central agency that sets production targets, income, and prices, and finds answers for the three basic questions. In a *laissez-faire (market) economy*, the three basic questions are answered through the operation of individual buyers and sellers following their own self-interest in markets.

All economies, in fact, are driven by a mixture of market forces and government intervention and regulation. Government intervention is felt to be necessary to correct *laissez-faire* "mistakes" such as an excessive inequality in the distribution of income and periodic spells of unemployment or inflation. (page 37)

PRACTICE

12. Advocates comparing the performance of a pure *laissez-faire* system with that of a command economy would claim that a pure *laissez-faire* system would do all of the following except
    A. promote efficiency.
    B. stimulate innovation.
    C. achieve an equal income distribution.
    D. be directed by the decisions of individual buyers and sellers.
    Answer: C. A pure *laissez-faire* system, which rewards those who contribute most, would have an unequal income distribution.

PRACTICE TEST

1. MUTIPLE CHOICE QUESTIONS.

Select the option that provides the single best answer.

_____ 1. Because the nation of Arboc is operating at a point inside its ppf, it
A. has full employment.
B. has unemployed or inefficiently employed resources.
C. must cut output of one good to increase production of another.
D. will be unable to experience economic growth.

_____ 2. Arboc commits more of its resources to capital production than does Arbez. _____ should experience a(n) _____ rapid rate of economic growth.
A. Arboc, more.
B. Arbez, more.
C. Arboc, less.
D. Both, equally.

_____ 3. Which of the following does not count as a productive resource?
A. Capital resources, such as a tractor.
B. Natural resources, such as a piece of farmland.
C. Financial resources, such as a twenty-dollar bill.
D. Human resources, such as a hairdresser.

Use the following diagram to answer the next four questions.

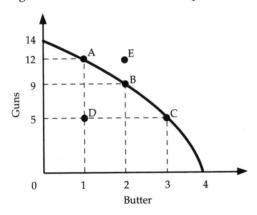

_____ 4. Point E might become attainable if this economy
A. reduces prices.
B. reduces wages.
C. improves the quality of its workforce.
D. encourages emigration.

_____ 5. A movement from A to B and then to C indicates that
A. the cost of additional butter is decreasing.
B. the cost of additional guns is increasing.
C. the economy is becoming more efficient.
D. the cost of additional butter is increasing.

_____ 6. To move from D to A indicates that
A. the opportunity cost would be zero.
B. some butter would have to be given up.
C. there would have to be an increase in the quantity of resources.
D. the opportunity cost would be 7 guns forgone.

_____ 7. The opportunity cost of producing another unit of butter is
A. higher at B than at C.
B. lower at D than at C.
C. higher at A than at B.
D. equal at D and at C.

_____ 8. A production possibility frontier diagram illustrates all of the following concepts except
A. scarcity.
B. unlimited wants.
C. opportunity cost.
D. constrained choice.

_____ 9. Of the following, the least serious problem for _laissez-faire_ economies is
A. unemployment.
B. income inequality.
C. inflation.
D. satisfaction of consumer sovereignty.

Use the following production possibility table to answer the next three questions. Suppose that wheat is on the Y-axis.

Alternative	A	B	C	D	E	F
Wheat	0	1	2	3	4	5
Tobacco	15	14	12	9	5	0

_____ 10. The opportunity cost of a unit of wheat as the economy moves from C to D is
A. ⅓ unit of tobacco production forgone.
B. 3 units of tobacco production forgone.
C. 9 units of tobacco production forgone.
D. 12 unit of tobacco production forgone.

_____ 11. The opportunity cost of a unit of tobacco as the economy moves from C to B is
A. ½ unit of wheat production forgone.
B. 1 units of wheat production forgone.
C. 2 units of wheat production forgone.
D. 12 unit of wheat production forgone.

_____ 12. An output of 3 units of wheat and 7 units of tobacco indicates that
A. this economy has poor technology.
B. resources are being used inefficiently.
C. tobacco is preferred to wheat.
D. it is not possible for this economy to produce at a point on the production possibility frontier.

_____ 13. Which of the following is most likely to shift the production possibility frontier outward?
A. A sudden expansion in the labor force.
B. An increase in stock prices.
C. A shift of productive resources from capital goods to consumer goods.
D. A general increase in the public's demand for goods.

_____ 14. Which of the following is not one of the basic economic questions?
A. What will be produced?
B. How much will be produced?
C. How will it be produced?
D. Who will get what is produced?

_____ 15. Private markets work best when
   A. they are competitive.
   B. they are regulated by a government agency.
   C. a monopolist is present.
   D. consumer sovereignty is restricted.

_____ 16. Arboc has an increasing-cost production possibility frontier. Its slope must be
   A. positive and increasing.
   B. positive and decreasing.
   C. negative and increasing.
   D. negative and decreasing.

_____ 17. For Jill to have a comparative advantage in the production of pins means that, relative to Jack, with the same resources
   A. Jill is relatively better at producing pins than at producing needles.
   B. Jill is relatively better at producing both pins and needles.
   C. Jill can produce fewer needles than Jack can produce.
   D. Jill can produce more pins than Jack can produce.

_____ 18. Each of the following is a basic concern of any economic system except
   A. the allocation of scarce resources among producers.
   B. the mix of different types of output.
   C. the distribution of output among consumers.
   D. the quality of resources allocated among consumers.

The following table shows the maximum output of each good in each country, e.g. maximum Arbezani production of goat milk is 3 units.

	Arboc	Arbez
Goat Milk	3	6
Bananas	5	2

_____ 19. According to the table above,
   A. Arboc has a comparative advantage in producing both goods.
   B. Arboc has a comparative advantage in the production of bananas, and Arbez has a comparative advantage in the production of goat milk.
   C. Arboc has a comparative advantage in the production of goat milk, and Arbez has a comparative advantage in the production of bananas.
   D. Arbez has a comparative advantage in the production of both goods.

_____ 20. The nation of Regit has a bowed-out production possibility frontier with potatoes on the vertical axis and steel on the horizontal axis. A movement down along the ppf will incur _____ costs; a movement up along the ppf will incur _____ costs.
   A. increasing, increasing.
   B. increasing, decreasing.
   C. decreasing, increasing.
   D. decreasing, decreasing.

II. APPLICATION QUESTIONS.

1. Farmer Brown has four fields that can produce corn or tobacco. Assume that the trade-off between corn and tobacco *within* each field is constant. The maximum yields for each field are given in the following table. Field A, for instance, can produce 40 units of corn and no tobacco or, as another alternative, no corn and 10 units of tobacco.

Field	A	B	C	D
Corn	40	30	20	10
Tobacco	10	20	30	40

   a. Draw Farmer Brown's ppf.
   b. To be on the ppf, what conditions must hold true?
   c. Brown is currently producing only corn: If he wants to produce some tobacco, in what order would he switch his fields from corn to tobacco production?
   d. Explain your answer to c.

2. Two countries, Arboc and Arbez, produce wine and cheese, and each has constant costs of production. The maximum amounts of the two goods for each country is given in the following table.

Arboc	Arbez	Goods
40	120	wine
20	30	cheese

   a. Draw the production possibility frontier for each country.

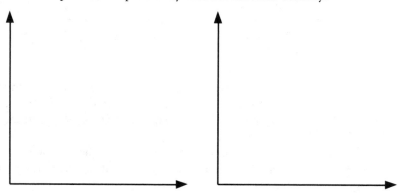

   b. Calculate the opportunity cost of wine in Arboc and in Arbez.
   c. In which country, then, is wine production cheaper?
   d. Answer questions b. and c. for cheese production—remember that the opportunity costs are reciprocals of one another.

Note that Arbez has an advantage in both goods in terms of total production, but a comparative advantage only in wine production.

Now assume that Arboc becomes more efficient and can double its output of both wine and cheese.

   e. Graph the new ppf on the diagram above.
   f. Which good should Arboc now produce?

Suppose, instead, that Arbez has a specific technological advance that permits it to increase cheese production to a maximum of 90.

   g. Now which nation should produce wine?

3. In a national contest, the first prize is a town. The winner receives a furnished house, a general store and gasoline station, a pick-up truck, and 100 acres of land. The store comes fully stocked with everything you might find in a country general store. The town is located 100 miles from a small city. It is the shopping center for about a thousand families who live in the countryside. In addition, the road through the town is fairly well traveled. Suppose you win the contest and decide to try running the town as a business for at least a year.
   a. Describe the resources available to the economy of your town. What is the potential labor force? What are the natural resources?
   b. Describe the capital stock of your town.
   c. List some of the factors that are beyond your control that will affect your income.
   d. List some of the decisions you must make that could affect your income, and explain what their effects might be.
   e. At the end of the year, you must decide whether to stay or go back to college. How will you decide? What factors will you weigh in making your decision? What role do your expectations play?

4. The following data give the production possibilities of an economy that produces two types of goods, guns (horizontal axis) and butter (vertical axis).

PRODUCTION POSSIBILITIES	GUNS	BUTTER
A	0	105
B	10	100
C	20	90
D	30	75
E	40	55
F	50	30
G	60	0

   a. Graph the production possibilities frontier.
   b. Explain why Point D is efficient while Point H (30 guns and 45 units of butter) is not.
   c. Calculate the per-unit opportunity cost of an increase in the production of guns in each of the following cases.
      i. From Point A to Point B?
      ii. From Point B to Point C?
      iii. From Point E to Point F?
      iv. From Point F to Point G?
   d. Calculate the per-unit opportunity cost of an increase in the production of butter in each of the following cases.
      i. From Point G to Point F?
      ii. From Point D to Point C?
      iii. From Point C to Point B?
      iv. From Point B to Point A?
   e. Using the production possibility frontier concept, explain what will happen if this nation declares war on one of its neighbors.

5. Draw a production possibilities frontier with farm goods (x-axis) and manufacturing goods (y-axis) on the axes. In each of the following cases, explain
   what will happen to the production possibilities frontier.

   a. There is an increase in the unemployment rate.
   b. There is an improvement in farming techniques.
   c. There is a decrease in quantity of physical capital.
   d. The productivity of workers doubles.
   e. The government requires farmers to slaughter a portion of their dairy
      herds.

6. Consider the following ppf diagram.

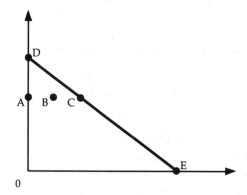

   a. Which point is "best?" and which is "worst?"
   b. Now suppose that you're told that the axes measure food (horizontal) and
      moonshine whisky (vertical). Would your answer be different?
   c. Point B may be preferable to Point D, although Point B in terms of pro-
      duction Point B is less efficient. Why might it be preferable?

7. The nation of Arbez can produce two goods, corn and steel. The table shows
   some points on the Arbezani ppf.

Alternative	A	B	C	D	E	F
Corn	0	1	2	3	4	5
Steel	20	16	12	8	4	0

a. Draw the ppf in the space below.

b. Moving from Alternative A to B, B to C, and so on, calculate the opportunity cost of each additional unit of corn. Going from F to E, E to D, and so on, calculate the opportunity cost *per unit* of steel. Confirm that the pairs of values are reciprocals of each other. (This must always be true.)

Opportunity Cost of 1 Unit of:

Alternative	Corn	Steel
A–B		
B–C		
C–D		
D–E		
E–F		

c. Consider each of the following situations.
   Situation X: Arbez is producing 4 units of corn and no steel. What is the opportunity cost of the next unit of corn? The next unit of steel?
   Situation Y: Arbez is producing 4 units of corn and 4 units of steel. What is the opportunity cost of the next unit of corn? The next unit of steel?

d. Why do you find a different set of answers in Situation X and Situation Y?

e. Now consider a new situation, Situation Z: Arbez is producing 3 units of corn and 5 units of steel. What is the opportunity cost of the next unit of corn? The next unit of steel?

f. Which Situation (X, Y, or Z) is the most productively efficient and which the least productively efficient?

g. On the Arbezani ppf, what is the cost of each unit of corn and what is the cost of each unit of steel?

The nation of Arboc also produces corn and steel. The following table shows some points on the Arbocali ppf.

Alternative	A	B	C	D	E	F
Corn	0	1	2	3	4	5
Steel	20	16	12	8	4	0

   h. On the Arbocali ppf, what is the cost of each unit of corn and what is the cost of each unit of steel?

   i. Point to ponder: Because steel is relatively cheaper to produce in Arboc/Arbez and corn is relatively cheaper to produce in Arboc/Arbez, might mutually beneficial trade be possible?

8. Refer to the following diagram.

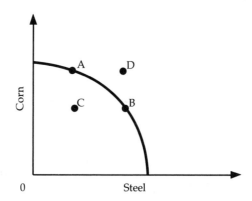

   a. Which point is unattainable?

   b. To achieve this currently unattainable production combination, what must happen (two possible answers)?

   c. Which point represents unemployment or inefficiency?

   d. Will a movement from B to A increase corn production or steel production?

   e. What is the opportunity cost of moving from C to B?

9. Draw the axes of a ppf. Use corn (on the vertical axis) and steel (on the horizontal axis) as the two goods.

Choose a point, A, that represents some corn and some steel production. Suppose that this point is on the ppf—it's a maximum point. Split the diagram up into quarters, with Point A in the center.

   a. Is a production mix to the south-west possible?

   b. Would such a mix be productively efficient?

   c. Would such a mix be economically efficient?

   d. Is a move to the north-east quadrant possible? What do you know about it?

Only the north-west and south-east quadrants are possible locations in which productively efficient output alternatives can occur.

   e. What would happen if the present level of corn production (at Point A) was reduced?

If steel production does not change, unemployment occurs. The unemployed resources can be absorbed by the steel industry and more steel can be produced. A parallel case can be made given cutbacks in steel production. Can you see how the ppf *must* have a negative slope and that it portrays the concept of opportunity cost?

10. Use the diagrams below to answer this question.

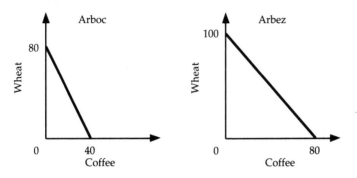

a. What is the opportunity cost of one unit of coffee in Arboc?
b. What is the opportunity cost of one unit of coffee in Arbez?
c. Which country has a comparative advantage in the production of coffee?
d. What is the opportunity cost of one unit of wheat in Arboc?
e. What is the opportunity cost of one unit of wheat in Arbez?
f. Which country has a comparative advantage in the production of wheat?
g. *Ceteris paribus*, ignoring other issues, which good should Arboc produce and which good should Arbez produce?

11. Draw a production possibility curve. Put guns on the vertical axis and butter on the horizontal axis. Suppose that the technology for producing butter improves but the technology for producing guns does not. Describe how your diagram would change. In general, how will this technological advance affect the opportunity cost of producing guns?

12. Jennie has set 10 hours this weekend to study for an Economics test and a Physics test. She believes that, with no studying at all, she would score 40 points on each test. Suppose that for each hour studying Econ. she can raise her Econ. score by 10 points, and that for each hour studying Physics she can raise her Physics score by 5 points.
    a. Draw a production possibility frontier graph and show all the points that are feasible if Jennie has 10 hours to divide between Econ. and Physics. Put "hours of study for Econ." on the vertical axis and "hours of study for Physics" on the horizontal axis.

b. Show Point A, where Jennie studies Econ. for 5 hours and Physics for 5 hours.

c. Show Point B, where Jennie studies Econ. for 0 hours and Physics for 10 hours.

d. True or false? Jennie can score 60 on the Econ. test and 80 on the Physics test.

e. True or false? Jennie is lying when tells us that, in fact, she scored 80 on both tests.

f. Jennie decides to spend 4 hours studying for the Econ. test. What's the highest score she can expect to get on the Physics test?

g. If Jennie was satisfied with 60 on both tests, how many hours would she have had to study?

h. True or false? If Jennie scored 70 on both tests we know that she did not study for the full 10 hours.

i. Draw a line (labeled EE) showing all the points which have exactly 2 hours of study time for the Econ. test.

ANSWERS AND SOLUTIONS

PRACTICE TEST

I. SOLUTIONS TO MULTIPLE CHOICE QUESTIONS

1. B. To be on the ppf, Arboc must have all of its resources fully and efficiently employed. Because it is operating inside the ppf, at least one of these conditions must have been violated.

2. A. If Arboc produces relatively more capital, then it is expanding its resource base more rapidly and, *ceteris paribus*, it will grow more rapidly.

3. C. Financial resources may be used to purchase real productive resources but are not themselves productive. Note that, to an economist, "investment" is the creation of real productive capacity, not merely the purchase of stock in a company.

4. C. To reach Point E the economy must grow, shifting out its ppf. This could occur if the labor force became more efficient.

5. D. This is an increasing-cost ppf. As we increase the production of one good (butter), the cost in terms of the other good increases. In this case, a one-unit increase in butter (A to B) costs 3 guns; the move from B to C costs more (4 guns).

6. A. Opportunity cost is defined (loosely) as the quantity of Good B given up to increase production of Good A. The quantity of butter remains at 1 unit while gun production is increased.

7. B. See the answer to Question 6. Opportunity cost of one unit of butter is zero at Point D. The opportunity cost of one unit of butter at Point C is 5 guns.

8. B. The ppf depicts what it is possible to produce but nothing about what is wanted.

9. D. *Laissez-faire* economies respond well to the needs of private consumers, in general.

10. B. A one-unit increase in wheat results in a three-unit decrease in tobacco production.

11. A. A two-unit increase in tobacco results in a one-unit decrease in wheat.

12. B. This point is inside the ppf. (We could be producing two more units of tobacco with the same amount of wheat production, for example.) This indicates that our resources are unemployed and/or inefficiently employed.

13. A. The labor-force expansion represents an increase in productive resources. Note that the ppf depicts what can be supplied—demand is not reflected in the diagram.

14. B. See p. 26 for a discussion of the three basic questions.

15. A. A general theme in economics is that private competition is highly efficient in providing most goods.

16. C. With scarce resources, the production possibility frontier will *always* have a negative slope. With an increasing-cost ppf, the cost of producing one good in terms of the other accelerates as production level increases.

17. A. Comparative advantage is a relative concept. If, relative to Jack, Jill is better at producing pins, then she has a comparative advantage in this.

18. D. The first three answers are statements of the three "basic" questions. In any case, resources are allocated among producers, not consumers.

19. C. The cost of one unit of goat milk in Arbez is 1 and ⅔ unit of bananas while the cost of one unit of goat milk in Arboc is ⅓ unit of bananas. Arboc has the advantage here. One unit of bananas in Arbez costs ⅗ unit of goat milk while one unit of bananas in Arboc costs 3 units of goat milk. Arbez has the advantage in bananas.

20. A. A bowed-out ppf indicates increasing costs; the costs increase whether the movement is down along the ppf or up along the ppf.

II. SOLUTIONS TO APPLICATION QUESTIONS

1. a. Your ppf should include the following points:

   | Corn | 100 | 90 | 70 | 40 | 0 |
   | Tobacco | 0 | 40 | 70 | 90 | 100 |

   There will be a straight line between each of the points.
   b. Resources fully employed, and employed in the more efficient activity. For example, Field A may be producing its maximum output of tobacco, but (since the opportunity cost of tobacco production in that field is high) it should be used to produce tobacco only after the other fields have been switched over to tobacco production. If it is switched before Field B, for instance, Brown will be producing inefficiently and inside his ppf.
   c. D, C, B, A.
   d. See the explanation for b.

2. a, e. See the following diagrams.

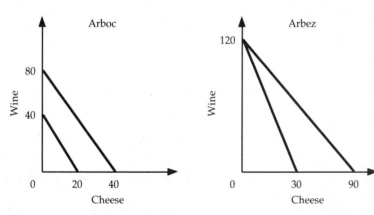

   b. 1 wine = ½ cheese, 1 wine = ¼ cheese.
   c. Arbez.
   d. 1 cheese = 2 wine (Arboc), 1 cheese = 4 wine (Arbez). Arboc can produce cheese more cheaply than Arbez can.
   f. Arboc should still produce cheese since the comparative costs have not changed.
   g. Arboc. Recompute the opportunity costs. Note that the relative steepness of the ppfs has changed.

3. a–b. This question is intended to get you to think about all of the decisions that must be made in an economic system. The owner has land, labor, and capital at his/her disposal. The capital stock includes the store, the gas station, inventories, trucks, the house, and so forth. The road is also capital even though it was produced by the government. We are not told much about the natural resources of the town. These would include the fertility of the land. The potential labor force includes some fraction of those who live nearby.
   c. The people who travel the road, the general economic circumstances of the people who live nearby, the weather, gasoline prices, the potential for competition from other stores, and so forth.
   d. What to sell, whether to advertise, what prices to change, whether to fix up the town, how many people to hire, and so forth.
   e. I will add up all the future income I will earn, net of costs. I must consider all the alternatives and my expectations about them. How much will I earn here? How much

will college cost? What am I likely to earn when I have graduated from college? I also need to consider carefully the personal pleasure I will derive from the two situations.

4. a. See the following diagram.

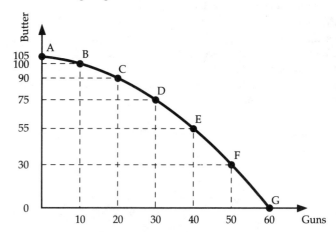

   b. Point D is on the ppf, indicating full employment of resources while Point H is inside the curve, indicating underproduction and an underutilization of scarce resources.
   c. i.   ½ unit of butter.
       ii. 1 unit of butter.
       iii. 2 ½ units of butter.
       iv. 3 units of butter.
   d. i.   ⅓ of a gun.
       ii. ⅔ of a gun.
       iii. 1 gun.
       iv. 2 guns.
   e. The ppf will not shift position! We would expect the balance of production to shift in favor of guns. If unemployment exists, indicated by a bundle of goods inside the ppf, war production will shift the economy towards the ppf.

5. a. No change in the position of the ppf.
   b. The end of the ppf on the x-axis will shift out. The end on the y-axis will not move.
   c. The ppf would shift inwards.
   d. The ppf would shift outwards.
   e. The end of the ppf on the x-axis will shift in. The end on the y-axis will not move.

6. a. You might think C and A are "best" and "worst," respectively—but the question is a trap! What do we mean by "best"? Perhaps a particular point inside the ppf is better than a particular point on it. There's not enough information to give a complete answer.
   b. Clearly, all points on the ppf are not created equal, and Point E might be the "best" choice of those depicted.
   c. The "best" output mix depends on what best meets society's wants. If you think about it, what society *wants* isn't shown on a ppf diagram—only what can be *produced*.

7. a. See the following diagram.

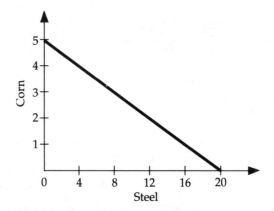

b.

Production	Opportunity Cost of 1 Unit of:	
Alternative	Corn	Steel
A–B	4 steel	¼ corn
B–C	4 steel	¼ corn
C–D	4 steel	¼ corn
D–E	4 steel	¼ corn
E–F	4 steel	¼ corn

c. Situation X: 0 steel; 0 corn.
   Situation Y: 4 steel; ¼ corn.
d. In Situation X there are still some unemployed (inefficiently used) resources. In Situation Y, Arbez is already utilizing all of its resources, and a trade-off is necessary. (Plot the points on the diagram to see the difference.)
e. Situation Z: 1 steel; 0 corn.
f. Situation Y is the most productively efficient. Either X or Z is the least productively efficient—we don't have enough information.
g. Each unit of corn costs 4 units of steel; each unit of steel costs ¼ unit of corn.
h. Each unit of corn costs 2 units of steel. Each unit of steel costs ½ unit of corn.
i. Arbez; Arboc. Yes, trade can be mutually beneficial.

8. a. D.
   b. The economy must either grow (more resources) or experience a technological improvement.
   c. C.
   d. Corn.
   e. There is no opportunity cost; more steel is produced without any reduction in corn production. Note that there are "free lunches" if the economy is operating at an inefficient point.

9. a. Yes.
   b. No, because it is possible to produce more of each good. Also some resources are unemployed.
   c. No, not relative to Point A, where consumers would have more of each good available to them.
   d. It is beyond the maximum level of production, given current resources and technology.
   e. Resources would be released and transferred to steel production.

10. a. 2 units of wheat.
    b. 1¼ units of wheat.
    c. Arbez.
    d. ½ unit of coffee.
    e. ⁸⁄₁₀ unit of coffee.
    f. Arboc.
    g. Arboc should specialize in wheat production and Arboc should specialize in coffee production.

11. The ppf would pivot at its "guns" endpoint and become flatter, which indicates that it is possible to produce a greater maximum quantity of butter than before, while still producing the same maximum quantity of guns. The slope of the ppf represents opportunity cost. Producing only guns means that we surrender a larger quantity of butter than before—the opportunity cost of guns has increased (and the opportunity cost of butter has decreased).

12. a. See the following diagram.

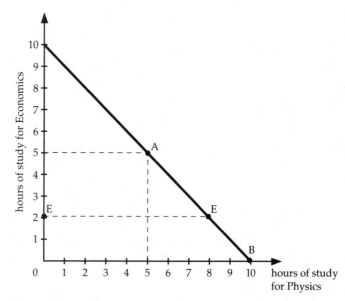

b. See the diagram above.
c. See the diagram above.
d. True. Economics: 40 + (10 × 2) = 60. Physics: 40 + (5 × 8) = 80.
e. True. Economics: 40 + (10 × 2) = 60. Physics: 40 + (5 × 8) = 80. If she gets 80 on the Physics test, 60 is the maximum she can get on the Economics test.
f. She has 6 hours for Physics. Physics: 40 + (5 × 6) = 70.
g. Economics: 40 + (10 × 2) = 60. Physics: 40 + (5 × 4) = 60. This totals 6 hours.
h. True. Economics: 40 + (10 × 3) = 70. Physics: 40 + (5 × 6) = 70. This totals 9 hours.
i. See the diagram above.

THE STRUCTURE OF THE U.S. ECONOMY: THE PRIVATE, PUBLIC, AND INTERNATIONAL SECTORS

OBJECTIVES: POINT BY POINT

After completing this chapter, you should be able to accomplish the objectives listed below.

General Comment

This chapter contains a lot of facts and numbers. Try to look past these to the broader issues. The topics that carry over most powerfully to later chapters are those dealing with the organization of industry—the four different "types"—and the major elements of government spending and tax collections. It will help if you split the chapter into its two main parts (pp. 48–52, pp. 55–61) and read each separately.

OBJECTIVE 1: Outline the private/public sector distinction in the U.S. economy. Indicate the elements each sector contains.

The *private sector* contains all decision-making units not owned by the government. These decision-making units in the private sector include households, nonprofit organizations, and firms. The *public sector* is comprised of federal, state, and local government.

The key private/public sector distinction is that decisions in the private sector are subject to independent choice and that resources are owned privately.   (page 45)

PRACTICE

1. The private sector would include each of the following except
   A. Lockheed-Martin.
   B. Boy Scouts.
   C. NASA.
   D. Nationsbank.
   Answer: C. Although it supplies military hardware to the government, Lockheed-Martin is a private corporation. NASA, on the other hand, is funded and run by the government.

2. The public sector would include each of the following organizations except
   A. the United Way, a charitable organization.
   B. the U.S. Air Force.
   C. the office staff of your local Senator.
   D. the District Court in your county.
   Answer: A. The United Way is a private nonprofit organization.

OBJECTIVE 2: List, and distinguish among, the three different legal categories of profit-making firms.

Sole proprietors have the disadvantage of unlimited liability—their personal assets, outside the firm, might be taken if their company runs up sufficiently high debts. Advantage: The sole proprietor is his or her own boss and free to follow his or her business instincts. Also, s/he keeps all of the profits s/he makes. Usually, *partner-*

ships have the same unlimited liability drawback. Indeed, perhaps it's worse—partners may be held responsible not only for their debts, but also those of their partners! Advantage: greater expertise and financial resources. *Corporations* have the advantage of limited liability because they exist as separate legal entities—XYZ, Inc. can be taken to court. If the firm runs up debts, the owners' maximum liability is the value of their stock investment. After-tax profits may be distributed as dividends or held by the company as retained earnings. A major disadvantage is that the corporation's management structure may become cumbersome. Also, owners of corporations are subject to double taxation. (page 46)

PRACTICE

3. The most common form of business organization is
   A. the proprietorship.
   B. the partnership.
   C. perfect competition.
   D. the corporation.
   Answer: A. Perfect competition is not a form of business organization—it is a market structure. Check the textbook for the distinction. In 1993, 74.5% of firms were proprietorships. See Table 3.1.

4. In terms of total sales, the most important form of business organization is
   A. the proprietorship.
   B. the partnership.
   C. monopoly.
   D. the corporation.
   Answer: D. Monopoly is not a form of business organization—it is a market structure. Check the textbook for the distinction. In 1993, 89.4% of total sales were accounted for by corporations. See Table 3.1.

5. The Cumfy Chair Corporation has a net income of $300,000 in 1999. Of this income, $160,000 is paid in taxes and $40,000 is retained to buy capital. The Cumfy Chair Corporation will pay dividends of
   A. $140,000.
   B. $120,000.
   C. $100,000.
   D. more than $100,000 but less than $140,000.
   Answer: C. Net income—the profits of a corporation—may be split up into corporate income tax payments, dividends, and retained earnings.

OBJECTIVE 3: Identify and distinguish among the four forms of market organization (structure).

Firms are organized along industry lines. Industries, which can be defined broadly or more narrowly, produce similar products. They can be classified as:
   a. perfectly competitive
   b. monopolistically competitive
   c. oligopolistic, or
   d. monopolistic.
In perfect competition, firms sell identical products and each is an insignificant player in the market. As a result no perfectly competitive firm can control the price it receives. However, the monopoly can—it is the industry supplier. The monopolistically competitive firm can, too—to the extent that it sells a differentiated product. The oligopolist can—the firm is a major market player, and its product may be differentiated, too. (page 48)

LEARNING TIP: Bring to mind a clear example of each of the four forms of market organization.

Perfect Competition—the usual example is agricultural products, but the stock market and the large numbers of typists and word processors around your college campus who produce resumes and term papers are good examples, too.

Monopolistic Competition—local radio stations, restaurants, shoe stores, and hairdressers are all "classic" examples of this category.

Oligopoly—the oil industry, the car industry.

Monopoly—the local electric company or water utility. If you don't buy electricity or water from them, you pretty much do without. (Most full-blown monopolies are closely controlled by the government and may be run by the state.) Cable TV is a private-sector example but, again, note that it is supervised by the government. Note, too, the definition of an "industry" (cable TV) is quite narrow.

LEARNING TIP: A "firm" is any unit engaged in production; it doesn't have to be a formal organization with special premises. A street entertainer (who produces "entertainment") is a firm.

LEARNING TIP: Study carefully Figure 3.1, which compares the characteristics of the four types of industry organization—Case and Fair devote *seven* chapters in the microeconomics section of the textbook to the distinctions summarized in this table! The concepts of perfect competition and monopoly frequently crop up in macroeconomics courses, too.

LEARNING TIP: The concept of an industry is a little fuzzy. We can talk about the electronics industry and the entertainment industry in general but we may wish to be more specific. Is there a Michael Jordan "industry," for example? Is there an alcohol "industry," or is it more sensible to split this up into the hard liquor, wine, and beer industries? You might be able to make a case for the view that the "light" beers represent a special market of their own and that nonalcoholic beers are another separate entity. Clearly, the concept of an industry (or market) is flexible.

PRACTICE

6. Each of the following is true for perfect competition except that
   A. there are many firms.
   B. new firms are excluded.
   C. firms market virtually identical products.
   D. individually, firms have no control over the market price.
   Answer: B. In perfect competition there are no *barriers to entry* into the industry, so new firms cannot be excluded.

7. Each of the firms in Industry A sells a slightly differentiated product. A seller wishing to enter this industry would find it easy to do so. This industry is
   A. perfectly competitive.
   B. monopolistically competitive.
   C. oligopolistic.
   D. monopolistic.
   Answer: B. This industry is not a monopoly since there is more than one firm. It is not an oligopoly since entry is easy. It is not perfectly competitive since there is some product differentiation.

8. Each of the following is true for monopoly except that
   A. there is one firm in the industry.
   B. barriers to entry exist that prevent new firms from entering the industry.
   C. only one close substitute exists for the monopolist's product.
   D. the monopolist has some control over the price of his product.
   Answer: C. In a monopoly, there are no close substitutes for the firm's product.

9. Each of the following is a characteristic of an oligopoly except that
   A. there are a few large firms.
   B. firms sell a standardized product.
   C. new entry of firms is difficult but not impossible.
   D. each firm typically behaves "strategically" with respect to other firms.
   Answer: B. In some oligopolistic industries, e.g., oil, the product is standardized, but this is not a requirement.

OBJECTIVE 4: Identify the major types of expenditure for the federal and state/local levels of government.

The government is a major employer of resources and purchaser of goods. The federal government is the largest and most rapidly growing branch of government. National defense and Social Security payments represent over 40% of federal spending while education, public welfare, health and hospitals, and highways are the main expenditure categories for state and local government.   (page 55)

> **LEARNING TIP:** Note the important distinction between government purchases and transfer payments—the former is a payment for goods and services received by the government; the latter is not. A welfare check is given precisely because the recipient is *not* providing a service.

PRACTICE

10. The salary of your local Senator is classified as
    A. a government transfer payment.
    B. a government interest payment.
    C. government spending.
    D. a government subsidy payment.
    Answer: C. Your local Senator's salary (which he or she has earned for work performed) is government spending. A transfer payment is a payment that requires no good or service in return. Your Senator would strongly resent the implication if you answered Option A!

OBJECTIVE 5: Identify the major sources of revenue for the federal and state/local levels of government.

The main sources of federal revenue are social insurance taxes and income taxes— individual income taxes and corporate income taxes. At the state and local levels, sales and property taxes are the main sources of revenue.   (page 59)

PRACTICE

11. The largest single source of federal revenue is
    A. sales taxes.
    B. property taxes.
    C. social insurance taxes.
    D. individual income taxes.
    Answer: D. See Table 3.10 and p. 60.

12. The largest single source of state and local revenue is
    A. sales taxes.
    B. property taxes.
    C. social insurance taxes.
    D. personal income taxes.
    Answer: A. See Table 3.11 and p. 61.

13. In 1991, taxes as a percentage of GDP were _____ in the United States than in Germany, and _____ in the United States than in Japan.
    A. higher, higher.
    B. higher, lower.
    C. lower, higher.
    D. lower, lower.
    Answer: D. See Figure 3.2 on p. 58.

OBJECTIVE 6: Describe and give reasons for the changing expenditure patterns within the federal government budget over the past decade.

The end of the Cold War signaled a decrease in defense spending. The "graying" of the population has resulted in increased expenditures on medical care and social security. In the early 1990s, falling interest rates slowed the rate of increase in interest payments, but persistent deficits have meant that federal government interest payments have risen over the past decade.   (page 57)

OBJECTIVE 7: Outline the trends that have occurred in international trade over the past three decades.

The *international sector* of the U.S. economy is growing in importance. The U.S. exports over 10% of its production and buys a similar amount of imports from foreigners.   (page 61)

PRACTICE

14. By 1996, exports were _____ of GDP and imports were _____ of GDP.
    A. 11.4%, 12.6%.
    B. 11.4%, 21.2%.
    C. 14.3%, 11.4%.
    D. 21.2%, 11.4%.
    Answer: A. See p. 62.

15. In 1996, the most important component of U.S. exports was
    A. industrial supplies and materials.
    B. capital goods (except automotive).
    C. consumer goods (except automotive).
    D. food, feeds, and beverages.
    Answer: B. See p. 62.

PRACTICE TEST

I. MULTIPLE CHOICE QUESTIONS.

Select the option that provides the single best answer.

_____ 1. Which of the following would not be included in the private sector?
A. AT&T.
B. Matthew Mark University, a Baptist seminary.
C. North Virginia State University.
D. The World Wildlife Fund, a nonprofit organization.

_____ 2. The type of business organization with limited liability from debt for its owner(s) is a
A. proprietorship.
B. partnership.
C. corporation.
D. company.

_____ 3. The restaurant industry in Hometown has many small establishments, each with its own "specialties" and atmosphere. This restaurant market is
A. perfectly competitive.
B. monopolistically competitive.
C. a monopoly.
D. an oligopoly.

_____ 4. Statement 1: "After all the corporation's expenses have been paid, the retained earnings are distributed to the stockholders." Statement 2: "Welfare checks are a part of transfer payments." Statement 1 is _____ ; Statement 2 is. _____
A. false, false.
B. true, true.
C. false, true.
D. true, false.

_____ 5. A(n) _____ _____ industry is the most likely industry to have substantial barriers to entry.
A. perfectly competitive.
B. monopolistic.
C. monopolistically competitive.
D. oligopolistic.

_____ 6. Government expenditures are made up of
A. government purchases, transfer payments, and interest payments.
B. government purchases, welfare payments, and national defense.
C. transfer payments, national defense, and social security payments.
D. transfer payments, tax payments, and interest payments.

_____ 7. For firms in perfect competition,
A. output is homogeneous.
B. each firm controls a relatively large portion of the market.
C. each firm is free to select its own price level.
D. advertising is essential to remain competitive.

_____ 8. In perfect competition, each firm
A. advertises aggressively to stay competitive.
B. controls a substantial share of its local market.
C. places importance on customers who have brand loyalty.
D. has to make do with the price arrived at by market forces.

_____ 9. The biggest single category of revenue-earner for the federal government is the
   A. individual income taxes.
   B. corporate income taxes.
   C. sales taxes.
   D. payroll taxes.

_____ 10. Of the following, the best example of an oligopoly is
   A. the U.S. automobile industry.
   B. your local electricity supplier.
   C. the shoe industry.
   D. clothing stores.

_____ 11. As a percentage of GDP, total government expenditures _____ and government employment _____ between 1970 and 1997.
   A. increased, increased.
   B. increased, decreased.
   C. decreased, increased.
   D. decreased, decreased.

_____ 12. Which of the following is not a government transfer payment?
   A. Social Security payments to the elderly.
   B. Unemployment compensation.
   C. Payments to the widow of a war veteran.
   D. Social insurance tax payment by an employee.

II. APPLICATION QUESTIONS.

1. Firms in both oligopolies and monopolistically competitive markets can have differentiated products, more than one seller, and some ability to enter or leave the industry. What, then, is the distinction between them?

2. Suppose that you're the Chair of the President's Council of Economic Advisers. The President is committed to balancing the budget before the next election and asks you how this can be achieved. (Remember, if the President isn't re-elected, you lose your job too!)

   Come up with three distinct policy recommendations. If the President cuts expenditures, where should the cuts fall? Be specific! Who would be hurt by such a proposal? Would it affect particular social or regional groups? Does the political power of a state, such as Texas or California, have any bearing on the political decision process? If taxes are to be raised, which ones? Again, who might be hurt by a specific tax hike? Should producers be taxed, or should consumers? Wage earners or investors? Are there any parts of the budget that are "not negotiable" (veterans' benefits or Medicare, for example)?

3. Give the advantages and disadvantages of organizing a firm as a
   a. proprietorship
   b. partnership
   c. corporation
   d. Give an example of each form of business organization.

4. You are considering setting up a small business. Which factors would you take into account when deciding whether to establish a single proprietorship or a partnership?

5. Think up a simple business enterprise—such as doing yard work, typing term papers, opening a hot dog stand, or selling vitamins—and decide which would be the most appropriate form of legal organization for your firm. Why is this form of organization the best choice? List the drawbacks that might occur. How might you solve the problems? What advantages do the other forms of organization offer, for example? If you have a proprietorship, how would you feel about giving up control/ownership of "your" business to a group of unknown shareholders and about making decisions by committee?

Major point: No single legal organization is always "best"—it depends upon the particular circumstances of the business and the objectives of the owner(s).

6. In a sense, the three levels of government specialize. For the federal government, defense and the postal service are major sources of employment. Why? Because there's a need for a "national" organization. At the state level, education and highways are the main sources of employment. At the local level, fire, police, and sanitation (all "local" issues) are prominent.

   Now do a thought experiment: Try to imagine what would happen if Washington tried to control fire, police, and sanitation, while turning national defense over to local government. Not very efficient! Also, observe that the public sector can *complement* private endeavors through the provision of so-called public goods (roads and education, for example) and through the enforcement of compliance with a legal system designed to protect the rights of private consumers and firms.

7. Make up a list of industries. Now categorize each of the industries you've named into one of the four market organizations (perfect competition, etc.). Do you see a pattern in the list? Most of the examples you've listed will be oligopolistic or monopolistically competitive industries and most will be heavily committed to TV advertising.

   Are all of your classifications unambiguous? How did you arrive at a decision in each case?

   Starting again, come up with your own examples for the "perfect competition" and "monopoly" categories. To get you started, I suggest the stock market, the local farmers' market, and typing services (perfect competition) and a local utility (monopoly).

8. What are the three kinds of legal organization for the firm? List them and give your own example of the sort of firm you'd expect to find in each category.

9. List the four categories of market organization. Into which market structure is entry easiest?

10. Which form of legal organization is most likely for each of the following businesses?
    a. Coca Cola   _____
    b. a medical practice   _____
    c. a legal firm   _____
    d. a plumbing firm   _____
    e. a car manufacturer   _____
    f. a small tobacco grower   _____
    g. a small country store   _____
    h. MTV   _____
    i. a law firm   _____
    j. McDonald's   _____

    In each case, which factors lead you to your answer and what do you think is the main advantage that each firm derives from this form of organization?

ANSWERS AND SOLUTIONS

PRACTICE TEST

I. SOLUTIONS TO MULTIPLE CHOICE QUESTIONS

1. C. A state university is financed by the government.
2. C. Corporations have limited liability. See p. 47. Note that a partnership may have limited liability, but only in some cases.
3. B. The "many firms" condition excludes monopoly and oligopoly. The presence of "differentiation" excludes perfect competition.

4. C. Retained earnings are just that—retained (by the corporation). Welfare checks are payments that do not require a service in return—i.e., transfers.

5. B. To maintain exclusive control, monopolies typically construct high barriers to entry from would-be competitors.

6. A. National defense is an element in government purchases, and welfare payments are included in the more general category of "transfer payments."

7. A. Because there is no product differentiation in perfect competition—output is homogeneous—there is no reason to advertise. Each firm is "small."

8. D. Each firm in perfect competition is a price taker, accepting the price established by market forces. Also see the answer to Question 7.

9. A. Individual income taxes are now the largest component of federal revenues. See Table 3.10.

10. A. Electricity is generated by a monopolist. Shoe production and retail clothing stores are monopolistically competitive. The auto industry has a few "big" firms.

11. B. See Table 3.6.

12. D. This is a tax payment by an individual to the government.

II. SOLUTIONS TO APPLICATION QUESTIONS

1. The distinction is that, in oligopoly, there are a few firms rather than many. Since each is a significant player in the marketplace, the actions of each may significantly influence the well-being of the others. A cut in prices may trigger a response, such as a price war. For examples, think of the airlines or the burger industry. Monopolistically competitive industries, on the other hand, have many firms, each with a quite small portion of the total market. Changes in price or promotion by Company A will have only a slight impact on Company Z.

2. The answer to this question is open to opinion. Most economists would claim that, to cut the deficit, the government must increase taxes or reduce transfer payments and expenditures.

3. a. proprietorship: advantages—the proprietor is his own boss, keeps all the profits, the firm is flexible, possible tax breaks
    disadvantages—munlimited liability, no pool of specialized experience at the top

    b. partnership: advantages—pool of expertise
    disadvantages—unlimited liability, less flexibility, greater need for consultation between partners

    c. corporation: advantages—limited liability, market power, political power
    disadvantages—possible lack of communication and coordination

    d. proprietorship: corner grocery store; partnership—law firm; corporation—Exxon.

4. The most important consideration is likely to be financial—can the business be started without outside help. Additionally, can the business be run effectively with only one individual in control—can a manager be hired?

5-7. The answer to each question is open to opinion.

8. Proprietorship, a family grocery store; partnership, a legal firm; corporation, a manufacturing firm.

9. Perfect competition; monopolistic competition; monopoly; oligopoly. Perfect competition is easiest for a firm to enter.

10. a. corporation.
    b. partnership.
    c. partnership.
    d. proprietorship.
    e. corporation.
    f. proprietorship.
    g. proprietorship.
    h. corporation.
    i. partnership.
    j. corporation.

DEMAND, SUPPLY, AND MARKET EQUILIBRIUM

4

OBJECTIVES: POINT BY POINT

After completing this chapter, you should be able to accomplish the objectives listed below.

General Comment

The single best piece of advice, particularly for this essential chapter, is "practice, practice, practice." A second piece of advice must be "draw, draw, draw." Don't be put off by the graphs—try to develop a solid intuitive feel for demand and supply by talking your way through how the market should behave.

In most of the multiple-choice questions in this chapter, the *first* thing to do is to start to sketch a demand and supply picture. Graphs are an effective and time-saving tool for organizing your analysis.

Get into the habit of asking "What should happen to demand?" and "Will this make supply increase or decrease?". Predict whether price should rise or fall in a given circumstance (common sense should carry you a long way here). Don't try to avoid graphs—they'll make your course a lot easier *and* more rewarding. If you have some initial problems, check the Appendix to Chapter 1 and the "Learning Tips" in this Guide.

OBJECTIVE 1: Define and apply quantity demanded and quantity supplied, and state the law of demand and the law of supply.

Quantity demanded is the amount of a product that a household would buy, in a given period, if it could buy all it wanted at the current price. *Quantity supplied* is the amount of a product that a firm would be willing and able to offer for sale at a particular price during a given time period. The *law of demand* states that there is a negative relationship between the price and the quantity demanded of a product. When the price of McDonald's fries increases, we buy less. The *law of supply* states that there is a positive relationship between the price and the quantity supplied of a product. When McDonald's raises its hourly wage, we want to work more hours there.   (page 70/80)

OBJECTIVE 2: Draw and interpret demand and supply graphs.

A *demand schedule* is a table showing how much of a given product households would be willing and able to buy at different prices in a given time period; a *demand curve* shows this relationship graphically. Demand curves slope downward.   (page 71)

A *supply schedule* is a table listing how much of a product a firm will supply at alternative prices in a given time period; a *supply curve*, shows this relationship graphically. Supply curves slope upward.   (page 81)

> **NOTE:** Demand and supply graphs *always* have price on the vertical axis and quantity (demanded or supplied, as appropriate) on the horizontal axis. It is a bad, though common, mistake to reverse the variables. Learn to draw the

demand and supply graphs quickly! A demand curve slopes down; a supply curve slopes up. Practice to increase your speed. Label each curve as you go. In diagrams where there are several curves, clear, consistent labeling is critical.

PRACTICE

1. At each price shown, estimate how many apples per month you might demand.

PRICE PER APPLE	QUANTITY DEMANDED
60¢	
50¢	
40¢	
30¢	
20¢	
10¢	

You have constructed a demand schedule. Now, in the blank space to the right of the demand schedule, draw vertical (price) and horizontal (quantity) axes. Plot your monthly demand curve for apples. Label the curve D_1.
Answer: This line is unlikely to be smooth like those in the textbook, but it should have a general downward slope—the lower the price, the more you're likely to buy. You should have the horizontal axis labeled "quantity demanded" and the vertical axis labeled "price."

2. In the diagrams below, match each of the numbers with the appropriate term below to produce a correct demand or supply diagram for apples.
   A. Price of apples.
   B. Price of apples.
   C. Quantity of apples supplied.
   D. Quantity of apples demanded.
   E. Demand curve.
   F. Supply curve.

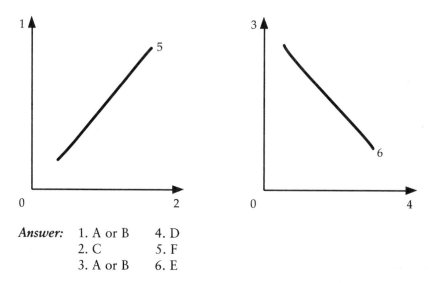

Answer:	1. A or B	4. D
	2. C	5. F
	3. A or B	6. E

OBJECTIVE 3: Identify the determinants of demand and supply and indicate how each must change for demand and supply to increase or decrease.

The willingness and ability of a household to buy units of a good (quantity demanded) are likely to depend principally on the price of the good itself. Other factors—including the household's income and wealth, the prices of other products, tastes and preferences, and expectations about price, income, and wealth—will influence demand.

   Comment: This section of the textbook will probably be your most frustrating section. Be patient—time spent understanding demand/supply analysis will serve you well in future chapters.

> **LEARNING TIP:** When analyzing the impact of change on demand and supply in a market, a golden rule to remember is that each curve will shift no more than once. It is the market price that is changed by shifts in the demand and supply curves, not the demand and supply curves that are changed by shifts in the market price.

A change in price does not cause the demand curve or the supply curve to shift position. Analyze the following sequence of events for errors. "Demand goes up. That makes price go up, which encourages sellers to supply more. But, when more is supplied, price goes down. When price goes down, demand goes up again, and so on."

   Answer: A demand increase from D_1 to D_2 will make price rise from P_1 to P_2. Sellers will supply more from Q_1 to Q_2—an increase in *quantity supplied*, not an increase in supply, as the statement claims. Price, therefore, will *not* go back down. The remainder of the statement is incorrect. Draw this example.

When you constructed your demand schedule and demand curve with varying price levels in Practice Question 1, you made assumptions about your income level, wealth, prices of other goods, and so on. Change the assumptions and you will change the diagram. The curve shifts position—a *change in demand.*

Factors that can cause a change in demand are:
   a.   income
   b.   wealth
   c.   prices of related products
   d.   tastes or preferences of the household
   e.   expectations.   (page 74)

Increases in income and wealth, improved preferences, or expectations of a higher price, income, or wealth will increase demand for normal goods. An increase in the price of a substitute product or a decrease in the price of a complementary product will also increase demand, i.e., the entire demand curve shifts to the right. Graphically, an increase in demand (D_1 to D_2) appears as shown below:

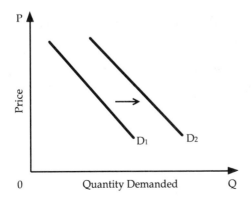

LEARNING TIP: When shifting the demand curve, you might naturally associate "rise" and "fall" with a vertical shift. This causes no problems in the case of demand, and you'd expect to be correct in using the same approach in the case of supply—but you'd be wrong! A vertical shift up in supply is a *decrease* in supply. When shifting the demand or supply curve, think in terms of the curve sliding *left* for a decrease (demand less or supply less) and *right* for an increase (demand more or supply more), *not* up and down.

The decision to supply is affected by the ability to earn profits (that is, the difference between revenues and costs). The willingness and ability of a firm to offer units of a good for sale (quantity supplied) are likely to depend principally on the price of the good itself. If other factors important to producers change, then the supply curve diagram will change. The supply curve shifts position—a *change in supply*.

Factors that can cause a change in supply are:
    a. changes in costs of production (input prices)
    b. new costs and market opportunities
    c. changes in prices of related products.   (page 80)

Improvements in technology, decreases in the costs of inputs and other costs of production, or increases in the price of complementary products will increase supply. Decreases in the price of substitute products will also increase supply, i.e., the entire supply curve will shift to the right. Graphically, an increase in supply (S_1 to S_2) appears as shown below:

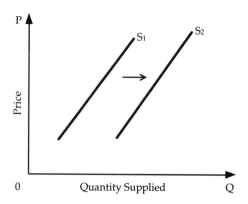

LEARNING TIP: When considering if a given factor will cause supply to increase or decrease, ask "Will this change increase or decrease profits?". Producers will want to supply more if their profits are rising—so, if the answer to the question is "increase profits," you should predict an increase (rightward shift) in supply.

LEARNING TIP: Keep these lists of factors that can change demand or supply in a place very close to your heart! Write them on an index card and review them frequently.

Demand: Do "thought experiments." Pick a good that you buy frequently (preferably a name brand), such as Exxon gasoline. What would you react if Exxon hiked the price of its gas? If your income fell? If the price of engine oil (a complement) increased? If the price of Mobil gas (a substitute) decreased?

Supply: Perhaps you have a part-time job—you supply labor. Which factors affect how many hours you would work per week. The wage (price) you earn affects the quantity of labor you supply. What other factors would make you more or less willing and able to work?

Supply will be analyzed in greater detail in Chapters 7, 8 and 9. Note the reference to the *short run* and the *long run* on page 82. These are important economic concepts that you'll meet later on. Essentially, suppliers will be more responsive to demand-side changes in a longer time period than they will be in a shorter time period.

LEARNING TIP: When you are told to imagine that income or some other variable has changed, imagine an *enormous* change—this will help you work out the effects. If a can of Pepsi has risen in price, suppose that it has tripled in price—it's easier to see what will happen to the quantity demanded or supplied of Pepsi and to the demand for Coke.

PRACTICE

3. A decrease in the supply of American cars might be caused by
    A. an increase in the price of imported Japanese cars.
    B. an increase in the wages of U.S. car workers.
    C. an increase in demand that causes car prices to rise.
    D. a reduction in the cost of steel.
    Answer: B. The supply of American cars will decrease if input prices, such as the wages of U.S. car workers, increase. See p. 80.

4. Energizer and Duracell's Coppertop batteries are substitutes. The Energizer Bunny cuts supply and increases the price of its batteries. Equilibrium price will _____ and quantity exchanged will _____ in the market for Duracell.
    A. rise, rise.
    B. fall, rise.
    C. fall, fall.
    D. rise, fall.
    Answer: A. If Energizer increases the price of its batteries, consumers will switch over to substitutes such as Duracell, increasing the demand for Duracell. This will raise both equilibrium price and quantity. See p. 74.

5. Barney's Bowling Balls and Fred's Bowling Shoes are complements. Fred notices a decrease in the quantity demanded of bowling shoes (a movement along his demand curve). This could have been caused by
   A. a decrease in the income of Fred's customers.
   B. an increase in the price of Fred's Bowling Shoes.
   C. an increase in the price of Barney's Bowling Balls.
   D. an increased expectation that Fred will reduce the price of his bowling balls in the near future.
   Answer: B. This is a change in quantity demanded, not a change in demand! The only thing that can cause a change in quantity demanded is a change in price. See p. 71.

6. As the price of oranges increases, orange growers will
   A. use more expensive methods of growing oranges.
   B. use less expensive methods of growing oranges.
   C. increase the supply of oranges.
   D. decrease the supply of oranges.
   Answer: A. An increase in price results in an increase in quantity supplied. Suppliers are able to produce more because, at the higher price, they can afford to hire more expensive resources. See p. 81.

7. The supply of oranges will shift to the right if
   A. very bad weather afflicts the Florida orange groves.
   B. oranges are rumored to have been treated with an insecticide that causes heart disease.
   C. the Florida government requires that all orange workers are given more substantial health benefits by employers.
   D. citrus growers see the price of grapefruits decreasing permanently.
   Answer: D. As the price of grapefruits falls, citrus farmers will switch over to another production option—oranges. See p. 83.

OBJECTIVE 4: Derive market demand and market supply curves from individual demand and supply schedules.

Market demand is the sum of all the quantities of a good or service demanded per period by all the households buying in the market for that good or service. The *market demand curve* is a summing of all the individual demand curves. At a given price level, the quantity demanded by each household is determined and the total quantity demanded is calculated.   (page 79/84)

The *market supply curve* is a horizontal summing of all the supply curves for a given product.

PRACTICE

8. If the firms producing fuzzy dice for cars must obtain a higher price than they did previously to produce the same level of output as before, then we can say that there has been
   A. an increase in quantity supplied.
   B. an increase in supply.
   C. a decrease in supply.
   D. a decrease in quantity supplied.
   Answer: C. Draw the supply curve. At the same output level and at a higher price, the supply curve has shifted to the left—a decrease in supply. See p. 84.

9. The market supply curve for wheat depends on each of the following except
   A. the price of wheat-producing land.
   B. the price of production alternatives for wheat.
   C. the tastes and preferences of wheat consumers.
   D. the number of wheat farmers in the market.
   Answer: C. Tastes and preferences are determinants of demand, not supply. See p. 80.

OBJECTIVE 5: Differentiate between a shift of a demand curve or supply curve and a movement along a curve, and depict these cases correctly on a graph.

When important factors other than the price of the product change, such as tastes or income, the entire demand curve shifts position. This is called a *change in demand* to distinguish it from a movement along the demand curve, which represents a *change in quantity demanded* and which can be caused *only* by a change in the price of the commodity. (page 76)

Similarly, when important factors other than price change for a producer, the amount of a given product offered for sale will change even if the price level is unchanged. This is a *change in supply*. If *only* the price of the product itself changes, there will be a movement along the original supply curve—a *change in quantity supplied*. (page 83)

> **GRAPHING POINTER: CHANGES IN QUANTITY DEMANDED (SUPPLIED) VS. CHANGES IN DEMAND (SUPPLY).** Most students experience confusion regarding the distinction between a "change in quantity demanded" and a "change in demand." The distinction is rather artificial; the six factors (listed on page 76) that affect demand do include price of the product. However, we regard the price-quantity demanded relationship as the most important and draw the demand curve with these two variables on the axes, assuming that all other factors are fixed at a "given" level. This is the *ceteris paribus* assumption.
>
> Look at a demand curve; price and quantity demanded can have a range of values while all other variables (income, other prices, etc.) are fixed at a particular level. If price changes, we move along the curve; if another factor changes, our *ceteris paribus* assumption is broken and we must redraw the price-quantity demanded relationship.
>
> The *only* thing that can cause a "change in the quantity demanded" of Pepsi is a change in the price of Pepsi—a movement from one point on the demand curve to another point on the same demand curve.
>
> If any other factor on the list changes we will have to redraw the entire diagram—a "change in demand"—because the "all else being equal" assumption has been broken.
>
> Similarly, a "change in the quantity supplied" of chicken can only be caused by a change in the price of chicken. A change in any other factor on the list on page 80 of the text causes a "change in supply."

LEARNING TIP: Here is an example that points up the difference between a "change in quantity demanded" and a "change in demand". In the diagram below, we have a demand curve for Ford Rangers on the left and a demand curve for Dodge Rams on the right.

Initially, the price of the Ranger is $17,000 and 2,000 are demanded per week. The Ram sells for $16,000 and has 2,500 demanders at that price. (Note: It's irrelevant whether the Ram's price is above, below, or equal to that of the Ranger—at any realistic prices, each truck will have some enthusiasts.)

Suppose that the price of Rangers decreases to $15,000. More truck-buyers will order Rangers—an increase in quantity demanded as there is a movement along the demand curve from A to B. Some of those new Ford customers would have bought the Dodge Ram but now will not. At the same price ($16,000) as before, demand for Rams has decreased, perhaps to 2,200. The entire demand curve for Rams has shifted.

PRACTICE

10. Return to Practice Question 1. Suppose that the prices of other fruits you might buy increase. What would happen to the number of apples you demand per month? Sketch this change on your diagram. Label the demand curve D_2. What is likely to happen to the price of apples?
    Answer: See your diagram for Practice Question 1. Presumably you'd demand more apples at each price. The demand curve shifts right, to D_2. Because apples are more popular now, the price of apples will likely rise.

11. A "change in demand" means
    A. the quantity demanded changes as price changes.
    B. a movement along a given demand curve or schedule.
    C. a shift in the position of the demand curve.
    D. a change in the shape of a demand curve.
    Answer: C. A "change in demand" means that, at every price level, more or less is being demanded. This is represented as a shift in the position of the demand curve. See p. 76.

12. Which of the following will cause a decrease in the demand for tennis racquets?
    A. A rise in the price of squash racquets.
    B. A rise in the price of tennis racquets.
    C. A rise in the price of tennis balls.
    D. A fall in the price of tennis shoes.
    Answer: C. A decrease in the demand for tennis racquets will occur if a complement (tennis balls) increases in price because fewer tennis balls will be bought. See p. 75.

OBJECTIVE 6: Provide explanations for the slope of a typical demand curve.

Demand curves slope down—as price rises, quantity demanded falls. We know this intuitively, but economists have explored this important "social law" more analytically. The higher the price of a good, lowfat milk for instance, the higher the opportunity cost of buying it, (i.e., the more of other goods we will give up, and the less willing we will be to buy lowfat milk).

Utility is a conceptual measure of satisfaction. Successive units of a good bestow satisfaction, but typically at a decreasing rate—the second cup of coffee may be less enjoyable than the first. Accordingly, the price we will be willing to pay will decrease. (page 72)

PRACTICE

13. The demand curve has
    A. "price" on the vertical axis, "quantity demanded per time period" on the horizontal axis, and an upward sloping demand curve.
    B. "price" on the horizontal axis, "quantity demanded per time period" on the vertical axis, and an upward sloping demand curve.
    C. "price" on the vertical axis, "quantity demanded per time period" on the horizontal axis, and a downward sloping demand curve.
    D. "price" on the horizontal axis, "quantity demanded per time period" on the vertical axis, and a downward sloping demand curve.
    Answer: C. See p. 71.

14. We are trying to explain the law of demand. When the price of pretzels rises,
    A. the opportunity cost of pretzels increases along the demand curve.
    B. sellers switch production and increase the quantity supplied of pretzels.
    C. income rises for producers of pretzels.
    D. the opportunity cost of other goods increases.
    Answer: A. See p. 72.

OBJECTIVE 7: Distinguish the relationship that exists between two goods that are substitutes and the relationship that exists between two goods that are complements.

If, when the price of Good A rises, the demand for Good B also rises, then A and B are *substitutes*; however, if the demand for B falls when the price of A rises, then A and B are *complements*. (page 74)

LEARNING TIP: Think of several ready-made examples of substitute goods and complementary goods from your own life. Working with your own examples (e.g., during an exam) makes it easier to work through the analysis correctly. Here are a few examples:

Substitutes: Coke and Pepsi, prerecorded audio tapes and CDs.

Complements: peanut butter and jelly, CDs and CD players, cars and gasoline, cameras and film, left and right shoes.

PRACTICE

15. The demand for JIF peanut butter will decrease if there is
    A. an increase in the price of JIF peanut butter.
    B. an increase in the price of Peter Pan peanut butter.
    C. a decrease in the demand for jelly.
    D. an increase in the price of bread.
    Answer: D. Bread and peanut butter are complements. An increase in the price of bread will result in less bread being bought and a lower demand for JIF to spread on it. See p. 75.

16. Good A and Good B are substitutes for one another. An increase in the price of A will
    A. increase the demand for B.
    B. reduce the quantity demanded of B.
    C. increase the quantity demanded of B.
    D. reduce the demand for B.
    Answer: A. Suppose A is Coke and B is Pepsi. If Coke rises in price, we would buy less Coke (a fall in quantity demanded of Coke) and more of Pepsi (an increase in the demand for Pepsi). See p. 75.

OBJECTIVE 8: Distinguish between a good that is normal and a good that is inferior.

When income increases, demand increases for *normal* goods. If demand for a good decreases when income increases, then the good is *inferior*.   (page 74)

> **LEARNING TIP:** Think of several ready-made examples of both normal goods and inferior goods from your own life. Working with your own examples (during an exam, for instance) makes it easier to work through the analysis correctly. Here are a few examples:
>
> **Normal goods:** movie tickets, steak, and more expensive imported beers.
>
> **Inferior goods:** second-hand clothes, store-brand (versus name-brand) foods, generic medicines, rice, beans, bus rides.

PRACTICE

17. If the economy's income rises by 10 percent then, *ceteris paribus*, we would predict
    A. a decrease in demand for a normal good.
    B. an increase in quantity demanded for a normal good.
    C. an increase in quantity demanded for an inferior good.
    D. a decrease in demand for an inferior good.
    Answer: D. See p. 74. Remember than a change in "quantity demanded" can only be due to a change in the price of the good.

18. The demand for Good A has been increasing over the past year. Having examined the following facts, you conclude that Good A is an inferior good. Which fact led you to that conclusion?
    A. The price of Good A has been increasing over the past year.
    B. An economic slowdown has reduced the income of the traditional buyers of Good A.
    C. Good B, a substitute for Good A, has cut its price over the last twelve months.
    D. Household wealth has increased among the traditional buyers of Good A.
    Answer: B. Inferior goods experience increasing popularity as income levels fall. See p. 74.

19. Turnips are available in both the United States and in Mexico. During the past year, incomes have grown by 10% in each country. The demand for turnips has grown by 12% in the United States and grown by 3% in Mexico. We can conclude that turnips are
    A. normal goods in the United States and normal goods in Mexico.
    B. normal goods in the United States and inferior goods in Mexico.
    C. inferior goods in the United States and normal goods in Mexico.
    D. inferior goods in the United States and inferior goods in Mexico.
    Answer: A. In each case, demand has increased as income has increased. See p. 74.

OBJECTIVE 9: Determine equilibrium price and quantity and detail the process by which the market moves from one equilibrium situation to another when demand or supply shifts.

In the market for a particular good or service, quantity demanded may be greater than, less than, or equal to quantity supplied. *Equilibrium* occurs when quantity demanded equals quantity supplied. There is no tendency for the price to change because, at that price, there is a perfect match between the quantity of the good demanded and the quantity supplied. (page 85)

LEARNING TIP: Equilibrium. The notion of equilibrium is important throughout the remainder of the course. The simple, less analytical, way to think about this concept is as "the point where the lines cross." It will help your understanding if you remember that equilibrium is the "balance" situation in which there is no tendency for change—unless some outside factor intervenes.

LEARNING TIP: Changes in Equilibrium Price and Quantity. Demand and supply may change position simultaneously. If the magnitudes of the shifts are unknown, then either the effect on equilibrium price or on equilibrium quantity *must* be uncertain. It's easy to forget this important fact. If demand and supply change position simultaneously, break down the situation into two separate graphs, one for the "demand shift" and the other for the "supply shift." In each case, decide the direction of change in price and quantity, and then add them together.

Example: Demand decreases and supply increases.

	PRICE CHANGE	QUANTITY CHANGE
Demand-side effect	decrease	decrease
Supply-side effect	decrease	increase
Total effect	decrease	uncertain

In this case, where demand decreases and supply increases, we predict a certain decrease in price and an uncertain change in equilibrium quantity.

Note: A change in price does not cause the demand curve or the supply curve to shift position. Analyze the following sequence of events for errors. "Demand goes up. That makes price go up, which encourages sellers to supply more. But, when more is supplied, price goes down. When price goes down, demand goes up again, and so on."

Answer: A demand increase from D_1 to D_2 will make price rise from P_1 to P_2. Sellers will supply more from Q_1 to Q_2—an increase in *quantity supplied*, not an increase in supply, as the statement claims. Price, therefore, will *not* go back down. The remainder of the statement is incorrect. Draw this example.

PRACTICE

20. Equilibrium quantity will certainly decrease if
    A. demand and supply both increase.
    B. demand and supply both decrease.
    C. demand decreases and supply increases.
    D. demand increases and supply decreases.
    Answer: B. A decrease in demand will decrease equilibrium quantity. Similarly, a decrease in supply will decrease equilibrium quantity.

21. The market for canned dog food is in equilibrium when
    A. the quantity demanded is less than the quantity supplied.
    B. the demand curve is downsloping and the supply curve is upsloping.
    C. the quantity demanded and the quantity supplied are equal.
    D. all inputs producing canned dog food are employed.
    Answer: C. A market is in equilibrium when price has adjusted to make the quantity demanded and the quantity supplied equal. See p. 86.

22. In the market for broccoli, the price of broccoli will certainly increase if
    A. the supply of broccoli increases and the demand for broccoli increases.
    B. the supply of broccoli increases and the demand for broccoli decreases.
    C. the supply of broccoli decreases and the demand for broccoli increases.
    D. the supply of broccoli decreases and the demand for broccoli decreases.
    Answer: C. An increase in demand will increase equilibrium price. Similarly, a decrease in supply will increase equilibrium price.

23. In the market for mushrooms, the price of mushrooms will certainly increase if
    A. the supply curve shifts right and the demand curve shifts right.
    B. the supply curve shifts right and the demand curve shifts left.
    C. the supply curve shifts left and the demand curve shifts right.
    D. the supply curve shifts left and the demand curve shifts left.
    Answer: C. When demand increases and supply decreases, both shifts are prompting a price increase.

24. In the market for broccoli, the equilibrium quantity of broccoli will certainly increase if the supply of broccoli _____ and the demand for broccoli _____
    A. increases, increases.
    B. increases, decreases.
    C. decreases, increases.
    D. decreases, decreases.
    Answer: A. An increase in supply will increase the quantity traded; similarly, an increase in demand will increase the quantity traded.

OBJECTIVE 10: Define excess demand (shortage) and excess supply (surplus) and predict their effects on the existing price level.

If the quantity demanded is greater than the quantity supplied of a good, there is *excess demand* (shortage), and we would expect the price of that good to rise. If quantity supplied is greater than the quantity demanded of a good, there is an *excess supply* (surplus), and we would expect the price of that good to fall.   (page 86/87)

PRACTICE

25. When there is a surplus, quantity supplied _____ quantity demanded. Price will _____
    A. exceeds, rise.
    B. is less than, fall.
    C. is less than, rise.
    D. exceeds, fall.
    Answer: D. A surplus (excess supply) occurs when quantity supplied exceeds quantity demanded. This surplus will force price down. See p. 87.

26. The equilibrium price of a gallon of unleaded gas is $1.10. At a price of 84¢
    A. quantity supplied will be less than quantity demanded, causing a shortage of unleaded gas.
    B. quantity supplied will be greater than quantity demanded, causing a surplus of unleaded gas.
    C. quantity supplied will be greater than quantity demanded, causing a shortage of unleaded gas.
    D. quantity supplied will be less than quantity demanded, causing a surplus of unleaded gas.
    Answer: A. If the current price is less than the equilibrium price, a shortage will occur (quantity supplied will be less than quantity demanded). This shortage will force price to increase.

OBJECTIVE 11: Understand the role of the *ceteris paribus* and time held constant assumptions in demand and supply analysis.

When dealing with changes in demand and/or supply determinants, it is crucial to treat each change in isolation—that is, to assume that no other change has occurred. It is also crucial to conduct supply and demand analysis in a given time period.

(page 77)

PRACTICE TEST

I. MULTIPLE CHOICE QUESTIONS.

Select the option that provides the single best answer.

_____ 1. Households are
    A. suppliers in the input market.
    B. demanders in the labor market.
    C. suppliers in the product market.
    D. demanders in the input market.

_____ 2. Good C increases its price. The demand for Good D increases. The goods are
    A. complements.
    B. substitutes.
    C. normal.
    D. inferior.

3. The demand for prerecorded tapes is downsloping. Suddenly the price of tapes rises from $8 to $10. This will cause
   A. demand to shift to the left.
   B. demand to shift to the right.
   C. quantity demanded to increase.
   D. quantity demanded to decrease.

4. All of the following will shift the supply curve of frisbees to the right except
   A. an increase in price of frisbees.
   B. an improvement in the production processes used to manufacture frisbees.
   C. a reduction in the price of plastic from which frisbees are made.
   D. an improvement in storage resulting in fewer defective frisbees.

5. Along a given supply curve for eggs,
   A. supply increases as price increases.
   B. supply increases as technology improves.
   C. quantity supplied increases as price increases.
   D. quantity supplied increases as technology improves.

6. Price is currently below equilibrium. There is a situation of excess _____ . We would expect price to _____
   A. demand, rise.
   B. demand, fall.
   C. supply, rise.
   D. supply, fall.

7. You expect your income to rise. For a normal good, this would result in
   A. an increase in quantity demanded and a fall in price.
   B. an increase in demand and a fall in price.
   C. an increase in quantity demanded and a rise in price.
   D. an increase in demand and a rise in price.

8. The price of frisbees (a normal good) will definitely increase if
   A. there is an improvement in the technology of making frisbees and frisbees become more popular.
   B. the cost of plastic used to produce frisbees increases and people have more leisure time to throw frisbees.
   C. frisbee workers negotiate a wage increase and boomerangs (a frisbee-substitute) decrease in price.
   D. a sales tax is imposed on frisbees and (because of widespread unemployment) incomes fall.

9. A rightward shift in the supply of U.S. cars might be due to
   A. an increase in the price of steel.
   B. a reduction in foreign competition.
   C. the introduction of cost-saving robots.
   D. increased popularity of foreign cars.

10. If the market is initially in equilibrium, a technological improvement will cause price to _____ and quantity demanded to _____
    A. fall, fall.
    B. rise, rise.
    C. fall, rise.
    D. rise, fall.

_____ 11. The price of beans rises sharply. Which of the following cannot be true?
   A. The supply of beans may have decreased with no change in the demand for beans.
   B. The demand for beans may have increased with no change in the supply of beans.
   C. The demand for beans may have increased with an increase in the quantity supplied of beans.
   D. The supply of beans may have increased with an increase in the quantity demanded of beans.

_____ 12. The market for peas is experiencing a surplus. You should predict that
   A. price will increase, quantity demanded will fall, and the quantity supplied will rise.
   B. price will increase, quantity demanded will rise, and the quantity supplied will fall.
   C. price will decrease, quantity demanded will rise, and the quantity supplied will fall.
   D. price will decrease, quantity demanded will fall, and the quantity supplied will rise.

_____ 13. Today, you change your expectations about your future income. In fact, you now believe that your future income will be significantly higher than you had previously expected. For a normal good, this would result in an increase in
   A. quantity demanded today.
   B. demand today.
   C. quantity demanded but only in the future.
   D. demand but only in the future.

_____ 14. If less demanded of a product at each possible price, then there has been
   A. a decrease in the quantity demanded.
   B. a decrease in demand.
   C. an increase in demand.
   D. an increase in the quantity demanded.

_____ 15. Chuck's Chips and Debi's Dip are complements. Costs of chip production fall. At the same time a government health report alleges that dip consumption causes bone cancer. For Debi's Dip, the equilibrium price will _____ and the equilibrium quantity will
_____
   A. fall, be indeterminate.
   B. be indeterminate, rise.
   C. be indeterminate, fall.
   D. be indeterminate, be indeterminate.

_____ 16. The market for legal secretaries is in equilibrium. Now there is a simultaneous increase in the demand for legal secretaries and a decrease in the supply of legal secretaries. If there is no change in the wage paid to legal secretaries
   A. there will be a shortage legal secretaries.
   B. there will be a surplus of legal secretaries.
   C. law firms will have no difficulty in hiring the desired number of legal secretaries at the current wage.
   D. the supply of legal secretaries will decrease even more.

Use the diagram below to answer the next six questions. The diagram refers to the demand for and supply of hot dogs. The hot dog market is initially in equilibrium at Point A. Assume that hot dogs are a normal good.

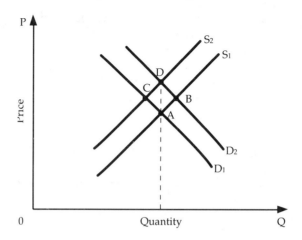

_____ 17. The hot dog market moves from Point A to a new equilibrium at Point B. There has been
   A. an increase in demand and an increase in supply.
   B. an increase in demand and an increase in quantity supplied.
   C. an increase in quantity demanded and an increase in quantity supplied.
   D. an increase in quantity demanded and an increase in supply.

_____ 18. The movement from Point A to Point B might have been caused by
   A. an increase in the price of hamburgers (a substitute for hot dogs).
   B. an increase in the price of fries (a complement for hot dogs).
   C. a new widespread belief that meat products are bad for the heart.
   D. a decrease in the price of ketchup (an ingredient used in making hot dogs).

_____ 19. The hot dog market moves from Point A to a new equilibrium at Point C. There has been
   A. a decrease in demand and a decrease in supply.
   B. a decrease in demand and a decrease in quantity supplied.
   C. a decrease in quantity demanded and a decrease in quantity supplied.
   D. a decrease in quantity demanded and a decrease in supply.

_____ 20. The movement from Point A to Point C might have been caused by a
   A. decrease in the price of hamburgers (a substitute for hot dogs).
   B. tightening of sanitary regulations required for the preparation of hot dogs.
   C. decrease in the wages of workers in the hot dog industry.
   D. decrease in the price of hot dog buns.

_____ 21. The hot dog market moves from Point A to a new equilibrium at Point D. There has been
   A. an increase in demand and an increase in supply.
   B. an increase in demand and a decrease in supply.
   C. a decrease in demand and an increase in supply.
   D. a decrease in demand and a decrease in supply.

_____ 22. The movement from Point A to Point D might have been caused by
   A. an increase in the price of hot dogs and no change in the equilibrium quantity of hot dogs.
   B. an expected increase in the income of hot dog consumers and a hike in the wages of hot dog preparers.
   C. an expected decrease in the price of hot dogs and an increase in the cost of making hot dogs.
   D. a decrease in the income of hot dog consumers and a reduction in the cost of making hot dogs.

_____ 23. Generic aspirin is an inferior good. As Jorge's income decreases we would expect
   A. a decrease in Jorge's demand for generic aspirin.
   B. an increase in Jorge's quantity demanded of generic aspirin.
   C. an increase in Jorge's demand for generic aspirin.
   D. a decrease in Jorge's quantity demanded of generic aspirin.

_____ 24. The supply of computer software packages increases. As a result, the demand for personal computers rises. These two goods are _____ . The price of microchips, used to produce personal computers, will _____
   A. substitutes, increase.
   B. substitutes, decrease.
   C. complements, increase.
   D. complements, decrease.

_____ 25. Along a given demand curve for corn, which of the following is not held constant?
   A. The price of corn.
   B. The income of corn farmers.
   C. The income of corn demanders.
   D. The price of wheat.

_____ 26. The law of demand is best illustrated by
   A. the price of Pepsi rising, leading consumers buy more Coke.
   B. increased purchases of Coke as the price of Coke decreases.
   C. an increase in income which results in reduced purchases of store-brand soft drinks.
   D. an increase in income which results in increased purchases of Coke.

Use the table below to answer the next three questions. The table refers to the demand for and supply of tuna.

Price of tuna	Quantity demanded	Quantity supplied
90¢	30	880
80¢	45	70
70¢	60	60
60¢	75	50
50¢	90	40
40¢	105	30

_____ 27. The equilibrium price is _____ and the equilibrium quantity is _____
A. 70¢, 60.
B. 60¢, 75.
C. 60¢, 50.
D. 70¢, 70.

_____ 28. There would be an excess demand for tuna if the price were at
A. 90¢.
B. 80¢.
C. 70¢.
D. 60¢.

_____ 29. If the price were 80¢, there would be
A. an excess demand of 70.
B. an excess demand of 25.
C. an excess supply of 25.
D. an excess supply of 70.

_____ 30. New costly regulations to protect workers are introduced in the production of tuna. We would expect the equilibrium price of tuna to _____ and the equilibrium quantity of tuna to _____
A. increase, increase.
B. increase, decrease.
C. decrease, increase.
D. decrease, decrease.

II. APPLICATION QUESTIONS.

1. Consider the following information regarding the quantity of corn demanded and supplied per month at a number of prices.

Price per bushel	Quantity demanded	Quantity supplied
40¢	39,000	83,000
35¢	48,000	78,000
30¢	58,000	74,000
25¢	67,000	67,000
20¢	75,000	62,000
15¢	81,000	59,000

a. What is the equilibrium price? What is the equilibrium quantity?
b. Describe the situation when the price is at 40¢ per bushel and predict what will happen.
c. Describe the situation when the price is at 15¢ per bushel and predict what will happen.
d. Explain what would happen if a serious transport strike reduced corn output (at each price) by 30,000 bushels.

2. DoughCrust Bread is a normal good produced by the DoughCrust Bakery. What will happen to the equilibrium price and quantity of DoughCrust Bread in each of the following situations?
    a. Due to a recession, households which buy DoughCrust experience a decrease in income.
    b. The cost of wheat used in DoughCrust increases significantly.
    c. DoughCrust buys improved ovens that reduce the costs of DoughCrust bread.
    d. Luvly Loaf, a rival, cuts the price of its bread.
    e. Consumers become health-conscious and switch to low-calorie breads.

3. How will each of the following changes affect the supply of hamburgers?
    a. There is an increase in the price of hamburger buns (used in the production of burgers).
    b. There is an increase in the price of hamburgers.
    c. Producers discover that the price of cheeseburgers is increasing.

4. Pietro Cavalini sells ice cream at the beach. He is in competition with numerous other vendors. How will each of the following changes affect the demand for Pietro's ice cream?
    a. Hot dog vendors reduce the price of hot dogs. Hot dogs are consumption substitutes for ice cream.
    b. The cost of refrigeration decreases.
    c. Fine weather attracts record crowds to the beach.

5. The market for videocassettes has supply and demand curves given by $Qs = 3P$ and $Qd = 60 - 2P$, respectively. Videocassettes are a normal good.
    a. Complete the following table.

Price	Quantity Demanded	Quantity Supplied
$30	_____	_____
$25	_____	_____
$20	_____	_____
$15	_____	_____
$10	_____	_____
$ 5	_____	_____
$ 0	_____	_____

   b. Calculate the equilibrium price and quantity. You can do this either by graphing the curves or algebraically.
   c. Suppose that the current market price is $20. Calculate the number of units that will be traded.
   d. Suppose that the demand equation changed to $Qd = 80 - 2P$. Is this an increase or a decrease in demand? Suggest what might have caused such a change.
   e. Calculate the new equilibrium price and quantity.

6. Here is a demand and supply schedule for bread in East Yeastville, Colorado.

PRICE ($)	QUANTITY DEMANDED	QUANITY SUPPLIED
5.00	1,000	6,000
4.50	1,300	4,500
4.00	1,600	4,000
3.50	2,000	3,500
3.00	3,000	3,000
2.50	3,200	2,700
2.00	4,000	2,200
1.50	4,500	1,800
1.00	5,400	1,400
.50	7,000	1,200

a. Find equilibrium price and equilibrium quantity.
b. Graph the demand (D_1) and supply (S_1) schedules in the space below and confirm the equilibrium values.

c. At a price of $1, is there an excess demand or supply? How great is the excess? Suppose supply increases by 1,800 units at each price level.
d. Draw the new supply curve (S_2) on the graph in b. above.
e. At the original equilibrium price level, is there an excess demand or an excess supply?
f. What will now happen to price, quantity demanded and quantity supplied?

7. The diagram below shows the labor market. D is the demand for labor and S is the supply. The minimum wage is $4.55 and unemployment is 150 workers.

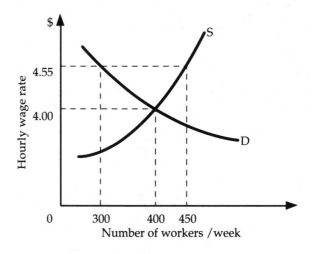

If the minimum wage law was revoked, the wage would fall to an equilibrium level of $4.00, and there would be no unemployment because quantity demanded would be equal to quantity supplied. However, the number of workers demanded would rise by only 100, not 150. Reconcile this apparent contradiction.

8. Here are the demand schedules for orange juice for 3 buyers in the orange juice market and the supply schedules for 3 sellers in the orange juice market.

Price/ gallon	Quantity demanded by:			Quantity supplied by:		
	Brown	Black	White	Gray	Green	Scarlett
$5	1	0	0	5	10	14
$4	3	2	0	4	7	9
$3	7	5	4	3	6	7
$2	9	9	5	0	4	5
$1	11	12	7	0	0	1

a. Graph market demand (D1) and market supply (S1).

b. Show equilibrium price (P*) and quantity (Q*).
c. Now suppose the farm workers who pick oranges are given a higher wage rate. Show on your graph the changes that will occur in the orange juice market. Label any new demand curve D_2 and supply curve S_2. Discuss why curves shift, why price changes, and the significance of any shortage or surplus. Note that you don't have the data to draw precise curves.
d. Suppose now that, in addition to the orange pickers' higher wage rate, All-Cola, a substitute for orange juice, reduces its price. Sketch in the new demand curve for orange juice (D_3), and explain the reason why you moved the curve as you did.

9. a. Draw a demand and supply graph for milk, and establish the equilibrium price (P*).

   b. There is an increase in demand for milk (from D_1 to D_2). How will this change affect the equilibrium price?
   c. In terms of the diagram you just sketched, what is the only way that the equilibrium price can increase, if the supply curve doesn't shift?
   d. Draw in the new demand curve. Now trace through the process by which a new equilibrium is established.

   On one diagram you can display the distinction between a change in demand and a change in quantity demanded.

10. Mooville is a small town in Texas. Assume that beef is a normal good. What happens to the amount of beef demanded or supplied in each of the following cases? Draw a separate demand and supply graph for each part of this question, label the axes, and show how the change will shift the demand and/or the supply curve. Explain any curve shifts in each case. Show initial and final equilibrium price (P* and P**) and initial and final equilibrium quantity (Q* and Q**) for beef.

   a. A subsidy that reduces production costs for beef producers.

   b. A reduced supply of fish (consumers view beef and fish as substitutes).

c. A rise in the wage in the beef industry.

d. A rise in income.

e. An improvement in the productivity of producing beef.

f. A bad tomato crop (beef and ketchup are complements and tomatoes are used to produce ketchup).

11. Think of some commodity that you like. Try to avoid "lumpy" things, like cars or houses, and pick something like coffee, movies, CDs, or long-distance phone calls.
   a. Roughly sketch your demand curve for this good. Does it intersect the price axis? Where? How much of this commodity would you buy at a zero price?

   b. Are there substitutes for this commodity? How does the availability of substitutes affect the shape of your curve?
   c. How would your demand curve change in response to an increase in the price of a substitute?
   d. How would your demand curve change if you won the lottery and were to receive $2,000 per week for life?

12. Assume that the Boston Red Sox baseball team charges $5 per ticket for all seats at all regular season games. Assume also that the capacity of their stadium, Fenway Park, is 35,000. In August, the Red Sox played games against the New York Yankees (a great rival) and the Cleveland Indians (a team in last place) on consecutive Sundays. All tickets to the Yankees game were sold out a month in advance, and many people who wanted tickets could not get them. At the Cleveland game, there were many vacant seats.
    a. Draw an imaginary demand and supply graph for the Yankees' game and another for the Indians' game.
    b. Is there a pricing strategy that would fill the stadium for the Cleveland game? Would such a policy bring the Red Sox higher, or lower, revenue?

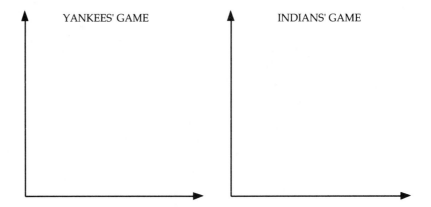

13. During the 1980s, home prices in the northeastern United States doubled. The result was a significant increase in new home construction and a large increase in the demand for labor in the region. At the same time, though, high home prices caused a drop in the supply of labor as people found it too expensive to live in the region. Draw a diagram of the labor market and discuss the impact of these events on wages and thus on the costs of doing business in the Northeast.

14. In London, cabbies must be able to demonstrate a knowledge of at least 400 streets in order to obtain a license. This is quite difficult, so the number of cabbies is rather limited.
    a. Draw a demand and supply diagram for taxi service in London. How has this diagram been affected by the presence of the test?

    b. How has the presence of the test affected usage of other forms of public transport—for example, the red double-decker buses and the "tube" (subway)? How have these prices responded?
    c. If the effect of restricting the numbers of cabbies is to reduce the number of customers, why might cabdrivers favor the restriction?

15. Indicate in each case whether demand for steak (a normal good) will increase (I), decrease (D), or remain unchanged (U) in the following cases.
    a. _____ Pork, a substitute for steak, decreases in price.
    b. _____ High levels of unemployment sweep the nation.
    c. _____ The price of steak falls.
    d. _____ The price of steak sauce increases dramatically.
    e. _____ A government report establishes a conclusive link between the consumption of steak and cancer.
    f. _____ New refrigeration techniques reduce spoilage of steaks before they reach the market.
    g. _____ It is expected that the price of steak will skyrocket within two months.

16. Indicate in each case whether the supply of beer will increase (I), decrease (D), or remain unchanged (U) in the following cases.
    a. _____ Wine coolers become more popular with consumers.
    b. _____ Beer decreases in price.
    c. _____ States impose a new tax on beer producers.
    d. _____ Beer workers' wages increase.
    e. _____ The price of hops, an important ingredient in brewing, decreases.
    f. Costs of transportation decrease.
    g. _____ Improved technology results in less waste of beer.
    h. _____ The economy enters a downturn and many beer-drinkers become unemployed.
    i. _____ Fuel costs rise at the brewery.

17. Indicate in each case whether the market price and quantity of popcorn will increase (I), decrease (D), or be uncertain (U) in the following cases. Assume that popcorn and lemonade are normal goods.

    Price   *Quantity*

    a. _____ _____ The price of lemonade, a complement of popcorn, rises while the harvest of popping corn is unusually poor this year.

    b. _____ _____ Consumers' income falls; low-cost migrant workers cause the cost of popping corn to decline.

    c. _____ _____ Oil, used in popcorn production, falls in price; consumers expect an imminent rise in the price of popcorn.

    d. _____ _____ Eating popcorn is shown to be healthy; new hybrid corn is less expensive to produce and provides higher yields.

18. Kornville is a small town in rural Virginia. Work out what will happen to the amount of corn supplied in each of the following cases and explain your answer.

    Result A = increase in the supply of corn.
    Result B = decrease in the supply of corn.
    Result C = increase in the quantity supplied of corn.
    Result D = decrease in the quantity supplied of corn.

    a. _____ A new government tax is imposed on corn.

    b. _____ Landlords raise the rent on land used for growing corn.

    c. _____ A new spray, effective in controlling insects harmful to corn plants, is made available.

    d. _____ The local senator campaigns effectively for an increase in the price of corn, which can be grown in Kornville.

    e. _____ The local senator campaigns effectively for a rise in the price of tobacco.

    f. _____ Many corn-growing farmers suffer bankruptcy.

    g. _____ The cost of diesel fuel, used in farm machinery, falls.

    h. _____ Red McPinkie unionizes agricultural workers and raises their wages.

    i. _____ Tougher laws stop foreign workers from working at harvest time.

    j. _____ Cornflakes (which are made from corn) become much more popular. (Careful!)

III. ECONOMICS EXPLORER.

Use the first module ("Market Analysis") from the Economics Explorer software to shift demand and supply curves and to explore concepts such as equilibrium through real-world applications. This module also prepares you for the material coming in Chapter 5, including elasticity and total revenue.

ANSWERS AND SOLUTIONS

PRACTICE TEST

I. SOLUTIONS TO MULTIPLE CHOICE QUESTIONS

1. A. In the input market, firms demand inputs and household supply inputs.

2. B. To check your answer, put in a pair of substitutes, such as Pepsi and Coke. If Pepsi increases in price, we will buy less Pepsi and the demand for Coke will increase.

3. D. A change in price leads to a movement along the demand curve. This is a "change in quantity demanded." An increase in price causes a decrease in quantity demanded.

4. A. A change in price leads to a movement along the supply curve. See p. 81.

5. C. A movement along a supply curve (a change in quantity supplied) can only be caused by a change in the price of the good itself. See p. 81.

6. A. Draw the demand and supply diagram. In equilibrium, quantity demanded equals quantity supplied. At lower prices, quantity demanded exceeds quantity supplied.

7. D. For a normal good, higher income will stimulate additional demand. Higher demand will cause the equilibrium price to rise. See p. 74.

8. B. If the cost of plastic increases, supply will decrease. If buyers have more leisure time, demand for leisure goods (like frisbees) will increase. A decrease in supply, coupled with an increase in demand, will push up the price.

9. C. A rightward shift—an increase in supply—will occur if costs are reduced.

10. C. A technological improvement will increase supply. This will drive down the equilibrium price. As the price decreases, quantity demanded will increase.

11. D. If the price of beans rises, then it cannot have been caused by an increase in the supply of beans.

12. C. A surplus means that quantity supplied is greater than the quantity demanded. To reduce the surplus, sellers will accept lower prices. As price falls, quantity demanded will increase and quantity supplied will decrease.

13. B. For a normal good, expected higher income will increase demand now and in the future.

14. B. Try drawing this. At each price level the demand curve will be further to the left.

15. D. Chip supply increases because costs have fallen. This will increase chip (and dip) demand. The health report will reduce demand for dip. Because we don't know which has the stronger effect on the demand for dip, the change in both equilibrium price and quantity is indeterminate.

16. A. Higher demand and less supply will lead to a shortage if the wage level doesn't increase.

17. B. The demand curve has shifted right from D_1 to D_2. As the price increased, quantity supplied increased.

18. A. There has been an increase in demand. This could have been due to an increase in the price of hamburgers because consumers would wish to buy fewer hamburgers and would switch over to demanding hot dogs.

19. D. The supply curve has shifted left, from S_1 to S_2. As the price increased, quantity demanded decreased.

20. B. There has been a decrease in supply. This could have been due to a tightening of the sanitary regulations required for the preparation of hot dogs (which would have increased costs and/or reduced the number of sellers).

21. B. The demand curve has shifted right, from D_1 to D_2, and the supply curve has shifted left, from S_1 to S_2.

22. B. An expected increase in the income of hot dog consumers will increase demand for a normal good, and a hike in the wages of hot dog preparers will increase costs and reduce supply. Option A is incorrect—it describes the effect rather than the cause.

23. C. As income changes, it changes the *demand* for a good. A decrease in income results in a decrease in the demand for a normal good. A decrease in income results in an increase in the demand for an inferior good. See p. 74.

24. C. If the supply of software increases, the price will fall. As one might expect, software and computers are complements—the evidence in the question bears this out. As the quantity of computers traded increases, the demand for microchips will increase, which pushes up their price. See p. 75.

25. A. A movement along a demand curve is a change in quantity demanded. The only factor that can cause such a change is a change in the price of the good. See p. 71.

26. B. The law of demand relates the relationship between the price of a good and the quantity demanded. See p. 71.

27. A. Equilibrium occurs where quantity demanded equals quantity supplied. See p. 86.

28. D. At 60¢, quantity demanded is 25 units greater than quantity supplied.

29. C. At 80¢, quantity supplied is 25 units greater than quantity demanded.
30. B. The new regulations will decrease the supply of tuna which, in turn, will increase the equilibrium price and decrease the equilibrium quantity.

II. SOLUTIONS TO APPLICATION QUESTIONS

1. a. 25¢. 67,000 bushels.
   b. There is a surplus of 44,000 bushels at a price of 40¢ per bushel. Pressure is present to force price down.
   c. There is a shortage of 22,000 bushels at a price of 15¢ per bushel. Pressure is present to force price up.
   d. Supply would shift to the left by 30,000 bushels. Equilibrium price would increase to 35¢ per bushel and the equilibrium quantity would be 48,000 bushels.
2. a. A decrease in income will reduce demand. Equilibrium price will fall and equilibrium quantity will fall.
   b. An increase in the cost of wheat will decrease supply. Equilibrium price will rise and equilibrium quantity will fall.
   c. A decrease in the cost of wheat will increase supply. Equilibrium price will fall and equilibrium quantity will rise.
   d. A fall in the price of a substitute will reduce the demand for DoughCrust. Equilibrium price will fall and equilibrium quantity will fall.
   e. There will be a decrease in demand. Equilibrium price will fall and equilibrium quantity will fall.
3. a. Supply will decrease—cost of inputs has increased.
   b. Supply will not change. A change in the price of a good results in a change in quantity supplied.
   c. Supply of hamburgers will decrease—producers will switch resources to cheeseburger production.
4. a. Hot dogs are substitutes for ice cream. Demand for ice cream will decrease.
   b. No effect on demand. Changes in the cost of refrigeration will affect supply.
   c. Demand will increase as the number of buyers increases.
5. a.

PRICE	QUANTITY DEMANDED	QUANTITY SUPPLIED
$30	0	90
$25	10	75
$20	20	60
$15	30	45
$10	40	30
$ 5	50	15
$ 0	60	0

   b. Equilibrium price is $12 and equilibrium quantity is 36.
      In equilibrium, Qd = Qs, therefore,

   $$60 - 2P = 3P$$

   $$60 = 5P \text{ and } P = 12.$$

      If P = 12, then Q = 60 − 2(12) = 36.
   c. At $20, there is an excess supply of 40 units. It's a buyers market—only 20 units will be traded.
   d. This is an increase in demand. Tastes might have changed, consumer incomes may have risen (if videocassettes are a normal good), and so on.
   e. Equilibrium price is $16 and equilibrium quantity is 48.
      In equilibrium, Qd = Qs, therefore,

   $$80 - 2P = 3P$$

   $$80 = 5P \text{ and } P = 16.$$

      If P = 16, then Q = 80 − 2(16) = 48.

6. a. $3; 3,000.
   b. See the diagram below.

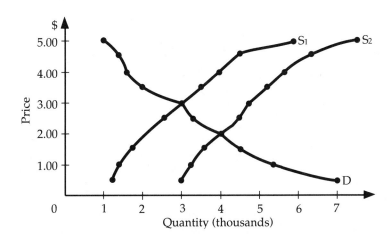

   c. There is an excess demand (shortage) equal to 4,000 units (5,400 − 1,400).
   d. See the diagram above ($2, 4,000).
   e. There will be an excess supply (surplus) of 1,800 units.
   f. Price will fall to $2; quantity demanded and supplied will move to 4,000 units.
7. The unemployment was removed because 100 extra jobs were created (increase in quantity demanded) and, because the wage had become too low, 50 workers decided to cease offering themselves for employment (decrease in quantity supplied).
8. a. See the diagram below.

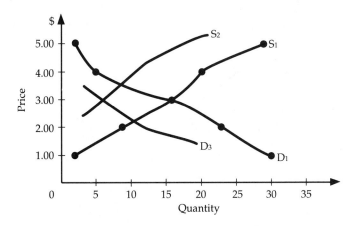

   b. P* = $3; Q* = 16.
   c. See the diagram above. There will be no change in demand! Costs have risen, reducing profits, so supply will shift to the left (although we can't say how far). At $3, a shortage now exists, which will push prices higher.
   d. See the diagram above. Demand for orange juice will fall (although we can't say by how much). Consumption of All-Cola will rise and some consumers of orange juice will substitute the relatively cheap All-Cola.

9. a. See the diagram below.

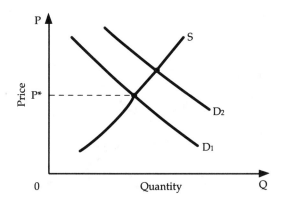

b. Increase.
c. The demand curve must shift to the right.
d. Excess demand, leading to pressure for price to rise, will cause a reduction in the quantity demanded and an increase in the quantity supplied. This will continue until a new equilibrium is established.

10. a. The subsidy will increase supply. Price will fall and output will rise.

b. The price of fish will increase and consumers will switch to beef. The demand for beef will increase. Price will rise and output will rise.

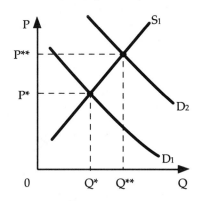

c. Costs of production have risen. This will decrease supply. Price will rise and output will fall.

d. Beef is a normal good. Higher incomes will cause the demand curve to shift right. Price will rise and output will rise.

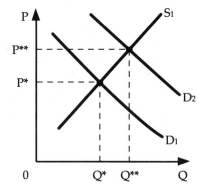

e. Costs of production will fall. Supply will shift to the right. Price will fall and output will rise.

f. A poor tomato crop will drive up the price of tomatoes (and ketchup). Less ketchup will be used so less beef will be demanded. Price and output will fall.

 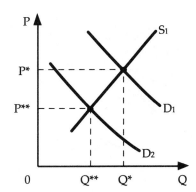

11. a. Presumably, your demand curve is downsloping and intersects the price axis at some point.
    b. With a greater number of substitutes, you will be more sensitive to changes in the price of your good. The curve will tend to be flatter. This refers to elasticity of demand, which we will discuss in Chapter 5.
    c. Presumably, the demand curve would shift to the right.
    d. If this is a normal good, demand would increase. If it is an inferior good, demand would decrease.

12. a. The supply curves are the same (vertical at 35,000). In the Yankees' case, at a price of $5 per ticket, there is an excess demand. In the Indians' case, at a price of $5 per ticket, because demand is so low, there is an excess supply. See the diagram below.
    b. To fill the stadium, let the ticket price fall to the equilibrium level. Whether this strategy will bring in more revenue will depend on the elasticity of the demand curve—see Chapter 5 for more on the concept of elasticity. Another strategy would be to charge $10 for a combined pass to both games. Fans wanting to see the Yankees would probably pay out more money and might also come to the second game.

13. Demand for labor would increase and, as workers moved away from the region, supply of labor would decrease. Wages, then, would increase and the costs of doing business in the Northeast would rise.

14. a. The test has reduced the supply of cabbies. This has forced up the price of taxi rides in London.
    b. Given the raised price of cab rides, the demand for substitutes will have increased. Other forms of public transportation will have been able to increase their prices.
    c. Cabbies who have passed the test and earned their license like the scheme because it reduces competition. This is especially true if the degree of substitutability with other types of public transportation is slight.

15. a. D   b. D   c. U   d. D
    e. D   f. I or U   g. I

16. a. U   b. U   c. D   d. D
    e. I   f. I   g. I   h. U
    i. D

17. a. U and D   b. D and U   c. U and I   d. U and I

18. a. B   b. B   c. A   d. C
    e. B   f. B   g. A   h. B
    i. B   j. C

THE PRICE SYSTEM, SUPPLY AND DEMAND, AND ELASTICITY

5

OBJECTIVES: POINT BY POINT

After completing this chapter, you should be able to accomplish the objectives listed below.

OBJECTIVE 1: Explain and demonstrate how the market uses the price-rationing mechanism to allocate resources and distribute output.

The price system has two important functions—it rations scarce output and determines how productive resources are allocated. Because of scarcity, rationing always occurs. Price rationing operates to distinguish those who are "willing and able" to buy from those who are only able but no longer willing, i.e., it allocates according to the willingness and ability of consumers to pay—those who are willing and able to pay as the price increases will get the good. Demand is constrained by income and wealth but, within those limits, individual preferences will prevail. If demand increases, price rises, signaling producers that profits may be made. More of the good will be produced with resources being switched from other lines of production.

(page 97)

> **LEARNING TIP:** Note the lobster example in the textbook, which describes the rationing and allocative roles that prices play in the marketplace.
>
> Note, too, that the profit motive is highly durable. Limitations (such as price ceilings or rationing) placed on the operation of the market can lead to black markets so that demand can be serviced.

PRACTICE

1. In a free market, either price must change or nonprice rationing must occur when _____ exists.
   A. a shortage.
   B. a surplus.
   C. a perfectly elastic demand.
   D. a perfectly inelastic demand.
   Answer: A. Given a shortage, either price will increase (price rationing) or nonprice rationing must be enforced.

2. In a free market, the rationing mechanism is
   A. price.
   B. quantity.
   C. demand.
   D. supply.
   Answer: A. Given an imbalance between quantity demanded and quantity supplied, a free market will adjust price to achieve equilibrium.

OBJECTIVE 2: List nonprice rationing policies designed to supplant the price rationing mechanism, identify the rationale behind these, and analyze their effects.

Price rationing may be considered "unfair"—poor people might be priced out of the market for some essentials—so other nonprice rationing methods, including queuing, ration coupons, favored customers, and lotteries, are applied. Such schemes usually involve hidden costs (queuing costs time, for example) that may make them inefficient. Note that different types of rationing benefit different groups of people.

(page 99)

At many colleges, basketball tickets are distributed on a first-come first-served basis—meaning that students must queue, perhaps for days, to get tickets to the big game. Not-so-hidden costs include the inconvenience, loss of study time, and possible health effects. As an example of a lottery, colleges may allocate dorm rooms, not by price or need, but by random number selection.

> **LEARNING TIP:** It may seem confusing—to have a ceiling below the equilibrium price. Remember that a price ceiling stops the price going higher (just like a ceiling in a room), while a price floor is a lower limit. To have an effect on equilibrium price, a ceiling must be set *below* the equilibrium price and a floor *above* the equilibrium price.
>
> **Comment:** The conceptual companion of a price ceiling is a price floor. A price ceiling sets a maximum price; a price floor sets a minimum price. The minimum wage is a price floor. An effective price ceiling creates a shortage; an effective price floor creates a surplus.
>
> A price ceiling need not be established below the equilibrium price, although a ceiling set *above* the equilibrium has no effect. If demand and/or supply conditions change however, the ceiling could become effective. For instance, adjustable rate mortgages have "caps" on how high the interest rate can move in response to market conditions—this is a price ceiling.

PRACTICE

3. A price ceiling is established below the equilibrium price. We can predict that
   A. quantity demanded will decrease.
   B. quantity supplied will be greater than quantity demanded.
   C. demand will be less than supply.
   D. quantity supplied will decrease.
   Answer: D. Price will be reduced by the price ceiling. A decrease in price causes quantity supplied to decrease (not a shift in the supply curve).

4. A price ceiling is established below the equilibrium price. We can predict that
   A. there will be a leftward shift in the demand curve.
   B. there will be a leftward shift in the supply curve.
   C. quantity demanded will be greater than quantity supplied.
   D. quantity supplied will be reduced to equal quantity demanded.
   Answer: C. A change in price does not cause the demand and/or supply curve to shift position! If price is "too low," a shortage (quantity demanded greater than quantity supplied) will occur.

5. Ticket scalping will be successful if
   A. demand is elastic.
   B. demand is inelastic.
   C. the official price is below the equilibrium price.
   D. the official price is above the equilibrium price.
   Answer: C. Elasticity is irrelevant in this case. The important issue is that a shortage of tickets exists because the official price has been set too low.

OBJECTIVE 3: Explain, using words and/or diagrams, how an oil import fee would affect the domestic production and total consumption of oil.

The text offers the imposition of a tax on imported oil (an oil import fee) as an example of the usefulness of demand and supply analysis. The analysis shows that a new tax will raise the domestic price of oil, cutting quantity demanded and encouraging domestic production. The size of these changes depends on the slopes of the demand and supply curves or, more accurately, the *elasticities* of demand and supply. Although the imposition of this tax would raise government revenues, reduce dependence on foreign oil, and stimulate domestic production of oil, inefficient domestic producers may be sheltered from lower-priced foreign competition.

(page 105)

Which consumers are most likely to be penalized by an oil import fee? Within the market, some buyers will have a relatively inelastic demand, while others will be more able to trim demand if price rises. Would a price hike discriminate more against the poor (who may have little choice in their fuel consumption) than against those who are better off (who can afford to buy other kinds of heating)?

PRACTICE

Refer to the following diagram for the next four questions. The world price of oil is $20 per barrel.

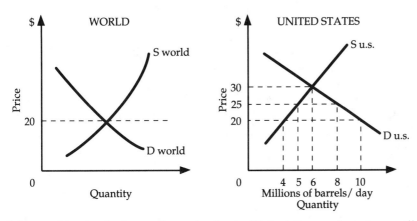

6. If the world price is the market price in the United States, then there will be a _____ million barrels per day.
   A. surplus of 10.
   B. surplus of 6.
   C. shortage of 10.
   D. shortage of 6.
   Answer: D. At $20 per barrel, quantity supplied is 4 million and quantity demanded is 10 million.

7. Suppose that the United States imposes a $5 per barrel import fee. This will result in each of the following except
   A. a decrease in imports to 3 million barrels per day.
   B. an increase in the quantity supplied of oil in the U.S. to 5 million barrels per day.
   C. a decrease in the quantity demanded of oil in the U.S. to 8 million barrels per day.
   D. a decrease in U.S. imports of oil by 2 million barrels per day.
   Answer: D. Oil imports had been 6 million barrels per day. After the imposition of the fee, oil imports are 3 million barrels per day. Imports decreased by 3 million barrels per day.

8. An import fee of $5 per imported barrel of oil will generate a tax revenue of
   A. $3 million per day.
   B. $5 million per day.
   C. $8 million per day.
   D. $15 million per day.

   Answer: D. Imports are 3 million barrels per day. Each barrel yields a tax revenue of $5.

9. Suppose that the United States wishes to become self-sufficient in oil. This could be done by
   A. establishing a price ceiling (maximum price) of $15 per barrel of oil.
   B. establishing a price ceiling (maximum price) of $30 per barrel of oil.
   C. imposing a fee of $10 per barrel on foreign oil.
   D. imposing a fee of $30 per barrel on foreign oil.

   Answer: C. A fee of $10 per barrel on foreign oil will result in equilibrium in the U.S. market.

OBJECTIVE 4: Define and use the elasticity of demand and use the midpoint formula or "percentage change" formula to measure elasticity.

For "elasticity" read "responsiveness." The elasticity concept is not limited to demand; it is a general concept. Elasticity changes continuously all the way along a straight-line curve, so using the slope of a demand or supply curve as a measure of elasticity is not a good idea; special formulas—such as the midpoint formula—must be used.

> **LEARNING TIP:** The best way to understand "elasticity" is to equate the term with "responsiveness." Select a good for which demand is fairly sensitive to price changes (prescription drugs, gasoline, college tuition) and one for which demand is quite sensitive (a particular brand of gasoline or soft drink). When you need to think through an elasticity problem, plug in your chosen example.

> **LEARNING TIP:** Here is a simple memory aid for elasticity graphs. The demand curve is vertical ($|$) for perfectly (I)nelastic demand, but horizontal (—) for perfectly (E)lastic demand.

Price elasticity of demand is the most frequently used measurement and sets a pattern for all the formulas: it is the percentage change in quantity demanded divided by the percentage change in price.   (page 106)

> **LEARNING TIP:** By canceling the 2's in the textbook formula, the midpoint elasticity formula can be simplified to:
>
> $$\frac{\dfrac{Q_1 - Q_2}{Q_1 + Q_2}}{\dfrac{P_1 - P_2}{P_1 + P_2}}$$
>
> Make sure you have the "quantity" term in the numerator and the "price" term in the denominator—we're measuring how much *quantity* (top) responds to a change in the *dollar* amount (bottom).

PRACTICE

Use the following information to answer the next three questions: Stellio's Pizzeria has been experimenting with the price of its Stellio's Supreme Pizza. At a price of $12, quantity demanded is 100. At $10, quantity demanded increases to 120 pizzas. When the price is $8, quantity demanded increases to 140 pizzas.

10. Using the midpoint formula, the price elasticity of demand between $12 and $10 is
    A. elastic with an elasticity value of −2.
    B. unitarily elastic with an elasticity value of −1.
    C. elastic with an elasticity value of −10.
    D. inelastic with an elasticity value of −.1.
    Answer: B. P_1 is 12; P_2 is 10; Q_1 is 100; Q_2 is 120. Plug the values into the formula. Note: Confirm your result using the total revenue test. See Objective 6.

11. Using the midpoint formula, the price elasticity of demand between $10 and $8 is
    A. elastic with an elasticity value of −13/9.
    B. elastic with an elasticity value of −9/13.
    C. inelastic with an elasticity value of −13/9.
    D. inelastic with an elasticity value of −9/13.
    Answer: D. P_1 is 10; P_2 is 8; Q_1 is 120; Q_2 is 140. Options B and C must be incorrect—an elastic demand cannot have an elasticity of −9/13. Note: Confirm your "inelastic" result using the total revenue test. See Objective 6.

12. Using the midpoint formula, the price elasticity of demand between $12 and $8 is
    A. elastic with an elasticity value of −5/6.
    B. elastic with an elasticity value of −6/5.
    C. inelastic with an elasticity value of −6/5.
    D. inelastic with an elasticity value of −5/6.
    Answer: D. P_1 is 12; P_2 is 8; Q_1 is 100; Q_2 is 140. Options B and C must be incorrect—an elastic demand cannot have an elasticity of −5/6 and an inelastic demand cannot have an elasticity of −6/5. Note: Confirm your "inelastic" result using the total revenue test. See Objective 6.

OBJECTIVE 5: Interpret the terms elastic, inelastic, and unitarily elastic in the context of price elasticity of demand.

Demand responsiveness may be classified as:
  a. perfectly elastic. The absolute price elasticity measure is infinity.
  b. elastic. The absolute price elasticity measure is >1.
  c. unitarily elastic. The absolute price elasticity measure is 1.
  d. inelastic. The absolute price elasticity measure is <1.
  e. perfectly inelastic. The absolute price elasticity measure is 0.   (page 108)

Recall that elasticity measures responsiveness. The more responsive a buyer is to a price change, the more elastic is demand and (in absolute terms) the larger is the price elasticity of demand.

PRACTICE

13. A 10% fall in the price of shampoo results in a 5% increase in the quantity of shampoo demanded. Demand is
    A. inelastic.
    B. elastic.
    C. unitarily elastic.
    D. perfectly elastic.
    Answer: A. See p. 109.

14. The price elasticity of demand can be calculated by
    A. multiplying the percentage change in quantity demanded by the percentage change in price.
    B. dividing the percentage change in quantity demanded by the percentage change in price.
    C. dividing the percentage change in price by the percentage change in quantity demanded.
    D. multiplying the percentage change in price by the percentage change in quantity demanded.
    Answer: B. See p. 109.

15. The supply of flapdoodles increases. There is no effect on the equilibrium quantity. Demand is
    A. perfectly inelastic.
    B. elastic.
    C. inelastic.
    D. perfectly elastic.
    Answer: A. If demand is completely unresponsive to a price change, it is perfectly inelastic—a vertical demand curve.

16. The demand for potato chips has a downsloping straight-line demand curve. As the price of chips increases, the price elasticity of demand
    A. becomes more elastic.
    B. becomes less elastic.
    C. remains constant—the slope of a straight line is constant.
    D. remains constant—each price increase causes an equal decrease in quantity demanded.
    Answer: A. Slope does not give a good guide to elasticity. A general rule, though, for a straight-line demand curve is that, as price rises, demand becomes more elastic.

17. A 10% increase in the price of video games results in a 5% decrease in the quantity of video games demanded. The price elasticity of demand is _____ and demand is _____
    A. −.5, elastic.
    B. −2.0, elastic.
    C. −.5, inelastic.
    D. −2.0, inelastic.
    Answer: C. Options A and D must be wrong—an "elastic" value must have an absolute value of more than 1 while an "inelastic" value must have an absolute value of less than 1. The relatively large price change prompts a relatively small quantity change—that's inelastic.

OBJECTIVE 6: Predict the effect on total revenue of a price change, given the elasticity of demand. Apply the total revenue test.

Total revenue is "price × quantity." The relationship between elasticity and total revenue, as price increases, may be classified as:
    a. Elastic if total revenue decreases,
    b. unitarily elastic if total revenue remains constant,
    c. inelastic if total revenue increases.

Given a good with an elastic demand (Pepsi), a small increase in price will trigger a relatively large decrease in quantity demanded, as consumers switch over to Coke and other close substitutes. Total spending on Pepsi will decrease.

Given a good with an inelastic demand (gasoline), even a large price hike will result in only a small decrease in quantity demanded, since consumers have few close substitutes for the product. Total spending on gas will increase. (page 116)

The *total revenue test* allows us to determine whether demand is elastic or inelastic when price changes. The following table gives a summary of this test.

Price	Quantity	Elasticity	Total Revenue
increase	decrease	perfectly elastic	falling to zero
increase	decrease	elastic	falling
increase	decrease	unitarily elastic	constant
increase	decrease	inelastic	rising
increase	no change	perfectly inelastic	rising

Note that usually you don't need to know the exact numerical elasticity values.

If you don't know the exact elasticity values, checking how total revenue is changing is an effective way to discover if the good has an elastic demand or not.

PRACTICE

18. The price of canned salmon increases; total spending on canned salmon remains unchanged. Canned salmon has a(n) _____ demand.
    A. perfectly inelastic.
    B. perfectly elastic.
    C. unitarily elastic.
    D. inelastic.
    Answer: C. Total revenue will increase if salmon has an inelastic demand and will decrease if salmon has an elastic demand. This is the middle case where the price change results in no change in total spending.

19. Total revenue will decrease if price _____ and demand is _____ .
    A. increases, inelastic.
    B. increases, unitarily elastic.
    C. decreases, inelastic.
    D. decreases, elastic.
    Answer: C. College tuition has an inelastic demand. Total revenue on tuition will increase if college administrators declare a price increase. By the same argument, if tuition rates are reduced, total revenue will decrease.

20. An excellent harvest causes apples to fall in price by 10%. Consumers buy 5% more apples. The price decrease has caused consumers to
    A. spend less on apples.
    B. spend more on apples.
    C. reduce the quantity of apples bought. We can't tell what has happened to spending.
    D. increase the quantity of apples bought. We can't tell what has happened to spending.
    Answer: A. The price elasticity of demand is −.5—inelastic. A decrease in price then, we know, will reduce the number of dollars spent.

OBJECTIVE 7: Explain the effects of the three determinants of price elasticity of demand.

The responsiveness of demand to changes in price is affected by the availability of substitutes, the fraction of total spending that a good absorbs, and the time factor. The elasticity of demand will *increase* if more substitutes become available, if the good commands a greater portion of the household's budget, or if the response time is longer rather than shorter. (page 117)

LEARNING TIP: To remember how price elasticity is influenced by its determinants (the availability of substitutes, the fraction of total spending that a good absorbs, and time), make up a few intuitive examples.

Substitutes: Exxon gas has an elastic demand because there are many substitutes (BP, Mobil, etc.); gasoline, in general, has few substitutes—elasticity will be lower. Pepsi has many substitutes, electricity has few.

As more substitutes become available, demand becomes more elastic. The drug that combats AIDS, AZT, at one time had no substitutes—inelastic demand. The producer was attacked for setting price too high and reaping substantial revenues. The emergence of substitutes will make AZT's demand more elastic.

Fraction of total spending: Suppose Bazooka Joe bubblegum (or salt, or pepper) doubled in price. It's such a small portion of expenditures for most people that the price increase would pass almost unnoticed and quantity demanded would respond only slightly—inelastic demand. In contrast, a doubling in the price of a good that is important in one's budget (gasoline, perhaps) will provoke a greater response.

Time: The longer the consumer has to "shop around" following a price increase, the more responsive he or she can be. In the late 1970s, for instance, gas prices rose rapidly. Initially, drivers planned trips more carefully. Then came carpooling. Eventually, as cars aged, newer, more fuel-efficient models were bought. Progressively, fuel consumption was reduced.

In each example, remember to apply the total revenue test. If gasoline increases in price, your gas bill will increase (inelastic demand). If Pepsi increases in price, your spending on Pepsi will decrease (elastic demand).

PRACTICE

21. Nita is a senior at East Dakota University. Probably, she will have the most elastic demand for
   A. East Dakota University tuition.
   B. warm clothing in December.
   C. Exxon gasoline.
   D. required prescription drugs.
   Answer: C. There should be many substitutes (other companies' gasoline), and Nita is likely to consider gas as an important part of her budget. Tuition may be important in Nita's budget, but few substitutes are likely to be available.

OBJECTIVE 8: Distinguish between and calculate cross-price elasticity of demand and income elasticity of demand.

Income elasticity of demand—which measures how much a demand curve shifts position when income level changes—measures whether goods are inferior, normal, or luxuries.
   a. inferior   negative elasticity
   b. normal   positive elasticity of less than one, or
   c. luxuries   positive elasticity of greater than one.   (page 119)

Cross-price elasticity of demand—which measures how the demand curve for Good A shifts when the price of Good B changes—measures whether a substitute relationship or a complement relationship exists.

   a. substitute   positive elasticity, or
   b. complement   negative elasticity.   (page 119)

The main point is the sign (positive or negative) of the relationship rather than the magnitude. If it is a positive relationship, the goods are substitutes; if it is negative, the goods are complements. As a secondary issue, the larger (in absolute terms) the elasticity, the more related are the two goods. For instance, a small decrease in the price of Pepsi may trigger a sizable decrease in the demand for Coke (close substitutes) but a smaller decrease in the demand for Yoo-Hoo Chocolate Drink.

> **LEARNING TIP:** Check these results by "plugging in" your own examples from Chapter 4.
>
> **Substitutes.** An increase in the price of Pepsi will lead to a decrease in the quantity demanded of Pepsi and an increase in the demand for Coke (positive sign).
>
> **Complements.** An increase in the price of CDs will lead to decrease in the demand for CD players (negative sign).
>
> **Inferior Goods.** Rice, beans, and generic aspirin are good examples of inferior goods. As your income increases, you will probably decrease your spending on such goods (negative sign).
>
> **Normal Goods.** As your income increases, you will probably increase your spending on soft drinks, books, clothes, CDs, etc. (positive sign).
>
> **Luxury Goods.** Home ownership might be a luxury. If your income is low, you can only rent. If your income rises, you may qualify for mortgage loans and enter the house-purchasing market. Expenditure on house purchases rises more than the increase in income in such a case.

> **LEARNING TIP:** Remember: put the "number" term (quantity) in the numerator and the "dollar" term (price or income) in the denominator.
>
> From this point it's easy to alter the original midpoint formula to introduce the concepts of income elasticity (measuring how much *quantity* responds to a change in *income*), or even cross-price elasticity (measuring how much *quantity demanded* of Good A responds to a change in the *price of Good B*).

PRACTICE

22. The cross-price elasticity of demand between Exxon gas and Havoline oil is −.7. Exxon gas and Havoline oil are _____ . The cross-price elasticity of demand between Exxon gas and BP gas will be _____ .
    A. substitutes, positive.
    B. substitutes, negative.
    C. complements, positive.
    D. complements, negative.
    Answer: C. A negative cross-price elasticity indicates that goods are complements. Because Exxon and BP are substitutes, the cross-price elasticity will be positive.

23. The income elasticity of demand for Havoline oil is .6. We can conclude that Havoline oil
    A. is an inferior good.
    B. is a normal good, but not a luxury.
    C. is a luxury.
    D. has a demand that is not very sensitive to changes in its price.
    Answer: B. An increase in income will raise demand for Havoline. The elasticity is positive but less than one, so it is not a luxury. Option D does not refer to income elasticity.

OBJECTIVE 9: Calculate and interpret given elasticity measures for the price elasticity of supply.

Price elasticity of supply looks at the responsiveness of suppliers to changes in price while price elasticity of labor supply does the same thing for the labor supply curve. The labor supply curve can be backward-bending (if price elasticity of supply is negative). (page 119)

PRACTICE

24. The price elasticity of labor supply is .7. Labor supply is _____ and _____
    A. elastic, upward sloping.
    B. elastic, downward sloping.
    C. inelastic, upward sloping.
    D. inelastic, downward sloping.
    Answer: C. The elasticity is positive—a rise in the wage results in an rise in the quantity of labor supplied. Since the elasticity has a value of less than one, a given percentage increase in wage will result in a smaller percentage increase in quantity of labor supplied—an inelastic response.

PRACTICE TEST

I. MULTIPLE CHOICE QUESTIONS.

Select the option that provides the single best answer.

_____ 1. Price elasticity of demand is −.50. Price increases by 10%. We would predict a
    A. 50% increase in quantity demanded.
    B. 20% decrease in quantity demanded.
    C. 5% increase in quantity demanded.
    D. 5% decrease in quantity demanded.

_____ 2. Sellers of frisbees want to raise their revenues. They should _____ price by 30¢ if they believe demand to be _____ in that price range.
    A. lower, elastic.
    B. lower, inelastic.
    C. raise, elastic.
    D. Two of the above are feasible scenarios.

_____ 3. A 10% fall in the price of apples results in a 20% increase in the quantity of apples demanded. Demand is
    A. inelastic.
    B. elastic.
    C. unitarily elastic.
    D. perfectly elastic.

_____ 4. Which of the following is NOT a determinant of price elasticity of demand for gasoline?
    A. the quantity of gasoline produced.
    B. the amount of time given to adjust to a price change.
    C. the availability of close substitutes.
    D. the importance of gasoline in one's budget.

_____ 5. Price elasticity of demand is a measure of the
    A. extent of competition in the market.
    B. percentage change in quantity times the percentage change in price.
    C. slope of the demand curve.
    D. degree of consumer responsiveness to changes in price.

_____ 6. The price elasticity of demand for Exxon gas will tend to be
A. less elastic, the lower the price of substitutes.
B. less elastic, the smaller the share of consumers' income spent on Exxon gas.
C. less elastic, the greater the availability of close substitutes for Exxon gas.
D. more elastic, the more urgently gas is needed.

_____ 7. Two goods are complements. Their cross-price elasticity of demand will be
A. a negative number.
B. a positive number.
C. a positive number greater than one.
D. one.

Use the graph below to answer the next two questions.

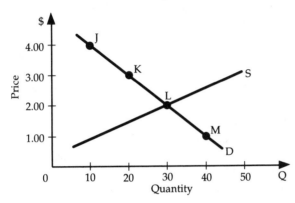

_____ 8. Which statement is false? "Demand for this product is _____ in the range _____ ."
A. elastic; J to K.
B. elastic; J to L.
C. inelastic; L to M.
D. elastic; K to L.

_____ 9. Suppose a price ceiling of $1.00 is set. This will cause a
A. surplus of 50 units.
B. shortage of 50 units.
C. shortage of 30 units.
D. surplus of 30 units.

_____ 10. The income elasticity of Good A is positive, and the cross-price elasticity between Good A and Good B is negative. Good A is a(n)
A. normal good and a substitute for Good B.
B. inferior good and a substitute for Good B.
C. normal good and a complement for Good B.
D. inferior good and a complement for Good B.

_____ 11. The price of a frisbee rises from $5 to $6. Total revenue falls from $400 to $360. We can conclude that price elasticity of demand is (roughly) _____ , which means that demand is _____ .
A. −.579, inelastic.
B. −1.571, elastic.
C. −.579, elastic.
D. −1.571, inelastic.

_____ 12. Good C has a *negative* income elasticity. Which of the following goods is most likely to be Good C?
A. Alfa Romeo sports car.
B. A vacation in Europe.
C. A compact disc.
D. A can of generic beer.

_____ 13. An increase in the labor costs of the sellers of a product, combined with a relatively inelastic demand curve, will result in
A. a relatively small reduction in output.
B. a relatively small increase in equilibrium price.
C. a rightward shift in the supply curve.
D. a leftward shift in the demand curve.

_____ 14. A leftward shift in the supply curve of Pan Galactic Gargle Blasters causes price to rise by 10%. Arthur Dent thereafter buys 20% fewer Gargle Blasters. The price rise has caused Arthur to
A. spend less on Gargle Blasters.
B. spend more on Gargle Blasters.
C. reduce the quantity bought. We can't tell what has happened to how much he spends.
D. increase the quantity bought. We can't tell what has happened to how much he spends.

_____ 15. Moo U. radio station reports that, since the college eatery, *The Five Beans*, raised the price of hot dogs, fewer hot dogs have been bought and *The Five Beans'* total revenue on hot dogs has been halved. This indicates that
A. the demand schedule for hot dogs at *The Five Beans* is horizontal.
B. at present, prices are in the elastic section of the demand schedule.
C. hot dogs are an inferior good.
D. the price elasticity of demand for hot dogs is .5.

_____ 16. The closer substitutes two goods are, the _____ will be their cross-price elasticity.
A. more positive.
B. more negative.
C. less positive.
D. less negative.

Use the diagram below to answer the next four questions. The world price for gasoline is 50¢ per gallon. The equilibrium price in the U.S. market is $1.50.

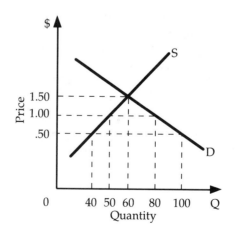

_____ 17. Assume that the U.S. neither imports nor exports gasoline. At the world price for gasoline, there is a _____ of gas in the U.S. market of _____ units.
A. surplus, 60.
B. surplus, 100.
C. shortage, 60.
D. shortage, 100.

_____ 18. Assume that the U.S. imports gasoline. The government imposes an import tax that raises the price of gas to $1.00 per gallon. Based on the diagram, we can infer that
A. demand is elastic.
B. demand is inelastic.
C. the market is now in equilibrium.
D. total revenue has increased to $80 million.

_____ 19. Assume that the U.S. imports gasoline. The government imposes an import tax that raises the price of gas to $1.00 per gallon. Based on the diagram, which of the following is true?
A. Supply is price-elastic between 50¢ and $1.00.
B. Government tax revenues will be 50¢ times 60 million.
C. Demand is price-inelastic between $1.00 and $1.50.
D. Equilibrium price is now $1.00.

_____ 20. The government has imposed an import tax that raises the price of gas to $1.00 per gallon. If the domestic supply of gas rose by 30 million gallons per day
A. the shortage of gas would be eliminated.
B. government tax revenues would be 30 million times 50¢.
C. quantity demanded would increase.
D. the equilibrium price would remain at $1.50.

_____ 21. The government has decided that the free market price for baby formula is "too high." Which of the following rationing proposals will result in the **least** misallocation of baby formula resources?
A. Proposal A: establish an official price ceiling, then let sellers decide how to allocate baby formula among customers.
B. Proposal B: issue coupons for baby formula that cannot be resold.
C. Proposal C: issue coupons for baby formula that can be resold.
D. Proposal D: establish a price ceiling and require purchasers to queue.

_____ 22. The cross-price elasticity between Wendy's Biggie Fries and Wendy's Frostie is _____ . The cross-price elasticity between Burger King's Whopper and McDonald's Big Mac is _____
A. positive, positive.
B. positive, negative.
C. negative, positive.
D. negative, negative.

_____ 23. A ticket to a concert by the Screeming Habdabs costs you $35. However, your roommate offers you the "scalping" rate of $100 for your ticket. Your opportunity cost of refusing the offer and attending the concert is
A. $35.
B. $65.
C. $100.
D. $135.

_____ 24. In a free market, health care costs are felt by the government to be too high. Accordingly, the government sets a maximum price per unit of health care that is below the equilibrium price. *Ceteris paribus,*
    A. the quantity of health care services received will increase.
    B. the quantity of health care services received will decrease.
    C. total spending on health care will increase if the demand curve is elastic.
    D. the health of the population will improve if the demand curve is elastic.

_____ 25. A government imposed **ceiling** on apartment rents, if set above the equilibrium rent level, would
    A. have no effect on the housing market.
    B. lead to a persistent shortage of apartments.
    C. lead to a persistent surplus of apartments.
    D. shift the supply curve for apartments to the right.

II. APPLICATION QUESTIONS.

1. You've just bought a company that publishes cookbooks. You consult your in-house economist. The conversation goes like this:
He tells you that the elasticity of demand for your cookbooks is −2.4.
Then you tell him that you want to maximize sales revenue.
Then he tells you that you should raise the price of the cookbooks.
Then you tell him that he is a useless collection of carbon-based molecules.
Explain your reaction.

2. The price of Good A and of Good B is $10, and both goods have a quantity demanded of 100 units/week. When the price of Good A falls to $9, the quantity demanded rises to 200 units/week. However, the price of Good B must fall to $8 in order to achieve sales of 200.
    a. In the price ranges given, which good has the more **elastic** demand?
    b. Use the total revenue test to confirm that both goods face elastic demand curves.
    c. Verify your answer by calculating the price elasticity for Good A and Good B.

3. The cross-price elasticity for Good X (to a change in Good Y's price) is −.7.
The cross-price elasticity for Good X (to a change in Good Z's price) is +.7.
Good X's income elasticity is −.7.
If Good X's producer wishes its demand to increase, which of the following scenarios is the most preferred?
    A. The economy experiences unexpected prosperity; the price of Good Y increases.
    B. The economy experiences an unexpected recession; the price of Good Y increases.
    C. The economy experiences unexpected prosperity; the price of Good Y decreases.
    D. The economy experiences an unexpected recession; the price of Good Z increases.
    E. The price of Good Y increases; the price of Good Z increases.
Explain your answer.

4. Consider the following diagram which shows the market for fluid milk. Quantity is in thousands of gallons.

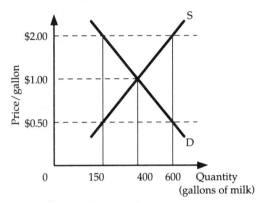

a. Calculate total income for dairy farmers.
b. Suppose that this income level is felt to be inadequate, and that a political decision is made to boost farm income to $1,200,000. Suppose the government establishes a price floor at $2.00, with the government buying the surplus. How much milk will be supplied?
c. Who gets the milk?
d. The plan achieves the income objective, but what else has it done? There are costs involved with tampering with the price mechanism. What are they?
Now suppose the government establishes a price ceiling of 50¢ per gallon.
e. How much milk would consumers actually receive?
f. Which plan is better for a milk consumer who pays no state tax? Why?

5. In the *Applications* section of Chapter 4, we examined the market for video-cassettes where the supply and demand curves are given by $Qs = 3P$ and $Qd = 60 - 2P$, respectively.
a. If the government imposes a price ceiling of $5 in this market, what will happen to the positions of the demand and supply curves?
b. Considering the demand curve in isolation, calculate the total revenue when price is $5 and when price is $10.
c. Considering the demand curve in isolation, calculate the total revenue when price is $20 and when price is $25.
d. Use the total revenue test to estimate the elasticity of demand between $5 and $10 and between $20 and $25.
e. Using the midpoint formula, calculate the price elasticity of demand between $5 and $10 and between $20 and $25.

6. In many Eastern European cities, there is a thriving market in farm produce.
a. Draw a demand and supply diagram below for the Warsaw egg market. Label the curves D_1 and S_1 respectively. Show the equilibrium price (P_1) and quantity (Q_1).

b. In August, the price of eggs now triples because of a decrease in supply caused of very hot weather. Show how the market changed in August. Label the new supply curve S_2. Show the new equilibrium price (P_2) and quantity (Q_2).

c. Is the Warsaw egg market operating efficiently?

d. Suppose the government decided to maintain the initial price (P_1). Should it impose a price ceiling or a price floor? Explain whether an excess demand or an excess supply will result.

e. Is the Warsaw egg market now operating efficiently?

f. How do you think suppliers might react to the price ceiling?

g. Suggest what nonprice methods might develop to circumvent the imbalance in this market.

7. a. Use the following demand schedule to complete the table.

Price	Quantity Demanded	Total Revenue	Elasticity (in words)	Elasticity Coefficient	As price rises, TR is:
$6	10	$ 60			
$5	20	$100			
$4	30	$120			
$3	40	$120			
$2	50	$100			
$1	60	$ 60	—	—	—

b. Work out a rule, based on your results in the last two columns, linking the change in total revenue and elasticity.

8. Use the information in the table to answer the questions below.

Month	Income per month	Quantity demanded of chicken per month	Quantity demanded of steak per month
1	$400	5 pounds	3 pounds
2	$800	3 pounds	5 pounds
3	$800	5 pounds	3 pounds

a. Using Months 1 and 2, is the income elasticity of chicken positive, negative, or zero? What kind of a good is chicken?

b. Using Months 1 and 2, estimate the income elasticity of steak. Is steak a normal good?

c. Intuitively, what sort of demand relationship do you think will exist between chicken and steak?

d. In Month 3 the price of steak rose from $2/pound to $3/pound. Estimate the cross-price elasticity to check your intuition.

9. On January 1, 1999, the Board of Aldermen of Dukeham, VT, doubled the rate it charged residents for water in order to pay for a new sewage-treatment plant. The table shows the Town Manager's predictions of revenues and the actual revenues collected. (Assume a straight-line demand curve throughout.)

Year	Price (/1000 gal)	Predicted Revenue	Actual Quantity Used	Actual Revenue
1999	$0.60	300,000	$180,000	
2000	$1.20	$300,000	200,000	$240,000

   a. What elasticity of demand (elastic/inelastic/unitarily elastic) did the Town Manager assume in her predicted revenue estimate?
   b. How can you tell that this was her assumption without first calculating the elasticity of demand?
   c. Using the midpoint formula, calculate the "predicted" elasticity of demand.
   d. Using the midpoint formula, calculate the "actual" elasticity of demand.

   Based on what happened, Alderman Phil E. Buster claims that water rate hikes are an easy way to increase town funds. He proposes that the water rate be raised to $5.00 per 1000 gallons.
   e. What do you think will happen to the position of the demand for water curve?
   f. Do you think the elasticity will be the same?
   g. Explain your answer to part f.

10. Here is some information about the demand for milk in Nollidge College.

Price/gallon	Quantity demanded
$1.50	6,000
$2.00	4,000

   Now, suppose the price of a gallon of milk rises from $1.50 to $2.00.
   a. Using the midpoint formula, calculate the elasticity of demand using the prices and quantities above.
   b. Calculate the change in the buyers' total expenditure.
   c. On the basis of your calculations, is demand elastic or inelastic, or neither, in this price range?
   d. Is your answer in part c consistent with your calculations in part a?

11. The freeze that destroyed much of the South American coffee crop in the mid-1970s increased the price of tea. Explain why, using supply and demand diagrams.

12. Illustrate the following with demand and/or supply curves.
   a. A perfectly inelastic supply curve.
   b. A labor supply curve along which labor supply elasticity is negative.
   c. A situation of excess demand created by a price ceiling.
   d. The effect of an increase in income on the price of an inferior good.
   e. The effect of a sharp increase in electricity rates on the demand for and price of air conditioners.

13. Use the following demand and supply schedule to answer the questions.

Price	Quantity Demanded	Quantity Supplied
$6	10	70
$5	20	60
$4	30	50
$3	40	40
$2	50	30
$1	60	20

    a. Calculate the equilibrium price and the equilibrium quantity.

    b. Now the government establishes a price ceiling of $2. Will this cause an excess supply or an excess demand? An excess of how many units?

III. ECONOMICS EXPLORER.

Use the first module ("Market Analysis") from the Economics Explorer software to explore concepts such as elasticity and total revenue. You can examine the impact of government intervention in competitive markets. Consumer surplus is also included.

ANSWERS AND SOLUTIONS

PRACTICE TEST

I. SOLUTIONS TO MULTIPLE CHOICE QUESTIONS

1. D. Price elasticity looks at the percentage change in quantity demanded divided by the percentage change in price. If $X/Y = -.5$ and Y equals 10%, then X equals 5%.

2. A. Check the total revenue test. If price is raised on a good with an elastic demand, many customers will stop buying it and revenue will fall. Therefore, cutting price on a good with an elastic demand will increase total revenue. See p. 116.

3. B. Price elasticity measures the percentage change in quantity demanded divided by the percentage change in price. Here, elasticity is -2.0, which is elastic.

4. A. A change in the quantity of gasoline produced is shown by a supply curve shift.

5. D. For "elasticity" read "responsiveness."

6. B. The elasticity of demand tends to be greater when an item represents a large part of our budget. An increase in its price hurts! If an item is insignificant, changes in its price are insignificant, too, and we are less sensitive to such changes. See p. 117.

7. A. Price of Good A rises, and quantity demanded falls. The other partner in the pair, Good B, experiences a decrease in demand. Cross-price elasticity measures the percentage change in quantity demanded of Good B divided by the percentage change in price of Good A—a negative divided by a positive.

8. D. Apply the total revenue test. When price is $2.00, total revenue is $60. When price is $3.00, total revenue is $60. Demand is unitarily elastic in this price range.

9. C. An effective price ceiling (set below the equilibrium price) will create a shortage. Quantity demanded is 40, but quantity supplied is only 10.

10. C. A positive income elasticity indicates that Good A is normal. A negative cross-price elasticity indicates that Good A is a complement of Good B. See p. 119.

11. B. If price rises and total revenue falls, we have a good with an elastic demand. Elasticity must be more negative than -1. (In fact, if you work out the value, it is -1.571, but this is not necessary to answer the question.)

12. D. A negative income elasticity indicates that Good C is inferior. For most people, the inferior good on the list would be the can of generic beer. See p. 119.

13. A. The increase in labor costs will make supply shift left. Price will rise and quantity demanded will fall. If demand is relatively inelastic, the increase in price will be relatively large and the decrease in quantity demanded relatively small.

14. A. Arthur's price elasticity is −2.0—elastic. An increase in price, then, will reduce the number of dollars he spends. See p. 116.

15. B. Price has risen and total revenue has fallen. Demand is elastic.

16. A. Substitutes have a positive cross-price elasticity. The closer they are, the more responsive buyers are to changes in price and the higher the elasticity will be. See p. 119.

17. C. The price is below the equilibrium price, with quantity demanded being 100 and quantity supplied being only 40. A shortage of 60 exists. See p. 101.

18. B. Apply the total revenue test. As price rises from 50¢ to $1.00, total revenue would rise from $50 million to $80 million. Note that total revenue is unable to rise like this because supply is restricted. See p. 116.

19. C. As price rises from $1.00 to $1.50, total spending would rise from $80 million to $90 million. Demand is inelastic if, when price rises, total spending rises.

20. A. The increase in supply would eliminate the shortage and eliminate government tax revenues.

21. C. Issuing coupons that can be resold will lead to a market for coupons with those willing and able to pay the most receiving the right to buy baby formula.

22. C. Wendy's products "go together"—a cut in the price of fries, for example, will encourage more customers to buy Frosties too. The Whopper and Big Mac are substitutes—a lower price for the Whopper will reduce demand for the Big Mac.

23. C. The opportunity cost is the value of the next best alternative given up, i.e., in monetary terms, whatever the $100 offered price would buy. The $35 has already been spent—it is a sunk cost.

24. B. A price ceiling is in effect and a shortage of health care has been created. Assuming an upward sloping supply curve, fewer health care services will be offered.

25. A. To be effective, a price ceiling must be set below the equilibrium price.

II. SOLUTIONS TO APPLICATION QUESTIONS

1. An elasticity of demand of −2.4 indicates that demand is elastic. When demand is elastic, an increase in price will cause total revenue to decrease.

2. Good A has the more elastic demand. The same "change in quantity" response is elicited with a lesser change in price.

   The total revenue test shows an elastic demand in each case. For Good A, a decrease in price, from $10 to $9, leads to an increase in total revenue from $1000 to $1800. For Good B, a decrease in price, from $10 to $8, leads to an increase in total revenue from $1000 to $1600.

   More formally, the midpoint formula for Good A is:

   $$\frac{(100 - 200)/[(100 + 200)/2]}{(10 - 9)/[(10 + 9)/2]}$$

   The price elasticity for Good A is −6.333.

   The midpoint formula for Good B is:

   $$\frac{(100 - 200)/[(100 + 200)/2]}{(10 - 8)/[(10 + 8)/2]}$$

   The price elasticity for Good B is −.3.000.

3. Option D is best. Good X and Good Y are complements. Good X and Good Z are substitutes. Good X is an inferior good. A recession will increase the demand for Good X; prosperity will not. An increase in the price of Good Z will reduce the quantity demanded of Y and increase the demand for substitute Good X. An increase in the price of Y will reduce the quantity demanded of Y and reduce the demand for complementary Good X.

4. a. $400,000.
    b. 600,000 gallons.
    c. 150,000 gallons for the consumer, and the rest is taken by the government.
    d. Many things—milk is now more expensive and less plentiful for consumers. Taxpayers—who needn't be milk consumers—will have to pick up the subsidy tab. There will be storage and administrative costs, too. Also, there is an overallocation of resources toward milk production.
    e. Consumers will receive 150,000 gallons. In this case there will be an excess demand.
    f. The second plan is better in that the price of milk is lower.

5. a. Nothing! A change in price leads to movements along the given demand and supply curves.
    b. When the price is $5, quantity is 50 units. Total revenue is $250. When the price is $10, quantity is 40 units. Total revenue is $400.
    c. When the price is $20, quantity is 20 units. Total revenue is $400. When the price is $25, quantity is 10 units. Total revenue is $250.
    d. As price increases from $5 to $10, total revenue increases from $250 to $400. Demand is inelastic. As price increases from $20 to $25, total revenue decreases from $400 to $250. Demand is elastic.
    e. The midpoint formula when price lies between $5 to $10 is:

$$\frac{(50 - 40)/[(50 + 40)/2]}{(5 - 10)/[(5 + 10)/2]}$$

The price elasticity in this price range is $-.333$.

The midpoint formula when price lies between $20 to $25 is:

$$\frac{(20 - 10)/[(20 + 10)/2]}{(20 - 25)/[(20 + 25)/2]}$$

The price elasticity in this price range is -3.000.

6. a. See the diagram below.

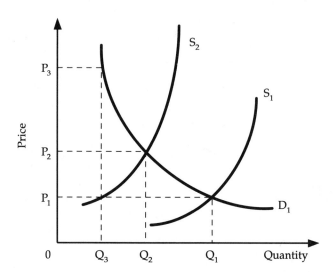

    b. See the diagram above.
    c. The market is efficient, in that it is reflecting the change in supply and equalizing quantity demanded and quantity supplied.
    d. The government should impose a price ceiling to place an upper limit on price. Quantity demanded will exceed quantity supplied—there will be an excess demand.
    e. This is now a seller's market. Output is restricted to Q_3. At that output, an excess demand exists.
    f. Suppliers may withdraw eggs from the controlled Warsaw market—selling them either outside Warsaw or on the black market within the city. Sub-standard (small or damaged) eggs may be offered for sale. Egg quality may be sacrificed.
    g. Other rationing methods, such as queuing or preferred customers, might be used. Black markets with higher prices are likely to develop. Eggs may be sold as part of a "package" of commodities.

7. a. See the table below.

Price	Quantity Demanded	Total Revenue	Elasticity (in words)	Elasticity Coefficient	As price rises, TR
$6	10	$ 60	elastic	$E_D = -3.667$	falls
$5	20	$100	elastic	$E_D = -1.800$	falls
$4	30	$120	unit elastic	$E_D = -1.000$	is constant
$3	40	$120	inelastic	$E_D = -0.555$	rises
$2	50	$100	inelastic	$E_D = -0.273$	rises
$1	60	$ 60	—	—	—

    b. As price rises, total revenue rises when demand is inelastic. Given a price increase, total revenue will decrease when demand is elastic.

8. a. As income rises, quantity demanded falls. Income elasticity is negative—chicken is an inferior good.
    b. As income doubles, quantity demanded rises but doesn't double. Steak's income elasticity is positive but less than one—steak is a normal good.
    c. They are likely to be substitutes.
    d. Quantity demanded of chicken rose as the price of steak rose. Cross-elasticity is positive—chicken and steak are substitutes.
    (For additional practice, calculate the numerical elasticity values that go along with your estimates.)

9. a. inelastic.
    b. An increase in price led to a (predicted) increase in total revenue.
    c. $-\frac{3}{11}$, or $-.2727$.
    d. $-\frac{3}{5}$, or $-.60$.
    e. The position of the curve will remain unchanged. A change in price causes a change in quantity demanded!
    f. No, given that we have assumed a straight-line demand curve.
    g. With a straight-line demand curve, movements along the curve to higher price levels lead to less inelastic (more elastic) regions.

10. a. $-\frac{7}{5}$ or -1.4.
    b. A fall of $1,000, from $9,000 to $8,000.
    c. Elastic. When price rises, total revenue falls.
    d. Both results indicate an elastic demand.

11. Higher coffee prices increased the demand for tea (a substitute). See the diagrams below.

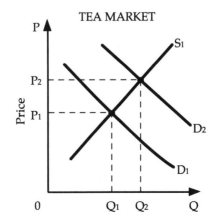

12. See the diagrams below.

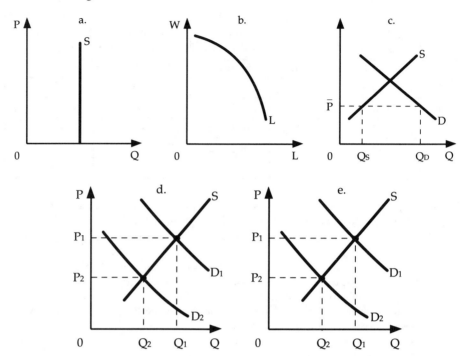

13. a. $3; 40.
    b. excess demand; 20.

COMPREHENSIVE REVIEW TEST FOR PART 1

The following questions provide a wide-ranging review of the material covered in Part 1 (Chapters 1–5) of the textbook. Each question deals with a topic or technique important for your understanding of economic principles. If you miss a question you should return to the relevant section of the chapter in the textbook and fine-tune your understanding.

PRACTICE TEST

MULTIPLE CHOICE QUESTIONS.

Select the option that provides the single best answer.

_____ 1. The Arbezani economy is operating at a point inside its ppf. This may be because
   A. the economy has very poor technological know-how.
   B. Arbez is a very small nation and can't produce much.
   C. Arbez has specialized in producing a good in which it has a comparative disadvantage.
   D. Arbez has some unemployment.

_____ 2. Movements along the production possibilities frontier illustrate
   A. the concept of opportunity cost.
   B. the operation of market forces.
   C. improvements in technology.
   D. changes in the resource mix.

_____ 3. The Arbezani economy can produce consumer goods and capital goods. There is a technological improvement in the production of consumer goods. Along the production possibilities frontier, the opportunity cost of consumer goods will
   A. increase.
   B. decrease.
   C. remain unchanged.
   D. be indeterminate.

Use the diagram for the next five questions. It illustrates the production possibilities frontier for Arbez.

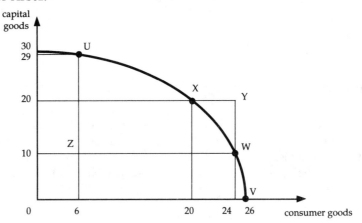

_____ 4. Which point implies the existence of unemployment?
   A. Z.
   B. V.
   C. U.
   D. Y.

_____ 5. Of those shown, with which combination of goods would the Arbezani economy grow most rapidly?
   A. Z.
   B. V.
   C. U.
   D. Y.

_____ 6. Which statement is true?
   A. The opportunity cost of capital goods is decreasing.
   B. The opportunity cost of consumer goods is constant.
   C. Producing at point V can never be economically efficient.
   D. The opportunity cost of consumer goods is increasing.

_____ 7. Arbez is at point W. The opportunity cost of increasing capital goods production by 10 is
   A. 24 consumer goods given up.
   B. 20 consumer goods given up.
   C. 14 consumer goods given up.
   D. 4 consumer goods given up.

_____ 8. Arbez is at point Z. The opportunity cost of increasing capital goods production by 20 is
   A. 24 consumer goods given up.
   B. 14 consumer goods given up.
   C. 6 consumer goods given up.
   D. 0 consumer goods given up.

_____ 9. The price of Pepsi decreases. This will cause
   A. an increase in the demand of Pepsi.
   B. an increase in the demand of Coke.
   C. a decrease in the demand of Pepsi.
   D. a decrease in the demand of Coke.

Each week, Jack and Jill can each produce vinegar and brown paper in the quantities shown in the following table. Constant costs apply for each individual.

	Jack	*Jill*
Vinegar	8	12
Brown Paper	10	24

_____ 10. According to the table,
   A. Jack has a comparative advantage in the production of both goods.
   B. Jack has a comparative advantage in the production of vinegar, and Jill has a comparative advantage in the production of brown paper.
   C. Jack has a comparative advantage in the production of brown paper, and Jill has a comparative advantage in the production of vinegar.
   D. Jill has a comparative advantage in the production of both goods.

_____ 11. If producers must obtain a higher price than previously in order to produce the same level of output as before, then we can say that there has been
   A. an increase in quantity supplied.
   B. an increase in supply.
   C. a decrease in supply.
   D. a decrease in quantity supplied.

_____ 12. The widget market is in equilibrium at a price where
   A. there is no shortage of the good.
   B. the demand curve is downsloping and the supply curve is upsloping.
   C. the quantity demanded and the quantity supplied are equal.
   D. there is no surplus of the good.

_____ 13. The market for peas is experiencing a shortage. You should predict that
   A. quantity demanded will decrease and quantity supplied will increase.
   B. demand will increase and supply will decrease.
   C. quantity demanded will increase and quantity supplied will decrease.
   D. demand will decrease and supply will increase.

_____ 14. Californian wine and Italian wine are consumption substitutes. The Italian wine industry decreases wine production following a drought. The equilibrium price will _____ and quantity traded will _____ for Californian wine.
   A. increase, increase.
   B. decrease, increase.
   C. decrease, decrease.
   D. increase, decrease.

_____ 15. Initially, the market for peas is in equilibrium. Suddenly, at the same price level, there is a surplus. This might have been caused by an increase in
   A. quantity demanded.
   B. quantity supplied.
   C. demand.
   D. supply.

_____ 16. Greaseboro's local coffeehouse _The Daily Grind_ cut the price of coffee and doughnuts by 6% and boosted the number of servings sold. _The Daily Grind's_ total revenue on coffee and doughnuts has risen by 3%. This information shows that
   A. the demand schedule for coffee and doughnuts at _The Daily Grind_ is horizontal.
   B. at present, prices are in the elastic section of the demand schedule.
   C. coffee and doughnuts are a normal good.
   D. the price elasticity of demand for coffee and doughnuts is −2.0.

_____ 17. The income elasticity of Good A is −.7, and the cross-price elasticity between Good A and Good B is −.7. Good A is a(n)
A. normal good and a substitute for Good B.
B. inferior good and a substitute for Good B.
C. normal good and a complement for Good B.
D. inferior good and a complement for Good B.

_____ 18. Costs of production decrease for Debi's Dip. At the same time a government health report alleges that dip consumption causes bone cancer. For Debi's Dip, the equilibrium price will _____ and the equilibrium quantity will _____
A. increase, be indeterminate.
B. decrease, be indeterminate.
C. be indeterminate, increase.
D. be indeterminate, decrease.

_____ 19. The Board of Aldermen of Polka, West Virginia implement a rent control—a ceiling on the maximum rent that can be charged for an apartment. As a result we would expect to see
A. an increase in the number of apartments supplied in order to meet the increased demand.
B. higher prices for single-family homes which will become more popular.
C. renters renting more expensive or poorer quality apartments outside Polka.
D. renters now able to find an adequate number of low-rent apartments.

_____ 20. An oil spill reduces lobster fishing off the Maine coast and, simultaneously, a recession reduces consumers' incomes. Compared to the equilibrium price and quantity in the market for lobster (a normal good) before these events, in the new equilibrium,
A. the price will be lower and the quantity will be lower.
B. the price will be higher and the quantity will be lower.
C. the price will be lower; the effect of the events on quantity cannot be determined without further information.
D. the effect of the events on price cannot be determined without further information; the quantity will be lower.

_____ 21. The law of demand is best illustrated by
A. the fact that, as the price of Pepsi rises, so consumers buy more Coke.
B. increased purchases of Coke as the price of Coke decreases.
C. an increase in income results in reduced purchases of store-brand soft drinks.
D. an increase in income results in increased purchases of Coke.

_____ 22. Price elasticity of demand is −.40. Price increases by 20%. We would predict a(n)
A. 20% increase in quantity demanded.
B. 20% decrease in quantity demanded.
C. 8% increase in quantity demanded.
D. 8% decrease in quantity demanded.

_____ 23. Each of the following will cause an increase in the demand for tennis racquets (a normal good) except
A. a decrease in the price of tennis racquets.
B. an increase in income.
C. a decrease in the price of tennis balls.
D. an increase in the number of persons playing tennis.

_____ 24. In the lettuce industry, an increase in the wage of lettuce harvesters will
   A. increase the supply of lettuce, as workers will work harder than before.
   B. increase the supply of lettuce, as more workers will be employed.
   C. decrease the supply of lettuce, as workers will not need to work as hard as before.
   D. decrease the supply of lettuce, as fewer workers will be employed.

_____ 25. The demand for Good A has been decreasing over the past year. Having examined the following facts, you conclude that Good A is a normal good. Which fact led you to that conclusion?
   A. The price of Good A has been decreasing over the past year.
   B. An economic slowdown has reduced the income of the traditional buyers of Good A.
   C. Good B, a substitute for Good A, has decreased its price over the last twelve months.
   D. Household wealth has decreased among the traditional buyers of Good A.

Use the diagram below to answer the next five questions. The diagram refers to the market for Vito's Vitamins (a good with a positive income elasticity of demand). Vito's Vitamins has a positive cross-price elasticity of demand with Vinnie's Vitamins. On demand curve D1, at a price of $5.00, price elasticity of demand is −2.0.

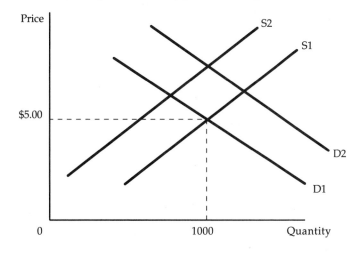

_____ 26. Given demand curve D_1, if supply moves from S_1 to S_2,
   A. supply has increased.
   B. demand has decreased.
   C. price has decreased.
   D. quantity demanded has decreased.

_____ 27. Given demand curve D_1, if supply moves from S_1 to S_2, we would expect Vito's
   A. total revenue to increase because demand is elastic.
   B. total revenue to increase because demand is inelastic.
   C. total revenue to decrease because demand is elastic.
   D. total revenue to decrease because demand is inelastic.

_____ 28. A change in supply from S_1 to S_2 might have been caused by
   A. an increase in the price of Vinnie's Vitamins.
   B. an increase in the demand for Vito's Vitamins.
   C. an improvement in the technology of manufacturing Vito's Vitamins.
   D. an increase in the production costs of Vito's Vitamins.

_____ 29. A change in demand from D_2 to D_1 could have been caused by
A. an increase in the price of Vito's Vitamins.
B. an increase in the consumption of Vito's Vitamins.
C. a decrease in the price of Vinnie's Vitamins.
D. an increase in the income of Vito's customers.

_____ 30. Demand moves from D_1 to D_2 while supply moves from S_1 to S_2. At the initial price level of $5.00 a _____ exists. Price will

_____.
A. shortage, increase.
B. shortage, decrease.
C. surplus, increase.
D. surplus, decrease.

APPLICATION QUESTION

The market for oil has supply and demand curves given by $Qs = -4 + P$ and $Qd = 28 - P$, respectively. Units are millions of barrels of oil per day.
1. Complete the following table.

PRICE (P)	QUANTITY DEMANDED (Qd)	QUANTITY SUPPLIED (Qs)
$20	_____	_____
$18	_____	_____
$16	_____	_____
$14	_____	_____
$12	_____	_____
$10	_____	_____
$ 8	_____	_____
$ 6	_____	_____

2. Determine the equilibrium price and quantity traded.

3. If the government imposes a price ceiling of $12 in this market, what will happen to the positions of the demand and supply curves?

4. If the government imposes a price ceiling of $12 in this market, what effect will this have on the market?

5. Considering the demand curve in isolation, calculate the total revenue when price is $8 _____ and when price is $10 _____

6. Use your knowledge of the relationship between price and total revenue to estimate the price elasticity of demand between $8 and $10.

7. Considering the demand curve in isolation, calculate the total revenue when price is $16 _____ and when price is $18 _____

8. Use your knowledge of the relationship between price and total revenue to estimate the price elasticity of demand between $16 and $18.

9. Use the midpoint formula to calculate the price elasticity of demand between $8 and $10 _____ between $16 and $18 _____

10. If the world price of oil is $10 per barrel, how many barrels will the United States import each day?

11. If the United States imposed a $4 per barrel tax on imported oil, how many barrels with the United States import each day?

12. If the United States imposed a $4 per barrel tax on imported oil, calculate the tax revenue that would be generated.

ANSWERS AND SOLUTIONS

ANSWERS TO REVIEW TEST FOR PART 1

MULTIPLE CHOICE

1. D. If the economy is producing inside its frontier there is an underuse of available resources.
2. A. At full capacity, an increase in the production of one good requires a reallocation of resources and a reduction in the production of the second good.
3. B. One way to look at this is to note that it now takes fewer resources to produce a given quantity of consumer goods—the amount of capital goods forgone is less than before. Recall that the slope of the ppf (which has changed) depicts opportunity cost.
4. A. See the answer to question 1.
5. C. The more heavily Arbez indulges in capital formation (rather than consumption) the more quickly will its resource base expand.
6. D. This ppf is bowed outwards: it is an increasing-cost ppf. As more of a good is produced the cost, in terms of the other good forgone, will increase.
7. D. Currently the economy is producing 10 capital goods and 24 consumer goods. To increase capital goods production by 10, the economy would have to be at point X, where 20 consumer goods are produced—a loss of 4 consumer goods.
8. C. Currently the economy is producing 10 capital goods and 6 consumer goods. To increase capital goods production by 20, the economy would have to be on the vertical axis, where no consumer goods are produced—a loss of 6 consumer goods.
9. D. If the price of Pepsi decreases, the quantity demanded of Pepsi will increase and the demand for the substitute good will decrease.
10. B. For Jack, the opportunity cost of a unit of vinegar is 1.25 units of brown paper. For Jill, the opportunity cost of a unit of vinegar is 2 units of brown paper. Jack has the comparative advantage in vinegar. For Jack, the opportunity cost of a unit of brown paper is .8 of a unit of vinegar. For Jill, the opportunity cost of a unit of brown paper is .5 of a unit of vinegar. Jill has the comparative advantage in brown paper.
11 C. Draw this if you got it wrong! Begin with a supply curve. At any given output the price will be higher than before. The entire price/quantity relationship has shifted.
12. C. Equilibrium occurs only at the price level at which all active buyers and sellers can have their needs satisfied.
13. A. To restore equilibrium, price must increase. As price increases, quantity demanded decreases (movement along the demand curve) and quantity supplied increases (movement along the supply curve).
14. A. The decrease in the supply of Italian wine will force up its price. Quantity demanded will fall. The demand for the substitute will increase.
15. C. Draw the diagram if you missed this one! Remember the distinction between a change in demand and a change in quantity demanded.
16. B. Price has risen and total revenue has risen. This is enough to confirm that demand is elastic.
17. D. A negative income elasticity indicates an inferior good. A negative cross-price elasticity occurs when the two goods are complements.
18. B. The decrease in production costs will increase profitability and increase supply. The report will reduce demand. Each factor decreases price but, while the increase in supply increases output the decrease in demand will reduce output. The net effect on output is uncertain.
19. C. The rent control is a price ceiling. Assuming that it is set below the equilibrium price, a shortage of rent-controlled housing will occur, forcing renters to take apartments that are not subject to rent control.
20. D. The oil spill will decrease supply (it is now more costly to catch lobsters). The recession will reduce demand for a normal good. Each factor decreases output but, while the decrease in supply increases price the decrease in demand will increase price. The net effect on price is uncertain.
21. B. Each of the other answers will shift the demand for Coke.
22. D. Price elasticity = percentage change in quantity/percentage change in price.

23. A. A decrease in the price of tennis racquets will cause a movement along the demand curve.
24. D. Higher costs reduce profitability and reduce supply.
25. B. If a good is a normal good, a decrease in income will reduce demand.
26. D. As supply decreases, price rises and there is a movement along the demand curve.
27. C. Price elasticity of demand is −2.0 (elastic). A good with an elastic demand will see total revenue fall as price increases.
28. D. If production costs increase, profitability will decrease, prompting a decrease in supply.
29. C. Vinnie's Vitamins is a substitute (positive cross-price elasticity). Vito's decrease in demand could have been prompted by a decrease in Vinnie's price.
30. A. Quantity demanded exceeds quantity supplied. Price will increase in this seller's market.

APPLICATION

1. See the following table.

PRICE (P)	QUANTITY DEMANDED (Qd)	QUANTITY SUPPLIED (Qs)
$20	8	16
$18	10	14
$16	12	12
$14	14	10
$12	16	8
$10	18	6
$ 8	20	4
$ 6	22	2

2. Equilibrium price is $16 and equilibrium quantity is 12. You can derive this by inspecting the demand and supply schedules, careful graphing, or algebra.
In equilibrium, Qd = Qs, therefore,
   28 − P = −4 + P
   32 = 2P and P = 16.
If P = 16, then Q = 28 − 1(16) = 12.

3. The curves will not change position. A change in price leads to movements along the given demand and supply curves. If you missed this, return to Chapter 4 and review the distinction between a "change in demand" and a "change in quantity demanded."

4. Quantity demanded will increase to 16 while quantity supplied will shrink to 8. There will be a shortage. Black markets may occur. Queuing is likely.

5. When the price is $8, quantity is 20 units. Total revenue is $160. When the price is $10, quantity is 18 units. Total revenue is $180.

6. As price increases from $8 to $10, total revenue increases from $160 to $180. Demand is inelastic.

7. When the price is $16, quantity is 12 units. Total revenue is $192. When the price is $18, quantity is 10 units. Total revenue is $180.

8. As price increases from $16 to $18, total revenue decreases from $192 to $180. Demand is elastic.

9. The midpoint formula when price lies between $8 to $10 is:
$$\frac{(20 - 18)/[(20 + 18)/2]}{(8 - 10)/[(8 + 10)/2]}$$
The price elasticity of demand in this price range is -.4737.
The midpoint formula when price lies between $16 to $18 is:
$$\frac{(12 - 10)/[(12 + 10)/2]}{(16 - 18)/[(16 + 18)/2]}$$
The price elasticity of demand in this price range is −1.5455.

10. If the price is $10, U.S. suppliers will offer 6 (million) barrels, but buyers will demand 18 (million) barrels. 12 (million) barrels will be imported.

11. If the price is $14, U.S. suppliers will offer 10 (million) barrels, but buyers will demand 14 (million) barrels. 4 (million) barrels will be imported.

12. $8 million—4 (million) barrels will be imported, yielding $2 each.

HOUSEHOLD BEHAVIOR AND CONSUMER CHOICE

6

OBJECTIVES: POINT BY POINT

After completing this chapter, you should be able to accomplish the objectives listed below.

OBJECTIVE 1: Draw and explain the meaning of a budget constraint diagram, given price and income data. Indicate the constraints that operate on a household's consumption choices and relate these to the concept of the opportunity set.

Each household operates within constraints (income, wealth, and the prices of goods) and, therefore, must make choices. Case and Fair narrow down these choices to three:
   a. which combination of goods to buy,
   b. how many hours of work to provide, and
   c. how much money to save rather than to spend.

To simplify the analysis, it is assumed in the analysis of household choice that there is perfect competition in all (input and output) markets, that price is governed by demand and supply, and that households are "informed"—they have perfect knowledge about the price, availability, and quality of goods, about wage rates, and (later) about interest rates.   (page 129)

Each semester, you must weigh up your own situation. How much money will the semester cost? What is essential (tuition, housing, food, textbooks, aspirin, coffee, No-Doz) and what is, perhaps, optional (movies, phone calls home)? How much do these items cost? How much spending power have you set aside from your summer job (wealth)? What income will you have during the semester, perhaps from a part-time job? In simplified form, the *budget constraint diagram* illustrates the limited set of opportunities available to you.

The *budget constraint* defines the maximum possible amount of goods that can be bought and is determined by the household's income and wealth, and prices. In a two-good situation, this constraint looks rather like a production possibility frontier—think of it as a "consumption" possibility frontier, if you will. The real cost of buying more of one good is the value of the other good that must be forgone. All points on and inside the constraint are combinations of goods that can be bought; they comprise the *opportunity (choice) set*. Points outside cannot be bought. The budget constraint will shift to the right—meaning that there is an increase in possible consumption levels—if income or wealth increases or if prices fall. If the price of one good falls, the budget constraint *swivels* and the slope of the constraint changes. The slope is determined by the relative prices of the two goods. Given the constraints, decisions depend on the preferences of the household.

> **LEARNING TIP:** The "Ann and Tom" example in the textbook is particularly effective in making the points you need to know. Be sure to cover it thoroughly.

PRACTICE

1. The budget constraint is the limit imposed on household choices by the household's
   A. expectations about future income, wealth, and prices.
   B. wealth.
   C. income, wealth, and prices.
   D. preferences and monthly spending plan.
   Answer: C. See p. 134. The basic analysis provided to this point has not yet incorporated expectations about future income, wealth, or prices.

2. Gretchen's opportunity set can be increased by
   A. a decrease in prices.
   B. a decrease in income.
   C. an increase in quantity demanded.
   D. a decrease in quantity demanded.
   Answer: A. The opportunity set defines what is available—rather than what is demanded. A decrease in prices will permit Gretchen to stretch her dollars further.

3. Jenny the Junior buys only two goods: meals and movies. This semester she has $500 in a savings account that she plans to spend, but no income. Meals cost $5 each and movies cost $10 each. Jenny's maximum spending on meals is _____ and her maximum spending on movies is _____
   A. $500, $0.
   B. $0, $500.
   C. $250, $250.
   D. $500, $500.
   Answer: D. At one extreme, Jenny could spend all of her resources on meals or, at the other, all of her resources on movies.

4. Jenny the Junior buys only two goods: meals and movies. This semester she has $500 in a savings account that she plans to spend, but no income. Meals cost $5 each and movies cost $10 each. Jenny can buy a maximum of _____ meals and a maximum of _____ movies.
   A. 100, 0.
   B. 100, 100.
   C. 0, 50.
   D. 100, 50.
   Answer: D. With $500 and facing a meal price of $5, Jenny could buy as many as 100 meals. With $500 and facing a movie price of $10, Jenny could buy as many as 50 movies.

5. Draw Jenny's budget constraint in the space below. Place "meals" on the horizontal axis and "movies" on the vertical axis. Write in the maximum value for meals and for movies at the appropriate places.

Answer: The budget constraint should be a downsloping straight line. The "meals" and "movies" endpoints should be 100 and 50, respectively.

6. The slope of Jenny's budget constraint is
   A. −2.
   B. −½.
   C. ½.
   D. 2.
   Answer: B. "Rise over run" is the formula for the slope of a straight line. If you are uncertain about this, check the textbook's Appendix to Chapter 1.

7. Refer to your diagram. Along the budget constraint, the opportunity cost of one movie is
   A. zero, since the goods have already been bought.
   B. ½ a meal.
   C. 1 meal.
   D. 2 meals.
   Answer: D. The $10 could have bought two meals.

8. Refer to your diagram. If _____ , Jenny's new budget constraint will _____
   A. the price of movies increases, shift out and be parallel to the initial budget constraint.
   B. her income increases, swivel inwards.
   C. her income decreases, swivel inwards.
   D. the price of movies decreases, swivel outwards.
   Answer: D. Income (or wealth) changes will cause a parallel shift in the budget constraint. A lower price of movies will increase the maximum number of movies it is possible for Jenny to attend but leave unaffected the maximum number of meals she may consume.

OBJECTIVE 2: Distinguish between total utility and marginal utility. State the law of diminishing marginal utility.

Utility (satisfaction) is derived from goods and services, including leisure. The *marginal utility* you derive from a good (potato chips, for example) is the additional satisfaction you get from each additional portion. The *total utility* is the sum of these additional contributions to your level of satisfaction. The *law of diminishing marginal utility* states that extra units of a good yield less and less extra satisfaction. While the first few potato chips may provide quite significant increases in utility, subsequent chips are likely to provide progressively less utility (as your hunger decreases and your guilt increases). (page 135)

PRACTICE

9. Regarding Hershey's Kisses, the marginal utility is the _____ satisfaction gained by eating _____
   A. total, all of the available Kisses.
   B. total, the last Kiss.
   C. additional, one more Kiss.
   D. additional, all of the available Kisses.
   Answer: C. For "marginal," read "additional" or "extra." Marginal utility is the additional satisfaction you get from each additional portion.

10. The law of diminishing marginal utility indicates that, after some point, marginal utility
    A. decreases at a constant rate.
    B. decreases at an increasing rate.
    C. decreases at a decreasing rate.
    D. decreases.
    Answer: D. The rate at which marginal utility diminishes will vary from person to person and from good to good. All we can claim is that marginal utility will decrease after some point.

11. Mario plays video games. Although he is experiencing diminishing marginal utility, his marginal utility remains positive. We can say that Mario's total utility is
    A. increasing at an increasing rate.
    B. increasing at a decreasing rate.
    C. decreasing at an increasing rate.
    D. decreasing at a decreasing rate.
    Answer: B. Because Mario's marginal utility is positive, each new game increases his total satisfaction, but at a decreasing rate of increase.

12. Candy has eaten ten Hershey's Kisses and admits that each additional Kiss has been less enjoyable than the previous one. We can deduce that, for Candy,
    A. the marginal utility of Kisses is positive but decreasing.
    B. the marginal utility of Kisses is negative.
    C. the total utility of Kisses is diminishing.
    D. the total utility of Kisses has peaked.
    Answer: A. This is an example of the law of diminishing marginal utility. Since Candy is still eating Kisses, she must still be deriving some (positive) marginal utility from them, so the total utility is increasing, but at a decreasing rate.

Use the table below to answer the next three questions.

Susan visits the state fair and rides the Ferris Wheel several times.

Number of Rides	Total Utility	Marginal Utility
1	10	
2	24	
3	34	
4		7
5	46	

13. The marginal utility of the first ride on the Ferris Wheel is
    A. 5.
    B. 10.
    C. 12.
    D. 14.
    Answer: B. The total utility derived from no rides must be zero. One ride added 10 units of utility.

14. The total utility of the fourth ride is
    A. 6.
    B. 7.
    C. 12.
    D. 41.
    Answer: D. The total utility derived from three rides is 34. The fourth ride added an additional 7 units of utility for a total utility of 41.

15. Diminishing marginal utility sets in after the _____ ride.
    A. first.
    B. second.
    C. third.
    D. fourth.
    Answer: B. The first ride adds 10 units of utility; the second, 14; the third, 10, so diminishing marginal utility sets in after the second ride.

OBJECTIVE 3: State the utility-maximizing rule in words and mathematically, and analyze how the consumer would respond to disequilibrium situations.

Assuming that households try to maximize their utility, they should select those goods that give the largest marginal utility per dollar. Utility will be maximized when the per-dollar marginal utility of the last unit of each good bought is equal. Formally it is stated:

$$MU_x / P_x = MU_y / P_y$$

All this means is that, to get the most satisfaction from one's money, the "extra benefit per dollar" must be equalized for all goods purchased.

An *imbalance* in the utility-maximizing condition, for example,

$$MU_x / P_x > MU_y / P_y$$

means that you could shuffle your income around—buying more of the good giving the greater marginal utility per dollar (X) and less of the other (Y)—and get a better deal. Buying more of X will reduce its marginal utility and buying less of Y will increase its marginal utility. So the imbalance is removed.   (page 138)

> **LEARNING TIP:** The idea of maximizing utility—despite the graphs and algebra—is fairly intuitive. You want to get the most satisfaction for your dollar ("bang for your buck"). You should choose the good that gives you the most extra satisfaction per dollar (MU/P). In economics, remember, choices are made at the margin. (If you've forgotten this important point, review Chapter 1.) In the final analysis, with perfectly divisible goods, this becomes the utility-maximizing rule:
>
> $$MU_x / P_x = MU_y / P_y$$
>
> where the marginal utilities per dollar are balanced.

PRACTICE

16. Arthur Dent is buying shirts and shoes such that the marginal utility of shirts is 12 and the marginal utility of shoes is 3. Shirts and shoes are priced at $8 and $2 respectively. It can be concluded that Arthur is
    A. spending too much on shirts and not enough on shoes.
    B. spending too much on shoes and not enough on shirts.
    C. spending his income on shirts and shoes in such a way as to maximize his satisfaction.
    D. failing to maximize his satisfaction.
    Answer: C. Arthur is complying with the utility-maximizing rule. The marginal utility per dollar of shirts (¹²⁄₈) equals the marginal utility per dollar of shoes (³⁄₂).

17. We discover that my $MU_{coffee} / P_{coffee} > MU_{tea} / P_{tea}$. This implies that
    A. switching some funds from coffee to tea will increase my utility.
    B. switching some funds from tea to coffee will increase my utility.
    C. coffee is more expensive than tea.
    D. tea is more expensive than coffee.
    Answer: B. The per dollar satisfaction from an extra cup of coffee is greater than the per dollar satisfaction from an extra cup of tea. I should spend less on tea and use the saved dollars to buy more coffee.

18. $MU_{Snickers} / MU_{Mars\ Bar} > P_{Snickers} / P_{Mars\ Bar}$. Given my income, to increase my utility, I should spend
    A. more on Snickers and more on Mars Bars.
    B. more on Snickers and less on Mars Bars.
    C. less on Snickers and more on Mars Bars.
    D. less on Snickers and less on Mars Bars.
    Answer: B. Given my income, I cannot buy more of both goods. Because the marginal utility of Snickers is relatively high, I should spend less on Mars Bars and use the saved dollars to buy more Snickers.

OBJECTIVE 4: Explain why the concept of utility is useful in demand analysis.

Utility analysis explains the downward slope of the demand curve. Since marginal satisfaction falls with each additional unit bought, price must fall to "encourage" additional purchases of a good. (page 139)

It is quite easy to see this "diminishing marginal utility" explanation in operation when one finds examples of "Buy the first, and get the second for half price."

PRACTICE

19. Angela will buy additional units of a good (apples) if the value of the good's
    A. total utility exceeds the price.
    B. total utility is less than the price.
    C. marginal utility exceeds the price.
    D. marginal utility is less than the price.
    Answer: C. If Angela's extra benefit is greater than the cost of the apple, then the purchase will be worthwhile.

20. Consider Good X. The law of diminishing marginal utility indicates that
    A. the individual's quantity demanded for Good X will increase as the price of Good X decreases.
    B. the individual's budget constraint is downward sloping.
    C. total utility decreases as an individual consumes more of a product.
    D. Good X is an inferior good.
    Answer: A. Option B is true but not related to the law of diminishing marginal utility.

OBJECTIVE 5: Distinguish between the income effect and the substitution effect and explain their role in the theory of household behavior.

The income effect and the substitution effect provide a second explanation for the downward slope of the demand curve. Most goods are *normal goods*. As the price of a normal good (lowfat milk, for instance) rises, you become poorer because your food dollar can't stretch as far as it did before (*income effect*), and you seek cheaper substitutes such as regular milk (*substitution effect*). Both effects result in a decrease in the quantity demanded of lowfat milk as its price increases.

Although the demand curve for *inferior goods* (Spam, perhaps), still slopes down, the income effect is reversed. As before, a rise in price of the good (Spam) makes you seek cheaper substitutes, such as other meats (substitution effect). But you're poorer because of the higher price—your food dollar can't stretch as far. In the case of an inferior good, however, the income effect results in more of the good being bought. Because you're poorer after a price rise, you may no longer be able afford that steak you were going to buy—Spam is the best you can manage. In general, the substitution effect (price higher—buy less) is stronger than the income effect (price higher—buy more), so, on balance, the quantity demanded falls when price rises.

(page 139)

PRACTICE

21. The substitution effect occurs when
    A. a decrease in the price of Good A makes the good relatively cheaper and encourages consumers to buy more.
    B. a decrease in the price of Good A encourages consumers to buy more of substitute Good B.
    C. a decrease in the price of Good A makes consumers better off so that they can buy more of the good.
    D. an increase in the price of Good A encourages consumers to buy less of substitute Good B.

    Answer: A. The substitution effect refers to the behavior of consumers of Good A when the price of that Good A itself changes.

22. The income effect helps to explain why
    A. the demand curve for a normal good shifts to the right when income increases.
    B. the quantity demanded of a good increases when the price of that good decreases.
    C. the demand curve of an inferior good shifts to the left when income decreases.
    D. normal goods have higher prices than inferior goods do.

    Answer: B. The income effect provides part of the explanation for the slope of the demand curve as the price of the good changes.

23. The substitution effect helps to explain why _____ when price of good A rises.
    A. sellers switch production and increase quantity supplied of good A.
    B. the demand curve for good A is sloped as it is.
    C. demand for another good, B, rises.
    D. price elasticity increases along the curve.

    Answer: B. Together, the income effect and the substitution effect offer an alternative explanation of the negative relationship between price and quantity demanded.

24. The price of Froot Loops cereal falls. Consumers switch over from other cereals to Froot Loops because its price is relatively lower. This is the _____ in operation.
    A. income effect.
    B. substitution effect.
    C. *ceteris paribus* effect.
    D. quantity demanded effect.

    Answer: B. The lower price is causing buyers to substitute Froot Loops for other cereals.

25. The price of Froot Loops cereal falls. Wanda finds that she has some money left over after buying her usual quantity of Froot Loops. She spends some of the extra money on more Froot Loops. This is the
    A. income effect in operation.
    B. substitution effect in operation.
    C. normal effect in operation.
    D. inferior effect in operation.

    Answer: A. The reduced price has increased Wanda's spending power—her income, in this sense, has increased. We can see that this good is a normal good for Wanda because she buys more.

OBJECTIVE 6: Define consumer surplus.

For the final unit of a good purchased, the price and the value derived should be equal. Previous units should be valued more highly but the same price charged. *Consumer surplus* is the difference between the value the purchaser places on his or her purchases of a product and the price he or she pays. Graphically, the consumer surplus is the triangle bounded by the demand curve, the vertical axis, and the product price. Changes in the triangle's area reflect changes in consumer well-being. Can you see that, if Steven's demand for steak increases, other things remaining unchanged, his consumer surplus will increase? (page 142)

PRACTICE

26. Given your demand curve for bananas, as the price of bananas decreases, your consumer surplus will
    A. increase, because the gap between the price you would pay and the price you do pay is greater than before.
    B. decrease, because marginal utility diminishes as more of a good is bought.
    C. remain constant, because the demand curve has not changed position.
    D. remain constant, because the maximum price you would pay has not changed.
    Answer: A. See the definition of consumer surplus on p. 144.

27. Diamonds are more expensive than water because the price of a product tends to reflect its
    A. total value.
    B. consumer surplus.
    C. marginal value.
    D. revealed preference.
    Answer: C. The consumer assesses whether to buy or not by comparing the price with the marginal utility. If the marginal utility is low, the price will need to be low to encourage purchase.

Use the diagram below to answer the following question.

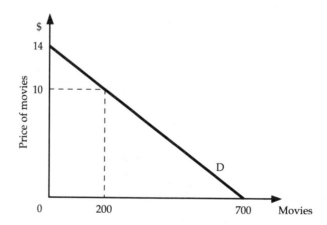

28. When the price of a movie is $10, the consumer surplus is
    A. $4.
    B. $200.
    C. $400.
    D. $800.
    Answer: C. Consumer surplus is the area between the demand curve and the price. With a straight line demand curve it is $\frac{1}{2}(P_{max} - P)Qd$. In this case, consumer surplus is $\frac{1}{2}(14 - 10)200$, or $400.

OBJECTIVE 7: Analyze the shape of the labor-supply curve using the income and substitution effects.

A household chooses how much labor to supply (and how much leisure and unpaid work time to relinquish). The opportunity cost of paid work is leisure and unpaid work. The wage rate can be thought of as the "price" of unpaid work or leisure. If the wage rate rises, the substitution effect would encourage supplying additional labor (the opportunity cost of leisure is now higher) but the income effect would discourage additional work (higher income would make the worker want to increase consumption of normal goods, including leisure). If the income effect is stronger than the substitution effect, the labor-supply curve will bend backwards.

(page 146)

> **LEARNING TIP:** Throughout the textbook, Case and Fair stress the links between the input and output markets. For you to make sense of the remainder of the book you have to develop a good understanding of the material on household behavior in the labor market.
>
> There is an interesting example of a strong income effect in operation in the Algerian labor market. To attract workers, U.S. companies in Algeria in the early 1960s paid wages that were about four times the local norm. To their dismay they found that, after a short time on the payroll, workers would not show up for work. The workers, who had earned a year's worth of income in a few months, simply chose to take the leisure time to enjoy their prosperity!

> **LEARNING TIP:** A good way to understand the section on labor supply is to turn the concept around and consider the amount of leisure demanded. As the "price" of leisure (the wage rate) increases, the quantity demanded of leisure will decrease (substitution effect). If higher wage rates increase income and if leisure is a normal good, the quantity demanded of leisure will increase (income effect). So two conflicting forces are in operation.

PRACTICE

29. In Crantown, an increase in the wage of deckhands results in an increase in the number of deckhands making themselves available for work. This indicates that the
    A. income effect is stronger than the substitution effect.
    B. substitution effect is stronger than the income effect.
    C. income effect is positive.
    D. substitution effect is negative.
    Answer: B. The supply of deckhands is upward sloping. This indicates that, although deckhands may wish to work less and enjoy leisure at higher wage rates (income effect), the substitution effect predominates.

Use the diagram below, which depicts Kevin's supply of labor mowing lawns during the summer, to answer the following question.

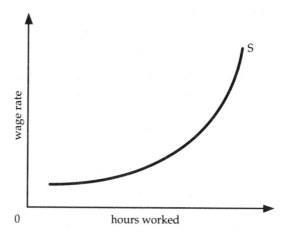

30. Along Kevin's labor supply curve,
    A. the income effect dominates the substitution effect as the wage rate increases.
    B. the substitution effect dominates the income effect as the wage rate increases.
    C. the substitution effect of a wage increase is zero.
    D. the income effect of a wage increase is zero.
    Answer: B. When the labor supply curve has its typical positive slope, the attractiveness of substituting labor for leisure outweighs the ability to take time off and enjoy the extra income.

OBJECTIVE 8: Explain why indifference curves are negatively sloped and cannot intersect.

Indifference curves plot bundles of goods giving equal satisfaction. If there is less of one good, the individual must be compensated by having more of the other good—a negative relationship. Indifference curves cannot intersect because this would imply that the same bundle of goods could give more than one level of satisfaction.
(page 153)

GRAPHING POINTER: You'll find it easier to draw an indifference curve tangential to a given budget constraint rather than to draw the indifference curve first.

Be careful when there is a price change: a price increase swivels the budget constraint inwards, and a price decrease swivels it outwards. This may be counterintuitive. For extra practice on this difficult topic, draw the diagram but have the budget constraint swivel from the horizontal rather than the vertical axis. Theoretically, the analysis is identical—visually, it becomes more challenging.

31. An indifference curve plots all the combinations of Good X and Good Y
    A. that may be bought with a given income level and given prices for Good X and Good Y.
    B. that give maximum satisfaction as income level changes.
    C. that give the same marginal utility.
    D. that give the same total utility.
    Answer: D. A movement along an indifference curve shows that the individual is gaining more of one good but losing some of the other. The gain in satisfaction from the former exactly equals the loss in satisfaction from the latter.

32. An indifference curve is downward sloping because
    A. more is preferred to less.
    B. preferences remain constant as income level increases.
    C. the marginal rate of substitution increases as one moves along the indifference curve.
    D. the marginal rate of substitution decreases as one moves along the indifference curve.

    Answer: A. Because more is preferred to less, an increase in the quantity of Good X consumed must be balanced by a decrease in the quantity of Good Y consumed. Option C refers to the curvature of an indifference curve, not to its slope.

OBJECTIVE 9: Derive a demand curve using indifference curve analysis.

The budget constraint diagram is combined with indifference curves in order to depict the utility-maximizing mix of purchases. Four assumptions are made, the main one being that the marginal rate of substitution is diminishing. An indifference curve maps all the combinations of goods that provide a particular level of utility. The curves are bent inwards because of the assumption that the rate of marginal substitution is diminishing. Higher (further right) indifference curves indicate higher levels of utility. (page 156)

The *marginal rate of substitution* is a ratio, the rate at which an individual is willing to surrender units of one good for units of the other. Put differently, it's the ratio of the marginal utility of one good to the marginal utility of the other. Formally the equation is stated:

$$MU_x / MU_y$$

In equilibrium, this ratio is equal to the price ratio, so that

$$MU_x / MU_y = P_x / P_y$$

for all pairs of goods.

The analysis makes two important points. First, utility will be maximized where the budget constraint is tangent to the highest possible indifference curve—this is where the price ratio equals the marginal rate of substitution. Second, by changing the price of one good, the quantity demanded can be shown to rise—another explanation of the downward sloping demand curve.

33. My marginal rate of substitution between a round of golf and a game of tennis is 6. This implies that
    A. a round of golf is 6 times more valuable to me than a game of tennis.
    B. a game of tennis is 6 times more valuable to me than a round of golf.
    C. tennis is 6 times as expensive as golf.
    D. golf is 6 times as expensive as tennis.

    Answer: A. The marginal rate of substitution represents the rate at which I am willing to substitute one good for another.

34. In a two-good world, Jason is in equilibrium when
    A. $MU_x / MU_y = Px/Py$.
    B. $MU_x / MU_y = Py (Px)$.
    C. $MU_x / MU_y = Py/Px$.
    D. $MU_x / MU_y = -Py/Px$.

    Answer: A. See p. 156.

PRACTICE TEST

I. MULTIPLE CHOICE QUESTIONS.

Select the option that provides the single best answer.

_____ 1. Good A and Good B cost $3 and $4, respectively. Jo, spending all of her income, buys 4 units of Good A and 3 units of Good B. The final unit of each good gives her 12 units of utility.
   A. Jo is maximizing her utility.
   B. Jo should buy more of Good A and less of Good B to maximize utility.
   C. Jo should buy less of Good A and more of Good B to maximize utility.
   D. Jo should buy less of both goods to maximize utility.

_____ 2. P_X is $12 and P_Y is $6. These prices indicate that the individual can
   A. trade 12 units of Good X for 6 of Good Y.
   B. trade 1 unit of Good X for 2 of Good Y.
   C. increase his utility by buying more units of the cheaper Good Y.
   D. increase his utility by buying more of the more highly-valued Good X.

_____ 3. A given budget constraint
   A. will swivel out if the price of one of the goods increases.
   B. will swivel in if income falls.
   C. will swivel out if income falls.
   D. will swivel in if the price of one of the goods increases.

_____ 4. If prices double and income doubles, the budget constraint
   A. will double.
   B. will move inward.
   C. will move outward by 50%.
   D. will not shift position.

_____ 5. Jill's consumer surplus for Good A will
   A. increase if the price of A increases.
   B. increase if the price of B, a substitute for A, falls.
   C. decrease if Jill's income falls and A is a normal good.
   D. decrease if the price of C, a complement for A, falls.

_____ 6. The wage rate rises. If the quantity of labor supplied falls, the most likely explanation is that
   A. the substitution effect and the income effect are both positive.
   B. the substitution effect is negative and the income effect is positive.
   C. the substitution effect and the income effect are both negative.
   D. the substitution effect is positive and the income effect is negative.

_____ 7. Higher interest rates cause
   A. future consumption to increase.
   B. current consumption to increase.
   C. current borrowing to increase.
   D. current saving to decrease.

_____ 8. Jill is maximizing her utility. The price of Good A falls. Jill will
   A. buy more of Good A because it is relatively cheaper—the substitution effect.
   B. buy less of Good A because her marginal utility is diminishing.
   C. buy more of Good A because her marginal utility is increasing.
   D. buy more of Good B—the substitution effect.

9. Fred has had 4 hamburgers and 2 hot dogs this week and is now indifferent between them. Hamburgers cost $2 and hot dogs cost $1. Currently
   A. Fred's marginal utility of hamburgers is double that of hot dogs.
   B. Fred's total utility of hamburgers is equal to that of hot dogs.
   C. Fred's total utility of hamburgers is double that of hot dogs.
   D. Fred's marginal utility of hamburgers is equal to that of hot dogs.

10. In a two-good analysis, the slope of the budget constraint is determined by
    A. the prices of the two goods.
    B. the income and wealth of the household.
    C. the income, but not the wealth, of the household.
    D. the income and wealth of the household and the prices of the two goods.

11. The wage rate can be seen as a measure of the opportunity cost of
    A. work.
    B. saving.
    C. leisure.
    D. future consumption.

12. The utility-maximizing combination of two goods (cakes and ale) occurs when the MRS of cakes for ale equals
    A. the MRS of ale for cakes.
    B. the ratio of MU of cakes / MU of ale.
    C. the ratio of the price of cakes to the price of ale.
    D. the ratio of the price of ale to the price of cakes.

13. A price decrease
    A. increases the choice set.
    B. decreases the opportunity set.
    C. makes utility-maximizers worse off.
    D. decreases the choice set.

14. "Utility"
    A. involves the subjective weighing of the satisfaction individuals receive from goods and services.
    B. is measurable.
    C. can be used to compare the likes and dislikes of different individuals.
    D. all of the above.

15. The diamond-water paradox is resolved recognizing that the price of a product tends to reflect its
    A. use value.
    B. total value.
    C. consumer surplus.
    D. marginal value.

16. When the price of pretzels rises, the "income effect" helps to explain why
    A. opportunity cost increases along the demand curve.
    B. sellers switch production and increase the quantity supplied of pretzels.
    C. income rises for producers of pretzels.
    D. the demand curve for pretzels is sloped as it is.

_____ 17. The market demand curve for pizza is given by $Qd = 400 - 25P$, where P is the price of pizza in dollars. If the price of pizza is $10, the consumer surplus is
A. $6.
B. $150.
C. $450.
D. $800.

_____ 18. Joe would pay $1.00 for his first cup of soda during the NCAA basketball championship game. He would pay 60¢ for his second, 50¢ for his third, and 40¢ for his fourth. If the price is
A. 50¢ per cup, Joe will buy 3 cups and have a consumer surplus of $2.10.
B. 50¢ per cup, Joe will buy 3 cups and have a consumer surplus of $1.60.
C. 55¢ per cup, Joe will buy 2 cups and have a consumer surplus of 50¢.
D. 55¢ per cup, Joe will buy 2 cups and have a consumer surplus of $1.05.

Use the following information for the next two questions. Kaori's income is $100; the price of apples is $5 per unit; the price of oranges is $10 per unit. Assume a consumer choice diagram with apples on the vertical axis and oranges on the horizontal axis.

_____ 19. If Kaori's income falls to $75, but the prices of apples and oranges remain unchanged, there will be
A. a parallel shift inwards of the indifference curves.
B. a parallel shift outwards of the budget line.
C. a parallel shift inwards of the budget line.
D. a decrease in Kaori's consumption of both apples and oranges.

_____ 20. If the price of apples increases to $10 per unit,
A. the budget line will rotate clockwise around the intersection of the budget line and the vertical axis.
B. the budget line will rotate counter-clockwise around the intersection of the budget line and the horizontal axis.
C. Kaori will be on the same indifference curve, but fewer apples will be consumed.
D. Kaori's consumption of apples will decrease.

_____ 21. An increase in the wage rate will _____ the quantity of labor supplied, according to the substitution effect, and will _____ the quantity of labor supplied, according to the income effect.
A. increase, increase.
B. increase, decrease.
C. decrease, increase.
D. decrease, decrease.

Use the following information for the next two questions. Currently, Zack is using his income to consume two goods, X and Y, in such a way that $MU_x / MU_y < P_x/P_y$.

_____ 22. To maximize his satisfaction, Zack should
A. increase consumption of Good X and increase consumption of Good Y.
B. increase consumption of Good X and decrease consumption of Good Y.
C. decrease consumption of Good X and increase consumption of Good Y.
D. decrease consumption of Good X and decrease consumption of Good Y.

_____ 23. As Zack moves towards equilibrium,
   A. he will move along the same indifference curve.
   B. he will move along the same budget constraint.
   C. the marginal utility of Good X will decrease.
   D. the marginal rate of substitution will decrease.

_____ 24. Lesley Behan can buy two goods, Good X and Good Y. Good X is
   represented on the horizontal axis. Which of the following will
   cause the budget constraint to increase its slope?
   A. An increase in the price of Good X.
   B. An equal increase in the price of both goods.
   C. An increase in Lesley's income.
   D. An increase in the price of Good Y.

II. APPLICATION QUESTIONS.

1. The indifference curve diagram below shows Jenny's utility-maximizing goods
   combinations (K and L) given two different prices of Good B. The vertical
   axis represents spending on all other goods.

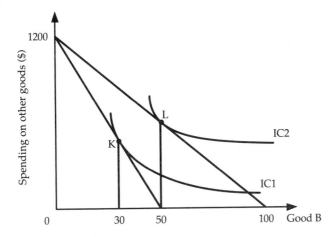

a. What is Jenny's income?
b. What is the price of Good B at point K?
c. What is the price of Good B at point L?
d. When in equilibrium at point K, how much will she spend on Good B?
e. When in equilibrium at point L, how much will she spend on Good B?
f. If Jenny has a straight, downward sloping demand curve for Good B, plot the
   two points on her demand curve that you know, showing price and quantity
   information. Sketch in the straight-line demand curve through these points.

g. Calculate her price elasticity of demand coefficient for Good B as the price changes from $12 to $24. Use the midpoint formula. (Hint: Refer to Chapter 5 if you are unsure of how to do this.)

h. In this price range, classify Jenny's elasticity of demand for Good B as "elastic," "inelastic," or "unit elastic."

i. Use the total revenue test to confirm your answer to part h.

j. Jenny's curve for Good B is given by Qd = 70 − (5/3)P, where P is the price of Good B in dollars. On the diagram you used in part f above, draw in Jenny's complete demand curve to both axes. Calculate the endpoints.

k. Calculate Jenny's consumer surplus when the price of Good B is $12.

l. Calculate Jenny's consumer surplus when the price of Good B is $24.

2. Suppose that we are told that the price of Good X and Good Y are $1 and $6 respectively, and that Marina's income is $300.

   a. Draw Marina's budget constraint (BB), clearly showing the maximum values of X and Y that can be purchased. Plot Y on the vertical axis and X on the horizontal axis.

   b. For Marina to maximize utility, what must be the marginal rate of substitution?

   c. If the price of Good X were to rise to $3 and the price of good Y were to rise to $10, what would happen to the marginal rate of substitution when Marina is maximizing her utility? What has happened to her opportunity set?

   d. If Marina's income had doubled simultaneously with the price changes, what would have happened to her opportunity set, relative to the situation in c. above?

   e. Suppose, instead, that the price of Good X had become $4 while that of Good Y had remained at $6. Now what is the utility-maximizing marginal rate of substitution?

   f. Given the new prices and an income of $300, draw Marina's new budget constraint (B'B') on the diagram in a. above.

   g. Make up a rule relating the slope of the budget constraint, the ratio of prices, and the utility-maximizing marginal rate of substitution.

3. Assume that consumers in Megropolis buy only two goods: bread (a necessity) and soufflés (a luxury). Lucretia Bourgeois has an income of 1,000 opeks per year. The price of a loaf of bread is 5 opeks, and the price of soufflés is 10 opeks.
   a. Sketch Lucretia's budget constraint (AA).

   b. Shade in Lucretia's opportunity set.
   c. If Lucretia were relatively poor in Megropolis, where on the budget constraint might you expect her choice to lie?
   d. Suppose that the price of soufflés were to fall from 10 opeks to 5 opeks. Sketch Lucretia's new budget constraint (AB). What happens to the size and position of Lucretia's opportunity set on the diagram in a. above?
   e. Suppose that prior to the price decrease a tax of 20% had been placed on luxury goods. Assume that the tax is paid by the consumer. Sketch the new budget constraint (AC) facing Lucretia.
   f. Suppose that Lucretia's income increases from 1,000 opeks to 2,000 opeks. Sketch the new budget constraint (DD).

4. The following diagram depicts Bill's budget constraint. Bill has $6 to spend on candy and cigarettes. Each candy bar costs 50¢ while each pack of cigarettes costs $2.

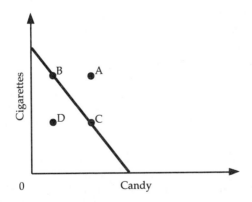

   a. How many candy bars could Bill buy? How many packs of cigarettes?
   b. Is the combination of goods represented by Point A attainable? Why?
   c. Is Point D attainable? What is the implication of choosing Point D?
   d. Which is better—the combination at Point B or that at Point C?
   e. What would happen to the maximum levels of consumption if Bill's income rose to $10?
   f. What would happen if cigarettes then increased in price to $5?

5. Billy-Bob spends all of his income on loaves of bread and two-liter bottles of Coke at prices of $1.00 and $1.50, respectively. At the moment, he is buying these two products in amounts such that the marginal utilities from the final units bought are 80 and 100 utils, respectively.
   a. Is Billy-Bob maximizing his utility? Explain your answer.
   b. If you feel that Billy-Bob could improve his utility, given the conditions, explain how he should adjust his expenditures.

6. Sally derives utility from pizza slices and hot dogs according to the following schedule. A slice of pizza costs $1.00 and a hot dog costs 50¢.

Pizza Slices				Hot Dogs		
TU	MU	MU/$	<-# consumed->	TU	MU	MU/$
20			1	12		
36			2	22		
50			3	31		
62			4	39		
72			5	45		
80			6	49		
86			7	52		
90			8	54		
91			9	55		

   a. Complete the "marginal utility" and "marginal utility per dollar" columns for each good.
   b. Sally's income is $8.00. Assuming that no half units may be bought, how many slices of pizza and how many hot dogs should she consume to maximize her utility?
   c. What would be Sally's total utility?
   d. Sally would not maximize her utility by buying 4 slices of pizza and 5 hot dogs. Why not?
   e. She wouldn't buy 5 slices of pizza and 7 hot dogs. Why not?
   f. It would be possible for Sally's total utility to increase if conditions changed. Give three examples of ways in which conditions could change so that Sally's utility would be greater than before.
   g. Derive "MU/$" values for pizza slices when the price/slice is 50¢, $1.00, $1.50, and $2.00. At each price level, work out the utility-maximizing combination of the two goods. Compare the "marginal utility/dollar" results with the formula in the textbook. Observe that the equality present in the utility-maximizing formula is an *ideal*—in the real world goods are "lumpy." Use the utility-maximizing numbers derived for pizza slices to complete the demand schedule in the following table. Changing prices, combined with utility-maximizing behavior, give us a demand curve.

Pizza Slices	
Price	Quantity demanded / week
50¢	
$1.00	
$1.50	
$2.00	

h. Return to the original situation where the price of pizza slices and hot dogs are $1.00 and 50¢, respectively. Sally's income rises from $8.00 to $10.50. Calculate the utility-maximizing combination of goods.

i. Are pizza slices "normal" goods for Sally?

7. Soon Woo has the following indifference curve map. Her income is 60 yuan. Cotton costs 5 yuan a unit and rice costs 10 yuan a unit.

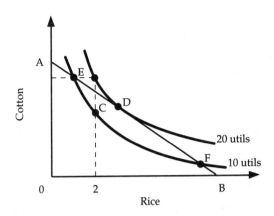

a. Calculate the maximum amount of cotton and the maximum amount of rice.

b. Soon would prefer to be at which point?

c. Suppose she buys 6 units of cotton at Point D. How many units of rice would she buy?

d. If Soon were at Point F, is she buying too much cotton or too much rice?

e. Suppose the government requires each individual to buy no more than 2 units of rice. Soon will buy _____ units of cotton and _____ units of rice. Describe where on the diagram her new combination of purchases will be. What has happened to her utility?

f. Given the government requirement, to restore her original level of utility, and be in equilibrium at that level, what would have to happen? (Careful!)

8. In 1981, Congress passed the Economic Recovery Tax Act. This legislation included, among other provisions, a major reduction in individual income tax rates. Proponents of the bill argued that the reduction in taxes would significantly increase the incentive to work, and they predicted that the result would be an increase in the labor supply. In fact, evidence suggests that for some groups labor supply actually declined. Using income and substitution effects, explain how this could be possible. (Hint: A decrease in taxes means that after-tax wages increase.) What determines whether or not labor supply will increase when tax rates are lower?

9. Suppose that two gourmet ice cream stores sell ice cream cones in your town. Tom and Jerry's cones sell for $1.25 and Johnson Howard's cones sell for $1.00. Suppose you love ice cream and have decided to budget $50 per month for ice cream cones.

a. Sketch your budget constraint and the opportunity set of combinations of Tom and Jerry's cones and Johnson Howard's cones available for $50.

b. Suppose that Tom and Jerry's cones and Johnson Howard's cones are perfect substitutes in your mind—you are indifferent between cones from either store. What point on your budget constraint will you choose?

c. Suppose that the total demand for Johnson Howard's cones is given by the equation $Q_j = 50 - 2P_j$. At $P_j = \$1$, calculate consumer surplus. Now suppose that Johnson Howard raises the price to $1.25. Find the new consumer surplus. What happens to the loss in surplus?

10. First, draw Georgia's indifference map for the two goods "leisure" and "goods." Maximum leisure time is 24 hours, the wage rate is $3/hour, and "goods" cost $6/unit. Now draw the budget constraint. What is the endpoint value for "goods"? Identify the equilibrium combination of leisure and "goods" as point A. Why is this the equilibrium?

Now suppose the wage rate increases to $4/hour. Draw in Georgia's new budget constraint. Why is the combination at point A no longer the equilibrium? Identify the new equilibrium as point B. What has happened to the amount of leisure time consumed? Is your answer affected by the position of your indifference curve? Experiment with the indifference curve "map" to see if you can produce a different result. Based on this example, discuss how the indifference curve diagram—and the income and substitution effects—might be used to explain the slope of the labor-supply curve.

III. ECONOMICS EXPLORER.

Use the second module ("Individual Choice") from the Economics Explorer software to investigate concepts such as consumer choice, budget constraints and indifference curves. Note that some of the material in this module is quite advanced, even going beyond the textbook, e.g., Engel curves and the price consumption curve.

ANSWERS AND SOLUTIONS

PRACTICE TEST

I. SOLUTIONS TO MULTIPLE CHOICE QUESTIONS

1. B. To maximize utility the marginal utility per dollar should be equal. Currently John is receiving greater marginal utility per dollar from Good A. He should increase consumption of A and reduce consumption of B.

2. B. Good X is worth twice as much as Good Y.

3. D. The budget constraint swivels with a price change. A price increase will make the budget constraint swivel in.

4. D. The doubling in prices will not affect the slope of the budget constraint. By doubling income, too, the budget constraint will not shift.

5. C. A decrease in income will reduce the demand for a normal good and, given the market price, consumer surplus will decrease.

6. D. A higher wage rate will encourage increased labor supply through the substitution effect and discourage labor supply through the income effect. In this case, the income effect dominates.

7. A. Higher interest rates encourage more current saving and less current consumption.

8. A. Marginal utility decreases with additional consumption. More will be bought since Good A is a better buy now, relative to other products—the substitution effect.

9. A. If Fred is indifferent between the two goods, then the marginal utility per dollar must be equal. Since the price of hamburgers is twice as great as the price of hot dogs, the marginal utility of hamburgers must be twice as great as that of hot dogs.

10. A. See p. 130.

11. C. Choosing not to work means that one surrenders the wage that could have been earned.

12. C. The utility-maximizing condition is MUc/MUa = Pc/Pa.

13. A. The price decrease will cause the budget constraint to swivel outwards.

14. A. Utility is subjective—comparison between individuals is not possible.

15. D. See p. 144.

16. D. The income effect and the substitution effect both help to explain the slope of the relationship between the price of pretzels and the quantity demanded of pretzels.

17. C. Given $Qd = 400 - 25P$, the maximum value for P is \$16 (i.e., $^{400}\!/_{25}$). When $P = 10$, $Qd = 150$. Consumer surplus is $\frac{1}{2}(P_{max} - P)Qd$. See p. 142.

18. C. Consumer surplus is the difference between the price and the demand curve. Joe would buy two sodas because the value of the third and subsequent sodas is less than the price. His consumer surplus is $(\$1.00 - 55¢) + (60¢ - 55¢)$.

19. C. Kaori can buy less of both goods—her opportunity set has been reduced.

20. B. When the price of a good increases there is a decrease in the maximum quantity that can be bought.

21. B. The substitution effect indicates that the wage rate increase will cause the opportunity cost of leisure to increase, discouraging leisure time—labor supplied increases—but the income effect indicates that the increase in the wage rate increases income, encouraging workers to consume more normal goods (including leisure).

22. C. See the diagram below. Zack is currently at point A. To maximize satisfaction, he needs to be at point B.

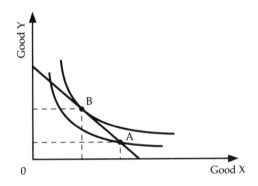

23. B. The marginal rate of substitution is less at point A (a flatter indifference curve) than at point B. It increases as we move to point B (along the budget line and to a new indifference curve).

24. A. Lesley will be able to buy less of Good A if its price increases. The endpoint of the budget constraint will move inwards, making the constraint steeper.

II. SOLUTIONS TO APPLICATION QUESTIONS

1. a. \$1200.
    b. $\$1200/50 = \$24$.
    c. $\$1200/100 = \$12$.
    d. Spending on Good B = price × quantity = $\$24 × 30 = \$720$.
    e. Spending on Good B = price × quantity = $\$24 × 30 = \$600$.
    f. See the diagram below.

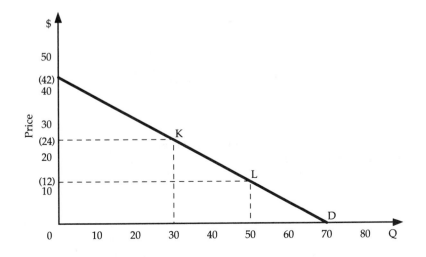

g. $[(50 - 30)/[(50 + 30)/2] / [(11 - 24)/[(12 + 24)/2] = -.75.$

h. An elasticity value with an absolute value of less than 1.00 indicates an inelastic demand.

i. As the price increases from $12 to $24, total revenue (spending) increases from $600 to $720. This indicates an inelastic demand.

j. See the diagram above. When Q is zero, P is 42. When P is zero, Q is 70.

k. Consumer surplus is the area between the demand curve and the price. With a straight line demand curve it is ½(P_{max} − P)Qd. Jenny's consumer surplus is ½(42 − 12)50, or $750.

l. Jenny's consumer surplus is ½(42 − 24)30, or $270.

2. a. See diagram below.

b. −⅙.

c. MRS would change to −³⁄₁₀ and Marina's opportunity set would shrink.

d. Marina's opportunity set would increase, the endpoints of the budget constraint being 200 (X) and 60 (Y).

e. −⅔.

f. See the diagram above.

g. The slope of the budget constraint is determined by the ratio of the prices. When maximizing utility, the MRS will also equal this ratio.

3. a-b. See the diagram below.

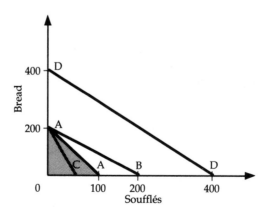

c. Presumably, Lucretia would mainly consume bread.

d-f. See the diagram above.

4. a. 12; 3.
   b. The combination at Point A is not attainable because Bill doesn't have enough money, given current prices.
   c. The combination at Point D is attainable. Choosing D would imply that Bill is not spending all of his income.
   d. Without knowing Bill's preferences (smoker or sweet-tooth) we can't say which combination (B or C) is preferable.
   e. Bill could buy as many as 5 packs of cigarettes or 20 candy bars.
   f. Bill would be able to buy no more than 2 packs of cigarettes; he could still buy as many as 20 candy bars. His budget constraint would swivel inwards.

5. a. Billy-Bob is not maximizing utility because
      $$MU_{bread} / P_{bread} \neq MU_{Coke} / P_{Coke}$$
   b. Since 80 utils/$1.00 > 100 utils/$1.50, he should allocate more of his income to buying bread and less to buying Coke.

6. a. See the table below.

Pizza Slices				Hot Dogs		
TU	*MU*	*MU/$*	*<-# consumed->*	*TU*	*MU*	*MU/$*
20	20	20	1	12	12	24
36	16	16	2	22	10	20
50	14	14	3	31	9	18
62	12	12	4	39	8	16
72	10	10	5	45	6	12
80	8	8	6	49	4	8
86	6	6	7	52	3	6
90	4	4	8	54	2	4
91	1	1	9	55	1	2

   b. 5 slices of pizza and 6 hot dogs.
   c. 121 utils (72 + 49).
   d. The "marginal utility per dollar" values are the same but Sally would not be spending all of her income.
   e. She doesn't have enough money.
   f. Sally's total utility would increase if her income rose, or if the price of pizza or the price of hot dogs fell.
   g. See the table below.

Pizza Slices	
Price	*Quantity demanded / week*
50¢	8
$1.00	5
$1.50	3
$2.00	2

   h. 7 slices of pizza and 7 hot dogs.
   i. Pizza slices are normal goods—demand increases as income increases.

7. a. 12 units of cotton; 6 units of rice.
    b. D.
    c. 3.
    d. Too much rice.
    e. 8; 2. This combination will be on the budget constraint between Point E and Point D. Her utility has been reduced.
    f. Cotton would have to fall in price and rice increase in price in such a way that the budget constraint would tilt to be tangent to the indifference curve.

8. The lower tax rate increases the after-tax wage rate. The substitution effect: Leisure is more expensive relative to other goods. Each hour of leisure requires a bigger sacrifice of other goods. Thus, you would expect people to consume less leisure and to work more. The income effect: Because the after-tax wage rate has increased, people have more income—they are better off. Assuming that leisure is a normal good, you would expect people to consume more of it along with the other things that their income can buy, and to work less. The two effects operate against each other.

9. a-b. You would choose 50 of Johnson Howard's cones since you are indifferent and we assume that more is better than less. See the diagram below.

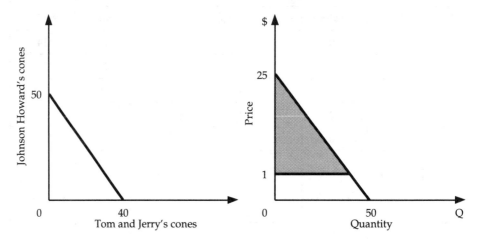

    c. At P = $1, the consumer surplus will be $576; at P = $1.25, consumer surplus will be $564.06. Approximately $12 is lost. Consumers receive less utility from consuming ice cream.

10. See the diagram below. Working 24 hours will earn Georgia $72. She would be able to buy 12 goods. Point A is the equilibrium because at that point the "price" ratio is equal to the marginal rate of substitution between goods and leisure.

    The new budget constraint swivels around with the goods endpoint being 16. Point A is no longer the equilibrium because the "price" ratio is no longer equal to the marginal rate of substitution between goods and leisure.

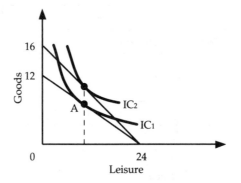

The amount of leisure time consumed may increase or decrease—it depends on the interplay between the income effect and the substitution effect. Shifting IC_2 to the left will decrease the amount of leisure and shifting it to the right will increase leisure time.

THE BEHAVIOR OF PROFIT-MAXIMIZING FIRMS AND THE PRODUCTION PROCESS

7

OBJECTIVES: POINT BY POINT

After completing this chapter, you should be able to accomplish the objectives listed below.

General Comment

This chapter moves from the decisions of utility-maximizing households to examine the factors governing the behavior of perfectly competitive profit-maximizing producers. It is a transition chapter that introduces many central topics, among which are productivity, costs, and economic profits. The topics introduced in this chapter will be reused in several subsequent chapters.

OBJECTIVE 1: State the two assumptions underlying the perfect competition model and relate these to the firm's role as a "price taker."

The basic assumptions used for the *perfectly competitive model* are: many small firms producing a homogeneous (standardized) product with easy entry into, and exit from, the market in the long run. These assumptions lead to two important implications. Each firm faces a perfectly elastic (horizontal) demand curve, and each firm is a price taker. (page 161)

A farmers' market is a reasonable example of a perfectly competitive market—tomatoes are a quite homogeneous product. No single farmer sets his/her own price independently. Any seller who prices above the going rate will make no sales.

> **LEARNING TIP:** Perfect competition is the basic model of industry type in microeconomics. Subsequent models will be developed and compared against this one. Learn the criteria that identify perfect competition.
>
> **Normal and Economic Profits:** Costs include an allowance for normal profits. The owner of a firm that is "breaking even" in an economic sense (total revenue equals total cost) will be quite well satisfied. Obviously, s/he would prefer even more profits, but the normal return is adequate to ensure continued production.
>
> **Examples of Perfect Competition:** The material in this chapter might put you off because of the lack of plausible examples of perfect competition—it may seem rather artificial. The traditional example is farming, while financial markets and telemarketing are others. At the schoolyard level, trading in baseball cards fits the criteria.
>
> A more recent major phenomenon, with the advent of fairly cheap computer technology, is word processing. Check by going over each of the criteria. Entry and exit into these markets are easy, the supplier not even having to surrender his regular job in many cases. In college towns, bulletin boards reveal large numbers of typists competing to produce term papers and resumes that must be executed according to established conventions, thus allowing little in the way of product differentiation.

PRACTICE

1. In a perfectly competitive industry, the market demand curve is
   A. vertical.
   B. horizontal.
   C. downward sloping.
   D. upward sloping.
   Answer: C. The market demand curve is downward sloping although for each individual producer the demand curve is horizontal.

2. Elmo sells in a perfectly competitive market. A perfectly elastic demand curve implies that Elmo
   A. can attract more customers by pricing below the market price.
   B. will lose all of his customers if he prices above the market price.
   C. can increase his total revenue by pricing above the market price.
   D. can increase his total revenue by decreasing his price below the market price.
   Answer: B. Raising his price will lose Elmo all of his customers and all of his revenue. Elmo can attract as many customers as he wishes at the going price-he doesn't need to cut his price. Recall that a perfectly elastic demand curve is horizontal.

3. In a perfectly competitive industry all of the following are true except that
   A. each firm faces a horizontal demand curve.
   B. there is easy entry into the industry.
   C. to survive in such a competitive environment, firms must advertise.
   D. firms sell identical products.
   Answer: C. Advertising is unnecessary. Because firms sell identical products, no firm can advertise its good as special.

4. Elmo's firm will find it difficult to make an excess profit in its perfectly competitive industry because
   A. his firm faces a perfectly elastic demand curve.
   B. his firm, and all other firms in the industry, are price takers.
   C. his firm, and all other firms in the industry, sell identical products.
   D. firms can enter and leave this industry easily.
   Answer: D. The key factor that squeezes out excess profits is the assumption that firms can enter and leave the industry easily affecting market supply, price, and profits.

5. Which of the following statements about the perfectly competitive firm is not true?
   A. The firm's demand curve is perfectly elastic.
   B. There is easy entry into, and exit from, the market.
   C. The firm advertises in order to distinguish its product from those of its competitors.
   D. The firm is one of many competing firms, each of which is a price taker.
   Answer: C. Firms produce homogeneous (identical) products. There is no point in advertising.

OBJECTIVE 2: Define economic profit, distinguish it from accounting profit, and discuss the meaning of positive, zero, and negative economic profit.

Profit equals total revenue minus total (economic) cost. Note that economists distinguish between accounting costs and economic costs. *Economic cost* includes the opportunity cost of all the factors of production and a normal rate of return for the owners of the firm. In this sense, cost includes a profit component. A normal rate of return is a reward sufficient to compensate the owners for the risk and effort they have undertaken. When total revenue just covers total cost (i.e., zero economic profit), owners are receiving an adequate reward. (page 163)

If you provided your (car repair) services to a friend "at cost," an accountant would claim that you broke even. Given that your time had some value (you might have serviced another customer, perhaps), an economist would say that you did not meet all your costs—you made a negative economic profit.

Positive economic profits (or excess profits) are a higher-than-normal reward. New firms are likely to be attracted to an industry by the presence of positive economic profits. In the long run, given negative economic profits (i.e., losses), firms will begin to leave the industry.

Nickie can earn $500 per month (after accounting costs) in Activity A. This $500 per month is the opportunity cost (the value of the next-best alternative, Activity B) for Nickie of Activity A. If, after accounting costs are paid, Nickie can clear more than $500 in Activity A, she should shift over to Activity A because she would be making positive economic profits.

PRACTICE

Use the following information for the next three questions. Jason has a plot of land that has three alternative uses: R, S, and T. The revenue from each use is $5, $6, and $8, respectively. The accounting cost of each use is zero.

6. The opportunity cost of using the land for Use S is
   A. $5, the value in Use R.
   B. $8, the value in Use T.
   C. $1, the difference in value between Use R and Use S.
   D. $2, the difference in value between Use T and Use S.
   Answer: B. Opportunity cost is the value of the next-best alternative, Use T.

7. The economic profit of using the land for Use S is
   A. -$8, the value in Use T.
   B. $8, the value in Use T.
   C. -$2, the difference in value between Use T and Use S.
   D. $2, the difference in value between Use T and Use S.
   Answer: C. Economic profit is total revenue (which for Use S is $6) minus total costs. Accounting costs are zero but economic (opportunity) costs are $8 (the revenue from Use T).

8. To maximize profits, Jason should utilize the land for _____ . If Jason is a typical producer in a perfectly competitive industry, we would expect firms to _____ this industry.
   A. Use S, enter.
   B. Use S, leave.
   C. Use T, enter.
   D. Use T, leave.
   Answer: C. Use T offers the highest profit ($2). In the long run, firms will be attracted to the industry by the positive economic profits.

Use the following information for the next two questions. Amos can sell as many cantaloupes as he wishes at the market price of $2.00 each. Total cost to Amos of carrying each cantaloupe to market is 50¢. He chooses to sell 10 cantaloupes.

9. His total revenue is
   A. $1.50.
   B. $2.00.
   C. $15.00.
   D. $20.00.
   Answer: D. Total revenue is price × quantity.

10. Amos is making
    A. a total economic profit of $15.00.
    B. a total economic profit of $20.00.
    C. a normal rate of return of 10%.
    D. a total economic profit of $1.50.
    Answer: A. Total economic profit is total revenue less total cost. For Amos, total revenue is $20.00 and total cost is $5.00.

11. Jocelyn Willetts starts a VCR repair service. She invests $60,000 in the business. The normal rate of return in the VCR repair trade is 12%. At the end of the first year, Jocelyn's economic profit is $5000. She should
    A. leave this industry. A normal profit is $60,000 × .12, i.e., $7200 which is more than $5000.
    B. probably leave this industry. She has ignored other costs of production.
    C. stay in the industry. She is earning more than the normal rate of return.
    D. probably stay in the industry. 8.33% rate of return is below average, but it might take more time to establish customer loyalty.
    Answer: C. If Jocelyn has an economic profit she must be earning more than the normal rate of return, i.e., she is earning more than enough to keep her interested. Option D is wrong twice over: in perfect competition, because as sellers' products are identical, there is no customer loyalty.

OBJECTIVE 3: Distinguish the short run from the long run.

The *long run* is a time period sufficiently long for the firm to alter any and all of its factors of production. The *short run* is any time period less than that—the period in which each firm has a fixed scale of production with at least one resource fixed in quantity. In the long run, new firms can enter or leave the market. In the short run, they can't. (page 165)

LEARNING TIP: Perhaps the best way to remember the difference between the short run and the long run is to understand the long run first. The long run is a period of time sufficiently long enough for the firm to alter all of its factors of production. Simply, the short run is any time period less than that.

In the long run, firms can enter or leave the industry. In the short run, a firm that want to leave the industry can reduce production to zero. (You'll find out in Chapter 8 that, since it still has some fixed resources, it still has bills to pay. In effect, the closed-down firm is still in existence.) A firm that wants to get into the industry hasn't had enough time to assemble all of its factors of production—maybe the machines and workers are ready but the factory hasn't been built yet.

Remember: The short run and long run are **conceptual** time periods—not a specific number of days or weeks. It will be quicker to reach the long run in some industries than in others—think of all the years of training it takes to enter the market as a dentist!

PRACTICE

12. In the short run
    A. firms may leave the industry.
    B. firms may enter the industry.
    C. there are no fixed resources.
    D. at least one resource is fixed.
    Answer: D. See p. 165.

13. In the long run
    A. the majority of resources are not fixed.
    B. all firms will make positive economic profits.
    C. a firm can vary all of its inputs, but can't change its mix of inputs.
    D. the firm can leave the industry if it so chooses.
    Answer: D. In the long run, a firm can vary all of its inputs and its mix of inputs. It can, indeed, vary the level of its inputs all the way to zero—that is, leave the industry.

14. In the short run a firm
    A. can shut down and leave the industry.
    B. can shut down but cannot leave the industry.
    C. cannot shut down.
    D. cannot vary its output level.
    Answer: B. The firm can vary its output level (perhaps by laying off workers or working overtime), and can reduce output to zero but, in the short run, the firm does not have enough time to sell off all its assets and, therefore, it remains within the industry.

OBJECTIVE 4: Understand how the production function relates inputs to outputs.

A *production function* is a mathematical or numerical representation of the relationship between inputs and outputs. Increasing the quantity of a variable input should cause total production to increase—marginal product is positive. *Marginal product* is the addition to total product due to the addition of a unit of an input.   (page 167)

Most students are concerned with grades—Ivan Exxum certainly is. For an upcoming economics test, Ivan has some fixed resources (his textbook and lecture notes) and some variable resources (particularly study time for economics). By increasing the study time for his economics test hour by hour, Ivan seeks to increase "production" (his score on the test). In some sense, Ivan has a production function (although it isn't explicit or mathematically precise). An extra hour of study should increase his score by some number of points—this is his marginal product. Ivan may choose to adopt a relatively labor-intensive approach (himself and his notes) or a more capital-intensive approach (viewing video tapes, getting help from a Study Lab, hiring "human capital" in the form of a tutor).

OBJECTIVE 5: State the law of diminishing marginal returns and explain why this phenomenon occurs only in the short run. Explain the relationships between marginal, total, and average product and, given the graph of a production function, interpret the behavior of marginal and average product from it.

The law of diminishing returns states that, when extra units of a variable input are combined with fixed inputs, the marginal product will decline. This is a short-run concept—in the long run there are no fixed inputs.   (page 169)

> **Comment:** When marginal product is increasing the slope of the production function is positive and increasing (rising at an increasing rate). When diminishing marginal returns set in the slope of the production function is positive but decreasing.

A frequently used illustration of the validity of the law of diminishing returns is a flowerpot. Space, in this case, is a fixed resource. If the law of diminishing returns did *not* hold, we could add larger and larger quantities of resources such as light and fertilizer, better hybrids and more effective insecticides, and feed everyone in the nation from the product of the one flowerpot. Clearly, the law of diminishing returns *does* apply.

The *average product* (of labor, for example) is the total product divided by the number of units (of labor), and is related to marginal product. If marginal product is more than average product, average product increases; if the marginal value is less than average value, the average value decreases. (page 169)

The Average-Marginal Rule: The relationship between marginal and average values is ruled by the laws of arithmetic. If your GPA is 3.0 and you get an "A" in this course, your average will rise. If you pick up a "D," your average will fall. If the extra (marginal) value is more than the average, the average rises; if the marginal value is less than the average, the average falls. This rule, you will discover, pops up throughout your microeconomics course.

LEARNING TIP: Diminishing Returns: The law of diminishing returns is easier to understand if you remember the "specialization effect" and the "congestion effect." (These are just made-up names; it's the idea that's important.)

First, imagine the inefficient use of resources if only one worker was allowed access to the (fixed) capital. Imagine adding a second worker, and a third. See how production increases vigorously? Each worker is still working up to capacity, and the underemployment of machines is being reduced. The extra (marginal) product is increasing as well as the total product. What should be happening to production level per worker? It'll be rising. Call this situation where marginal product is rising the *specialization effect*.

Carry the story further. Imagine the small factory swarming with workers. What has happened? The machines are being worked up to capacity, but workers are having to wait idly to use equipment. Average product and marginal product must be falling. An extra worker will make little contribution to production. Call this the *congestion effect*.

The specialization and congestion effects coexist at all levels of factor usage. At first the benefits from the specialization effect are stronger but, as overcrowding intensifies, the congestion effect begins to prevail. Diminishing returns have set in!

PRACTICE

Use the following table to answer the next five questions.

Labor (workers)	Total Product	Marginal Product	Average Product
0	0	—	—
1	15		
2	32		
3	48		
4	60		
5		10	
6			13

15. Total product, if 6 workers are employed, is
    A. 70 units of output.
    B. 73 units of output.
    C. 78 units of output.
    D. 86 units of output.
    Answer: C. Total product is average product times the number of workers (13 × 6).

16. Average product, if 5 workers are employed, is
    A. 10 units of output.
    B. 12 units of output.
    C. 14 units of output.
    D. 15 units of output.
    Answer: C. With 4 workers, total product is 60 units. The fifth worker adds 10 more units to make a total of 70. Average product is total product divided by the number of workers (70/5).

17. Diminishing returns set in with the _____ worker.
    A. first.
    B. second.
    C. third.
    D. fourth.
    Answer: C. The marginal products of the first, second, and third workers respectively are 15, 17, 16. The decline begins with the third worker.

18. Average product begins to decrease with the _____ worker.
    A. first.
    B. second.
    C. third.
    D. fourth.
    Answer: D. The average products of the first, second, third, and fourth workers respectively are 15, 16, 16, 15. The decline begins with the fourth worker.

19. The marginal product of the sixth worker is
    A. 8 units of output.
    B. 13 units of output.
    C. 14 units of output.
    D. 78 units of output.
    Answer: A. Total product of 5 workers is 70. Total product of 6 workers is 78. The sixth worker adds 8 units of output.

20. When marginal product is decreasing, average product is
    A. decreasing.
    B. increasing.
    C. negative.
    D. none of the above.
    Answer: D. Average product may be increasing or decreasing but, without additional information, we can't say for certain.

OBJECTIVE 6: Explain and, given a numerical example with prices, select the least-cost production technology for a firm.

Choosing the least-cost (profit-maximizing) method of production depends on the available techniques of production and the prices of the factors of production.

(page 171)

For a given output level, the producer should attempt to employ the least-cost method of production. One gets the best "value for money" by hiring resources to equalize the marginal product per dollar of each resource.

> **LEARNING TIP:** The logic here is the same as we saw in Chapter 6 where consumers attempt to maximize utility by equating the marginal utility per dollar of each good purchased. Go back and review that discussion, if the similar point here is unclear to you.

PRACTICE

Use the following information for the next four questions. Each technology produces the same amount of output.

Technology	Units of Capital	Units of Labor
A	2	15
B	5	8
C	9	3
D	14	1

21. The price of both labor and capital is $1 per unit. Which is the optimal production technique?
    A. A.
    B. B.
    C. C.
    D. D.
    Answer: C. Technique C is best (least-cost). The total cost is $12.

22. If the price of labor remains at $1 per unit and the price of capital rises to $10 per unit, which is the optimal production technique?
    A. A.
    B. B.
    C. C.
    D. D.
    Answer: A. The total cost is $35. The next best is B with a total cost of $58.

23. If the price of capital is $1 per unit and the price of labor is $5 per unit, which is the optimal production technique?
    A. A.
    B. B.
    C. C.
    D. D.
    Answer: D. The total cost is $19. The next best is B with a total cost of $24.

24. Which production technique is the most labor intensive?
    A. A.
    B. B.
    C. C.
    D. D.
    Answer: A. Technique A uses more units of labor than any of the other techniques.

OBJECTIVE 7: Use the isoquant-isocost diagram to identify the optimal capital-labor mix for a given production level.

The appendix to Chapter 7 develops two new graphical tools: the isoquant and the isocost line. By combining these it becomes possible to work out the least costly (and profit-maximizing) combination of two inputs, given a particular output level.

(page 177)

Isoquants are lines plotting all the combinations of two inputs that will produce a particular level of production. In general, they are downward sloping—the more labor we use, the less capital we need. The slope of the isoquant is the *marginal rate of technical substitution* (MRTS), the rate at which we can surrender workers and hire new machines while holding production constant. Higher levels of production are represented by isoquants that are further from the origin.   (page 177)

Isocosts are lines plotting all the combinations of labor and capital that can be hired for a given amount of money. In general, isocost lines are downward sloping—the more labor we hire, the less money there is left to hire capital. The slope of the line is determined by the relative costs of labor and capital. A higher level of expenditure is represented by an isocost line that is further from the origin.   (page 178)

Given the trade-off between labor and capital, and the relative prices of the two inputs, the producer's goal is to find the lowest possible cost for producing a chosen level of production. This must also represent the *profit-maximizing* input mix. Equilibrium occurs when the lowest possible isocost line is just tangential to the given isoquant. Formally, the equilibrium condition is stated:

$$MPL / PL = MPK / PK$$

> **LEARNING TIP:** You should see the relationship between the material in the appendix of this chapter and in that of Chapter 6. Economists lack imagination and tend to use the same ideas over and over again! For "isoquant," read "indifference curve." For "isocost line," read "budget line." And, of course, the marginal rate of technical substitution is the production-side version of the marginal rate of substitution. If you're a little confused by the appendix of Chapter 7, review the appendix of Chapter 6.

PRACTICE

25. A graph showing all the combinations of labor and capital that can be used to produce a given level of output is called
    A. an isocost line.
    B. an isoquant.
    C. an isotech line.
    D. a production function.
    Answer: B. There's no such thing as an isotech line. See p. 177 for the discussion of isoquants.

Use the following information to answer the next five questions.

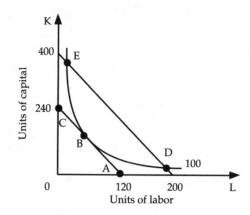

26. If the price of labor is $12 per unit, the total cost along isocost line AC
    A. is $10.
    B. is $12.
    C. is $1440.
    D. depends on the price of capital too.
    Answer: C. Each unit of labor costs $12, and 120 can be bought.

27. If the price of labor is $12 per unit, then the price of a unit of capital is
    A. $2.
    B. $6.
    C. $12.
    D. $1440.
    Answer: B. Labor costs $12 per unit and twice as many units of capital can be bought.

28. If the firm chooses to produce 100 units of output, its least-cost mix of labor and capital is represented by point
    A. B.
    B. D.
    C. E.
    D. A.
    Answer: A. Point B is the least-cost mix because it is on the lowest possible isocost line that can achieve 100 units of output.

29. The slope of the isoquant in the diagram above is given by
    A. −TPL/TPK.
    B. −TPK/TP.
    C. −APL/APK.
    D. −MPL/MPK.
    Answer: D. Slope is "rise over run." See p. 178.

30. Considering the isocost line that passes through point D: if the price of labor is still $12, the total cost must be _____ and the price of capital must be _____
    A. $2400, $6.
    B. $4800, $6.
    C. $2400, $12.
    D. $4800, $12.
    Answer: A. Twice as much capital can be bought as labor, so capital must be half the price of labor. Total cost is $12 × 200.

PRACTICE TEST

I. MULTIPLE CHOICE QUESTIONS.

Select the option that provides the single best answer.

_____ 1. Four workers produce 160 units of output and 5 workers produce 180. The marginal product of the fifth worker is
   A. 32 units of output.
   B. 4 units of output.
   C. 20 units of output.
   D. 36 units of output.

_____ 2. The return on investment that is just sufficient to satisfy the owners of a business is called
   A. normal profit.
   B. marginal profit.
   C. economic profit.
   D. excess profit.

_____ 3. The law of diminishing returns
   A. applies in the short run but not in the long run.
   B. requires that all factors of production must diminish in equal proportions.
   C. requires that all factors of production must diminish in unequal proportions.
   D. states that marginal product must always be less than average product.

_____ 4. The demand curve faced by a perfectly competitive firm is
   A. always downward sloping.
   B. horizontal.
   C. perfectly inelastic.
   D. downward sloping if the law of demand applies.

_____ 5. The short run is a period of time during which
   A. all resources are fixed.
   B. all resources are variable.
   C. the scale of production is fixed.
   D. the scale of production is variable.

_____ 6. If diminishing returns have set in, a firm that doubles the number of workers will see total production
   A. decrease.
   B. less than double.
   C. more than double.
   D. decrease by 50%.

_____ 7. Andy increases the amount of capital his workers use. The average product of labor will _____ and the marginal product of labor will _____
   A. increase, increase.
   B. decrease, decrease.
   C. increase, decrease.
   D. decrease, increase.

_____ 8. Which of the following is most likely to reach the long run soonest?
   A. An ice cream vendor.
   B. An aircraft manufacturer.
   C. A private college.
   D. A state university.

Use the following table to answer the next two questions.

Number of Workers	Marginal Product
1	19
2	26
3	24
4	20
5	18

_____ 9. Total product, if 4 workers are employed, is
A. 20 units of output.
B. 69 units of output.
C. 89 units of output.
D. 107 units of output.

_____ 10. Average product, if 3 workers are employed, is
A. 24 units of output.
B. 23 units of output.
C. 26 units of output.
D. 8 units of output.

_____ 11. Each of the following is a decision that must be made by a perfectly competitive firm except
A. which price level to set for its output.
B. how much of each input to demand.
C. how to produce its output.
D. how much output to supply.

_____ 12. In the short run which of the following is incorrect?
A. Existing firms cannot leave the industry.
B. New firms cannot enter the industry.
C. The firm is operating under a fixed scale of production.
D. Firms have no variable factors of production.

_____ 13. The cost-minimizing combination of labor and capital occurs when the MRTS of capital for labor equals
A. the MRTS of labor for capital.
B. the ratio of MPL / MPK.
C. the ratio of the price of labor to the price of capital.
D. the ratio of the price of capital to the price of labor.

_____ 14. On a given isoquant a firm is hiring too much capital (and not enough labor).
A. The firm is failing to minimize costs.
B. The marginal product of capital is greater than the marginal product of labor.
C. The price of capital will fall.
D. The marginal product of capital is less than the marginal product of labor.
Note: Try drawing this one!

Use the following diagram to answer the next four questions.

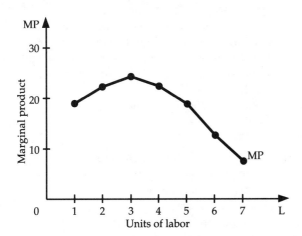

_____ 15. Based on the diagram above, the marginal product of labor for the fifth worker is
   A. 22 units of output.
   B. 19 units of output.
   C. 13 units of output.
   D. 5 units of output.

_____ 16. Based on the diagram above, the total product of labor when there are 2 workers is
   A. 22 units of output.
   B. 38 units of output.
   C. 41 units of output.
   D. 44 units of output.

_____ 17. Based on the diagram above, the average product of labor when there are 4 workers is
   A. 5.5 units of output.
   B. 6 units of output.
   C. 21.75 units of output.
   D. 87 units of output.

_____ 18. Based on the diagram above, diminishing returns set in with the
   A. first worker.
   B. second worker.
   C. third worker.
   D. fourth worker.

_____ 19. The cost-minimizing equilibrium condition is
   A. $MP_L/P_L = MP_K/P_K$.
   B. $-MP_L/MP_K = -P_L/P_K$.
   C. $-MP_L/P_L = MP_K/P_K$.
   D. $P_K/P_L = -MP_L/MP_K$.

_____ 20. When marginal product is zero, total product is _____ and average product is _____
   A. maximized, maximized.
   B. maximized, decreasing.
   C. decreasing, maximized.
   D. decreasing, decreasing.

_____ 21. The perfectly competitive firm has no choice regarding
   A. the price that may be charged.
   B. how much output to produce.
   C. the choice of technology.
   D. how much of each input to hire.

_____ 22. Ms. Prudence Juris decides to open a law office. She quits her job as an assistant district attorney (annual salary: $25,000), borrows $50,000 at 10% annual interest, hires a secretary at $20,000/year and rents office space at $55,000/year. During her first year, she receives revenues of $100,000. Assuming costs and revenues as represented, what is her **economic profit** for the year?
A. $20,000.
B. zero, but she does earn a normal profit.
C. −$5,000.
D. −$50,000.

_____ 23. Because of the law of diminishing returns, the general appearance of the production function graph is that it
A. increases at an increasing rate.
B. increases at a decreasing rate.
C. decreases at an increasing rate.
D. decreases at a decreasing rate.

Use the following information for the next two questions. Russell is making plans to open a car wash. His research has isolated four distinct methods of production, each of which will produce the same number of gleaming clean cars.

Technology	Units of Capital	Units of Labor
A	2	20
B	4	15
C	6	11
D	8	8

_____ 24. If the hourly price of a unit of capital is $60 and the hourly wage is $6, which production technology should Russell choose in order to minimize costs?
A. A.
B. B.
C. C.
D. D.

_____ 25. Which is the most labor-intensive method of production?
A. A.
B. B.
C. C.
D. D.

II. APPLICATION QUESTIONS.

1. Here are three different mixes of capital and labor and how they change as output level increases.

Output	—Mix 1—		—Mix 2—		—Mix 3—	
	K	L	K	L	K	L
11	6	1	4	4	2	7
12	7	3	6	6	3	10
13	9	5	8	8	4	14
14	12	7	10	10	5	20
15	15	9	12	12	6	26
16	21	11	14	14	7	32

a. In general, which input mix is the most desirable?
b. Which input mix will be chosen if the firm wishes to produce 11 units of output and the price of capital is $4/unit and the price of labor is $2/unit?
c. Will this still be cheapest if the input prices change to $3 and $3, respectively?
d. Or $2 and $4, respectively?
e. For each of the three sets of prices in b., c., and d. above, establish which input mix is cheapest at each output level. To do this you will have to calculate total costs. Note that no one technology, capital-, or labor-intensive, or intermediate, is always cheapest.

2. Total cost is $200. The price of a unit of labor is $10 and the price of a unit of capital is $20. See the diagram below.

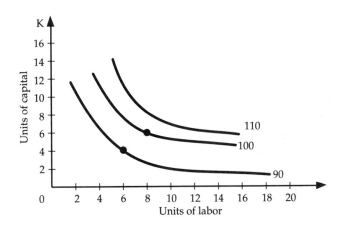

a. Draw the isocost line. Call the point of tangency Point A.
b. What is the maximum output level attainable?
c. How many units of labor and capital are used?
d. Check that this solution complies with the total cost of $200.
e. At Point A, is the marginal product of the last unit of labor greater than or less than the marginal product of the last unit of capital.
f. Graph the effect of an increase in the price of labor to $20.
g. Calculate the new cost-minimizing combination of inputs.

3. Billy Bob is a highly-paid economics professor making $15,000 per year. He thinks that there must be a better way to make a living and decides to go into hog farming. Billy Bob resigns his teaching job, rents some land, and hires an agricultural college graduate to help around the farm, drive the tractor and slop the hogs.

   At the end of the year, Billy Bob has incurred the following explicit costs:

Labor	$20,000
Rent	$40,000
Fuel, feed, seed, fertilizer, piglets	$33,000

   As for revenue, Billy Bob sold 110 pigs during the year for an average revenue of $1000 each. How much *economic* profit did the farm earn? Assuming that teaching is his only option, should he continue in the hog business?

4. Below is the production function for Wilma's Wicker Baskets.

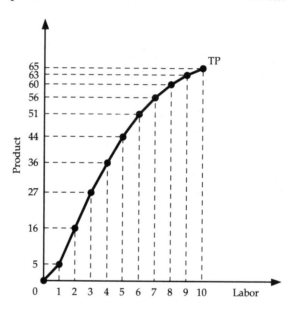

   a. Compute the marginal product and average product values in the table below.

LABOR	TOTAL PRODUCT	MARGINAL PRODUCT	AVERAGE PRODUCT
1	_____	_____	_____
2	_____	_____	_____
3	_____	_____	_____
4	_____	_____	_____
5	_____	_____	_____
6	_____	_____	_____
7	_____	_____	_____
8	_____	_____	_____
9	_____	_____	_____
10	_____	_____	_____

   b. With which worker do diminishing returns occur?

5. Consider the following diagram which shows isoquants and an isocost constraint. The price of a unit of capital is $20 and the price of a unit of labor is $10.

a. Calculate the total cost of producing Q2 units of output.
b. Calculate the slope of the isocost line.
c. Describe what is happening to output if output changes from Q2 to Q1.
d. At point A, compare the marginal rate of technical substitution to the input price ratio. If this information was all that the producer had, how should he adjust his input mix while maintaining the output level? Why?
e. Consider the movement from point C to point A. Can this move takes place in the short run, or can it only occur in the long run?

6. A perfectly competitive firm can sell as much as it wants at the going market price. The price is $10 per unit.

Quantity	Total Revenue	Marginal Revenue
1		
2		
3		
4		
5		

a. Fill in the total revenue column.
b. If you graphed these numbers, what sort of slope would total revenue have?

Marginal revenue is the extra revenue brought in by selling one more unit of production (coming up in Chapter 8).

c. Use this information to fill in the marginal revenue column.
d. If you were to graph the marginal revenue numbers, how would the graph look?

7. Use the following table for this question.

Number of Workers	Marginal Product	Total Product	Average Product
1	12		
2	16		
3	14		
4	13		
5	10		

a. Complete the total product and average product columns.
b. With which worker do diminishing returns occur?
c. Graph the marginal and average product curves.

8. The diagram below is a short-run production function.

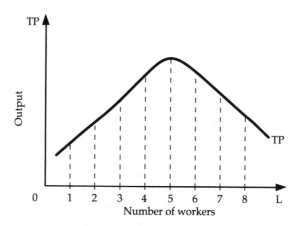

a. There exists a unique quantity of labor that no rational, profit-maximizing firm will exceed. Find and label that quantity of labor.
b. Explain why a firm would never use more than that amount.
c. What must be happening to the marginal product of labor after this point?

9. The diagram below is a marginal product of labor diagram, showing its three distinct phases, with increasing, decreasing/positive, and decreasing/negative marginal product. These are labeled Phases 1, 2, and 3, respectively.

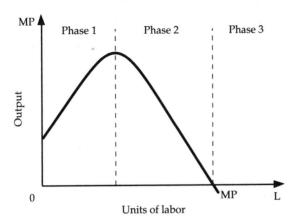

   a. In which phase(s) are increasing returns occurring?
   b. Explain why increasing returns are occurring.
   c. What is happening to total product and to average product in Phase 1?
   d. In which phase(s) are marginal returns diminishing?
   e. Go to Phase 3. What is happening to marginal product?
   f. In Phase 3, what must be happening to total product?
   g. In Phase 3, what must be happening to average product?
   h. What is happening to marginal, average, and total product in Phase 2?
   i. Why does average product show this behavior in Phase 2?

10. The diagram below shows the various combinations of capital and labor that can be used to produce 100 units of output.

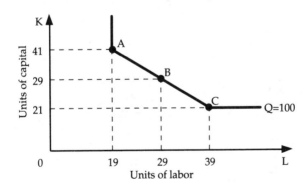

   a. Consider the techniques represented by points A, B, and C. If the price of labor and capital were $2 each and the firm decided to produce 100 units of output, which technique would the firm employ?
   b. If a payroll tax were imposed that pushed the price of labor up to $3 but left the price of capital at $2, which technique would the firm choose?
   c. If a profits tax pushed the price of capital up to $3 but left the price of labor at $2, which technique would the firm choose?

11. Assume that wooden chairs can be produced using two different techniques, A and B. The following table provides data on the total input requirement of each at four different output levels.

Technique	Q = 1		Q = 2		Q = 3		Q = 4	
	K	L	K	L	K	L	K	L
A	5	2	8	4	11	5	15	5
B	3	3	6	5	8	7	11	10

a. If labor costs $2 per unit and capital costs $3 per unit, what is the minimum cost of producing:
   1 chair?
   2 chairs?
   3 chairs?
   4 chairs?

b. Graph total cost of production as a function of output. (Put output on the X axis and cost on the Y axis.)

c. How much does it cost a profit-maximizing firm to go from an output of:
   one chair to an output of two chairs?
   two chairs to an output of three chairs?
   three chairs to four chairs?

12. The following example gives some practice in working out which input mix is the most desirable.

Output	—Mix 1—		—Mix 2—		—Mix 3—	
	K	L	K	L	K	L
11	7	2	4	4	2	7
12	8	4	6	6	3	8
13	9	6	8	8	4	13
14	12	8	10	10	5	19
15	15	10	12	12	6	25
16	21	12	14	14	7	31

a. Which input mix will be chosen if the firm wishes to produce 11 units of output, the price of capital is $4/unit, and the price of labor is $2/unit?

b. Will this mix still be cheapest if the per-unit input prices change to $3 for capital and $3 for labor?

c. Will this mix still be cheapest if the per-unit input prices change to $2 for capital and $4 for labor?

No one technology, capital-, or labor-intensive, or intermediate, is always the cheapest.

III. ECONOMICS EXPLORER.

Use the third module ("Production and Costs") from the Economics Explorer software to investigate essential concepts such as marginal product, average product, and the production function in the short run. This module also introduces the material you will encounter in textbook Chapter 8. The long run is dealt with in Module 5.

ANSWERS AND SOLUTIONS

PRACTICE TEST

I. SOLUTIONS TO MULTIPLE CHOICE QUESTIONS

1. C. Marginal product is the change in total product that occurs when an additional unit of a resource is added.

2. A. See p. 163.

3. A. This law requires that a variable resource is added to a given quantity of a fixed resource. Fixed resources can occur only in the short run.

4. B. Each firm is a price taker facing a perfectly elastic (horizontal) demand curve.

5. C. In the short run, at least one factor must be fixed, thus locking the firm into a given scale of production.

6. B. Unless marginal product is negative (which is unlikely), an increase in resources will result in an increase in output. Because each new worker is producing less than previous workers, output will increase but not double.

7. A. Each worker will become more productive, causing marginal product to increase. If each worker produces more, average product will also increase.

8. A. The ice cream vendor has few resource requirements and those s/he does have can be adjusted rapidly, as opposed to, say, a college, which may have severe limitations on land availability.

9. C. Total product is the sum of the preceding marginal products— 19 + 26 + 24 + 20.

10. B. Average product is total product divided by the number of workers— (19 + 26 + 24)/3 = 23.

11. A. The perfectly competitive firm is, by definition, a price taker and cannot set the price for its output.

12. D. In the short run firms can neither enter nor leave an industry, nor can they adjust their scale of production. However, not all resources are fixed.

13. C. The MRTS equals -MPL/MPK. See p. 178.

14. A. We don't know anything about the marginal product of capital relative to the marginal product of labor. However, the marginal product per dollar for capital is less than the marginal product per dollar of labor. The firm could achieve the same level of output by reducing capital and increasing labor.

15. B. The diagram graphs marginal product. Read off the value for the fifth worker which is 19.

16. C. Add the contributions of the first two workers (19 + 22).

17. C. Total product is 87 (19 + 22 + 24 + 22). Average product is 87/4.

18. D. The third worker contributes 24 extra units of output; the fourth worker's contribution is only 22.
19. A. See p. 180.
20. B. When marginal product becomes negative, total product passes its peak and begins to fall. Given that average product has been positive, an extra (non-productive) worker will drag down the average.
21. A. The perfectly competitive firm is a price taker.
22. C. Prudence makes an economic loss of $5000. Her costs are $(25,000 + 5,000 + 20,000 + 55,000).
23. B. Although initially the production function may increase at an increasing rate, because of the law of diminishing returns it increases at a decreasing rate.
24. A. The total cost is $[(2 × 60) + (20 × 6)], or 240.
25. A. See p. 167.

II. SOLUTIONS TO APPLICATION QUESTIONS

1. a. You can't tell which is the "best" (cheapest) mix without input price information and, even then, there may not be a single correct answer.
   b. Mix 3 is cheapest at $22.
   c. Mix 1 is cheapest at $21.
   d. Mix 1 is cheapest at $16.
   e. See the tables below.

Capital at $4, and labor at $2.

Output	—Mix 1—	—Mix 2—	—Mix 3—
11	26	24	**22**
12	34	36	**32**
13	46	48	**44**
14	62	60	**60**
15	78	**72**	76
16	106	**84**	92

Capital at $3, and labor at $3.

Output	—Mix 1—	—Mix 2—	—Mix 3—
11	**21**	24	27
12	**30**	36	39
13	**42**	48	54
14	**57**	60	75
15	**72**	**72**	96
16	96	**84**	117

Capital at $2, and labor at $4.

Output	—Mix 1—	—Mix 2—	—Mix 3—
11	**16**	24	32
12	**26**	36	46
13	**38**	48	64
14	**52**	60	90
15	**66**	72	116
16	86	84	142

2. a. See the diagram below.

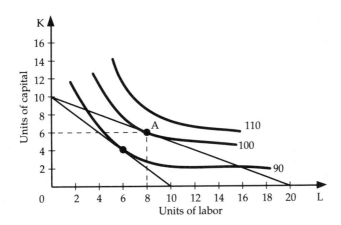

b. 100 units.
c. 8 labor; 6 capital.
d. (8 × $10) + (6 × $20) = $200.
e. greater than. MPL/PL = MPK/PK in equilibrium. Because the price of labor is less than the price of capital, the marginal product of labor exceeds the marginal product of capital.
f. See the diagram in part a. above.
g. 6 units of labor and 4 units of capital.

3. Billy-Bob's revenue is $110,000. His accounting cost is $93,000, as indicated by the table. However, he has an opportunity cost too—the $15,000 he could have made teaching. His total (economic) cost is $108,000. Since his total revenue exceeds his total cost, he should stay in farming. He is earning an economic profit of $2,000.

4. a. See the table below.

LABOR	TOTAL PRODUCT	MARGINAL PRODUCT	AVERAGE PRODUCT
1	5	5	5.0
2	16	11	8.0
3	27	11	9.0
4	36	9	9.0
5	44	8	8.8
6	51	7	8.5
7	56	5	8.0
8	60	4	7.5
9	63	3	7.0
10	65	2	6.5

b. Diminishing returns set in with the fourth worker.

5. a. Total cost is $1000.
    b. −½.
    c. A movement from Q2 to Q1 is a decrease in output.
    d. At point A, the marginal rate of technical substitution is less than the price ratio. The firm should reduce its labor input and increase its capital input because the final dollar spent on labor provides a lower marginal product than the final dollar spent on capital provides.
    e. The movement from point C to point A requires that the quantities of both labor and capital change. In the short run, at least one input must be fixed. Only in the long run can the quantities of all inputs vary.

6. The price is $10 per unit.

Quantity	Total Revenue	Marginal Revenue
1	$10	$10
2	$20	$10
3	$30	$10
4	$40	$10
5	$50	$10

    a. See the table above.
    b. Total revenue would graph as a straight, upward sloping line.
    c. See the table above.
    d. Marginal revenue would graph as a horizontal line, equal to price.

7. a. See the table below.

Number of Workers	Marginal Product	Total Product	Average Product
1	12	12	12
2	16	28	14
3	14	42	14
4	13	55	13.75
5	10	65	13

    b. Diminishing returns set in with the third worker.
    c. See the diagram below. [Note that marginal curves are drawn halfway between the quantity values.]

8. a.   5 workers.
    b.   Hiring more than 5 workers will cause total production to fall.
    c.   Marginal product of labor not only is diminishing, it is *negative*.

9. a.   Phase 1.
    b.   The "specialization effect" is stronger than the "congestion effect."
    c.   Average product is rising but is less than marginal product. Total product is rising rapidly.
    d.   Over the remainder of the diagram—Phases 2 and 3.
    e.   Marginal product has become negative.
    f.   Total product must be falling.
    g.   Average product must be falling.
    h.   Marginal product is falling because the congestion effect has prevailed; total product is rising; average product is rising and then falling.
    i.   This is an example of the "average-marginal rule."

10. a.   If the price of capital (P_K) and the price of labor (P_L) are both $2, Technique B is the least expensive. 100 units cost $116, while costs are $120 for both Technique A and Technique C.
    b.   When PL = $3, Technique A wins with a cost of $139.
    c.   When PK = $3, Technique C wins with a cost of $141.

11. a.   In each case, Technique B is the less expensive.

Technique	Q = 1	Q = 2	Q = 3	Q = 4
A:	$19	$32	$43	$55
B:	$15	$28	$38	$53

    b.   See the diagram below.

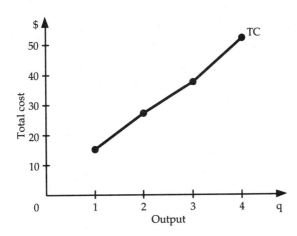

    c.   The marginal cost of increasing production from 1 chair to 2 chairs is $13; from 2 to 3 it is $10; from 3 to 4 it is $15.

12. a.   Mix 3, with a total cost of (2 × 4) + (7 × 2) = 22.
    b.   Mix 2, with a total cost of (4 × 3) + (4 × 3) = 24.
    c.   Mix 1, with a total cost of (7 × 2) + (2 × 4) = 22.

SHORT-RUN COSTS AND OUTPUT DECISIONS | 8

OBJECTIVES: POINT BY POINT

After completing this chapter, you should be able to accomplish the objectives listed below.

General Comment

Throughout this chapter keep in mind that the authors are dealing only with the short run. Fixed resources have costs—and those costs don't change. Because fixed costs don't change, they don't enter into the decision whether or not to produce. In that sense, in the short run fixed costs don't matter—variable costs (and so, marginal costs) do.

There are a lot of definitions and a lot of graphical relationships to learn in this chapter. However, the cost relationships will be recycled through the next several chapters so your "time investment" will be worthwhile. Your ultimate goal is to master Figures 8.9 and 8.10—these are the diagrams that you will be using most. Remember that if you know the "average" values and the quantity produced then you can work back to the "total" cost values.

OBJECTIVE 1: Define, distinguish, and explain the relationships among total cost, total fixed cost and total variable cost; and average total cost, average fixed cost, and average variable cost. Interpret cost diagrams.

In the short run, the costs of fixed resources are called *fixed costs* and those of variable resources are called *variable costs*. Added together they are *total costs*. In the short run, total fixed costs (TFC) are unavoidable and must be paid—even if the firm has ceased production. In the long run, however, all resources and all costs are variable. Total variable cost (TVC) is the cost associated with the cheapest combination of inputs at each level of production. (page 184)

Average fixed cost (TFC ÷ q) graphs as a downward sloping line—as output increases the overheads are being spread out over more units. *Average variable cost* (TVC ÷ q) is U-shaped and it is influenced by the marginal cost curve because of the "average-marginal" rule. *Average total cost* is TC ÷ q or AFC + AVC. (page 185)

> **LEARNING TIP:** To establish the distinction between fixed and variable costs, consider your own situation in college. Your output is knowledge (measured by GPA, perhaps). Fixed costs are the costs you must pay even if nothing is produced. Tuition, dorm room rent, living expenses, and perhaps a PC are examples of fixed costs. Variable costs are those incurred while increasing knowledge. Books, pencils, notepads, library fines, some traveling expenses, and perhaps floppy disks, black coffee, and aspirins are examples. Because costs, to an economist, need not be financial outlays, the opportunity cost of the time spent studying and in class should be included too.

PRACTICE

1. Which of the following statements about fixed costs is true?
   A. Fixed costs increase as time goes by.
   B. Average fixed cost graphs as a U-shaped curve.
   C. Fixed costs are zero in the long run.
   D. Fixed costs are zero when the firm decides to produce no output.
   Answer: C. All resources (and all costs) are variable in the long run.

2. As output increases, total fixed costs
   A. increase.
   B. remain constant.
   C. decrease.
   D. decrease and then increase.
   Answer: B. Because fixed resources are a given quantity, the costs of those resources are a given quantity too.

3. The _____ curve decreases continuously as output increases.
   A. average fixed cost.
   B. average variable cost.
   C. total fixed cost.
   D. total variable cost.
   Answer: A. Total fixed cost remains constant as output increases. AFC (TFC/q) is reduced as quantity increases.

4. Of the following, _____ is the most likely to be a variable cost.
   A. the wage of a security guard.
   B. the firm's rent on its factory building.
   C. the firm's electricity bill.
   D. the firm's interest payment on a bank loan.
   Answer: C. In the other three cases, as output level changes, the cost is unlikely to change.

5. As output level increases, the difference between average total cost and average variable cost
   A. increases, because total cost includes fixed costs.
   B. decreases, because additional units of output spread fixed cost over a larger number of units and reduce its importance.
   C. remains constant, because total fixed cost (which is included in total cost) is a constant.
   D. decreases and then increases, because they are U-shaped curves.
   Answer: B. See the reason given. ATC = AVC + AFC. AFC decreases as output level increases.

6. If labor is a variable resource and the wage rate increases, then the total variable cost curve will _____ and the total cost curve will _____
   A. shift upwards at all levels of output, shift upwards at all levels of output.
   B. shift upwards at all levels of output, pivot upwards.
   C. pivot upwards, shift upwards at all levels of output.
   D. pivot upwards, pivot upwards.
   Answer: D. When output is zero, variable cost is zero. Both curves will pivot upwards from their point of intersection with the vertical axis.

7. Complete the following table. Total fixed cost is $10.

q	TC	TFC	TVC	ATC	AFC	AVC
0	$10	_____	_____	—	—	—
1	$18	_____	_____	_____	_____	_____
2	$24	_____	_____	_____	_____	_____
3	$30	_____	_____	_____	_____	_____
4	$36	_____	_____	_____	_____	_____
5	$40	_____	_____	_____	_____	_____
6	$45	_____	_____	_____	_____	_____
7	$70	_____	_____	_____	_____	_____

Answer: See the *Answers and Solutions* section.

8. Eva and ZsaZsa own small factories producing decorative boxes. Eva uses a production process that has high fixed costs and low variable costs while ZsaZsa uses a process that has low fixed costs and high variable costs. Each factory is producing 100 boxes per week and the total costs are equal. If each firm increases output by 10 boxes per week
    A. Eva's total cost will increase more than ZsaZsa's.
    B. Eva's total cost will increase less than ZsaZsa's.
    C. Eva's total fixed cost will increase more than ZsaZsa's.
    D. Eva's total fixed cost will increase less than ZsaZsa's.

    Answer: B. An increase in output will increase variable costs and ZsaZsa's variable costs, which are higher, will increase more. Total fixed costs do not change as output changes.

OBJECTIVE 2: Define and graph marginal cost. Explain the shape of the marginal cost curve, using your knowledge of marginal product. Relate marginal cost to total variable cost and total cost.

Marginal cost is the increase in total cost—and total variable cost—of hiring resources that occurs when an extra unit of output is produced. In the short run, because of the given fixed resources that the firm has, marginal cost will eventually increase because the law of diminishing returns will apply and marginal productivity will decrease. (page 187)

Each NASCAR driver has a pit crew that services his car when he stops during a race. What an extra crew member produces, in effect, is "seconds of time saved." If Jeff Gordon has no pit crew (and has to do all servicing himself) the gain from hiring a helper would be quite significant. From Chapter 7 (diminishing returns), we know that additional crew members might exhibit increasing marginal productivity initially but that, after some point, the contribution to "time saved" by extra workers would decrease. However, crew members are all paid the same wage. The addition to total cost is the same each time an extra worker is hired, but his addition to total product is less than those who have already been hired. Because of diminishing returns, the marginal cost of additional "time saved" is increasing.

The marginal cost curve intersects the average variable cost curve and average total cost curve at the lowest point of each.

> **LEARNING TIP:** As in Chapter 7, the "average-marginal rule" applies to the relationship between the marginal (extra) value and the average value. Remember that marginal cost indicates how total cost has changed as output changes. Because total fixed cost doesn't change, it has no effect at all on marginal cost.

LEARNING TIP: The cost diagram represented by AVC, ATC, and MC is important in this and subsequent chapters and it's crucial that you learn to draw it correctly. Your note-taking and understanding will improve if you can draw and interpret the diagram quickly and accurately. Practice drawing the diagram! It's not merely a collection of randomly positioned U-shaped curves. The marginal cost curve must cut through the other two at their minimum value. Always draw the ATC curve above the AVC curve—total cost must be larger than any single component of costs. The vertical gap between ATC and AVC represents the level of AFC.

The easiest way to draw the diagram correctly is to draw the MC curve first, then the ATC curve. Be sure that the ATC curve bottoms out just as it meets the MC curve (because of the "average-marginal rule"). Finally, draw in the AVC curve—it also bottoms out when it reaches the MC curve. Be careful that you draw the AVC curve so that it gets closer to the ATC curve as quantity increases—the difference between ATC and AVC (that is, AFC) decreases as AFC decreases.

Caution: Be careful of misinterpreting the box on p. 203! It is true that MC = ΔTVC, but *only* when $\Delta q = 1$. As is stated, more generally, MC = ΔTVC/Δq.

PRACTICE

9. Marginal cost can be defined as
   A. the value of total cost divided by the value of quantity produced.
   B. the change in total variable cost divided by the change in quantity produced.
   C. the change in average total cost divided by the change in quantity produced.
   D. the change in average variable cost divided by the change in quantity produced.
   Answer: B. Marginal cost reports how much total cost (or total variable cost) changes as output level changes.

10. When average cost is greater than marginal cost,
    a. average cost is rising.
    b. average cost is falling.
    c. marginal cost is rising.
    d. marginal cost is falling.
    Answer: B. This is an application of the "average-marginal rule." If the extra value is less than the average value, the average is pulled down. Option C is quite good but MC does decrease before it increases.

11. As marginal product decreases,
    A. marginal cost increases.
    B. marginal cost decreases.
    C. average cost increases.
    D. average cost decreases.
    Answer: A. As productivity falls, the cost of making extra units rises.

12. Refer to the table you completed in Practice Question 7 above. The marginal cost of the fourth unit of output is
    A. $6.
    B. $10.
    C. $26.
    D. $36.
    Answer: A. Total (variable) cost changes by $6 ($36 − $30) while quantity changes by 1.

OBJECTIVE 3: Define marginal revenue and explain why it is constant in perfect competition.

The demand curve faced by the perfectly competitive firm is perfectly elastic (horizontal) and is identical to the marginal revenue curve. Total revenue is price × quantity sold, while *marginal revenue* is how much total revenue changes as an extra unit is sold. In perfect competition, marginal revenue equals price (because each extra unit sold increases total revenue by the amount of the price). (page 195)

> **LEARNING TIP:** Mathematically, *marginal revenue* is change in total revenue (TR) divided by change in quantity. Total revenue is price times quantity, and "change in total revenue" is "change in price × change in quantity." However, in perfect competition, price remains constant as the firm's output level changes. The only way that total revenue can change, then, is through a change in quantity. The marginal revenue formula becomes
>
> MR = (Price × change in quantity) / change in quantity
>
> Because the "change in quantity" terms cancel, we can see that MR equals price (and demand) and, therefore, is constant.

PRACTICE

13. Marginal revenue is defined as
    A. total revenue divided by quantity.
    B. total revenue divided by change in quantity.
    C. change in total revenue divided by quantity.
    D. change in total revenue divided by change in quantity.
    Answer: D. "Marginal" concepts refer to changes. See p. 197.

OBJECTIVE 4: State how firms determine the profit-maximizing level of output and explain why profit is maximized at that production level.

To maximize profits, the firm should produce at the level of production where price (or marginal revenue) is equal to marginal cost. The profit-maximizing condition, then, is MR = MC. (page 197)

> **LEARNING TIP:** To simplify your study, you can immediately adopt the "MR = MC" profit-maximizing formula, instead of the "P = MC" formula used in Chapter 8. Either formula is correct for perfect competition, but the "MR = MC" formula applies in *all* the cases you will encounter (e.g., monopoly, monopolistic competition). Knowing how to find the profit-maximizing level of output is one of your most powerful tools in microeconomics.
>
> When MR exceeds MC, output should be increased—the marginal unit brings in more revenue than it costs. When MR is less than MC, output should be decreased—the marginal unit costs more than it earns in revenue.
>
> In general, the firm first locates the profit-maximizing level of production—*quantity* is decided first. In perfect competition, the firm is a price taker. In other market structures, you will discover, the price is specified *following* the selection of the level of production.
>
> To see the profit-maximization process in a way you've seen it before, re-read Application 8 (Deal B) in Chapter 1 of this Guide.

PRACTICE

14. Complete the following table based on the information given. The price of this product is $10 per unit.

q	TC	TR	MC	MR
0	$10	_____		
1	$18	_____	_____	_____
2	$24	_____	_____	_____
3	$30	_____	_____	_____
4	$36	_____	_____	_____
5	$40	_____	_____	_____
6	$54	_____	_____	_____
7	$70	_____	_____	_____

Answer: See the *Answers and Solutions* section.

15. Referring to the table above, what is the profit-maximizing output level?
    A. 3 units.
    B. 5 units.
    C. 6 units.
    D. 7 units.
    Answer: B. Five units is the last output level at which marginal revenue exceeds marginal cost.

16. Referring to the table above, the maximum total profit is
    A. zero.
    B. $6.
    C. $10.
    D. $50.
    Answer: C. At 5 units, total revenue is $50 and total cost is $40.

17. Jill and John Pantera produce earthenware mugs. They can sell their mugs at $2 each. They find that the marginal cost of production for the first, second, third, fourth, and fifth mug is 50¢, $1.00, $1.50, $2.00, and $2.50 respectively. Assuming that Jill and John do produce some mugs, which of the following statements is true?
    A. The profit-maximizing output level is 3 mugs.
    B. Jill and John can make a positive profit from selling their mugs.
    C. Jill and John should produce the fourth mug.
    D. Because marginal cost is increasing by 50 cents per mug, there is a constant rate of increase in total cost.
    Answer: C. The fourth mug allows the Panteras to maximize profits (assuming that profits are made). Option B is wrong because we have no information about total cost, only how it's changing. Option D is incorrect—see the information in the next question.

Use the following information about the Panteras' enterprise, Mugs-R-Us, for the next four questions. Total fixed cost is $4.00. Mugs sell for $2.50 each.

q	TC	TR	MC	MR
0	$4.00	_____	$ .50	
1	_____	_____	$1.00	_____
2	_____	_____	$1.50	_____
3	_____	_____	$2.00	_____
4	_____	_____	$2.50	_____
5	_____	_____	$3.00	_____
6	_____	_____		_____

18. Total revenue for 4 mugs is _____ and total cost is _____
    A. $2.50, $
    B. $10, $9.
    C. $2.50, $9.
    D. $10, $4.
    Answer: B. TR = $2.50 × 4 = $10. TC = $4 + .50 + 1.00 + 1.50 + 2.00 = $9.

19. At 3 units of output, marginal revenue _____ marginal cost. To maximize profits, Mugs-R-Us should _____ production.
    A. exceeds, increase.
    B. exceeds, decrease.
    C. is less than, increase.
    D. is less than, decrease.
    Answer: A. MR = P = $2.50. MC = $1.50. They should increase production.

20. To maximize profits, Mugs-R-Us should produce _____ mugs. Jill and John Pantera will make a total economic profit of _____
    A. 4, $1.
    B. 4, −$1.
    C. 5, $1.
    D. 5, −$1.
    Answer: C. MR = MC at 5 units of output. TR = $12.50 and TC = $11.50.

21. If the total fixed cost of production increased to $6.00, Mugs-R-Us should produce _____ mugs. Jill and John Pantera will make a total economic profit of
    _____
    A. 4, $1.
    B. 4, −$1.
    C. 5, $1.
    D. 5, −$1.
    Answer: D. MC will not be affected by the change in fixed cost, so the profit-maximizing output level will remain at 5 units. TR will still be $12.50 but TC will now be $13.50.
    Note: See the completed table in the *Answers and Solutions* section.

OBJECTIVE 5: Explain why the marginal cost curve represents the firm's short-run supply curve above the AVC curve.

Marginal cost is identified with the firm's short-run supply curve. As price (and marginal revenue) increase, the firm will increase production. The determining factor is the behavior of marginal cost.

Note that for a portion of its length—the portion where MC lies below AVC—the marginal cost curve is not the firm's short-run supply curve. In the case where the price is so low that the firm is unable to cover its variable costs, it will close down. The MC curve is therefore the short-run supply curve above the AVC curve.   (page 200)

In the Mugs-R-Us example above, if the price of mugs was $1.00, Jill and John would sell only 2 mugs to maximize profits (or, in this case, to minimize losses). If the price was $1.50, they would sell 3. If the price was $2.00, 4 mugs would be sold.

LEARNING TIP: Table 8.5 (p. 199) in the text offers a convenient summary of many of the points made in the chapter.

The Supply Curve and Marginal Cost: Think back to Chapter 4 and the factors that determine the position of the supply curve—revenues and *costs*. Read pages 80–84 again, keeping the definition of marginal cost in your mind. The decision to produce is based on price (marginal revenue) and the extra cost of production (marginal cost).

PRACTICE

Refer to the following table used for the next four questions.

q	TC	MC
0	$ 3.00	
1	$ 4.50	$1.50
2	$ 5.50	$1.00
3	$ 7.00	$1.50
4	$ 9.00	$2.00
5	$11.50	$2.50
6	$14.00	$3.00
7	$17.50	$3.50
8	$21.50	$4.00

22. Given the cost information in the table, if the market price is $1.00, the profit-maximizing quantity produced is _____ and the economic profit is _____
   A. 0, −$3.00.
   B. 0, −$2.00.
   C. 2, −$3.50.
   D. 2, −$4.50.
   Answer: A. Producing any quantity will result in a greater economic loss than no production at all. When the firm closes down, its loss will equal its fixed costs.

23. Given the cost information in the table, if the market price is $1.50, the profit-maximizing quantity produced is _____ and the economic profit is _____
   A. 0, −$3.00.
   B. 2, $2.50.
   C. 3, −$2.50.
   D. 3, $−5.50.
   Answer: C. If the firm closes down, it will lose $3.00. Producing 3 units will generate $4.50 in total revenue which will partly offset the total cost of $7.00.

24. Given the cost information in the table, if the market price is $3.00, the profit-maximizing quantity produced is _____ and the economic profit is _____
   A. 5, $3.50.
   B. 6, $4.00.
   C. 7, $4.00.
   D. 8, $2.50.
   Answer: B. Total revenue is $3.00 × 6 = $18.00. Total cost is $14.00.

25. Based on your calculations above, fill in the following table.

PRICE	OUTPUT
$1.00	_____
$1.50	_____
$2.00	_____
$2.50	_____
$3.00	_____
$3.50	_____
$4.00	_____

Note: See the completed table in the *Answers and Solutions* section.

PRACTICE TEST

I. MULTIPLE CHOICE QUESTIONS.

Select the option that provides the single best answer.

_____ 1. The TVC of 11 units is $100. The TVC of 12 units is $120. Marginal cost of the 12th unit is
   A. $60.
   B. $10.
   C. $120.
   D. $20.

_____ 2. The short-run supply curve for a perfectly competitive firm is upward sloping because, as production increases
   A. the firm must pay higher hourly wages to its workers.
   B. total fixed costs increase.
   C. the firm is able to assign its work force to specialized tasks.
   D. the marginal productivity of additional workers decreases.

_____ 3. In the short run, which of the following is possible?
   A. AFC may be greater than ATC.
   B. MC may intersect ATC when ATC is decreasing.
   C. AFC may be greater than AVC.
   D. TFC falls as output rises.

_____ 4. ABC Corp. and XYZ Corp. have identical total variable costs. ABC's total fixed costs are $10,000/month higher than XYZ's are. ABC's MC curve
   A. is identical to that of XYZ.
   B. has the same shape, but is higher than that of XYZ.
   C. has the same shape, but is lower than that of XYZ.
   D. is higher than that of XYZ, and need not have the same shape.

_____ 5. The firm is at the output level where marginal cost intersects average variable cost. We can infer that
   A. average variable cost is rising.
   B. average variable cost is falling.
   C. average total cost is falling.
   D. average total cost is rising.

_____ 6. The firm's total cost curve is a straight line sloping up to the right. The marginal cost is
   A. upward sloping as output increases.
   B. downward sloping as output increases.
   C. horizontal.
   D. horizontal and equal to zero.

_____ 7. In the short run, profits will be maximized at the output level where
   A. price is equal to marginal revenue.
   B. marginal cost is equal to average variable cost (which is when AVC is minimized).
   C. average total cost is minimized (and is equal to marginal cost).
   D. marginal cost is equal to price (which is equal to marginal revenue).

_____ 8. At the current production level, ATC is increasing. Of the following situations, we should consider increasing production if
   A. price is less than average total cost.
   B. price is greater than average total cost.
   C. price exceeds average variable cost, but less than average total cost.
   D. price is equal to average total cost.

_____ 9. In the short run, profits will be maximized at that output level where
A. total revenues are maximized.
B. total costs are minimized.
C. marginal costs and marginal revenues are equalized.
D. variable costs are minimized.

_____ 10. HAL Corp., a perfectly competitive firm, is currently producing 20 units. The price is $10 per unit, total fixed costs are $10, and average variable costs are $3. The firm
A. is making a total profit of $130.
B. is maximizing profit.
C. is making a loss of $3 per unit.
D. is making a profit of $7 per unit.

Use the following information for the next four questions.

Notebooks sell for $4 apiece. Write On Inc. can produce 1 notebook for a total cost of $3, 2 notebooks for a total cost of $6, 3 for $10, 4 for $15, and 5 for $21. Total fixed cost is $1.

_____ 11. The marginal revenue of the fourth unit is
A. $2.
B. $3.
C. $4.
D. $5.

_____ 12. The marginal cost of the second unit is
A. $2.
B. $3.
C. $4.
D. $6.

_____ 13. To maximize profits, Write On will produce
A. 2 units.
B. 3 units.
C. 4 units.
D. 5 units.

_____ 14. The average variable cost of 5 units is
A. $20.
B. $4.
C. $21.
D. $6.

Use the following information for the next two questions. Total fixed cost is $20.

OUTPUT	ATC
2	$20
3	$15
4	$14
5	$16

_____ 15. Which of the following statements is false?
A. The total cost of producing 4 units is $56.
B. The marginal cost of the fifth unit is $2.
C. The average variable cost of the fifth unit is $12.
D. The marginal cost of the third unit is $5.

_____ 16. If the price of this product was $10, _____ units should be pro-
duced. _____ profit would be made.
A. 3, $15.
B. 3, −$15.
C. 4, $16.
D. 4, −$16.

Use the following diagram, which refers to Jill and John's Jugs, to answer the next
six questions.

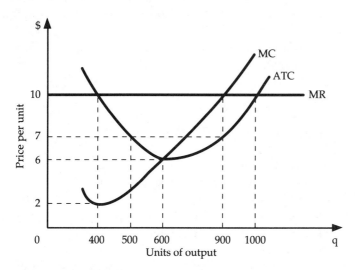

_____ 17. In the diagram above, the profit-maximizing output level is
A. 400 jugs.
B. 600 jugs.
C. 900 jugs.
D. 1000 jugs.

_____ 18. In the diagram above, if the firm produces 600 jugs, its profit will be
A. zero.
B. $2400.
C. $3600.
D. $6300.

_____ 19. In the diagram above, if the firm produces 400 jugs, its total cost
will be
A. $10.
B. $400.
C. $800.
D. $4000.

_____ 20. In the diagram above, if the firm is producing 600 jugs it should
_____ to maximize profits.
A. increase output to 900 jugs.
B. increase output to 1000 jugs.
C. maintain its current output level.
D. increase price to $20 and increase output to 1000 jugs.

_____ 21. In the diagram above, if the firm produces 900 jugs, total revenue is
A. $2700.
B. $5600.
C. $6300.
D. $9000.

_____ 22. In the diagram above, if the firm expands production from 600 jugs to 900 jugs, profit will
  A. increase from zero to $2700.
  B. decrease from $2400 to zero.
  C. decrease from $2400 to $1800.
  D. increase from $2400 to $2700.

Use the following information to answer the next three questions.

Freda's Flip-Flops, a perfectly competitive firm, is producing 10 units of output (pairs of flip-flops). The market price is $6.00 per pair, average variable costs are $3.50, and total fixed costs are $10.00.

_____ 23. The firm will make a total economic profit of
  A. $15.00.
  B. $1.50.
  C. −$7.50.
  D. −$75.00.

_____ 24. To maximize profits, this firm should
  A. increase output.
  B. decrease output.
  C. maintain its current level of production.
  D. Additional information is needed to answer the question.

_____ 25. Freda now tells you that she is considering increasing production to 11 pairs of flip-flops. AVC will increase to $4.00 per pair. Should she expand output?
  A. Yes, because Freda will make an economic profit of $22.00.
  B. Yes, because the marginal cost of the eleventh pair of flip-flops is less than the marginal revenue.
  C. No, because the marginal cost of the eleventh pair of flip-flops exceeds the marginal revenue.
  D. No, because Freda's average profit will decrease.

II. APPLICATION QUESTIONS.

1. Here is a production function for XYZ Incorporated.

# OF WORKERS	OUTPUT	TVC	TFC	TC	AVC	AFC	ATC	MC
0	0	___	___	___	—	—	—	
1	12	___	___	___	___	___	___	___
2	31	___	___	___	___	___	___	___
3	41	___	___	___	___	___	___	___
4	50	___	___	___	___	___	___	___
5	58	___	___	___	___	___	___	___
6	64	___	___	___	___	___	___	___
7	67	___	___	___	___	___	___	___

The firm's overheads/day are:
  Taxes $ 15
  Rent $ 50
  Machines $ 45
  Total/day $110
The variable costs/day are the $30 wage for each worker hired.
  a. The firm is operating in the short run. How can you tell?
  b. What is happening to marginal product? Why? (Refer to Chapter 7 if you're uncertain.) At which output level is marginal product greatest?
  c. Use the figures given to derive the cost information for the table.

d. Use the figures to sketch diagrams of the average cost curves and marginal cost. (Remember that the "average-marginal rule" guarantees that MC will intersect AVC and ATC at their minimum points!)

e. Compare the output level where MP peaks with the output level where MC bottoms out. Why are they the same?

2. You are hired as a consultant by Ken's Cuddly Critters, a manufacturer of soft toy animals. Ken has the most modern equipment and a well-motivated work force, but he is not sure whether he is maximizing his profits. You are given the following information about Ken's costs and the market he faces. Ken informs you that production comes in "batches" of 100 animals.

Note: The "Other Costs" category includes items like rent, interest on bank loans incurred by Ken, and an allowance for capital depreciation.

ANIMALS PER WEEK	LABOR COSTS PER WEEK	MATERIAL COSTS PER WEEK	OTHER COSTS PER WEEK	SALES REVENUE PER WEEK
0	$ 200	$ 0	$300	$ 0
100	$ 250	$ 150	$300	$ 430
200	$ 350	$ 320	$300	$ 860
300	$ 470	$ 510	$300	$1290
400	$ 610	$ 720	$300	$1720
500	$ 770	$ 950	$300	$2150
600	$ 950	$1200	$300	$2580
700	$1150	$1470	$300	$3010

a. What is the price per stuffed animal?
b. Calculate Ken's total fixed cost.
c. Calculate Ken's marginal costs per animal and complete the following table.

ANIMALS PER WEEK	MARGINAL COSTS PER WEEK
0–100	_____
101–200	_____
201–300	_____
301–400	_____
401–500	_____
501–600	_____
601–700	_____

    d. Having compiled your information, you ask Ken for his present output level and are told that output is 200 animals per week. Ken asks if this the profit-maximizing output level and, if not, how he should adjust his production. How should you respond?

    e. Before he makes his decision to accept your recommendation, Ken asks what the maximum economic profit will be.

    f. Ken now tells you that his landlord is proposing a rent increase to $200 per week, effective next week. How does this change in Ken's costs affect your recommendations?

3. Examine the following data:

    q = 50 units   TVC = $750   AVC = $15
    TC = $1,000   TFC = $250   AFC = $5

    The cost of producing the 51st unit is $25.

    Sketch the AFC, AVC, ATC, and MC curves as they would be at an output level of 50 units.

4. Average total cost is $300, total fixed cost is $2,000, and total cost is $6,000. Calculate the average variable cost.

5. Total fixed cost is $20, average variable cost is $10, and average total cost is $11. Calculate total variable cost, total cost, and the output level.

    TVC _____   TC _____   q _____

    Extra practice: In each case, sketch the cost curves and indicate the given level of production.

6. Following is the Average Total Cost schedule for the Watergate Tape-Erase Corp.

QUANTITY	ATC
200	$200
201	$201
202	$202

    The firm is currently maximizing profits by selling 201 tape erasers. The president of the corporation, Silas S. Golden, is approached by the White House with an urgent request for an additional tape eraser. He is offered $300.

    Assume that the additional sale will not influence present market sales.

    If his only criterion is maximizing profits, should he fill the order? Why?

7. Examine the following information about two methods of producing basket-balls.

Output	Method 1 Capital	Method 1 Labor	Method 2 Capital	Method 2 Labor	Costs TVC	Costs TC
11	7	2	2	6		
12	8	4	3	9		
13	10	6	4	13		
14	12	9	7	18		
15	15	11	10	25		
16	19	14	13	31		

Overheads are $40. Machines and workers cost $4 and $2 respectively.
a. Work out the total costs and total variable costs of production. Which method of production is cheaper?
b. Which method is cheaper at low levels of production?
c. When should the firm switch to the other method?
Note that, if input prices for capital and labor were $2 and $4 respectively, different conclusions about the methods of production would be drawn.
d. If the price of a basketball is $13, how many should the firm produce to maximize profits? _____
e. Given your answer in Part d, how much profit is made? _____

8. Suppose that the total costs of a purely competitive firm are as follows:

Output	TFC	MC	TVC	TC	TR	P (MR)	Profit
0	$20	0					
1		$10					
2		$20					
3		$30					
4		$40					
5		$50					
6		$60					

a. Complete the TVC and TC columns.
b. The price of the product is $30. Fill in the TR column.
c. Compare the TC and TR columns to fill in the profit column.
d. To maximize profits, what output should the firm choose? _____ What will be the firm's total profit? _____
e. Fill in the P (MR) column. Using the P = MC (profit maximization) rule, what output should the firm choose? _____
f. What do you predict will happen to the number of firms in this industry? In that case, what will happen to supply and to the market price?
g. Now work out the profit-maximizing output levels when price is $20 _____ $40 _____ $50 _____ $60 _____

h. Graph these points on the diagram below. It's a marginal cost curve, and—because it shows how much will be supplied at each price level—a supply curve too.

9. ABC Baseball Corp. checks its production costs. Its overheads are $200 daily, and 3 workers (the only variable resource) are hired daily, each for $25. Production is running at 500 units per day. If a fourth worker is employed, production would rise to 550 units per day.

a. Calculate the marginal product of the fourth worker and the (approximate) marginal cost of the 550th unit.

b. Sketch the MC, AVC, and ATC curves for the firm, based on your knowledge and the information given.

c. If the price of baseballs is $1 each, is this firm at its profit-maximizing output level? If not, why not? Should the firm increase or decrease its level of production? Explain. Calculate total profit at output levels of 500 and 550.

10. The table includes information about a perfectly competitive firm.

OUTPUT	TOTAL COST
0	10
1	40
2	60
3	90
4	130

Use the table to find the following values.

a. Marginal cost of the third unit _____
b. Total fixed cost _____
c. AVC if 4 units are produced _____
d. The number of units the firm should produce if the price is $30 each? _____
e. The firm's maximum profit _____

11. a. If average total costs are $500, total fixed costs are $4,000, and total costs are $10,000, calculate the AVC. _____

b. If total fixed costs are $30, average variable costs are $28, and average costs are $31, calculate TVC _____ and the output level. _____

c. If average total costs are $300, total fixed costs are $2000, and total costs are $6000, calculate the AVC. _____

d. If total fixed costs are $20, average variable costs are $10, and average total costs are $11, calculate TV _____ and the output level. _____

12. ABC Baseball Corp. checks its costs of production. Total fixed costs are $100 daily, and 3 workers (the only variable resource) are hired daily, each for $20. Production is running at 400 units per day. If a fourth worker is employed, production would rise to 440 units per day.
    a. Calculate the marginal product of the fourth worker.
    b. Calculate the marginal cost of the 440th unit.
    c. If the price of baseballs is $2 each, is this firm at its profit-maximizing output level? If not, why not?
    d. Should the firm increase or decrease its level of production? Explain.
    e. Calculate total profit at output levels of 400 and 440.

13. In Chapter 7 we visited Wilma's Wicker Baskets and found the production information below. Now suppose that each worker costs $24 to hire. In addition, Wilma's Wicker Baskets has total fixed costs of $30.
    a. Insert the total fixed cost, total variable cost and total cost values in the table below.

LABOR	TOTAL PRODUCT	TOTAL FIXED COST	TOTAL VARIABLE COST	TOTAL COST
0	0	_____	_____	_____
1	5	_____	_____	_____
2	16	_____	_____	_____
3	27	_____	_____	_____
4	36	_____	_____	_____
5	44	_____	_____	_____
6	51	_____	_____	_____
7	56	_____	_____	_____
8	60	_____	_____	_____
9	63	_____	_____	_____
10	65	_____	_____	_____

    b. Insert the average fixed cost, average variable cost, average total cost and marginal cost values in the table below.

LABOR	TOTAL PRODUCT	AVERAGE FIXED COST	AVERAGE VARIABLE COST	AVERAGE TOTAL COST	MARGINAL COST
0	0	—	—	—	—
1	5	_____	_____	_____	_____
2	16	_____	_____	_____	_____
3	27	_____	_____	_____	_____
4	36	_____	_____	_____	_____
5	44	_____	_____	_____	_____
6	51	_____	_____	_____	_____
7	56	_____	_____	_____	_____
8	60	_____	_____	_____	_____
9	63	_____	_____	_____	_____
10	65	_____	_____	_____	_____

    c. At a price of $3.00, how many baskets of output will Wilma produce to maximize profits?
    d. At a price of $3.00, determine how much of an economic profit or loss the firm will make in the short run.
    e. At a price of $4.80, how many baskets of output will Wilma produce to maximize profits?
    f. At a price of $4.80, determine how much of an economic profit or loss the firm will make in the short run.

III. ECONOMICS EXPLORER.

Use the third module ("Production and Costs") from the Economics Explorer software to investigate essential concepts such as marginal cost and the family of average cost curves. You should also do the Theory lectures and Problems in Module 4 which looks at short-run profit-maximization.

ANSWERS AND SOLUTIONS

ANSWERS TO PRACTICE QUESTIONS

7.

q	TC	TFC	TVC	ATC	AFC	AVC
0	$10	$10	$ 0	—	—	—
1	$18	$10	$ 8	$18.00	$10.00	$8.00
2	$24	$10	$14	$12.00	$ 5.00	$7.00
3	$30	$10	$20	$10.00	$ 3.33	$6.67
4	$36	$10	$26	$ 9.00	$ 2.50	$6.50
5	$40	$10	$30	$ 8.00	$ 2.00	$6.00
6	$54	$10	$44	$ 9.00	$ 1.67	$7.33
7	$70	$10	$60	$10.00	$ 1.43	$8.57

14.

q	TC	TR	MC	MR
0	$10	$ 0		
1	$18	$10	$ 8	$10
2	$24	$20	$ 6	$10
3	$30	$30	$ 6	$10
4	$36	$40	$ 6	$10
5	$40	$50	$ 4	$10
6	$54	$60	$14	$10
7	$70	$70	$16	$10

18–21.

q	TC	TR	MC	MR
0	$ 4.00	$ 0		
1	$ 4.50	$ 2.50	$ .50	$2.50
2	$ 5.50	$ 5.00	$1.00	$2.50
3	$ 7.00	$ 7.50	$1.50	$2.50
4	$ 9.00	$10.00	$2.00	$2.50
5	$11.50	$12.50	$2.50	$2.50
6	$14.50	$15.00	$3.00	$2.50

25.

PRICE	OUTPUT
$1.00	0
$1.50	3
$2.00	4
$2.50	5
$3.00	6
$3.50	7
$4.00	8

PRACTICE TEST

I. SOLUTIONS TO MULTIPLE CHOICE QUESTIONS

1. D. Marginal cost is the change in total cost ($20) divided by the change in quantity produced (1).

2. D. The shape of the marginal cost curve is affected by marginal productivity. The upward sloping section of the MC curve is related to diminishing returns as additional units of variable inputs (workers) are added.

3. C. When low levels of output are produced, few variable resources are hired and fixed costs can exceed variable costs.

4. A. Fixed costs (which do not change as output level changes) have no effect on the value of marginal cost.

5. C. AVC will be at its minimum value and neither rising nor falling. Because marginal cost is lower than ATC, ATC will be decreasing.

6. C. MC is the change in total cost divided by the change in quantity produced, i.e., the slope of the TC curve. With a straight-line TC curve, MC is constant.

7. D. In perfect competition, price and marginal revenue have the same value. To maximize profits, the firm should produce at the level of output where MR = MC.

8. B. If ATC is rising, MC must be above it. In perfect competition, price equals MR. The profit-maximizing firm should increase production only if MR exceeds MC. This *may* be the case only if price (MR) exceeds ATC. In all other cases, MR is less than MC and output should be reduced. Draw the diagram to verify this.

9. C. The profit-maximizing condition is that MR should equal MC.

10. A. TR = P × q = $10 × 20 = $200. TVC = AVC × q = $3 × 20 = $60. TC = TFC + TVC = $10 + $60 = $70. Total economic profit = TR − TC = $200 − $70 = $130.

The following table applies to the next four questions.

q	0	1	2	3	4	5
TC	$1	$3	$6	$10	$15	$21
MC	—	$2	$3	$ 4	$ 5	$ 6
MR	—	$4	$4	$ 4	$ 4	$ 4

11. C. Marginal revenue is a change in total revenue divided by the change in quantity and is constant for all output levels.

12. B. See the table above.

13. B. Write On should produce at the level of output where MR = MC.

14. B. TVC = TC − TFC = $21 − $1 = $20 AVC = TVC/q = $20/5 = $4.

15. B. TC at 4 units of output is $56 ($14 × 4). TC at 5 units of output is $80 ($16 × 5). MC = $24/1 = $24.

16. B. At 3 units, MR = $10 and MC = $5. At 4 units, MR = $10 and MC = $11. At 3 units, TR = $30 and TC = $45.

17. C. MR = MC when the output level is 900.

18. B. TR = $10 × 600 = $6000. TC = $6 × 600 = $3600.

19. D. TC = ATC × q = $10 × 400 = $4000.

20. A. MR = MC at 900 units of output. Note: The perfectly competitive firm is a price taker and cannot increase its price.

21. D. TR = P × q = $10 × 900 = $9000.

22. D. At 600, TR − TC = $6000 − $3600 = $2400. At 900, TR − TC = $9000 − $6300 = $2700.

23. A. Total economic profit is total revenue minus total cost. Total revenue is $6.00 × 10 = $60.00. Total cost is TVC plus TFC. TVC is AVC × quantity, or $35.00 ($3.50 × 10). TFC is $10.00.

24. D. Surprisingly, in fact, none of the other options is certainly true. To maximize profits, this firm needs to know the relationship between marginal revenue, which is $6.00, and marginal cost, which is unknown. Because the firm is making an economic profit, the shut-down case (see Chapter 9) is ruled out.

25. C. Freda's average profit will decrease (Option D) but this is not relevant to her decision—total profit may increase even when average profit is decreasing. Freda must compare marginal revenue and marginal cost. Total variable cost of 10 units is $35.00; total variable cost of 11 units is $44.00. MC is $9.00. MR is $6.00. Because MR is less than MC, the eleventh unit should not be produced.

II. SOLUTIONS TO APPLICATION QUESTIONS

1. a. There are some fixed costs. That can happen only in the short run.
   b. Marginal product is decreasing as production increases. This is happening because of diminishing marginal productivity. Marginal productivity is greatest with the second worker (19 units).
   c. See the table below.

# OF WORKERS	OUTPUT	TVC	TFC	TC	AVC	AFC	ATC	MC
0	0	$ 0	$110	$110	—	—	—	
1	12	$ 30	$110	$140	$2.50	$9.16	$11.67	$ 2.50
2	31	$ 60	$110	$170	$1.94	$3.55	$ 5.48	$ 1.58
3	41	$ 90	$110	$200	$2.20	$2.68	$ 4.88	$ 3.00
4	50	$120	$110	$230	$2.40	$2.20	$ 4.60	$ 3.33
5	58	$150	$110	$260	$2.59	$1.90	$ 4.48	$ 3.75
6	64	$180	$110	$290	$2.81	$1.72	$ 4.53	$ 5.00
7	67	$210	$110	$320	$3.13	$1.64	$ 4.78	$10.00

   d. See the diagram below. Note that marginal curves are drawn halfway between the quantity values.

   e. The two levels are the same. At that output level, the extra worker is the most productive of all, so the extra hiring cost is spread over the largest number of extra units.

2. a. $4.30.
    b. Ken's total fixed cost includes any costs that are present when output is zero, therefore, total fixed cost equals $500.

    c.

ANIMALS PER WEEK	MARGINAL COSTS PER WEEK
0–100	$2.00
101–200	$2.70
201–300	$3.10
301–400	$3.50
401–500	$3.90
501–600	$4.30
601–700	$4.70

    d. If output is 200, marginal cost is $2.70. Because the price is $4.30, the marginal revenue is also $4.30. Because marginal cost is less than marginal revenue, Ken should increase output. In fact, the profit-maximizing output level is 600.
    e. Ken's maximum profit is TR − TC = $2,580 − $2,450 = $130.
    f. This change in Ken's costs will not affect the profit-maximizing output level. Rent is a fixed cost which, therefore, does not influence marginal cost.

3. See the diagram below.

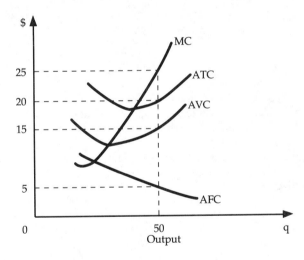

4. TVC = TC − TFC = 6,000 − 2,000 = 4,000
    q = TC / ATC = 6,000 / 300 = 20
    So, AVC = 4,000 / 20 = 200.
5. AFC = ATC − AVC = 11 − 10 = 1
    q = TFC / AFC = 20 / 1 = 20
    TVC = AVC × q = 10 × 20 = 200
    TC = TVC + TFC = 200 + 20 = 220.
6. Silas should not produce the extra tape eraser. To determine this, we need to know marginal revenue and marginal cost information. The marginal revenue is $300. The marginal cost is $401.

QUANTITY	ATC	TC	MC
200	$200	$40,000	
201	$201	$40,401	$401
202	$202	$40,804	$403

Because the marginal cost of the extra unit exceeds $300, Silas's total economic profit would be reduced by filling the order.

7. a. See the table below. Neither is always cheaper.
    b. Method 2 is cheaper up to and including 14 units of output.
    c. After producing the 14th unit of output, Method 1 is cheaper.

	Method 1		Method 2		Costs	
Output	Capital	Labor	Capital	Labor	TVC	TC
11	7	2	2	6	$ 20	$ 60
12	8	4	3	9	$ 30	$ 70
13	10	6	4	13	$ 42	$ 82
14	12	9	7	18	$ 64	$104
15	15	11	10	25	$ 82	$122
16	19	14	13	31	$104	$144

    d. Produce 13 units.
    e. Total profit would be ($13 × $13) − $82 = $87.
8. a. See the table below.

Output	TFC	MC	TVC	TC	TR	P (MR)	Profit
0	$20	0	0	$ 20	0	$30	−$20
1	$20	$10	$ 10	$ 30	$ 30	$30	0
2	$20	$20	$ 30	$ 50	$ 60	$30	$10
3	$20	$30	$ 60	$ 80	$ 90	$30	$10
4	$20	$40	$100	$120	$120	$30	0
5	$20	$50	$150	$170	$150	$30	−$20
6	$20	$60	$210	$230	$180	$30	−$50

    b. See the table above.
    c. See the table above.
    d. The firm should produce 3 units for a total profit of $10.
    e. See the table. The firm will choose to produce 3 units.
    f. There should be an increase in the number of firms in the long run. Supply will shift to the right, making the market price fall.
    g. When price is $20, the profit-maximizing output level is 2 units; at $40, it's 4; at $50, it's 5; and at $60, it's 6.
    h. See the diagram below.

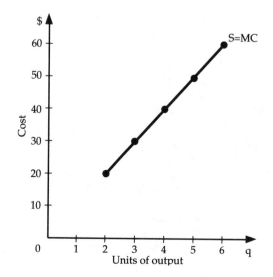

9. a. Marginal product of the fourth worker is 50 units (550 − 500). The approximate marginal cost of the 550th unit is 50¢. $25 wage ÷ 50.

    b. See the diagram below. Note that this diagram shows only the parts of the curves about which we have information—some guesswork is involved. ATC is falling, from 55¢ (275/500) to 54.54¢ (300/550), indicating that MC is below ATC. AVC is rising, from 15¢ (75/500) to 18.2¢ (100/550), indicating that MC is above AVC.

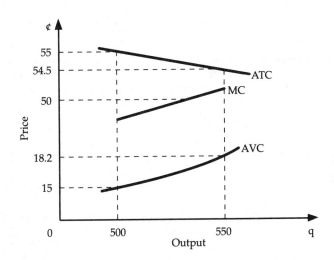

    c. Price (marginal revenue) is greater than marginal cost. To maximize profit it should increase production until P = MC. At 500 units the firm's profit is $225, and at 550 units its profit is $250.

10. a. Marginal cost is change in total cost ($90 − 60) divided by change in quantity (1). MC = $30.

    b. When no output is produced, no variable resources are hired and all costs are fixed. TFC = $10.

    c. TVC = TC − TFC. At 4 units, TVC = 130 − 10 = $120. AVC = TVC/q = 120/4 = $30.

    d. If the price is $30, then MR is also $30. The firm should produce up to the output level where MC is $30—that is, 3 units.

    e. TR = P × q. At 3 units, TR = $30 × 3 = $90. TC = $90. The firm is earning a normal profit.

11. a. TC = ATC × q = 10,000 = 500 × q => q = 20
        TVC = TC − TFC = 10,000 − 4000 = 6000
        AVC = TVC/q = 6000/20 = 300.

    b. AFC = ATC − AVC = 31 − 28 = 3
        TFC = AFC × q => 30 = 3 × q => q = 10
        TVC = AVC × q = 28 × 10 = 280.

    c. TC = ATC × q = 6000 = 300 × q => q = 20
        TVC = TC − TFC = 6000 − 2000 = 4000.
        AVC = TVC/q = 4000/20 = 200.

    d. AFC = ATC − AVC = 11 − 10 = 1
        TFC = AFC × q => 20 = 1 × q => q = 20.
        TVC = AVC × q = 10 × 20 = 200.

12. a. MP = change in total product (40) divided by change in quantity of input (1) = 40.

    b. MC = change in total cost ($20) divided by change in quantity of output (40) = 50¢.

    c. The firm is not at its profit-maximizing output level because marginal revenue ($2.00) is not equal to marginal cost (50¢).

    d. The firm should increase production. The 441st baseball, for instance, will increase profits by $1.50.

    e. Total profit = total revenue − total cost.

       At 400 units of output:

         TR = P × q = $2 × 400 = $800

         TC = TFC + TVC = $100 + $60 = $160

         Total profit = $800 − $160 = $640.

       At 440 units of output:

         TR = P × q = $2 × 440 = $880

         TC = TFC + TVC = $100 + $80 = $180

         Total profit = $880 − $180 = $700.

13. a. See the table below.

LABOR	TOTAL PRODUCT	TOTAL FIXED COST	TOTAL VARIABLE COST	TOTAL COST
0	0	$30	$ 0	$ 30
1	5	$30	$ 24	$ 54
2	16	$30	$ 48	$ 78
3	27	$30	$ 72	$102
4	36	$30	$ 96	$126
5	44	$30	$120	$150
6	51	$30	$144	$174
7	56	$30	$168	$198
8	60	$30	$192	$222
9	63	$30	$216	$246
10	65	$30	$240	$270

    b. See the table below.

LABOR	TOTAL PRODUCT	AVERAGE FIXED COST	AVERAGE VARIABLE COST	AVERAGE TOTAL COST	MARGINAL COST
0	0	—	—	—	
1	5	$6.00	$4.80	$10.80	$ 4.80
2	16	$1.88	$3.00	$ 4.88	$ 1.60
3	27	$1.11	$2.67	$ 3.78	$ 2.18
4	36	$ .83	$2.67	$ 3.50	$ 2.67
5	44	$ .68	$2.73	$ 3.41	$ 3.00
6	51	$ .59	$2.82	$ 3.41	$ 3.43
7	56	$ .54	$3.00	$ 3.54	$ 4.80
8	60	$ .50	$3.20	$ 3.70	$ 6.00
9	63	$ .48	$3.43	$ 3.91	$ 8.00
10	65	$ .46	$3.69	$ 4.15	$12.00

    c. At a price of $3.00, Wilma will produce 44 baskets. This output is where her marginal revenue and marginal cost are equal.

    d. At a price of $3.00, Wilma will earn an economic loss of $18, because total revenue is only $132 while total cost is $150.

    e. At a price of $4.80, Wilma will produce 56 baskets.

    f. At a price of $4.80, Wilma will earn an economic profit of $70.80, because total revenue is $268.80 while total cost is $198.

COSTS AND OUTPUT DECISIONS IN THE LONG RUN

9

OBJECTIVES: POINT BY POINT

After completing this chapter, you should be able to accomplish the objectives listed below.

OBJECTIVE 1: Graph a firm in short-run equilibrium that is making profits (losses) and identify those profits (losses). Explain the rationale behind the decision to shut down or not to shut down when short-run losses occur.

In the short run, the firm must be

   (1)   making an economic profit;
   (2)   breaking even, i.e., making a normal profit; or
   (3)   making a loss. This firm will continue to produce, if it can cover its operating expenses, or shut down.   (page 208)

In the long run, each of the cases above produces a different response.

   (1)   The firm making an economic profit will try to expand; new firms, attracted by the extra profits, will enter the industry.
   (2)   The firm making a normal profit will maintain its production level; no incentive exists for firms to enter or leave the industry.
   (3)   The firm making a loss will leave the industry.   (page 214)

> **LEARNING TIP:** As a general point, the diagrams in this chapter are especially detailed. Practice is essential! Redraw each of the four short-run cases—(1) making economic profits, (2) breaking even, (3) making a loss but producing, and (4) making a loss and closing down.

> **GRAPHING POINTER:** Always start with the "short-run cost diagram" comprised of AVC, ATC, and MC, because this is the most difficult part to draw correctly. The trick then is to position the horizontal price (marginal revenue) line to get the particular result you want.

LEARNING TIP: Here is an extended graphical example giving each of the possible short-run cases covered by the textbook.

Initially, you're interested only in the "average" curves. For (1), make the price line slice through the ATC curve. For (2), the price line just grazes the ATC curve at its minimum point. For (3), the price line slices through AVC but "misses" ATC. For (4), the price line "misses" AVC entirely.

After you've drawn the price line, seek out the profit-maximizing (loss-minimizing) P = MC intersection point. Where these curves intersect—that's the profit-maximizing quantity (q*).

Next, work out the total economic profit (Case 1) or loss (Case 3). Find the difference between price and ATC at q*, then multiply by the number of units produced. That gives total profit (or loss). Case 2 gives normal profit. Case 4 gives a loss equal to total fixed costs.

PRACTICE

Use the following diagram, which describes cost and revenue information for Jill and John Pantera's Mugs-R-Us pitchers, for the next fifteen questions.

1. If the market price of pitchers is $14.22, Mugs-R-Us should produce _____ pitchers in the short run.
   A. 70.
   B. 80.
   C. 90.
   D. 100.
   Answer: C. The profit-maximizing MR = MC point would be at this output level.

2. If the market price of pitchers is $15.00, Mugs-R-Us should produce _____ pitchers in the short run.
   A. 70.
   B. 80.
   C. 90.
   D. 100.
   Answer: D. The profit-maximizing MR = MC point would be at this output level.

3. If the market price of pitchers is $8.90, Mugs-R-Us should produce _____ pitchers in the short run.
   A. 70.
   B. 80.
   C. 90.
   D. 100.
   Answer: B. The profit-maximizing MR = MC point would be at this output level.

4. If the market price of pitchers is $7.00, Mugs-R-Us should produce _____ pitchers in the short run.
   A. 70.
   B. 80.
   C. 90.
   D. 100.
   Answer: A. The profit-maximizing MR = MC point would be at this output level.

5. If the market price of pitchers is $6.00, Mugs-R-Us should produce _____ pitchers in the short run.
   A. 70.
   B. 80.
   C. 90.
   D. none of the above.
   Answer: D. In fact, Mugs-R-Us should cease operations in the short run because it is not covering its AVC.

6. If the market price of pitchers is $15.00, Mugs-R-Us can earn a _____ economic profit of _____
   A. positive, $50.
   B. positive, $1500.
   C. negative, $50.
   D. negative, $1450.
   Answer: A. TR = $15 × 100 = $1500. TC = 14.50 × 100 = $1450. Also, you can use price and ATC. At 100 pitchers, P exceeds ATC by 50¢ per unit. This is the "per unit profit". With 100 units, total profit is $50.

7. If the market price of pitchers is $14.22, Mugs-R-Us can earn an economic profit of _____
   A. zero.
   B. -$90.
   C. -$560.
   D. -$540.
   Answer: A. P = ATC = MC = $14.22.

8. If the market price of pitchers is $8.90, Mugs-R-Us can earn a _____ economic profit of _____
   A. positive, $478.80.
   B. positive, $112.
   C. negative, $448.
   D. negative, $425.60.
   Answer: C. TR = $8.90 × 80 = $712. TC = $14.50 × 80 = $1160.

9. At an output level of 70 pitchers, total variable cost is _____ and total fixed cost is _____
   A. $490, $560.
   B. $490, $1050.
   C. $560, $490.
   D. $560, $1050.
   Answer: A. TC = TVC + TFC => ATC × q = AVC × q + (ATC − AVC) × q = 15 × 70 = (7 × 70) + (15 − 7)70 = 490 + 560.

10. At an output level of 70 pitchers, with a price of $7, Mugs-R-Us makes an economic loss of _____ . If it closes down, Mugs-R-Us will make an economic loss of _____
    A. $490, $490.
    B. $490, $560.
    C. $560, $490.
    D. $560, $560.
    Answer: D. If Mugs-R-Us chooses to produce, TR will be $7 × 70 = $490. TC will be $15 × 70 = $1050. Mugs-R-Us will lose $560. If it closes down, TR will be zero and it will have to pay its fixed costs ($560).
    Note: At any price less than $7 it is better off closing down.

OBJECTIVE 2: Explain why the firm's short-run supply curve is the section of the MC curve above AVC. Derive the industry supply curve and explain the factors that shift the industry supply curve in the long run.

In the short run, the border between producing at a loss and shutting down occurs where average variable cost is at its minimum (and where marginal cost intersects it). If the price per unit isn't high enough to cover even these minimum average operating expenses, the firm should shut down. Any price above the minimum AVC value will lead to "profit-maximizing" behavior, producing where P = MC. Therefore, the portion of the MC curve above its intersection with the AVC curve is the firm's short-run supply curve. (page 213)

The industry supply curve is derived by aggregation. In the short run anything that affects marginal cost and in the long run alters the number of firms in the industry can shift the industry supply curve. (page 213)

LEARNING TIP: Table 9.4 in the text is an excellent summary. Refer to it often throughout this chapter.

PRACTICE

11. Use the answers to questions 1–5 above to construct a short-run supply schedule for Mugs-R-Us pitchers.

PRICE	OUTPUT
$15.00	_____
$14.22	_____
$ 8.90	_____
$ 7.00	_____
$ 6.00	_____

Answer: See the *Answers and Solutions* section.

12. A firm makes an operating loss if
    A. price is less than average total cost.
    B. price is less than average total cost but greater than average variable cost.
    C. price is less than average variable cost.
    D. price is less than average fixed cost.
    Answer: C. Variable costs are the ones that are actively incurred during the firm's operation.

13. If Mugs-R-Us shuts down in the short run, then
    A. total revenue will be zero and total cost will be zero.
    B. total revenue will be zero but total fixed costs will still have to be paid.
    C. total revenue will be zero but total variable costs will still have to be paid.
    D. total profit will be zero and total costs will be positive.
    Answer: B. In the short run there are some fixed resources (and some fixed costs).

14. If Mugs-R-Us faces a price of $8.90, it will experience an operating
    A. profit of $112.
    B. profit of $448.
    C. loss of $112.
    D. loss of $448.
    Answer: A. Operating profit or loss depends on price and AVC (times quantity). See p. 210.

15. In the short run, Mugs-R-Us will earn a positive economic profit as long as the price is greater than _____ and will produce as long as the price is greater than _____
    A. $7.00, $7.00.
    B. $7.00, $14.22.
    C. $14.22, $7.00.
    D. $14.22, $14.22.
    Answer: C. Economic profit occurs as long as price is greater than the minimum ATC value. The firm will continue in operation as long as operating profits can be made (as long as price is greater than the minimum AVC value).

OBJECTIVE 3: Explain why the long-run average cost curve is U-shaped. Distinguish between, and outline, the short-run explanation and the long-run explanation of U-shaped average cost curves. Provide examples of factors that would cause internal economies or diseconomies of scale. Indicate the long-run profit-maximizing level of production.

A U-shaped long-run average cost curve can't be due to diminishing returns because the concept of diminishing returns is purely short-run. The long-run average cost curve is U-shaped because of internal economies and diseconomies of scale. In the presence of economies of scale, average costs decrease as output rises; in the presence of diseconomies of scale, average costs increase as output rises.

Internal economies of scale (increasing returns to scale) are revealed when the firm's long-run average costs fall as its production increases. If a firm doubles all inputs, it will more than double output. Such cost-reducing improvements might be due to standardization or bulk buying. *Internal diseconomies of scale* (decreasing returns to scale) occur when the firm's long-run average costs increase as its production expands. Diseconomies are most frequently blamed on managerial inefficiency as a business becomes too large and unwieldy to operate effectively. Constant returns to scale are a third possibility. (page 215)

Long-Run Diagrams: As with the short-run diagrams, it's important to draw the long-run diagram and work though the adjustment process for the firm and industry. This is fairly complicated, since your depiction depends on the assumptions you make about internal and external returns to scale. To start, the simplest assumption is to suppose that the firm faces a U-shaped long-run average cost curve and constant external returns to scale. See Application question 9 for some guided practice.

Economies and Diseconomies of Scale: Learn the "other names" for internal economies and diseconomies of scale—increasing returns and decreasing returns, respectively. This material is intended to explain the downward- and the upward-sloping long-run average cost curve—why it is U-shaped. As with diminishing returns in the short run (see the Learning Tip in Objective 5 in Chapter 7), you can think of economies and diseconomies fighting for dominance as the firm increases output. Initially, economies of scale represent the stronger effect and push average costs down but, as output rises, the diseconomies begin to prevail and costs start to rise.

> **LEARNING TIP:** Keep this material separate from *external* economies and diseconomies of scale. They're there to explain why the firm's LRAC curve might shift position (falling in the presence of external economies and rising in the presence of external diseconomies) as output rises. A quick example: As an industry expands, the skilled workers it needs will be able to command higher wages, pushing costs up for each firm. This will affect even those firms that are not expanding production.

PRACTICE

16. If a firm experiences constant returns to scale, its long-run average cost curve will be
    A. horizontal.
    B. U-shaped.
    C. upward sloping.
    D. downward sloping.
    Answer: A. See p. 219.

17. Each point on the long-run average cost curve indicates, at the given output level, the
    A. minimum possible average cost when the scale of production can be changed.
    B. minimum possible average cost when the scale of production is fixed.
    C. average cost due to economies of scale.
    D. average cost due to diseconomies of scale.
    Answer: A. See p. 217.

18. Vigor Vitamins discovers the following long-run information. When it produces 100 units, its total cost is $50; when it produces 200 units, its total cost is $76; and when it produces 300 units, its total cost is $99. Vigor is exhibiting _____ between 100 and 200 units of output and _____ between 200 and 300 units of output.
    A. economies of scale, economies of scale.
    B. economies of scale, diseconomies of scale.
    C. diseconomies of scale, economies of scale.
    D. diseconomies of scale, diseconomies of scale.
    Answer: A. At 100 units, LRAC is 50¢; at 200 units, LRAC is 38¢; at 300 units, LRAC is 33¢. LRAC is decreasing.

In the diagram below, cost and revenue information is presented for Vigor Vitamins, a typical firm in the vitamin industry. In the short run, Vigor's total fixed costs are $10. Assume that Vigor is currently producing 200 units. Initially the market price is 38¢ per unit. Use the diagram below to answer the next three questions.

19. The market price per unit is 38¢ per unit. If the firm is producing 200 units, we can say that, in the short run, the firm
    A. is earning a normal profit.
    B. is earning a positive economic profit.
    C. is earning a negative economic profit.
    D. should close down.
    Answer: C. The SRAC of 40¢ is greater than 38¢ at 200 units of output. This firm is not maximizing profits in the short run because MR (38¢) does not equal SRMC.

20. The market price per unit is 38¢ per unit. In the short run, at 200 units of output, Vigor is making an operating _____ ; in the long run, market price will _____
    A. profit, increase.
    B. profit, decrease.
    C. loss, increase.
    D. loss, decrease.
    Answer: B. Vigor's total cost is $80 and total fixed cost is $10. TVC is $70 while TR is $76. In the long run, price will be driven down to the lowest point on the LRAC.

21. In the long run, Vigor will _____ its scale of operations and price will _____
    A. increase, increase.
    B. increase, decrease.
    C. decrease, increase.
    D. decrease, decrease.
    Answer: B. To survive in this industry, Vigor must become more efficient by adjusting its scale of production. As Vigor and others become more efficient, price will decrease (to 33¢).

OBJECTIVE 4: State the conditions that hold for the firm in long-run competitive equilibrium.

In the long run, firms will maximize profits (MR = LRMC) and make zero economic profit (P = LRAC). However, profit-maximizing occurs in the short run too, where MR = SRMC. If the firm is in long-run equilibrium, earning normal profit, then this condition also applies in the short run (P = SRAC). In perfect competition, where price always equals marginal revenue, the complete long-run equilibrium condition holds: P = SRMC = SRAC = LRAC. (page 220)

> **Long-Run Competitive Equilibrium: P = SRMC = SRAC = LRAC.** This is an important result that will be used in later chapters, and it may be dissected to advantage. You know the first three elements from Chapter 8.
>
> The firm maximizes profits where P (or MR) = SRMC. MC = SRAC reveals that unit costs are minimized and that average productivity is maximized—inputs are being allocated efficiently. (Recall that the SRMC and SRAC curves intersect at the minimum point on the average cost curve.)
>
> Competition requires that only normal profits be made in the long run, so P = LRAC. In the short run, a similar logic holds, so P = SRAC. You may question this—can't economic profits occur in the short run? Yes, but to achieve long-run equilibrium, they must have been competed away in a perfectly competitive industry. Notice that, in equilibrium, the typical firm produces at the lowest possible cost per unit in the short run and in the long run. This result occurs because of easy entry into and exit from the market, forcing the firm to the most cost-efficient output level.
>
> Why is this an equilibrium? Because there's no incentive to change. No new firms want into the industry (forcing price down); no existing firms are dissatisfied with their normal profits and seeking to leave (forcing price up).

PRACTICE

In the diagram below, cost and revenue information is presented for Pastry Pie Bakery, a typical firm in the pastry industry. In the short run, Pastry Pie's total fixed costs are $1000. Assume that there are no external economies or diseconomies of scale. Use the diagram to answer the next five questions.

22. Diseconomies of scale set in after
    A. 600 units.
    B. 1000 units.
    C. 1250 units.
    D. 1300 units.
    Answer: B. Diseconomies make the LRAC curve slope upwards.

23. In the long run, the equilibrium price will be _____ and the equilibrium output level will be _____
    A. $2, 1200 units.
    B. $2, 1000 units.
    C. $3, 1200 units.
    D. $3, 1000 units.
    Answer: B. In the long run, the equilibrium price and equilibrium output level will be depend on the minimum point of the LRAC curve.

24. Suppose that Pastry Pie's SRAC curve is SRAC3. The market price is $4.00. In the long run,
    A. firms will enter the industry and price will rise because each firm is experiencing internal diseconomies of scale.
    B. Pastry Pie will increase its scale of production because it is earning excess profits.
    C. Pastry Pie will decrease its scale of production to increase its economic profits.
    D. Pastry Pie will reduce its output and the industry will increase output.
    Answer: D. Pastry Pie will be forced to earn normal profits at the minimum LRAC point. Because more firms enter the industry, production will increase. Pastry Pie can't earn economic profits in the long run. The scale of production will decrease (Option C) but economic profit will be zero in the long run.

25. Suppose that Pastry Pie's SRAC curve is SRAC2. Demand decreases and the market price falls to $1.50.
    A. In the short run, Pastry Pie should shut down.
    B. In the long run, the industry supply curve will shift left.
    C. In the long run, market demand will increase because the market price has fallen.
    D. In the long run, the industry supply curve will not change position.
    Answer: B. The industry supply curve will shift left because firms are leaving the industry.
    Note: Because Pastry Pie has fixed costs of $1000, it is worth its while to remain in business in the short run. At an output of 1000, TC is $2000, $1000 of which is TVC. Because Pastry Pie can earn $1500, it can cover its operating costs.

26. Suppose that Pastry Pie's SRAC curve is SRAC3. The market price is $3.00. Also suppose that this is an increasing-cost industry. In the long run, the equilibrium price will certainly be
    A. $3.00.
    B. more than $2.00.
    C. more than $3.00.
    D. between $3.00 and $4.00.
    Answer: B. More than $2.00 is the best answer. If there were constant costs, the equilibrium price would be $2.00. Because of profits, the industry will grow, pushing up the LRAC curve. Equilibrium price will certainly be greater than $2.00.

OBJECTIVE 5: Explain the factors that cause increasing-cost, constant-cost, and decreasing-cost industries. Distinguish external from internal economies and diseconomies of scale and explain their role in determining average costs in an industry. List and explain the factors that influence the long-run industry supply curve.

An industry may be decreasing-cost (which means that it benefits from external economies of scale and has a downward sloping long-run industry supply curve), increasing-cost (which means that it suffers from external diseconomies of scale and has an upward sloping long-run industry supply curve), or constant-cost (where the long-run industry supply curve is horizontal). (page 215)

External economies of scale are caused by growth in the entire industry and result in decreases in the firm's long-run average costs. If industry growth results in increases in long-run average costs, an *external diseconomy of scale* is present. The *long-run industry supply curve,* which shows how price and total output change as an industry expands in response to an increase in demand, depends on whether external economies or external diseconomies are present.   (page 229)

PRACTICE

27. The typical firm in a perfectly competitive increasing-cost industry is making economic profits. Predict what will happen in this industry in the long run.
    A. Firms will enter this industry. The industry supply curve will shift to the right and the LRAC curve will shift down.
    B. Firms will enter this industry. The industry supply curve will shift to the right and the LRAC curve will shift up.
    C. Firms will leave this industry. The industry supply curve will shift to the right and the LRAC curve will shift down.
    D. Firms will leave this industry. The industry supply curve will shift to the right and the LRAC curve will shift up.
    Answer: B. Profits attract firms to the industry and supply will increase. Extra competition for scarce resources will make long-run average costs increase.

28. At all points along the long-run industry supply curve
    A. industry price level is constant.
    B. all firms earn a normal profit.
    C. all firms earn an economic profit.
    D. industry output level is constant.
    Answer: B. In the long run, firms can only earn a normal profit.

29. Refer to the diagram for Vigor Vitamins above, (at question 19). Between output levels 300 and 400 the firm is experiencing
    A. internal economies of scale.
    B. internal diseconomies of scale.
    C. external economies of scale.
    D. external diseconomies of scale.
    Answer: B. LRAC is increasing. This indicates diseconomies of scale within the firm. See p. 219.

30. Vigor is currently producing 300 units and is in long-run equilibrium. Suddenly demand increases. In the long run, the industry's new equilibrium price stabilizes at 35¢ per unit. This indicates that the industry has experienced external _____ . The long-run industry supply curve is _____
    A. economies of scale, upward sloping.
    B. economies of scale, downward sloping.
    C. diseconomies of scale, upward sloping.
    D. diseconomies of scale, downward sloping.
    Answer: C. The long-run equilibrium price was 33¢ (minimum LRAC). As the industry grew, price increased. This must be due to external diseconomies.

PRACTICE TEST

I. MULTIPLE CHOICE QUESTIONS.

Select the option that provides the single best answer.

_____ 1. ABC Corp. cuts usage of all inputs by 50%. Production falls by more than 50%. This firm is experiencing
A. external economies of scale.
B. external diseconomies of scale.
C. increasing returns to scale.
D. decreasing returns to scale.

_____ 2. In the short run, a perfectly competitive firm incurring losses should still produce if it can cover its
A. average costs.
B. variable costs.
C. fixed costs.
D. economic costs.

_____ 3. An industry has external economies of scale. In the long run, an increase in demand will
A. decrease price.
B. increase price.
C. not change price.
D. cause an indeterminate change in price.

_____ 4. Suddenly there is an increase in the demand for frisbees. The most likely result would be
A. higher prices in the short run, followed by an increase in production in the long run that would cause prices to decline somewhat.
B. higher prices in the short run, followed by larger long-run price increases as the stock of frisbees is depleted.
C. higher prices in the short run because of greater sales volume, and even higher prices later on as plant sizes are increased.
D. lower prices in the short run because of higher sales, but higher prices in the long run as the stock of frisbees is depleted.

_____ 5. In the long-run perfectly competitive equilibrium, each of the following conditions will hold, except
A. $P = MR$.
B. $P = SRMC$.
C. LRAC is minimized.
D. SRMC is minimized.

_____ 6. An increasing-cost industry experiences external _____ of scale and has a(n) _____ long-run industry supply curve.
A. economies, upward sloping.
B. economies, downward sloping.
C. diseconomies, upward sloping.
D. diseconomies, downward sloping.

Use the following table to answer the next seven questions. The data refer to a perfectly competitive firm.

Output	Marginal Cost	AVC	ATC
1	$6.00	$6.00	$24.00
2	$4.00	$5.00	$14.00
3	$2.00	$4.00	$10.00
4	$4.00	$4.00	$8.50
5	$6.00	$4.40	$8.00
6	$8.00	$5.00	$8.00
7	$10.00	$5.72	$8.30

_____ 7. The total fixed cost at 6 units of output is
A. $24.00.
B. $8.00.
C. $18.00.
D. $3.00.

_____ 8. The firm will shut down in the short run if the price falls below
A. $8.00.
B. $4.00.
C. $2.00.
D. $6.00.

_____ 9. The price is currently $7.70. In the short run, to maximize profits, the firm should
A. produce 6 units.
B. produce 7 units.
C. produce 5 units.
D. shut down.

_____ 10. At this price ($7.70), the firm will make a short-run
A. profit of $1.50.
B. profit of $2.00.
C. loss of $1.50.
D. loss of $2.00.

_____ 11. At this price ($7.70), the firm will make a short-run operating
A. profit of $1.50.
B. profit of $16.50.
C. loss of $1.50.
D. loss of $16.50.

_____ 12. In the long run, firms will _____ this industry and the price will probably _____
A. enter, increase.
B. enter, decrease.
C. leave, increase.
D. leave, decrease.

_____ 13. If this is an industry that is experiencing external diseconomies of scale, the long-run price could be
A. $7.70.
B. $8.00.
C. $8.30.
D. $9.00.

_____ 14. A perfectly competitive decreasing-cost industry in long-run equilibrium experiences a permanent decrease in market demand. When the industry reaches its new long-run equilibrium, the equilibrium price of its good will be _____ than before and the equilibrium industry output will be _____ than before.
  A. higher, higher.
  B. higher, lower.
  C. lower, higher.
  D. lower, lower.

_____ 15. A firm will not produce where MR = MC when
  A. it is earning positive economic profits.
  B. it is making an operating loss.
  C. it is earning negative economic profits.
  D. it is making an operating profit.

_____ 16. Jenny's Gemstones is making an operating loss. It should _____ in the short run and _____ in the long run.
  A. shut down, leave the industry.
  B. leave the industry, shut down.
  C. increase its price, leave the industry.
  D. increase its price, reduce production.

_____ 17. Jenny's Gemstones is making an operating loss. The industry supply curve will shift _____ in the _____
  A. right, short run.
  B. right, long run.
  C. left, short run.
  D. left, long run.

_____ 18. Lambert's Lamps finds that when it increases its inputs by 20%, its output increases by 25%. It can conclude
  A. that it is operating in an increasing-cost industry.
  B. that it is operating in a decreasing-cost industry.
  C. that it is operating in a constant-cost industry.
  D. none of the above.

_____ 19. A perfectly competitive firm sells its output for $40 per unit. Its current output is 1,000 units. At that level, its marginal cost is $50 and increasing, average variable cost is $35, and average total cost is $60. To maximize short-run profits, the firm should
  A. increase production.
  B. increase price.
  C. decrease production.
  D. shut down.

Use the following information to answer the next three questions. A perfectly competitive firm, operating in an industry that is experiencing external diseconomies of scale, Johnny's T-shirts, is in long-run equilibrium producing 500 t-shirts per week. Suddenly, the price of all variable factors of production falls. Also, market demand for t-shirts increases.

_____ 20. In the short run, Johnny's T-shirts will
  A. produce more t-shirts, but the effect on profits is uncertain.
  B. produce fewer t-shirts, and possibly close down.
  C. earn positive (economic) profits, but the effect on output is uncertain.
  D. produce more t-shirts and earn positive (economic) profits.

_____ 21. In the long run, Johnny's T-shirts will
   A. produce more than 500 t-shirts per week, but the effect on profits is uncertain.
   B. produce fewer than 500 t-shirts per week, and earn normal profits.
   C. earn normal profits, but the effect on output is uncertain.
   D. earn positive (economic) profits, but the effect on output is uncertain.

_____ 22. The short-run industry supply curve will have shifted to the _____ and the long-run industry supply curve is _____
   A. right, upward sloping.
   B. right, downward sloping.
   C. left, upward sloping.
   D. left, downward sloping.

_____ 23. When P < LRAC, we would expect _____ and _____ firms in this industry.
   A. investment, more.
   B. investment, fewer.
   C. disinvestment, more.
   D. disinvestment, fewer.

Use the following diagram, which refers to Jill and John's Jugs, to answer the next two questions. LRAC is minimized at 600 units of output.

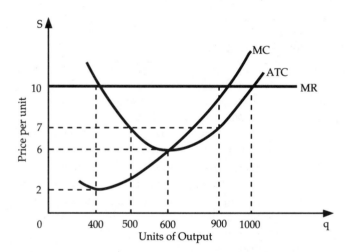

_____ 24. Assume that this firm is maximizing profit in an industry that is experiencing neither external economies nor diseconomies of scale. In the long run,
   A. each existing firm will expand production and new firms will enter the industry.
   B. each existing firm will expand production and new firms will leave the industry.
   C. each existing firm will reduce production and firms will enter this industry.
   D. each existing firm will reduce production and firms will leave this industry.

_____ 25. Assume that this firm is operating in an industry that is experiencing external economies of scale. In the long run,
   A. price will be $6 per unit.
   B. price will be between $10 per unit and $6 per unit.
   C. price will be less than $6 per unit.
   D. price will be $10 per unit.

II. APPLICATION QUESTIONS.

1. Check your understanding of the short-run relationships among costs, revenue, and the behavior of the firm in the table below.
   Treat each of the examples as a *separate* case.
   Assume that MC is increasing as output is increasing. The asterisk (*) indicates that the value given is the *minimum* ATC or AVC.
   Fill in the spaces and enter in the "response" column one of the responses provided.

Firm	P	q	TR	TC	TFC	TVC	ATC	AVC	MC	Response
Firm A	10		500				12*	9		
Firm B	10	200			300			8*		
Firm C	10		1000		200			4	10	
Firm D			2000		1500	1400		7	4	
Firm E	10		700				8	6	7	
Firm F	10		1000				12*	11		
Firm G	10	100			300			9*		
Firm H	10		1000		200			12	8	

Response	Meaning
1	the firm is now at the profit-maximizing output level.
2	the firm should increase output to maximize profits.
3	the firm should decrease output to maximize profits.
4	the firm should close down operations.

Sketch the diagram for Case A.

2. Suppose you are a consultant for ABC Inc., a firm in a perfectly competitive industry. Your research reveals two facts: (1) that the cost of producing the final unit of output is just equal to the market price, and (2) that the firm's total revenue is greater than its total variable cost and less than its total fixed cost. What would you recommend ABC do in the short run and in the long run?

   Now XYZ, a firm in the same industry, requests your advice. Your research reveals that: (1) the cost of producing the final unit of output is just equal to the market price, and (2) the firm's total revenue is greater than its total fixed cost and less than its total variable cost. What would you recommend XYZ do in the short run and in the long run?

3. Currently your firm is losing $2,000 per month. Variable costs are running at $1,200 per month. Your economist advises you to shut down. Why or why not should you accept her advice? The economist adds that your firm is experiencing diminishing marginal product but increasing returns to scale. Isn't there an inconsistency here? Should you fire her?

4. You have been hired as a consultant for DEF, Inc., a firm in a perfectly competitive industry with no external economies or diseconomies of scale. You have developed the following total cost information, based on three feasible plant sizes ("small", "medium", and "large").

q	TCSmall	TCMedium	TCLarge
0	$1.00	$3.40	$5.00
1	$5.00	$7.40	$12.00
2	$8.00	$10.40	$18.00
3	$9.60	$12.90	$21.00
4	$12.00	$15.00	$23.60
5	$16.00	$16.00	$25.00
6	$20.40	$16.80	$25.80
7	$28.00	$17.50	$26.67
8	$44.80	$18.00	$27.60
9	$68.40	$22.50	$28.71
10	$96.00	$30.00	$30.00
11	$127.60	$41.25	$31.35
12	$163.20	$57.00	$33.00
13	$202.80	$78.00	$36.40
14	$252.00	$112.00	$42.00

a. Calculate the average total cost information and complete the table below.

q	ATCSmall	ATCMedium	ATCLarge
1	___	___	___
2	___	___	___
3	___	___	___
4	___	___	___
5	___	___	___
6	___	___	___
7	___	___	___
8	___	___	___
9	___	___	___
10	___	___	___
11	___	___	___
12	___	___	___
13	___	___	___
14	___	___	___

b. Calculate the marginal cost information and complete the table below.

q	MCSmall	MCMedium	MCLarge
1	_____	_____	_____
2	_____	_____	_____
3	_____	_____	_____
4	_____	_____	_____
5	_____	_____	_____
6	_____	_____	_____
7	_____	_____	_____
8	_____	_____	_____
9	_____	_____	_____
10	_____	_____	_____
11	_____	_____	_____
12	_____	_____	_____
13	_____	_____	_____
14	_____	_____	_____

c. The market price is $2.40. Based on the information you have, and knowing that DEF is intending to produce 4 units of output, in which plant size, if any, would you advise the firm to invest?

d. The market price is $2.40. If DEF wishes to maximize profits, which is the optimal plant size, in your opinion? How many units should be produced? Calculate the firm's economic profit.

e. Draw DEF's short-run average cost curves and then the long-run average cost curve.

    f.   Over what range of output is DEF experiencing internal economies of scale? Internal diseconomies?

    g.   Consider your answer to part d. Is this the end of the adjustments that DEF will face? Describe any further changes that will occur in this industry. Draw a diagram with market demand and supply curves and the long-run industry supply curve.

5.   In the following diagram, draw the firm's demand curve.

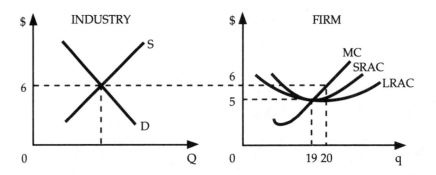

Determine the market price. The firm will make a short-run _____ (profit/loss) of $ _____ . Determine the short-run profit-maximizing output level. We would expect firms to _____ (enter/leave) this industry.

6.   Draw the "short-run cost diagram" comprised of AVC, ATC, and MC.

    a.   Draw in a horizontal demand curve (D_a) such that economic profits can be earned. Pick out the profit-maximizing output level (q_a).

    b.   Repeat the process, drawing the demand curve (D_b) so that only normal profits occur (q_b).

    c.   Repeat the process, drawing the demand curve (D_c) so that a loss is made but the firm continues to produce (q_c).

    d.   Draw in the demand curve (D_d) which would just permit the firm to cover its operating expenses (q_d).

    e.   Lastly, present the "shut down" case (D_e).

    f.   Highlight all the points on the MC curve where production will occur. Confirm that it's the short-run supply curve.

7. Examine the following diagram.

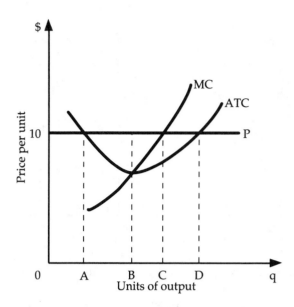

a. What can you tell from it? Is it short-run or long-run? Can profits be made or are losses inevitable? Should the firm shut down? At which output level would profits be maximized?

b. At Point A, price is equal to average total cost. How much profit is being made here? Is this a long-run equilibrium? If not, how about Point D?

c. Suppose this is a constant-cost industry. Can you say anything definite about the price level? The number of firms in the market?

8. Interpret the following diagram, and predict what will happen in this industry.

a. In the short run, at 100, are any profits being made?

b. In the long run, what will happen in this industry?

9. Study the following diagram. Assume constant costs for the industry. The firm's long-run average cost curve is $LRAC_1$.

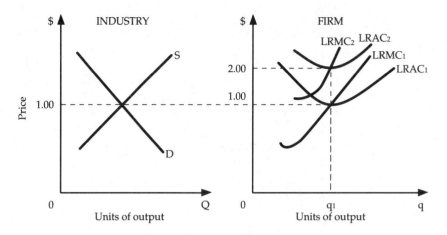

a. Verify that the firm is making normal profits and that it is in long-run equilibrium at a price of $1.
b. Suppose that there is an increase in average costs to $LRAC_2$. What will happen to the average and marginal cost curves?
c. What will happen to the short-run profits of the typical firm in this industry?
d. What will happen to output in the short run and why?
e. What will happen to industry supply in the long run and why?
f. If this had been an increasing-cost industry, would average cost be experiencing a pressure to rise or fall?

10. The following diagram, which is for a firm operating in a constant-cost industry, the initial curves have the notation "1"—e.g., demand curve D1. The firm is at q1.

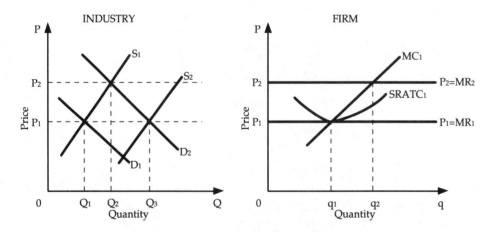

a. What will this typical firm will do in the short run?
b. Now suppose demand rises to D2. What are the immediate effects on the industry and on the firm?
c. In the short run the firm will produce _____ units and the industry will produce _____ units.
d. Examine the graph. Does your answer in part c represent an equilibrium?
e. Depict the firm's short-run profits on your diagram.
f. Explain your answer to part d.
g. What will happen to this industry in the long run? How far will price fall?

Note that, although more is being supplied by more firms, the size of the typical firm has not changed—because of the assumption of a constant-cost industry.

11. You can display the relationship between SRAC curves and the LRAC quite simply. Consider the following information about the average costs of three short-run methods of production. In each case one resource is fixed; others are variable.

OUTPUT	METHOD 1	METHOD 2	METHOD 3
	—AVERAGE COST—		
100	10.00	13.00	17.00
200	9.00	11.50	14.30
300	8.50	9.75	12.50
400	8.30	8.40	10.80
500	8.40	8.10	9.60
600	8.90	7.50	8.60
700	9.60	7.30	8.10
800	11.70	7.60	7.80
900	14.80	8.10	8.00
1000	17.00	8.90	8.30
1100	23.00	10.20	9.00

a. Is each curve a "typical" short-run ATC curve?
b. Which method should be used if an output of 100 is desired?
c. Which method should be used if an output of 500 is desired?
d. Which method should be used if an output of 1000 is desired?
e. Plot each of the curves on a single piece of graph paper.
f. You're using Method 1. If you want to move from an output level of 100 units to 1000 units, what would happen to average cost, in the short run?
g. In the long run, what would be your lowest-cost strategy?
h. What does this firm's LRAC curve look like?
i. Why is this the *long-run* AC curve?
j. When output was doubled from, say 300 to 600, average costs fell, in the long run. What does this information tell you about returns to scale in this part of the firm's LRAC curve?

12. There are 100 firms in the perfectly competitive "beanie bear" industry. Each firm has identical costs. The total costs of one such perfectly competitive firm (Barney's Beanie Bears) are as follows:

TOTAL OUTPUT	TOTAL COST	AVERAGE VARIABLE COST	AVERAGE TOTAL COST	MARGINAL VARIABLE COST	COST
0	$10	_____	—	—	—
1	$22	_____	_____	_____	_____
2	$28	_____	_____	_____	_____
3	$38	_____	_____	_____	_____
4	$50	_____	_____	_____	_____
5	$64	_____	_____	_____	_____
6	$80	_____	_____	_____	_____
7	$100	_____	_____	_____	_____
8	$126	_____	_____	_____	_____

a. Complete the TVC, AVC, ATC, and MC columns.
b. If the price of the product is $12, what output should the firm choose?
c. At a price of $12, how much will be the firm's total economic profit?
d. Calculate the firm's total economic profit if the price is $6, $10, $16, or $10, respectively.

OUTPUT	PROFIT WHEN PRICE = $6	PROFIT WHEN PRICE = $10	PROFIT WHEN PRICE = $16	PROFIT WHEN PRICE = $20
0	_____	_____	_____	_____
1	_____	_____	_____	_____
2	_____	_____	_____	_____
3	_____	_____	_____	_____
4	_____	_____	_____	_____
5	_____	_____	_____	_____
6	_____	_____	_____	_____
7	_____	_____	_____	_____
8	_____	_____	_____	_____

e. Collect your answers from the previous question in the following table. At each price level, indicate which case is present, e.g., loss-minimization, shut-down.

PRICE	QUANTITY SUPPLIED	CASE
$ 6	_____	_____
$10	_____	_____
$12	_____	_____
$16	_____	_____
$20	_____	_____

f. Based on your answers to the previous questions, derive values for the "beanie bear" industry supply curve.

PRICE	QUANTITY SUPPLIED	CASE
$ 6	_____	_____
$10	_____	_____
$12	_____	_____
$16	_____	_____
$20	_____	_____

g. Based on your previous analysis, if the price level is currently $12, predict what will happen to the industry supply curve and to the price level in the long run.

13. In Chapters 7 and 8 we examined the production and cost conditions facing Wilma's Wicker Baskets. The production information is summarized below. Each worker costs $24 to hire and Wilma has total fixed costs of $30.

LABOR	TOTAL PRODUCT	TOTAL COST	AVERAGE VARIABLE COST	AVERAGE TOTAL COST	MARGINAL COST
0	0	$30	—	—	—
1	5	$54	$4.80	$10.80	$4.80
2	16	$78	$3.00	$4.88	$1.60
3	27	$102	$2.67	$3.78	$2.18
4	36	$126	$2.67	$3.50	$2.67
5	44	$150	$2.73	$3.41	$3.00
6	51	$174	$2.82	$3.41	$3.43
7	56	$198	$3.00	$3.54	$4.80
8	60	$222	$3.20	$3.70	$6.00
9	63	$246	$3.43	$3.91	$8.00
10	65	$270	$3.69	$4.15	$12.00

a. If the price is $1.60, how many baskets should Wilma produce in the short run? What will be her economic profit?

b. What is the lowest price at which Wilma will produce in the short run?

c. If the price is $3.43, how many baskets should Wilma produce in the short run? What will be her economic profit?

d. At a price of $3.00, predict what will happen to the number of firms in this industry in the long run. Explain your prediction.

e. Wilma operates in an industry with no external economies or diseconomies. At a price of $3.00, predict what will happen market price in this industry in the long run. Explain your prediction.

f. At a price of $6.00, determine how many units Wilma will produce in the short run.

III. ECONOMICS EXPLORER.

Use the fifth module ("The Long Run") from the Economics Explorer software. This module focuses on important long-run concepts—including economies of scale. The complex process that moves the industry to long-run equilibrium is portrayed in this module.

ANSWERS AND SOLUTIONS

ANSWERS TO PRACTICE QUESTIONS

11.

PRICE	OUTPUT
$15.00	100
$14.22	90
$8.90	80
$7.00	70
$6.00	0

PRACTICE TEST

I. SOLUTIONS TO MULTIPLE CHOICE QUESTIONS

1. C. External (dis)economies of scale refer to industry-wide changes. See p. 229.

2. B. If a firm can earn an operating profit it will minimize losses by producing.

3. A. See p. 230.

4. A. Initially, existing firms will increase production as higher prices earn them greater profits. In the long run, new firms will enter the industry, increasing supply and decreasing the price level.

5. D. In the long run, price will equal the minimum value of average cost. See Figure 9.7 on p. 221.

6. C. As the number of firms increases, costs increase. This pushes up the price charged by the industry.

7. C. At one unit of output, TC = ATC × q = $24.00 and TVC = AVC × q = $6.00. TFC = TC − TVC.

8. B. If price is less than the minimum AVC ($4.00), then the firm should shut down.

9. C. P = MR = $7.70. To maximize profits, increase production where MR is equal to or exceeds MC.

10. C. When the output is set at 5 units, TR = $7.70 × 5 = $38.50. TC = ATC × q = $8.00 × 5 = $40.00. The firm will make a negative economic profit of $1.50.

11. B. TR = $7.70 × 5 = $38.50. TVC = $4.40 × 5 = $22.00.

12. C. Because losses are being experienced, firms will leave the industry. Market supply will decrease, causing the price to increase (unless there are external economies of scale resulting in a downward sloping industry supply curve).

13. A. At a price of $7.70, firms will leave this industry in the long run. In an industry experiencing external diseconomies of scale, this reduction in output will reduce average cost from $8.00 and reduce equilibrium price.

14. B. In a decreasing-cost industry, costs decrease as output increases and they increase as output decreases.

15. B. A firm that is making an operating loss will close down. Note: Making a negative economic profit is not an adequate answer because the firm could still be making an operating profit.

16. A. Perfectly competitive firms can't change the price they face—they are price takers. Because Jenny can't cover her variable costs, she should shut down in the short run and leave the industry in the long run.

17. D. Firms will leave the industry in the long run.

18. D. The behavior of costs for an individual firm (its internal economies of scale) are no guide to the behavior of costs for the entire industry (its external economies of scale).

19. C. If price is $40, then marginal revenue is also $40. MR is less than MC—the firm's output level is too high. It should not shut down as it can cover its variable costs.

20. D. Marginal cost is affected by the behavior of variable costs. A decrease in variable costs will decrease marginal cost. An increase in price will increase marginal revenue. Together, these effects will increase the profit-maximizing output level. In long-run equilibrium, Johnny's T-shirts was earning a normal profit. With higher prices and lower costs, the firm will earn an economic profit.

21. C. In the long run, the competitive firm always earns normal profits. As the industry expands, external diseconomies (increasing costs) are experienced, reducing the firm's profit-maximizing output level. Without extra information we cannot say whether the final output level will be greater than, equal to, or less than 500 t-shirts.

22. A. New firms have entered this industry, shifting the short-run supply curve to the right. The long-run industry supply curve is upward sloping because of the external diseconomies of scale.

23. D. If price is less than long-run average cost, disinvestment will occur and firms will leave the industry in search of normal profits in other activities.

24. C. New firms will enter, attracted by the economic profits, pushing down the price. As price falls, existing firms will cut back production.

25. C. As firms enter the industry, external economies of scale will reduce costs. The minimum average cost will be less than $6. In equilibrium, price equals average cost.

II. SOLUTIONS TO APPLICATION QUESTIONS

1. See the following table.

Firm	P	q	TR	TC	TFC	TVC	ATC	AVC	MC	Response
Firm A	10	50	500	600	150	450	12*	9	12	3
Firm B	10	200	2000	1900	300	1600	9.5	8*	8	2
Firm C	10	100	1000	600	200	400	6	4	10	1
Firm D	10	200	2000	2900	1500	1400	14.5	7	4	2
Firm E	10	70	700	560	140	420	88	6	7	2
Firm F	10	100	1000	1200	100	1100	12*	11	12	3 or 4
Firm G	10	100	1000	1200	300	900	12	9*	9	2
Firm H	10	100	1000	1400	200	1200	14	12	8	2 or 4

A (fairly complex) sketch that would describe the situation in Case A is presented below. (For more practice, try to do the other cases—without first peeking at the sketches on the following page!)

Note: Case F and Case H have two possible outcomes, depending on the behavior of AVC. Again, try sketching these cases and try to get the different results.

2. ABC. Fact 1 means that MR = MC. Fact 2 means that the firm is making an eco-
    nomic loss but, because it is covering its variable (operating) costs, it should continue
    to produce in the short run. In the long run, the firm should leave the industry.

    XYZ. Fact 1 means that MR = MC. Fact 2 means that the firm is making an eco-
    nomic loss and that it is not covering its variable (operating) costs—it should cease
    production in the short run. In the long run, the firm should leave the industry.

3. The first question to ask is: Am I maximizing profits? If the firm is not producing
    where MR = MC, then the situation might be completely turned around by adjusting
    output. If the firm is currently producing where MR = MC, then price is clearly less
    than short-run ATC. However, it is not clear whether an operating profit is being
    made. In Case A, below, the firm should shut down; in Case B, because it can cover
    its variable costs, it should not.

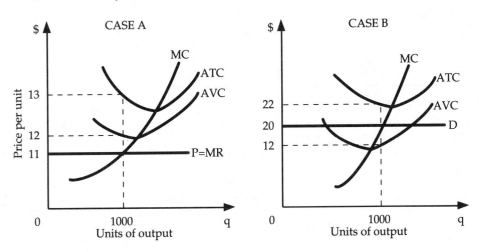

Regarding diminishing returns and increasing returns to scale, there is no inconsistency. The former is a short-run concept (and, in fact, applies for almost all producers) while the latter is a long-run concept.

4. a. See the table below.

q	ATCSmall	ATCMedium	ATCLarge
1	$5.00	$7.40	$12.00
2	$4.00	$5.20	$9.00
3	$3.20	$4.30	$7.00
4	$3.00	$3.75	$5.90
5	$3.20	$3.20	$5.00
6	$3.40	$2.80	$4.30
7	$4.00	$2.50	$3.81
8	$5.60	$2.25	$3.45
9	$7.60	$2.50	$3.19
10	$9.60	$3.00	$3.00
11	$11.60	$3.75	$2.85
12	$13.60	$4.75	$2.75
13	$15.60	$6.00	$2.80
14	$18.00	$8.00	$3.00

b. See the table below.

q	MCSmall	MCMedium	MCLarge
1	$4.00	$4.00	$7.00
2	$3.00	$3.00	$6.00
3	$1.60	$2.50	$3.00
4	$2.40	$2.10	$2.60
5	$4.00	$1.00	$1.40
6	$4.40	$0.80	$0.80
7	$7.60	$0.70	$0.87
8	$16.80	$0.50	$0.93
9	$23.60	$4.50	$1.11
10	$27.60	$7.50	$1.29
11	$31.60	$11.25	$1.35
12	$35.60	$15.75	$1.65
13	$39.60	$21.00	$3.40
14	$49.20	$34.00	$5.60

c. The firm should not produce. Even in the case of the small plant, the firm will incur a loss because $2.40 × 4 is less than $12. If the firm had committed to the small plant, in the short run it should shut down because it cannot cover its variable costs. Note that total fixed costs are only $1.00, with variable costs accounting for the remainder.

d. The medium plant is best, with the lowest total costs. Neither of the two other plant sizes has an average cost as low as the price. Producing up to the output where price equals (or is greater than) marginal cost, DEF should produce 8 units of output. The firm's economic profit is ($2.40 − $2.25) × 8, or $1.20.

e. See the diagram below.

f. Internal economies of scale occur until the minimum point of the long-run average cost curve, i.e., at 8 units, after which point diseconomies take over.

g. Because DEF is earning an economic profit, new firms will enter the industry. There are no external economies or diseconomies of scale, so the firm's long-run average cost curve will not change position. For the same reason, the long-run industry supply curve is horizontal. As new firms enter, market supply increases from S1 to S2 and the market price will decrease from 2.40 to $2.25 at which point the process will cease because the market price has reached the minimum long-run average cost. Economic profits have been competed away. Given DEF's marginal cost values, the firm's output will remain at 8 units.

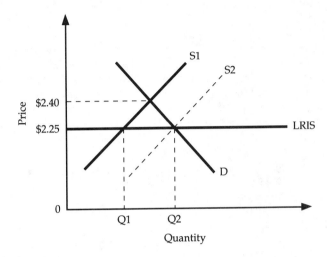

5. The firm's demand curve graphs as a horizontal line. It is set at the industry level by the forces of demand and supply at a level of $6.

   The market price is $6. The firm will make a short-run profit of $20 at an output level of 20 units. We would expect firms to enter this industry.

6. See the diagram below.

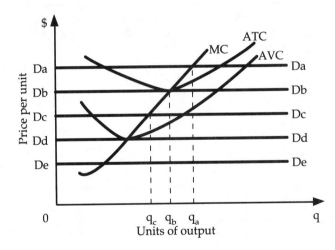

7. a. This is a short-run diagram (because there are economic profits) for a perfectly competitive firm (because the demand curve is horizontal). Price is $10 and the profit-maximizing output level is output level C.
   b. The firm is earning normal profit at both Point A and Point D. Neither is a long-run equilibrium, however, because other firms can enter the market and make economic profits.
   c. Price will fall and the number of firms will increase.

8. a. The firm is making normal profits (P = ATC), but is not maximizing profits because it is not producing where MR = MC.
   b. In the long run, since price is greater than the minimum LRAC point, firms will enter the industry, forcing price to fall.

9. a. Check that P = MR = SRMC = SRAC = LRAC.
    b. Average and marginal cost curves will rise.
    c. Short-run losses will be encountered.
    d. Some firms will shut down in the short run and supply will fall for the industry.
    e. Supply will decrease as firms exit the industry.
    f. Fall! As output rises for an increasing-cost industry, costs rise. Here output is shrinking, and costs would fall.

10. a. Stay as it is, since it is already profit-maximizing.
    b. Price and quantity supplied increase in each case, and the number of firms is unchanged.
    c. q2; Q2.
    d. Yes in the short run; no in the long run.
    e. The profit-maximizing output level occurs where MR = MC.
    f. In the short run the firm is maximizing profits, but in the long run the economic profits will attract new competitions and a change in price will occur.
    g. Entering firms will push the supply curve to the right (to S2), and price will decline. Price will fall back to its initial level since, at any other price, profits or losses will be made.

11. a. Yes, each ATC is U-shaped.
    b. Method 1, which is cheapest until about 425 units.
    c. Method 2 is cheapest from about 425 units until about 875.
    d. Method 3 is cheapest from about 875 units on.
    f. ATC would rise to $17.00.
    g. Maintain Method 1 until production has grown to 425 units, then switch to Method 2. Maintain Method 2 until production has grown to 875 units, then switch to Method 3. In effect you are tracing out the LRAC for this firm.
    h. U-shaped, *in this case.*
    i. We release the fixed resource constraint as we move from one method of production to the next.
    j. The firm has increasing returns to scale (economies of scale).

12. a. See the following table.

TOTAL OUTPUT	TOTAL COST	AVERAGE VARIABLE COST	AVERAGE TOTAL COST	MARGINAL VARIABLE COST	COST
0	$10	$ 0	—	—	—
1	$22	$12	$22.00	$12.00	$12.00
2	$28	$18	$14.00	$ 9.00	$ 6.00
3	$38	$28	$12.67	$ 9.33	$10.00
4	$50	$40	$12.50	$10.00	$12.00
5	$64	$54	$12.80	$10.80	$14.00
6	$80	$70	$13.33	$11.67	$16.00
7	$100	$90	$14.29	$12.86	$20.00
8	$126	$116	$15.75	$14.50	$26.00

    b. The firm should produce 4 units of output, where MR = MC.
    c. The firm's total revenue is $48; the firm's total cost is $50. It will make an economic loss of $2.

d. See the following table.

OUTPUT	PROFIT WHEN PRICE = $6	PROFIT WHEN PRICE = $10	PROFIT WHEN PRICE = $16	PROFIT WHEN PRICE = $20
0	−$10	−$10	−$10	−$10
1	−$16	−$12	−$6	−$2
2	−$16	−$8	$4	$12
3	−$20	−$8	$10	$22
4	−$26	−$10	$14	$30
5	−$34	−$14	$16	$36
6	−$44	−$20	$16	$40
7	−$58	−$30	$12	$40
8	−$78	−$46	$2	$34

e. See the following table.

PRICE	QUANTITY SUPPLIED	CASE
$6	0	Shut-down
$10	3	Loss-minimization
$12	4	Profit-maximization
$16	6	Profit-maximization
$20	7	Profit-maximization

f. See the following table. There are 100 identical firms. As price increases, output level increases as determined by the behavior of marginal cost.

PRICE	QUANTITY SUPPLIED
$6	0
$10	300
$12	400
$16	600
$20	700

g. If the price is $12, economic profits are being earned by the typical firm. New firms will enter the industry, shifting the industry supply curve to the right. Consequently, the price will fall.

13. a. Wilma will close down. Her loss will equal her total fixed costs of $30.
   b. Wilma will produce as long as the price is $2.67 or more. $2.67 is the minimum average variable cost value.
   c. At a price of $3.43, Wilma will produce 51 baskets and earn an economic profit of 93¢ ($174.93 − $174.00).
   d. At a price of $3.00, Wilma will produce 44 baskets and make an economic loss of $18. If the typical firm in an industry is making an economic loss, firms will leave the industry in the long run, in search of more attractive profits elsewhere.
   e. As firms leave the industry, the industry supply curve will shift to the left and the market price will increase.
   f. At a price of $6.00, Wilma will produce 60 baskets.

INPUT DEMAND: THE LABOR AND LAND MARKETS

10

OBJECTIVES: POINT BY POINT

After completing this chapter, you should be able to accomplish the objectives listed below.

General Comments

While there is much new material in this chapter, there is also a lot of familiar material, too. The discussion of the input markets reuses tools that you have already developed—e.g. profit-maximization, marginal product, demand curves, and elasticity. Take this as a reminder that (for better or for worse) economics is a cumulative discipline—new material doesn't supplant earlier material, it builds on it.

Keep in mind too that, although the chapter talks mostly in terms of labor demand, the conclusions apply equally to other inputs, including capital.

OBJECTIVE 1: Explain why input demand is a "derived" demand.

When the management of the Chicago Bulls signs Michael Jordan to a contract, it does so because of the "output" (points and excitement) that Jordan can produce for the team. The demand for his labor services is a demand *derived* from the demand for the team's output by its public. This specific conclusion is true generally for the demand for all types of input. (page 233)

> **LEARNING TIP:** The main theme of this chapter is that the value of any input depends on society's valuation of the output produced by that input. Inputs will be hired as long as their contribution to the value of production is greater than their cost. Keep this point in mind as you go through the chapter.

PRACTICE

1. Which of the following is a "derived demand"?
   A. The demand by your *Study Guide*'s author for a word processor.
   B. The demand for Cracker Jacks at the ball game.
   C. The demand for tax-free municipal bonds by a highly paid executive seeking to reduce her tax payments.
   D. The demand for wood to help you build a doghouse for your new puppy.
   Answer: A. This option is the only one involving the demand for an input by a producer. Cracker Jacks and bonds are not inputs. Wood, bought by a construction firm, is an input; bought by an end-user, it is not.

OBJECTIVE 2: Explain why inputs are simultaneously complements and substitutes.

Although fans of the Bulls might disagree (for them, the only valid product is a "W" in the win column), the product of the Chicago Bulls is "entertainment"—the Bulls compete with movies, rock concerts, and so on for the public's leisure dollars. The facilities in the Bulls' stadium add to the entire entertainment package (inputs are complements) but they may be seen as substitutes for Michael Jordan (a team without a Michael Jordan may be able to attract fans by offering other facilities instead). At the team level, one player can assist (complement) another's play and can also substitute for that player. (page 235)

PRACTICE

2. Which of the following is true about input markets?
   A. Firms demand inputs in the labor market and supply inputs in the capital market.
   B. Firms supply inputs in the labor market and demand inputs in the capital market.
   C. Households supply inputs in the labor market and demand inputs in the capital market.
   D. Households supply inputs in the labor market and supply inputs in the capital market.
   Answer: D. Households supply inputs to all resource markets; firms demand in all resource markets.

3. To produce cloth, a mill owner must hire a weaver and a loom. The weaver and the loom are
   A. substitutable inputs.
   B. complementary inputs.
   C. both substitutable and complementary inputs.
   D. not inputs—they are factors of production.
   Answer: B. To produce cloth, both inputs are required. Note: Factors of production are inputs.

4. To mine coal, a mine owner can use a robotic drill or a team of coal miners. The drill and the coal miners are
   A. substitutable inputs.
   B. complementary inputs.
   C. both substitutable and complementary inputs.
   D. unrelated inputs.
   Answer: A. This is an either/or situation. The inputs are substitutes in this case.

5. To mine coal, a mine owner can use a robotic drill or a team of coal miners. Within the group, the coal miners are
   A. substitutable inputs.
   B. complementary inputs.
   C. both substitutable and complementary inputs.
   D. unrelated inputs.
   Answer: C. Each miner helps the others to produce coal (complements), and each can take over from another worker (substitutes). See p. 235.

OBJECTIVE 3: Define and calculate marginal revenue product (MRP). Find the profit-maximizing hiring level for an input, given MRP and input price information. Explain why the MRP curve is identical to the input demand curve.

Marginal revenue product (MRP) is the addition to total revenue attributable to the hiring of an additional input. It can be defined as the extra units of output (marginal product) times the price of the product. Marginal revenue product of labor is the addition to revenue that occurs when an additional worker is hired—it's the dollar value of the extra merchandise he produces, i.e., (MP_L.P). In the short run, as extra workers are hired, MRP falls because of diminishing marginal productivity. The MRP curve is typically downward sloping. (page 236)

To maximize profits, the employer should hire each input up to the point at which MRP equals the cost of hiring that input. For labor, wage will equal MRP. (page 239)

The MRP curve for a factor of production is identical with the demand curve for that factor. The demand curve for labor is the marginal revenue product of labor curve. (page 240)

> **Profit Maximization and the Hiring Decision:** Two rules from earlier chapters crop up in the "hiring decision." The logic of profit-maximization (P = MC) leads to Wage = MRP_L. No profit-maximizing employer will hire a worker who doesn't pay his or her way.
>
> Recall the rule developed to describe the consumer's utility-maximizing mix of purchases: the final dollar spent on each good must provide the same utility. The same logic applies to profit maximization. It shows up as: $MP_L/P_L = MP_K/P_K = MP_A/P_A$—the final dollar spent on each input must generate the same amount of additional production.

PRACTICE

Tom grows tomatoes, which he sells for 75¢ per pound. His variable resource is labor and he has recorded the productivity of his workers in the table below.

NUMBER OF WORKERS	TOTAL PRODUCT	MARGINAL PRODUCT	MARGINAL REVENUE PRODUCT
0	0	—	—
1	10	_____	_____
2	25	_____	_____
3	38	_____	_____
4	48	_____	_____
5	56	_____	_____

6. Fill in the marginal product and marginal revenue product columns.
   Answer: See the *Answers and Solutions* section.

7. Graph the marginal product curve for the first 5 workers on part a of the diagram.

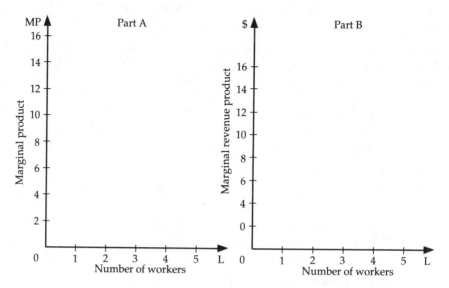

Answer: See the *Answers and Solutions* section.

8. If the wage is $10, Tom should hire
   A. 2 workers.
   B. 3 workers.
   C. 4 workers.
   D. 5 workers.
   Answer: A. To maximize profits, Tom should not hire any worker whose MRP is less than $10. The MRP of the third worker is $9.75.

9. The maximum wage that Tom would pay if he were to hire 3 workers is
   A. $9.75.
   B. $7.50.
   C. $10.00.
   D. $11.25.
   Answer: A. To maximize profits, Tom should not hire the fourth worker (whose MRP is $7.50) at any wage above $7.50.

OBJECTIVE 4: Identify the factors that affect the position of an input demand curve and explain how each factor may shift the curve.

A profit-maximizing employer will hire any worker who pays his/her way. As the wage changes, the hiring level will change too, based on the MRP schedule—the demand for the input and the MRP curve are identical. Each point on the demand schedule equates input price and MRP. The equilibrium hiring condition is: W = MRP. It is equivalent to the P = MC profit-maximization rule in output markets. The input demand curve will shift right if marginal productivity increases or if the price of the product increases. (page 247)

PRACTICE

10. Graph the MRP curve on Part B of the previous diagram.
    Answer: See the *Answers and Solutions* section.

11. If tomatoes sell for 75¢ a pound, Tom's demand for labor curve will have the same *shape* as the
    A. marginal product curve.
    B. total product curve.
    C. product demand curve.
    D. marginal cost curve.
    Answer: A. See the diagram you've drawn above.

12. Petra's Portland Cement is a perfectly competitive firm. Cement sells at $4 per bag. Petra employs 15 workers at a wage of $12 per hour. The marginal revenue product of the 15th worker is $8 per hour. To increase profits, Petra should
    A. increase employment until the MRP of labor equals $12. B. decrease employment until the MRP of labor equals $12.
    C. increase the price of cement to at least $8 per bag.
    D. increase the price of cement to at least $12 per bag.
    Answer: B. In a perfectly competitive industry, the producer has no control over price. Because wage exceeds MRP, Petra should reduce her labor force.

13. The supply of labor falls in the fishing industry. Which of the following events will occur? The wage rate will _____ and firms will _____ employment until MRP equals the new wage.
    A. increase, increase.
    B. increase, decrease.
    C. decrease, increase.
    D. decrease, decrease.
    Answer: B. See Figure 10.3 on p. 238. A decrease in supply increases the price of labor (wage). To restore equality, MRP must increase. To accomplish this, fewer workers will be hired.

14. We saw in Chapter 8 (p. 189) that there is a link between marginal cost and marginal product of labor; in fact, $MC = W/MP_L$. We now know that $MRP_L = MP_L.P$. If DoughCrust Bakery's marginal revenue product of labor is greater than the wage, it must be the case that
    A. total revenues exceed total costs.
    B. the wage is greater than the marginal cost.
    C. DoughCrust's price exceeds its marginal cost.
    D. DoughCrust's price is less than its marginal cost.
    Answer: C. We know that $MRP_L = MP_L.P$ and are told that $MRP_L > W$, so $MP_L.P > W$. We know that $MC = W/MP_L$ so $MP_L.MC = W$. If $MP_L.P > W$ and $MP_L.MC = W$ then $P > MC$.

OBJECTIVE 5: In a world with more than one variable resource, derive and explain the factors influencing the demand curve for each input.

The same profit-maximizing principles are applied with two variable factors of production as with one variable factor of production. However, when more than one factor is involved, an increase in the price of an input has a factor substitution effect and an output effect. These effects explain why, as wage increases the quantity demanded of labor decreases. As the wage rises, capital is substituted for the now relatively more expensive labor—the factor substitution effect. Also, higher wages may mean higher production costs, lower production and less use of all inputs, including labor—the output effect.   (page 242)

LEARNING TIP: You can depict the factor substitution effect and the output effect on a diagram. Draw a labor demand curve. Suppose the price of robot car-machines decreases and that there is job loss on the assembly line. In the labor market, which factor is stronger, the factor substitution effect or the output effect?

The lowered price of robots will increase management's desire to substitute capital for labor. The labor demand curve will decrease—this represents the factor substitution effect. Because production costs have fallen (cheaper robots), the company will wish to expand production because, with lower costs and the same selling price, the company will earn higher profits. Expanding production means that the demand for labor will increase—this is the output effect. If labor demand fell, on balance, the factor substitution effect would be stronger.

The firm's input demand curve will shift position if demand for the firm's product changes (causing its price to change); if the amount, productivity, or price of other inputs change; or if the state of technology changes. Each of these changes will affect MRP—the dollar value of the extra merchandise produced by an additional unit of an input.

(page 243)

PRACTICE

15. The tendency of firms to move away from usage of a factor whose price has increased is called the
    A. output substitution effect.
    B. factor substitution effect.
    C. complementarity effect.
    D. income effect.
    Answer: B. See p. 243.

16. The output effect indicates that the quantity demanded of labor
    A. will increase if the price of the final product increases.
    B. will decrease when the price of other factors increases.
    C. will increase if the price of labor increases.
    D. will increase if the price of labor decreases.
    Answer: D. The output effect helps explain why the quantity of labor demanded increases as the price of labor decreases.

17. Labor is a normal input. If the price of labor increases, the factor substitution effect will cause the demand for labor to _____ and the output effect will cause the demand for labor to _____
    A. increase, increase.
    B. increase, decrease.
    C. decrease, increase.
    D. decrease, decrease.
    Answer: D. Other resources will be used instead of the more expensive labor (factor substitution effect). Because costs of production have risen, less will be produced and less labor will be demanded (output effect).

18. The wage of workers (a variable resource) is increased. This will cause each of the following to occur except
    A. the firm's profit-maximizing output level will decrease.
    B. the firm will substitute away from labor to capital.
    C. the output effect will lead to a decrease in the demand for capital as well as labor.
    D. the MRP of the final worker hired will decrease.
    Answer: D. Fewer workers are being hired. As extra workers are hired, MRP decreases; as fewer are hired, the MRP of the final worker increases.

19. The demand for labor will increase if
    A. the wage paid to labor increases.
    B. the wage paid to labor decreases.
    C. there is an increase in the amount of capital used.
    D. there is a decrease in the amount of capital used.
    Answer: C. Additional capital (machinery) will let workers be more productive, thus affecting MRP.

20. A technological advance increases labor productivity. This will cause
    A. an increase in the demand for labor.
    B. an increase in the supply of labor.
    C. a decrease in the demand for labor.
    D. a decrease in the supply for labor.
    Answer: A. MRP_L (MP_L .P) has increased.

21. Mauro uses labor and capital to produce soccer balls. He finds that as the price of capital rises, he hires more workers and cuts back on the use of capital. This behavior is consistent with
    A. labor and capital being complementary inputs.
    B. the factor substitution effect.
    C. the increasing marginal productivity of labor.
    D. the dominance of the factor substitution effect over the output effect for capital.
    Answer: B. Simply, Mauro is switching from one input to the other to reduce costs.

22. The demand for soccer balls decreases. This will cause Mauro to _____ his demand for labor and _____ his demand for capital.
    A. increase, increase.
    B. increase, decrease.
    C. decrease, increase.
    D. decrease, decrease.
    Answer: D. Mauro will produce less because his costs have risen. He will need fewer workers and less capital.

OBJECTIVE 6: Explain what is meant by the term "pure rent" and explain why it arises.

The market for land is similar to the market for labor but differs in one important respect: land prices are demand-determined, due to the fact that land is strictly fixed in supply. The return to any factor of production in fixed supply is called a *pure rent*. Any site has a variety of uses and should be allocated to the user who is willing to pay the most. (page 244)

LEARNING TIP: Pure rent emerges when *any* factor (not just land) is fixed in supply. Any payment greater than zero is a "bonus."

Example: Suppose that Marlene has a PC she's willing to lend out (lease, if you want) to her suitemates, Charlene, Arlene, and Darlene. Each has a term paper due tomorrow morning and is willing to pay for the use of the PC (which is the only one available at such short notice). Marlene would take $6, but asks for bids. Charlene offers $7, Arlene, $8, and Darlene, $10. Darlene would have the use of the PC, and Marlene would receive a pure rent of $4.

PRACTICE

23. The supply of land of a particular quality at a given location is
    A. perfectly elastic.
    B. perfectly inelastic.
    C. unitarily elastic.
    D. dependent on demand.
    Answer: The supply of land isn't dependent on demand—the price is. The supply, however, is perfectly insensitive to changes in price.

24. A tax on landowners will _____ the quantity of land supplied and will _____ rents charged.
    A. decrease, decrease.
    B. decrease, not affect.
    C. not affect, decrease.
    D. not affect, not affect.
    Answer: D. The supply, however, is perfectly insensitive to changes in price or taxes. Because the rent charged is demand-driven, rents will not change. Economic rent will be reduced.

OBJECTIVE 7: In a world with more than one variable resource, state and interpret the conditions necessary for profit maximization.

The profit-maximizing equilibrium is to "balance the margins" according to the following rule: $MRP_L/P_L = MRP_K/P_K = MRP_A/P_A = 1$ (the marginal revenue product/dollar of the final unit of each input should be equal and have a value of one). Put differently, $MP_L/P_L = MP_K/P_K = MP_A/P_A$. (page 246)

PRACTICE

25. Sellco finds that its workers have an average revenue product of $20 (the final worker adding $10) and its machines have an average revenue product of $100 (the final machine adding $60). Workers earn $15 and machines cost $50. Assuming that Sellco is at the profit-maximizing output level, it should hire _____ workers and hire _____ machines.
    A. more, more.
    B. more, fewer.
    C. fewer, more.
    D. fewer, fewer.
    Answer: C. Compare MRP (not average revenue product) with the price of the input. MRP_L is less than P_L and MRP_K is greater than P_K.

At the conclusion of Chapter 10, Case and Fair have demonstrated how competitive firms decide how much of each resource to hire, how to combine those resources, and how much output to produce. Income distribution is determined by the marginal revenue product of resources.

PRACTICE TEST

I.   MULTIPLE CHOICE QUESTIONS.

Select the option that provides the single best answer.

_____ 1. The firm has two inputs, capital and labor. Economic theory suggests that
   A. these are complementary but not substitutable.
   B. these are substitutable but not complementary.
   C. these are both complementary and substitutable.
   D. labor is complementary, while capital is substitutable.

_____ 2. Labor demand is a "derived" demand because
   A. it is derived from the demand for capital.
   B. it depends on the demand for outputs.
   C. it is derived from firms.
   D. it is derived from marginal revenue product.

_____ 3. The firm has one variable input, labor. The demand for labor is labor's
   A. total product curve.
   B. productivity times the wage rate.
   C. marginal product curve.
   D. marginal revenue product curve.

_____ 4. The firm is hiring labor and capital such that $MRP_L = P_L$ and $MRP_K < P_K$. The firm should certainly hire
   A. more labor and more capital.
   B. less capital.
   C. less labor and less capital.
   D. less labor and more capital.

_____ 5. You are told that $MP_L/MP_L > MP_K/P_K$. Given a fixed amount of funds to produce more output, the firm should
   A. shift dollars away from labor and toward capital.
   B. shift dollars away from capital and toward labor.
   C. hire more capital to increase MP_K.
   D. hire more capital to decrease MP_K.

_____ 6. Downtown land is a normal input. If the price of downtown land decreases, then the factor substitution effect will _____ the quantity demanded and the output effect will _____ the quantity demanded.
   A. increase, increase.
   B. increase, decrease.
   C. decrease, increase.
   D. decrease, decrease.

_____ 7. The firm has two variable inputs, labor and capital. Now the price of labor falls. The output effect indicates that
   A. output will fall.
   B. fewer of all factors will be demanded.
   C. more labor will be demanded.
   D. less labor will be demanded.

_____ 8. A firm has one variable input, labor. An increase in the price of the output will
   A. increase the demand for labor.
   B. decrease the demand for labor.
   C. cause the factor substitution effect to outweigh the output effect.
   D. cause the output effect to outweigh the factor substitution effect.

_____ 9. The total product from 3 workers is 32 units and that from 4 is 40 units. Output is selling at $2. What is the maximum the firm would be willing to pay the fourth worker?
   A. $10.
   B. $8.
   C. $16.
   D. $20.

_____ 10. The firm has two variable inputs, labor and capital. Now the price of labor rises. The factor substitution effect indicates that
   A. the marginal product of labor will fall.
   B. the marginal product of capital will fall.
   C. more labor will be demanded.
   D. less capital will be demanded.

_____ 11. Tennis players earn more than economics professors. This is best explained by noting that
   A. consumers are willing to spend more to watch a tennis match than to listen to an economics professor.
   B. tennis players are more athletic.
   C. economics professors last longer—their income is spread out more.
   D. the demand for economics professors is more inelastic.

Use the following information to answer the next two questions.

There are five apartment buildings in town. Each year the non-land cost of Building #1 is $10,000; for Building #2, it's $20,000; for Building #3, it's $30,000; and so on.

_____ 12. If each apartment building could generate $100,000 of revenues each year, how much is the pure economic rent of Building #1?
   A. $100,000.
   B. $90,000.
   C. $50,000.
   D. $40,000.

_____ 13. If each apartment building could generate $40,000 in revenues each year, which building would earn zero pure economic rent?
   A. Building #4.
   B. Building #3.
   C. Building #5.
   D. All plots will earn pure rents.

Use the following information to answer the next five questions.

Rhonda grows peaches, which she sells for $2 per pound. Her variable resource is labor and she has recorded the productivity of her workers in the table below.

NUMBER OF WORKERS	TOTAL PRODUCT	MARGINAL PRODUCT	MARGINAL REVENUE PRODUCT
0	0	—	—
1	15	_____	_____
2	40	_____	_____
3	60	_____	_____
4	75	_____	_____
5	85	_____	_____

_____ 14. The marginal product of the fifth worker is
  A. 10.
  B. 15.
  C. 17.
  D. 19.

_____ 15. The marginal revenue product of the second worker is
  A. $25.
  B. $30.
  C. $40.
  D. $50.

_____ 16. If the wage is $36, Rhonda should hire
  A. 2 workers.
  B. 3 workers.
  C. 4 workers.
  D. 5 workers.

_____ 17. The wage is $36. Currently, Rhonda is employing two workers. If she hires a third worker her profits would
  A. increase by $4.
  B. increase by $6.
  C. decrease by $4.
  D. decrease by $6.

_____ 18. The maximum wage that Rhonda would pay if she were to hire 3 workers is
  A. $20.
  B. $30.
  C. $35.
  D. $40.

_____ 19. The price of labor decreases. The quantity demanded of labor will
  A. increase, because capital will be substituted for labor.
  B. increase, regardless of the relative strengths of the output effect and the factor substitution effect.
  C. be indeterminate—the factor substitution effect and the output effect work in opposite directions.
  D. decrease—if the output effect dominates the factor substitution effect.

Use the following diagram to answer the next four questions.

Drushka has a small firm that manufactures *matrushka* dolls. His variable resource, labor, exhibits the marginal productivity behavior shown in the diagram below.

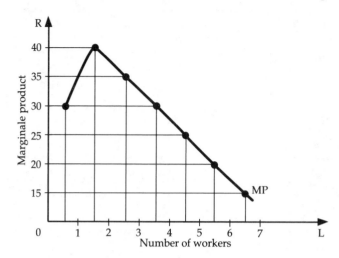

_____ 20. Each *matrushka* doll sells for 2 rubles. The marginal revenue product of the third worker is
   A. 35 rubles.
   B. 30 rubles.
   C. 60 rubles.
   D. 70 rubles.

_____ 21. If the wage is 40 rubles, Drushka should hire
   A. 3 workers.
   B. 4 workers.
   C. 5 workers.
   D. 6 workers.

_____ 22. The wage is 50 rubles. Currently, Drushka is employing 5 workers. If he hires a sixth worker his profits would
   A. increase by 5 rubles.
   B. increase by 10 rubles.
   C. decrease by 5 rubles.
   D. decrease by 10 rubles.

_____ 23. The maximum wage that Drushka would pay if he were to hire 4 workers is
   A. 30 rubles.
   B. 40 rubles.
   C. 50 rubles.
   D. 60 rubles.

_____ 24. Hitoshi, the owner of a Japanese restaurant, tells you that, because of an increase in the wage rate, he has sold the tables and chairs he used for outside seating and has reduced his hours of business. In economic terms, you could tell him each of the following except that
   A. he might have made a mistake. The factor substitution effect should have led him to substitute away from labor and to increase his capital.
   B. he has made a smart move. The wage hike has caused higher costs which should lead him to cut production according to the output effect.
   C. he has made a smart move. The output effect of the wage hike has caused less demand for all inputs.
   D. he might have made a mistake. He should have increased output and hired more of all inputs to cover the increased labor costs.

_____ 25. The price of labor increases. The demand for capital will
   A. increase, because capital will be substituted for labor.
   B. increase, if the output effect dominates the factor substitution effect.
   C. be indeterminate—the factor substitution effect and the output effect work in opposite directions.
   D. decrease—higher costs will reduce output and less capital will be needed.

II. APPLICATION QUESTIONS.

1. Palmer's flour mill operates in a perfectly competitive market and employs labor and capital. Labor costs $30 per day. Machines cost $36 per day. Currently, Palmer's has six machines and the marginal revenue product of capital is $30. Output sells at $5 per unit. Palmer's hires you as a consultant and provides you with the following production function.

WORKERS	TOTAL OUTPUT
1	9
2	17
3	24
4	30
5	35
6	39
7	42

   a. In the short run, how many workers do you recommend Palmer's should hire per day?
   b. Is Palmer's maximizing profit? How can you tell?
   c. In the short run, how can Palmer's improve its profitability?
   d. In the long run, if Palmer's maintains its current output level, how can the firm improve its profitability?
   e. Given your answer to part d, explain how the marginal revenue product values of labor and capital will change.
   f. Explain to Dusty Palmer, the owner of the mill, why your answer to part d is not the end of the analysis.

2. The number of haircuts given by Shear Delight each day is given by the equation $q = 10L - .5L^2$, where L is the number of hours of labor. MP_L is $10 - L$. The haircut industry is perfectly competitive with a price of $10 per haircut.
   a. What is the firm's demand for labor schedule?
   b. How many hours of labor will be hired at a wage of $20 per hour? A wage of $40 per hour?
   c. If the price of haircuts rose to $20, and the wage was $40 per hour, calculate the number of hours of labor hired and the number of haircuts provided.
   d. Given your answer to part c, calculate Shear Delight's daily profit.

3. The city of Greaseboro contains three firms, each of which operates in a perfectly competitive industry. The three firms are a fireworks factory, a poultry processing plant, and a textiles mill. Each firm employs unskilled workers who can move easily between firms.

The price of output is given in the following table.

FIRM	OUTPUT PRICE
Fireworks Factory	$8
Poultry Plant	$1
Textiles Mill	$2

Weekly marginal productivity information is given in the following table. Assume that marginal productivity diminishes at a constant rate between each set of data points.

	——MARGINAL PRODUCT PER WORKER——		
WORKERS	FIREWORKS FACTORY	POULTRY PLANT	TEXTILE MILL
0	—	—	—
100	100	1200	500
200	90	1000	450
300	80	800	400
400	70	600	350
500	60	500	300
600	50	400	250
700	40	300	200
800	30	200	150
900	20	100	100
1000	10	0	50

a. Calculate the marginal revenue product values and include them in the following table.

	——MARGINAL REVENUE PRODUCT PER WORKER——		
WORKERS	FIREWORKS FACTORY	POULTRY PLANT	TEXTILES MILL
100	_____	_____	_____
200	_____	_____	_____
300	_____	_____	_____
400	_____	_____	_____
500	_____	_____	_____
600	_____	_____	_____
700	_____	_____	_____
800	_____	_____	_____
900	_____	_____	_____
1000	_____	_____	_____

b. Calculate the total demand for labor in Greaseboro at each of the weekly wage rates in the following table.

WAGE	FIREWORKS FACTORY	POULTRY PLANT	TEXTILES MILL	TOTAL LABOR DEMAND
$800	_____	_____	_____	_____
$700	_____	_____	_____	_____
$600	_____	_____	_____	_____
$500	_____	_____	_____	_____
$400	_____	_____	_____	_____
$300	_____	_____	_____	_____
$200	_____	_____	_____	_____

c.

WAGE	TOTAL SUPPLY
$800	_____
$700	_____
$600	_____
$500	_____
$400	_____
$300	_____
$200	_____

As the wage level increases the quantity of labor supplied in Greaseboro increases, as shown in the equation, $Q = 1100 + 2W$, where W is the weekly wage. Complete the table above.

d. Graph the labor demand and labor supply curves below. Determine the equilibrium wage and level of employment.

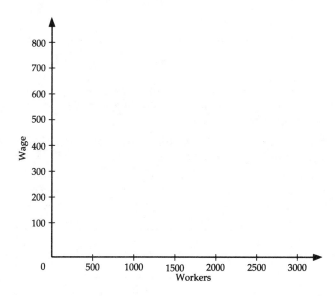

e. Calculate the level of employment in each industry.

FIRM	EMPLOYMENT
Fireworks Factory	_____
Poultry Plant	_____
Textiles Mill	_____

f. Verify that the profit-maximizing equilibrium conforms to the rule:
$MRP_{ff}/P_{ff} = MRP_{pp}/P_{pp} = MRP_{tm}/P_{tm} = 1$.

4. In a central area of the city of Fairview there are 300 vacant lots suitable for development. As the price per lot increases, the quantity demanded decreases, as indicated in the following table.

PRICE PER LOT	LOTS DEMANDED
$30,000	0
$25,000	100
$15,000	300
$10,000	400
$5,000	500

a. Graph the market for vacant lots in Fairview. Show the equilibrium price.

b. Suppose that the city government imposed a maximum price per lot of $10,000. What effect will this have on the number of lots available? What allocation problems will occur?

5. Suppose that ABC Corporation sells audio cassettes in a perfectly competitive market at a price of $1 per unit and that the wage rate is $15.

Labor	MP	TP	TR	MRP
1	10			
2	20			
3	25			
4	23			
5	20			
6	18			
7	15			
8	12			

a. Calculate total product, total revenue and MRP.

b. Draw the MRP schedule below and plot the wage too.

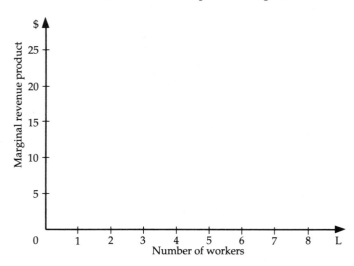

c. Note that MRP *rises* initially. Why?

d. Consider the first worker. Should she be hired, if the wage rate is $15?

e. Which is the first worker who won't be hired?

f. Make up a "hiring rule of thumb" for the profit-maximizing employer.

g. Confirm that MRP depicts the quantity of labor demanded at different wage levels.

6. Examine the following production function for ABC Corporation, which sells audio cassettes in a perfectly competitive market at a price of $2 per unit. Labor is the only variable input. The wage rate of labor is $16.

Labor	MP	TP	TR	MRP
1	19			
2	17			
3	15			
4	12			
5	10			
6	7			
7	5			

a. Calculate total product, total revenue and MRP.

b. How many workers should be hired?

7. Your firm is currently hiring labor and capital. The MRP of labor is $80 and that of capital is $120. Price of the final product is $2. The price of labor is $10 per unit and the price of capital is $20 per unit.

a. Is your firm maximizing profits? Explain.

b. Given your current budget, what should you do?

c. What will happen to the marginal productivity of capital? The marginal productivity of labor?

8. Assume that shoes are produced with one variable factor of production, labor. Using the following production function, estimate the amount of labor that a competitive firm would hire, assuming that labor is available for $35 per day and that shoes sell for $10 per pair. (Hint: First determine the MRP schedule.)

UNITS OF LABOR (DAYS)	TOTAL OUTPUT (PAIRS OF SHOES)
1	5
2	9
3	12
4	14
5	15

9. In the three preceding chapters we have visited Wilma's Wicker Baskets, a competitive firm that has the following production information. Suppose the price of a basket is $6.00.

   a. Complete the table below.

LABOR	TOTAL PRODUCT	MARGINAL PRODUCT OF LABOR	TOTAL REVENUE	MARGINAL REVENUE PRODUCT
0	0	—	0	—
1	5	5	_____	_____
2	16	11	_____	_____
3	27	11	_____	_____
4	36	9	_____	_____
5	44	8	_____	_____
6	51	_____	_____	_____
7	56	_____	_____	_____
8	_____	4	_____	_____
9	63	3	_____	_____
10	65	2	_____	_____

   b. If the wage per unit of labor is $24, determine how many workers the firm should hire. Why? How many baskets should be produced?

III. ECONOMICS EXPLORER.

Use the sixth module ("Leisure and Labor") from the Economics Explorer software to improve your grasp of the labor supply decision. Much of this material, especially the applications, is quite demanding.

ANSWERS AND SOLUTIONS

I. ANSWERS TO PRACTICE QUESTIONS

Select the option that provides the single best answer.

6.

NUMBER OF WORKERS	TOTAL PRODUCT	MARGINAL PRODUCT	MARGINAL REVENUE PRODUCT
0	0	—	—
1	10	10	$ 7.50
2	25	15	$11.25
3	38	13	$ 9.75
4	48	10	$ 7.50
5	56	8	$ 6.00

7–10. See the diagrams below.

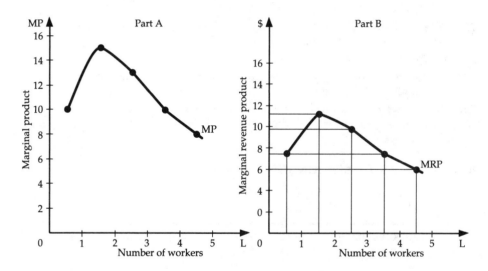

PRACTICE TEST

I. SOLUTIONS TO MULTIPLE CHOICE QUESTIONS

1. C. See p. 235.
2. B. See p. 233.
3. D. The value of production by each additional worker determines how much s/he will be paid.
4. B. The marginal revenue product of the final machine is less than the cost of hiring it. The businessperson should cut back on capital usage.
5. B. Per dollar, labor is contributing more than capital is.
6. A. When the price of a normal input decreases, the factor substitution effect and the output effect both increase the quantity demanded. See p. 243.
7. C. Total cost of production is reduced because of the factor price decrease. More output is produced and more of all factors (including labor) is hired.
8. A. An increase in the price of output will increase the input's MRP. MRP is the demand for the input.
9. C. Marginal product of the fourth worker is 8 units. MRP = MP × P = 8 × $2 = $16. This worker is worth as much as $16.

10. B. As less labor is hired, the marginal productivity of labor will increase. More of the relatively cheaper capital will be hired, resulting in a decrease in its marginal productivity.

11. A. Earnings depend on MRP. MRP depends on the selling price of output.

12. B. With a normal profit, Building #1 should earn $10,000. The additional $90,000 is economic rent.

13. A. With a normal profit, Building #4 should earn $40,000. If revenue is $40,000, this building earns zero economic rent.

14. A. Recall that MP is the change in total product (85 − 75) divided by the change in the number of workers (1).

15. D. MRP = MP × P. See p. 235.

16. B. To maximize profits, Rhonda should not hire any worker whose MRP is less than $36. Point to ponder: What about the first worker?

17. A. The worker costs $36 and contributes $40, a gain of $4.

18. D. The third worker's MRP is $40. To maximize profits, Rhonda should not hire the fourth worker (whose MRP is $30) at any wage above $30.

19. B. Both effects work in the same direction.

20. D. MP is 35. MRP = MP × P = 35 × 2 rubles = 70 rubles.

21. D. MRP of the sixth worker is 40 rubles.

22. D. The sixth worker's MRP is 40 rubles and s/he would cost 50 rubles to hire. Drushka would lose 10 rubles.

23. D. The fourth worker's MRP is 60 rubles.

24. D. Both the factor substitution effect and the output effect indicate that the quantity of labor demanded should decrease as the wage increases.

25. C. Demand for capital will tend to increase because labor is now more costly (factor substitution effect) *and* tend to decrease because the firm will want less of all inputs (output effect).

II. SOLUTIONS TO APPLICATION QUESTIONS

1. a. See the table below. Palmer's should hire until MRP_L = wage, i.e., up to and including the fourth worker.

WORKERS (DAYS)	TOTAL OUTPUT	MARGINAL PRODUCT	MRP	WAGE
1	9	9	$45	$30
2	17	8	$40	$30
3	24	7	$35	$30
4	30	6	$30	$30
5	35	5	$25	$30
6	39	4	$20	$30
7	42	3	$15	$30

   b. Palmer's is not maximizing profit. The profit-maximizing input combination follows the rule that the marginal revenue product/dollar of the final unit of each input should be equal. This is not so in this case because $MRP_L/P_L > MRP_K/P_K$.

   c. Palmer's can't improve its profitability in the short run—it's tied to the decisions it has made.

   d. Because $MRP_L/P_L > MRP_K/P_K$, Palmer's should reduce its capital. If the output level is maintained, and labor and capital as substitutes, more labor should be hired. The effect will be to reduce total cost and, therefore, to increase profit.

   e. *Ceteris paribus*, as additional workers are added, marginal revenue product of labor will decrease. *Ceteris paribus*, as fewer machines are hired, marginal revenue product of capital will increase. Both movements will help correct the imbalance between the ratios of MRP per dollar.

f. In part d you note that, given the same output level, the firm should hire more workers and fewer machines and reduce total cost. Another way to look at this is to maintain the total cost and increase output. Output will increase because inputs are being allocated more efficiently than before. However, with less than 6 machines, the marginal productivity of *labor* will fall, making the rise in labor less than that predicted by the answer to part d. Similarly, with more than 4 workers, the marginal productivity of *capital* will increase, making the decrease in capital less than that predicted by the answer to part d.

2. a. MP_L is $10 - L$, and $P = \$10$, then $MRP_L = \$10 \times [10 - L] = \$100 - \$10L$. The demand for labor schedule is given by $MRP_L = W$. Substituting W for MRP_L in the equation gives us the demand for labor schedule, $W = \$100 - \$10L$.

   b. If $W = \$20$, then $\$20 = \$100 - \$10L$, therefore $L = 8$. If $W = \$40$, then $\$40 = \$100 - \$10L$, therefore $L = 6$.

   c. MP_L is $10 - L$, and $P = \$20$, then $MRP_L = \$20 \times [10 - L] = \$200 - \$20L$. The demand for labor schedule is given by $MRP_L = W$. Substituting W for MRP_L in the equation gives us the demand for labor schedule, $W = \$200 - \$20L$. If $W = \$40$, then $\$40 = \$200 - \$20L$, therefore $L = 8$. If $L = 8$, the equation $q = 10L - .5L^2$ gives $q = 80 - 32$, or 48 haircuts (i.e., 6 per hour).

   d. Labor is the only input: total cost is $\$40 \times 8$, or $\$320$. Total revenue is $\$20 \times 48$, $\$960$. Profit is $\$640$.

3. a.

WORKERS	—MARGINAL REVENUE PRODUCT PER WORKER—		
	FIREWORKS FACTORY	POULTRY PLANT	TEXTILES MILL
100	$800	$1200	$1000
200	$720	$1000	$900
300	$640	$800	$800
400	$560	$600	$700
500	$480	$500	$600
600	$400	$400	$500
700	$320	$300	$400
800	$240	$200	$300
900	$160	$100	$200
1000	$80	$0	$100

b.

WAGE	FIREWORKS FACTORY	POULTRY PLANT	TEXTILES MILL	TOTAL LABOR DEMAND
$800	100	300	300	700
$700	225	350	400	975
$600	350	400	500	1250
$500	475	500	600	1575
$400	600	600	700	1900
$300	725	700	800	2225
$200	850	800	900	2550

c.

WAGE	TOTAL LABOR SUPPLY
$800	2700
$700	2500
$600	2300
$500	2100
$400	1900
$300	1700
$200	1500

d. See the following diagram.

The equilibrium wage is $400 per week and 1900 workers will be employed each week.

e.

FIRM	EMPLOYMENT
Fireworks Factory	600
Poultry Plant	600
Textiles Mill	700

f. The profit-maximizing equilibrium rule is that the marginal product/dollar of the final unit of each input should be equal. In each case, MRP is $400 and the wage is $400.

4. a. See the diagram below. The equilibrium price is $15,000.

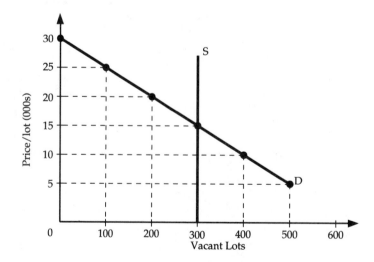

b. The number of lots available will remain at 300. However, because of the lower price, there has been an increase in quantity demanded to 400 and an excess demand exists. Because market price is no longer able to perform its rationing function, some other method of allocating lots to demanders will have to be found, e.g., first-come, first-served, special government permit, bribery, waiting lists, a tedious application process.

5. a. See the table below.

Labor	MP	TP	TR	MRP
1	10	10	$ 10	$10
2	20	30	$ 30	$20
3	25	55	$ 55	$25
4	23	78	$ 78	$23
5	20	98	$ 98	$20
6	18	116	$116	$18
7	15	131	$131	$15
8	12	143	$143	$12

   b. See the diagram below. Note that marginal values are typically shown between units because they indicate change.

   c. Increasing productivity.
   d. Yes! Although ABC will take a loss because MRP is only $10, the first worker must be hired to hire subsequent, "profitable," workers.
   e. The eighth worker won't be hired.
   f. Hire any input that at least pays its way.
   g. Yes, it does. At a wage of $15, for example, 7 workers are demanded; at $18, 6 workers are demanded.

6. a. See the table below.

Labor	MP	TP	TR	MRP
1	19	19	$ 38	$38
2	17	36	$ 72	$34
3	15	51	$102	$30
4	12	63	$126	$24
5	10	73	$146	$20
6	7	80	$160	$14
7	5	85	$170	$10

   b. 5 workers should be hired.

7. a. No. The final dollar spent on each input must generate the same additional production. We should hire such that $MP_L/P_L = MP_K/P_K$.
   b. Cut back on capital and hire more workers.
   c. Rise; fall.

8. If we assume that shoes sell for $10 per pair over and above the cost of leather and materials, we can derive the following table.

UNITS OF LABOR (DAYS)	TOTAL OUTPUT (PAIRS OF SHOES)	MARGINAL PRODUCT	MRP
1	5	5	$50
2	9	4	$40
3	12	3	$30
4	14	2	$20
5	15	1	$10

The firm will hire 2 workers. A third worker would have an MRP of $30, which is less than the $35 wage rate.

9. a. See the table below.

LABOR	TOTAL PRODUCT	MARGINAL PRODUCT OF LABOR	TOTAL REVENUE	MARGINAL REVENUE PRODUCT
0	0		0	
1	5	5	$ 30	$30
2	16	11	$ 96	$66
3	27	11	$162	$66
4	36	9	$216	$54
5	44	8	$264	$48
6	51	7	$306	$42
7	56	5	$336	$30
8	60	4	$360	$24
9	63	3	$378	$18
10	65	2	$390	$12

   b. If the wage per unit of labor is $24, Wilma should hire 8 workers because the value of the marginal product of labor up to this point is equal to or greater than the marginal cost of hiring the workers. The firm should produce 60 baskets. Note that a wage of $24 per worker was established in Chapter 7. At a price of $6.00 per basket, we saw in Chapter 9 that the firm should produce 60 baskets. We have come full circle to the same conclusion by consideration of the input market.

INPUT DEMAND: THE CAPITAL MARKET AND THE INVESTMENT DECISION

11

OBJECTIVES: POINT BY POINT

After completing this chapter, you should be able to accomplish the objectives listed below.

General Comment

In approaching this chapter, note the similarities between the conclusions reached about hiring decisions in the labor and land markets and those in the capital market. Capital may seem different because of the time dimension but businesspeople still weigh the benefits and the costs of employing new resources. The time element makes the calculations more difficult—both revenues and costs may extend into the future. Also, note that capital accumulation is not undertaken only by the business community; households, the government, and you (human capital!) make capital-investment decisions.

OBJECTIVE 1: Distinguish between stocks and flows and relate them to tangible and intangible capital, investment, and depreciation. Define depreciation and identify two reasons why a capital asset depreciates.

Capital goods are those goods that can be used as inputs into the production process now and in the future. Capital may be *tangible* (machines, all construction, and inventories) or *intangible* (human capital, goodwill, brand loyalty). Capital accumulation occurs not only in the business sector but also in the public sector (social capital, such as interstate highways) and in the households sector.   (page 254)

Stocks are variables that are measured at a point in time (capital stock) while *flows* are measured over a period of time (earnings per month, investment per quarter, depreciation per year). *Investment* has a specific meaning for economists—investment is the creation of capital. It is *not* financial purchases, even the purchase of stock in a corporation.

Depreciation (a flow) is the decline in the economic value of an asset over time—think of it as an aging process. A unit of capital (a machine, perhaps) might depreciate simply because of wear and tear or because new technology renders it obsolete.
(page 256)

> **LEARNING TIP:** It's easy to overlook the importance of **intangible capital.** Choose a business with which you are familiar and identify all the types of intangible capital in use—goodwill, name recognition, human capital of managers and employees. If, overnight, the firm's intangible capital evaporated, production and sales would shudder to a halt. Even with an excellent product, a salesperson who fails to "connect" with a customer will be ineffectual—trust is as important as it is intangible.
>
> **Capital:** Because capital is so diverse it is measured by its dollar value. However, keep in mind at all times that capital should be thought of as a physical factor of production and not as a monetary unit.

PRACTICE

1. The construction of a new house is investment in
   A. social capital.
   B. a consumer durable good.
   C. tangible capital.
   D. human capital.
   Answer: C. All construction (including residential construction) is classified as capital. Social capital is usually state-provided.

2. HAL Corp. institutes a training program to introduce its employees to the new Orange computer. This should increase productivity. This is an investment in
   A. tangible capital.
   B. human capital.
   C. social capital.
   D. infrastructure capital.
   Answer: B. The quality of the labor force is being improved.

3. Which of the following is not an example of capital?
   A. An IBM warehouse.
   B. A Macintosh computer used by an IBM employee.
   C. A car used by an IBM service representative.
   D. The revenue earned by IBM this year.
   Answer: D. Money is not capital! See p. 256.

4. Capital is a _____ , investment is a _____ , and depreciation is a _____
   A. stock, stock, stock.
   B. stock, flow, stock.
   C. flow, flow, stock.
   D. stock, flow, flow.
   Answer: D. The capital *stock* is measured at a point in time. Investment takes place over time, as does depreciation.

5. A columnist once argued that his educated brain cells were part of his _____ capital and that, as time passed, the rate at which they were being depleted should be counted as _____ (for tax purposes).
   A. social, investment.
   B. depreciation, depreciation.
   C. human, investment.
   D. human, depreciation.
   Answer: D. The quality of human resources counts as human capital. Wear and tear (and the death of brain cells through the passage of time) is depreciation. Note: The IRS is not convinced by this argument.

6. Which of the following is not an act of investment?
   A. A marketing firm buys a new automated mailing machine.
   B. Pat Doyle's college education is paid for by his parents.
   C. Federal Express delivers the mail.
   D. The Doyles build a new vacation home.
   Answer: C. Mail delivery is a productive activity, but Federal Express is not increasing its productive capacity in the process. Note that a new vacation home is construction of a residential structure—the use to which it will be put is not considered.

OBJECTIVE 2: Explain the role of interest and profit in capital accumulation.

Ownership of capital generates *capital income* (usually profit and interest), which rewards households for postponing consumption and channeling resources instead into investment. Capital markets act as one method of channeling these funds to investment purposes. Capital income is the income flow paid to the owners of capital that induces them to supply funds. It is also the spur that provokes the process of capital allocation and accumulation. (page 257)

> **LEARNING TIP:** Nature abhors a vacuum. It's the same with profit opportunities in an efficient market. The presence of economic profits in an industry will draw in resources, including capital.

PRACTICE

7. The two most important types of capital income are
   A. investment and saving.
   B. profit and interest.
   C. dividends and rents.
   D. pure economic rent and disposable income.
   Answer: B. See p. 258.

8. The ultimate suppliers of financial capital are
   A. households.
   B. the private banking sector.
   C. the central bank (the "Fed").
   D. businesses.
   Answer: A. Ultimately, all income—and therefore all funds for investment purposes—derives from households.

9. Walt asks Virginia to lend him $3,000 for 12 months. Walt agrees to pay Virginia $3,150 at the end of that time. The interest rate that Virginia could have earned if she had not loaned to Walt is 6%. Virginia has earned an economic profit of
   A. −$30.
   B. $30.
   C. $150.
   D. −$9.
   Answer: A. Virginia earned $150 in interest. She could have earned $180 ($3,000 × 1.06). The loan to Walt cost her $30.

Use the following information to answer the next three questions.

Eight-year-old Josh has discovered that the price his friends can charge while selling lemonade on the sidewalk has doubled because of the hot summer weather. Lemonade selling is a perfectly competitive industry and, previously, the reward was not quite enough to encourage Josh to participate. Now, however, he rushes home to borrow ingredients from his parents, build a lemonade stand, and write out a price list.

10. Josh's ingredients are _____ capital and his lemonade stand and price list are _____
    A. inventory, durable equipment.
    B. inventory, nonresidential construction.
    C. intangible, durable equipment.
    D. intangible, nonresidential construction.
    Answer: A. Stocks of inputs or unsold output is inventory. The lemonade stand is durable.

11. Josh promises his parents, using his candy allowance as collateral, to repay the face value of his borrowed ingredients. He is financing his investment with
    A. venture capital.
    B. economic profits.
    C. retained earnings.
    D. a zero-interest direct loan.
    Answer: D. If Josh repays the full value of the ingredients he pays no interest. This is the equivalent of a direct loan. If Josh writes out the promise to pay, he has issued a bond.

12. As a result of the existence of economic profits caused by increased demand, resources allocated to the lemonade industry have _____ . Lemonade prices will _____
    A. increased, increase.
    B. increased, decrease.
    C. decreased, increase.
    D. decreased, decrease.
    Answer: B. More lemonade will be available and, consequently, prices and economic profit will decrease.

Use the following information to answer the next two questions.

The health club industry is perfectly competitive and in long-run equilibrium. As the baby boomers age and sag, the demand for health clubs increases.

13. Existing health clubs will earn _____ economic profits. We would predict _____ investment in the health club industry.
    A. short-run, increased.
    B. short-run, decreased.
    C. long-run, increased.
    D. long-run, decreased.
    Answer: A. Higher demand will lead to higher profits in the short run: recall that economic profits are zero in the long run for competitive firms. As existing firms expand and as firms enter the industry, capital accumulation will occur.

14. Firms outside the health club industry (but using similar resources) will see their costs _____ and will _____ the quantity of resources they use.
    A. increase, increase.
    B. increase, decrease.
    C. decrease, increase.
    D. decrease, decrease.
    Answer: B. Recall that "costs" to an economist are opportunity costs—the value of the next best alternative forgone. Cost depends on the reward that can be earned in an alternative activity, e.g., provision of health club services As those earnings rise, costs increase for non-participants, profits decrease, and resources will be reallocated to the health club industry.

OBJECTIVE 3: Define the investment demand schedule and discuss the factors that influence its shape and position. Outline how changes in the market interest rate influence the investment decision.

The firm must form an expectation of the future earnings and costs of a project. The difference between expected future earnings and the costs of a project, expressed as a percentage of the project cost, is the *expected rate of return*. The investment decision turns on how this rate compares against the cost (interest) of providing capital for investment. If the expected rate of return exceeds the interest rate, then the investment project should be undertaken. As the interest rate rises, profitable projects become unprofitable and the demand for funds is reduced.

By ranking the expected yield on projects, the investment demand schedule is developed. The shape and slope of the investment demand curve depend critically on the expectations of those making investment decisions—anything that affects expectations may affect investment. (page 263)

The profit-maximizing firm will employ capital up to the point at which its marginal revenue product is equal to its price, i.e., it will invest whenever the expected rate of return exceeds the interest rate. (page 266)

> **LEARNING TIP:** The logic behind the investment demand curve is identical to that of other demand curves. The interest rate is the "price" of investment and the expected rate of return plays the role of "other factors" which influence investment. As before, if the interest rate changes you move along the curve; if at a given rate of interest, the expected rate of return changes, you shift the curve.

PRACTICE

Use the following table for the next four questions.
Sellco has the following list of investment projects to consider.

PROJECT	TOTAL INVESTMENT AMOUNT	EXPECTED RATE OF RETURN (%)
A. New corporate headquarters	$300,000	20
B. Personal computers for salesforce	$ 60,000	16
C. Training for employees	$140,000	10
D. Wellness program	$ 60,000	9
E. Employee leisure facility	$ 80,000	5
F. New canteen	$ 40,000	5

15. If the interest rate is 14%, Sellco would fund
    A. only Project A.
    B. Projects A and B.
    C. Projects A, B, and C.
    D. Projects D and E only.
    Answer: B. Projects A and B have expected rates of return exceeding the interest rate—they are worthwhile.

16. If the interest rate is 21%, Sellco would fund
    A. only Project A.
    B. Projects B, D, and E only.
    C. Projects B and E only.
    D. none of the above.
    Answer: D. No project offers a high enough expected rate of return to justify the expense.

17. At an interest rate of 14%, Sellco's total investment would amount to
    A. zero, since no project has a return equal to 14%.
    B. $360,000.
    C. $500,000.
    D. $200,000.
    Answer: B. $300,000 (Project A) + $60,000 (Project B).

18. If the interest rate is 5%, Sellco would fund
    A. Project E only.
    B. Project F only, because it is less expensive than Project E.
    C. Projects E and F only, because their expected rate of return is equal to 5%.
    D. all the projects.
    Answer: D. The rule is that the firm should undertake any and all projects that have an expected rate of return equal to or greater than the interest rate.

19. The expected cost of an investment
    A. depends on the interest rate.
    B. is zero if the firm uses its own funds.
    C. is zero if the investment is undertaken by the government.
    D. is inversely related to its expected income stream.
    Answer: A. See p. 264.

20. An increase in the market interest rate will cause
    A. a rightward shift in the investment demand curve.
    B. a leftward shift in the investment demand curve.
    C. a movement up the investment demand curve.
    D. a movement down the investment demand curve.
    Answer: C. See p. 266.

21. Firms become quite pessimistic because the Administration has announced higher business taxes. This will cause the investment demand curve to shift _____ and the level of investment to _____
    A. right, increase.
    B. right, decrease.
    C. left, increase.
    D. left, decrease.
    Answer: D. See p. 266.

22. Sellco is a perfectly competitive profit-maximizing firm. It will invest in new capital up to the point at which
    A. the rate of return equals the expected interest rate.
    B. the expected rate of return equals the interest rate.
    C. the expected rate of return equals the expected interest rate.
    D. the rate of return equals the interest rate.
    Answer: B. The interest rate is incurred today, at the time of the investment; the earnings will accrue in the future and, today, they are estimates.

23. Part of the "Republican Revolution" of 1995 was a commitment to reduce corporate taxes. If business leaders believed this pledge then, *ceteris paribus*, it would most likely cause firms to
    A. plan to increase investment because of the expectation that interest rates would be lower.
    B. plan to increase investment because of the expectation of higher after-tax benefits.
    C. plan to decrease investment because less effort would be needed to achieve a given level of after-tax income.
    D. plan to leave investment unchanged because business tax cuts would not affect the demand for their product and, ultimately, the demand for an input is a "derived" demand.
    Answer: B. Lower taxes lead to higher after-tax profits and higher expected rates of return.

OBJECTIVE 4: Calculate and evaluate the present discounted value and the rate of return on a project. Explain how higher interest rates reduce present values.

When considering discounting and the role of *present (discounted) value* in evaluating investment projects, remember that future dollars are worth less than dollars in hand today and should be discounted in value. Discounting puts dollars of all vintages on a common basis—present value. The discount rate is the interest rate and the formula used is:

$$PV = R \div (1 + r)^t$$

where R is the future value of payments, r is the interest rate, and t is the number of time periods. Investment should go ahead if the present value of the expected stream of earnings is greater than the cost of the project. The rate of return and present value methods of evaluation are equivalent.   (page 270)

Discounting the value of future income by the market interest rate gives that income's value in today's dollars. If the expected future income of a project shows a present value that is greater than the cost of the investment, then it should be undertaken.

Note: The formula tells us that, as interest rates rise, the present value of a project will fall and the project will be less likely to be undertaken. This is the same conclusion that we arrived at with the method using investment demand and the expected rate of return.

Present Value Example: What is the opportunity cost of removing, for a year, $100 from your bank account? The interest rate. If it is 10%, then the opportunity cost is $10.00. The $100 be worth $110 at the end of the year if left in the bank. $100 today equals $110 in a year. Turn this the other way: $110 future dollars are worth $100 today, given the interest rate—that is, $110 \div (1 + .1) = $100.

What would that $100 be worth at the end of two years if it were left in the bank? $121.00 or $100 \times 1.1 \times 1.1. Or, $121 two years in the future is worth $100 today. Formally, this relationship is:

$$\text{Present Value} = \text{Future Value} \div (1 + \text{interest rate})^t$$

A Present Value Table: Here is a table showing the present value of $100 payable at various dates and at various interest rates. Example: The promise of $100 two years from today has a present value of $90.00 if the interest rate is 6 percent.

INTEREST RATE (r)	1 YEAR	2 YEARS	3 YEARS	10 YEARS	20 YEARS
.03	97.09	94.26	91.51	74.41	55.37
.04	96.15	92.46	88.90	67.56	45.64
.05	95.24	90.70	86.38	61.39	37.69
.06	94.34	90.00	83.96	55.84	31.18
.07	93.46	87.34	81.63	50.83	25.84
.08	92.59	85.73	79.38	46.32	21.45

LEARNING TIP: Remember that future dollars are worth less—we *discount* their value.

PRACTICE

24. The market interest rate is 25% The present value of $500 in one year is
   A. $400.
   B. $125.
   C. $625.
   D. $2000.
   Answer: A. PV = R $\div$ (1 + r)^t = 500 $\div$ 1.25^1 = $400.

25. Sellco should invest in a project if the present value of its income stream
    A. is greater than the full cost of the project.
    B. is greater than (or equal to) the full cost of the project.
    C. is greater than the interest rate.
    D. is greater than (or equal to) the interest rate.
    Answer: B. If the value today of the project's earnings is greater than or at least equal to the cost of implementing the project, Sellco will make a profit.

PRACTICE TEST

I. MULTIPLE CHOICE QUESTIONS.

Select the option that provides the single best answer.

_____ 1. In 1994–95, the central bank (the "Fed") repeatedly hiked interest rates in order to dampen rising prices. Which of the following explanations best describes the Fed's view of the economy?
    A. An increase in interest rates will reduce investment which, in turn, will reduce production, making the economy's expansion less rapid. A less rapid expansion will put less upward pressure on the national price level.
    B. Higher interest rates lead to higher expectations about profits, which shifts the investment demand curve out.
    C. Lower prices will lead to a lower marginal revenue product of capital, which will discourage investment. Because the demand for investment goods is part of national demand, national demand (and the national price level) will be lower than otherwise.
    D. Higher interest rates make fewer investments profitable and, because the demand for investment goods is part of national demand, national demand (and the national price level) will be lower than otherwise.

_____ 2. A frequently heard argument is that government deficits cause higher interest rates. Assuming that this is so, then, *ceteris paribus*, reducing the government deficit should
    A. increase investment and increase the marginal revenue product of capital.
    B. increase investment and decrease the marginal revenue product of capital.
    C. decrease investment and increase the marginal revenue product of capital.
    D. decrease investment and decrease the marginal revenue product of capital.

_____ 3. Changes in the physical capital stock are caused by
    A. investment and stock purchases.
    B. investment and depreciation.
    C. obsolescence and interest rate changes.
    D. accumulation and discounting of value.

_____ 4. Which of the following is not an act of investment?
    A. Paying for courses at a technical college.
    B. Construction of a bridge by the state government.
    C. The purchase of new solar technology by a business.
    D. Buying a government bond.

_____ 5. Which of the following is not an example of capital?
 A. an office block owned by IBM.
 B. brand loyalty of consumers to IBM.
 C. a share of IBM stock.
 D. an IBM computer.

_____ 6. In which case will investment be greatest?

	MARKET INTEREST RATE	INFLATION RATE
A.	8	7
B.	9	0
C	6	2
D.	7	3

_____ 7. A new machine will yield $500 a month in earnings for one year. The machine's maintenance is estimated to cost $2,000 a year. Its scrap value will be zero. If the current market interest rate is 8%, the firm would be willing to pay _____ to get the machine.
 A. $62,500.
 B. $6,250.
 C. $50,000.
 D. $75,000.

_____ 8. Billy-Bob knows that he will buy a new Jeep either this month or a year from now. The current price is $10,000 and next year he estimates that it will be $12,000. If his discount rate is 10% he should
 A. not buy either this year or next.
 B. buy now.
 C. buy next year.
 D. be indifferent, since both options have the same present value.

_____ 9. The expected rate of return on an investment depends on all of the following except
 A. the expected interest rate.
 B. the amount of revenue attributable each year to the project.
 C. the length of time that the project provides additional cost savings or revenue.
 D. the price of the investment.

_____ 10. Investment projects will be funded up to the point where
 A. the interest rate and the expected rate of return are equal.
 B. the expected rate of return is zero.
 C. the rate of return is maximized.
 D. the expected rate of return is maximized.

_____ 11. A bond pays $1,000 in one year (and nothing else before or after). The interest rate is 20%. The most one should pay for this bond is
 A. $1,200.
 B. $800.
 C. $909.09.
 D. $833.33.

_____ 12. The expected cost of an investment is _____ if the funds are borrowed and is _____ if the project is self-financed.
 A. positive, positive.
 B. positive, zero.
 C. zero, positive.
 D. zero, zero.

_____ 13. Goodwill _____ a form of capital and inventory _____ a form of capital.
   A. is, is.
   B. is, is not.
   C. is not, is.
   D. is not, is not.

_____ 14. As the interest rate increases, the cost of new investment projects becomes _____ and the number of profitable investment projects becomes _____
   A. higher, higher.
   B. higher, lower.
   C. lower, higher.
   D. lower, lower.

_____ 15. When the interest rate increases, the expected rate of return of an investment _____ and the present value of the investment _____
   A. decreases, decreases.
   B. decreases, does not change.
   C. does not change, decreases.
   D. does not change, does not change.

II. APPLICATION QUESTIONS.

1. Camille has an important career decision to make. She intends to retire in five years. If she stays in her present job, she expects to earn $22,000 per year for the five years. However, she has been offered the opportunity to take a two-year training program, after which she will earn $40,000 per year for the remaining three years of her work-life. The training program is free but Camille will be unable to work during the two-year period. She has sufficient savings to tide her over the two-year training period.
   a. Camille has asked her sister Clarissa which option she should take. Clarissa said that she should go for the training program because, after all, $22,000 times 5 is less than $40,000 times 3. Camille is still unconvinced and asks your opinion. What would you advise?
   b. Explain to Camille the problem with the basis of Clarissa's advice.
   c. Suppose the interest rate is 10%. Can you now offer Camille a definitive answer to her career choice?
   d. The training program is an investment in human capital as is a college education for high school graduates. If the government wished to encourage additional investment in human capital, should it increase or decrease the interest rate?
   e. Based on your answer to part d, should the government adopt a "high-interest rate" strategy or a "low-interest rate" strategy if it wished to encourage long-term rather than short-term investment projects?

2. Two of your assistants, Judy and Jody, have each devised an investment project costing $750 and earning a total income of $1000. Judy's project will return a steady stream of income, $200 per year, for five years. Jody's project starts more slowly, with $100 in each of the first three years, then $300 and $400 in the last two. The interest rate is 10%. How can you explain, nontechnically, to Jody why his project is unacceptable, although Judy's has been given the go-ahead? If he pressed you for proof, what would you do?

3. In July, 1993, excitement in the nation was high because the Powerball lottery prize was $100 million. The prize would be disbursed to the winner at a rate of $5 million per year for 20 years. Given these numbers, did the winner really win $100 million?

4. Many alumni donate funds to their college or university.
   a. G. P. A. Crammer has just pledged $500,000 payable on his retirement which will be in 20 years time. In present value terms, if the interest rate is 7%, how much did Crammer pledge? _____ Use the present value table in the *Point By Point* section (Objective 4).
   b. If the interest rate falls to 3%, what is the present value of Crammer's pledge?

5. The Johnson family decides to have a house built that costs $100,000. This year the Johnsons have a disposable (after-tax) income of $40,000, of which $25,000 is spent on current consumption and the rest is used as a down payment on the house. The additional $85,000 is borrowed from aged Aunt Agatha who earns no income and currently lives off her wealth. Assume that Aunt Agatha sells some shares of stock to acquire the cash for the loan. Jack Diamond, who earned $200,000 last year, buys the stock from Aunt Agatha for $85,000 and spends $115,000 on current consumption.

   For each of the three parties, calculate:
   a. The amount of saving during the period.

Johnsons	Aunt Agatha	Jack Diamond
_____	_____	_____

   b. The quantity of investment during the period.

Johnsons	Aunt Agatha	Jack Diamond
_____	_____	_____

   c. Any change in net worth.

Johnsons	Aunt Agatha	Jack Diamond
_____	_____	_____

   d. Any change in capital stock.

Johnsons	Aunt Agatha	Jack Diamond
_____	_____	_____

6. Imagine a 10-year bond issued by ABC Corp., with a face value of $1,000 and an interest rate of 12%.
   a. What is the annual interest payment? _____
   b. How much would you pay for the bond if the bond had 3 years to maturity and the market interest rate is 12%? _____
   c. If the market rate was _____ , the bond would be less attractive, and its price would _____ .
   d. If the market rate changed to 8%, and the bond had 3 years to maturity, the value of the bond would _____ to _____ .
   e. When the market rate is below the interest rate of the bond, the market price of the bond will be _____ than its face value. When the market rate is above the interest rate of the bond, the market price of the bond will be _____ than its face value.

7. Consider the investment demand schedule. Indicate if investment would increase (I) or decrease (D) in the following cases.
   a. _____ an increase in interest rates
   b. _____ the development of a new technology
   c. _____ the expectation of new technological developments
   d. _____ the expectation of a corporate tax increase
   e. _____ the expectation of more generous tax write-offs for depreciation
   f. _____ a new product line is introduced
   g. _____ the industry is experiencing short-run economic losses
   h. _____ the industry is encountering diseconomies of scale

8. Judy and Jody each devise an investment project costing $900 and earning a total income of $1,200. Judy's project will return a steady stream of income, $300 per year, for 4 years. Jody's project starts more slowly, with $100 in each of the first 3 years, then $900 in the last year. The interest rate is 10%.

Use present value to decide if either project should be undertaken.

9. A dollar today and a dollar next year have different values. Discounting puts dollars of all vintages on a common basis—present value. The following case exemplifies this and highlights the importance of the market interest rate.

Here are two projects. Each has the same total cost and revenue.

| | **Project 1** | | **Project 2** | |
Year	Costs	Revenues	Costs	Revenues
1	$700	$ 0	$300	$100
2	$100	$100	$300	$600
3	$ 0	$900	$200	$300
	$800	$900	$800	$900

a. Is the rate of return equal for both projects?
b. Intuitively, which project is the better investment?
c. Suppose the interest rate is 10%. Which project is the better investment?
d. What else is revealed?

10. Consider the investment demand schedule.
a. What economic variables does it relate?
b. What determines its slope and its position?
c. It is said that investment is volatile. Do you think that this is reflected by the shape of the curve, by its position, or by both?

Explain how investment behavior would be affected by:
d. a cut in interest rates.
e. the development of a new technology.
f. the expectation of new technological developments.
g. the expectation of a corporate tax increase.

III. ECONOMICS EXPLORER.

Use the seventh module ("Investment") from the Economics Explorer software to help analyze the investment decision. This module brings present value to the center of its analysis—this material shows up in the Appendix in the textbook.

ANSWERS AND SOLUTIONS

PRACTICE TEST

I. SOLUTIONS TO MULTIPLE CHOICE QUESTIONS

Select the option that provides the single best answer.

1. D. Given the investment demand schedule, higher interest rates prompt less investment, lower demand in the economy, and prices that are lower than would otherwise be the case.

2. B. Reducing the government deficit should decrease interest rates and increase investment. As investment increases, the marginal revenue product of capital will decrease because marginal productivity will decrease.

3. B. The capital stock increases through investment and decreases through wear and tear (depreciation).

4. D. Investment is the creation of new productive capacity. Option A represents an improvement in human capital. Option D is the transfer of a financial asset.

5. C. A share of IBM stock is a financial asset. Brand loyalty is a type of "goodwill."

6. A. Investment will be greatest when the real interest rate is lowest. The real interest rate is the market interest rate minus the inflation rate.

7. C. Earnings are $6000 per year and costs are $2000. The expected profit is $4000. Cost = expected profit divided by interest rate = $4000/.08 = $50,000.

8. B. PV of purchase today = $10,000. PV of purchase next year = $12,000/1.1 = $10,909.09. Because the PV today is less, he should buy today.

9. A. The current market interest rate is the key factor, not the expected interest rate.

10. A. See p. 266.

11. D. Price of bond = future value/(1 + r) = $1000/(1.2) = 833.33.

12. A. Even if a project is self-financed there is an opportunity cost—the interest rate forgone. See p. 264.

13. A. Goodwill is intangible capital; inventory is tangible capital. See p. 254.

14. B. In general, the higher the interest rate, the cost of new investment projects will be higher and the number of profitable investment projects will be fewer. Note that the investment demand curve is downward sloping.

15. C. Present value is affected by interest rate changes, expected rate of return is not.

II. SOLUTIONS TO APPLICATION QUESTIONS

1. a. Clarissa's advice may be sound, but for the wrong reason. You really can't give Camille much help, without knowing the interest rate.

    b. Clarissa is assuming a dollar today and a dollar five years in the future are identical in value. She is ignoring present value (or assuming that the interest rate is 0%).

    c. Camille should not accept the offer of the training program.
    The present value of $22,000 per year for five years is:
    $22,000/1.1 + 22,000/(1.1^2) + 22,000/(1.1^3) + 22,000/(1.1^4) + 22,000/(1.1^5) = \$20,000.00 + \$18,181.81 + \$16,528.93 + \$15,026.30 + \$13,660.27 = \$83,387.31$.
    The present value of $40,000 per year for the three final years is:
    $40,000/(1.1^3) + 40,000/(1.1^4) + 40,000/(1.1^5) = \$30,052.59 + \$27,320.54 + \$24,836.85 = \$82,209.98$.
    Because the present value of the current position exceeds that of the "training plus new position," Camille is better advised to retain her present position.

    d. To encourage investment of any kind, the government should decrease the interest rate. At the extreme, using Clarissa's assumption of a 0% interest rate, the PV of the training program would exceed the PV of the 5-year position ($120,000 exceeds $110,000).

    e. A "low-interest rate" strategy will promote longer-term investments—the "discount" applied to future earnings is smaller. Lowering the interest rate makes the present value of all future income streams higher, but the effect is more pronounced over longer time periods.

2. Although each project earns a total income of $1000, the present value of Jody's project is lower. This is because each dollar earned 5 years from now is worth less than each dollar earned 1 year from now. Judy's project accumulates revenue faster.

    If Jody demanded proof, set up the following table calculating present values. Judy's project has a present value of $758.16, while Jody's trails at $701.96.

Year	Judy's Project Income	Judy's Project PV	Jody's Project Income	Jody's Project PV
1	$ 200	$181.82	$ 100	$ 90.91
2	$ 200	$165.29	$ 100	$ 82.64
3	$ 200	$150.26	$ 100	$ 75.13
4	$ 200	$136.60	$ 300	$204.90
5	$ 200	$124.18	$ 400	$248.37
	$1000	$758.16	$1000	$701.96

3. No, the winner didn't really win $100 million in current dollars. If the interest rate is assumed to be 5% (for example), the final $5,000,000 would be worth only(!) $1,884,447 in present value terms $(5,000,000/1.05^{20})$.

4. a. Given an interest rate of 7%, $100 would be worth $25.84. $500,000 would be worth $129,200.
   b. Given an interest rate of 3%, $100 would be worth $55.37. $500,000 would be worth $276,850.

5.

		Johnsons	Aunt Agatha	Jack Diamond
a.	Saving	$15,000	can't tell	$85,000
b.	Investment	$100,000	0	0
c.	Change in net worth	$15,000	0	$85,000
d.	Change in capital stock.	$100,000	0	0

6. a. $120.
   b. $120/1.12 + 120/(1.12^2) + 120/(1.12^3) + 1,000/(1.12^3) = \$107.14 + \$95.66 + \$85.14 + \$711.78 = \$1,000.00$.
   c. higher; fall.
   d. rise; $120/1.08 + 120/(1.08^2) + 120/(1.08^3) + 1,000/(1.08^3) = \$111.11 + \$102.88 + \$95.26 + \$793.83 = \$1,103.08$.
   e. higher; lower.

7. a. D b. I c. I or D d. D
   e. I f. I g. D h. D

8. Judy's project should be undertaken. Present value is $950.96, which is greater than the $900 cost, but Jody's project would bring in only $863.40 in present value.

9. a. No!
   b. Project 2.
   c. Project 2 is clearly superior, once all the values have been converted to a common basis. Some calculation can be avoided by looking at the net cash flow (revenue − cost).

	Project 1			Project 2		
Year	Cash Flow ÷	Conversion	PV	Cash Flow ÷	Conversion	PV
1	−$700	1.1	−$636.36	−$200	1.1	−$181.82
2	0	1.21	0.00	$300	1.21	$247.93
3	$900	1.331	$676.18	$100	1.331	$ 75.13
			$ 39.82			$141.24

   d. Both projects are profitable, so the rate of return exceeds 10%.

10. a. Investment demand relates the market interest rate (the cost of borrowing funds) to the quantity of new capital (investment) demanded.
   b. The investment demand curve's slope and position are critically affected by the expectations of those making investment decisions. Expectations can be influenced by political events, circumstances abroad, or changes in the domestic economy.
   c. Volatility is reflected by both the shape and position of the curve. If demand is elastic, changes in the interest rate will provoke large changes in the level of investment. The curve will shift position, perhaps dramatically, as expectations change.
   d. When there is a cut in interest rates, the cost of financing a new project falls. Given that the revenue from the project remains unchanged, profits will rise. More projects will become profitable and more investment will occur.
   e. The development of a new technology may make the existing capital stock obsolete (or less competitive), forcing a wave of new investment.
   f. If new technological developments are expected, firms may delay investment, because they don't want to lock into an old technology. Investment will fall.
   g. If there is an expectation that corporate taxes will increase, there is an expectation that after-tax profits will decrease. This is likely to dampen investment.

GENERAL EQUILIBRIUM AND THE EFFICIENCY OF PERFECT COMPETITION

12

OBJECTIVES: POINT BY POINT

After completing this chapter, you should be able to accomplish the objectives listed below.

General Comment

This chapter plays three major roles. First, while presenting a general equilibrium model, it serves as a review chapter for all of the partial equilibrium material developed for the perfectly competitive model from Chapter 6 onwards. Second, it establishes an "efficiency" benchmark against which subsequent market structures (monopoly, etc.) and related topics will be measured. Last, Chapter 12 previews the upcoming chapters, 13 through 17, in a sense providing a convenient "road map" for the remainder of your micro principles course. Chapter 12 is both a beginning and an end.

The first half of the chapter is pretty much a review of previous material. Use it as such. The wine industry example gives you a chance to check up on your understanding of changes in demand, cost curves, the role of profit and loss, and long-run adjustments.

Although a formal proof of general equilibrium is mathematically complex, you can see the big picture if you use your intuition. If you've done a little physics or chemistry, thinking of a system in equilibrium will help. When the system is shocked, all portions of it will adjust until "balance" is restored.

OBJECTIVE 1: Define general equilibrium and distinguish it from partial equilibrium. Distinguish the effects on a general equilibrium of a given change in one market.

Firms and households make simultaneous decisions in output and input markets, trying to maximize profit and utility, respectively. A *partial equilibrium* approach looks at individual markets for specific goods, but some issues require a broader view—a *general equilibrium* perspective. Changes in one market will affect other markets—products have substitutes and complements, for example. General equilibrium analysis corrects this inadequacy. (page 275)

If a hard frost damages the Florida orange crop, it is easy to go beyond partial equilibrium analysis (the price of oranges will increase) to a wider analysis (the price of orange juice will increase, as will the price of substitutes such as grapefruit juice). In real life, we do this all the time, especially when moving from input markets to product markets. It was easy to predict that the 1991 Gulf War would affect the pump price of gasoline. The more closely related two markets are, the more significant the effect on one if there is a change in the other.

> **LEARNING TIP:** Trace through the implications of the textbook's extended example on the wine industry (pp. 278–281). It is, simultaneously, a good review of partial equilibrium concepts and a good example of general equilibrium analysis.

> **LEARNING TIP:** Use Application 6 below as a review of the equilibrium concepts developed in the partial equilibrium analysis of previous chapters.

PRACTICE

1. General equilibrium analysis ignores which of the following questions?
   A. Are equilibria in different markets compatible?
   B. Can all markets achieve equilibrium simultaneously?
   C. How will a change in demand in Market A affect circumstances in other markets?
   D. What are the equilibrium conditions for markets other than Market A?
   Answer: D. General equilibrium analysis is not concerned with single markets.

2. General equilibrium exists whenever
   A. normal profits are being earned.
   B. total excess demand equals total excess supply.
   C. quantity demanded equals quantity supplied in each market.
   D. income is allocated equitably.
   Answer: C. See p. 275.

Use the following information for the next four questions:

Arboc has only two products, ground nuts and goat cheese. These goods are substitutes and are produced by perfectly competitive firms. Initially, both markets are in long-run equilibrium. Now consumer preferences shift away from goat cheese and toward ground nuts.

3. Given the information above, which of the following will not occur?
   A. In the short run, goat cheese producers will incur losses.
   B. In the short run, there will be an increase in the demand for ground nut workers.
   C. In the long run, more firms will enter the ground nut industry.
   D. More capital will flow into the production of goat cheese.
   Answer: D. Less capital will flow into the production of goat cheese.

4. Given the information above, we would expect
   A. short-run profits in the ground nut industry.
   B. long-run losses in the goat cheese industry.
   C. long-run profits in the ground nut industry.
   D. short-run losses in the ground nut industry.
   Answer: A. You can't get long-run profits or losses.

5. As a goat cheese producer, your best short-run strategy is to
   A. leave the industry and enter the ground nut industry.
   B. switch over to ground nut production.
   C. set your output level to equalize marginal cost and the market price.
   D. cut your price to become more competitive and to increase your market share.
   Answer: C. To maximize profits, produce where P = MC. If you can't cover your operating costs, you'd be better off closing down.

6. The demand for inputs used in goat cheese production will _____ and the demand for inputs used in ground nut production will _____
   A. increase, increase.
   B. increase, decrease.
   C. decrease, increase.
   D. decrease, decrease.
   Answer: C. Input demand, recall, is influenced by the price of the final product. As goat cheese producers scale back operations, they will cut their demand for inputs. Ground nut producers will increase their input demand.

OBJECTIVE 2: Define allocative, or Pareto, efficiency. Outline why we know that resources are allocated efficiently, outputs are distributed efficiently, and the correct output mix is achieved in a perfectly competitive economy.

Efficiency is one criterion for evaluating any given economic system or market and for flagging potential problems in the perfect operation of the market system. An allocatively efficient economy produces, as cheaply as possible, the commodities that consumers want. A change is *efficient* if at least one person is made better off and no person is made worse off as a result of that change. Sometimes this is called Pareto efficiency. An efficient economy is one in which no such change is possible. Even if a change "hurts" some individuals, it is still *potentially efficient* if the gains outweigh the losses. (Gainers could bribe losers and still come out ahead.)   (page 281)

> **Efficiency:** You may have some difficulty with the concept of efficiency. One way to assess an economy's performance is in terms of how well it meets the needs of its consumers. The efficiency concept captures this notion. The major point to take away from this chapter is that perfectly competitive markets result in maximum allocative efficiency—the "best" mix of outputs, produced as cheaply as possible. Movements away from the perfectly competitive ideal (externalities, for example) lead to distortions—either too much or too little of a good is produced, or the price or cost is too high.

PRACTICE

7. Pareto optimality is present in Robinson Crusoe Land when
   A. any improvement in the welfare of Robinson reduces the welfare of Friday.
   B. the benefits from production are divided evenly.
   C. an improvement in the welfare of Robinson does not reduce the welfare of Friday.
   D. the benefits from production are divided according to effort.
   Answer: A. Pareto optimality pertains to any situation where making one or more persons better off has an adverse impact on the welfare of another.

8. On Mindy's Milk Farm, overtime (which runs to 20 hours per week) has traditionally been awarded on the basis of seniority. Old Joshua Merriweather (who has been on the farm since he was a lad, 80 years ago) invariably does all the overtime himself. The four other farm workers (who want to work some overtime) propose a "fair shares for all" method of allocating overtime. We can conclude that
   A. the new method is certainly Pareto optimal.
   B. the traditional method is certainly Pareto optimal.
   C. both methods are certainly Pareto optimal.
   D. neither method is certainly Pareto optimal.
   Answer: D. An increase in the welfare of the four workers will reduce Joshua's welfare. The traditional method is not certainly optimal because the four workers' loss in welfare may exceed Joshua's increase in welfare.

9. You own a calculus book from a course you took last semester. You paid $40 for it as a used textbook at the college bookstore. You value it at $15, but its sell-back value at the bookstore is only $10. Is selling the book to the bookstore Pareto efficient?
    A. Yes, because $10 is better than nothing and you could use the cash.
    B. Yes, because it is a voluntary exchange—no one is twisting your arm.
    C. No, because the market price of the book is $40.
    D. No, because the $10 is less that the $15 value you place on the book.
    Answer: D. Selling for $10 an item that you value at $15 results in a loss. If, as in Option A, you could use the cash, this should have affected your valuation of the book.

10. You have a calculus book from a course you took last semester. You paid $40 for it as a used textbook at the college bookstore. Because its sell-back value is only $10 and you value it at $15, you have decided to keep it. Now Arnold (a math major who values the book at $25) offers you $20. Is selling the book to Arnold Pareto efficient?
    A. Yes, because both you and Arnold have gained from the trade.
    B. Yes, because Arnold has compensated you for the loss imposed by the college bookstore sell-back policy.
    C. No, because you are still selling a book that costs $60 for $20.
    D. No, because you could have got $5 more—Arnold would have paid as much as $25.
    Answer: A. A voluntary exchange must make at least one of the participants better off. In this case, you dispose of a book worth $15 to you for $20 (gain) and Arnold receives a book worth $25 to him for $20 (gain). Note that, given the decision not to sell to the bookstore, that transaction becomes irrelevant.

OBJECTIVE 3: List each of the assumptions underpinning the perfectly competitive model and indicate how perfect competition produces efficiently.

The perfectly competitive model developed over the previous chapters leads to an efficient (optimal) allocation of resources. The system works because resources are allocated among firms efficiently, final products are allocated among households to maximize utility, and the system produces the goods and services (including leisure) that society wants. (page 283)

EFFICIENT OUTPUT MIX—P = MC: It's important to grasp that, by operating where P = MC, firms produce the most efficient combination of outputs. The logic is displayed graphically in Figure 12.4—take some time to get a good understanding of the diagram. You saw the right-hand side of the diagram in Chapter 6, and the left-hand side in Chapter 10. Now is a good time to go back and review that material.

Remember, too, that the marginal cost of Good X embodies the opportunity cost of the next most preferred alternative forgone, say Good Y. If the price that consumers are willing to pay for Good X is less than that, i.e., the value of Good Y—then producing the extra unit of Good X must reduce their utility. If the marginal cost of producing Good X is lower than the price of Good X, then more of Good X should be produced.

Finally, don't forget that perfect competition extends to input markets—workers and employers are both price takers in the labor market, for instance. If the equilibrium condition—$W = MRP_L$—doesn't hold, there will be inefficiency.

PRACTICE

11. If an economy has competitive input and output markets, and firms who maximize profits, the economy will
    A. achieve an efficient allocation of resources.
    B. achieve an equitable distribution of income.
    C. minimize differences between the marginal revenue products of different types of inputs.
    D. allow the marginal utility of consumers to be maximized.
    Answer: A. In the absence of "market failures" (discussed in the textbook on p. 287), these economic conditions will result in an efficient allocation of resources.

12. The condition that ensures that consumers get the goods they want is
    A. MR = M
    B. P = MC.
    C. MR = P.
    D. P = ATC.
    Answer: B. In this case, the marginal cost of a good for society is equal to the value placed on that good by society.

13. The price of jelly beans is $1.00. The total cost of producing 24 units of jelly beans is $24.75. The total cost of producing 25 units of jelly beans is $25.25. The total cost of producing 26 units of jelly beans is $26.00. Currently, 25 units of jelly beans are being produced. Society would benefit
    A. if the 26th unit of jelly beans is produced.
    B. if production is kept at 25 units.
    C. if the price of jelly beans is increased.
    D. if production is reduced to 24 units of jelly beans.
    Answer: A. MC of the 26th unit is 75¢. Because price exceeds MC, the 26th unit should be produced.

14. The social value of a unit of jelly beans is
    A. the price of the unit of jelly beans.
    B. the marginal revenue of the unit of jelly beans.
    C. the marginal cost of the unit of jelly beans.
    D. the total cost of the unit of jelly beans.
    Answer: A. Price reflects the value society puts on a good. See p. 285.

15. Marginal cost of a unit of jelly beans is a measure of
    A. the value society places on a unit of jelly beans.
    B. society's net gain when the unit of jelly beans is produced.
    C. society's net loss when the unit of jelly beans is produced.
    D. what society gives up to produce the unit of jelly beans.
    Answer: D. Marginal cost measures the opportunity cost to society of the resources used in producing the jelly beans.

16. Dot and Ted Sfeir own a firm ("Dotted Spheres") that produces size 3 soccer balls in a perfectly competitive market. They produce 60 balls a week at a cost of $7 per ball, which is the lowest possible long-run average cost. The market price is $10. Which of the following is true?
    A. Dotted Spheres' current output level is efficient because average cost is minimized.
    B. Society would be better off if Dotted Spheres increased its current output level because price exceeds marginal cost.
    C. Society would be better off if Dotted Spheres increased its current output level because price exceeds average cost.
    D. Society would be better off if Dotted Spheres decreased its current output level because this will increase the firm's profits.
    Answer: B. If average cost is minimized at $7, then marginal cost is also $7. (If you're uncertain on this, review Chapter 8.) Price, then, exceeds the cost of producing an extra ball, so more should be produced.

OBJECTIVE 4: Identify four causes of market failure and describe how they arise. Explain the results each market failure presents and suggest how each might be rectified.

In the real world, the stringent conditions of the perfectly competitive model might not be met. In such a situation a *market failure* occurs and inefficiencies creep into the system of unregulated markets. (page 287)

a. *Imperfect competition*, such as monopoly, arises when firms have some measure of control over price and/or competition. Economic profits may be maintained indefinitely if competition can be barred from entry. The consequences are more restricted production and higher prices than would occur in a competitive environment—consumers lose.

b. *Public goods* provide benefits to more than one consumer at a time. Because one can consume without having to pay, there is a powerful incentive to be a free rider. Although private firms might produce most public goods, the problem is that they will not produce enough of them, because they cannot compel consumers to pay their fair share. By using tax dollars, the government can produce public goods and improve efficiency.

c. *Externalities*, which are costs or benefits encountered by a party outside a transaction, do not enter into the calculations of profit- and utility-maximizing firms and consumers. If externalities *are* a factor, the allocation of resources is likely to be suboptimal.

d. *Misinformation or poor information* affects the market participant's ability to make an informed choice. The less informed he or she is, the more likely a suboptimal outcome is.

Inefficient Output Mix—P ≠ MC: Although in different ways, the efficient P = MC condition is infringed in each of the four cases.

PRACTICE

17. In the market for apples there is a consumer surplus and a short-run economic profit is being made. This is conclusive evidence of
    A. externalities.
    B. market failure.
    C. apples being a public good.
    D. none of the above.
    Answer: D. Consumer surplus and short-run economic profits are possible in a perfectly competitive industry. See p. 144 in the textbook to review the concept of consumer surplus.

18. The firms in a perfectly competitive industry merge into one big firm and impose barriers to entry into the industry. We can say that
    A. we can expect that externalities will begin to appear.
    B. the product of this industry is a public good.
    C. the price of the product will be higher, and the output lower, than the values under perfect competition.
    D. this firm will be unable to maximize profits.
    Answer: C. Imperfect markets are a source of inefficiency. See p. 287.

19. The production of Good Z involves positive externalities. A perfectly competitive industry will _____ this good; a monopoly will _____ this good.
    A. overproduce, overproduce.
    B. overproduce, underproduce.
    C. underproduce, overproduce.
    D. underproduce, underproduce.
    Answer: D. The presence of a positive externality means that the market does not capture the full benefits to society flowing from this good.

20. Public goods are a source of market failure because
    A. they permit economic profits to occur in the long run.
    B. they are provided by government agencies.
    C. their benefits cannot be limited to those who purchase them.
    D. they can be produced more cheaply by private firms.
    Answer: C. Because benefits cannot be limited to those who purchase them, the demand for public goods does not reflect their social value.

21. The production of Good Y imposes a cost on the purchaser. Good Y
    A. has negative externalities.
    B. has positive externalities.
    C. is a public good.
    D. is a typical good.
    Answer: D. All goods involve costs (and benefits). Only those goods that pass costs (or benefits) on to third parties exhibit externalities.

22. The licensing of cosmetologists is an attempt to
    A. control provision of a public good.
    B. improve the imperfect information for buyers of this service.
    C. impose externalities on potential competitors.
    D. correct an imperfectly competitive market structure.
    Answer: B. Licensing offers buyers the benefit of knowing that practitioners have achieved a given quality of performance. It may also operate as a barrier to entry (not an externality).

23. Ground nuts are sold by a monopoly and goat cheese is sold by perfectly competitive firms. When both markets are in equilibrium,
    A. P > MC for both goods.
    B. P = MC for both goods.
    C. P = MC for ground nuts and P > MC for goat cheese.
    D. P > MC for ground nuts and P = MC for goat cheese.
    Answer: D. In perfect competition, MR = P = MC. In monopoly, P > MR = MC.

24. Levees along the Mississippi are a _____ . The free market will _____ them.
    A. private good, overproduce.
    B. private good, underproduce.
    C. public good, overproduce.
    D. public good, underproduce.
    Answer: D. Levees provide benefits for all residents. The free market will tend to build too few.

25. A museum in Britain once mounted a display of Roman coins. After some time, a small boy approached the curator and pointed out that one of the "coins" was, in fact, a dirty plastic bottletop! An economist would say that
    A. society lost, because the value of the exhibit was reduced.
    B. society lost, because, although the exhibit might never be sold, society now knew that the coin was a fake.
    C. society gained, because better information about the exhibit was now available.
    D. society gained, because now the remaining coins were even more rare.
    Answer: C. See p. 290.

A Look Ahead

The previous chapters have set up the perfectly competitive framework—the economist's version of the best of all possible worlds. If perfect competition cannot be attained in the market, though, neither can allocative efficiency. Imperfections—externalities, public goods, inadequate information, monopoly power—occur in the real world and mess things up. The conclusions reached in this and the preceding chapters will be used to assess the performance of markets where imperfections exist.

PRACTICE TEST

I. MULTIPLE CHOICE QUESTIONS.

Select the option that provides the single best answer.

_____ 1. Which of the following indicates that we have an efficient output market?
A. Wage equals marginal revenue product of labor.
B. Price of the output equals the marginal cost of the output.
C. Price of the output equals the marginal revenue product.
D. Marginal utility is greater than the price of the output.

Use the following information to answer the next five questions.
Chicken and beef are the only goods produced in the economy. Each is a constant-cost industry and each is currently in equilibrium. Suddenly there is a permanent shift in the preferences of consumers in favor of chicken and away from beef.

_____ 2. We would expect
A. short-run losses in the beef industry.
B. long-run losses in the beef industry.
C. short-run losses in the chicken industry.
D. long-run losses in the chicken industry.

_____ 3. Relative to the current price, the price of chicken would _____ in the short run and _____ in the long run.
A. rise, remain unchanged.
B. fall, remain unchanged.
C. rise, fall.
D. fall, rise.

_____ 4. As a beef producer, in the short run, your best strategy is to
A. shut down immediately.
B. keep operating as long as you can cover your fixed costs.
C. keep operating as long as you can cover your variable costs.
D. cut the price of your beef to win your customers back.

_____ 5. As a chicken producer, in the short run, your best strategy is to
A. increase your beef-producing facilities.
B. cut price to increase market share.
C. expand production until marginal cost is again equal to price.
D. buy more of every input to expand production.

_____ 6. As the economy moves from the initial long-run equilibrium to the final long-run equilibrium we would expect that, with respect to inputs,
A. each industry will continue to use the same amounts of inputs because these are constant-cost industries.
B. all input markets will be affected.
C. the labor market will not be affected.
D. only the labor and capital markets will be affected because land is fixed in supply.

_____ 7. Sellco introduces a new policy that reduces the cost of joining the company club but limits how frequently club members can use the facilities. As a result, some employees will lose and some will gain. On balance, the new plan bestows benefits of $1000 at a cost of $300. The company's previous policy was _____ . The new policy is _____
A. inefficient, potentially efficient.
B. Pareto optimal, potentially efficient.
C. efficient, Pareto optimal.
D. inefficient, Pareto optimal.

_____ 8. Barriers to entry are most closely linked with
A. externalities.
B. public goods.
C. monopolies.
D. perfect competition.

_____ 9. Pollution is an example of
A. a public good.
B. an externality.
C. imperfect competition.
D. imperfect information.

_____ 10. The milk industry is perfectly competitive, selling its product at $2.00 per gallon. The marginal cost of milk at Dana's Dairy is $1.50. Dana should price her product at
A. $2.00.
B. $1.50.
C. 50¢.
D. $1.75.

_____ 11. Mike's Milkery is able to exclude other firms from entering its market. This is an example of
A. externalities.
B. external competition.
C. a monopoly.
D. a public good.

_____ 12. All of the following are sources of market inefficiency except
A. public goods.
B. externalities.
C. monopolistically competitive firms.
D. lack of control by individual firms over price.

_____ 13. Relative to perfect competition, imperfect competition will produce
A. lower prices and more output.
B. lower prices and less output.
C. higher prices and more output.
D. higher prices and less output.

_____ 14. A market is efficient if
A. any change that improves the welfare of one individual reduces the welfare of another.
B. income is equally distributed.
C. output is equally distributed.
D. it produces any mix of output at the lowest cost.

_____ 15. Which of the following activities is least likely to generate an externality?
A. Wearing perfume.
B. Smoking a cigarette.
C. Reading a comic book.
D. Plowing snow from a road.

_____ 16. Ruth tithes (i.e., gives one tenth of her income) to her church. Which of the following is true?
   A. This exchange is Pareto optimal, because Ruth can use this charitable contribution as a tax deduction.
   B. This exchange is Pareto optimal, otherwise the two parties would not voluntarily agree to the exchange.
   C. This exchange is not Pareto optimal because, as the church has no option but to accept the money, it is not a voluntary exchange.
   D. This exchange is not Pareto optimal because Ruth does not necessarily receive any good or service in exchange.

_____ 17. The hog industry, a highly competitive industry, is booming in the southeastern states. Opponents, however, point out the presence of negative externalities that firms ignore. When deciding how much to produce, the typical firm will
   A. produce more than the efficient output level.
   B. produce less than the efficient output level.
   C. produce the efficient output level because the firm is competitive.
   D. produce the efficient output level because the industry is competitive.

Use the following information for the next three questions. Tobacco Belt land can be used for the production of tobacco or soy beans. The Surgeon General finds definitive evidence that cigarette smoking shortens a smoker's life. This leads to a shift in preferences away from tobacco products and towards soy bean consumption.

_____ 18. As the Tobacco Belt economy moves from the initial equilibrium to the new equilibrium, we would predict that
   A. all input markets will be affected.
   B. all input markets, except land (which can be used for both tobacco and soy beans), will be affected.
   C. the land market will not be affected because tobacco and soy beans require different farming techniques.
   D. the labor market will not be affected because unskilled workers are employed in both types of product.

_____ 19. As the Tobacco Belt economy moves from the initial equilibrium to the new equilibrium, we would predict all of the following except that
   A. farms producing tobacco will experience short-run losses.
   B. farms producing soy beans will experience short-run profits.
   C. more farmers will switch over to soy bean production and away from tobacco production.
   D. additional capital will move into tobacco production to make up for the loss of land resources.

_____ 20. Sarah Quinn owns a soy bean farm. Her best profit-maximizing strategy is to
   A. cut her prices to increase her market share of the expanding industry.
   B. plant tobacco because, as fewer farmers plant tobacco, its price will rise.
   C. increase soy bean production to earn short-run economic profits.
   D. decrease soy bean production to force the price higher.

II. APPLICATION QUESTIONS.

1. Two refugees, Alex (who likes candy) and Branko (who likes to smoke), have found their way to a Red Cross camp in Eastern Europe. They each receive a Red Cross parcel containing 20 cigarettes and 20 pieces of candy.

	ALEX		BRANKO	
	CIGARETTES	CANDY	CIGARETTES	CANDY
Red Cross	20	20	20	20
Experiment	12	30	24	10
Trade I	_____	_____	_____	_____
Trade II (Pavel)	_____	_____	_____	_____

Suppose you (an entrepreneur) are also in the refugee camp and that you know the preferences of your two colleagues. As an "experiment," you ask Alex how many cigarettes he would trade in order to receive 10 more units of candy—Alex replies 8. You ask Branko how many cigarettes he would need to be induced to trade 10 units of candy—he replies 4.

   a. Suppose you act as a middleman and reallocate the candy and cigarettes between Alex and Branko according to the numbers provided by the experiment. Who gains? Does anyone lose? Is this a Pareto optimal action?

   b. Can you see any way of profiting from the present situation? If so, how? Write the results of the trade in the table above. You have provided a service. Assuming no half cigarettes or half pieces of candy, derive the maximum possible profit. Call this "Trade I." Who gains? Does anyone lose? Is this a Pareto optimal action?

   c. Suppose a rival trader (Pavel) observes the economic profits that you are earning and decides to undercut you when the next Red Cross parcels are distributed to Alex and Branko. Assuming no half cigarettes or half pieces of candy, derive the maximum possible profit for Pavel. Call this "Trade II."

   d. When will this process end and who are the major winners?

2. There is certainly a demand for, and supply of, aerosol sprays. Suppose they are produced by a perfectly competitive industry. Evidence suggests that aerosols may be responsible in part for increasing world temperatures, i.e. "the greenhouse effect." Does the presence of this side effect pose any problems for our analysis?

3. Consider the market for personal computers that began booming in the early 1980s. In what ways did that boom affect the labor market? What new skills were demanded? How were those skills produced? Suppose Andrea Hacker just bought a PC for $2000. If PCs didn't exist, how might Andrea have spent the same $2000? What happens to employment in the sectors where these items are produced?

4. If I buy a good—for example, a new CD—and share it with my friend, allowing her to tape from it, does my action improve or diminish the allocative efficiency of the economic system? Why?

   Suppose, instead, I resell the CD to my friend. Does this affect your answer?

5. We have an economy which produces only two goods—guns and butter. Each industry is perfectly competitive and there are constant returns to scale. You have been appointed as assistant to the Assistant Secretary of Commerce. Because of a reduction in geo-political tensions, the demand for guns is expected to decrease quite substantially in the near future while, because of

the peaceful climate, the demand for butter will increase. The Assistant Secretary has asked you to prepare a report on the full effects of this change. What will be the effect on:

a. the price and quantity of guns?
b. the price and quantity of butter?

6. Given the profit-maximizing output level, a firm will seek to minimize costs— you can't earn maximum profits if you allow a more costly than necessary method of production. The connection between utility maximization and profit maximization is less evident. The following example lets you work through the link between the maximizing behavior of households and of firms.

   a. What, in words, is the utility-maximizing rule? (Check back to Chapter 6 for the "household equilibrium condition" if you're not too sure.)
   b. With only two goods, A and B, what is the utility-maximizing formula?

   The ratio $MU_A/MU_B = P_A/P_B$ must be true for every pair of goods. If you want, put in numbers to confirm the ratios.

   c. What, in words, is the profit-maximization rule?
   d. Write down an interpretation of the meaning of MC.
   e. Now write down the profit-maximizing formula. Does it hold for all profit maximizers?
   f. Let's generalize by noting that $P_A = MC_A$ and $P_B = MC_B$.

   Observe that the two results combined give:
   $MU_A/MU_B = MC_A/MC_B$.

   The perfectly competitive model results in the production of exactly those quantities of each of the goods requested by consumers, given their opportunity costs—i.e. the optimal output mix.

   Now let's violate the equalities in this formula to check understanding. Suppose, for example, that Good A is apples and Good B is butter and the following is true:

   $MU_A = 50$, $MC_A = 40$ and $MU_B = 60$, $MC_B = 30$

   Substitute these values into the formula. What does the inequality tell you?
   g. What should be the response?
   h. What will happen to each of the 4 values?
   Here is evidence that profit maximizers will respond to consumer demands to produce the desired product mix.

7. Match up the "market failure" with the infringed "perfectly competitive" assumption and the correct example.

	MARKET FAILURE	ASSUMPTION	EXAMPLE
a.	Externality	_____	_____
b.	Imperfect competition	_____	_____
c.	Public goods	_____	_____
d.	Partial information	_____	_____

Assumptions
A. all participants will be price takers
B. all costs and benefits will be borne by producers and consumers
C. perfect knowledge
D. to benefit from consumption one must pay the supplier

Examples
National defense
Monopoly
"Lemons" in the car market
Noise pollution

III. ECONOMICS EXPLORER.

Use the eighth module ("The Broader Picture") from the Economics Explorer software. This module focuses on equilibrium in a perfectly competitive environment.

ANSWERS AND SOLUTIONS

PRACTICE TEST

I. SOLUTIONS TO MULTIPLE CHOICE QUESTIONS

1. B. See p. 285.
2. A. A reduction in demand will reduce profits in the beef industry.
3. A. The demand for chicken has increased. In the short run, this will result in higher prices and higher profits. In the long run, new firms will enter the industry, increasing supply and reducing price. Because the industry is constant-cost, price will return to the original level.
4. C. In the short run you have fixed costs to consider. If you can cover your variable (operating) costs, you should produce.
5. C. The profit-maximizing rule is to set production at the level where P (MR) = MC.
6. B. One industry has expanded and the other has contracted, so they would not maintain the same usage of inputs. We should see all input markets being impacted by the change in demand for outputs.
7. A. The previous plan was inefficient because the benefits of the new plan outstrip the costs. We can't say that the new plan is Pareto optimal because further changes might improve the welfare of employees still more.
8. C. See p. 287.
9. B. See p. 289.
10. A. The profit-maximizing rule is to set production at the level where P (MR) = MC. Dana is a (perfectly competitive) price taker. She should increase production.
11. C. If Mike can exclude others from his market, he has established a monopoly through the use of barriers to entry.
12. D. Lack of control over price is a hallmark of perfect competition.
13. D. Typically, imperfectly competitive producers will restrict output and charge higher prices.
14. A. See p. 281.
15. C. See p. 289.
16. B. Because the exchange takes place and is voluntary, neither party is hurt and at least one of the two parties must gain.
17. A. Even if an industry is perfectly competitive, when the social cost of a negative externality is ignored by the producer, production will be too high.
18. A. See p. 280.
19. D. There should be a general decline in the quantity of all resources used in tobacco production.
20. C. As price rises, it will be greater than marginal cost at the initial output level, so Sarah should increase production until P = MC once more. A perfectly competitive firm is a price taker.

II. SOLUTIONS TO APPLICATION QUESTIONS

1. a. If you merely replicate the experiment, no one gains! Alex and Branko get different, but no more satisfying, allocations. The experiment, recall, asked what an *equivalent* allocation would be. Because you have taken some trouble to effect the exchange, but have received no reward for your enterprise, you have lost. This exchange is not a Pareto optimal action.

	ALEX CIGARETTES	CANDY	BRANKO CIGARETTES	CANDY
Red Cross	20	20	20	20
Experiment	12	30	24	10
Trade I	12	30	24	10
Trade II (Pavel)	13	30	24	10

   b. In general, given identical initial parcels of goods, different preferences, and zero transactions costs, trade will *always* be beneficial. It's easy to forget that you, as facilitator, need a reward.
   Trade I: "Borrow" 10 pieces of candy from Branko, promising him cigarettes in return. Give Alex the 10 pieces of candy and take 8 cigarettes in return—Alex has not lost. "Pay" Branko 4 cigarettes for the borrowed candy—Branko has not lost. You have gained 4 cigarettes. Because no one has lost and you have gained, this is a Pareto optimal action.

   c. Trade II: Pavel "borrows" 10 pieces of candy from Branko, promising him cigarettes in return. Pavel gives Alex the 10 pieces of candy and generously takes 7, not 8, cigarettes in return—Alex has gained. "Pay" Branko 4 cigarettes for the borrowed candy—Branko has not lost. Pavel has gained 3 cigarettes. No one has lost and Pavel and Branko have gained, this is a Pareto optimal action. Note: You have not lost because you were not a participant in this round of trading.

   d. The process ends when profits are pushed so low that they can be pushed no lower, i.e., normal profits are being earned. As the entrepreneurs take less of a cut, the consumers, Alex and Branko, keep more and, therefore, gain.

   Note: Alex and Branko gain because of competition. You and Pavel have an incentive to collude and/or impose barriers to entry to reduce competition and keep profits high. Such action reduces market efficiency.

2. The basic conclusion in this chapter is that perfect competition will provide the "best" allocation of resources. However, we should recall that the presence of externalities undermines this conclusion. Aerosols may, indeed, produce externalities that our perfectly competitive producers choose to ignore.

3. Demand for technically trained labor increased. Programmers, designers, systems analysts of all kinds, and skilled assembly workers experienced an increase in demand. Technical schools and major universities began training programs. Firms did on-the-job training. Andrea might have done any number of things, like buying a (used) car or some new clothes or traveling. Employment falls in those sectors.

4. Home taping of CDs reduces economic efficiency. It represents an externality. The market demand for CDs does not accurately represent the true demand for CDs. Because the market for new CDs is affected by the market for used CDs, resale does not reduce efficiency.

5. a. The demand for guns will shift to the left—the price and quantity traded will decrease in the short run. Firms will leave the industry because short-run economic losses are being made. This exodus of firms will make the market supply curve shift to the left. This movement will continue until normal profits are achieved. Given constant returns to scale, the long-run industry supply curve will be horizontal, and the initial price level will be restored. The quantity of resources allocated to this industry will be reduced.

b. The demand for butter will shift to the right—the price and quantity traded will increase in the short run. Firms will enter the industry because short-run economic profits are being made. The additional firms will make the market supply curve shift to the right. This movement will continue until normal profits are achieved. Given constant returns to scale, the long-run industry supply curve will be horizontal, and the initial price level will be restored. The quantity of resources allocated to this industry will be increased.

6. a. The last dollar spent on each good should purchase an equal amount of marginal utility.
   b. $MU_A/P_A = MU_B/P_B$.
   c. Produce until the quantity is reached where marginal revenue is inadequate to cover marginal cost.
   d. Marginal cost is the opportunity cost of the resources used to produce the final unit of output—the value of the other goods that we could have produced instead.
   e. $P = MR = MC$. This is true for all profit maximizers in perfect competition.
   f. The per dollar cost of the last units of satisfaction from apples is relatively too high ($50/40 < 60/30$).
   g. Spend less on apples and reallocate funds to butter.
   h. Diminishing marginal utility will drive MU_A up and MU_B down, while decreasing marginal productivity will make MC_A fall and MC_B rise until a balance is struck.

7. a. B   Noise pollution
   b. A   Monopoly
   c. D   National defense
   d. C   "Lemons" in the car market

COMPREHENSIVE REVIEW TEST FOR PART 2

The following questions provide a wide-ranging review of the material covered in Part 2 (Chapters 6–12) of the textbook. Each question deals with a topic or technique important for your understanding of economic principles. If you miss a question you should return to the relevant section of the chapter in the textbook and fine-tune your understanding.

PRACTICE TEST

MULTIPLE CHOICE QUESTIONS.

Select the option that provides the single best answer.

_____ 1. Denny has a straight, downsloping demand curve for cookies. A decrease in the price of cookies
   A. will make Denny's budget constraint swivel inwards.
   B. will result in an increase in the absolute value of Denny's price elasticity for cookies.
   C. shift Denny's demand curve for cookies to the right.
   D. will increase Denny's consumer surplus.

Use the following information for the next two questions.

Joe's recreation budget is $120 per month which he divides between attending movies (which cost $10) and buying CDs (which cost $15). Joe finds that the satisfaction derived from the final movie of the month is 50 units while the satisfaction from the final CD is 60 units. Assume diminishing marginal utility is present.

_____ 2. How should Joe adjust his spending pattern on movies and CDs?
   A. Joe should attend more movies and buy fewer CDs because the marginal utility of movies is more than that of CDs.
   B. Joe should attend more movies and buy fewer CDs because the marginal utility per dollar of movies is more than that of CDs.
   C. Joe should attend fewer movies and buy more CDs because the marginal utility of CDs is more than that of movies.
   D. Joe should attend fewer movies and buy more CDs because the marginal utility per dollar of CDs is more than that of movies.

3. As Joe adjusts his purchases of movies and CDs to achieve maximum satisfaction, the marginal utility of movies will
   A. increase because he is attending more movies.
   B. increase because he is attending fewer movies.
   C. decrease because he is attending more movies.
   D. decrease because he is attending fewer movies.

4. There is an increase in the interest rate. The operation of the substitution effect will _____ current saving. The operation of the income effect will _____ current saving.
   A. increase, increase.
   B. increase, decrease.
   C. decrease, increase.
   D. decrease, decrease.

5. There is an increase in the interest rate. The operation of the income effect will _____ current saving because _____ .
   A. increase, at higher interest rates the individual earns more from previously saved income.
   B. increase, the opportunity cost of each dollar spent has increased.
   C. decrease, at higher interest rates the individual earns more from previously saved income.
   D. decrease, the opportunity cost of each dollar spent has increased.

6. Sam's demand curve for kiwi fruit is given by the equation $Qd = 50 - 2P$. Now her demand changes to $Qd = 100 - 2P$. Assuming that the market price is unchanged, this implies that her price elasticity of demand for kiwi fruit will become _____ elastic and her consumer surplus will _____ .
   A. more, increase.
   B. more, decrease.
   C. less, increase.
   D. less, decrease.

7. In perfect competition, the industry's demand curve is _____ ; the firm's demand curve is _____ .
   A. horizontal, horizontal.
   B. horizontal, downward sloping.
   C. downward sloping, horizontal.
   D. downward sloping, downward sloping.

8. The consumption level maximizing utility from goods A and B is indicated by the formula
   A. MR = MC.
   B. P = MC.
   C. P = ATC (min).
   D. $MU_A/Price_A = MU_B/Price_B$.

9. Jill's consumer surplus for Good A will decrease if
   A. the price of A decreases.
   B. the price of B, a substitute for A, rises.
   C. Jill's income falls and A is a normal good.
   D. Jill's demand for A becomes more inelastic.

_____ 10. The total value Paul places on one apple a day is $2.00. The total value of two apples a day is $3.10; of three apples a day, $3.70; of four apples, $4.00; and of five apples, $4.20. Apples cost 50¢ each. To maximize his consumer surplus, how many should Paul buy?
   A. At least five.
   B. Five.
   C. Four.
   D. Three.

_____ 11. The income effect for normal Good A occurs when
   A. a decrease in income makes the consumer buy more of Good A.
   B. a decrease in income encourages consumers to buy more of substitute Good B which is inferior.
   C. a decrease in the price of Good A makes consumers better off so that they can buy more of the Good A.
   D. an increase in the price of Good A encourages consumers to buy more of inferior Good B.

_____ 12. Labor is the variable resource in a basketball factory. At the point where diminishing returns are beginning to occur
   A. the average product of labor is maximized.
   B. the average product of labor is minimized.
   C. the long-run average cost curve is at its minimum.
   D. the average product of labor is increasing.

_____ 13. A factory reorganizes production and finds that the marginal productivity of its variable resource (labor) has increased in the short run. We would expect that the factory's
   A. marginal cost has increased at each output level.
   B. marginal cost has decreased at each output level.
   C. average variable cost has increased at each output level.
   D. average total cost has increased at each output level.

_____ 14. Which of the following is the best explanation for the fact that the marginal revenue that perfectly competitive Farmer Gustafson receives from an additional bushel of wheat is constant and equal to its price.
   A. Gustafson supplies an insignificant fraction of the total market supply of wheat.
   B. The market demand curve for wheat is downward-sloping.
   C. There are few good substitutes for wheat.
   D. In the short run no new firms can enter this industry.

_____ 15. Walt's Widgets is a perfectly competitive firm. In the long run, if Walt earns zero economic profit, he will
   A. shut down.
   B. decrease his output level but may not shut down.
   C. increase his output level to attract more business.
   D. remain at his current output level.

Use the following diagram to answer the next six questions.

_____ 16. The short-run profit-maximizing output level is
   A. 80.
   B. 100.
   C. 120.
   D. 150.

_____ 17. The short-run profit-maximizing price is
   A. $14.00.
   B. $13.50.
   C. $10.00.
   D. $7.00.

_____ 18. In the short run, maximum economic profit is
   A. −$420.
   B. −$400.
   C. $200.
   D. $420.

_____ 19. Total fixed cost
   A. is $600.
   B. is $800.
   C. is $1400.
   D. cannot be calculated from the information given.

_____ 20. At 120 units of output, marginal cost is _____ than marginal revenue. Economic profit can be increased by _____ output.
   A. greater, increasing.
   B. greater, decreasing.
   C. less, increasing.
   D. less, decreasing.

_____ 21. We would expect firms to
   A. enter this industry in the short run.
   B. enter this industry in the long run.
   C. leave this industry in the short run.
   D. leave this industry in the long run.

_____ 22. A perfectly competitive firm's short-run supply curve is that part of its marginal cost that is
A. upward sloping.
B. above the average total cost curve.
C. above the average variable cost curve.
D. above the average fixed cost curve.

_____ 23. In the short run, a perfectly competitive firm can earn economic profits if the market price is greater than
A. average total cost.
B. average fixed cost.
C. average variable cost.
D. marginal cost.

_____ 24. The government requires all the firms in the perfectly-competitive widget industry to adopt antipollution equipment that increases production costs. We would expect
A. the market demand for widgets to decrease.
B. the market supply curve for widgets to shift left in the long run.
C. firms to leave the industry in the short run.
D. the long-run economic profits of the typical firm to be reduced.

_____ 25. The wheat industry is perfectly competitive and is in long-run equilibrium. Which statement best describes the short-run effects of a decrease in the demand for wheat? The price of wheat will _____ ; quantity traded will _____ ; the output of the typical farmer will _____ .
A. increase; increase; increase.
B. increase; increase; decrease.
C. decrease; decrease; increase.
D. decrease; decrease; decrease.

_____ 26. When a firm experiences "economies of scale" _____ as output increases.
A. its fixed costs decrease.
B. its average costs decrease.
C. its total costs decrease.
D. the marginal productivity of its fixed inputs increase.

_____ 27. Which of the following indicates that we have an economically efficient market?
A. Wage equals marginal product of labor.
B. Price of the product equals the marginal cost of the product.
C. Price of the product equals the marginal revenue of the product.
D. Marginal utility of the product is greater than the price of the product.

_____ 28. Which of the following would *not* shift a competitive firm's labor demand curve to the right?
A. An increase in the price of the firm's output.
B. A decrease in the wage rate.
C. An increase in the productivity of labor.
D. A decrease in the cost of other inputs complementary to labor.

_____ 29. *To Air is Humane* is currently producing 5000 units of output, using 25 units of labor and 20 units of capital. The marginal product of labor is 200, while the marginal product of capital is 100. The price of labor is $2, and the price of capital is $3. Given this information, which of the following is true?
A. The firm is currently using the optimal mix of labor and capital.
B. The firm should increase labor and reduce capital.
C. The firm should reduce labor and increase capital.
D. The firm should increase labor and increase capital.

_____ 30. DEF, Corp. is employing 100 units of labor and 50 units of capital to produce 2000 widgets. Labor costs $10 per unit and capital costs $30 per unit. For the quantities of inputs employed, the marginal product of labor is 3 and the marginal product of capital is 10. At this output level, the firm
A. is producing at the lowest possible cost.
B. could lower production costs by using more capital and less labor.
C. could increase its profit by using more labor and less capital.
D. could lower production costs by using more labor and less capital.

APPLICATION QUESTION

Here is some production information for the Smiley-Smile Mouthwash Company.

Number of Workers	Marginal Produce	Total Product	Average Product
0	—		
1	12		
2	14		
3	22		
4	12		
5	10		
6	8		
7	6		
8	4		
9	2		

1. Complete the Total Product and Average Product columns.
2. With which worker do diminishing returns begin to occur?
3. When the marginal product of labor is positive and increasing, is total product rising or falling?
When marginal product of labor is positive and decreasing, is total product rising or falling?
4. If marginal product of labor became negative, what would happen to total product?

Each worker costs $10 to hire. In addition, Smiley-Smile has total fixed costs of $60.

5. Use the information from the table above to help you complete the following table.

Total Product	Total Cost	ATC	AVC	AFC	MC
		—	—	—	—

6. Make up a rule: "When marginal cost is rising, average total cost is RISING / FALLING / CAN'T TELL"

7. Make up a rule: "When average variable cost is falling, average total cost is RISING / FALLING / CAN'T TELL"

8. How can you tell that Smiley-Smile is operating in the short run?

Smiley-Smile is a perfectly competitive profit-maximizing firm.

9. If the market price is $1.00 per unit, how many units of output (bottles of mouthwash) will the firm produce?

10. At a price of $1.00, calculate the firm's total economic profit or loss.

11. At a price of $1.00, should Smiley-Smile stay in business in the short run? Why?

12. At a price of $1.00, what will happen in the long run to the number of firms, the position of the industry supply curve, and the market price?

13. If the market price is $2.50 per unit, how many units of output (bottles of mouthwash) will the firm produce?

14. At a price of $2.50, calculate the firm's total economic profit or loss.

15. You have the information to derive Smiley-Smile's supply schedule for the prices given below.

PRICE/ BOTTLE	SMILEY-SMILE'S SUPPLY SCHEDULE	MARKET SUPPLY
$3.50	_____	_____
$3.00	_____	_____
$2.50	_____	_____
$2.00	_____	_____
$1.50	_____	_____
$1.00	_____	_____

16. Suppose that there are 100 identical firms in the market. Calculate total market supply.

Below is the market demand schedule in the mouthwash market.

PRICE/ BOTTLE	MARKET DEMAND
$3.50	4800
$3.00	6800
$2.50	8800
$2.00	10,800
$1.50	12,800
$1.00	14,800

17. Determine the short-run equilibrium price and equilibrium quantity traded.

18. Confirm that, when the market price is $2.50, the marginal revenue product of the last worker hired is equal to the wage.

ANSWERS AND SOLUTIONS

ANSWERS TO REVIEW TEST FOR PART 1

1. D. There is an increase in the difference between how much Denny would pay and how much she does pay for cookies (the triangular area between price and the demand curve). Answer C is a serious error. A change in price does not cause a shift in the position of a demand curve. Movement down a straight-line demand curve result in a less elastic demand.

2. B. Compare the marginal utility per dollar values. Movies offer more utility per dollar.

3. B. As more of a good is purchased, marginal utility decreases; as less of a good is purchased, the marginal utility of the last item consumed must increase.

4. B. See Chapter 6, p. 148.

5. C. Higher interest rates will generate more interest on existing saved funds, so less will need to be saved now to achieve a given income level in the future.

6. B. The per dollar satisfaction from an extra cup of coffee is greater than the per dollar satisfaction from an extra cup of tea. I should spend less on tea and use the saved dollars to buy more coffee.

7. C. The industry demand curve is a normal downsloping curve—competition makes the demand curve facing each firm horizontal.

8. D. To maximize utility, one should try to equalize the satisfaction per dollar from each good.

9. C. Consumer surplus is depicted by the triangular space between price and the demand curve. The space will diminish as the demand curve shifts left, as will happen for a normal good if income level falls.

10. D. Paul should buy up to the point where price equals marginal benefit. The marginal benefit of the third apple is 60¢ while the marginal benefit of the fourth apple is 30¢.

11. C. The income effect occurs when, as price changes, spending power (income) changes, and the consumer's purchasing level is influenced.

12. D. Marginal product of labor is at a maximum when diminishing returns are just beginning to emerge, o the average product of labor is still rising. See the diagram on p. 170.

13. B. With one variable resource, when marginal product increases, marginal cost decreases—the denominator of the marginal cost formula has increased.

14. A. Gustafson has no control over price.

15. D. Although economic profit is zero, a normal rate of return is included in costs. In addition, in long run equilibrium, economic profits *must* be zero.

16. B. This is the output level at which marginal revenue equals marginal cost.
17. C. $10.00 is the market price, based on the demand curve.
18. B. At the profit-maximizing output level, average total cost is $14, while the price is $10. There is a $4 loss on each of the 100 units produced.
19. A. When output is 100 units, average fixed cost is $6 (ATC − AVC).
20. B. Output should be reduced to 100 units, where marginal revenue equals marginal cost.
21. D. Firms cannot enter or leave in the short run. If this is a typical firm and it is making an economic loss, firms will leave the industry in the long run.
22. C. See p. 200.
23. A. See p. 197.
24. B. Profitability has been reduced, resulting in some firms leaving the industry in the long run.
25. D. Draw a demand and supply diagram to verify this.
26. B. There are no fixed inputs in the long run! Economies of scale yield decreasing average costs.
27. B. Price represents the marginal benefit of the product. Economic inefficiency occurs if production is at any level other than where marginal benefit equals marginal cost.
28. B. A change in the wage rate will cause a movement along the labor demand curve.
29. B. The optimal combination of resources equalizes the marginal product per dollar of each input. In the given situation the marginal product of labor per dollar was lower than that of capital.
30. B. The optimal combination of resources equalizes the marginal product per dollar of each input. In the given situation the marginal product of capital per dollar was lower than that of labor.

APPLICATION

1. See the following table.

Number of Workers	Marginal Produce	Total Product	Average Product
0	—	0	—
1	12	12	12
2	14	26	13
3	22	48	16
4	12	60	15
5	10	70	14
6	8	78	13
7	6	84	12
8	4	88	11
9	2	90	10

2. Diminishing returns begin with the fourth worker.
3. When marginal product is positive, total product will always increase.
4. If marginal product of labor became negative, total product would decrease.

5. See the following table.

Total Product	Total Cost	ATC	AVC	AFC	MC
0	$ 60.00	—	—	—	—
12	$ 70.00	$5.83	$0.83	$5.00	$0.83
26	$ 80.00	$3.08	$0.77	$2.31	$0.71
48	$ 90.00	$1.88	$0.63	$1.25	$0.45
60	$100.00	$1.67	$0.67	$1.00	$0.83
70	$110.00	$1.57	$0.71	$0.86	$1.00
78	$120.00	$1.54	$0.77	$0.77	$1.25
84	$130.00	$1.55	$0.83	$0.71	$1.67
88	$140.00	$1.59	$0.91	$0.68	$2.50
90	$150.00	$1.67	$1.00	$0.67	$5.00

6. When marginal cost is rising, average total cost could be either rising or falling. "Can't tell" is the best answer.

7. "When average variable cost is falling, average total cost is falling."

8. Smiley-Smile has some fixed resources, which cannot occur in the long run when all resources are variable.

9. If the market price is $1.00 per unit, then marginal revenue is $1.00 per unit. To maximize profit the firm should produce where MR = MC, i.e., at an output level of 70.

10. At a price of $1.00, total revenue is $70 while total cost is $110. Smiley-Smile will make an economic loss of $40.

11. Smiley-Smile should stay in business in the short run, making a loss of $40 because, if it shut down it would make a loss of $60 (its fixed costs).

12. In the long run, firms will leave this industry, industry supply will decrease and market price will increase.

13. If the market price is $2.50 per unit, then marginal revenue is $2.50 per unit. To maximize profit the firm should produce where MR = MC, i.e., at an output level of 88.

14. At a price of $2.50, total revenue is $220 while total cost is $140. Smiley-Smile will make an economic profit of $80.

15. See the following table.

PRICE/ BOTTLE	SMILEY-SMILE'S SUPPLY SCHEDULE	MARKET SUPPLY
$5.00	90	9000
$2.50	88	8800
$1.67	84	8400
$1.25	78	7800
$1.00	70	7000

16. See the preceding table.

17. The equilibrium price is $2.50 and equilibrium quantity traded is 8800 bottles.

18. When the market price is $2.50, the marginal revenue product of the last worker hired (the eighth) is $2.50 × 4. This equals the wage which is given as $10.00.

MONOPOLY

OBJECTIVES: POINT BY POINT

After completing this chapter, you should be able to accomplish the objectives listed below.

OBJECTIVE 1: List the "perfectly competitive" assumptions that are not met by a monopolist and relate these to the features found in such a market. Name three types of barrier to entry.

Travel to Europe and experience "Bed and Breakfast" in a private household offering cheap overnight accommodation to tourists. This feature of tourist travel is a reasonable approximation of a perfectly competitive market. The key elements include (1) many sellers and buyers; (2) fairly homogeneous products; and (3) ease of entry (all you need is a spare bed!). Private motels at the beach are a similar example in the United States. When these competitive elements are absent, imperfect competition (monopoly, oligopoly, or monopolistic competition) is present. (page 297)

The college dorm for a first-semester freshman is close to being a monopoly. S/he may be required to reside in a dorm. A *pure monopoly* occurs when there is a single firm in an industry producing a product with no close substitutes (in this case, campus accommodation). *Barriers to entry* are the reason that this situation can arise and endure. Different forms of barriers to entry are: legal (franchises, patents), economies of scale, and exclusive ownership of a necessary input. Government franchises and economies of scale are typical reasons for the emergence of natural monopolies. (page 298)

> **LEARNING TIP:** You have already derived the cost curves for a perfectly competitive firm and industry. The cost curves used in this, and subsequent, chapters are the *same* as those that you've seen before. Most people find it easier to draw the "cost diagram" first and then put in the demand and marginal revenue curves afterwards. The **only** differences occur in the revenue parts of the diagram. Demand for the firm is the same as the market demand—there is only one firm. For a straight-line demand curve, the marginal revenue curve is a straight line whose slope is twice as steep as that of the demand curve.

PRACTICE

1. A pure monopoly is an industry with a single firm that produces a product that has _____ close substitutes and in which there are _____ barriers to entry.
   A. many, significant.
   B. many, no.
   C. no, significant.
   D. no, no.
   Answer: C. See p. 298.

2. Peter's Pan Pizzeria operates in an imperfectly competitive market. Which of the following statements does not apply to this firm?
   A. Peter's Pan Pizzeria has some control over the price it charges.
   B. Peter's Pan Pizzeria has a downward sloping demand curve.
   C. Peter's Pan Pizzeria does not compete with the other pizzerias in town.
   D. Peter's Pan Pizzeria has some market power.
   Answer: C. If other pizzerias produce substitutes for Peter's pizza, Peter's is a monopolistically competitive firm and does compete.

3. Your local electric company maintains its monopoly because of
   A. a patent.
   B. product differentiation.
   C. ownership of a scarce resource.
   D. a government franchise.
   Answer: D. Cable TV and local telephone companies are other examples. See p. 298.

4. The _____ broadly we define an industry, the _____ substitutes it has, and the _____ elastic the demand for its products.
   A. more, more, more.
   B. more, fewer, less.
   C. less, more, less.
   D. less, fewer, less.
   Answer: B. The broader the definition of an industry, the more difficult it is to find a substitute and the less elastic the demand. See p. 298.

OBJECTIVE 2: Define marginal revenue and explain why the monopolist's marginal revenue decreases as output increases.

In imperfect competition, *marginal revenue is less than price* because, to sell an extra unit, the firm must cut price and the price cut applies to all units bought. The addition to revenue from selling the extra unit is less than the price charged. When few items are affected by the price cut, the increase in sales increases total revenue, and marginal revenue is positive. However, as progressively more items suffer a lower price, the increase in revenue from the new sales is offset by the decrease in revenue from existing sales and total revenue decreases—marginal revenue becomes negative.

(page 302)

LEARNING TIP: In order to understand what is happening to revenue as price and quantity change, examine the following diagram.

When price is $11 and $10, respectively, total revenue is $77 and $80, respectively. Marginal revenue is $3. Now consider area A and area B. Verify that they are $7 and $10 respectively. Area A represents the revenue lost because of the price change while area B represents the revenue gained. Comparing the two, let us calculate MR visually. As price falls and output expands, the one-unit revenue increase dwindles in importance beside the multi-unit revenue decrease—imagine the difference in areas if, rather than 7 and 8 units, the diagram showed 1007 and 1008 units.

LEARNING TIP: Review Chapter 5's section on price elasticity and the total revenue test. Note that as price decreases, total revenue increases when demand is elastic (MR is positive), and that total revenue decreases when demand is inelastic (MR is negative).

PRACTICE

5. In a monopoly,
   A. the market demand curve is above, and parallel to, the marginal revenue curve.
   B. the marginal revenue curve is downward sloping.
   C. increasing price will not result in a decrease in quantity demanded.
   D. we assume that the demand curve is unknown.
   Answer: B. See p. 303. Note: The market demand curve is above, but is not parallel to, the marginal revenue curve.

Use the following table to answer the next four questions. The Uretown Yokels ice hockey team is the only live sports entertainment in Uretown. Here is some information about their ticket prices and attendance at their games.

TICKET PRICE	TOTAL ATTENDANCE	TOTAL REVENUE	MARGINAL REVENUE
$14	100	_____	
$12	200	_____	_____
$10	300	_____	_____
$ 8	400	_____	_____
$ 6	500	_____	_____
$ 4	600	_____	_____

6. Fill in the total revenue and marginal revenue columns in the table above then graph the demand and marginal revenue curves above.
   Answer: See the *Answers and Solutions* section.

7. At a price of $12 per ticket, the Yokels attract 200 spectators. For the Yokels to attract 300 spectators, they would have to _____ price. Total revenue would _____
   A. increase, increase.
   B. increase, decrease.
   C. decrease, increase.
   D. decrease, decrease.
   Answer: C. See the table above.

8. When the Yokels decrease price from $12 to $10 to attract 300 spectators, total revenue increases, indicating that demand is _____ and that marginal revenue is _____
   A. elastic, positive.
   B. elastic, negative.
   C. inelastic, positive.
   D. inelastic, negative.
   Answer: A. See p. 305 and Figure 13.4.

9. If the Yokels cut price from $12 to $10 per ticket, each new customer will _____ and each regular customer will _____
   A. increase total revenue by $10, increase total revenue by $2.
   B. increase total revenue by $10, decrease total revenue by $2.
   C. decrease total revenue by $10, increase total revenue by $2.
   D. decrease total revenue by $10, decrease total revenue by $2.
   Answer: B. MR = 600. TR increases by 100 × $10 (new customers) and decreases by 200 × $2 (regular customers).

OBJECTIVE 3: Draw and interpret a diagram representing the price and output choices of a profit-maximizing monopolist.

Monopolists (and other types of imperfectly competitive firm) must decide how much output to produce, how to produce it, and how much of each input to hire, just as a perfectly competitive firm must do. However, monopolists must also decide which price to set. This is determined by the "MR = MC" rule. The "demand side," then, limits the monopolist. The firm can't charge any price, because they are limited by the demand for their product.   (page 306)

Marginal Revenue and the Profit-Maximizing Rule: MR = MC: Marginal revenue—the amount by which total revenue changes as output increases by one unit—is a key concept that you've seen before. Perfect competition is a special case, where P = MR. For any firm with a downward sloping demand curve, price is greater than marginal revenue. The profit-maximizing output level can *always* be found by equating marginal revenue and marginal cost (MR 5 MC). The monopolist, therefore, doesn't charge the highest price to get the most profit—s/he takes both cost and revenue (demand) information into account.

> **GRAPHING POINTER:** Having found where MR = MC, it is a common error to move immediately to the vertical axis and identify that value as the price, e.g., OF in the diagram in the Practice questions below. However, you must always refer to the demand curve to determine the correct price. Draw a line up from the intersection of marginal revenue and marginal cost to the demand curve and then over to the vertical axis.

PRACTICE

10. A monopoly produces where marginal revenue exceeds marginal cost.
    A. The firm could increase profits by increasing output.
    B. The firm could increase profits by decreasing output.
    C. The firm is making an economic profit.
    D. The firm is earning a negative economic profit (loss).
    Answer: A. The firm should produce at the output level where MR = MC. Because we don't know anything about the relationship between price and ATC we can't say whether or not a profit is being made (Option C).

Use the following diagram to answer the next three questions.

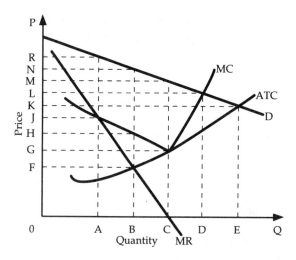

11. The profit-maximizing output level is
   A. OA.
   B. OB.
   C. OD.
   D. OE.
   Answer: B. This is the output level where MR = MC.

12. The profit-maximizing price is
   A. OF.
   B. OG.
   C. OH.
   D. ON.
   Answer: D. At output level OF, the demand curve shows that the price can be as high as ON.

13. The firm's maximum profit is
   A. OB × HN.
   B. OC × GM.
   C. OB × FN.
   D. OC × HN.
   Answer: A. Total profit is (price − ATC) × Q.

OBJECTIVE 4: Draw a diagram to compare a monopolist relative to the effects of a perfectly competitive firm in terms of price, output, and the effect on income distribution.

In terms of welfare and efficiency, monopoly compares poorly with perfect competition. Assuming similar costs, the monopolist will overprice and underproduce. The monopolist is not efficient because output is not set where P = MC, the firm does not use the lowest-cost production method, and the distribution of income is altered (through the appropriation of excess profits, which is like a private tax).

If a competitive industry were to become a monopoly, price would increase and quantity would decrease. Consumers would lose through the higher prices and reduced level of production—in general, society loses when a monopoly replaces perfect competition.   (page 309)

> **Monopoly:** Remember the long-run perfectly competitive equilibrium result: P = MC = LRAC (minimum) = SRAC (minimum). First, in monopoly, the firm will not minimize average costs. Second, the monopolist will not produce the output society considers to be optimal (where P = MC).

Natural monopoly can avoid these criticisms because of the benefits derived from economies of scale. Demand just isn't sufficient to warrant producing where costs are minimized.

Comment: Figure 13.9 on p. 312 is *extremely important* for this and subsequent chapters. Use it as a review of your knowledge of profit maximization (MR = MC), the meaning of the demand (marginal benefit) curve, consumer surplus, and the essential meaning of marginal cost—the opportunity cost of production. The finding of a welfare loss (and higher prices and restricted output) is a theoretical basis for the antitrust policies and regulation detailed in following chapters.

PRACTICE

Use the following table, which provides *long-run* information about the market for apples, to answer the next four questions. Price is price per pound of apples.

QUANTITY (POUNDS)	PRICE PER POUND	MARGINAL REVENUE	MARGINAL COST	AVERAGE TOTAL COST
100	$1.40	—	—	$2.00
200	$1.07	$ .74	$ .50	$1.50
300	$ .92	$ .62	$ .46	$ .75
400	$ .80	$ .44	$ .44	$ .70
500	$ .66	$ .10	$ .43	$ .65
600	$ .50	−$ .30	$ .50	$ .50
700	$ .30	−$ .80	$ .59	$1.00

14. Given the *cost* information above, a perfectly competitive industry would charge a price of _____ per pound and produce _____ pounds of apples.
    A. 80¢, 400.
    B. 44¢, 400.
    C. 50¢, 600.
    D. 30¢, 600.
    Answer: C. The perfectly competitive industry will produce at the lowest point on its long-run average cost curve. Because price and marginal revenue are identical in perfect competition, and MR must equal MC to maximize profits, the price will also be 50¢.

15. Given the cost information above, a monopoly would charge a price of _____ per pound and produce _____ pounds of apples.
    A. 80¢, 400.
    B. 44¢, 400.
    C. 50¢, 600.
    D. 30¢, 600.
    Answer: A. The monopolist will produce where MR = MC. Price is then determined.

16. Given the information above, a profit-maximizing monopoly would earn an economic profit of
    A. $144.
    B. $40.
    C. zero.
    D. −$104.
    Answer: B. Economic profit is (P − ATC) × Q. In this case, (80¢ − 70¢) × 400 = $40.

17. From the previous questions, we can formulate the following long-run rule: The monopolist will produce _____ and charge _____ than the perfectly competitive industry.
    A. more, more.
    B. more, less.
    C. less, more.
    D. less, less.
    Answer: C. If this is still unclear, review the answers to the three previous questions and read pp. 309–311 in the textbook.

Use the following diagram, which shows the revenue and cost curves for coffee, to answer the next two questions. Initially, this is a perfectly competitive industry.

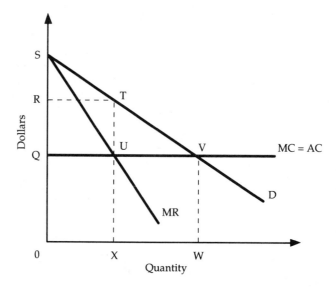

18. If the coffee industry becomes a monopoly, the loss in social welfare is equal to _____ . The monopolist will be willing to spend an area equal to _____ to preserve the monopoly.
    A. TUV, QRTV.
    B. TUV, QRTU.
    C. QRTU, TUV.
    D. >QRTV, TUV.
    Answer: B. The perfectly competitive firm would produce W units at a price of Q dollars. The monopolist will reduce output to X units and charge the higher price of R dollars. The welfare loss due to the decrease in output and the increase in price is TUV. The monopolist's profit [(price − average cost) × quantity], i.e., QRTU, is the amount s/he is willing to spend to maintain the monopoly.

19. If the coffee industry becomes a monopoly, the loss in consumer surplus will be
    A. TUV.
    B. RST.
    C. QRTU.
    D. QRTV.
    Answer: D. With perfect competition, the consumer surplus would be QSV. With monopoly, the consumer surplus shrinks to RST. QRTV represents the difference in consumer surplus. See the textbook's p. 149 to review this concept.

OBJECTIVE 5: Distinguish a natural monopoly from other monopolies.

A *natural monopoly* occurs where average costs decrease as output levels rise because of long-lasting economies of scale. In such circumstances, a single-firm industry can be the most efficient way to organize production. Here it would be undesirable to break up the monopoly because having one producer is the "best" way to organize the market. Such an industry is usually regulated.   (page 315)

PRACTICE

20. If a natural monopoly is split into a number of smaller competing firms, price will
    A. increase, because smaller firms will have higher average costs.
    B. increase, because each firm will experience diseconomies of scale.
    C. decrease, because additional competition is taking place.
    D. increase in the short run because of the disruption, but decrease in the long run because of the additional competition.
    Answer: A. Each firm is driven up along the average cost curve as output level falls. The firms don't experience diseconomies of scale—they aren't large enough.

21. For the typical natural monopolist, in the short run, fixed costs are relatively _____ and marginal costs are relatively _____
    A. high, high.
    B. high, low.
    C. low, high.
    D. low, low.
    Answer: B. See p. 315.

OBJECTIVE 6: Define monopsony. Calculate marginal factor cost given input supply information, and explain why the monopsonist's marginal factor cost (MFC) is an upward sloping curve.

Monopsony is the situation in which there is only one buyer in the input market. The employer faces an upward sloping input supply curve—he is not an input price taker. To attract extra workers, for example, the wage must be increased. Since the wage increase applies to all workers, the extra cost of hiring a worker is greater than the wage that worker receives. *Marginal factor cost* (of labor) measures the extra cost of hiring one extra worker and is also upward sloping. As in perfect competition, the monopsonist will hire workers until the marginal revenue product equals the marginal factor cost.   (page 317)

> **Monopsony:** There are parallels between downward sloping output demand curves and marginal revenue curves, and upward sloping input supply curves and marginal factor cost curves. If you can understand why MR is less than demand, extend your insight to explain why MFC is more than supply. Just as P > MR translates into a graph where the demand curve is above the MR curve, MFC > W is graphed with the MFC curve above the labor supply curve.

PRACTICE

Use the following table about labor supply to answer the next five questions. Maxine is a monopsonistic employer in Uretown.

WAGE	WORKERS	TOTAL FACTOR COST	MARGINAL FACTOR COST
$14	7	_____	
$12	6	_____	_____
$10	5	_____	_____
$ 8	4	_____	_____
$ 6	3	_____	_____
$ 4	2	_____	_____

22. Complete the table.
    Answer: See the *Answers and Solutions* section.

23. At a wage of $10, Maxine the Monopsonist can hire 5 workers. For Maxine to hire 6 workers, she would have to _____ wage. The total wage bill (factor cost) would _____
    A. increase, increase.
    B. increase, decrease.
    C. decrease, increase.
    D. decrease, decrease.
    Answer: A. See the table above.

24. If Maxine increases the wage from $10 to $12, the new worker will increase total factor cost by _____ and each previous worker will increase total factor cost by _____
    A. $12, $12.
    B. $12, $2.
    C. $2, $12.
    D. $2, $2.
    Answer: B. MFC = 22 leq $12 (the new worker) + $2 × 5 (other workers).

25. At the profit-maximizing hiring level for labor for a monopsonist,
    A. the marginal factor cost is equal to the marginal revenue product and is less than the wage.
    B. the marginal factor cost is greater than the marginal revenue product and is equal to the wage.
    C. the marginal factor cost is less than the marginal revenue product and is greater than the wage.
    D. the marginal factor cost is equal to the marginal revenue product and is greater than the wage.
    Answer: D. See p. 318.

26. We know that marginal revenue product of labor decreases as additional workers are hired. See Chapter 10 if you're unsure about this point. In this question, however, assume that MRP is constant at $14. Maxine will hire _____ workers and pay a wage of _____
    A. 4, $8.
    B. 4, $14.
    C. 7, $12.
    D. 7, $14.
    Answer: A. Maxine will hire until MFC is equal to MRP. She will not hire the fifth worker. The labor supply curve indicates that she can hire 4 workers for $8 each.

PRACTICE TEST

I. MULTIPLE CHOICE QUESTIONS.

Select the option that provides the single best answer.

_____ 1. A pure monopoly is best defined as a firm
   A. selling a product for which there are no close substitutes.
   B. making short-run economic profits.
   C. with a degree of market power.
   D. with a downward sloping demand curve.

_____ 2. Which of the following is not a barrier to entry?
   A. Ownership of patent rights.
   B. Ownership of private property.
   C. The possession of a government franchise.
   D. Substantial economies of scale.

_____ 3. Monty the Monopolist is seeking to maximize profits. Currently, he is producing where marginal revenue is less than marginal cost. He should
   A. increase production.
   B. reduce price.
   C. reduce production.
   D. produce where price is equal to marginal cost.

_____ 4. The profit-maximizing monopolist must decide all of the following except
   A. output level.
   B. price level.
   C. the wage level.
   D. the combination of inputs.

_____ 5. A monopolist is currently maximizing profits. We can conclude that
   A. he is maximizing total revenue and minimizing total cost.
   B. he has reduced the difference between marginal revenue and marginal cost to zero.
   C. he is maximizing total revenue and marginal revenue.
   D. he is producing where marginal revenue equals average cost.

_____ 6. Manuel the Monopolist sells at a price of $4. His marginal cost is $3 and the price elasticity of demand is $-.6$. We can conclude that Manuel
   A. is maximizing profit.
   B. should increase output.
   C. should decrease output.
   D. should decrease price.

_____ 7. Mandy the Monopolist operates a firm that is not a natural monopoly. Relative to a perfectly competitive industry, we would expect Mandy to have
   A. lower prices and lower output.
   B. lower prices and higher output.
   C. higher prices and higher output.
   D. higher prices and lower output.

Use the diagram below to answer the next six questions. The cost information and the industry demand curve apply in both perfect competition and monopoly.

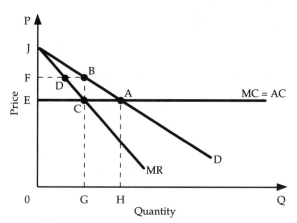

_____ 8. This perfectly competitive industry becomes a monopoly. Price will _____ , quantity will _____
A. fall to E, fall to G.
B. fall to E, rise to H.
C. rise to F, rise to H.
D. rise to F, fall to G.

_____ 9. With a profit-maximizing monopolist, the net loss of social welfare is shown by area
A. FBCE.
B. BAC.
C. EABF.
D. BCD.

_____ 10. To preserve the monopoly, this firm would be willing to spend up to
A. FBCE.
B. BAC.
C. EABF.
D. ABDC.

_____ 11. If this industry were initially perfectly competitive and then became a monopoly, the amount of consumer surplus transferred to the monopolist is shown by the area
A. DBC.
B. ABC.
C. FBCE.
D. FBAE.

_____ 12. If this industry were perfectly competitive, consumer surplus would be shown by the area
A. ABC.
B. JEA.
C. FBCE.
D. FBAE.

_____ 13. If this industry were a monopoly, consumer surplus would be shown by the area
A. ABC.
B. HEA.
C. JFB.
D. ECBH.

_____ 14. The labor hiring rule for Mickey the Monopolist, who hires in a perfectly competitive labor market, is to hire that amount of labor for which the wage equals
A. marginal revenue.
B. marginal revenue product.
C. marginal product.
D. marginal factor cost.

_____ 15. The Snow White Mining Corporation, a monopsonist, hires 6 dwarfs for a total factor cost of $98. If a seventh dwarf, Dopey, is hired, the total factor cost rises to $140. When 7 dwarfs are hired the wage per worker is _____ and the marginal factor cost of the seventh dwarf is _____
A. $140, $20.
B. $20, $42.
C. $20, $20.
D. $140, $42.

_____ 16. Mike the Monopolist produces where marginal revenue equals marginal cost equals average total cost. His economic profits will be
A. positive.
B. negative.
C. zero.
D. indeterminate—it depends on demand conditions too. (Try sketching this one.)

_____ 17. A monopsonist will hire _____ workers and pay them _____ wages than would a price-taking employer.
A. more, more.
B. fewer, less.
C. more, less.
D. fewer, more.

_____ 18. Use the following information for Firm A. Total revenue = $1,200. Total cost = $400. Price = $12. MR = $10. Total variable cost = $300. MC = $6. This is a _____ firm currently in a _____ situation.
A. perfectly competitive, short-run.
B. monopolistic, short-run.
C. monopolistic, long-run.
D. perfectly competitive, long-run.

_____ 19. Molly the Monopolist faces an elastic demand curve. If she decreases price, marginal revenue will be _____ and total revenue will _____
A. positive, rise.
B. positive, fall.
C. negative, rise.
D. negative, fall.

_____ 20. The additional cost of using an additional unit of an input is
A. marginal cost.
B. marginal revenue.
C. marginal revenue product.
D. marginal factor cost.

_____ 21. Myron the Monopolist owns two plants. The profit-maximizing condition is best expressed as
A. SMR = MC1 = MC2.
B. SMC = MR1 = MR2.
C. minimum MC = MR1 = MR2.
D. SMC = MR. Note: The symbol Σ indicates a summation.

II. APPLICATION QUESTIONS.

1. In 2000, the U.S. airline industry is radically transformed. Following a vicious price war and a series of mergers, one company (Untied Airlines) has emerged as the sole survivor. Untied adopts a new slogan (*Fly Untied—or Walk*) and hires you as a consultant on pricing policy. Untied offers a one-way trip from Atlanta to Washington. The marginal cost for each passenger is $40. Fixed cost is $500,000. Demand information is shown below. Note: The demand and marginal revenue curves are linear.

PRICE OF ONE-WAY TRIP TICKETS	ONE-WAY TRIPS DEMANDED PER YEAR (THOUSANDS)	MARGINAL REVENUE
_____	_____	_____
_____	_____	_____
_____	_____	_____
$140	6	_____
$130	8	_____
$120	10	_____
$110	12	_____
$100	14	_____
$ 90	16	_____
$ 80	18	_____
$ 70	20	_____

a. Complete the table.
b. Give the demand equation in the form $P = X + YQd$, where X and Y are numbers and Qd is the quantity demanded.
c. Calculate the quantity demanded when the price is zero.
d. Give the marginal revenue equation in the form $MR = X - Qd$, where X and Y are numbers and P is the price of a one-way ticket.
e. Calculate the quantity demanded when the marginal revenue is zero. Careful!

Suppose that Untied's corporate chiefs wish to charge a single, profit-maximizing ticket price for all their Atlanta-Washington customers.

f. Which price will maximize profits?
g. Calculate Untied's total cost at the profit-maximizing output level.
h. Calculate Untied's economic profits.
i. Draw a diagram showing the demand, marginal revenue and marginal cost curves.
j. Calculate the consumer surplus and interpret your finding for Untied's top brass.
k. Determine the efficient output level and price.
l. A noted economist, Dr. Faircase, who is opposed to Untied's monopoly position, has claimed that the loss in social welfare caused by Untied has a monetary value of $300,000. How would you advise Untied to reply?
m. Is it coincidental that the welfare loss and the consumer surplus values are identical?
n. A campaign is being waged to split up Untied into smaller independent units. The management wants to know the maximum amount they should allocate to a "war chest" to lobby and to buy political favors.
o. Calculate Untied's economic profits at the efficient output level.
p. If the government required that Untied price tickets at the efficient price, what would be Untied's long-run response?
q. Suppose the government requires that the price be set at the efficient level, but will offer Untied a subsidy to maintain the flight. How great a subsidy per passenger would the government have to offer Untied to induce them to keep the flight open?

2. Veterinary services can be provided at any level for an opportunity cost of $60,000 per vet. Yearly demand for veterinary services is given by P = $300,000 − 4Qd. (P is the dollar price per vet.)

   a. Calculate the marginal revenue equation.
   b. In the space below, graph the demand, MR, MC and AC curves for veterinary services. Put in numerical values where possible.

   c. The American Veterinary Association operates as a profit-maximizing monopoly. Calculate the price and output level in this industry.
   d. Calculate the total economic profit per vet.
   e. If entry into this industry was unrestricted, state the price and output level that would emerge.

3. You are a profit-maximization consultant specializing in monopolies. Three firms seek your advice but, in each case, the information the firm can provide is incomplete. You will be able, however, to recommend one of the following **short-run** actions and write a justification of your proposal. To verify your answer and for some additional graphing practice, try sketching the diagram in each case.

   Recommended actions

   1. Remain at current output level.
   2. Increase output.
   3. Decrease output.
   4. Shut down.
   5. Uncertain—the figures provided cannot possibly be correct.

FIRM	PRICE	MR	TR	Q	TC	MC	ATC	AVC
A	6.40	3.10	_____	1000	6400	3.00	_____	3.24

Recommendation: _____
Justification:

FIRM	PRICE	MR	TR	Q	TC	MC	ATC	AVC
B	12.80	_____	_____	2000	_____	12.80	12.00	9.2

Recommendation: _____
Justification:

FIRM	PRICE	MR	TR	Q	TC	MC	ATC	AVC
C	5.00	4.00	30,000	_____	_____	4.00	5.10	5.05

Recommendation: _____
Justification:

4. a. Fill in the blanks in the table which refers to a monopolist.

Price	Quantity	TR	MR
$8	2		—
$7		$21	
$6	4		
$5			$1
$4	6		
$3		$21	

   b. Why, when price falls from $6 to $5, does total revenue increase by only $1?

5. The food service at your university is run by a single firm (Food Service). The table below shows the monthly demand for meals and total costs.
   a. Complete the table.

Sales (units)	Price (per meal)	Total Cost	MR	MC
4,000	$1.50	$ 6,100		
5,000	$1.40	$ 6,400		
6,000	$1.30	$ 6,800		
7,000	$1.20	$ 7,300		
8,000	$1.10	$ 8,000		
9,000	$1.00	$ 9,000		
10,000	$0.90	$10,200		

   b. If Food Service tries to maximize profits, it will set the price per meal at _____ (of the choices given here).
   c. Students form a committee to regulate the food service. They want to maximize consumers' welfare, given that total costs are covered. The price they set should be _____ .
   d. Between which two price levels is the market demand curve unitarily elastic?

6.

> **GRAPHING POINTER:** This diagram is meant to depict a monopoly in long-run equilibrium. P* and Q* are equilibrium quantity and price, respectively. However, if this is the situation that is meant to be shown, there are several errors in the graph. Indicate as many errors as possible and explain, based on your economic understanding, *why* they are errors.

7. The following example lets you use your intuition to construct a diagram for a monopoly.

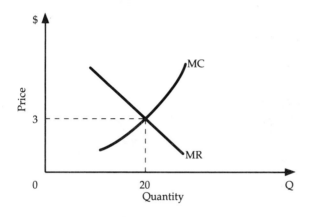

  a. Where on the diagram will the firm maximize profits (or minimize losses)?
  b. What is the price?
  c. Draw your own demand curve on the diagram. Now work out price.
  d. Finally, sketch in an average cost curve. Is this firm making a profit or a loss?
  e. Are losses feasible in long-run equilibrium?

8. A mind-bender: Suppose the monopolist's demand curve is *not* a straight line but a rectangular hyperbola—i.e., a line with the same area underneath it at all points.
  a. What does this tell you about total revenue?
  b. What do you think the marginal revenue values will be? What will the MR curve look like?
  c. What will be the elasticity along this demand curve?

    d. Use the following table to confirm your predictions.

Price	Quantity	TR	MR
$24	1		—
$12	2		
$ 8	3		
$ 6	4		
$ 4	6		
$ 3	8		
$ 2	12		

    e. Now graph demand and marginal revenue.

    f. Define "marginal cost." Can MC ever be zero?
    g. Now, on your diagram, draw a "typical" marginal cost curve. Where will the profit-maximizing output level be?

III. ECONOMICS EXPLORER.

Use the ninth module ("Monopoly") from the Economics Explorer software to compare monopoly and perfect competition. This module derives the monopolist's marginal revenue curve and allows you to determine the profit-maximizing price and output. The other problems take you beyond the textbook material in this chapter. Price discrimination is dealt with in Chapter 15.

ANSWERS AND SOLUTIONS

ANSWERS TO PRACTICE QUESTIONS

6.

TICKET PRICE	TOTAL ATTENDANCE	TOTAL REVENUE	MARGINAL REVENUE
$14	100	$1400	
			$10
$12	200	$2400	
			$ 6
$10	300	$3000	
			$ 2
$ 8	400	$3200	
			–$ 2
$ 6	500	$3000	
			–$ 6
$ 4	600	$2400	

Note: Recall that marginal revenue is found by dividing the change in total revenue by the change in quantity.

22.

WAGE	WORKERS	TOTAL FACTOR COST	MARGINAL FACTOR COST
$14	7	$98	
			$26
$12	6	$72	
			$22
$10	5	$50	
			$18
$ 8	4	$32	
			$14
$ 6	3	$18	
			$10
$ 4	2	$ 8	

PRACTICE TEST

I. SOLUTIONS TO MULTIPLE CHOICE QUESTIONS

1. A. Monopoly means "single seller." See p. 298.
2. B. There are no barriers to entry into a perfectly competitive industry although the means of production may be privately owned.
3. C. To maximize profits, the firm should produce where MR = MC. When marginal revenue is less than marginal cost, too much is being produced.

4. C. The labor market determines the wage level, and this market may be perfectly competitive. The monopolist would be a wage taker with no control.

5. B. To maximize profits, the firm must be producing where MR = MC.

6. C. If MR is −.6, demand is inelastic and MR is negative. If so, MC must exceed MR, and Manuel should reduce output.

7. D. See Figure 13.9 on p. 312. Note: The natural monopolist is an exception to this rule.

8. D. In the perfectly competitive industry, output is established where P = MC. In the monopoly, output is where MR = MC. Given the demand curve, price will rise.

9. B. See Figure 13.9 on p. 312.

10. A. The monopolist's economic profit is (P − AC) × Q. S/he would be willing to sacrifice all of this in order to maintain the monopoly.

11. C. See Figure 13.9 on p. 312.

12. B. See p. 312.

13. C. See p. 312.

14. B. If Mickey were a monopsonist as well as a monopolist, the wage would equal marginal factor cost. In this case (perfect competition in the labor market), the wage will equal the marginal revenue product of labor.

15. B. The wage per worker is the total factor cost divided by the number of workers. The marginal factor cost is the change in the total factor cost as an additional worker is hired.

16. A. For the monopolist, the demand curve is above the MR curve. If MR = ATC, the price exceeds ATC and Mike is earning an economic profit.

17. B. All firms will hire until marginal factor cost equals MRP. For the monopsonist, MFC is upward sloping; for the perfectly competitive employer, MFC is horizontal.

18. B. Price is not equal to MR—Firm A is not perfectly competitive. Because total costs are greater than variable costs, there must be fixed costs—a short-run phenomenon.

19. A. A decrease in price represents a movement down Molly's demand curve. When demand is elastic, marginal revenue (addition to total revenue) is positive and, given a decrease in price, total revenue will increase.

20. D. See p. 317.

21. D. To maximize profits, the monopolist follows the MR = MC rule. In a multi-plant situation, the relevant marginal cost is the sum of the marginal costs of the individual plants. See p. 309.

II. SOLUTIONS TO APPLICATION QUESTIONS

1. a. See the table below.

PRICE OF ONE-WAY TRIP TICKETS	ONE-WAY TRIPS DEMANDED PER YEAR (THOUSANDS)	MARGINAL REVENUE
$170	0	—
$160	2	$160
$150	4	$140
$140	6	$120
$130	8	$100
$120	10	$ 80
$110	12	$ 60
$100	14	$ 40
$ 90	16	$ 20
$ 80	18	$ 0
$ 70	20	−$ 20

   b. P = 170 − 5Qd. The slope is rise/run. As price falls by $10, quantity rises by 2—the slope is −5. The vertical intercept, i.e., when Qd is zero, occurs when price is 170. We get the equation P = 170 − 5Qd.

   c. Given P = 170 − 5Qd, when P = 0, 170 = 5Qd, therefore Qd = 34.

d. MR = 170 − 10Qd. Recall that the marginal revenue curve has the same vertical intercept as the demand curve, i.e., $170. The slope is twice as steep as that of the demand curve, i.e., −10.

e. Given MR = 170 − 10Qd, when MR = 0, 170 = 10Qd, therefore Qd = 17. Comment: Note that the table seems to give the value as 18. This apparent discrepancy is because the table reports the marginal revenue in the range from 16 to 18. The table reports discrete values, while the formula is a continuous function.

f. Set MR = MC, i.e., 170 − 10Qd = 40. Qd = 13. When Qd = 13, P = $105.

g. TC = TFC + TVC. TFC is given as $500,000. To get TVC, recall that MC is the addition to total cost as extra units are produced, i.e., variable cost. TVC = $40 × 13,000 = $520,000. TC = $500,000 + $520,000 = $1,020,000.

h. Economic profits = TR − TC. TR = P × Q = $105 × 13,000 = $1,365,000. TC = $1,020,000. Economic profits = $345,000.

i. See the diagram below.

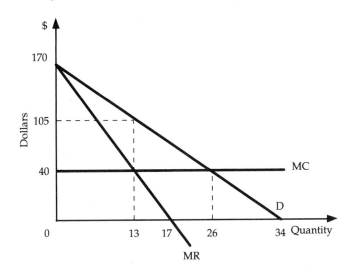

j. Consumer surplus is the area between price and the demand curve, i.e., .5(170 − 105) × 13,000 = $422,500. Consumer surplus refers to difference between the value of the extra benefits derived by customers and the price they paid.

k. The efficient output level is where P = MC. Because MC is constant at $40, P must equal $40. Substituting that price into the demand equation, we get output to be 26.

l. The social loss is .5($105 − $40) × (26,000 − 13,000), or $422,500. This, in fact, is greater than the value given by Faircase. It's probably best, therefore, to make no comment. If comment is required, either Untied should not dispute Faircase's claim or, in an attempt to confuse the issue, mention the consumer surplus value which exceeds $300,000. This is, of course, a complete red herring!

m. Given straight line curves, it's not a coincidence. Because the MR curve is twice the slope of the demand curve, it bisects MC. From that point, geometry requires identical triangles for the two concepts. Other examples, and the real world, are not so clear cut.

n. Rent-seeking behavior tells us that the firm can allocate all of their economic profits ($345,000) to defeat the campaign.

o. Economic profits = TR − TC. TR = P × Q = $40 × 26,000 = $1,040,000. TC = TFC + TVC. TFC = $500,000. TVC = $40 × 26,000 = $1,040,000. TC = $500,000 + $1,040,000 = $1,540,000. Economic profits = −$500,000.

p. Untied would stop offering this flight—no firm will make an economic loss indefinitely.

q. The economic loss is −$500,000 to fly 26,000 passengers. The subsidy would be $19.23 (approximately).

2. a. MR = $300,000 − 8Qd. Recall that the marginal revenue curve has the same vertical intercept as the demand curve, i.e., $300,000. The slope is twice as steep as that of the demand curve, i.e., −8.

   b. See the diagram below.

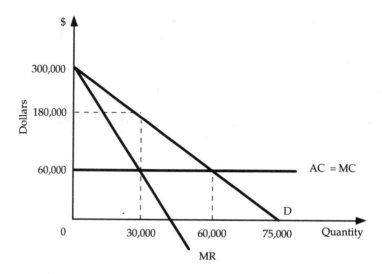

   c. The profit-maximizing output level is where MR = MC, i.e., where Q = 30,000. When Q is 30,000, P is $180,000.

   d. Total economic profit = TR − TC. TR = P × Q = $180,000 × 30,000 = $5,400,000,000. TC = AC × Q = $60,000 × 30,000 = $1,800,000,000. Total economic profit equals $3,600,000,000. Per vet, this is $120,000.

   e. In perfect competition, economic profits would be driven to zero. The price would be $60,000 (i.e., equal to marginal cost). When P = $60,000, quantity is 60,000.

3. See each of the cases below.

FIRM	PRICE	MR	TR	Q	TC	MC	ATC	AVC
A	6.40	3.10	6400	1000	6400	3.00	6.40	3.10

Recommendation: 2

Justification: Firm A is earning a normal profit, even when not maximizing profit. Because MR > MC, the firm should expand production.

FIRM	PRICE	MR	TR	Q	TC	MC	ATC	AVC
B	12.80	<12.80	25,600	2000	24,000	12.80	12.00	9.24

Recommendation: 3

Justification: MR is less than price and, therefore, less than 12.80. MR < MC. The firm should reduce output. It should not close down, however, because an economic profit can be earned.

FIRM	PRICE	MR	TR	Q	TC	MC	ATC	AVC
C	5.00	4.00	30,000	6,000	30,600	4.00	5.10	5.05

Recommendation: 4

Justification: MR = MC. The firm should shut down because it is unable to cover its variable costs of production.

4. a. See the table below.

Price	Quantity	TR	MR
$8	2	$16	—
$7	3	$21	$5
$6	4	$24	$3
$5	5	$25	$1
$4	6	$24	–$1
$3	7	$21	–$3

   b. Total revenue rises by only $1 (MR = $1) because price had to fall to $5 to increase sales by one unit. $5 of extra revenue were generated by selling the extra unit. Unfortunately, though, the other 4 units, each of which could have been sold at $6, had to have $1 trimmed off their price tag. So the seller lost $4 on those. Net gain was $1.

5. a. See the table below.
   b. $1.20, where MR < MC for the next step of 1000 units.
   c. $1.00, where P = MC.

Sales	Price (per meal)	Total Cost	MR	MC
4,000	$1.50	$ 6,100	—	—
5,000	$1.40	$ 6,400	$1.00	$0.30
6,000	$1.30	$ 6,800	$0.80	$0.40
7,000	$1.20	$ 7,300	$0.60	$0.50
8,000	$1.10	$ 8,000	$0.40	$0.70
9,000	$1.00	$ 9,000	$0.20	$1.00
10,000	$0.90	$10,200	$0.00	$1.20

   d. Between 90¢ and $1.00. The demand curve is unitarily elastic where MR is zero. Confirm this with the total revenue test—as price increases, total revenue remains constant in this price range.

6. The cost diagram: MC doesn't intersect AVC or ATC at their minimum points. The diagram shows a short-run situation, since ATC − AVC = AFC. Fixed costs can show up only in the short run.

   The revenue diagram: The downsloping MC curve should be labeled MR.

   MR = MC tells us that this firm is maximizing profits—as we'd expect. At that output level (Q*), price equals average cost. Normal profits are being earned. However, a section of the demand curve lies above ATC, which must mean that economic profits are possible. Therefore, the demand and the marginal revenue curves don't agree.

7. a. Where MR = MC.
   b. It is unknown because there is no demand curve shown.
   c. The demand curve is downward sloping and above the MR curve. (Note for perfectionists: With a straight-line demand curve, the slope of MR is twice as steep as that of the demand curve.) Remember that the quantity variable is *already determined*: only that knife-edge vertical line rising from the "20 units" output level is of any significance. Read off the price when output is 20 units.
   d. The final diagram may reveal normal *or* economic profits *or* losses being made— it depends on where you've positioned the demand curve and the ATC curve.
   e. No! The monopolist would leave the industry. Only two cases are possible, the one with economic profits being the typical representation of a monopolist.

8. a. Total revenue is the same at all price levels.
    b. Marginal revenue will be constant at zero. This would be shown as a horizontal line drawn *on* the quantity axis!
    c. Because, as price rises, TR neither rises (inelastic demand) nor falls (elastic demand), demand is unitarily elastic at all points.
    d. See the table below.

Price	Quantity	TR	MR
$24	1	24	—
$12	2	24	0
$ 8	3	24	0
$ 6	4	24	0
$ 4	6	24	0
$ 3	8	24	0
$ 2	12	24	0

    e. See the diagram below.

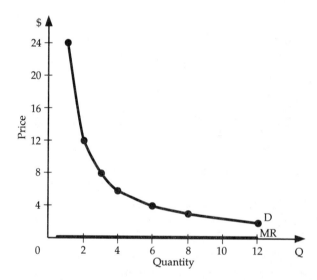

Demand has a regular shape (downward sloping) although it is a curving line instead of a straight line. Marginal revenue, though, is unusual—it graphs along the horizontal axis, because it is always zero.

    f. Marginal cost is the additional cost caused by increasing output by one unit. It can't be zero (if, as is usually assumed, inputs are infinitely divisible).
    g. Do you see a problem? In this unusual case, MR doesn't seem to equal MC at *any* level of output! The solution? The firm gets the same total revenue at each output level so, to maximize profits, it will produce one unit—enough to get the revenue but where total costs are minimized. Think about it: MR for the first unit is $24, since TR must be zero when none are sold. (Notice we've broken the "rectangular hyperbola" assumption.) Rest assured that your "MR = MC" profit-maximization rule will work for all cases you'll have to analyze. This example is merely to challenge your understanding.

MONOPOLISTIC COMPETITION AND OLIGOPOLY | 14

OBJECTIVES: POINT BY POINT

After completing this chapter, you should be able to accomplish the objectives listed below.

General Comment

As you read through this chapter, you will find it helpful to keep in mind the classifications made by **industrial organization** economists. They classify their investigations into an industry under three broad categories:

a. Market structure: How many firms are there? Are there economies of scale? How big are the four, or eight, largest firms?

b. Conduct: How do firms behave? How are prices set? Do firms advertise?

c. Performance: Is the industry efficient? Does it promote growth?

Pose questions like these as you examine monopolistic competition and oligopoly (and monopoly).

OBJECTIVE 1: Identify the features that characterize a monopolistically competitive firm and industry.

Monopolistic competition is characterized by a large number of firms, none of which can control market price, but which produce differentiated products. There are no barriers to entry in monopolistic competition. Restaurants are an excellent example.

Product differentiation (making one's product appear unique) is important in monopolistic competition and advertising can be an important aid in making the firm's or industry's demand curve less elastic. Supporters of advertising argue that the firm must make consumers aware of their products and differentiate its product from those of its competitors; opponents claim that advertising contains little information, distorts consumer preferences, and is wasteful. There is no clear answer one way or the other.   (page 323)

> **Right Answers in Economics:** President Truman once wished for a "one-handed economist." On all issues his economic experts invariably told him "on the one hand this, but on the other hand, that." Economics often gives "maybe" answers—in the current chapter, for example, advertising has benefits *and* costs.

> **Product Differentiation:** Advertising and expectations play a powerful role in product differentiation, as the following (true) story shows. Regulars in a bar were firm supporters of one or other of the two brands of cheap Scotch offered. Sometimes, the bar would run out of the favorite brand of one faction and its patrons would unwillingly have to consume the other. Invariably, expressing dissatisfaction, they swore that they could tell the difference. The point is that they drank with their eyes: both bottles contained the *same* brand of Scotch. The barman topped them up before opening time—using a third, even cheaper, brand!

Local radio is another good example of monopolistic competition—the airwaves are abuzz with radio stations claiming that they're the answer to your listening requirements. In 1992, KLAX in Los Angeles, was languishing at the lower end of the top forty stations with a playlist that was indistinguishable from that of its competitors. Changing formats, KLAX zoomed to the city's premier station within three months, claiming the loyalty of one million listeners. KLAX found a "new" product—*ranchera* and *banda* (Mexican country music). As we would expect, because barriers to switching formats in the radio industry are low, other stations challenged for a share of this market which is estimated at between three and five million listeners.

> **LEARNING TIP:** Monopoly has *one* firm, oligopoly a *few*, perfect competition and monopolistic competition *many*. The distinguishing characteristic of monopolistic competition is **product differentiation**. Except for the downward sloping demand and marginal revenue curves, the perfectly and monopolistically competitive short-run and long-run stories are very similar. Monopolistic competition differs from monopoly and oligopoly in that firms in these industries can't affect the market price by virtue of their size. The oligopolist may or may not differentiate its product—as with most things in oligopoly, it depends.

> **LEARNING TIP:** Keep in mind clear examples of each market structure:
>
> a. Perfect competition: the stock market (unless there is insider trading), word processing.
> b. Monopolistic competition: your local restaurant scene.
> c. Oligopoly: De Beers, the diamond cartel that functions almost like a monopoly; OPEC, the cartel with a fairly homogeneous product (oil); the U.S. car industry, which tries to differentiate.
> d. Pure monopoly: Burroughs-Wellcome, the developers of the first anti-AIDS drug, AZT.

PRACTICE

1. Each of the following is a characteristic of monopolistic competition except
   A. many firms.
   B. product differentiation.
   C. no barriers to entry.
   D. mutual interdependence.
   Answer: D. See p. 323. Mutual interdependence characterizes oligopoly.

2. In monopolistic competition, firms achieve some market power
   A. by growing larger.
   B. by merging with other firms into a cartel.
   C. by establishing barriers to exit from the industry.
   D. through product differentiation.
   Answer: D. See p. 325.

3. Monopolistic competition differs from perfect competition because in monopolistic competition
   A. there are few firms.
   B. there are no barriers to entry.
   C. there are many firms.
   D. firms can differentiate their products.
   Answer: D. See the list of characteristics on p. 323.

OBJECTIVE 2: Explain the arguments for and against product differentiation and advertising

Proponents of product differentiation believe that consumers' tastes differ and that they prefer variety over sameness. In addition, higher quality (or more efficiently produced) goods should prevail over inferior rivals, resulting in greater efficiency in the use of scarce resources. However, consumers need to know about the choices open to them: advertising is necessary. (page 325)

Opponents of product differentiation argue that differentiation and advertising squander resources highlighting small or non-existent distinctions between brands. Advertising shapes consumer preferences and may reduce the buyer's ability to choose rationally. In addition, advertising costs may represent a barrier to entry that reduces competition. (page 327)

OBJECTIVE 3: Interpret the graph of a profit-maximizing monopolistically competitive firm, indicating the profit-maximizing output level and price. Explain why the monopolistically competitive firm will make normal profits in long-run equilibrium.

Graphically, monopolistic competition is similar to Chapter 13's monopoly picture. Demand is downward sloping, as in monopoly, but more elastic because of the many close substitutes for the monopolistic competitor's product. Profit maximization occurs at the production level where marginal revenue is equal to marginal cost. Short-run profits or losses are possible. In long-run equilibrium, normal profits must prevail due to easy entry into, and exit from, the industry. Economic profits attract new firms which, in turn, lessen the demand for each firm's product, driving the demand curve leftward towards the average cost curve and normal profits. (page 328)

> **LEARNING TIP:** The "cost diagram" for monopolistic competition and oligopoly is the same as that for perfect competition and monopoly—it's the demand side that's different. Draw the cost curves first, then fit in the demand and marginal revenue curves to suit your needs.

> **GRAPHING POINTER:** In monopolistic competition, the long-run graph *must* have the demand curve just touching the average cost curve. This is the profit-maximizing output level so, to be consistent, MR must equal MC at that same output level, too!

PRACTICE

4. Monopolistic competition differs from perfect competition because, unlike the perfect competitor, the monopolistically competitive firm
   A. faces a perfectly inelastic demand curve.
   B. can earn positive economic profit in the short run and in the long run.
   C. cannot earn positive economic profit even in the short run.
   D. does not have the same marginal revenue at every output level.
   Answer: D. Because demand is downward sloping for the monopolistically competitive firm, marginal revenue will lie below it.

5. Unlike a monopolist, a monopolistically competitive firm
   A. can earn positive economic profit in the short run but not in the long run.
   B. has a downward sloping marginal revenue curve.
   C. can never cover its minimum average cost in the long run.
   D. may sell to many buyers.
   Answer: A. Easy entry into the market will compete away any short-run economic profits.

6. In monopolistic competition, when profits are being maximized, the price
   A. equals marginal revenue.
   B. exceeds marginal cost.
   C. is less than marginal revenue.
   D. equals marginal cost.
   Answer: B. To maximize profits, MR = MC. Because price exceeds MR, price exceeds MC.

7. The monopolistically competitive firm's demand curve will be _____ elastic than that of the perfectly competitive firm. The monopolistically competitive market demand curve will be downward sloping, _____ the market demand curve in perfect competition.
   A. more, like.
   B. more, unlike.
   C. less, like.
   D. less, unlike.
   Answer: C. Given product differentiation, the degree of substitutability will be less than it is in perfect competition. The market demand curve is downward sloping in both market structures. The *firm's* demand curve is horizontal in perfect competition.

Use the following diagram to answer the next eight questions. This diagram depicts a monopolistically competitive firm.

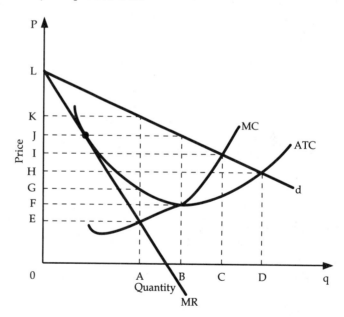

8. The profit-maximizing output level is
   A. OA.
   B. OB.
   C. OC.
   D. OD.
   Answer: A. This is the output level where MR = MC.

9. The profit-maximizing price is
    A. OE.
    B. OF.
    C. OG.
    D. OK.
    Answer: D. Use the demand curve to determine price.

10. This firm will earn a total economic profit of
    A. OA × OG.
    B. OA × OK.
    C. OA × GK.
    D. OA × EK.
    Answer: C. Total economic profit equals (P − ATC) × q.

11. This diagram depicts a monopolistic competitor in the
    A. short run, because marginal cost is less than average total cost at the profit-maximizing output level.
    B. short run, because economic profits are being earned.
    C. long run, because no fixed costs are shown.
    D. long run, because the firm is maximizing its profits.
    Answer: B. As shown in Question 10, this firm is earning an economic profit. Because of easy entry into the industry, such a circumstance cannot be maintained in the long run.

12. In the long run, firms will _____ this industry and, for the typical firm, demand will equal _____
    A. enter, marginal cost.
    B. enter, average total cost.
    C. exit, marginal cost.
    D. exit, average total cost.
    Answer: B. Firms enter, attracted by short-run economic profits. See p. 331.

13. In the long run, this firm's demand curve will shift to the _____ and become more _____
    A. right, inelastic.
    B. right, elastic.
    C. left, inelastic.
    D. left, elastic.
    Answer: D. Each firm will lose some of its market share as firms enter the industry. Demand will become more elastic because of the larger number of substitutes.

14. In the long run, this firm's marginal revenue curve will shift to the _____ and become more _____
    A. right, inelastic.
    B. right, elastic.
    C. left, inelastic.
    D. left, elastic.
    Answer: D. See the answer to Question 13 above. Demand and marginal revenue are linked. If you can't see why, review pp. 303–306.

15. Assuming that the cost curves of this typical firm remain unchanged, in the long run there will be _____ firms in this industry, each producing _____ output.
    A. more, more.
    B. more, less.
    C. fewer, more.
    D. fewer, less.
    Answer: B. Given short-run profits, more firms will enter the industry. If MR shifts left and MC remains unchanged, the profit-maximizing output level will decrease.

OBJECTIVE 4: Identify and analyze the factors in monopolistic competition that cause inefficiency and resource misallocation.

The presence of monopolistic competition has some welfare consequences. Because the firm produces where MR = MC and, because price is greater than MR, price is greater than marginal cost at the profit-maximizing output level. This is inefficient because society wants production to occur up to the point where P = MC. In the long run, because demand is downward sloping, average cost is not minimized—or, to put it another way, resources are not used to their maximum efficiency—there is excess plant capacity. Note, though, that despite the inefficiencies generated by this market structure, there are benefits springing from an extensive menu of choices. (page 332)

PRACTICE

16. Peter's Pan Pizzeria is a monopolistically competitive firm. In the short run, Peter is earning a positive economic profit by producing at the output that minimizes his long-run average cost. In the long run, Peter will _____ production and average cost will _____ (assuming constant returns to scale in the pizza industry).
    A. increase, increase.
    B. increase, remain unchanged.
    C. decrease, increase.
    D. decrease, remain unchanged.
    Answer: C. Try drawing this one. Peter is earning economic profits so other firms will enter the industry. Peter's market share will contract and his average costs will increase.

17. Monopolistic competition
    A. is efficient because entry is unrestricted and only normal profits can be earned in long-run equilibrium.
    B. is efficient because society receives as much of the good as is demanded.
    C. is not efficient because too little output is produced at too high a cost.
    D. is not efficient because there are too many small firms, each involved with a small share of the entire market.
    Answer: C. In long-run equilibrium, the typical firm does not operate where its costs per unit are minimized. Also, the profit-maximizing output level results in too little of the good being produced. Options A and D also describe perfect competition.

OBJECTIVE 5: Identify the features that characterize an oligopolistic firm and industry. Identify and discuss the behavioral implications of the models of oligopoly presented in the textbook.

Oligopoly is the market structure with a "few" interdependent firms, each having market power and exerting strong barriers to entry. The behavior of one firm in an oligopolistic industry depends on the reactions of the others. Because the actions of each firm depend on the expected reactions of its rivals, this market structure is notoriously complex. Models, such as the kinked demand curve model, have been devised to display the interdependence. Collusion and price leadership are attractive strategies. The concept of a "perfectly contestable market" suggests that, if there is easy entry into and exit from the industry and that capital is very mobile, the oligopolists will behave like perfectly competitive firms. (page 333)

L-tryptophane. In Chapter 13, the pros and cons of patents were discussed. L-tryptophane is a naturally occurring amino acid found in food (such as turkey and milk). For years it was manufactured for use in the treatment of chronic insomnia. One foreign supplier devised a new fermentation process. Unfortunately, the L-tryptophane produced was found to cause a rare disease (EMS) and all L-tryptophane was banned by the Food and Drug Administration until its use could be proved to be safe and effective. A market exists for L-tryptophane and it meets a need. However, a producer might have to spend millions of dollars on research to convince the FDA that the drug is both safe and effective. No producer is willing to undertake the expense because L-tryptophane occurs in nature and, therefore, it cannot be patented. The producer would not have a monopoly. Indeed, given that drug companies can transfer production facilities between different uses, the market would become close to a perfectly contestable market. In the meantime, L-tryptophane remains unavailable.

LEARNING TIP: The best way to see why the MR curve must have a gap in the kinked demand curve model is by extending the two demand curves back to the "price" axis and then drawing the associated MR curves from there. Remember that the MR curve is twice as steep as the demand curve, so the demand curve will, in each case, hit the horizontal axis at a quantity twice as great as that for marginal revenue. The existence of the gap is then a matter of geometry.

PRACTICE

18. Monopolistically competitive firms differ from oligopolists in that each monopolistically competitive firm
    A. faces a downward sloping demand curve, but an oligopolist does not.
    B. tries to differentiate its products from those of its rivals, but an oligopolist does not.
    C. may compete with others on price, but an oligopolist never does.
    D. is small relative to the size of its industry; an oligopolist frequently is large relative to the size of its industry.
    Answer: D. There are many firms in monopolistic competition, few in oligopoly.

19. Olga, an oligopolist, faces a kinked demand curve for her good. She believes that her competitors will _____ their prices if she lowers her price and will _____ their prices if she raises her price.
    A. lower, raise.
    B. lower, not raise.
    C. >not lower, raise.
    D. not lower, not raise.
    Answer: B. If Olga lowers her price, her rivals may lower price too—she gains a few extra customers. If Olga raises her price, her rivals may not—she loses many customers.

20. If profit-maximizing oligopolists collude, the result is the same as if the industry were
    A. monopolistically competitive.
    B. perfectly competitive.
    C. a monopoly.
    D. using price leadership.
    Answer: C. Several profit-maximizing oligopolists operating together are the equivalent of a monopolist. See p. 334.

21. For a cartel to operate,
    A. the members must be producing a homogeneous (standard) product.
    B. demand for the cartel's product must be elastic.
    C. demand for the cartel's product must be inelastic.
    D. there must be a single dominant firm.
    Answer: C. If many substitutes are available, customers can go elsewhere when there is a price hike.

22. The demand faced by the dominant firm in the price-leadership model is
    A. established first, then the demand for other firms is determined based on total market demand.
    B. equal to the sum of the demand curves of the smaller firms.
    C. determined by subtracting the supply of the smaller firms from the market demand curve.
    D. determined by subtracting the demand of the smaller firms from the market supply curve.
    Answer: C. The smaller firms are allowed to satisfy part of market demand—the dominant firm handles the rest. See p. 336.

23. A market is perfectly contestable if
    A. it contains many firms, each with a standardized product.
    B. entry to and exit from the industry are costless.
    C. each firm has a small share of the market and only normal profits are earned in long-run equilibrium.
    D. only normal profits are earned in the short run and in long-run equilibrium.
    Answer: B. The main point about contestable markets is that it is easy to get into them and to get out of them.

24. Of the following, which is most likely to have contestable markets?
    A. Nuclear power generation.
    B. Trucking.
    C. Dentistry.
    D. Automobile manufacturing.
    Answer: B. It is fairly cheap to enter and leave the trucking industry.

Use the following information and payoff matrix to answer the two questions. Lewis and Clark each run a cement business. Demand is not strong enough to justify raising price, so each is limited to maintaining the current price or reducing it. The following table gives the payoff matrix.

		Clark's Action	
		Cut price	*Maintain price*
Lewis's Action	*Cut price*	Lewis' profit $80,000	Lewis' profit $40,000
		Clark's profit $80,000	Clark's profit $60,000
	Maintain price	Lewis' profit $60,000	Lewis' profit $20,000
		Clark's profit $40,000	Clark's profit $20,000

25. Lewis's dominant strategy
    A. is to wait and see what Clark does.
    B. is to maintain her price.
    C. is to cut her price.
    D. is unknown, because it depends on her risk preference.
    Anwer: C. If Lewis maintains her price, her profit may be as low as $20,000. If she cuts her price, the lowest profit she should get is $40,000. Clark's position is identical. We are looking at a potential price war.

26. If Lewis and Clark agree to collude to improve each firm's payoff the best short-run profit-maximizing strategy for Lewis is to agree that
    A. neither firm will cut price and then to honor the agreement.
    B. neither firm will cut price and then cut price anyway.
    C. both firms will cut price and to honor the agreement.
    D. both firms will cut price and then cut price anyway.
    Answer: B. If Clark maintains his price and Lewis cheats, Lewis gains. If Clark cheats (and cuts price), then Lewis's lowering of her price is still the optimal choice for her. (Note: In the long run, Lewis and Clark would be better advised to honor their collusive agreement.)

OBJECTIVE 6: Describe ways in which an oligopolistic industry may be inefficient.

There is some debate regarding the efficiency of oligopolists. Oligopoly tends to be inefficient because output is restricted to less than that which society would prefer ($P > MC$). Firms may end up in wasteful deadlocks. Product differentiation and advertising may also be wasteful. Although they may reap economies of scale and foster technological improvements, the balance of opinion is that oligopolies allocate resources inefficiently.   (page 341)

PRACTICE

27. In oligopoly, an inefficient output level will occur except in the
    A. cartel model.
    B. perfectly contestable market model.
    C. Cournot model.
    D. kinked demand curve model.
    Answer: B. Because it is easy to enter and leave the industry, the threat of competition forces oligopolists to behave efficiently. See p. 339.

28. In the kinked demand curve model, the oligopolist is
    A. efficient, because s/he can maintain a stable price even if average cost increases.
    B. efficient, because s/he can maintain a stable price even if marginal cost increases.
    C. inefficient, because s/he fails to produce the output level at which society's welfare is maximized.
    D. inefficient, because changes in demand are not reflected by changes in price and output level.
    Answer: C. The oligopolist will produce where MR = MC. This is not where P = MC.

PRACTICE TEST

I. MULTIPLE CHOICE QUESTIONS.

Select the option that provides the single best answer.

_____ 1. In the long run, economic profits earned in a monopolistically competitive industry will cause _____ the industry and a _____ shift of the typical firm's demand curve.
A. entry into, rightward.
B. entry into, leftward.
C. exit from, rightward.
D. exit from, leftward.

_____ 2. Industrial organization economists analyze industries by considering three broad categories. Which of the following is not one of those categories?
A. Behavior.
B. Market structure.
C. Performance.
D. Efficiency.

_____ 3. Each of the following is a characteristic of monopolistic competition except
A. products are differentiated.
B. there is a large number of sellers.
C. firms will charge the same price.
D. each firm has some degree of market power.

_____ 4. Each of the following is an example of product differentiation except
A. advertising.
B. after-sales service.
C. development of "new and improved" products.
D. producing where marginal revenue equals marginal cost.

Bonnie and Clyde are caught robbing a store. They may be charged with armed robbery—a more serious crime. The police can't prove armed robbery unless one of the pair confesses to it. The following table gives the "punishment matrix."

		Clyde's Action	
		Don't Confess	*Confess*
Bonnie's Action	*Don't Confess*	Both get 2 years in jail	Clyde gets 6 months / Bonnie gets 10 years
	Confess	Clyde gets 10 years / Bonnie gets 6 months	Both get 6 years in jail

_____ 5. If both Bonnie and Clyde adopt the strategies that minimize the damage that the other can do, then
   A. neither will confess.
   B. both will confess.
   C. only Clyde will confess.
   D. only Bonnie will confess.

_____ 6. Price leadership
   A. makes tacit collusion difficult to detect.
   B. is a strategy used in monopolistic competition.
   C. is possible only when homogeneous goods are marketed.
   D. is possible only when differentiated goods are marketed.

_____ 7. A kinked demand curve
   A. discourages nonprice competition.
   B. should make prices more stable.
   C. should make prices less stable.
   D. is present only in the case of two firms—a duopoly.

_____ 8. All oligopolistic industries
   A. have significant barriers to entry.
   B. practice product differentiation.
   C. have fewer than sixteen firms.
   D. have firms large enough to exercise some control over the market price.

_____ 9. A group of firms that get together to set price and output jointly is called
   A. an oligopoly.
   B. a duopoly.
   C. a cartel.
   D. a price-leadership industry.

_____ 10. An oligopoly in which entry or exit is costless fits which theory best?
   A. The kinked demand curve model.
   B. The perfectly contestable market.
   C. Game theory.
   D. Collusion.

_____ 11. For a cartel to operate, which of the following conditions need not be present?
   A. The members must comply with the cartel's rules.
   B. The members must be firms of similar size.
   C. Demand must be inelastic.
   D. There must be few substitutes for the cartel's product.

_____ 12. The Cournot model assumes all of the following except that
   A. each firm anticipates the price movements of the other.
   B. there are only two firms in the industry.
   C. both firms maximize profits.
   D. each firm takes the output of the other as given.

The following diagram is for a typical firm in a monopolistically competitive industry. Use it to answer the next six questions.

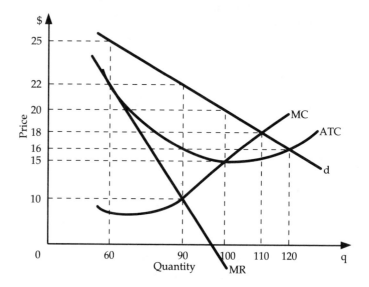

_____ 13. The profit-maximizing price is
   A. $10.
   B. $15.
   C. $18.
   D. $22.

_____ 14. The equilibrium output for this firm is
   A. 60.
   B. 90.
   C. 100.
   D. 110.

_____ 15. This firm is making an economic profit of
   A. $540.
   B. $1,040.
   C. $420.
   D. $630.

_____ 16. In the long run, we would expect to see the
   A. demand curve shift to the right and the average total cost curve shift down.
   B. demand curve shift to the left and the marginal cost curve shift up.
   C. marginal revenue curve shift to the left and the average total cost curve shift up.
   D. marginal revenue curve shift to the left and the demand curve shift to the left.

_____ 17. The efficient output level (the one that would maximize consumer welfare) is
   A. 60 units.
   B. 90 units.
   C. 100 units.
   D. 110 units.

_____ 18. In long-run equilibrium the firm produces an output of 70 units. Assuming no change in the position of the cost curves, the firm's excess capacity is
   A. 10 units.
   B. 20 units.
   C. 30 units.
   D. 40 units.

_____ 19. Advertising should make the monopolistically competitive firm's demand curve _____ and marginal revenue curve _____
   A. flatter, flatter.
   B. flatter, steeper.
   C. steeper, flatter.
   D. steeper, steeper.

_____ 20. In the kinked demand curve model, demand is relatively _____ at prices above the kink because competitors are expected _____ to a price increase.
   A. elastic, to respond.
   B. elastic, not to respond.
   C. inelastic, respond.
   D. inelastic, not to respond.

Use the following information to answer the next two questions. The Upper Crust Bakery Company, a monopolistically competitive firm, produces 10,000 loaves per day at a price of $2.00 per loaf. Marginal revenue and marginal cost are each $1.70. At that production level, total cost is $30,000, and total fixed cost is $7500.

_____ 21. Upper Crust should
   A. maintain the current output level, making short-run economic profits.
   B. maintain the current output level, despite making short-run economic losses.
   C. increase output level to the point where price equals marginal cost.
   D. shut down.

_____ 22. Relative to the individual firm's demand curve in the short run, we would predict that the surviving bakeries will face demand curves that are
   A. further to the right and more elastic.
   B. further to the right and less elastic.
   C. further to the left and more elastic.
   D. further to the left and less elastic.

_____ 23. The only oligopoly model in which price equals marginal cost in the long run is
   A. the Cournot model.
   B. the contestable markets model.
   C. the price-leadership model
   D. the kinked demand curve model.

_____ 24. A firm which makes decisions according to the maximin criterion chooses the strategy which gives the
   A. highest possible maximum loss to the firm.
   B. highest possible minimum payoff to the firm.
   C. lowest possible maximum loss to the firm.
   D. lowest possible minimum payoff to the firm.

_____ 25. You are the manager of a monopolistically competitive office-cleaning firm. The firm is in long-run equilibrium. In an effort to boost sales and to distinguish your firm from its rivals, you launch an advertising campaign. What will be the effects of the advertising campaign (assuming that it is successful) as the firm moves to a new long-run equilibrium?

A. Average cost will increase; demand and marginal revenue curves will shift right and become more elastic; price will increase.

B. Average cost will increase; demand and marginal revenue curves will shift right and become less elastic; price will increase.

C. Marginal cost will shift to the right; demand and marginal revenue curves will shift right and become more elastic; price will increase.

D. Marginal cost will shift to the right; demand and marginal revenue curves will shift right and become less elastic; price will increase.

II. APPLICATION QUESTIONS.

1. Often, economists don't have complete demand schedules and cost curves—they must make do with a few numbers. Suppose that you have the following numbers for Rose's Tea Shop, a firm in a monopolistically competitive industry.

Total Revenue = $1,200	Total Cost = $700	Price = $12
Marginal Revenue = $10	Total Variable Cost = $300	MC = $6

Explain how you know that:

a. This firm is imperfectly competitive.

b. This firm is not maximizing profit.

c. This firm is operating in the short run.

d. The demand curve is further right than it will be in the long run.

e. There is excess capacity.

f. Sketch the diagram for this firm based on your information and your economic knowledge of cost and revenue curves. Put in numerical values where you can.

2. Suppose that you have the following table of numbers for a firm. You know that the firm is operating in a monopolistically competitive industry.

OUTPUT	TOTAL COST	MARGINAL COST	QUANTITY DEMANDED	PRICE	MARGINAL REVENUE
0	$28	_____	0	$30	_____
1	40	_____	1	28	_____
2	50	_____	2	26	_____
3	58	_____	3	24	_____
4	68	_____	4	22	_____
5	80	_____	5	20	_____
6	94	_____	6	18	_____
7	110	_____	7	16	_____
8	130	_____	8	14	_____
9	160	_____	9	12	_____

a. Calculate the marginal cost and marginal revenue values at each output level and enter them in the table.
b. Determine the profit-maximizing price and output level.
c. Calculate total economic profit.
d. Describe what will happen to the number of firms in this industry in the long run, and explain why.
e. Describe what will happen to this firm's demand curve in the long run, and explain why.

3. Watch ten ads on TV; listen to ten on the radio; read ten in a weekly magazine and another ten in the daily newspaper. Does the amount of *information* in each differ? Which medium seems to contain the most information? Which the least? Do the different media attract a similar mix of monopolistically competitive and oligopolistic firms? In which medium is oligopoly most prominent? In which are monopolistically competitive firms most important? Why do you think these differences occur?

4. Suppose you obtain a license to sell ice cream on the beach. There is only one other licensed seller of ice cream on the beach. How would you respond to her/his presence? Where would you locate? How would you make your pricing decisions? Would you compete?

5. Lou and Howard own a small monopolistically competitive pizza parlor—The Nice Slice. Because of declining sales they have hired you as a consultant to examine their pricing and advertising strategy. You are provided with some information regarding daily demand at The Nice Slice under three conditions—when there is no advertising (which is the current situation); when only The Nice Slice advertises; when all pizzerias advertise. You are also told that, when The Nice Slice advertises, it costs a flat fee of $20 per day.

PRICE/ PIZZA	NO ADVERTISING		NICE SLICE ADVERTISES		ALL PIZZERIAS ADVERTISE	
	QUANTITY DEMANDED	MARGINAL REVENUE	QUANTITY DEMANDED	MARGINAL REVENUE	QUANTITY DEMANDED	MARGINAL REVENUE
$16	3		7		5	
$15	4	_____	8	_____	6	_____
$14	5	_____	9	_____	7	_____
$13	6	_____	10	_____	8	_____
$12	7	_____	11	_____	9	_____
$11	8	_____	12	_____	10	_____
$10	9	_____	13	_____	11	_____

a. Complete the table.

Now that you have the revenue information, you ask Lou and Howard about their costs. Howard tells you that each pizza costs a constant $4 to make. Advertising costs are not included.

b. Determine the profit-maximizing daily output level and price for The Nice Slice under each of the three advertising conditions.

CONDITION	PRICE	OUTPUT
No advertising	_____	_____
Nice Slice advertises	_____	_____
All pizzerias advertise	_____	_____

c. Calculate economic profit of The Nice Slice under each of the three conditions.

CONDITION	TR	TC	PROFIT
No advertising	_____	_____	_____
Nice Slice advertises	_____	_____	_____
All pizzerias advertise	_____	_____	_____

d. Complete your assignment by writing a brief report to Lou and Howard advising them on the best advertising strategy to adopt.

6. You have been called in to analyze the pricing strategy of Chewsday Gum, a brand of bubble gum operating in an oligopolistic non-collusive industry. You are given the following information regarding the firm's demand schedule. The firm's price is currently $1.40 per pack of gum. If the firm assumes that a price change will provoke no matching price change from rivals, the demand schedule is d1. If, however, any price change prompts a retaliatory price change from rivals, the relevant demand schedule is d2.

	(d1)		(d2)	
PRICE	QUANTITY DEMANDED	MARGINAL REVENUE	QUANTITY DEMANDED	MARGINAL REVENUE
$2.20	0		0	
$2.10	25	_____	0	_____
$2.00	50	_____	0	_____
$1.80	100	_____	0	_____
$1.60	150	_____	0	_____
$1.50	175	_____	100	_____
$1.40	200	_____	200	_____
$1.30	225	_____	300	_____
$1.20	250	_____	400	_____
$1.00	300	_____	600	_____

a. Complete the table.

b. Draw the kinked demand curve diagram below.

Jack and Ruby, the owners of Chewsday, tell you that their marginal cost is constant at $1.20. Total fixed costs are an additional $50.

c. Are Jack and Ruby making an economic profit?

d. Are Jack and Ruby maximizing profit?

e. Jack and Ruby ask for your recommendations. What would you suggest?

   i. Should they close down in the short run? Why?

   ii. What might happen if they raise their price by 10¢?

7. Examine the following graph, which depicts a monopolistically competitive firm.

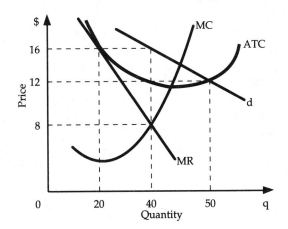

The profit-maximizing output level is _____ . The price is $ _____ . Marginal revenue is $ _____ . Total revenue is $ _____ . Total cost is $ _____ . Total profit is $ _____ .

8. The firm represented by the following diagram is either monopolistically competitive or a monopoly. The firm is currently producing at output level A.

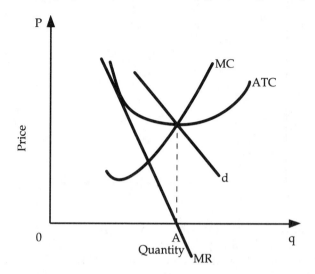

a. At output level A, is the firm maximizing profits?
b. What price is this firm charging currently? (Sketch your answer on the graph and label the price P_1.)
c. If different from P_1, sketch in the profit-maximizing price as P_2.
d. Is this a short-run or long-run situation, or can't you tell?
e. This is an *imperfectly* competitive firm. How do you know?
f. If this is the long run, what kind of imperfectly competitive industry is this, or can't you tell?
g. If the firm rises production past level A, what will happen to total revenue?

9. This exercise is a check on your understanding of graphs, the concept of the long run, and of monopolistic competition.

The following diagram is meant to depict a monopolistically competitive firm in long-run equilibrium (i.e. when MR = MC, ATC = Price) with p* and q* being the equilibrium quantity and price respectively. However, if this is the situation that is meant to be shown, there are several errors. Find as many errors as possible and explain, based on your economic understanding, why they are errors.

10. Here is a list of the major companies in the fast-food industry:
    a. McDonald's
    b. Burger King
    c. Wendy's
    d. KFC
    e. Hardee's

    Here is a list of characteristics for each fast-food restaurant chain:
    U. The restaurant with the best breakfasts.
    W. The place to get chicken.
    X. The fast-food place that kids love. The number one fast-food restaurant.
    Y. The fast-food restaurant for those without children looking for good values.
    Z. The other big fast-food restaurant.

    Note that the list of characteristics does not include advertising slogans, names of products, or corporate symbols. Despite that, match up the restaurant chain with its description.

III. ECONOMICS EXPLORER.

Use the tenth module ("Strategy and Choice") from the Economics Explorer software if you wish to do more work on game theory.

ANSWERS AND SOLUTIONS

PRACTICE TEST

I. SOLUTIONS TO MULTIPLE CHOICE QUESTIONS

1. B. Economic profits attract new firms. Each firm will have a smaller market share, depicted by a leftward shift of the demand curve.
2. D. Efficiency is a yardstick of performance, rather than an organizational classification.
3. C. Typically, monopolistic firms, e.g., restaurants, do not charge the same price.
4. D. Producing where MR = MC is a guide to maximizing profits. It has nothing to do with product differentiation.
5. B. If Bonnie confesses, Clyde would minimize the damage by having confessed too. Six years is better than 10. Bonnie would argue similarly.
6. A. See p. 336.
7. B. The profit-maximizing oligopolist will produce where MR = MC. Because the MR curve has a gap at the existing output level, MC can increase or decrease and the same profit-maximizing output level and price will be sustained.
8. D. Influence over market price is a common feature. Many oligopolistic models assume high barriers to entry—the perfectly contestable markets model does not.
9. C. See p. 334. See OPEC!
10. B. In this theory, firms must have mobile and transferable resources that can be switched from one use, and one industry, to another. See p. 339.
11. B. In OPEC (a very successful and long-lasting cartel), some member countries, such as Saudi Arabia, are very large oil producers while others, such as Gabon and Ecuador, are comparatively small.
12. A. In the Cournot model, output is given. The two firms in the duopoly do not guess each other's price movements.
13. D. Profits are maximized where MR = MC. Given the output level, the equilibrium price, based on the position of the demand curve, will be $22.
14. B. Profits are maximized at the output level where MR = MC.
15. A. Economic profit = (P − ATC) × q = ($22 − $16)90 = $540.

16. D. The typical firm is earning an economic profit in the short run. The presence of economic profits will attract new firms, resulting in a reduction in each firm's market share. This change will affect demand and marginal revenue. See p. 331.

17. D. Consumer welfare is maximized at the output level where P = MC.

18. C. Average costs are minimized at an output level of 100 units. If, in the long run, the firm produces only 70 units, it has an excess capacity of 30.

19. D. Advertising is intended to make consumers more interested in purchasing a product and in making other rivals appear less attractive. At a given output level, demand should become less elastic (steeper curve), and this will have a similar effect on marginal revenue.

20. B. If the firm increases price, the assumption is made that rivals will not increase price. This would lead consumers to leave the firm that has raised its price in search of relatively low price alternatives.

21. D. TVC = TC − TFC = $30,000 − $7500 = $22,500. AVC = TVC/q = $22500/10,000 = $2.25. Because P is less than AVC, the firm should shut down.

22. B. As firms, such as Upper Crust, leave the industry, the market will be divided among a smaller number of firms, each with fewer substitutes.

23. B. See p. 339.

24. C. See p. 339.

25. B. Average cost will increase; demand and marginal revenue curves will shift right and become less elastic as the firm becomes more "different" from its rivals; price will increase (because costs have risen).

II. SOLUTIONS TO APPLICATION QUESTIONS

1. Total Revenue = $1200   Total Cost = $700   Price = $12
   Marginal Revenue = $10   Total Variable Cost = $300   MC = $6

   a. This firm is imperfectly competitive because the demand curve is downward sloping. (P > MR)

   b. This firm is not maximizing profit because MR ≠ MC. (Because MR is greater than MC, the firm should expand production.)

   c. We know that this firm is operating in the short run for two reasons. First, there are fixed costs (which can occur only in the short run) because TC − TVC. Second, this monopolistically competitive firm is making economic profits, which can only happen in the short run.

   d. The demand curve is further right than it will be in the long run because, as new firms enter attracted by the economic profits, the firm's market share will erode.

   e. There is excess capacity because the firm is not producing where average cost is minimized. If P = $12 and TR = $1200, the firm must be selling 100 units. If TC = $700, average total cost must be $7, which is higher than MC. If the extra cost is less than the average cost, then the average cost must be falling and, therefore, not being minimized.

   f. See the diagram below.

2. a. See the table below.

OUTPUT	TOTAL COST	MARGINAL COST	QUANTITY DEMANDED	PRICE	MARGINAL REVENUE
0	$ 28		0	$30	
		12			$28
1	$ 40		1	$28	
		10			$24
2	$ 50		2	$26	
		8			$20
3	$ 58		3	$24	
		10			$16
4	$ 68		4	$22	
		12			$12
5	$ 80		5	$20	
		14			$ 8
6	$ 94		6	$18	
		16			$ 4
7	$110		7	$16	
		20			$ 0
8	$130		8	$14	
		30			$−4
9	$160		9	$12	

  b. 5; 20.

  c. $20 ($100 − $80).

  d. In the long run, firms will enter this industry, attracted by the higher-than-normal profits.

  e. The demand curve will shift over to the left and become less inelastic because of the presence of more (and closer) substitutes. This move will continue until the demand curve is just tangential to the average total cost curve and the firm is earning normal profits.

3. You should find that different companies and different types of companies use different media. National oligopolies (Coke, Exxon, Procter and Gamble) use TV and magazines, for instance. Radio and newspapers tend to attract more local and more monopolistically competitive advertisers. Advertising represents a barrier to entry; by advertising lavishly, perhaps oligopolies prevent the entrance of credible rivals.

4. f you believe your ice cream to be as good as, or better than, that of your competitor, you should locate in the middle of the beach. This should be the most convenient spot for your customers and should not give your rival an overall advantage. You should get a 50% share of the customers. Any other location will bring you fewer customers. If you fear that you might lose in a price war with your rival, a quiet piece of negotiation might produce a cartel from which both sellers would gain.

5. a.

PRICE/ PIZZA	NO ADVERTISING QUANTITY DEMANDED	MARGINAL REVENUE	NICE SLICE ADVERTISES QUANTITY DEMANDED	MARGINAL REVENUE	ALL PIZZERIAS ADVERTISE QUANTITY DEMANDED	MARGINAL REVENUE
$16	3		7		5	
		$12		$ 8		$10
$15	4		8		6	
		$10		$ 6		$ 8
$14	5		9		7	
		$ 8		$ 4		$ 6
$13	6		10		8	
		$ 6		$ 2		$ 4
$12	7		11		9	
		$ 4		$ 0		$ 2
$11	8		12		10	
		$ 2		$−2		$ 0
$10	9		13		11	

  b. See the table below. Values are derived by setting MR = MC = 4.

CONDITION	PRICE	OUTPUT
No advertising	$11	8
Nice Slice advertises	$13	10
All pizzerias advertise	$12	9

c.

CONDITION	TR	TC	PROFIT
No advertising	$ 88	$32	$56
Nice Slice advertises	$130	$40 + $20	$70
All pizzerias advertise	$108	$36 + $20	$52

d. If The Nice Slice chooses to advertise, its short-run profits will be $70 per day, up from the current level of $56 per day. However, this is based on the assumption that the rival pizzerias do not retaliate by advertising too. If they do retaliate, The Nice Slice will end up with an economic profit of $52 per day, *less* than the current level of $56 per day. Because the downside loss is slight ($4 per day) and the gain substantial ($14 per day), advertising is a good strategy. The less probable it is that rivals will retaliate, the more advisable it is to advertise.

6. a.

PRICE	(d1) QUANTITY DEMANDED	MARGINAL REVENUE	(d2) QUANTITY DEMANDED	MARGINAL REVENUE
$2.20	0		0	
$2.10	25	$2.10	0	
$2.00	50	$1.90	0	
$1.80	100	$1.60	0	
$1.60	150	$1.20	0	
$1.50	175	$0.90	100	$1.50
$1.40	200	$0.70	200	$1.30
$1.30	225	$0.50	300	$1.10
$1.20	250	$0.30	400	$0.90
$1.00	300	$0.00	600	$0.60

b. See the diagram below.

c. TC = TFC + TVC. TFC = $50. TVC = $1.20 × 200 = $240. TC = $290. TR = P × q = $1.40 × 200 = $280. Chewsday is making an economic loss of $10.

d. Yes. MR is in the range between $0.70 and $1.30, as is MC ($1.20).

e.   i.   They should not close down in the short run—their price is high enough to cover their variable costs.

   ii.   If they raise their price by 10¢, it is difficult to predict what will happen. It depends on the reaction of their rivals.

   If their rivals do not react, they will operate along demand curve d1, with quantity demanded of 175, and marginal revenue of 90¢.

   TC = TFC + TVC. TFC = $50. TVC = $1.20 × 170 = $210. TC = $260.
   TR = P × q = $1.50 × 175 = $262.50.
   Chewsday, which is not maximizing at this point, (MR < MC) would make an economic loss of $20.00.

   If their rivals do react, they will operate along demand curve d2, with quantity demanded of 100, and marginal revenue of $1.50.
   TC = TFC + TVC. TFC = $50. TVC = $1.20 × 100 = $120. TC = $170.
   TR = P × q = $1.50 × 100 = $150.
   Chewsday, which is not maximizing at this point, (MR < MC) would make an economic loss of $20.00.

   Raising price by 10¢ will still result in losses. How great those losses will be depends on the reaction of Chewsday's rivals.

7.   a.   q* = 40. p* = $16. MR = $8. TR = P × q = $16 × 40 = $640. TC = ATC × q = $12 × 40 = $480. Economic profit = TR − TC = $640 − $480 = $160.

8.   a.   No. (MR ≠ MC)
   b.   See the following diagram.
   c.   See the following diagram.

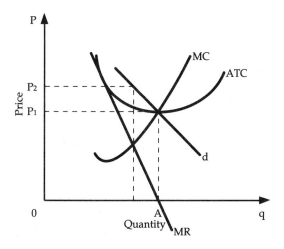

   d.   We can't tell yet if it's a long-run or short-run situation. See answer f below.
   e.   The demand curve is downward sloping, so it can't be perfectly competitive.
   f.   It must be a monopoly. Monopolistically competitive firms make only normal profits in long-run equilibrium.
   g.   Total revenue will fall because marginal revenue is negative.

9.   Error 1: The MC curve should intersect both the ATC and the AVC curves at their minimum points. The "average-marginal" rule determines this.

   Error 2: The profit-maximizing output level (q*, not Q*) occurs, as shown, where MR = MC, but the demand and ATC intersection is inconsistent. At higher output levels, demand exceeds ATC, indicating economic profits whereas, at "Q*," only normal profits occur.

   Error 3: The existence of economic profits indicates that this is not a long-run situation. The existence of fixed costs (ATC − AVC) also reveals this to be a short-run diagram.

   Note: If you had trouble with this problem, review Application 5 in Chapter 13.

10. Here is my list, based on my perceptions.
    a. X.   b. Z.   c. Y.   d. W.   e. U.

    Even if your selections differ from those given here, it is of interest that you could distinguish among restaurant chains. What differences do you perceive and *where* do you think these differing perceptions have come from? They have probably been guided by effective Madison Avenue advertising campaigns. Burger King's apparent lack of image may pose a problem to the company.

ANTITRUST POLICY AND REGULATION

15

OBJECTIVES: POINT BY POINT

After completing this chapter, you should be able to accomplish the objectives listed below.

General Comment

There's a lot of history and detail in this chapter—avoid being caught up in it. Make a time-line of the main pieces of antitrust legislation; note the practices they tried to outlaw, and tie these into your knowledge of monopoly and oligopoly behavior. Government bodies and subsequent acts to plug loopholes can be added to your potted history. This will help you to detect the evolution in antitrust legislation. Note the general pattern of increased legislative activity followed by more recent declines, especially in regulation.

Remember: antitrust is meant to promote competition; regulation intends to restrict competition. Both policies are intended to promote economic efficiency.

OBJECTIVE 1: Identify the two major policy positions adopted by the government with respect to promoting/restricting competition within an industry exhibiting monopoly characteristics.

When imperfect competition fails to produce the efficient level of output, the government may choose to intervene to improve the allocation of society's resources. There are two apparently conflicting government stances—first, promotion of competition and restriction of market power through *trustbusting legislation*, and second, restriction of competition by *regulation* of industries.   (page 347)

PRACTICE

1. The policy positions taken by the government with respect to imperfectly competitive industries are to _____ competition through antitrust legislation and to _____ competition through regulation.
    A. promote, promote.
    B. promote, restrict.
    C. restrict, promote.
    D. restrict, restrict.
    Answer: B. Broadly, antitrust legislation breaks up large companies into smaller units or prevents mergers, while regulation establishes a single supplier of a product and then controls the firm's behavior.

OBJECTIVE 2: List and explain the contributions of the various pieces of antitrust legislation passed since the Civil War. Name the two government organizations charged with combating antitrust violations. Give examples of outlawed antitrust conduct and explain how each restrains competition.

Antitrust legislation began in 1887 with the creation of the Interstate Commerce Commission, which monitored the railroads, and the Sherman Act of 1890, which made monopoly and trade restraints illegal. The 1914 Clayton Act strengthened

Sherman and made clear which forms of trade restraint were illegal. The Federal Trade Commission was also created at this time to investigate unfair competition. Several lesser pieces of legislation addressed other specific issues. (page 349)

Enforcement of antitrust laws is done by the FTC and the Antitrust Division of the Justice Department. Private citizens can also bring antitrust suits. The courts can impose civil and criminal penalties and specifically forbid illegal actions in the future. (page 354)

LEARNING TIP: Two big chunks of the chapter list the arguments for and against antitrust enforcement and regulation. Simply make lists of these.

PRACTICE

2. The _____ Act (1890) declared monopoly and trade restraints illegal.
   A. Sherman.
   B. Clayton.
   C. Wheeler-Lea.
   D. Willis-Graham.
   Answer: A. See p. 349.

3. The _____ Act restricted mergers and outlawed price discrimination, and tying contracts.
   A. Sherman.
   B. Clayton.
   C. Wheeler-Lea.
   D. Willis-Graham.
   Answer: B. See p. 350.

4. False and deceptive advertising is prosecuted by the
   A. Federal Trade Commission.
   B. Federal Truth in Advertising Commission.
   C. Federal Drug Administration.
   D. Trade Section of the Justice Department.
   Answer: A. See p. 350.

5. A merger of firms producing goods at the same stage in the production process is
   A. a horizontal merger.
   B. a conglomerate merger.
   C. an illegal merger.
   D. a vertical merger.
   Answer: A. See the definition given with the Celler-Kefauver Act.

6. Jason Wool Spinners merges with Argonaut Wool Spinners; this is a _____ merger. Todd Wool Spinners merges with Golden Fleece Wool Farms; this is a _____ merger.
   A. horizontal, horizontal.
   B. horizontal, vertical.
   C. vertical, horizontal.
   D. vertical, vertical.
   Answer: B. Jason and Argonaut are at the same stage in the production process. Todd and Golden Fleece are at different stages in production.

7. Antitrust laws are based on the premise that
   A. regulation is the most efficient form of market control.
   B. competition is the best way to achieve efficiency.
   C. public ownership of the private means of production gives superior results than ownership by self-interested profit-maximizers.
   D. as a firm increases its market share, it is able to reap the benefits of economies of scale.
   Answer: B. See p. 360.

8. The result of perfect price discrimination by a monopolist is
   A. less efficient than if all customers were charged the same price.
   B. more efficient because the monopolist's profits increase.
   C. the most efficient output level, with consumer surplus being zero.
   D. the most efficient output level, with consumer surplus being maximized.
   Answer: C. See p. 360.

OBJECTIVE 3: Explain what the Herfindahl-Hirschman Index is, how it is calculated, and how it is used in antitrust matters.

The *Herfindahl-Hirschman Index* (HHI) is a measure of competition and market structure and is used as a guide to decide whether mergers are permitted. The percentage market share of each firm is squared, and the values totaled. In general, the higher the score, the greater the degree of concentration. If the score is less than 1000, the industry is thought of as unconcentrated—mergers would go unopposed. In the range 1000 to 1800, any proposed merger that would increase the index by 100 or more would be challenged. In an industry with an HHI of greater than 1800 (a concentrated industry), any merger pushing the index up by 50 points or more would be challenged. (page 352)

> **Example:** Industry A has 100 firms, each having a 1% share. The HHI is 100 and a merger between any two firms would be unopposed. Industry B has 100 firms, with 99 each having a .5% share and the other having a 50.5% share. The HHI would be 2575. A merger between the big firm and any one other firm would be challenged because it would increase the index by 50.5.

PRACTICE

9. The HHI for refrigerators is 2253 while that for women's dresses is 20. A merger between refrigerator producers would _____ be challenged. A merger between producers of women's dresses would _____ be challenged.
   A. certainly, certainly.
   B. certainly, not.
   C. not, certainly.
   D. not, not.
   Answer: B. If the HHI exceeds 1800, a merger is automatically challenged. If the HHI is less than 1000, the merger will be unopposed.

10. Leonard, Adolph, Julius, Herbert, and Milton each run one of the 5 firms in Industry A. The firms have equal market shares. The Herfindahl-Hirschman Index is
    A. 25.
    B. 100.
    C. 500.
    D. 2000.
    Answer: D. $20^2 \times 5 = 2000$.

11. Leonard, Adolph, Julius, Herbert, and Milton each run one of the 5 firms in Industry A. The firms have equal market shares. A merger between Julius and Milton would be
   A. automatically challenged by the Justice Department.
   B. challenged by the Justice Department if the HHI rose by more than 100.
   C. challenged by the Justice Department if the HHI rose by more than 200.
   D. unopposed.
   Answer: A. Because the HHI is greater than 1800, the merger would be challenged automatically.

OBJECTIVE 4: Outline the avenues for the enforcement of antitrust law. State the arguments for and against enforcement.

Antitrust actions may be initiated by the Justice Department, the Federal Trade Commission, or private citizens. Many suits are settled with the signing of a consent decree. Penalties for breaches of antitrust law include fines and imprisonment. (page 354)

Lobbyists acting together, labor unions, sports organizations, and regulated industries are exempt from antitrust laws.

Proponents of more aggressive enforcement argue that anticompetitive behavior, such as price fixing, price discrimination, and unfair or deceptive practices, reduces the benefits flowing from the market system.

Opponents of vigorous antitrust action argue that enforcement is directed against firms that have gained an advantage through successful competition—a "hot" example in 1998 is the case of Microsoft's free provision of its browser. In addition, by weakening large domestic firms, antitrust enforcement may make global competition more difficult.

OBJECTIVE 5: Discuss the types of price discrimination and their consequences.

With *third-degree price discrimination*, the seller identifies different groups of sellers and charges different prices for the same good. The price differences may be called discounts or bonuses, implying that the buyer is getting a good or service for less than others who must pay the regular price. *Perfect price discrimination* occurs when a seller charges each buyer the maximum price that s/he would pay—consumer surplus is completely removed. (page 360)

To work well, the seller must be able to prevent resale and must be able to identify buyers who will pay different prices. Doctors and lawyers, who provide personal services, often charge clients different prices. Senior citizens or students may receive discounts at local stores.

> **LEARNING TIP:** Think of price discrimination as a way of removing consumer surplus. Consumer surplus, which is the triangular area between the price and the demand curve, indicates how much the buyer would pay if s/he had to. The more effectively the firm can identify buyers who value its good highly, the more chance it has to collect the surplus.

PRACTICE

12. Which of the following is not an example of price discrimination?
    A. Different prices are charged for first-class and second-class mail.
    B. Children are admitted free to the circus but adults must pay the full price.
    C. Military personnel receive a 10% discount in a local steakhouse.
    D. Gamma Airlines offers "frequent fliers" a reduced price on selected flights.
    Answer: A. Different services are being offered. In the other cases, the same good or service is being sold at different prices.

Use the following diagram, which shows revenue and cost information for Gamma Airlines, to answer the next question.

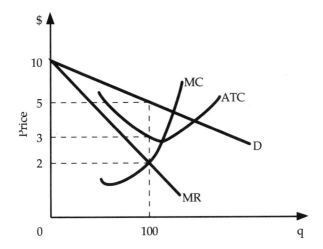

13. If Gamma maximizes its profits without price discrimination, economic profits will be _____ . With third-degree price discrimination, economic profits could be as great as _____
    A. $200, $450.
    B. $200, $700.
    C. $300, $550.
    D. $300, $800.
    Answer: A. Output is 100 where MR = MC and price is $2 higher than ATC. With price discrimination, the consumer surplus "triangle," which represents additional revenue of $250, can be collected at no additional cost.

OBJECTIVE 6: Detail the approaches the government can take to regulate monopolies and the problems behind the regulation of monopolies. Give the arguments for and against regulation of monopolies and indicate the recent trend in the conduct of regulation.

Given large economies of scale, efficiency would require having only one firm—a natural monopoly—and then regulating it to prevent abuse of its monopoly power. With a natural monopoly, the government has three options:
    a. set the efficient price (P = MC) and provide a subsidy, or
    b. set price equal to average cost, or
    c. impose a two-part tariff on each user of the monopoly's good or service.

There are problems, however—trucking, airlines, and telecommunications (among others) have all been regulated although none, in fact, is a natural monopoly. Lack of information, lack of incentives to be efficient, and a surfeit of nonprice competition dog the regulated industries. The Averch-Johnson effect refers to the tendency of a monopoly to accumulate excessive amounts of capital. Regulation has fallen from favor and gone into a decline in recent years—even the classic natural monopoly, electricity, is slated for deregulation. (page 364)

Effectiveness: Don't assume that government intervention always has the desired effect—the Averch-Johnson effect should warn you that it may not!

Here's another example. The Robinson-Patman Act (1936) or "Chain Store Law" was a legitimate attempt to enhance competition by supporting small retailers. The Act made it illegal to give quantity discounts or extra service to large retail buyers such as Sears because small stores wouldn't be able to compete. The intent of the law was good, but think about it—small, inefficient firms were being guaranteed a place in the market. The Robinson-Patman Act (1936) is a classic example of good intentions gone wrong.

PRACTICE

14. The exception to the rule that competitive markets are the most efficient markets is that of the
    A. contestable market.
    B. natural monopoly.
    C. monopolistically competitive firm that does not practice price discrimination.
    D. cross-subsidizing oligopolist.
    Answer: B. Natural monopolies gain benefits from economies of scale that, with competition, would be lost.

15. The _____ involves setting price equal to marginal cost and providing a subsidy out of general government revenues.
    A. average-cost pricing strategy.
    B. efficient price strategy.
    C. third-degree price discrimination strategy.
    D. fixed cost service charge.
    Answer: B. See p. 365.

16. The Averch-Johnson effect occurs in the presence of
    A. privatization, as stockholders attempt to maximize dividends.
    B. horizontal mergers, as firms accumulate additional productive capacity.
    C. the threat of antitrust action, as firms scale back profits.
    D. regulation, as the firm builds more capital than is necessary.
    Answer: D. The Averch-Johnson effect refers to the tendency of regulated monopolies to accumulate more capital than is needed.

17. The Averch-Johnson effect typically occurs if
    A. profits are high enough in a regulated industry to justify additional capital accumulation.
    B. profits are so low in a regulated industry that additional capital accumulation is necessary.
    C. the regulated industry's rate of return is based on a percentage of fixed costs.
    D. the regulated industry's rate of return is based on a percentage of variable costs.
    Answer: C. See p. 366.

A Look Ahead: Government Intervention

Antitrust enforcement and regulation are only two roles that the government plays in the economy. The next three chapters explore other areas of government involvement: externalities and public goods (Chapter 16), income distribution (Chapter 17), and taxation (Chapter 18).

PRACTICE TEST

I. MULTIPLE CHOICE QUESTIONS.

Select the option that provides the single best answer.

_____ 1. Which of the following is not definitely illegal under antitrust statutes?
A. Tying contracts.
B. Collusion to fix price.
C. Horizontal mergers.
D. Purchase of the physical assets of a competing firm to lessen competition.

_____ 2. The Wheeler-Lea Act
A. caused specific merger guidelines to be issued by the Supreme Court.
B. reaffirmed the right of "benevolent" monopolies to exist.
C. made illegal "deceptive" methods of competition.
D. made price discrimination, in some instances, illegal.

_____ 3. The Clayton Act outlawed each of the following except
A. tying contracts.
B. vertical mergers.
C. horizontal mergers.
D. price discrimination.

_____ 4. A Herfindahl-Hirschman Index of 900 would classify an industry as
A. unconcentrated.
B. mildly concentrated.
C. moderately concentrated.
D. concentrated.

_____ 5. For third-degree price discrimination to be effective, all of the following conditions must be present except
A. the ability to prevent resale.
B. the ability to identify correctly different groups of consumers.
C. a downward sloping demand curve.
D. an ATC which reaches its minimum point at some output greater than the profit-maximizing output.

_____ 6. An industry has a Herfindahl-Hirschman Index of 1600. A merger would be
A. unopposed.
B. opposed, if it raised the index by more than 50.
C. opposed, if it raised the index by more than 100.
D. opposed in all circumstances.

_____ 7. Regulation is made more difficult by of each of the following except
A. lack of information about the industry.
B. lack of incentives to be efficient.
C. excessive nonprice competition.
D. horizontal mergers.

_____ 8. Supporters of antitrust legislation suggest each of the following is a benefit except
A. antitrust laws operate as a deterrent to actions against the public interest.
B. price discrimination intended to lessen competition is illegal.
C. the tendency to accumulate more capital than needed is outlawed.
D. deliberate deception is illegal.

_____ 9. Opponents of antitrust enforcement have suggested that it does all of the following except
   A. penalize success.
   B. reduce the ability to compete against domestic companies.
   C. reduce the ability to compete against foreign companies.
   D. limit the ability or willingness to undertake research and development.

_____ 10. In recent years, which one of the following has been least influenced by deregulation and the reduction of monopoly power due to technological change?
   A. The Interstate Commerce Commission.
   B. The Civil Aeronautics Board.
   C. The Federal Energy Regulatory Commission.
   D. The state public utility commissions.

_____ 11. Most natural monopolies have _____ fixed costs and _____ marginal costs.
   A. high, high.
   B. high, low.
   C. low, high.
   D. low, low.

_____ 12. Jack Swindell of Swindell and Chita (attorneys) charges $500 to attend to some probate matters for Olaf Olson. He charges Olga Oppenheimer $100 for the same services. This is an example of
   A. price fixing.
   B. competitive pricing.
   C. price discrimination.
   D. sex discrimination.

_____ 13. Supporters of the breakup of AT&T have claimed all of the following except that
   A. long-distance rates have fallen sharply since the breakup.
   B. long-distance subsidies to AT&T increased AT&T's efficiency.
   C. local subsidies have been eliminated over time.
   D. regulators had built local subsidies into long-distance rates.

Use the following diagram, of a natural monopoly, to answer the next three questions.

_____ 14. The profit-maximizing output level is _____ units, with a price of
   A. 60, $4.
   B. 80, $3.
   C. 100, $2.
   D. 120, $1.

_____ 15. At the most efficient output level, ATC is $1.75. To produce at this level the company would require a subsidy of at least
   A. $75.00
   B. $90.00.
   C. $150.00
   D. $350.00.

_____ 16. At the output level where the company just receives a normal return on invested capital, the price would be $ _____ and _____ units would be produced.
   A. 4, 60.
   B. 3, 80.
   C. 2, 100.
   D. 1, 120.

_____ 17. In an industry where 1 firm has a 40% market share and 2 others each have a 30% market share, the Herfindahl-Hirschman Index is
   A. 300.
   B. 2500.
   C. 3400.
   D. 5200.

_____ 18. The cable television industry is regulated according to the principle of average cost pricing. A firm in this industry
   A. will earn economic profits, although less than the amount it would have received without regulation.
   B. will produce at the efficient output level.
   C. will require a subsidy to continue in operation.
   D. will earn a rate of return equal to normal profits.

_____ 19. Price discrimination is illegal under the Clayton Act because
   A. it is unfair.
   B. it is inefficient.
   C. it requires the prevention of voluntary exchange.
   D. it reduces competition.

_____ 20. Which of the following is exempt from antitrust legislation?
   A. Sam's Tomato Farm (a proprietorship).
   B. Swindell and Chita (a law partnership).
   C. Exxon.
   D. National Football League.

II. APPLICATION QUESTIONS.

1. In 1996, the U.S. airline industry is radically transformed. Following a vicious price war and a series of mergers, one company (Untied Airlines) has emerged as the sole survivor. Untied offers a one-way trip from Orlando to Washington. The marginal cost for each passenger is $40. Total fixed costs are $500,000.

Because of your previous success with Untied (Chapter 13), the company once more hires you as a consultant on pricing policy. Your research identifies two types of passenger—well-paid executives and frugal students/tourists. The demand by each of these types of customer is shown below.

PRICE OF ONE-WAY TRIP TICKETS	ONE-WAY TRIPS DEMANDED PER YEAR			"TOTAL" DEMAND'S MARGINAL REVENUE
	EXECUTIVES	STUDENTS/TOURISTS	TOTAL	
$140	7,000	0	___	
$130	8,000	0	___	___
$120	9,000	1,000	___	___
$110	10,000	2,000	___	___
$100	11,000	3,000	___	___
$ 90	12,000	4,000	___	___
$ 80	13,000	5,000	___	___
$ 70	14,000	6,000	___	___
$ 60	15,000	7,000	___	___

Note: In each case, the demand curve is a straight line and can extend beyond this price range.
a. Complete the table by calculating total demand by both types of passenger and the associated marginal revenue values.
b. Determine the profit-maximizing output level and price.
c. Calculate the number of executives who will fly at this price.
d. Calculate the monetary value of the executives' consumer surplus.
e. Calculate the number of students/tourists who will fly at this price.
f. Calculate the monetary value of the students/tourists' consumer surplus.
g. Calculate the total monetary value of the passengers' consumer surplus.
h. Determine the level of economic profits.

Untied wishes to change its "one price for all" pricing policy in order to increase profits.

i. State, in words, a feasible policy to maximize Untied's profits. (Hint: Think of Untied as two firms, one servicing executives, the other servicing students and tourists.)
j. Complete the following table.

PRICE OF ONE-WAY TRIP TICKETS	ONE-WAY TRIPS DEMANDED PER YEAR		EXECUTIVE MARGINAL REVENUE	STUDENT/TOURIST MARGINAL REVENUE
	EXECUTIVES	STUDENT/TOURISTS		
$140	7,000	0		
$130	8,000	0	___	___
$120	9,000	1,000	___	___
$110	10,000	2,000	___	___
$100	11,000	3,000	___	___
$ 90	12,000	4,000	___	___
$ 80	13,000	5,000	___	___
$ 70	14,000	6,000	___	___
$ 60	15,000	7,000	___	___

k. Determine the profit-maximizing output level and price for executives.
l. Calculate the monetary value of the executives' consumer surplus.
m. Determine the profit-maximizing output level and price for students/tourists.
n. Calculate the monetary value of the students/tourists' consumer surplus.

    o. Calculate the total monetary value of the passengers' consumer surplus.

    p. Determine the level of economic profits derived from executives.

    q. Determine the level of economic profits derived from students/tourists.

    r. Determine the overall level of economic profit and compare this with the results before price discrimination.

    s. Write a brief report to Untied's board of Directors explaining why, or why not, you believe price discrimination is a plausible option.

Suppose that Untied's Board of Directors rejects the price discrimination scheme for fear of attracting adverse public scrutiny. Nonetheless, the government decides to regulate Untied.

    t. If the regulators require that Untied produces at the efficient output level, what price will be established?

    u. At the efficient output level, how many passengers will Untied carry? (Hint: Remember that the demand curve for each class of passenger is a straight line.)

    v. How can you tell that demand is inelastic at this price level?

    w. Calculate Untied's economic profit under this regulatory requirement.

    x. What will be Untied's short-run and long-run responses under this regulatory requirement?

    y. If the regulators require that Untied produces at an output level that will provide a normal rate of return on invested capital, how great an economic profit (or loss) will Untied make?

2. The Arbezani Construction Group, a monopoly, manufactures prefabricated storage buildings and sells them in the domestic market for $700 each. The company is maximizing its profits. The marginal cost of each building is $300.

   The neighboring nation of Arboc has traditionally kept the price of storage buildings low but excluded imports. The present maximum price, which is $400, has resulted in an excess demand for storage buildings in Arboc of 100 units.

   As a consequence of trade talks, the two countries have formed AAFTA (Arboc-Arbez Free Trade Association) and Arboc has agreed to the importation of Arbezani storage buildings. Assume that Arbocali builders have been denied access to the Arbezani market—Arbezanis are notoriously hard bargainers and the Arbezani Construction Group is a powerful political force.

       a. Should the Arbezani Construction Group export storage buildings to Arboc and, if so, how many? Ignore transportation costs.

       b. Comment on the efficiency consequences of this action.

3. Industry A has 100 firms. 99 of the firms have a .5% share of the market each and the other, Red Inc., has a 50.5% share.

       a. Red Inc. proposes a horizontal merger with one of the other firms. Would the Justice Department challenge the merger? Explain.

       b. Suppose, instead, that 7 of the small firms propose a merger. Would this be opposed?

   Industry B has 2 firms, with a 20% market share each, 3 firms with 10% each, and 6 firms with 5% each.

       c. Calculate the Herfindahl-Hirshman Index for Industry B.

       d. Now two of the firms controlling 10% of the market propose a merger. Calculate the HHI if the merger took place.

       e. Why or why not would the merger be opposed?

4. A telephone system is to be established in Magropolis (a new city in Nevada). The initial capital investment of $80 million will be financed by issuing 7% bonds. Fixed costs would be $5.6 million ($80 million × .07). The variable costs are calculated to be 10¢ per call.

a. Fill in the cost table.

Total Quantity	Total Fixed Cost	Total Variable Cost	Total Cost	Marginal Cost	Average Total Cost
0				—	—
20 mill.					
40 mill.					
60 mill.					
80 mill.					
100 mill.					
120 mill.					

b. Graph your information about average total cost and marginal cost.

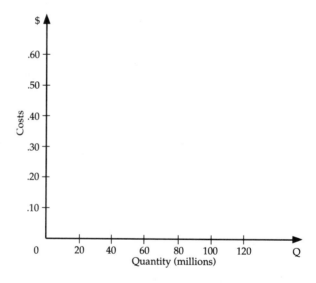

c. Suppose the price per call is set by the regulators at 10¢. What will happen if the residents of Magropolis make 40 million calls?

d. What would happen if 100 million calls were made at a price per call of 10¢?

e. Now sketch in a demand curve, starting at 60¢ on the vertical axis and ending at 120 million on the horizontal axis. Draw in the associated marginal revenue curve—remember that MR's slope is twice that of the demand curve.

f. What is the profit-maximizing price and output level?

g. What is the "average cost" price and output level?

h. What is the efficient price and output level (approximately)?

5. Water in the town of Santa Mira, California, is provided by a private company, Water King, which is a monopoly. Water rates are regulated by the California Public Utility Commission, whose chairman is Jack Finney. Rates are currently established at $.0055 per gallon. Water King supplies water to 8000 customers, each of whom uses an average of 61,200 gallons of water per year. Variable costs are $.00258 per gallon and fixed costs total $799,632 per year. Capital invested by the stockholders of Water King amounts to $6 million. Water King has applied to Jack for permission to increase the water rate. Jack's PUC is committed to a normal profits policy, where a fair return on capital is 12%.
   a. What is Water King's total variable cost?
   b. What is Water King's total cost?
   c. What is Water King's total revenue?
   d. Calculate Water King's total return.
   e. Calculate Water King's rate of return.
   f. Should Jack recommend a rate increase? If so, what should the price per gallon of water be in order to give a 12% rate of return?

6. Match up the piece of legislation with the description.

LEGISLATION	DESCRIPTION
a. Sherman Act	_____
b. Clayton Act	_____
c. Celler-Kefauver Act	_____
d. Willis-Graham Act	_____
e. Wheeler-Lea Act	_____
f. Hart-Scott-Rodino Act	_____

Description
A. Act that exempted from review mergers between firms in the telecommunications industry.
B. Act that extended legislation to include "deceptive" methods of competition.
C. Act that extended the government's authority to the blocking of vertical mergers.
D. Act that extended antitrust laws to proprietorships and partnerships and that required all proposed mergers to be reported to the Department of Justice.
E. Act clarifying the "rule of reason" and outlawing several specific practices such as tying contracts and price discrimination.
F. Act that declared monopoly and trade restraints illegal.

III. ECONOMICS EXPLORER.

Use the ninth module ("Monopoly") from the Economics Explorer software to investigate price discrimination.

ANSWERS AND SOLUTIONS

PRACTICE TEST

I. SOLUTIONS TO MULTIPLE CHOICE QUESTIONS

1. C. A horizontal merger may be permissible. It depends on the effect it will have on competition within the industry. See p. 351.
2. C. Wheeler-Lea added "deceptive" to "unfair" competition. See p. 351.
3. B. Celler-Kefauver, not Clayton, considered vertical mergers.
4. A. See Table 15.1 on p. 352.
5. D. See p. 360.
6. C. An HHI of 1600 lies in the middle region. It would be opposed if the index were raised "too much," i.e., by more than 100. See Table 15.1 on p. 352.
7. D. See the discussion on p. 366.
8. C. Antitrust legislation does not outlaw capital accumulation. See p. 360.
9. B. See the discussion on p. 362.
10. D. See p. 398.
11. B. The extra cost of generating an extra unit of electricity at a nuclear power station is low; the sunk (fixed) costs of establishing the generating capacity are very high.
12. C. Swindell might be practicing sex discrimination (we don't know why Olaf was charged more), but he is certainly discriminating in terms of price.
13. B. Supporters of the breakup argued that subsidies increased inefficiency.
14. A. Profit maximizing occurs where MR = MC, at 60 units. Given that output level and the demand curve, the price will be $4.
15. B. The most efficient output level is where P = MC, at 120 units. Price is $1.00. If ATC is $1.75, a subsidy of $(1.75 - 1.00) \times 120$ is required.
16. C. Normal return on invested capital occurs where P = ATC, at 100 units. P = $2.00.
17. C. The industry has only three firms, because 40% + 30% + 30% = 100%. HHI = $40^2 + 30^2 + 30^2 = 3400$.
18. D. Economic profit = (price − average cost)quantity. With average cost pricing, P = ATC, therefore economic profit is zero, i.e., the firm earns a normal profit.
19. D. The terms of Clayton are stated on p. 350.
20. D. Sports organizations are exempt. See p. 357.

II. SOLUTIONS TO APPLICATION QUESTIONS

1. a. See the following table.

PRICE OF ONE-WAY TRIP TICKETS	ONE-WAY TRIPS EXECUTIVES	DEMANDED PER YEAR STUDENTS/TOURISTS	TOTAL	"TOTAL" DEMAND'S MARGINAL REVENUE
$140	7,000	0	7,000	$80
$130	8,000	0	8,000	$60
$120	9,000	1,000	10,000	$80
$110	10,000	2,000	12,000	$60
$100	11,000	3,000	14,000	$40
$ 90	12,000	4,000	16,000	$20
$ 80	13,000	5,000	18,000	0
$ 70	14,000	6,000	20,000	−$20
$ 60	15,000	7,000	22,000	−$40

b. Profit-maximization occurs where MR = MC. MC is $40; MR is $40 when 14,000 passengers fly and the price is $100.

c. 11,000 executives.

d. $.5($210 − $100) \times 11,000 = $605,000$.

e. 3,000 students/tourists.

f. $.5($130 − $100) \times 3,000 = $45,000$.

g. $650,000.
h. When 14,000 passengers fly, total revenue is $100 × 14,000, or $1,400,000. Total cost includes total fixed cost and total variable cost. TFC = $500,000. TVC = $40 × 14,000 = $560,000. TC = $1,060,000. Economic profit = TR − TC = $340,000.
i. Untied should determine the marginal revenue values for each type of passenger separately and set price according to the MR = MC rule in each case.
j. See the following table.

PRICE OF ONE-WAY TRIP TICKETS	ONE-WAY TRIPS EXECUTIVES	DEMANDED PER YEAR STUDENTS/TOURISTS	EXECUTIVE MARGINAL REVENUE	STUDENT/TOURIST MARGINAL REVENUE
$140	7,000	0	$80	0
$130	8,000	0	$60	0
$120	9,000	1,000	$40	$120
$110	10,000	2,000	$20	$100
$100	11,000	3,000	0	$ 80
$ 90	12,000	4,000	−$20	$ 60
$ 80	13,000	5,000	−$40	$ 40
$ 70	14,000	6,000	−$60	$ 20
$ 60	15,000	7,000	−$80	0

k. Following the MR = MC rule, and recalling that MC = $40, 9,000 executives will fly at a price of $120.
l. .5($210 − $120) × 9,000 = $405,000.
m. Following the MR = MC rule, and recalling that MC = $40, 5,000 students/tourists will fly at a price of $80.
n. .5($130 − $80) × 5,000 = $125,000.
o. $530,000. Note that, by price discrimination, a portion of the consumer surplus has been appropriated by Untied.
p. Economic profit = TR − TC. TR = $120 × 9,000 = $1,080,000. TC = TFC + TVC. TVC = $40 × 9,000 = $360,000. TFC is a bit trickier because the $500,000 shouldn't be applied in total to executives. The total number of passengers is 14,000, of which 9/14 are executives. 9/14 of $500,000 is $321,428.57. TC = $681,428.57. Economic profit = $398,571.43.
q. Economic profit = TR − TC. TR = $80 × 5,000 = $400,000. TC = TFC + TVC. TVC = $40 × 5,000 = $200,000. 5/14 of $500,000 is $178,571.43. TC = $378,571.43. Economic profit = $21,428.57.
r. $398,571.43. + $21,428.57 = $420,000. Using price discrimination, Untied can increase its profits by $80,000.
s. The option of third-degree price discrimination is plausible because Untied should be able to prevent resale of tickets. Students, in particular, can be asked to show a valid student ID. Identifying a traveler as a tourist may be more problematical. In terms of public relations, it is advisable to advertise the $120 ticket as the "regular" price, with the $80 ticket offered as a special, discounted price.
t. The efficient output level is where P = MC and, because MC = $40, P = $40.
u. The demand schedule table can be extended.

PRICE OF ONE-WAY TRIP TICKETS	ONE-WAY TRIPS EXECUTIVES	DEMANDED PER YEAR STUDENTS/TOURISTS	TOTAL	"TOTAL" DEMAND'S MARGINAL REVENUE
$70	14,000	6,000	20,000	−$ 40
$60	15,000	7,000	22,000	−$ 80
$50	16,000	8,000	24,000	−$120
$40	17,000	9,000	26,000	−$160

Untied will carry 17,000 executives and 9,000 students/tourists.
v. When marginal revenue is negative (when P = $40, MR = −$160), demand is inelastic. See Chapter 13.
w. Untied will make an economic loss of $500,000. TR = $1,040,000 and TC = $500,000 + ($40 × 26,000).

x. In the short run, Untied will continue to provide service because its revenue can (just) meet its variable costs. In the long run, Untied will stop providing the service. If a subsidy equal to the loss were offered, Untied would continue to offer the service.

y. If Untied is receiving a normal rate of return on invested capital, it is earning a normal profit.

2. a. The Arbezani Construction Group should "fill the gap" in the market and export 100 units. Profits will be increased because the Arbocali price ($400) exceeds the Group's marginal cost ($300). Note that as each of the units can be sold for $400, marginal revenue is also $400. There is, in fact, additional scope for the Arbezani Construction Group to penetrate this market to a greater extent—we just don't have enough information.

b. Efficiency is unaffected in Arbez but is improved for Arbocali consumers. The situation is not Pareto optimal because trade is restricted between the two economies and is restricted within Arboc (because of the price ceiling). Complete liberalization of the market forces would improve efficiency.

3. a. The Justice Department would challenge the merger of Red Inc. and another firm, since the HHI is over 1800 (a concentrated industry) and would rise by more than 50.

   HHI (before merger) $= 50.5^2 + [(.5^2) \times 99] = 2575$
   HHI (after merger) $= 51.0^2 + [(.5^2) \times 98] = 2625.5$ (assuming the merged firms retained their market shares).

b. HHI (before merger) $= 50.5^2 + [(.5^2) \times 99] = 2575$
   HHI (after merger) $= 50.5^2 + 3.5^2 + [(.5^2) \times 92] = 2585.5$
   The HHI would rise by less than 50; the merger would not be opposed.

c. HHI $= 20^2 + 20^2 + [(10^2) \times 3] + [(5^2) \times 6] = 1250$.

d. HHI (after merger) $= [20^2 \times 3] + 10^2 + [(5^2) \times 6] = 1450$.

e. The HHI would rise by more than 100; the merger would be opposed.

4. a. See the table below.

Total Quantity	Total Fixed Cost	Total Variable Cost	Total Cost	Marginal Cost	Average Total Cost
0	$5.6 mill.	0	$ 5.6 mill.	—	—
20 mill.	$5.6 mill.	$ 2 mill.	$ 7.6 mill.	10¢	38.0¢
40 mill.	$5.6 mill.	$ 4 mill.	$ 9.6 mill.	10¢	24.0¢
60 mill.	$5.6 mill.	$ 6 mill.	$11.6 mill.	10¢	19.3¢
80 mill.	$5.6 mill.	$ 8 mill.	$13.6 mill.	10¢	17.0¢
100 mill.	$5.6 mill.	$10 mill.	$15.6 mill.	10¢	15.6¢
120 mill.	$5.6 mill.	$12 mill.	$17.6 mill.	10¢	14.7¢

b. See the diagram below.

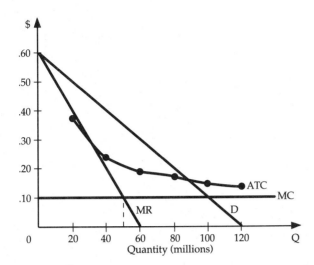

c. The phone company will lose 14¢ per call, or $5.6 million. The company would be wise to shut down.

d. The phone company will lose 5.6¢ per call, or $5.6 million. The company will lose its fixed costs whatever the number of calls is, if price is made to equal marginal cost. (Think about the link between marginal cost and variable cost for a moment to verify this.)

e. See the diagram above.

f. 35¢ per call and 50 million calls.

g. About 16.65¢ and 85 million calls.

h. 10¢ and 100 million calls—the $5.6 million loss would be made in this case.

5. a. TVC = AVC × Q = $.00258 × 61,200 × 8,000 = $1,263,168.

    b. TC = TVC + TFC = $1,263,168 + $799,632 = $2,062,800.

    c. TR = $.0055 × 61,200 × 8,000 = $2,692,800.

    d. TR − TC = $2,692,800 − $2,062,800 = $630,000.

    e. $630,000 ÷ $6,000,000 = .105 = 10.5%.

    f. 10.5% is less than the desired rate of 12%, so a rate increase is justified. Return should be .12 × $6,000,000 = $720,000. Given total cost ($2,062,800), TR must be $2,062,800 + $720,000 = $2,782,800. Price per gallon should be $2,782,800 ÷ (61,200 × 8,000) = .005684.

6. a. F

    b. E

    c. C

    d. A

    e. B

    f. D

EXTERNALITIES, PUBLIC GOODS, IMPERFECT INFORMATION, AND SOCIAL CHOICE

16

OBJECTIVES: POINT BY POINT

After completing this chapter, you should be able to accomplish the objectives listed below.

General Comment

Keep in mind that this chapter examines examples of market failure. The past three chapters have looked at only one aspect—imperfect competition. The cases in the present chapter can occur even in perfectly competitive industries. Go back and review Chapters 13, 14, and 15. In Chapter 12, review Figure 12.5—note how externalities upset the scales in this diagram. The benefits of perfect competition ensue only if the equilibrium output level is also the efficient output level. The firm maximizes profits in response to private marginal costs and benefits; if society's marginal costs and benefits are otherwise, inefficiency results.

OBJECTIVE 1: Define and list three sources of market failure.

Externalities, public goods, and imperfect information are major sources of *market failure*—that is, a situation when the perfectly competitive market is unable to reach an allocatively efficient competitive equilibrium.   (page 373)

PRACTICE

1. In perfect competition, a market failure occurs when, in the long run, the industry
   A. produces so much that average costs are minimized.
   B. produces so much that total profits are maximized.
   C. produces so much that the marginal benefit of the last unit produced exceeds its marginal cost.
   D. increases production past the output level where price is first equal to marginal revenue.
   Answer: C. The industry should produce until marginal benefit equals marginal cost. If marginal benefit does not equal marginal cost, a market failure has occurred. All other options refer to long-run equilibrium conditions in perfect competition.

OBJECTIVE 2: Define externality and explain why externalities are a source of market failure. Explain the terms marginal damage cost, marginal social cost, and marginal private cost. Explain why social costs and private costs may differ, and give examples.

Externalities occur when the actions or decisions of one agent impose a cost, or bestow a benefit, on second or third parties. There is no incentive to figure these costs (or benefits) into the decision to act. With a negative externality a wedge is driven between marginal cost, as faced by producers or consumers, and price. Producers look only at *marginal private cost*. A broader view would encompass all extra costs of production—*marginal social costs*. The difference between the two is *marginal damage cost.* When we fail to consider these additional costs (or benefits) to society, inefficient outcomes emerge—even in perfect competition. When external costs are present, more production occurs than society would prefer. When external benefits are present, the market, on its own, will produce less than society would like. Pollution is the "classic" example of an external cost. (page 374)

> **LEARNING TIP:** Keep in mind an example of a good having an external cost (a paper mill producing effluent), and an example of a good having an external benefit (the CD you borrow from a friend and then tape).

> **LEARNING TIP:** Calling externalities "spillover costs" and "spillover benefits" will help you. An externality exists whenever marginal social benefit differs from marginal private benefit or marginal social cost differs from marginal private cost. Externalities may occur during the production of a good or during its consumption.
>
> The concept of externalities is easy to grasp—pollution is all around us. Think of some topical and local examples of your own. Don't forget externalities providing benefits! Many goods provide both external costs and benefits. The classic example is the beekeeper and his neighbor, the apple-grower—the bees sting the workers, yet pollinate the apple trees, and the beekeeper receives "free" honey.
>
> What is less obvious is that the quantification of externalities (and so, claims for compensation) is extremely difficult—almost any position can be plausibly defended. Take the local examples you've thought of, and look for the counterargument (the "silver lining" to a negative externality).

PRACTICE

2. Assume there are no externalities. If price exceeds marginal cost, the benefits to consumers are _____ than the cost of resources needed to produce the good. _____ should be produced.
   A. greater, More.
   B. greater, Less.
   C. less, More.
   D. less, Less.
   Answer: A. If the price exceeds the cost of the final unit produced, society is deriving extra benefits. Production should increase until P = MC.

3. _____ is the sum of the marginal costs of producing a good and the correctly measured damage costs involved in the process of production.
   A. Marginal damage cost.
   B. Marginal social cost.
   C. Marginal private cost.
   D. Marginal external cost.
   Answer: B. MSC (marginal social cost) includes both the internal and external costs of production. See p. 376.

4. When marginal social cost exceeds the firm's marginal private cost, the industry's supply curve is too far to the _____ and _____ is being produced.
    A. right, too much.
    B. right, too little.
    C. left, too much.
    D. left, too little.
    Answer: A. Marginal cost is underestimating the true cost to society. Recall that the firm's (and the industry's) supply curve is based on MC.

5. As production increases, marginal damage costs are likely to
    A. remain constant.
    B. increase.
    C. decrease.
    D. become negative.
    Answer: B. See p. 381 and Figure 16.3 in the textbook.

6. An individual will continue an activity until
    A. marginal benefit equals marginal social cost.
    B. marginal benefit equals marginal damage cost.
    C. marginal social cost equals marginal private cost.
    D. marginal benefit equals marginal private cost.
    Answer: D. The individual will compare the marginal benefit with the extra privately-borne cost.

OBJECTIVE 3: Draw a graph depicting a negative externality. Explain why the presence of a negative (positive) externality will lead to an overproduction (underproduction) of the good. Evaluate five different methods of internalizing an externality.

Externalities may be controlled in a variety of ways, although no one way works in all circumstances. Five remedies for the problem of externalities are possible. These are:
    a. government-imposed taxes and subsidies,
    b. private bargaining and negotiation (the Coase Theorem),
    c. legal rules and procedures (such as injunctive relief and liability rules),
    d. the sale or auctioning of rights to impose externalities, and
    e. direct government regulation.   (page 381)

LEARNING TIP: Think of the Coase Theorem as another application of the idea of "balancing the margins." In this case, once the property rights to a good are defined and the true marginal benefit and marginal cost determined, an efficient equilibrium can be established.

PRACTICE

Use the following diagram, which depicts information for the chemical producer, Tox Inc., for the next five questions.

7. The firm depicted in the diagram is operating in a(n) _____ competitive industry. External _____ are present.
   A. perfectly, benefits.
   B. perfectly, costs.
   C. imperfectly, benefits.
   D. imperfectly, costs.
   Answer: B. Demand is horizontal—perfect competition. MSC is higher than MC—marginal damage costs are present.

8. The profit-maximizing firm will produce
   A. 60 units of output.
   B. 70 units of output.
   C. 80 units of output.
   D. 90 units of output.
   Answer: C. The firm will produce where P (MR) = MC.

9. The efficient output level is
   A. 60 units of output.
   B. 70 units of output.
   C. 80 units of output.
   D. 90 units of output.
   Answer: B. The efficient output level is where MSC = MB (as represented by price).

10. The marginal damage cost imposed by this firm is
    A. $4 per unit of output.
    B. $6 per unit of output.
    C. $10 per unit of output.
    D. $14 per unit of output.
    Answer: A. Marginal damage cost is the difference between the marginal social cost and the marginal cost. In the diagram, at 80 units of output, MSC is $14 and MC is $10.

11. To achieve an efficient output level, the government could impose a tax of
    A. $4 per unit.
    B. $6 per unit.
    C. $10 per unit.
    D. $14 per unit.
    Answer: A. This tax will increase the (private) production costs and make them the same as the marginal social costs.

OBJECTIVE 4: Identify the two critical characteristics of public goods. Explain why a free market would underproduce public goods and identify the two "problems" associated with the production of public goods.

Public goods are goods whose benefits are received collectively by all members of society (nonrival) and/or whose benefits can be denied to no one (nonexcludable), even if they refuse to pay. Because of these characteristics, public goods will either be underproduced or not produced at all if the private sector is made responsible for their provision. Two problems of public goods are the free-rider problem and the drop-in-the-bucket problem. (page 387)

The legal system is a classic example of a public good. What would society be like without known and enforced laws? Much of the framework of the market economy would collapse. Property rights and possessions would be endangered. There would be an unwillingness to trade by mail, to accept checks, or to offer trade credit. We derive benefits from law enforcement, but what choices do we have as individuals? We could each hire our own law enforcer in the "law market," but that wouldn't entirely solve the problem because enforcement would be neither uniform nor just. In addition, there would still be no mechanism for establishing laws, except by precedent and tradition.

The only effective solution is for society to act as a unit, levying taxes to pay for a system of justice. This publicly provided good does not erode the free-market system; rather, it *enhances* it. The justice system is nonexcludable and nonrival in consumption (unless there is a sudden crime wave). Also, note that the "drop-in-the-bucket" and "free-rider" problems are present. A town that is crime-free when a new resident moves into it doesn't experience extra costs from his relocation. His tax dollars will make no great difference in the fight against crime, and if he avoids payment he will still receive protection.

Not all goods provided by the government are public goods, as far as economists are concerned. The heart of the public goods issue is that the market fails to provide an adequate amount of such goods because there is neither an incentive to buy nor to sell privately. Consumers can "free ride," and the provision of a unit of the good, given nonrivalry in consumption, will service purchasers and free riders alike.

> **LEARNING TIP:** Keep in mind a clear example of a public good (a lighthouse or, better still, national defense). Confirm that, for a good to be a public good, consumption is nonrival and that consumers can't be excluded from the benefits provided.

PRACTICE

12. Public goods are _____ in consumption and non-purchasers _____ be excluded from their benefits.
    A. rival, can.
    B. rival, cannot.
    C. nonrival, can.
    D. nonrival, cannot.
    Answer: D. These are the two characteristics of public goods. Plug in an example (national defense) to see how they relate. See p. 387.

13. Because public goods are nonexcludable, individuals are usually unwilling to pay for them. This characteristic is known as the
    A. drop-in-the-bucket problem.
    B. impossibility theorem.
    C. Coase Theorem.
    D. free-rider problem.
    Answer: D. See p. 388.

14. As the number of recipients of a public good increases, the number of free riders will tend to
    A. increase because, as the size of the group increases, it is more difficult to detect free riders.
    B. increase because, as the size of the group increases, individuals become rivals for the benefits of the good.
    C. decrease because, as the size of the group increases, the per person payment will decrease.
    D. decrease because, as the size of the group increases, it is easier to exclude non-contributors.
    Answer: A. See p. 388.

OBJECTIVE 5: Outline Samuelson's theory of the optimal provision of public goods. Describe why government provision of public goods is likely to lead to dissatisfaction.

To determine the optimal (most efficient) level of provision, Samuelson devised the demand curve for public goods. The price each consumer is willing to pay is summed at each output level. An efficient provision of public goods will still leave many consumers dissatisfied, however, because some will prefer more and others less. To ensure an efficient level of provision, the preferences of each consumer would have to be revealed, which is possible only in theory because of the incentive not to reveal one's preferences. In practice, imperfect social choice mechanisms, such as majority rule, are used.

The Tiebout hypothesis offers the possibility that an efficient mix of public goods may be produced if consumers make their preferences known by changing location in response to government-offered goods. (page 389)

PRACTICE

15. The optimal level of provision of a public good occurs when society's _____ is equal to the _____ of the good.
    A. total willingness to pay, total cost.
    B. total willingness to pay, marginal cost.
    C. marginal willingness to pay, total cost.
    D. marginal willingness to pay, marginal cost.
    Answer: B. The demand curve totals the willingness to pay and this is equated with the marginal (social) cost to determine the optimal output level.

Use the following table for the next three questions. Society consists of two persons—Robinson and Friday. The table shows the quantity demanded by each of units of a public good—defense. Assume that each person's demand curve is a straight line.

PRICE	ROBINSON'S QUANTITY DEMANDED	FRIDAY'S QUANTITY DEMANDED
$3.00	3	1
$2.00	5	2
$1.00	7	3

16. Each of the following is a point on society's demand curve for defense except
    A. 1 unit at a price of $7.00.
    B. 3 units at a price of $4.00.
    C. 5 units at a price of $2.00.
    D. 7 units at a price of $2.00.
    Answer: D. The demand curve must be summed vertically, i.e., at each output level. Example: Friday will pay $3.00 to receive one unit and Robinson will pay $4.00 to receive one unit (Robinson's demand curve is a straight line). One unit, not two, is produced to be shared.

17. Complete the following demand schedule.

SOCIETY'S QUANTITY DEMANDED	PRICE
7	___
6	___
5	___
4	___
3	___
2	___
1	___

   Answer: See the *Answers and Solutions* section.

18. The marginal cost of each unit of defense is $4.00. What is the optimal number of units of defense that should be provided?
    A. 2 units.
    B. 3 units.
    C. 4 units.
    D. 5 units.
    Answer: B. Society should produce until P = MC.

OBJECTIVE 6: Indicate how imperfect information may interfere with market efficiency.

In a voluntary exchange with imperfect information, trade becomes inefficient. A participant may make an adverse selection if s/he has less information than the other party involved. In the real world, where information is not perfect, consumers and firms gather information up to the point where the marginal benefits and marginal costs of additional search are equal. In some cases it is necessary for the government to collect and disperse information.   (page 393)

Society attempts to reduce the threat of imperfect information. The buyer is protected by "truth in lending" and "truth in advertising" legislation, for instance, and consumer organizations may pressure corporations to improve information. Risks remain and they reduce the willingness of individuals to trade.

> There is a joke about an economics professor who accepted her boyfriend's marriage proposal by telling him that her decision was based on the belief that the marginal benefit of a continued search had become less than its marginal cost.

Moral hazard occurs in the insurance market. By reducing the cost of one's undesirable action, the insurance policy may encourage such action.

PRACTICE

19. Consumers should continue to search out information until the _____ benefit from the search equals the _____ cost of the search.
    A. total, total.
    B. total, marginal.
    C. marginal, total.
    D. marginal, marginal.
    Answer: D. This is entirely a marginal decision.

20. In the used car market, there are lemons and cherries and, although buyers cannot distinguish between them, sellers can. We would expect _____ lemons to enter the market and _____ cherries to enter the market.
    A. too many, too many.
    B. too many, too few.
    C. too few, too many.
    D. too few, too few.
    Answer: B. See p. 394 for a discussion of this example.

OBJECTIVE 7: Outline the issues involved in social choice.

Arrow's impossibility theorem illustrates the difficulty of establishing a consistent consensus given a lack of unanimity. The impossibility theorem proves that it can't be done. The voting paradox is an example of this theorem. Due to a lack of incentives and take on tough choices, government may be inefficient. However, the ultimate question remains *how much* government involvement is required, not *whether* it is required. (page 395)

PRACTICE

21. The demonstration that majority-rule voting can produce contradictory and inconsistent results is known as
    A. the impossibility theorem.
    B. the voting paradox.
    C. adverse selection.
    D. moral hazard.
    Answer: B. The voting paradox exemplifies the impossibility theorem.

Use the following information to answer the next two questions. Axl, Brigitta, and Carl have to choose one of four options (A, B, C, D). Individual preferences, from highest to lowest, are shown below. Majority voting will be used by pairing options, the loser being excluded from further consideration.

AXL	BRIGITTA	CARL
A	B	C
B	C	A
C	A	D
D	D	B

22. If A is first paired against B, then the winner against C, and then that winner against D, the option finally selected will be
    A. A.
    B. B.
    C. C.
    D. D.
    Answer: C. Carl will vote for A over B. Pairing A and C, Brigitta will cast the swing vote for C. Everyone prefers C over D.

23. If B is first paired against C, then the winner against D, and then that winner against A, the option finally selected will be
    A. A.
    B. B.
    C. C.
    D. D.
    Answer: A. Axl will vote for B over C. Pairing A and B, Carl will cast the swing vote for A. Everyone prefers A over D.

ENDPOINT: Intervention or Not?

Be aware that, during the last several chapters, a battle has been raging between those who believe that the free market works efficiently and those who believe that more structured control is required. You might pigeonhole the two camps as the "Small Government" and "Big Government" schools of public policy.

In this chapter "Big Government" is drawing attention to ways in which the free market fails if left uncorrected. For externalities, "Small Government" retaliates with the Coase Theorem and the private sale or auction of externality rights. For public goods, the debate tends to center on the question of which goods are clearly public goods. The "Small Government" school also retaliates with such concepts as "the voting paradox" and "the impossibility theorem"—hoping to undermine the belief that the government allocates efficiently.

The battle continues in Chapter 17 . . .

PRACTICE TEST

I. MULTIPLE CHOICE QUESTIONS.

Select the option that provides the single best answer.

_____ 1. Which of the following is not a good example of an externality?
    A. A hamburger.
    B. Noise pollution.
    C. Jack's cigarette smoke for Jill, who also smokes.
    D. Jack's cigarette smoke for Jane, who doesn't smoke.

_____ 2. For the Coase theorem to work, all of the following must be true except
    A. the basic rights at issue must be understood.
    B. the majority of concerned individuals participate.
    C. there must be no impediments to bargaining.
    D. only a few people can be involved.

_____ 3. Which one of the following is not advanced as a method of remedying an externality?
    A. Government subsidies.
    B. Private taxation.
    C. Private bargaining.
    D. Direct government regulation.

_____ 4. Firm A is producing at an output level where the marginal benefits to consumers are less than the marginal cost. Assuming no externalities, the price
    A. equals marginal cost.
    B. is less than marginal cost.
    C. is greater than marginal cost.
    D. is less than marginal damage cost.

_____ 5. When the marginal social cost of a good exceeds its marginal private cost,
A. too many units will be produced by the market.
B. the market price will be too high.
C. it is an example of a beneficial externality.
D. too few resources will be allocated to its production.

_____ 6. The production of a good imposes external costs on society. If these costs are not internalized then, from society's point of view, the firm is likely to
A. underproduce.
B. allocate too many resources to the production of the good.
C. charge too high a price.
D. make economic profits in the long run.

_____ 7. Your campus radio station is best described as an example of
A. an external cost.
B. a good that is nonrival in consumption but that generates benefits which are excludable.
C. a good that is nonrival in consumption and that generates benefits which are nonexcludable.
D. a public good plagued by the easy-rider problem.

_____ 8. Which of the following is the best example of a public good?
A. A hamburger.
B. A high school.
C. Police protection.
D. A toll bridge.

_____ 9. All of the following are true about the voting paradox except that
A. it is an example of the impossibility theorem.
B. it demonstrates the power wielded by the one who sets the voting agenda.
C. it shows that, when preferences for public goods differ, any attempt to add the preferences can lead to inconsistencies.
D. with majority rule, logrolling is necessary to get things done.

Use the following information to answer the next two questions.

Arboc is an economy comprised of three individuals: Ed, Ted, and Ned. The table shows the maximum price that each will pay for various quantities of a good.

Quantity	Ed	Ted	Ned
1	$7	$10	$17
2	$5	$ 9	$15
3	$4	$ 7	$11
4	$3	$ 4	$10

_____ 10. The maximum price that the private market would pay for the third unit is
A. $4.
B. $7.
C. $11.
D. $22.

_____ 11. Now suppose that the good is a *public* good. The maximum price that society would pay for the third unit is
A. $7.
B. $7.33 (approximately).
C. $11.
D. $22.

_____ 12. If there are external costs and these are not considered by perfectly competitive firms then, at the equilibrium output level,
A. P = MC and P = MSC.
B. P = MC and P < MSC.
C. P < MC and P = MSC.
D. P < MC and P < MSC.

_____ 13. The two problems in the provision of public goods are
A. nonrivalry in consumption and the drop-in-the bucket problem.
B. externalities and nonexcludability.
C. nonexcludability and moral hazard.
D. free riders and the drop-in-the bucket problem.

_____ 14. To derive the market demand for a public good, we sum the
A. quantity demanded by each consumer at each possible price level.
B. demand curve of each consumer horizontally.
C. amounts that each consumer is willing to pay at each level of output.
D. marginal social cost curve of each producer vertically.

_____ 15. There are external costs and these are not considered by perfectly competitive firms. The government imposes a tax so that the market is producing at the efficient output level. We can say that
A. P = MSC and MDC = 0.
B. P = MSC and MDC > 0.
C. P < MSC and MDC = 0.
D. P < MSC and MDC > 0.

_____ 16. Your local public television station is having a fund drive. Public TV is the only TV station you watch. You rationalize your failure to contribute by telling yourself that your pledge would make no difference one way or the other. This is an example of the _____ problem. Because you will still be able to tune in whether you pledge or not, you are a(n)
A. free-rider, free rider.
B. free-rider, externality.
C. drop-in-the-bucket; free rider.
D. drop-in-the-bucket, externality.

_____ 17. Hugo is selling his Yugo in the used car market, a market with imperfect information. The going price for a Yugo is $1000 and this is Hugo's asking price. Sadly, Hugo's Yugo is a "lemon." If price is used by buyers as an indication of quality in this market, Hugo should
A. keep his asking price at $1000.
B. raise his asking price above $1000.
C. lower his asking price below $1000.
D. withdraw his car from the market.

Use the following information to answer the next three questions.

Research has shown that Hayley Mills Incorp., a firm in the perfectly competitive paper industry, also produces pollution in the nearby Chicken River. The following table has been compiled showing the marginal cost (MC) and marginal social cost (MSC) of paper production. The market price of paper is $600 per ton.

TONS OF PAPER	MC	MSC
1	$400	$ 500
2	$500	$ 600
3	$600	$ 800
4	$700	$1100

_____ 18. The marginal damage cost borne by society from the production of 4 tons of paper is
   A. $1100 per ton.
   B. $275 per ton.
   C. $400 per ton.
   D. $100 per ton.

_____ 19. Hayley is able to ignore the damage costs. The firm will produce _____ tons of paper; the efficient output level is _____ tons.
   A. 2, 2.
   B. 3, 2.
   C. 3, 3.
   D. 4, 3.

_____ 20. To force this firm to produce at the efficient level, the government should
   A. impose a tax of $100 per ton.
   B. impose a tax of $200 per ton.
   C. grant a subsidy of $100 per ton.
   D. grant a subsidy of $200 per ton.

II. APPLICATION QUESTIONS.

1. From the rubble of disowned economic dogmas and disenchanted citizens, a new state has been built in Eastern Europe—Freedonia. The newly-elected Freedonian government is, naturally, keen to avoid the pitfalls of its predecessors, but it does realize that some (public) goods and services should be provided by the state. Jan Lipska, the Minister for Public Goods, has devised the following matrix, using the characteristics of public goods that she has read about in an economics textbook by Case and Fair.

	PUBLIC/PRIVATE GOOD MATRIX	
	RIVAL	NONRIVAL
Excludable	I	II
Nonexcludable	III	IV

The minister now calls in a top western economic adviser (you!) to interpret the matrix.

   a. Ms. Lipska asks you what sort of good would be included in Category I, asks for examples, and asks how the government should treat these goods.

b. Ms. Lipska now asks about the kind of good that should be included in Category IV, asks for examples, and asks how the government should treat these goods.

c. Ms. Lipska now asks about the kind of good that should be included in Categories II and III, asks for examples, and asks how the government should treat these goods.

d. The Minister considers Category I (pure private goods) and focuses on a particular industry—steel. She points out that steel is traditionally a polluter of the environment. Assuming that the government should do "something" about this issue on behalf of injured citizens, what might that "something" be?

e. Some goods, the Minister muses, can generate undesirable side-effects at the consumption stage—a car, for example, can pollute. You see the way the Minister's mind is working. You set up a matrix for externalities.

	EXTERNALITY PRODUCTION	MATRIX CONSUMPTION
Negative Externality	I	II
Positive Externality	III	IV

Interpret the matrix for the Minister.

f. Ms. Lipska asks what actions the government might take in each of these categories. How would you reply?

2. The inhabitants of the city of Croatoan, Virginia, have for years been coping with a transportation problem. The city is on an isthmus, and to connect it to the rest of civilization, there is one rocky, treacherous road that, almost invariably, is closed during the winter months. The proposed solution is to build a bridge to link Croatoan to the "mainland" more directly. John White, the City Manager, has hired you to conduct an analysis of the costs and benefits of this project. He points out that the project is all-or-nothing—you can't build half a bridge. Having taken an introductory economics course in college, he agrees with you when you suggest that the community's consumer surplus of the bridge should be figured into the calculations.

After some work, you have estimated the demand schedule below.

TOLL FEE	USAGE PER YEAR	ANNUAL REVENUES	CONSUMER SURPLUS	TOTAL ANNUAL BENEFITS
$1.00	0	_____	_____	_____
$0.80	20,000	_____	_____	_____
$0.60	40,000	_____	_____	_____
$0.40	60,000	_____	_____	_____
$0.20	80,000	_____	_____	_____
$0.10	90,000	_____	_____	_____
$0.00	100,000	_____	_____	_____

a. Complete the table.

The City Manager now tells you that the building and maintenance of the bridge can be financed through a loan that will cost $40,000 per year, regardless of the amount of traffic. (Ignore present value considerations.)

b. Left to a free market and the demand curve above, would the bridge be built? Why?

c. Comparing the total annual benefit and the total annual cost, do you recommend that Croatoan goes ahead with the project?

d. If White's objective is to maximize social welfare, should he impose a toll fee? If so, how much? Why?

e. If White wishes to offset as much of the cost as possible through toll revenues, which toll level should he set?

f. The strategies developed in part d and part e still leave Croatoan with an unpaid bill for the bridge. Recommend a method of deriving funds.

g. White, who is familiar with Freedonian politics (see Application Question 1 above), asks where the Croatoan bridge would fit into the "public/private goods matrix." How would you reply?

There remains an unresolved issue. The bay, and the land surrounding it, over which the bridge is to be built, is owned by five families. The right to build the bridge must be bought from them. The bridge will certainly reduce the amenity of the exceptionally fine shoreline. $10,000 per year has been budgeted as compensation for the five families to be divided equally.

Each family places a monetary value on the amenity of the bay. Four different possible sets of values (A 2 D) are given in the following table. The higher the monetary value, the greater the amenity and the greater the loss of amenity if the bridge is built.

The amenity of the bay is a public good for the five families (none can be excluded, and the scenery is nonrival), so the compensation should be accepted only if the value of the compensation exceeds the value of the bay.

	DISTRIBUTIONS			
FAMILY	A	B	C	D
Dare	$1,500	$3,000	$5,000	$2,500
Howe	$1,500	$3,000	$3,000	$2,500
Archard	$1,500	$3,000	$1,000	$2,500
Harvie	$1,500	$3,000	$1,000	$ 500
Viccars	$1,500	$1,000	$1,000	$ 500

h. In which of the four cases should the compensation be accepted by the five families, allowing Croatoan's bridge project to go forward?

The families get together and, in true Croatoan fashion, decide to abide by majority rule.

i. Using majority rule, in which of the four cases will the compensation be accepted by the five families?

j. In which cases will the compensation be accepted even though its benefits do not adequately compensate the five families?

k. Majority rule may result in inefficient choices. In some sense, an enforced decision that affects one adversely is like a negative externality—the actions of others adversely affect the individual. Referring to your answer to part i and to the Coase Theorem, how might the families negotiate among themselves, and with what result regarding the offered compensation?

3. We can move from the textbook discussion of externalities to a graphical presentation. Recall the concepts of marginal social cost and marginal (private) cost—MSC and MPC, respectively. Similarly, define marginal social benefit and marginal private benefit—MSB and MPB, respectively. MPC and MPB are the same as the supply and demand curves with which you're familiar.

In the graph below, without externalities, MSC = MPC and MSB = MPB. P1 and Q1 indicate the price and quantity of widgets traded in a free market. Because all costs and benefits are internalized, there is no market failure.

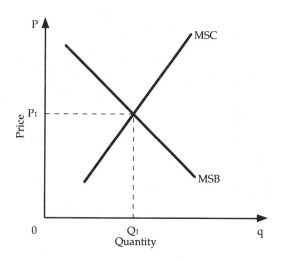

a. Negative externalities in production: What will happen if some of the costs are passed on to a third party? Draw the MPC curve. What effect have the spillover costs had? Can you think of an example of this situation?

b. Negative externalities in consumption: Return to the original diagram. Suppose that the consumption of widgets reduces the well-being of others. Why might this occur? Where will the MPB curve be, in relation to MSB, and what is the effect on resource allocation?

c. Positive externalities in consumption: Return to the original diagram. Suppose that the benefits from widgets accrue to persons other than the purchasers. What will happen to the diagram? What will be the effect on price and resource allocation? Can you think of any examples?

d. Positive externalities in production: Return to the original diagram. Suppose that the firm pays the cost of resources from which it derives no use. Can you think of an example? What will be the relationship between MSC and MPC?

4. We have a society with three individuals—Ted, Ned, and Fred. The following table lists the maximum price each will pay for various quantities of a public good.

Quantity	Ted's Price	Ned's Price	Fred's Price
1	$9	$12	$16
2	$7	$10	$12
3	$5	$ 6	$ 9
4	$3	$ 4	$ 6
5	$1	$ 2	$ 3

   a. How much will society pay for the second unit of the good?
   b. Graph society's demand curve for this public good.

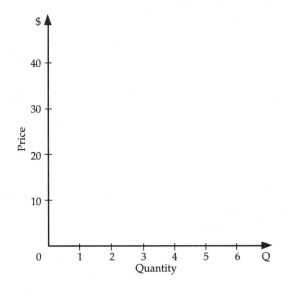

   c. Suppose that the marginal cost of producing this good is $14 for each additional unit of output. What is the efficient level of provision?
   d. Graph marginal cost to confirm your result.
   e. If each person is charged an equal amount to cover the cost of provision, will any of them be happy with the situation?

5. What do you think is the best way to deal with the following situations? Choose one of the following options.

   Situations
   a. a smoky factory
   b. noise pollution from a recently-built airport
   c. pornographic magazines
   d. noise from car exhaust systems
   e. unsightly billboards
   f. noise pollution from a building site
   g. your roommate always parties on the night before your exams

   Options
   A. tax or subsidy
   B. bargaining and negotiation
   C. legal rules
   D. direct regulation

6. Jilly, Lilly, and Billie are roommates. Each likes a different kind of music. Jilly loves jazz, tolerates loud rock, and hates bluegrass. Lilly loves loud rock, is impartial to bluegrass, but loathes jazz. Billie adores bluegrass, can live with jazz, and despises loud rock. Their apartment has one (communally-owned) radio. Billie asks your advice—how can she guarantee that only bluegrass will be played?

7. We have a society with two consumers—Liz and Boris. The following table lists how much each will demand of a good at various prices.

Price	Liz's Quantity	Boris' Quantity
$10	0	0
$ 8	2	0
$ 6	4	0
$ 4	6	4
$ 2	8	8
$ 0	10	12

a. If this good is marketed as a private good, complete the following table.

Price	Total Quantity
$10	
$ 8	
$ 6	
$ 4	
$ 2	
$ 0	

b. If the marginal cost of this good is constant at $4, how much will be traded?
c. If this good is marketed as a public good, complete the following table.

Price	Quantity
$16	
$13	
$10	
$ 7	
$ 4	
$ 1	
$ 0	

d. If the marginal cost of this good is constant at $4, how much will be traded?

8. What would be the implications if Joe Pacifist were allowed to refuse to pay taxes earmarked for the defense budget? Should Joe be permitted a free ride on a bus, which is obliged to run in any case? Are the two cases the same? Should we have compulsory taxation to pay for defense? What other options might be feasible?

ANSWERS AND SOLUTIONS

ANSWERS TO PRACTICE QUESTIONS

17. See the following demand schedule.

SOCIETY'S QUANTITY DEMANDED	PRICE	ROBINSON	FRIDAY
7	$1.00	$1.00	—
6	$1.50	$1.50	—
5	$2.00	$2.00	—
4	$2.50	$2.50	—
3	$4.00	$3.00	$1.00
2	$5.50	$3.50	$2.00
1	$7.00	$4.00	$3.00

PRACTICE TEST

I. SOLUTIONS TO MULTIPLE CHOICE QUESTIONS

1. A. There is no external cost or external benefit attached to the production and/or consumption of a hamburger.
2. B. See p. 384 for a discussion of the three requirements.
3. B. See p. 382 for a summary of the methods of remedying an externality.
4. B. See p. 374.
5. A. The additional (external) costs reduce society's welfare, indicating that too much is being produced. See p. 381.
6. B. See p. 381.
7. C. Your consumption of the radio station does not reduce its availability for others, nor can the radio station exclude any listeners.
8. C. Public goods are nonrival and nonexcludable. Police protection is a community-wide service that is available to all.
9. D. In the voting paradox example, things get done, but outcomes needn't be consistent.
10. C. In the private market, sum the demands vertically at each output level. Ned would be willing to pay $11 to buy the third unit.
11. D. Sum the demand information vertically at each output level for a publicly-provided good. Price will be $22 ($4 + $7 + $11).
12. B. In perfect competition, the firm will set P (MR) = MC to maximize profits. If there are external costs, MC will be less than MSC, therefore P
13. D. See p. 387.
14. C. See p. 391.
15. B. If there are externalities, MDC is positive. The profit-maximizing firm produces where P = MC which, with the tax, is equal to MSC.
16. C. See p. 388.
17. B. If Hugo raises his asking price, he is signaling to gullible buyers that his car is not a "lemon."
18. C. Marginal damage cost is MSC − MC. See p. 381.
19. B. The firm will produce where P = MC while the efficient output level is where P = MSC.
20. A. At the efficient output level of 2 tons, the government must increase the firm's private cost from $500 to $600.

II. SOLUTIONS TO APPLICATION QUESTIONS

1. a. Category I includes pure private goods—goods that are rival in consumption and excludable. Freedonian sausage, clothing, and private cars would be examples. The government should leave well alone and let market forces provide this type of good.

   b. Category IV includes pure public goods—goods that are nonrival in consumption and nonexcludable. Clean air, national defense, police protection, the legal system, public health, and fire protection would be examples. The government should provide this type of good.

   c. Categories II and III are where the government needs to be careful because they include goods possessing one or other of the characteristics of public goods. The private sector can produce those goods in Category II because free riders can be excluded, but the private sector might underproduce, i.e., exclude those who are unwilling to pay even though their inclusion is virtually costless. Examples include the post office, public transport, and cable television. The private sector is unable to produce goods in Category III because free riders cannot be excluded. There is rivalry, so public provision might best have a user fee included. National parks during peak season or highways at rush hour are examples.

   d. Given a negative externality in production, the offending firm will tend to overproduce. The government could impose a quota on production, or set a tax that would equate the marginal (private) cost and the marginal social cost.

   e. Category I includes firms that impose spillover costs, such as the polluting steel industry.

   Category II includes those goods that impose spillover costs when used by consumers—Ms. Lipska's car, or noise pollution from a loud radio.

   Category III includes firms that provide spillover benefits: a beekeeper's bees provide pollination services; a new tourist attraction will draw visitors who spend money at restaurants and other local businesses; the training of entry-level employees who might be "pirated" by other firms/industries/regions.

   Category IV includes consumption that provides beneficial side effects. Examples may be less obvious for this case. Higher education, which might make students more responsible citizens, is an example. The purchase of medical injections for an infectious disease, careful tending of the weeds in your garden, or allowing someone to listen to or tape your CDs are other examples.

   f. In the presence of negative externalities, the typical government policy is to tax to the extent of the marginal damage cost. Example: a high sales tax might be imposed on noisy boom boxes. In the presence of beneficial externalities, the government might provide a subsidy to stimulate production. Example: grants, or low-interest loans, for higher education.

2. a.

TOLL FEE	USAGE PER YEAR	ANNUAL REVENUES	CONSUMER SURPLUS	TOTAL ANNUAL BENEFITS
$1.00	0	—	—	—
$0.80	20,000	$16,000	$2,000	$18,000
$0.60	40,000	$24,000	$8,000	$32,000
$0.40	60,000	$24,000	$18,000	$42,000
$0.20	80,000	$16,000	$32,000	$48,000
$0.10	90,000	$9,000	$40,500	$49,500
$0.00	100,000	—	$50,000	$50,000

   Example of consumer surplus calculation. When the fee is $.40, the consumer surplus is $.5(1.00 - .40) \times 60,000$, or $18,000. See p. 142.

   b. The bridge would not be built. The maximum possible revenue that can be obtained is $25,000, with a toll of 50¢. Because the cost is $40,000, a private firm would make an economic loss of at least $15,000.

   c. Croatoan should proceed because the total benefit exceeds the total cost.

    d. The City Manager should not impose a toll fee. Any fee will reduce the total benefits from its maximum of $50,000. Suppose the toll were $1.00—no revenue would be raised. No benefits would accrue to Croatoan. By paying the bridge bill, the city would simply have lost $40,000. If, however, the toll were $0.00—no revenue would be raised but $50,000 in consumer surplus would accrue. By paying the bridge bill, the city would gain $10,000.

    e. If a fee were to be charged, a toll of 50¢ would be preferred because revenues would be maximized at $25,000.

    f. Using the answer to part d, where no toll is charged, Croatoan will need to raise $40,000. Increasing taxes by $40,000 within the community would achieve the result. Note: issuing bonds within the community is preferred because individuals can choose whether or not to buy the bonds.

    g. A bridge is a "mixed" good and should be located in Category II. It is mixed because, although it is nonrival (public), it is excludable (private)—Croatoan can charge a toll and exclude free riders, for example.

    h. Compensation will be accepted with Distribution A and, if negotiation and trade between families is allowed, Distribution D. See the table below. The total value of the bay's amenity is less than $10,000 in each of these cases.

FAMILY	DISTRIBUTIONS			
	A	**B**	**C**	**D**
Dare	$1,500	$ 3,000	$ 5,000	$2,500
Howe	$1,500	$ 3,000	$ 3,000	$2,500
Archard	$1,500	$ 3,000	$ 1,000	$2,500
Harvie	$1,500	$ 3,000	$ 1,000	$ 500
Viccars	$1,500	$ 1,000	$ 1,000	$ 500
Total value of Amenity	$7,500	$13,000	$11,000	$8,500
Voting to Accept	Yes 5/No 0	Yes 1/No 4	Yes 3/No 2	Yes 2/No 3
Decision	Accept	Reject	Accept	Reject
Efficient Choice	Efficient	Efficient	Inefficient	Inefficient

    i. The compensation will be accepted with Distributions A and C. See the table above.

    j. Distribution C. See the table above.

    k. With Distribution C, the families would accept compensation of $10,000, although the loss of amenity is valued at $11,000—a bad choice, especially for Dare and Howe. Coase's Theorem suggests that these two families could bribe one other (e.g., Archard) to vote with them. If Archard were given $1,000, his would become the swing vote. Even if Harvie and Viccars retaliated, the higher values placed on amenity by Dare and Howe would reverse the decision. The bridge project would not go through.

3.   a. The MSC curve will no longer represent all the costs borne by the firm. MPC will be lower.

      Lower price, more resources allocated to widget production.

      Pollution.

    b. Noise pollution from a loud radio, air pollution from cars.

      MSB will be lower than MPB.

      Price will be higher, and more resources than the optimal amount will be allocated to widgets.

c. MSB will be higher than MPB.
Prices will be lower, and less than is socially optimal will be allocated.

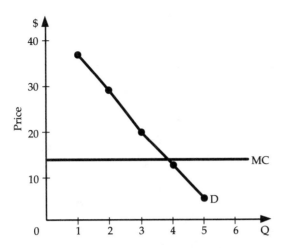

Purchase of medical injections for an infectious disease, careful tending of the weeds in your garden, or allowing someone to listen to or tape your CDs.

d. Training entry-level employees who are subsequently "attracted away" by other firms/industries/regions.
MPC will be higher, and production will be less than the socially optimal level.

4. a. $29. Add Ted, Ned, and Fred's price together for the second unit of the good.
b. See the diagram below.
c. 3 units.
d. See the diagram above.
e. No one will be really happy. Each consumer would prefer to have more of the good produced, given its current price and their revealed preferences.

5. a. D or A (regulation or taxation).
b. D (regulation of flight patterns and jet engines and damages).
c. D (regulation).
d. D (regulation about mufflers).
e. A (license fee—i.e., a tax).
f. C (injunction).
g. B (bargaining).
Most of these have several possible remedies. If your answers differ from these, re-assess the pros and cons of each option.

6. First off, it's unlikely that Billie will prevent the others from having some say in what's played. She might, however, offer to buy them off, essentially renting the radio for her own use. The cost will depend on the preferences of her roommates.

Perhaps you could suggest a cheaper alternative. Billie could request a round-table discussion and vote on the single kind of music acceptable to all. She should rig the voting sequence so that the first vote is jazz vs. loud rock. Jazz would win—Jilly and Billie vs. Lilly. The second vote should be between jazz and bluegrass. Bluegrass will win. Billie should then promptly adjourn the meeting before the others have time to think about the guile of their manipulative roommate.

7. a. See the table below.

Price	Total Quantity
$10	0
$ 8	2
$ 6	4
$ 4	10
$ 2	16
$ 0	22

b. 10 units.
c. See the table below.

Price	Quantity
$16	0
$13 (8 + 5)	2
$10 (6 + 4)	4
$ 7 (4 + 3)	6
$ 4 (2 + 2)	8
$ 1 (0 + 1)	10
$ 0	12

d. 8 units.

8. If Joe can refuse to pay taxes earmarked for defense, so can we all. If Joe rides the bus free, then other (paying) passengers would see an incentive to do the same. Revenues would decrease, and bus service might cease. The two cases, though, are not the same. In the former case, Joe is trying to opt out; in the latter, he is trying to opt in. The traditional response to financing defense expenditures has been taxation and, because voluntary taxes are unlikely to raise much revenue, they must be compulsory. It's difficult to imagine other options for financing this public good.

INCOME DISTRIBUTION AND POVERTY $\boxed{17}$

OBJECTIVES: POINT BY POINT

After completing this chapter, you should be able to accomplish the objectives listed below.

General Comment

Much of the material in this chapter is descriptive rather than theoretical. Aim to have a general idea about the sources of income in the economy, the trend in poverty, the major income-redistribution programs, and the arguments for and against them.

> **LEARNING TIP:** The entire chapter deals with the question of equity, rather than with the efficiency criterion which has dominated the previous chapters. The introductory section distinguishes between the equity (or fairness) criterion and the efficiency criterion for income distribution and draws attention to three questions:
> a. What causes inequality?
> b. How can it be measured?
> c. What is the appropriate role for the government?
>
> Use this three-part scheme to make sense of the material being presented in this chapter.

> **LEARNING TIP:** Do not equate equity or fairness with equality. It may be very equal if your professor gives everyone the same grade on your next exam, but it's unlikely to be fair or equitable!

OBJECTIVE 1: Outline the factors that cause differences in household income.

Several factors may produce inequalities in income distribution. Wage and salary differences may arise because of the nature (quality) of the worker—skills, level of education or training, physical ability—or from the nature of the job—degree of risk, difficulty, or glamour. The distribution of unemployment and the number of wage earners in the family will also have an effect. Property income and transfer payments are also unevenly distributed, with wealthier families tending to have more income-earning property than do poorer families. The concept of human capital is important—we can "invest" in job skills and education.   (page 405)

Certainly, accidents of birth may affect income distribution because property (and property income) can be passed on from one generation to the next. Socialist or Marxist economies, in particular, levy high "death duties" or estate taxes to reduce this source of inequality. An interesting example of this issue emerged in Britain in 1993 when Queen Elizabeth (reputedly the world's richest woman) "volunteered" to pay income taxes for the first time.

PRACTICE

1. Branka earns a degree in electrical engineering. This is an example of
    A. investment in human capital.
    B. wealth accumulation.
    C. income redistribution.
    D. a compensating differential.
    Answer: A. The degree improves Branka's knowledge and skills.

2. The major source of household income is
    A. wages and salaries.
    B. government payments.
    C. property income.
    D. inheritances and bequests.
    Answer: A. See p. 405.

3. In some jobs, workers earn "danger money." Danger money is an example of
    A. payment for human capital.
    B. a compensating differential.
    C. an equity differential.
    D. a bonus.
    Answer: B. Compensating differentials are paid to reward workers who undertake dangerous or unpleasant jobs.

4. Compensating differentials are best described as
    A. government transfer payments to poor families to increase their standard of living.
    B. wage differences caused by differences in human capital.
    C. wage differences caused by differences in working conditions.
    D. wage differences caused by differences in worker productivity.
    Answer: C. See p. 406.

5. _____ comprise property income.
    A. Economic profits and economic rents.
    B. Profits, rents, interest earnings, and dividends.
    C. Profits and dividends.
    D. Unearned interest payments and dividends.
    Answer: B. See p. 408.

6. Which of the following statements is false?
    A. Transfer payments reduce income inequality.
    B. Transfer payments are payments to individuals or households who provide no good or service in exchange.
    C. Transfer payments are used by the government to alleviate poverty.
    D. Eligibility for transfer payment is restricted to those in poverty.
    Answer: D. Almost all workers are eligible for social security.

7. In 1993, Congress passed a $6 billion flood-relief package for Midwest families affected by the flooding of the Mississippi. This is
    A. a compensating differential.
    B. a transfer payment.
    C. property income (rent).
    D. sweat equity.
    Answer: B. No good or service is required in return for the benefits received.

OBJECTIVE 2: Describe the current pattern of income distribution. Identify the information provided by the Lorenz curve and the Gini coefficient.

The distribution of income in the United States has remained quite stable for several decades. The *Lorenz curve* is a graphical device for describing the distribution of income in an economy. The *Gini coefficient* is a numerical measure of income inequality. A Gini coefficient of zero indicates a perfectly equal income distribution while the maximum score (one) indicates perfect inequality. If income were distributed equally, the Lorenz curve would be a 45° line. The more unequal distribution is, the more the curve bends below the 45° line, and the greater the Gini coefficient will be. U.S. income distribution is affected by race and size of household.   (page 408)

PRACTICE

8. The amount of money a household can spend without changing its net assets is called its
   A. money income.
   B. net property income.
   C. economic income.
   D. after-tax (disposable) income.
   Answer: C. See the definition on p. 408.

9. According to the textbook, in 1997 the top 5% of households earned about _____ times as much total income as the bottom 20%.
   A. three
   B. four.
   C. six.
   D. seven.
   Answer: D. See p. 409 and Table 17.1.

10. A Gini coefficient of one means that
    A. income is distributed equally.
    B. all income is earned by one individual.
    C. 50% of income is earned by the poorest 50% of the population.
    D. 20% of income is earned by the richest 20% (quintile) of the population.
    Answer: B. If the Gini coefficient is one, one individual earns all the income. The Lorenz curve would lie along the horizontal axis until 100%.

11. In the bottom 10% of families, transfers account for more than _____ of income.
    A. 20%.
    B. 50%.
    C. 75%.
    D. 80%.
    Answer: D. See p. 409.

12. The Gini coefficient indicates
    A. the percentage of households below the poverty line.
    B. the extent of income inequality in the economy.
    C. the proportion of households with below-average earnings.
    D. the proportion of money income that is in the form of transfer payments.
    Answer: B. The Gini coefficient is a measure of income inequality.

OBJECTIVE 3: Give the official definition of poverty. Describe the trend in poverty in the United States over the past three decades and distinguish between the poverty rates of different groups within the economy.

Poverty may be measured in either absolute or relative terms. The official U.S. poverty line is three times the cost of a nutritionally sound minimum "bundle" of food. A total of 38.1 million persons were below the poverty line in 1995, compared with 40.0 million in 1960 and 35.8 million in the 1980s. The poverty rate is higher among blacks and Hispanics than among whites, and women without husbands form the group with the highest poverty rate. The only group experiencing an increasing poverty rate is children.   (page 412)

Poverty: As you read through the statistics and assess the effectiveness the income-redistribution programs outlined in this chapter, bear in mind the following: the poor are most often the children of the poor and the rich are most often the children of the rich. Poverty is strongly linked to family background. Additionally, most of those in poverty have failed to complete ten years of schooling. What should this tell you about the importance of *human capital*?

Keep in mind the *underclass*, that group which even the statistics fail to measure, or the programs to help, simply because they have dropped out of the system. Do our poverty and income distribution figures record people such as teenage runaways, the rural unemployed, undocumented aliens, deinstitutionalized mental patients, or drug addicts? Are these groups part of the poverty problem?

PRACTICE

13. Of the following groups, the one with the highest poverty rate is
    A. Hispanics.
    B. women living in households with no husband present.
    C. children.
    D. senior citizens.
    Answer: B. See p. 414.

14. If the Department of Agriculture determines that the cost of a minimum food bundle is $5,000 per year, the poverty line is established at
    A. $5,000 per year.
    B. $10,000 per year.
    C. $15,000 per year.
    D. $20,000 per year.
    Answer: C. The official poverty line is determined by multiplying the cost of the food bundle by three. See p. 412.

OBJECTIVE 4: State the arguments for and against redistribution of income. Summarize the theories underlying these arguments.

The main argument *against income redistribution* is that one should be allowed to retain one's earnings—for Angela to receive extra income, for example, Bill must lose some of his. A disincentive to work may exist both for the individual who loses income *and* for the transfer's recipient. It is argued that the U.S. economic system is based on private property ownership and freedom of contract. Redistribution might undermine the system and reduce incentives to improve oneself.   (page 414)

The main argument *in support of income distribution* is a moral appeal—the rich should help those less fortunate than themselves to enjoy the necessities of life. The utilitarians, Rawls, and Marx have all constructed quite sophisticated philosophical formulations in support of this view.   (page 415)

In practice, most countries undertake some redistribution of income and wealth. Usually this is done through a progressive income tax system—where progressively higher tax rates are applied to the incomes of individuals with higher incomes—and through government payments (transfers). In the United States the overall tax system is only mildly progressive, but the transfer programs—including, among others, social security, "welfare," unemployment compensation, Medicare and Medicaid—do pay most benefits to those in lower income brackets.

PRACTICE

15. "A dollar is worth less to a rich person than to a poor person." This is a basic belief of
    A. utilitarian justice.
    B. Rawlsian justice.
    C. Marxian justice.
    D. social justice.
    Answer: A. Utilitarians would argue that redistribution from rich to poor increases society's total utility. See p. 416.

16. _____ is a theory of income distribution that claims that the social contract emerging from the original position would maximize the well-being of the _____
    A. Utilitarian justice, most typical member of society.
    B. Utilitarian justice, worst-off member of society.
    C. Rawlsian justice, most typical member of society.
    D. Rawlsian justice, worst-off member of society.
    Answer: D. In the original position, each member of society, according to Rawls, will be concerned about the position of the least fortunate.

17. Each of the following is an assumption in Rawls' theory except that
    A. individuals are risk averse.
    B. individuals may become rich.
    C. individuals may become poor.
    D. individuals may opt out of the social contract.
    Answer: D. Bargaining will continue until all members of society agree upon a contract. See p. 416.

18. Marx argued that _____ value derives from labor and that profits were
    A. all, a necessary return for ownership of resources and risk-taking.
    B. all, an expropriation of surplus value.
    C. some, a necessary return for ownership of resources and risk-taking.
    D. some, an expropriation of surplus value.
    Answer: B. According to Marx, the value of production depends solely on the amount of labor required to produce it.

OBJECTIVE 5: Describe the two major government redistribution programs and the groups that they seek to reach.

The government has used two broad sets of programs to affect the distribution of income, taxes and expenditure programs.   (page 417)

   a. *The tax system.* The progressivity of the income tax system is set against evidence that the U.S. tax system overall is almost proportional—each taxpayer, regardless of income, pays pretty much the same percentage of her or his income to the government. Conclusion: There's little income distribution being caused by the tax system.

   b. *Transfer and other expenditure programs.* Despite the purpose and scope of government expenditure programs, poverty has increased in recent years. Whether this is due to inadequate economic growth or inadequate redistribution programs remains an open question.

Welfare has been under increasing attack in recent years. The system may reduce incentives to work, be unfair to those who do work but receive low pay, and it may undermine "family values." Opponents also contend that the welfare has failed in its goal—the number of households in poverty is higher than ever. Finally, if poverty is relative (see p. 412), it may make more sense to dismantle the single national system and place responsibility at the state/local level.   (page 418)

Welfare Cadillacs: Abuses exist in government transfer programs—we are tempted to believe that "welfare" recipients are spongers. A report in the early 1990s indicated that 41.7% of poor people had a job and that only one third of poor people received welfare. The same report indicated that 20 million Americans suffered from hunger each month.

PRACTICE

19. _____ is the transfer program given the credit for significantly reducing poverty among senior citizens.
    A. Medicare.
    B. Social security.
    C. Food Stamps.
    D. Temporary Assistance for Needy Families.
    Answer: B. See p. 418.

20. The social security system includes all of the following programs except
    A. unemployment compensation.
    B. disability insurance program.
    C. health insurance program.
    D. OASI.
    Answer: A. See p. 418. Unemployment compensation is part of the public assistance (welfare) program.

> **LEARNING TIP:** This is the last chapter in the sequence examining the advantages and disadvantages of the market system. Chapter 18 begins a sequence of "topics" chapters. It's a good time to review your notes and summarize what has been covered. You may find it useful to re-read Chapters 1 and 2.

Conclusion

The chapter ends by pulling together some of the themes developed during earlier chapters. A market system, operating with complete efficiency, may still not be considered fair because some people—through handicap or inborn talent, luck, lack of education, or unemployment—will have more or less than others. In theory, efforts at redistribution should be aimed at redistributing well-being or *utility*, which (unfortunately) is neither observable nor measurable. Income and wealth are substitute measures of utility. The government's income-redistribution program itself is an imperfect instrument, and the debate continues as to the appropriate extent of government intervention in the economy.

  PRACTICE TEST

I. MULTIPLE CHOICE QUESTIONS.

Select the option that provides the single best answer.

_____ 1. Inefficiency is shown in a utility possibilities frontier diagram by
    A. a point inside the curve.
    B. a point outside the curve.
    C. the point where the curve reaches the vertical axis.
    D. any point not on the curve.

2. If the Gini coefficient is equal to zero, all of the following certainly are true except
   A. the Lorenz curve graphs as a straight line.
   B. income is equally distributed.
   C. the lowest quintile of the population will receive as many dollars as the highest quintile.
   D. we have an efficient distribution of income.

3. Society consists of two individuals, Richie Rich, (a millionaire who is so obsessed with money that his marginal utility of income increases with each extra dollar he gets) and Kermit the Hermit (a recluse who has rejected money and other earthly goods and finds that his marginal utility of income decreases with each extra dollar he gets). If income is transferred from the rich to the poor, we can say that society's
   A. total utility will increase.
   B. total utility will decrease.
   C. total utility will remain unchanged.
   D. total utility will change, but the net effect is uncertain.

4. Government retraining programs can be viewed as
   A. an inefficient method of income redistribution.
   B. an investment in human capital.
   C. a movement away from the utility possibilities frontier.
   D. regressive programs.

5. Which of the following is not a reason for variations in income from wages and salaries?
   A. Ownership of differing amounts of human capital.
   B. Compensating differentials.
   C. Unemployment.
   D. Ownership of differing amounts of real capital.

6. A politician promising to support greater equality of property income on one hand, and a more efficient allocation of resources on the other, may well be committed to
   A. two conflicting objectives. Equality and efficiency are not the same.
   B. two conflicting objectives. To achieve efficiency it may be necessary to let investors earn large rewards from their investment.
   C. two complementary objectives. Efficiency and equality must go hand in hand in a growing market economy.
   D. two complementary objectives. The more efficient and rewarding the property market is, the more participants there will be.

7. If the resource markets work correctly, then rewards are based on productivity. Therefore,
   A. because capital adds to the productivity of labor, owners of capital should earn a higher return.
   B. because labor is essential to all production processes, labor should be paid a higher rate of return.
   C. wages and salaries should be paid in accordance with the marginal productivity of workers.
   D. because there are more workers than machines, labor should be cheaper to hire and so earn less.

_____ 8. Income redistribution is considered to be a public good. Which of the following is a problem for implementing income redistribution as it relates to public goods?
A. People see no point in contributing voluntarily because their contribution will be insignificant.
B. People deserve to retain the fruits of their labors.
C. Giving people handouts may reduce their incentives to work and save.
D. The poor are often "free riders" living on welfare.

_____ 9. The income tax system is "progressive." This means that
A. progressively more persons are taxed each year.
B. those with higher income pay a higher percentage of it in taxes.
C. if a person earning $10,000 pays $3,000 in taxes, a person earning $20,000 would pay twice as much ($6,000) in taxes.
D. the more you earn, the more you pay.

_____ 10. Which of the following is not an argument against income redistribution?
A. Everyone is entitled to keep the fruits of his or her own efforts.
B. Freedom of contract.
C. Society has a moral obligation to provide for the basic needs of all citizens.
D. Redistribution reduces incentives to work, save, and invest.

_____ 11. In successive decades, Country A records a Gini coefficient of .3 (1960s), .7 (1970s), and 1.0 (1980s). Population has remained stable throughout the time period. We can state that
A. Country A's income distribution has become more equal as time has passed.
B. Country A had fewer poor people in the 1980s than in the 1960s.
C. the top 20% of income was earned by a smaller number of families in the 1980s than in the 1960s.
D. the gap between Country A's Lorenz curve and the 45° line has decreased as time has passed.

_____ 12. Jackie Blue is a police officer who patrols a dangerous high-crime neighborhood. Jackie earns more than officers who work in low-crime neighborhoods. This is an example of
A. a return on human capital.
B. a compensating differential.
C. a productivity differential.
D. a compensating productivity differential.

_____ 13. If we plot a Lorenz curve for U.S. income and another for U.S. wealth, the Lorenz curve for income will be _____ bowed; its Gini coefficient will be _____
A. more, larger.
B. more, smaller.
C. less, larger.
D. less, smaller.

_____ 14. The U.S. government could probably reduce the Gini coefficient by
A. reducing government spending on welfare programs.
B. eliminating student loan programs.
C. increasing taxes on inherited wealth.
D. cutting the capital gains tax rates.

_____ 15. If the area between the Lorenz curve and the line of perfect equality
became larger, we could conclude that the distribution of income
had become
A. more unequal.
B. less unequal.
C. more inefficient.
D. less inefficient.

_____ 16. According to Marx, the major source of inequality in the distribu-
tion of income is
A. property income.
B. labor income.
C. human capitalism.
D. social contracts.

_____ 17. Alice and Betty have trained as nurses in Memphis. Alice moves to
New York to work in a private hospital and earns $30,000. Betty
moves to New Orleans to work as a community health nurse and
earns $15,000. The cost of living is about 15% higher in New York
than in New Orleans. Which of the following is true?
A. Alice is better off than Betty, because she earns $15,000 more.
B. Betty must be better off, because she did not need to take the
job for $30,000.
C. Alice must be better off, because her earnings are double those
of Betty but the cost of living in New York is less than double
that in New Orleans.
D. We cannot determine who is better off, because income is an
imperfect measure of utility.

Use the following utility possibilities frontier to answer the next question.

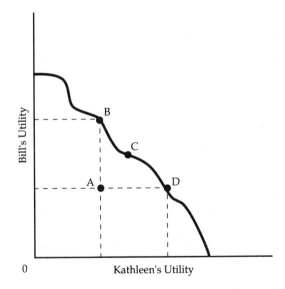

_____ 18. Which of the following moves is (are) efficient?
A. A to B.
B. A to C.
C. A to D.
D. All of the above moves are efficient.

Use the following Lorenz curve for the nation of Arboc to answer the next two questions.

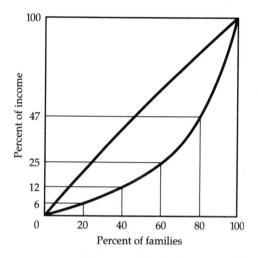

_____ 19. The top fifth of Arbocali families earn _____ % of income.
A. 20.
B. 47.
C. 53.
D. 80.

_____ 20. The third fifth of families earn _____ % of income.
A. 6.
B. 12.
C. 13.
D. 25.

II. APPLICATION QUESTIONS.

1. Use the following income distribution for the nation of Arboc.

Personal income class	% of all families in this class	% of total income received by this class	% of all families in this and all lower classes	% of total income received by this and all lower classes
Under $5,000	20	2	20	2
5,000–9,999	10	5	30	7
10,000–14,999	12	10		
15,000–19,999	15	15		
20,000–24,999	20	15		
25,000–49,999	13	22		
50,000 and over	10	30	100	100

a. Complete the table above.
b. Households earning less than $10,000 make up the lowest _____ % of the population and receive _____ % of the income, while those earning $25,000 or more make up _____ % of the population and receive _____ % of the income.

c. Use the information in the table to plot a Lorenz curve in the space below. Remember to plot the zero-zero point and to draw as smooth a curve as possible. Shade in the area on the graph that indicates inequality in income.

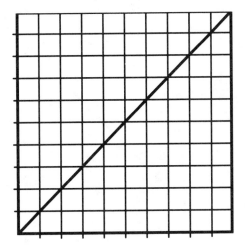

2. A tax is progressive (p. 418) if those with higher incomes pay a higher percentage of their income in tax. The opposite is called a regressive tax, i.e., those with higher incomes pay a lower percentage of their income in tax.

   a. A progressive tax will make income distribution _____ (more/less) equal.

   Three sales tax proposals have come before your state government. In each case, identify whether the tax will be progressive or regressive and, therefore, the effect on the distribution of income.

   b. A 20% sales tax on fur coats.
   c. A 12% sales tax on groceries.
   d. A general sales tax of 6% on all goods.

3. The Department of Agriculture has determined that a nutritionally sound minimum food bundle costs $23 per week per person.

   a. Calculate the poverty line for a family of four.

   The U.S. Bureau of the Census provides the following information for four-person families. There are 14,556,000 four-person families in the United States.

INCOME	PERCENTAGE OF FAMILIES	PERCENTAGE OF INCOME (CUMULATIVE)
$75,000 and over	15.3	100.0
$50,000 − $74,999	22.5	37.5
$35,000 − $49,999	22.9	25.0
$25,000 − $34,999	14.9	17.5
$15,000 − $24,999	12.4	12.5
$10,000 − $14,999	4.8	7.5
$5,000 − $9,999	4.6	5.0
Under $5,000	2.7	2.5

b. Using the data points you have, plot a Lorenz curve for four-person families.

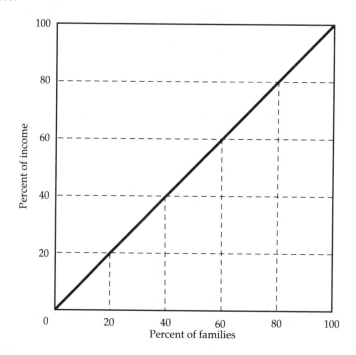

c. Draw a line (AB) perpendicular to the 45° line to the lower right-hand corner of the Lorenz curve diagram. The portion of this line between the Lorenz curve and the 45° line (AC), when divided by AB, gives an approximate estimate of the Gini coefficient. Estimate the Gini coefficient for this economy.

d. Given the income distribution above, calculate the poverty rate for four-person families. The poverty rate is the percentage of four-person families with incomes below the poverty line.

Mona Gregson is a twenty-five year old unmarried mother with three children, Rachel, 8, Peter, 7, and Michael, 2. Mona dropped out of high school when she became pregnant with Rachel and never graduated. She has no marketable job skills and has never had a job. Each month, Mona receives $800 in Temporary Assistance for Needy Families and $300 in Food Stamps. She has applied for a housing subsidy but has been rejected. The family is eligible for Medicaid. Assume that she pays no taxes.

e. What is the Gregsons' money income? In the income distribution above, where does Mona's family fit? Are they poor?

f. What is Mona's annual economic income?

g. Mona's Food Stamp allowance is increased to $400 per month. How does this affect her economic income? Her money income? Her position in the income distribution?

The state government has instituted a 15-week vocational training program. The participant's welfare benefits are maintained and s/he receives a modest travel allowance. Day care facilities are available during the program and for the first year after the trainee begins to work.

On completion of the program, the graduate will receive a $7.25 per hour clerical job with the state government. Monthly income is $1200. However, 7.65% will go to FICA (Federal social security payroll tax) and 1.35% will go to state payroll tax. Annual Federal and state income tax payments will be $660. Commuting/parking fees amount to $25 per month.

h. If Mona completes the program and gets the promised clerical job, will the Gregsons still be below the poverty line?

i. Are the Gregsons better off with Mona employed or on welfare?
j. Calculate the "tax" imposed on Mona as she moves from welfare to work.
k. If Mona wishes to maximize her net income, should she stay on welfare or enter the training program?

The state government implements a 15% tax on food items.

l. How will this new tax affect the distribution of income in Mona's state? How will the Gini coefficient change?

You decide to contribute $100 to help alleviate poverty. Family A and Family B are identical in all respects except that Family A is much poorer than Family B.

m. Would you be happier seeing your $100 go to Family A or to Family B?
n. Would you be happy if you kept your money and someone else contributed $100 to Family A?

Case and Fair suggest that income redistribution is a public good (p. 417). My increased happiness, caused by reduced income inequality does not interfere with your increased happiness—nonrivalry. If income distribution becomes more equal, I cannot be excluded from the benefits—nonexcludability.

Two points arise: Contributions may provide (some) satisfaction for the donor but, acting independently, probably the donor's benefits will be less than his costs. As the income level of the recipient rises, the marginal benefit derived *by the donor* from extra contributions decreases. The MB (marginal benefit) curve in the diagram below reflects these conclusions. The marginal cost of a dollar donated is a dollar for the contributor. The *MC private* curve reflects this conclusion.

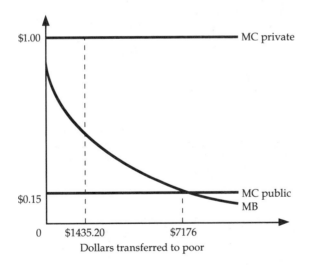

The poverty line is drawn at $14,352 and about 12% of families are "poor." Suppose that the average income of "poor" households is $14,352/2, or $7176. The distribution above shows that 60% of families (the "well-off") earn $35,000 or more.

o. Each poor family requires how much, on average, to reach the poverty line? Ignore taxes and so on.
p. If each "well-off" family contributes an equal amount, how much would they have to contribute to alleviate poverty?
q. Explain why each well-off family, acting independently, will not contribute the amount you determined in part p. Use the diagram above.
r. The well-off families get together and sign a binding contract to contribute $1435.20 each to help alleviate poverty. Explain why each well-off family will find it worthwhile to contribute.
s. Explain why such a contract is unlikely to be enacted.

4. Suppose that you lose your job (either real or imagined). Although you still have whatever savings and other assets you previously had, you have no other immediate source of income, including welfare checks or parents. You still have any financial commitments previously contracted. How would you react to this financial crisis? As the days pass, you may begin to see the real distress concealed behind unemployment and poverty statistics and the genuine relief offered by government programs.

5. To get a feel for poverty, volunteer at a local soup kitchen.

6. Suppose that, in a two-person economy, there exists the following utility possibilities frontier.

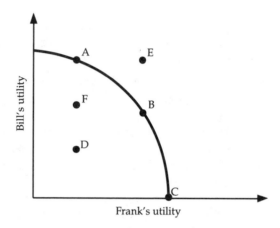

a. Which of the points is currently unattainable?
b. Which point would Bill prefer, B or F?
c. Which points represent maximum efficiency?
d. Why would Bill and Frank welcome a move from point D to point B on the curve?
e. Why would there be opposition to a move from D to C, but no opposition to a move from D to A?

7. What is the meaning of equity and why might economists study it? Why might it be difficult to study? Is a more equal distribution of income also more equitable? Do you think that there might be a trade-off between equality and equity? If so, given your knowledge of the present distribution of income in the United States, would you favor more equality or more equity?

ANSWERS AND SOLUTIONS

PRACTICE TEST

I. SOLUTIONS TO MULTIPLE CHOICE QUESTIONS

1. A. A point inside the curve indicates that individual I or J, or both, could increase satisfaction without the other individual losing anything.
2. D. The income distribution is certainly equal, but it doesn't follow that it is efficient.
3. B. This is the opposite case to the one suggested by the utilitarians. See p. 416.
4. B. Training or retraining programs develop the talents and improve the skills of the labor force—i.e., they are an investment in human capital.
5. D. Ownership of real capital will result in nonwage income.
6. B. The politician is dealing with the arguments for and against redistribution (p. 414). One argument against redistribution is that it reduces incentives to work and, therefore, reduces efficiency.
7. C. Note, though, that this is not the Marxian view.
8. A. This is the "drop-in-the-bucket" problem. See p. 417.

9.   B. With a progressive tax system, extra earnings are taxed at higher rates. Option D is true whenever the marginal tax rate is positive, even if the tax system is not progressive.
10. C. Option C is an argument often used by those who favor income redistribution.
11. C. As the Gini coefficient increases, income inequality increases.
12. B. Because Jackie has a more dangerous, less attractive "beat," the extra payment she receives is a compensating differential. See p. 406.
13. D. U.S. income is more evenly distributed than U.S. wealth is, so the Lorenz curve for income will be less bowed. The gap between the 45° line and the Lorenz curve (the Gini coefficient) will be smaller.
14. C. Taxing inheritances would reduce property income for subsequent generations.
15. A. The greater the gap, the greater the inequality.
16. A. See p. 416.
17. D. "It is important that you remember throughout this chapter—that income and wealth are imperfect measures of well-being." See p. 404.
18. D. A move is efficient if the utility of one individual increases without a decrease in the utility of the other.
19. C. 80% of families earn 47% of the income, the remaining 53% of income is earned by the top 20%.
20. C. The lowest 40% earn 12% of income. The lowest 60% earn 25%. By subtraction, the third fifth of families earn 13%.

II. SOLUTIONS TO APPLICATION QUESTIONS

1.   a.   See the table below.

Personal income class	% of all families in this class	% of total income received by this class	% of all families in this and all lower classes	% of total income received by this and all lower classes
Under $5,000	20	2	20	2
$5,000–9,999	10	5	30	7
$10,000–14,999	12	10		
$15,000–19,999	15	15		
$20,000–24,999	20	15		
$25,000–49,999	13	22		
$50,000 and over	10	30	100	100

b.   30; 7; 23; 52.
c.   See the diagram below.

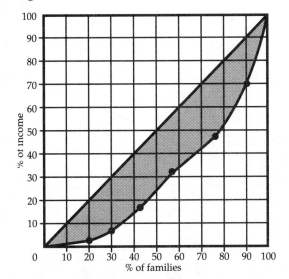

2. a. more.
    b. Progressive. Fur coats are bought predominantly by rich individuals so poor families will be unaffected while rich purchasers will pay the tax.
    c. Regressive. A 6% sales tax on groceries must be paid by all households, but the poor spend a relatively larger proportion of their income of groceries so, relatively, their tax payment will be greater.
    d. Regressive. A general sales tax is more broadly based than a food tax but, because poor households spend most or all of their income while rich households do not, the relative tax payment of the poor will be greater.

3. a. $23 \times 4 \times 52 \times 3 = \$14,352$.
    b. See the diagram below.

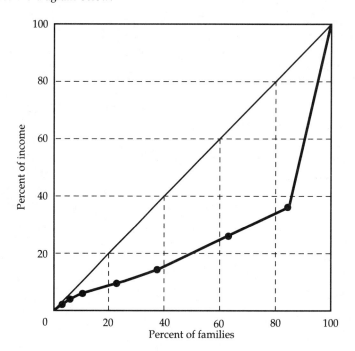

    c. The Gini coefficient $= AC/AB = 11/28 = .39$. See the diagram below.

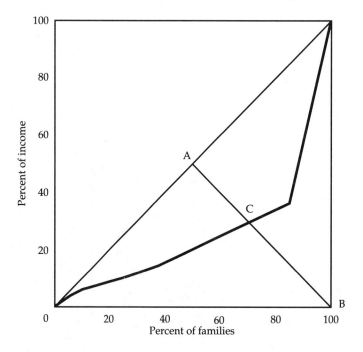

CHAPTER 17: INCOME DISTRIBUTION AND POVERTY **395**

d. $14,352 is about 87% of the way through the third class. Correspondingly, 4.18% is about 87% of 4.8%.
   2.7 + 4.6 + 4.18 = 11.48% of four-person families are in poverty. This amounts to 1,671,029 four-person families in poverty.

e. The Gregsons are below the poverty line. Their yearly income is $800 × 12, or $9,600. Food Stamps, which are in-kind transfers are not figured in. In the table above, the Gregsons would be in the third lowest category.

f. Economic income would include both the cash and in-kind payments. The Gregsons' annual economic income would be ($800 + $300) × 12 = $13,200.

g. Mona's economic income will rise by $100 per month. Annual economic income is $14,400. Her money income and her position in the income distribution are unchanged.

h. Mona's annual income will be $1200 × 12 = $14,400. This is (just) above the poverty line.

i. The Gregsons are worse off. Their income is $14,400. Deductions include payroll taxes of (.0765 + .0135) × $14,400, or $1296, income taxes of $660, and commuting/parking fees of $300. Total deductions are $2256. The Gregsons' income, after deductions, is $12,144 which is less than her economic income from welfare ($14,400).

j. Taxes while on welfare = $0. Taxes while working = $1956. Change = $1956. Welfare income = $14,400. Work income: $14,400. Change = $0.
   Mona's income didn't change, but her tax liability increased by $1956. This is a clear disincentive to work. Note that she also loses Medicaid benefits.

k. Unless she wishes to feel self-supporting, or she believes that the starting-level job will lead to higher-wage positions, Mona should stay on welfare.

l. The distribution of income will become less equal. See the answer to part c. The Gini coefficient will move closer to a value of 1.00.

m. Most persons would agree that the $100 would be worth more to Family A and that helping that family would provide the greater satisfaction.

n. Most persons derive satisfaction from the alleviation of poverty, especially if they don't have to pay for it. We cannot be excluded from this benefit if we refuse to contribute.

o. If the average income of "poor" households is $7176, each family needs an additional $7176 on average.

p. (12%/60%) × $7176 = $1435.20 per "well-off" household.

q. The marginal benefit of transferring $1435.20 is less than the private marginal cost.

r. The families will find contributing $1435.20 worthwhile because, by acting as a group, the marginal cost of transferring $7176 dollars has been reduced for each family.

s. Poverty alleviation is a public good. If every other well-off family contributes and I don't, I get the benefits without the cost. If each family follows the same logic, no one will sign.

4–5. The answers to these Applications are left to your own initiative.

6. a. E.
   b. F.
   c. A and C. Any point on the frontier is a point of maximum efficiency.
   d. There would be an increase in utility for each.
   e. A move from D to C would reduce Bill's utility—he would certainly oppose this. However, a move from D to A would increase Bill's utility without reducing Frank's. (In terms of efficiency, what does this mean?)

7. An equitable distribution of income is a fair distribution. One's opinion of what is fair is likely to be shaped by one's position in society and what one has to gain or lose from change. (Rawls attempted to address this issue.) Is it fair, for example, for some workers to be employed for 40 hours each week and for other, equally capable, workers to be unemployed? Are inheritances fair? Certainly, equity and equality are not identical concepts. It is not equitable to force all individuals to have the same income and wealth, if needs differ (e.g., if there are special medical expenses).

COMPREHENSIVE REVIEW TEST FOR PART 3

The following questions provide a wide-ranging review of the material covered in Part 3 (Chapters 13–17) of the textbook. Each question deals with a topic or technique important for your understanding of economic principles. If you miss a question you should return to the relevant section of the chapter in the textbook and fine-tune your understanding.

PRACTICE TEST

MULTIPLE CHOICE QUESTIONS.

Select the option that provides the single best answer.

_____ 1. Monty the Monopolist is seeking to maximize profits. Currently, he is producing where marginal revenue is more than marginal cost. He should
A. increase production.
B. increase price.
C. reduce production.
D. produce where price is equal to marginal cost.

_____ 2. The total cost to Walt's Widget Works of producing 1 widget is $24. The total cost of producing 2 widgets is $36. The total cost of producing 3 widgets is $50. Currently, MR = MC at 2 widgets. Which of the following is *certainly* true when 2 widgets are produced?
A. The demand for Walt's widgets is elastic.
B. Walt is making an economic profit.
C. Walt is making an economic loss but should produce.
D. Walt is making an economic loss and should shut down.

Use the following information to answer the next three questions. Marcel the Monopolist has a constant marginal cost of $3. Fixed costs are $4.

PRICE	QUANTITY DEMANDED
$10	0
$9	1
$8	2
$7	3
$6	4
$5	5
$4	6
$3	7

_____ 3. Given the demand schedule and cost information, Marcel will maximize profits by setting a price of
   A. $8.
   B. $7.
   C. $6.
   D. $5.

_____ 4. At the profit-maximizing output level, Marcel's economic profit will be
   A. $12.
   B. $10.
   C. $8.
   D. $6.

_____ 5. Currently, Marcel is producing at the output level where price equals marginal cost. Which of the following strategies will increase Marcel's profits?
   A. Maintain price and output—Marcel is already maximizing profit.
   B. Increase price and decrease output.
   C. Decrease price and increase output.
   D. Decrease price and decrease output.

Use the following diagram, which shows the revenue and cost curves for coffee, to answer the next two questions. Initially, this is a perfectly competitive industry.

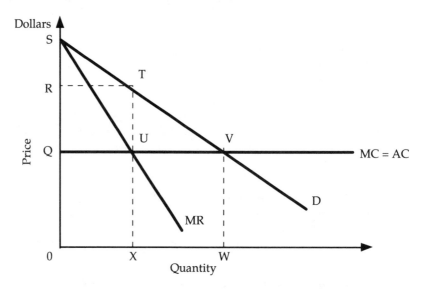

_____ 6. If the coffee industry becomes a monopoly, the loss in consumer surplus will be
   A. TUV.
   B. RST.
   C. QRTU.
   D. QRTV.

_____ 7. If the coffee industry becomes a monopoly, the net loss in social welfare is equal to _____ . The monopolist will be willing to spend an area equal to _____ to preserve the monopoly.
   A. TUV, QRTV.
   B. TUV, QRTU.
   C. QRTU, TUV.
   D. QRTV, TUV.

_____ 8. The Averch-Johnson effect usually occurs in
   A. oligopolies. It is an underinvestment in capital.
   B. regulated monopolies. It is an overinvestment in capital.
   C. monopolistically competitive firms. It is an underinvestment in capital.
   D. public goods. It is an overinvestment in capital.

_____ 9. Price exceeds marginal revenue for Mose the Monopolist because
   A. Mose's firm faces a perfectly elastic demand curve.
   B. Mose must reduce price on all units if he wants to attract more customers.
   C. the demand exceeds average total cost at the profit-maximizing output level.
   D. of economies of scale.

_____ 10. Wallace Gromits Incorp. is a natural monopoly if
   A. the firm holds patents that protect it from potential rivals.
   B. the government has issued Wallace an exclusive license to produce gromits.
   C. Wallace has sole ownership of toastite, an essential mineral in the production of gromits.
   D. economies of scale permit Wallace to produce gromits at a lower average cost than potential rivals.

Use the following diagram to answer the next four questions which depicts an monopolistically competitive firm.

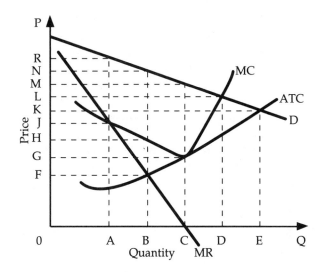

_____ 11. The profit-maximizing output level is
   A. OA.
   B. OB.
   C. OD.
   D. OE.

_____ 12. The profit-maximizing price is
A. OF.
B. OG.
C. OH.
D. ON.

_____ 13. The firm's maximum short-run profit is
A. OB × HN.
B. OC × GM.
C. OB × FN.
D. OC × HN.

_____ 14. In the short run firms will _____ this industry. In the long run firms _____ this industry.
A. enter, enter
B. enter, not enter
C. not enter, enter
D. not enter, not enter

_____ 15. Which statement is false? For the monopolistically competitive firm, economic profits
A. will never occur, because it is easy for firms to enter the industry.
B. attract new firms, causing each existing firm's demand curve to shift left.
C. attract new firms, causing each existing firm's demand curve become more elastic.
D. will be zero in long-run equilibrium.

_____ 16. In long-run equilibrium, monopolistic competition is
A. efficient because easy entry and exit eliminate economic profit.
B. efficient because firms produce where marginal revenue and long-run average cost are equal and where average revenue and long-run average cost are equal.
C. not efficient because too little output is produced—marginal cost is less than demand and average cost is not minimized.
D. not efficient because too little output is produced—marginal cost is still increasing.

_____ 17. Mando the Monopolist is producing where demand is inelastic. An increase in price will
A. increase total revenue, increase total cost and increase profit.
B. increase total revenue, decrease total cost and increase profit.
C. decrease total revenue, increase total cost and decrease profit.
D. decrease total revenue, decrease total cost and increase profit.

_____ 18. "Many sellers each offering a somewhat differentiated product" is a description of
A. perfect competition
B. monopoly.
C. monopolistic competition.
D. oligopoly.

_____ 19. A perfectly competitive firm maximizes profit by producing where _____ ; an imperfectly competitive firm maximizes profit by producing where _____ .
A. P = MC; P = MC
B. P = MC; P > MC
C. MR = MC; P < MC
D. MR = MC; P = MC

_____ 20. A market is contestable if
A. entry and exit are costless.
B. entry is easy but exit is restricted.
C. entry is restricted but exit is easy.
D. entry and exit are restricted.

_____ 21. To achieve the efficient output level, we must equate marginal benefit with
A. marginal damage cost.
B. marginal social cost.
C. marginal private cost.
D. marginal external cost.

_____ 22. It is assumed that the marginal benefit of consumption _____ as additional units are consumed while the marginal private cost _____ as additional units are consumed.
A. remains constant, increases.
B. remains constant, remains constant.
C. decreases, increases.
D. decreases, remains constant.

_____ 23. Papyrus Paper Mill is producing where its marginal revenue equals its marginal private cost. Marginal social cost exceeds Papyrus' marginal private cost. Papyrus is an example of
A. an externality.
B. a monopoly.
C. a public good.
D. regulated monopoly.

_____ 24. Country A has a Gini coefficient of .3 while Country B has a Gini coefficient of .7. We can state that Country A has
A. more poor people than Country B.
B. fewer poor people than Country B.
C. a more equal distribution of income than Country B.
D. a less equal distribution of income than Country B.

_____ 25. The essence of the utilitarian argument in favor of income redistribution is that a dollar transferred from a rich person to a poor person will increase total utility because the marginal utility of a poor person
A. increases faster than that of a rich person.
B. increases more slowly than that of a rich person.
C. is higher than that of a rich person.
D. is lower than that of a rich person.

Use the following diagram to answer the next five questions.

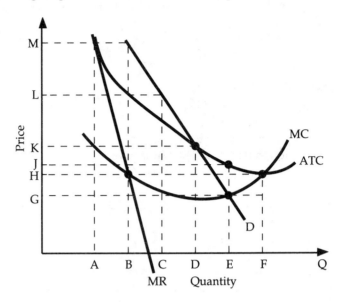

_____ 26. The type of industry depicted in the diagram above is best described as
A. a pure monopoly.
B. a natural monopoly.
C. imperfectly competitive.
D. an artificial monopoly.

_____ 27. At the most efficient output level, this firm would earn an economic
A. profit of OB × HM.
B. profit of OE × GJ.
C. loss of OB × HM.
D. loss of OE × GJ.

_____ 28. If Max, the owner of this firm, could choose his own output and price levels, he would choose an output of _____ and a price of

_____
A. OB, OM.
B. OD, OK.
C. OE, OG.
D. OF, OH.

_____ 29. If a price ceiling were imposed at OG, Max would
A. still produce OB units because this is where MR = MC.
B. have to receive a subsidy of HM dollars per unit.
C. have to receive a subsidy of GJ dollars per unit.
D. earn an economic profit of OE × GJ.

_____ 30. If a price ceiling were imposed at OK,
A. Max would earn an economic profit of OD × GJ.
B. the government would have to subsidize Max to the tune of KG dollars per unit.
C. Max would produce OB units because this is where MR = MC.
D. Max would make a normal profit and remain in the industry.

APPLICATION QUESTION.

Here is some information for the Hour Time Together Clock Company. HTT is in an industry with no external economies or diseconomies of scale.

Number of Workers	Marginal Product	Total Product		Price	Total Revenue	Marginal Revenue
0	—	0		—	—	—
1	20			$30.00		
2	30			$29.00	$1450	
3	28	78		$28.00		
4		104		$27.00		
5		125		$26.00		
6	19			$25.00		
7	10			$24.00		
8	8			$23.00		
9		168		$22.00		
10	2	170		$21.00		

1. Complete the table.
2. In the $27 − $28 price range, estimate the price elasticity of demand. Is it elastic, inelastic, unitary elastic, or can't you tell?
3. Is this firm perfectly competitive or imperfectly competitive? How can you tell?

Hour Time Together has total fixed costs of $2100. The wage of each (variable) worker is $120. Let us now suppose that Hour Time Together is a firm in a monopolistically competitive industry.

4. Complete the following table.

Number of Workers	Marginal Product	Total Cost	Average Total Cost	Average Variable Cost	Marginal Cost
0	—		—	—	—
1	20				
2	30		$46.80		
3	28	$2460			
4					
5					
6	19				
7	10				
8	8			$5.93	
9					
10	2				

5. Find the profit-maximizing output level (of the output levels given).
6. What price should be charged to maximize economic profit? What will be the maximum economic profit?
7. Predict what will happen to the number of firms in this industry in the short run.
8. Predict what will happen to the number of firms in this industry in the long run. Explain your answer.

Assume that the minimum short-run average cost (in the table) is also its minimum average cost in the long run.

9. Describe what will happen to the position of its demand curve in the long run.
10. Describe what will happen to the elasticity of its demand curve in the long run.
11. Of the output levels given, what would be the price and output level of a perfectly competitive firm in the long run?
12. Explain why (or why not) the firm's marginal cost curve will be steeper in the long run than in the short run.

ANSWERS AND SOLUTIONS

ANSWERS TO REVIEW TEST FOR PART 3

1. A. If marginal revenue is more than marginal cost, Monty should increase production until marginal revenue equals marginal cost.
2. A. The marginal cost of the second widget is $12. Marginal revenue, therefore, is $12. When marginal revenue is positive, the firm is operating in the elastic portion of its demand curve. If you missed this, review price elasticity in Chapter 5.
3. C. Marginal revenue is $3 and equal to marginal cost at 4 units of output. Refer to the following table.

PRICE	QUANTITY DEMANDED	TOTAL REVENUE	MARGINAL REVENUE	TOTAL COST	MARGINAL COST
$10	0	$ 0	—	$ 4	—
$9	1	$ 9	$9	$ 7	$3
$8	2	$16	$7	$10	$3
$7	3	$21	$5	$13	$3
$6	4	$24	$3	$16	$3
$5	5	$25	$1	$19	$3
$4	6	$24	−$1	$22	$3
$3	7	$21	−$3	$25	$3

4. C. At 4 units of output, total revenue is $24 and total cost is $16.
5. B. Price equals marginal cost at 7 units. Marginal revenue is less than marginal cost, therefore Marcel should cut production. He is then able to increase the price he charges.
6. D. The consumer surplus under perfect competition was SQV—the gap between the demand curve and price. Under a monopoly, this area shrinks to SRT, a loss of QRTV.
7. B. Area QRTU represents the firm's economic profit. To maintain its monopoly the firm will surrender up to this amount. Area TUV is the dead-weight loss, neither benefiting the monopolist as profit nor the consumers as consumer surplus.
8. B. See p. 366.
9. B. Demand is downsloping for the firm. Consequently, additional units sold bring in less total revenue—marginal revenue decreases.
10. D. The distinguishing feature of natural monopolies is long-lasting economies o scale which serve as a barrier against competition.
11. B. OB is the output level at which MR = MC.
12. D. At output level OB, the firm's demand curve allows it to charge a price of ON.
13. A. Maximum short-run profit is the output level (OB) times the difference between the price and average total cost (HN).
14. C. Firms, attracted by economic profit, can not enter an industry in the short run but can do so in the long run.
15. A. It is easy for firms to enter a monopolistically competitive industry—but only in the long run. Economic profits can be earned in the short run.

16. C. Monopolistically competitive firms are inefficient because they underproduce and produce at too high an average cost.
17. B. If demand is inelastic then marginal revenue is negative. Marginal cost, therefore, must exceed marginal revue. An increase in price will reduce output towards the profit-maximizing (MR = MC) output level.
18. C. Neither monopoly nor oligopoly have many sellers. Perfect competition has a standardized product.
19. B. Profit maximization involves producing where MR = MC. In perfect competition P = MR while, in imperfect competition, P > MR.
20. A. See p. 339.
21. B. Marginal social cost shows the true internal and external costs to society.
22. D. See Figure 16.3 on p. 381 in the textbook.
23. A. Papyrus is generating externalities. The difference between marginal social cost and marginal private cost is marginal damage cost.
24. C. Country A has a more equal distribution of income but that doesn't mean that it has fewer poor people. A hypothetical Third World nation might have a Gini coefficient of zero (perfectly equal), but all of its inhabitants might live at subsistence level.
25. C. Marginal utility decreases. The core of the utilitarian argument is that the marginal utility of a dollar given to a poor person is higher than the marginal utility of that dollar to a rich person.
26. B. For all relevant levels of demand, the long-run average cost curve slopes downward.
27. D. The most efficient output level is where P = MC. At that level (OE), price is less than average cost—the firm will make a loss.
28. A. Max will produce where MR = MC.
29. C. The price ceiling establishes a price that is less than the average cost of production.
30. D. At OK the price and average cost are equal.

APPLICATION

1. See the following table.

Number of Workers	Marginal Product	Total Product	Price	Total Revenue	Marginal Revenue
0	0	0	—	0	—
1	20	20	$30	$ 600	$30.00
2	30	50	$29	$1450	$28.33
3	28	78	$28	$2184	$26.21
4	26	104	$27	$2808	$24.00
5	21	125	$26	$3250	$21.05
6	19	144	$25	$3600	$18.42
7	10	154	$24	$3696	$ 9.60
8	8	162	$23	$3726	$ 3.75
9	6	168	$22	$3696	−$ 3.75
10	2	170	$21	$3570	−$61.00

2. As the price increases from $27 to $28, total revenue decreases. This relationship indicates that demand is elastic. If you are unsure why this is the case, check p. 116 in the textbook.

3. This is an imperfectly competitive firm. It has a downward-sloping demand curve or, alternatively, price is not equal to marginal revenue (as would be the case for a perfectly competitive firm).

4.   See the following table.

Number of Workers	Marginal Product	Total Cost	Average Total Cost	Average Variable Cost	Marginal Cost
0	0	$2100	—	—	—
1	20	$2220	$111.00	$6.00	$ 6.00
2	30	$2340	$ 46.80	$4.80	$ 4.00
3	28	$2460	$ 31.54	$4.62	$ 4.29
4	26	$2580	$ 24.81	$4.62	$ 4.62
5	21	$2700	$ 21.60	$4.80	$ 5.71
6	19	$2820	$ 19.58	$5.00	$ 6.32
7	10	$2940	$ 19.09	$5.45	$12.00
8	8	$3060	$ 18.89	$5.93	$15.00
9	6	$3180	$ 18.93	$6.43	$20.00
10	2	$3300	$ 19.41	$7.06	$60.00

5.   Ideally, the firm should produce where marginal revenue equals marginal cost. In this case, the best the firm can do, of the options available, is to produce 144 units. Any greater level of output would make marginal cost exceed marginal revenue.

Number of Workers	Total Product	Total Cost	Marginal Cost	Marginal Revenue
0	0	$2100	—	—
1	20	$2220	$ 6.00	$30.00
2	50	$2340	$ 4.00	$28.33
3	78	$2460	$ 4.29	$26.21
4	104	$2580	$ 4.62	$24.00
5	125	$2700	$ 5.71	$21.05
6	144	$2820	$ 6.32	$18.42
7	154	$2940	$12.00	$ 9.60
8	162	$3060	$15.00	$ 3.75
9	168	$3180	$20.00	−$ 3.75
10	170	$3300	$60.00	−$61.00

6.   Maximum economic profit is $780, which is achieved at a price of $25.

7.   The number of firms will remain unchanged. Firms can neither enter nor leave an industry in the short run!

8.   The number of firms will increase because new firms will enter the industry attracted by the economic profits.

9.   New firms will enter the industry, reducing Hour Time Together's market share and shifting its demand curve to the left until it is tangent with the long-run average cost curve.

10.   There will be more substitutes in the long run. Hour Time Together's demand will become more elastic.

11.   The perfectly competitive firm is forced to produce at its minimum average cost output level. In our example this occurs at an output level of 162 units. Price will be $18.89.

12.   The firm's marginal cost curve will be steeper—there are fewer constraints in the long run for any given change in output level.

PUBLIC FINANCE: THE ECONOMICS OF TAXATION 18

OBJECTIVES: POINT BY POINT

After completing this chapter, you should be able to accomplish the objectives listed below.

General Comment

There are many previously-developed concepts at work in this chapter—demand and supply, consumer surplus, elasticity, income and substitution effects, marginal thinking, opportunity costs, etc. For example, with respect to increasing the incentive to save: By cutting the marginal tax rate, the opportunity cost of a dollar spent is increased, so fewer dollars will be spent and more will be saved.

OBJECTIVE 1: Distinguish between the tax base and the tax rate structure. Distinguish among progressive, proportional, and regressive taxes.

Ultimately all taxes are paid by households. Each tax has two components: a *base*—the value on which the tax is levied—and a *rate structure*. The tax base of an income tax is income. Three candidates for "best" tax base are consumption, income, and wealth. A given tax may be progressive, proportional, or regressive. A *progressive* (*regressive*) tax takes a larger (smaller) fraction of income from a high-income person than from a low-income person. A *proportional* tax takes the same fraction of income from everyone, regardless of income. With progressive taxes, the marginal tax rate is higher than the average tax rate. With regressive taxes, the marginal tax rate is lower than the average tax rate.   (page 429)

> **LEARNING TIP:** Perhaps the single most important paragraph in Chapter 18 occurs on page 430, where marginal and average tax rates are distinguished. Keep in mind that it's the *marginal* tax rate that influences an individual's behavior—his or her outlook on working, saving, and investing a bit more or a bit less.

PRACTICE

1. The measure or value on which a tax is levied is called the
   A. tax burden.
   B. tax structure.
   C. tax base.
   D. tax incidence.
   Answer: C. See p. 430.

2. A regressive income tax has a(n) _____ marginal tax rate and a(n) _____ average tax rate.
   A. increasing, increasing.
   B. increasing, decreasing.
   C. decreasing, increasing.
   D. decreasing, decreasing.
   Answer: D. As income increases, more taxes must be paid, but a relatively smaller fraction of income is taxed away.

3. We have a progressive income tax system. Jack earns $20,000 and pays $6,000 in taxes. Jill earns $40,000. She could pay _____ in taxes.
   A. $6,000.
   B. $9,000.
   C. $12,000.
   D. $14,000.
   Answer: D. Jill's income is double Jack's. In a progressive tax system, her tax liability will be more than double that of Jack.

Use the following table to answer the next four questions.

INCOME	TOTAL TAXES
$10,000	$1,000
$20,000	$4,000
$30,000	$7,000
$40,000	$12,000

4. As income increases from $20,000 to $30,000, the marginal tax rate is
   A. 10%.
   B. 20%.
   C. 25%.
   D. 30%.
   Answer: D. Marginal tax rate is change in total tax/change in income. $(7,000 - 4,000)/(30,000 - 20,000) = 30\%$.

5. As income increases from $20,000 to $40,000, the marginal tax rate is
   A. 20%.
   B. 25%.
   C. 30%.
   D. 40%.
   Answer: D. Marginal tax rate is change in total tax/change in income. $(12,000 - 4,000)/(40,000 - 20,000) = 40\%$.

6. When the income level is $20,000, the average tax rate is
   A. 10%.
   B. 20%.
   C. 25%.
   D. 30%.
   Answer: B. Average tax rate is total tax/income. $4,000/20,000 = 20\%$.

7. The tax structure in this example is
   A. progressive.
   B. proportional.
   C. regressive.
   D. progressive at first, then regressive.
   Answer: A. Average tax rates increase as income level increases.

OBJECTIVE 2: Distinguish between the benefits-received principle and the ability-to-pay principle of taxation.

Two principles are used to judge whether a tax is "fair":
   a. the *ability-to-pay principle* suggests that those who are more able to pay should pay more.
   b. the *benefits-received principle* suggests that those who receive the benefits of the expenditures financed by a tax should be the ones to pay.

(page 432)

> **LEARNING TIP:** Make up a list of taxes and try to determine which principle is present. You should find that the ability-to-pay principle is favored in the United States.
>
> Note the disincentives that can occur with the ability-to-pay principle—the harder you work, the more you earn, and the more you pay! On the other hand, the "benefits-received" option implies that the poor and/or unemployed should be the ones to pay for their own income-support programs.

PRACTICE

8. A _____ is the tax most likely to ensure vertical equity.
   A. progressive income tax.
   B. regressive income tax.
   C. sales tax on alcohol.
   D. head tax of $100 per citizen.
   Answer: A. Vertical equity is related to the ability-to-pay principle.

9. Which of the following taxes is based on the benefits-received principle?
   A. A progressive property tax if the revenue is used to finance public education.
   B. A regressive property tax if the revenue is used to finance public education.
   C. A progressive property tax if the revenue is used to finance national defense.
   D. A flat-rate tax on car owners used to maintain and improve roads.
   Answer: D. Those who pay the tax are the ones who derive the benefit in terms of improved driving conditions.

OBJECTIVE 3: Evaluate the merit of consumption expenditures, income, and wealth as candidates for the "best" tax base.

Three candidates for the most appropriate tax base are consumption, economic income, and wealth. The arguments for and against each are presented in the textbook.

Note that the effect of a tax on savings is important in this discussion. A consumption tax, such as a national sales tax, would tax savings once while an income tax affects savings twice. (page 433)

> **LEARNING TIP:** Avoid the temptation to declare all taxes to be bad. Read through this section in the textbook critically. Which tax system would be least burdensome for you, personally, at the present time? Which would be least burdensome after you graduate? How does each affect you as a senior citizen? Last, are your needs and society's needs unchanged in each case?

PRACTICE

Use the following information to answer the next two questions.

Brenda, an unmarried banker, rents her apartment and earned $40,000 last year. Her firm paid her medical insurance worth $5,000 and contributed $4,000 to her retirement plan. Brenda's rich aunt sent a check for $5,000 for her birthday. Brenda's hobbies include gardening—last year she grew $100 of produce. She has no time to do anything with her stock market portfolio and its value fell from $8,000 to $6,000 last year.

10. Which of the following items would not be included in Brenda's economic income?
    A. The $8,000 in her stock market portfolio.
    B. The unearned gift of $5,000 from her uncle.
    C. The $100 of produce that never reached a market.
    D. The decrease of $2,000 in the value of Brenda's stock portfolio.
    Answer: A. This is wealth, not income.

11. The best estimate of Brenda's economic income is
    A. $46,100.
    B. $52,100.
    C. $54,100
    D. $60,100.
    Answer: B. Each item above should be included. The change in the value of the stock portfolio must be subtracted.

OBJECTIVE 4: Explain why households are the ultimate payers of all taxes—i.e., bear the incidence of the tax. Comment on the factors affecting the incidence of a particular tax, such as a payroll tax or corporation profits tax.

The ultimate distribution of a tax is called the *tax incidence*. Often, taxes can be passed on (shifted) to other individuals—this is *tax shifting*. Taxes can distort economic decisions and change behavior. Demand and supply can both be affected by the presence of a tax, as can prices. Payroll taxes are largely shifted to workers, and are regressive. Corporate tax seems to be borne by the owners of companies, with only slight impact on workers—tax-shifting is less successful in this case. State and local taxes are mildly regressive, but federal taxes are mildly progressive. The U.S. tax system is proportional or very mildly progressive. (page 436)

The notion that households ultimately bear the burden of all taxes may seem difficult to grasp. The burden from sales taxes, property taxes, and personal income taxes is fairly easy to see. Capital gains taxes or corporate profit taxes, though, are also borne by households—households, in the final analysis, own the firms.

> **LEARNING TIP:** Check your own list of taxes to see in which cases tax shifting is possible. Remember that taxes change behavior and that, eventually, the tax burden is borne by households.

PRACTICE

12. The incidence of a tax refers to
    A. the structure of the tax.
    B. how frequently the tax is collected.
    C. who bears the economic burden of the tax.
    D. the impact of the tax on prices or wages.
    Answer: C. See p. 436 for the definition.

13. The government imposes a tax on oranges. Most households reduce their purchases of oranges and buy other fruits instead. Their behavior is an example of
    A. tax incidence.
    B. tax shifting.
    C. tax restructuring.
    D. tax evasion.
    Answer: B. Tax shifting occurs when a taxpayer changes her/his behavior to avoid a tax.

14. Of the following, _____ would be the easiest to shift.
    A. a $100 tax per citizen.
    B. a 10% excise tax on oranges.
    C. a proportional income tax.
    D. a 5% consumption tax.
    Answer: B. It would be fairly easy to avoid the tax by not purchasing oranges.

Use the following diagram to answer the next three questions. The diagram shows the demand (D) and supply (S) curves in the labor market. A payroll tax of $1.00 is imposed.

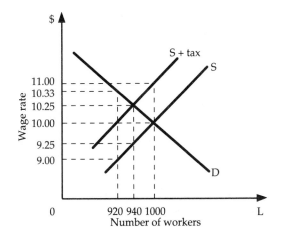

15. Before the imposition of the payroll tax, the equilibrium wage rate was _____ and the equilibrium level of employment was _____
    A. $10.00, 1,000.
    B. $10.00, 940.
    C. $10.25, 1,000.
    D. $10.25, 940.
    Answer: A. This is where the labor demand curve and the original labor supply curve intersect.

16. After the tax is imposed, _____ workers will each take home _____
    A. 1,000, $10.00.
    B. 1,000, $11.00.
    C. 940, $10.25.
    D. 940, $9.25.
    Answer: D. Equilibrium hiring level is 940. At this level, firms will pay no more than $9.25 per worker.

17. The workers' share of the tax burden is _____ ; the employer's share is _____
    A. $235, $235.
    B. $235, $705.
    C. $705, $235.
    D. $705, $705.
    Answer: C. Tax revenues are $940. Each worker lost 75¢ in wages; each employer has to pay 25¢.

18. The imposition of a corporate income tax will _____ profits in the corporate sector and _____ profits in the noncorporate sector.
    A. increase, increase.
    B. increase, decrease.
    C. decrease, increase.
    D. decrease, decrease.
    Answer: D. Competitive forces will equalize profits throughout the economy. Higher taxes will reduce profits in all sectors.

19. The _____ labor supply is, the _____ the proportion of a payroll tax will be borne by employees.
    A. more elastic, greater.
    B. less elastic, less.
    C. more inelastic, greater.
    D. more inelastic, less.
    Answer: C. In the extreme case, when labor supply is perfectly inelastic, all of a payroll tax will be borne by the workers.

OBJECTIVE 5: Explain the principle of tax neutrality. Explain the principle of second best and provide an example where this principle might be applied.

The *excess burden* of a tax is the amount by which the burden of a tax exceeds the total revenue collected. Given two taxes, the preferred tax is the one that imposes the smaller excess burden. *Neutral taxes*—which are most likely to be broad-based—are preferred on the grounds that they do not hurt efficiency. Additionally, the *principle of second best* is important: Sometimes—as in the case of an externality or in the presence of another distortionary tax—a new tax can correct the existing distortion, reduce the excess burden, and improve efficiency.   (page 442)

> **LEARNING TIP:** Note that when Case and Fair look at the size of excess burdens, the logic they use is the same as that you encountered in Chapter 13 when looking at the welfare loss from monopoly.

PRACTICE

20. We would most likely wish to impose a nonneutral tax if _____ are present.
    A. externalities and public goods.
    B. inelastic demand and other distortionary taxes.
    C. externalities and other distortionary taxes.
    D. inelastic demand and public goods.
    Answer: C. The adverse effects of both externalities and other distortionary taxes can be offset by nonneutral taxes.

21. The principle of the second best states that
    A. taxes should be neutral.
    B. excess burdens will be minimized if demand is perfectly inelastic.
    C. a distortionary tax can improve economic efficiency if imposed in a situation where previous distortions were present.
    D. a broad-based tax is preferable to a tax on a specific product.
    Answer: C. The principle of the second best is based on the argument that distortion may be corrected by the imposition of offsetting distortions.

Use the following information to answer the next three questions.

In the production of sweatbands, the current lowest-cost mix of labor and capital costs $6.00 per 10 sweatbands. A 50¢ tax is imposed per unit of labor. Producers react by switching to a different input mix, using only 5 units of labor to produce 10 sweatbands. The new input mix increases the cost of producing 10 sweatbands to $9.00.

22. If 1000 sweatbands are sold, the total tax revenue collected is
    A. $30.00.
    B. $25.00.
    C. $250.00.
    D. $300.00.
    Answer: C. Total tax on 10 sweatbands = 5 × 50¢ = $2.50. Total tax on 1000 sweatbands = $2.50 × 100 = $250.

23. If 1000 sweatbands are sold, the total tax burden is
    A. $30.00.
    B. $45.00.
    C. $300.00.
    D. $450.00.
    Answer: C. Total tax burden = ($9.00 − $6.00) x100 = $300.

24. If 1000 sweatbands are sold, the excess burden of the tax is
    A. $30.00.
    B. $50.00.
    C. $250.00.
    D. $300.00.
    Answer: B. The excess burden = the total tax burden − tax revenue = $300 − $250.

OBJECTIVE 6: Demonstrate, using graphs, the presence of the excess burden following the imposition of a tax, linking the resulting distortion to the relative elasticity of demand.

The shifting of taxation can impose an *excess burden* (over and above the revenues collected) on society. The size of the burden depends on the responsiveness of buyers and sellers, as measured by price or income elasticity.   (page 446)

LEARNING TIP: You'll get more out of the section on tax neutrality if you reread Chapter 12 first. Many of the concepts developed there are reused in this section.

PRACTICE

25. A broad-based tax, such as a general energy tax, tends to distort choices _____ and impose _____ excess burdens than a specific tax, (i.e., a gasoline tax) does.
    A. more, higher.
    B. more, lower.
    C. fewer, higher.
    D. fewer, lower.
    Answer: D. The specific tax is more shiftable, leading to more distortions and greater excess burdens.

26. The total burden of a tax can be described as
    A. the tax revenue minus the after-tax consumer surplus.
    B. the before-tax consumer surplus minus the after-tax consumer surplus.
    C. the tax revenue minus the excess burden.
    D. the excess burden minus the tax revenue.
    Answer: B. The total burden is measured by how much consumer welfare has been reduced.

27. In two communities, Balado and Clathy, the level of demand for gasoline is identical but it is more elastic in Balado. Marginal cost is assumed to be constant. The imposition of a gasoline tax will cause a greater decrease in consumption in _____ and a greater excess burden in _____
    A. Balado, Balado.
    B. Balado, Clathy.
    C. Clathy, Balado.
    D. Clathy, Clathy.
    Answer: A. As demand is more elastic in Balado, the tax-induced price hike will result in a larger decrease in consumption.

 PRACTICE TEST

I. MULTIPLE CHOICE QUESTIONS.

Select the option that provides the single best answer.

_____ 1. The government imposes a new tax on Savings and Loans.
           Economic theory suggests that, ultimately, the tax will be paid by
           A. the owners of the Savings and Loans.
           B. the employees of the Savings and Loans.
           C. the banking sector.
           D. households, some of whom may not even have S&L deposits.

Use the following information to answer the next three questions.

An economy has two sectors, agricultural and manufacturing, made up of farms and firms, respectively. In each sector capital earns a normal rate of return equal to 10%. The government imposes a 50% surtax on accounting profits in the manufacturing sector.

_____ 2. After the economy has fully adjusted to the new tax, who is the least likely to bear any of the tax burden?
           A. Owners of firms.
           B. Owners of farms.
           C. Consumers who buy mainly agricultural goods.
           D. Consumers who buy mainly manufactured goods.

_____ 3. After the economy has fully adjusted, we would expect
           A. after-tax return to capital to be greater for firms than for farms.
           B. after-tax return to capital to be greater for farms than for firms.
           C. after-tax return to capital to be the same for both firms and farms.
           D. before-tax return to capital to be greater for farms than for firms.

_____ 4. If the demand for manufactured goods is very inelastic, the increase in tax rate will be paid
           A. equally by firms and their customers.
           B. equally by farms and firms.
           C. mainly by firms.
           D. mainly by buyers of manufactured goods.

_____ 5. The "excess burden" of a tax
   A. is equal to the tax revenues collected by it.
   B. occurs whenever the imposition of a tax distorts economic behavior.
   C. is equal to the consumer surplus.
   D. is equal to the increase in price caused by the tax increase.

_____ 6. In the United States, most of the payroll tax is borne by workers because
   A. the elasticity of labor demand is close to zero.
   B. the elasticity of labor demand is close to one.
   C. the elasticity of labor supply is close to zero.
   D. the elasticity of labor supply is close to one.

_____ 7. The cardinal principle of tax analysis is that
   A. the burden of a tax is borne by individuals or households.
   B. institutions are the final payers of taxes.
   C. wage earners are the final source of taxes.
   D. the incidence of a tax cannot be shifted.

_____ 8. A new labor tax is levied on employers—the tax is $1 per unit of labor. The wage rate falls by 30¢. We can conclude that
   A. the income effect is stronger than the substitution effect.
   B. employees pay the bulk of the tax.
   C. the amount of labor used by firms has increased.
   D. the result would have been the same if the tax had been imposed on the workers, not the employers.

Use the following diagram to answer the next four questions.

The diagram shows the demand (D) and supply (S1) curves for ball bearings which are produced in a perfectly competitive industry.

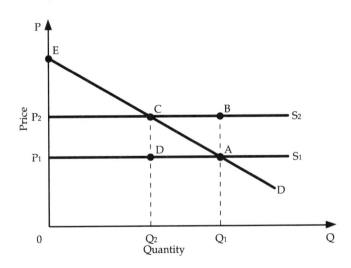

_____ 9. Their price is P_1. Which area represents the consumer surplus?
   A. P_1AE.
   B. ACD.
   C. P_1P_2CD.
   D. P_2EC.

_____ 10. Now a tax of $T is imposed that raises the price to P_2. Which area represents the tax revenue?
   A. $0P_1DQ_2$.
   B. P_1P_2CD.
   C. Q_1Q_2AC.
   D. $ABCD$.

_____ 11. Which area represents the excess burden of the tax to the consumer?
   A. ABC.
   B. CDA.
   C. Q_1Q_2AC.
   D. Q_1Q_2AD.

_____ 12. The total burden of the tax is
   A. Q_2CAQ_1.
   B. Q_2CBQ_1.
   C. P_2CAP_1.
   D. P_1ABP_2.

_____ 13. An income tax that "double taxes" saving tends to _____ the proportion of income consumed and _____ the proportion saved.
   A. increase, increase.
   B. increase, decrease.
   C. decrease, increase.
   D. decrease, decrease.

_____ 14. Most of a payroll tax is borne by _____ because labor supply is quite _____
   A. employers, elastic.
   B. employers, inelastic.
   C. employees, elastic.
   D. employees, inelastic.

_____ 15. Your boss explains that she will have to cut your wages by 10% because the local government has hiked her property taxes by 20%. This is an example of
   A. tax shifting.
   B. a regressive taxation.
   C. a progressive taxation.
   D. tax evasion.

_____ 16. Which of the following is a tax levied on a flow?
   A. A tax on interest earned on savings in your bank account.
   B. A property tax.
   C. A tax on the savings in your bank account.
   D. A tax on the value of the stocks you own.

Use the following information to answer the next four questions.

A basketball, which is produced in a perfectly competitive industry, can be produced using either of two processes as summarized in the table. Currently, the price of a unit of labor is $2 and the price of a unit of capital is $2. Demand is perfectly inelastic at a quantity of 100 basketballs. Assume that costs are constant.

	UNITS OF CAPITAL	UNITS OF LABOR
Process A	5	4
Process B	2	8

_____ 17. The long-run market price of a basketball is
   A. $12.
   B. $18.
   C. $22.
   D. $24.

_____ 18. Now the government imposes a $1 per unit tax on each unit of capital used. The long-run market price of a basketball will be
   A. $16.
   B. $22.
   C. $23.
   D. $24.

_____ 19. The government imposes a $1 per unit tax on each unit of capital used. The government's tax revenue is
   A. $4.
   B. $100.
   C. $200.
   D. $400.

_____ 20. The government imposes a $1 per unit tax on each unit of capital used. The excess burden of the tax is
   A. $100.
   B. $200.
   C. $300.
   D. $400.

II. APPLICATION QUESTIONS.

1. Jack and Jill are twins. They have identical salaries and, at birth, each was given a $100,000 bond (which would pay $10,000 each year) by Dame Dobb. Jack lives in a condominium with a rent of $10,000 each year. He uses the interest from the bond to pay his rent. Jill lives in an identical condo next door but she sold the bond, bought the condo, and pays no rent. In terms of income taxes, which twin is the better off?

2. The phenomenon of "bracket creep" has become less important, in terms of personal income tax, because of the reduction in the number of tax brackets. It is still present for other tax bases, however, the effect being to increase the fraction of the tax base claimed by the government as inflation occurs.

   A numerical example will quickly clarify this issue. Suppose that the marginal tax rate (MTR) is 30% on all income up to $30,000, and 50% on all income above that. Initially, Fred Fiscal earns $30,000.
   a. How much does he pay in taxes?

   Now suppose that there is a sudden doubling of all values denominated in dollars.
   b. Will there be any distributional effects?
   c. Calculate Fred's new tax liability.

   Note that prices have doubled but that Fred's take-home pay has failed to keep pace: Spending power has been redistributed from Fred to Washington.

3. A successful computer consultant, Mike Macintosh, charges a fee of $50 per hour. The personal income tax system has very progressive marginal tax rates: The rate that he faces is 75%.
   a. How much does he earn per hour after tax?

   Mike's house needs some work. In addition to the materials, the painter, Peter, will charge for labor at a rate of $30 per hour.
   b. Should Mike hire Peter or should he paint the house himself?
   c. Mike discovers that Peter's marginal tax rate is 25%. How might Mike and Peter attempt to circumvent the tax system?
   d. What other possibilities exist in this situation?
   e. Mike and Peter agree to barter services. Painting the house takes 4 hours while the computer services take 2 hours. How is this beneficial for both?

4. A hearing aid can be produced in one of two ways, as shown in the table. Assume that the marginal cost of additional hearing aids is constant.

	Units of Capital	*Units of Labor*
Process A	6	3
Process B	4	6

The price of capital is $1 and the price of labor is $1. Demand is perfectly inelastic at a level of 100 units.

a. The long-run price in this unregulated competitive industry will be $ _____ , and Process _____ will be chosen.

b. Now the government imposes a $1 tax per unit of capital used. Price now would be $ _____ using the original process, and $ _____ using Process _____ . The preferred process will be Process _____ .

c. Tax revenue will be $ _____ . The excess burden of the tax will be $ _____ . The total burden of the tax is $ _____ .

5. The graph below gives the labor demand and supply curves before and after the imposition of a $1.00 payroll tax.

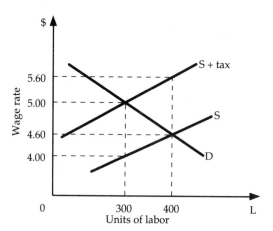

What was the original equilibrium wage rate and employment level? After the tax is imposed, the equilibrium wage and hiring level are $ _____ and _____ jobs. Total tax revenue is $ _____ . The share of the tax paid by employees is $ _____ and that paid by employers is $ _____ .

6. Sketch a Lorenz curve, showing some income inequality, in each of the three diagrams below. (If necessary, check back to Chapter 17 to review the Lorenz curve.)

    a. In the diagram below, show how the curve would change if the government introduced a more progressive tax system.

    0

    b. In the diagram below, show how the curve would change if the government introduced a more regressive tax system.

    0

    c. In the diagram below, show how the curve would change if the government introduced a proportional tax system.

    0

7. Following is a tax table, showing average and marginal tax rates. However, there are some blanks.

   a. Use your economic knowledge to complete the table.

TOTAL INCOME	TOTAL TAXES	AVERAGE TAX RATE	MARGINAL TAX RATE
$ 5,000	$750	_____	_____
$10,000	_____	_____	.090
$15,000	_____	.100	_____
$20,000	$1,600	_____	_____
$25,000	_____	_____	.130
$30,000	_____	.110	_____

   b. Is this system progressive, regressive, or proportional?

ANSWERS AND SOLUTIONS

PRACTICE TEST

I. SOLUTIONS TO MULTIPLE CHOICE QUESTIONS

1. D. Ultimately, all taxes are paid by households. See p. 436.
2. C. Certainly firms and their customers will lose. Farms will lose because manufactured goods are part of their inputs. Farm customers will be most insulated from the new tax. Note that the less elastic the demand for farm products, the more of the tax will be borne by farm customers.
3. C. Competitive forces will equalize the after-tax returns in the two sectors.
4. D. Because the purchase of manufactured goods is difficult to avoid, manufacturers will be able to pass on the tax to their customers will little decrease in sales.
5. B. See p. 442.
6. C. The elasticity of labor supply is close to zero, meaning that the labor is fairly insensitive to decreases in wage caused by the imposition of the payroll tax.
7. A. Ultimately, all taxes are paid by households. See p. 436.
8. D. See p. 439 for a discussion of this issue.
9. A. Consumer surplus is the (triangular) area between the price and the demand curve.
10. B. Tax revenue depends on the tax rate (the distance P_1P_2) and the quantity sold.
11. B. Total revenue collected is P_1P_2CB. The loss in consumer surplus is P_1P_2CA. The difference is the excess burden of the tax.
12. C. The total burden is the tax burden (P_1P_2CD) plus the excess burden (CDA), or, looked at another way, the decrease in consumer surplus.
13. B. Because the benefits from saving are reduced, taxpayers will tend to consume more and save less of their income.
14. D. When labor supply is inelastic, employers are more able to pass on the burden of the payroll tax to employees. See p. 439.
15. A. Tax shifting occurs when a tax is avoided, perhaps (as in this case), by passing on the burden to another party.
16. A. Interest is earned during a period of time, i.e., it is a flow variable. Each of the other tax bases is a stock measured at a point in time.
17. B. The lower-cost input mix (A) will be chosen. The cost of production is (2×5) + (2×4) = $18.
18. B. Process A now costs $23 per ball while Process B costs only $22 per ball.

19. B. Total tax = 100 (basketballs) $\times$ 2 (units of capital) $\times$ \$1 = \$200.
20. B. Excess burden = total burden − tax revenues collected. Total burden = tax-induced increase in price $\times$ quantity sold = (\$22 − \$18) $\times$ 100 = \$400. Taxes collected = \$200.

II. SOLUTIONS TO APPLICATION QUESTIONS

1. Jill has made the wiser move, at least in terms of income taxes. Jack earns \$10,000 more income than Jill and he will be taxed on this. If, however, property taxes are present, the situation changes, and Jack may be relatively better off than Jill.

2. a. \$9,000.
   b. Yes! See the table below.

PRE-TAX INCOME	MTR	TAX LIABILITY	AFTER-TAX INCOME
\$30,000	30%	\$ 9,000	\$21,000
\$60,000	50%	\$24,000	\$36,000

   c. \$24,000 = \$9,000 + (\$30,000 $\times$ .5).

3. a. \$12.50.
   b. Mike should paint his house himself—this is an example of a tax distortion! His after-tax income is \$12.509 per hour; he is better employed in an activity that saves him \$30 per hour. (The price system is signaling that Mike's efforts are worth \$50 per hour, yet he is rational in allocating time to an activity saving him \$30 per hour.)
   c. Mike could offer Peter a "cash basis" transaction. If Peter's marginal tax rate is 25%, the \$30 pre-tax income is the equivalent of \$22.50 after tax. Peter gains if he negotiates an "off-the-books" price of \$25, and Mike's bill is lower.
   d. One possibility is that Mike and Peter can barter services although this is unlikely given Mike's occupation, which is not easy to barter. Perhaps Mike can computerize Peter's billing and accounting system in exchange for the painting services.
   e. Painting the house takes 4 hours and the computer services take 2 hours. Mike has saved 4 hours (\$12.50 $\times$ 4 = \$50) at the cost of 2 hours (worth \$25.00). Similarly, Peter has worked 4 hours for a reward of \$30 $\times$ 4 $\times$ .75 = \$90 but received services that would have cost him \$100 on the open market. Mike can gain, as can Peter, who can also avoid tax payments. The "underground economy" is created, in part, by a desire to avoid taxes.

4. a. \$9. Average cost and marginal cost will both be \$9. In perfect competition, P = MR, and, to maximize profits, MR = MC. Therefore, P = MC = \$9. Process A is cheaper, given the price of labor and capital.
   b. \$15, because 6 units of capital are used. The entire tax hike will be passed on to the consumer because demand is perfectly inelastic. \$14, (\$10 + \$4), will be the price using Process B. Process B is cheaper.
   c. Tax revenue = \$4 x 100 units = \$400. The excess burden of the tax = tax burden − revenues = \$500 − \$400 = \$100. The total burden of the tax = (new price − initial price) $\times$ 100 = (\$14 − \$9) $\times$ 100 = \$500.

5. Original equilibrium wage is \$4.60 with 400 jobs. The new equilibrium wage is \$4.00 with 300 jobs. Total tax revenue is \$300. The share of the tax paid by employees is \$180 and that paid by employers is \$120.

6. See the diagrams below.

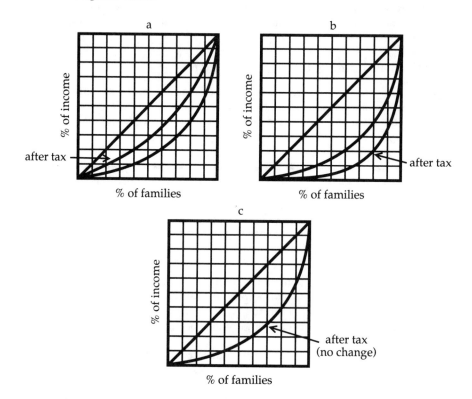

7. a.

TOTAL INCOME	AVERAGE TOTAL TAXES	MARGINAL TAX RATE	TAX RATE
$ 5,000	$ 750	.150	.150
$10,000	$1,200	.120	.090
$15,000	$1,500	.100	.060
$20,000	$1,600	.080	.020
$25,000	$2,250	.090	.130
$30,000	$3,300	.110	.210

b. This system is regressive until one's income reaches $20,000, after which it becomes progressive.

THE ECONOMICS OF LABOR MARKETS AND LABOR UNIONS

19

OBJECTIVES: POINT BY POINT

After completing this chapter, you should be able to accomplish the objectives listed below.

OBJECTIVE 1: Outline the basic determinants of the demand for labor and the supply of labor. Define human capital and describe the factors that affect the investment decision.

The *demand for labor* depends on the marginal productivity of labor; a worker is hired only for what s/he can produce. More precisely, the demand for labor depends on the marginal revenue product of labor. Workers may increase their human capital (making them more productive) through education, on-the-job training, or by other means. (page 452)

When you decide to go to college (invest in human capital), you are making a decision regarding benefits and costs. The explicit costs (tuition, books, and so on) are fairly obvious. Loss of earnings over four years is a less obvious factor. The benefits from a degree have been much more difficult to pin down but, in January 1993, the Census Bureau estimated that a college degree is worth $1,039 per month in extra pay ($9,351 per year after tax). The explicit costs of college can be reclaimed before the end of two years. If the total costs of college are $20,000 per year, the typical college student makes a return of 46.7% on her/his investment.

> **LEARNING TIP:** Review Application Question 1 in Chapter 11 for more on the decision to invest in human capital.

Labor supply depends on household preferences regarding work and leisure. It can be affected by the wage rate, nonlabor income, and wealth. A reduction in the tax rate (which would increase the after-tax wage rate) may cause labor supply to increase (if the substitution effect is larger than the income effect) or decrease (if the substitution effect is smaller than the income effect). According to labor-market studies, women seem to be more responsive than men to changes in wage rates. (page 453)

A curious example of the power of the income effect in determining labor supply was encountered by U.S. managers in North Africa. Local workers seemed loyal and dependable when employed by locally-run businesses but, despite offering somewhat higher wages and better working conditions, turnover rates of local workers were quite high when working for U.S. firms. Even higher wages exacerbated the problem. Investigation revealed that workers worked up to a particular "acceptable" income level and would then quit to enjoy their earnings. By quadrupling wage rates, foreign firms quadrupled the turnover rate.

LEARNING TIP: The first part of this chapter is purely a review and a great chance to check on what you've learned during your microeconomics course. Make up a list of topics that are reused in this chapter. Go back and read over Chapter 10 and, for the income and substitution effects that influence labor supply, Chapter 6, p. 146.

LEARNING TIP: The examples given in this chapter (Cathy, McDonald's, and David) feature the sort of questions labor economists address. More important for you, they use "economic thinking." Try making analyses like these for yourself, applying economic concepts and logic, perhaps based on your own labor market experiences.

Labor Supply: The study of labor supply is made complicated because supplying labor involves two decisions: whether to work or not and (once the decision to work is made) how many hours to work. Keep in mind that the decision to increase the number of hours worked means a decision to reduce the amount of leisure. When tracing through the effects of wage increases or reductions in tax rates, it can be easier to think of the decision in terms of leisure.

PRACTICE

1. For the perfectly competitive firm, the marginal revenue product of labor is equal to the
   A. marginal physical product times the price of labor.
   B. marginal physical product times the price of output.
   C. change in the wage bill divided by the number of workers.
   D. change in the wage bill divided by change in the number of workers.
   Answer: B. See p. 452.

2. Marginal revenue product of labor will increase if
   A. labor productivity improves.
   B. the wage rate decreases.
   C. the demand for output decreases.
   D. the supply of labor increases.
   Answer: A. MRP is dependent upon marginal physical product and the price of final output.

Use the following labor market diagram to answer the next four questions.

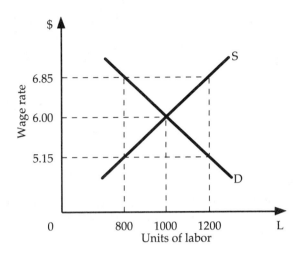

3. Refer to the diagram above. If the wage rate is currently $5.15, there is an excess _____ labor equal to _____ units of labor.
   A. demand for, 400.
   B. demand for, 1200.
   C. supply of, 400.
   D. supply of, 800.
   Answer: A. The wage rate is below the equilibrium wage rate, causing quantity demanded to exceed quantity supplied by $1,200 - 800$.

4. The labor market is in equilibrium. If labor productivity increased, we would expect the wage rate to _____ and employment to _____ 1,000.
   A. rise above $6, exceed.
   B. rise above $6, be less than.
   C. fall below $6, exceed.
   D. fall below $6, be less than.
   Answer: A. The current equilibrium situation is a wage rate of $6 and a hiring level of 1,000. The improved productivity will increase the demand for labor.

OBJECTIVE 2: Public Policy. Present the theoretical case for and against the minimum wage. Present the theoretical case for and against the effectiveness of a reduction in marginal tax rates for increasing employment. Summarize and interpret the findings of studies on labor supply elasticity. Describe the issues involved in the debate over the disincentives caused by income maintenance programs.

As a result of the *minimum wage,* those who work receive higher wages but those who lose their jobs are worse off. The more elastic the demand for labor, the greater will be the unemployment. Some evidence suggests only slight job-loss from increasing the minimum wage.   (page 457)

Cutting the marginal tax rate has a substitution effect (which raises labor supply) and an income effect (which reduces labor supply).   (page 460)

There seems to be a gender difference with respect to the elasticity of labor supply. Males are very unresponsive to changes in wage rates, while female workers respond positively. Although conventional wisdom and theory maintain that income maintenance programs (welfare) create a disincentive to work, recent evidence shows that most workers prefer to lose benefits and work if they can.   (page 460)

> **LEARNING TIP:** There is no single correct answer to the minimum wage issue. There is a trade-off involved—workers with jobs gain, those who lose their jobs lose.

PRACTICE

5. Refer to the diagram above. If a minimum wage of $6.85 were imposed, there would be an _____ workers and the wage rate would _____
   A. excess demand for, increase.
   B. excess demand for, decrease.
   C. excess supply of, increase.
   D. excess supply of, decrease.
   Answer: C. The equilibrium wage is $6. The minimum wage imposition sets up a disequilibrium, forcing the wage rate higher and creating an excess supply of 400 workers.

6. Refer to the diagram above. If the minimum wage is set below the equilibrium wage, at $5.15,
   A. there will be an excess demand for labor of 400.
   B. there will be an excess supply of labor of 400.
   C. the equilibrium wage rate will move from $6.
   D. there will be no effect on the labor market.
   Answer: D. A minimum wage places a lower limit on the wage rate. In this market, given demand and supply conditions, the lowest the wage will go is $6.

7. Wage elasticity of labor supply is (+).10. Assume labor demand is perfectly inelastic and that the labor market is in equilibrium with 100,000 workers employed. If a minimum wage is imposed that is 10% higher than the equilibrium wage, unemployment will
   A. increase by 1,000.
   B. decrease by 1,000.
   C. increase by 10,000.
   D. decrease by 10,000.
   Answer: A. A 10% wage increase will increase labor supply by 1%. 100,000 × .01 = 1,000.

8. As the wage increases, the _____ effect will encourage workers to supply _____ labor and the _____ effect will encourage workers to supply less labor.
   A. income, more, substitution.
   B. income, less, substitution.
   C. substitution, more, income.
   D. substitution, less, income.
   Answer: C. As the wage rises, the opportunity cost of leisure increases and the substitution effect will encourage workers to supply more labor. The income effect makes leisure more attractive and reduces labor supply.

9. Empirical studies show that, when there is a wage increase, the _____ dominates for males, and the _____ dominates for females.
   A. income effect, income effect.
   B. income effect, substitution effect.
   C. substitution effect, income effect.
   D. substitution effect, substitution effect.
   Answer: B. The income effect operates to reduce labor supply when there is a wage increase. See p. 460.

10. The wage elasticity of women is $+.94$. This means that a 10% increase in wage will result in a _____ increase in the supply of female labor.
    A. .094%.
    B. .6%.
    C. .94%.
    D. 9.4%.
    Answer: D. The wage elasticity formula is "change in labor supply/change in wage."

11. The benefits from income maintenance programs are increased. We would expect the income effect to _____ labor supply, and the substitution effect to _____ labor supply.
    A. increase, increase.
    B. increase, decrease.
    C. decrease, increase.
    D. decrease, decrease.
    Answer: D. Both effects operate in the same direction. See p. 460.

12. An increase in unemployment insurance payments will _____ job search time by _____
    A. increase, increasing expected benefits.
    B. increase, reducing search costs.
    C. decrease, increasing expected benefits.
    D. decrease, reducing search costs.
    Answer: B. See p. 463.

13. As the wage increases, the _____ effect indicates that leisure becomes _____ expensive.
    A. income, more.
    B. income, less.
    C. substitution, more.
    D. substitution, less.
    Answer: C. See p. 460.

14. An increase in the marginal tax rate will _____ labor supply according to the income effect and will _____ labor supply according to the substitution effect.
    A. increase, increase.
    B. increase, decrease.
    C. decrease, increase.
    D. decrease, decrease.
    Answer: B. A tax rate increase reduces earnings per hour and, therefore, reduces the opportunity cost of leisure. Workers substitute leisure for work. As earnings have fallen, though, poorer workers will wish to work more.

15. Gordo Delgado is unemployed. He should continue to search for a job as long as the expected gains from continuing to search
    A. are positive.
    B. are greater than zero.
    C. are greater than the additional costs of searching.
    D. are greater than the total costs of searching.
    Answer: C. As in much of economics, search decisions are based on marginal considerations. See p. 463.

OBJECTIVE 3: Outline the reasons for the diversity in wages and how labor market discrimination causes welfare losses.

Reasons for the diversity in wages include compensating differentials, occupational segregation, and discrimination. Discrimination occurs when an identifiable group of workers receives inferior treatment because of some characteristic irrelevant to job performance. Such treatment might include being barred from particular occupations, receiving lower wages, or having fewer promotion prospects.   (page 463)

An interesting example of segregation showed up in the former Soviet Union—at one point 70% of all Soviet medical doctors were female. By comparison, less than 20% of U.S. doctors are female and less than a third of medical school graduates in the United States are women.

PRACTICE

16. Labor market discrimination, which restricts access to black workers but not to whites, reduces the economy's welfare because the marginal product of blacks is reduced
    A. more than the marginal product of whites is increased.
    B. more than the marginal product of whites is reduced.
    C. less than the marginal product of whites is increased.
    D. less than the marginal product of whites is reduced.
    Answer: A. See p. 464.

OBJECTIVE 4: Discuss the effects of collective bargaining on wage negotiations with perfectly competitive employers and with monopsonistic employers. Describe the positive and negative effects of unions on the economy.

Unions may try to restrict the supply of labor or to increase the demand for labor in order to force up wages. Working conditions and numbers of jobs are other areas of union concern. However, there is a conflict of interest—higher wages reduce the quantity of labor demanded and union members might lose their jobs.

(page 465)

Featherbedding is a tactic intended to reduce job loss. It may be disguised as a concern for customer safety—e.g., the required use of a third pilot or navigator in a two-pilot plane. The Musicians Union requires that Broadway orchestras cannot have fewer than a specified number of members—the pit size determines orchestra size.

Traditionally, it has been argued that unions may represent a labor market imperfection , hiking wages and reducing U.S. competitiveness. On the other hand, when there is one hirer of labor (a monopsonist), unions may exert countervailing power, thus resulting in a *more* efficient wage rate and hiring level than would otherwise have arisen. Alongside the common gloomy view of the impact of unions, there is some recent evidence that suggests that unions may boost productivity, and increase the communication between workers and management.

(page 470)

> **Point to Ponder:** Are the benefits of a union a public good? Better conditions and higher wages are nonexcludable and nonrival, so a non-union worker can be a free rider. S/he is also subject to the drop-in-the-bucket argument. Does one additional union member make any difference?

PRACTICE

Use the following diagram to answer the next four questions.

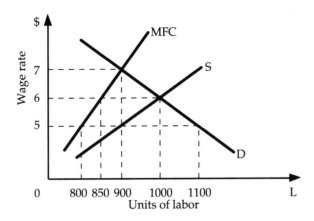

17. In the diagram above, the competitive wage rate is
    A. $5.
    B. $6.
    C. $7.
    D. indeterminate.
    Answer: B. In perfect competition, demand and supply will determine the wage.

18. A monopsonist will pay a wage of
    A. $5.
    B. $6.
    C. $7.
    D. between $5 and $7.
    Answer: A. The monopsonist will hire where marginal factor cost equals marginal revenue product. The wage is then determined by the labor supply curve.

19. If this labor market ceases to be perfectly competitive and becomes monopsonistic, the employment level will
    A. increase from 900 to 1000.
    B. increase from 900 to 1100.
    C. decrease from 1000 to 900.
    D. decrease from 1000 to 850.
    Answer: C. In perfect competition, demand and supply will determine employment level. The monopsonist will hire until marginal factor cost equals marginal revenue product.

20. If a union enters the monopsonistic market, the wage rate will be
    A. between $5 and $6.
    B. between $5 and $7.
    C. between $6 and $7.
    D. $7.
    Answer: B. The result will be indeterminate, depending on the relative negotiating strengths of the two sides.

PRACTICE TEST

I.   MULTIPLE CHOICE QUESTIONS.

Select the option that provides the single best answer.

_____ 1. Wage elasticity of labor demand is (−).05. Wage elasticity of labor supply is (+).15. The labor market is in equilibrium with 1,000,000 workers employed. If a minimum wage is imposed that is 10% higher than the equilibrium wage, layoffs will be _____ and there will be _____ unemployed new entrants.
   A. 5,000, 15,000.
   B. 5,000, 150,000.
   C. 50,000, 15,000.
   D. 50,000, 150,000.

_____ 2. The price of leisure may be measured by
   A. the marginal physical product of labor.
   B. the wage rate.
   C. the slope of the supply curve.
   D. the average product of labor.

_____ 3. If welfare benefits are increased, the income effect will operate to _____ labor supply, and the substitution effect will operate to _____ labor supply.
   A. increase, increase.
   B. decrease, increase.
   C. increase, decrease.
   D. decrease, decrease.

_____ 4. While male workers have access to either Occupation A or B, female workers are forced into Occupation B. Labor market discrimination
   A. has no effect on efficiency if workers are paid according to their marginal revenue product.
   B. will distort wage levels. Wages in Occupation A will be higher than otherwise.
   C. is inefficient. The high wages in Occupation A will cause unemployment.
   D. has no effect on efficiency. All workers will be able to find a job.

_____ 5. Unemployment benefits tend to _____ the cost of the job search and _____ job search time.
   A. decrease, decrease.
   B. decrease, increase.
   C. increase, decrease.
   D. increase, increase.

_____ 6. Which of the following is least likely to be a union strategy for raising wages?
   A. Encouraging capital investment to boost labor productivity.
   B. Restricting the supply of labor through pressure on legislators.
   C. Imposing a union wage through threat of striking.
   D. Advertising the product produced by union members.

_____ 7. Which of the following is incorrect?
   A. "Yellow-dog contracts" are contracts signed by workers who promise not to join a union.
   B. "Featherbedding" is the imposition of racial and/or gender barriers to restrict union membership.
   C. "Right-to-work" rules are passed and enforced by the states.
   D. The Wagner Act guaranteed workers the right to join unions.

_____ 8. The Dog Catchers Union has successfully negotiated a wage increase and an increase in employment for its members. The union has
   A. increased the demand for union labor.
   B. decreased the demand for union labor.
   C. increased the supply of union labor.
   D. decreased the supply of union labor.

_____ 9. A key Reagan Administration belief, echoed by the Republican Congressional majority in 1995, was that marginal tax rates should be _____ so that labor _____ would increase.
   A. lowered, supply.
   B. lowered, demand.
   C. raised, demand.
   D. raised, supply.

_____ 10. Bill has a job but is considering investing in additional education. A cut in Bill's marginal tax rate would _____ the cost and _____ the net benefits from the extra education.
   A. decrease, decrease.
   B. decrease, increase.
   C. increase, decrease.
   D. increase, increase.

_____ 11. Empirical reports suggest that a net increase in the wage would _____ the quantity supplied of male labor and _____ the quantity supplied of female labor.
   A. increase, increase.
   B. increase, decrease.
   C. decrease, increase.
   D. decrease, decrease.

_____ 12. The Republican "Contract with America" proposed cutting marginal tax rates for workers earning less than $200,000. This change would make leisure _____ expensive relative to work, and _____ the labor supply.
   A. more, increase.
   B. more, decrease.
   C. less, increase.
   D. less, decrease.

_____ 13. Marginal tax rates are reduced and the tax base is expanded simultaneously. Leisure should
   A. increase, because these actions result in only a substitution effect.
   B. increase, because the income effect will dominate the substitution effect.
   C. decrease, because these actions result in only a substitution effect.
   D. decrease, because the substitution effect always exceeds the income effect.

_____ 14. The Republican "Contract with America" proposed cutting income maintenance programs. The substitution effect of this proposal causes labor supply to _____ because the change in the implicit tax rate _____ the opportunity cost of leisure relative to work.
   A. increase, increases.
   B. increase, decreases.
   C. decrease, increases.
   D. decrease, decreases.

_____ 15. Women tend to earn lower wages than men. One possible explanation is discrimination. The marginal product of women will be _____ than otherwise, and that of men will be _____ than otherwise.
   A. greater, greater.
   B. greater, less.
   C. less, greater.
   D. less, less.

_____ 16. There is an increase in benefits from income maintenance programs. The income effect would predict a(n) _____ in work effort; the substitution effect would predict a(n) _____ in work effort.
   A. increase, increase.
   B. increase, decrease.
   C. decrease, increase.
   D. decrease, decrease.

_____ 17. Suppose that, in the labor market for professional baseball players, team owners operate as a monopsony. If players form a union, we would expect to see wages _____ and the market becoming _____ efficient.
   A. increasing, more.
   B. increasing, less.
   C. decreasing, more.
   D. decreasing, less.

_____ 18. Recent studies have shown that the labor supply is _____ than it would be in the absence of all income maintenance programs.
   A. 4.8% higher.
   B. 4.8% lower.
   C. 9.4% higher.
   D. 9.4% lower.

_____ 19. Unions often seek to increase the demand for goods made by union members. This is intended to _____ employment and _____ wages.
   A. increase, increase.
   B. increase, decrease.
   C. decrease, increase.
   D. decrease, decrease.

_____ 20. In a monopsonistic labor market, the entrance of a labor union may result in _____ wages, _____ employment, and _____ efficiency.
   A. higher, more, greater.
   B. higher, less, greater.
   C. higher, less, less.
   D. lower, more, less.

II. APPLICATION QUESTIONS.

1. The nation of Arbez has 600 native Arbezani workers and 2,400 immigrant Arbocali workers. The wage elasticity of labor demand in Occupation A is −.40, while the wage elasticity of labor demand in Occupation B is −.20. Assume that labor supply is perfectly inelastic. In equilibrium, 1,000 workers are employed in Occupation A and 2,000 are employed in Occupation B; the equilibrium wages are equal at 10 opeks per worker.
    a. Draw diagrams of the initial situation in Occupation A and Occupation B. Designate the supply of labor curves as S_{A1} and S_{B1}, respectively.

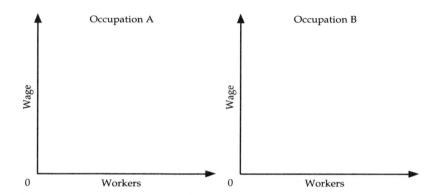

Now, native Arbezani workers are able to limit entry into Occupation A exclusively to native Arbezanis, of which there are 600.
    b. Describe what will happen to wages in Occupation A and Occupation B.
    c. Calculate (approximately) the new wage and employment levels in Occupation A and Occupation B.
    d. Draw the new situation in Occupation A and Occupation B on the previous diagram. Designate the supply of labor curves as S_{A2} and S_{B2}, respectively.
    e. We know that MRP (marginal revenue product) represents the change in production caused by a change in the number of workers. (If you're unsure, check out Chapter 10.) Using the diagram above, can you show the production loss caused by Arbezani discrimination.

2. Below is a labor demand schedule for lifeguards.

WAGE PER HOUR	HOURS DEMANDED PER WEEK	NUMBER OF 50-HOUR WORKERS DEMANDED	TOTAL WEEKLY INCOME OF LIFEGUARDS	WEEKLY INCOME PER LIFEGUARD
$5	100,000	_____	_____	_____
$6	80,000	_____	_____	_____

The lifeguards' union has established wage and work conditions in negotiation with employers. The contracted wage is $5 per hour with a required work week of 50 hours.
    a. Fill in the blanks in the table.

The union now wishes to renegotiate to get a wage of $6 and hires you as an advisor.

b. From the calculations you made to complete the table, you should be able to estimate whether the wage elasticity of demand for lifeguards is elastic or inelastic.

The union leadership has reviewed your information and is dismayed at the probable job losses.

c. Suggest a proposal that will increase the wage to $6, but not result in job loss.

3. The following application uses indifference curve analysis. If this has become unfamiliar to you, review the Appendix to Chapter 6 in the textbook.

The diagram below shows the indifference curve map for Cosmo Kramer. Hours of leisure are plotted on the horizontal axis. Income is plotted on the vertical axis.

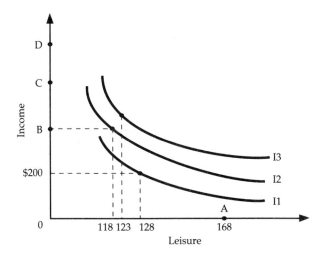

a. Calculate the maximum number of hours of leisure per week for Kramer.
b. If Kramer is offered $5 per hour, calculate his maximum income per week.
c. Kramer works 40 hours per week, at $5 per hour. Calculate his income per week. Draw in Kramer's budget constraint and label it AB.
d. If Kramer is offered $6 per hour, calculate his maximum income per week.
e. Kramer works 50 hours per week, at $6 per hour. Calculate his income per week. Draw in Kramer's budget constraint and label it AC.
f. An increase in wage has increased Kramer's number of hours worked. Which is stronger, the income effect or the substitution effect? How do you know?
g. If Kramer is offered $7 per hour, calculate his maximum income per week.
h. Kramer works 45 hours per week, at $7 per hour. Calculate his income per week. Draw in Kramer's budget constraint and label it AD.
i. Interpret the effect of the wage increase from $6 to $7 on the number of hours Kramer will work. Which is stronger, the income effect or the substitution effect? How do you know?

j. Graph Kramer's labor supply curve on the graph below.

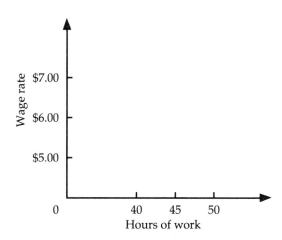

Note that the results you have found are the equivalent of a sequence of flat-tax rate changes. If the pre-tax wage rate is $8 but the marginal tax rate is 37.5%, after-tax wage is $5. If the tax rate is reduced to 25%, after-tax wage is $6. If the tax rate is reduced to 12.5%, after-tax wage is $7. Changing the marginal tax rate may increase or decrease the quantity of labor supplied, as determined by the income and substitution effects.

4. Suppose that Jack and Jill are "typical" male and female workers. Jill earns $12,000 and Jack $20,000, ignoring taxes. (Note: In the real world, full-time female pay is about 60% of full-time male pay. You might wish to ponder on the reasons for the persistence of this differential.)

   a. A new job, offering a 10% wage increase, would translate into $ _____ for Jill and $ _____ for Jack. (Note: The expected gains are greater for the man.)

   b. Which of the two would be more aggressive in the job search?

   c. Why?

   d. Now suppose that Jack and Jill are equally well qualified and both are laid off. The explicit costs of retraining/education are equivalent. Under prevailing labor market conditions, who will gain the higher expected reward from human capital investment?

5. Use the information in the table to answer questions about a profit-maximizing firm.

# of workers	Total Product	Product Price	MPP	Total Revenue Product($)	MRP($)	Wage	MFC($)
0	0	$2.10	—	0	—	—	—
1	15	$2.00				$2.00	
2	28	$1.90				$3.00	
3	39	$1.80				$4.00	
4	48	$1.70				$5.00	
5	55	$1.60				$6.00	
6	60	$1.50				$7.00	

a. Complete the table above. Calculate total revenue product to get the marginal revenue product. Similarly, calculate total resource cost to get the values for marginal factor cost.
b. How many workers will this firm choose to employ? (Assume that the firm can hire only "whole" workers.) How many units of output will the firm produce?
c. Explain how you arrived at your answers.
d. What is the equilibrium wage? What is the selling price of the product?
e. The resource market is (perfectly/imperfectly) competitive and the product market is (perfectly/imperfectly) competitive.
f. Explain how you arrived at your answer.
g. Draw a sketch of the labor market diagram for this firm. Include MRP and MFC curves, the equilibrium wage, and quantity of workers hired.

6. Let's try to analyze the issue of countervailing power in the labor market. First, sketch demand and supply of labor curves. Keep it simple—assume that the supply curve is not backward-bending. Suppose that perfect competition is present in the output market and in the input market. What does this mean, though?
   a. There is perfect competition in the output market for the goods produced by the workers. If more workers are hired by a company, what will happen to the price of output?
   b. What, then, is the relationship between the demand for labor curve and the marginal revenue product curve?
   c. Turning to supply, in perfect competition, what is the relationship between the supply curve and the marginal factor cost curve?

   The perfectly competitive wage rate is where demand and supply intersect. Call the wage W1 and number of workers hired Q1.

   d. How does your diagram change if you now assume that the employer is a monopsonist?
   e. The employer will hire up to the point where _____ equals _____ . The new wage will be _____ (higher/lower) than W1 and the hiring level will be _____ (higher/lower) than Q1.
   f. Explain why the monopsonist's MFC lies above the supply curve.
   g. A union may be able to _____ (increase/decrease) wages while potentially achieving a _____ (more/less) efficient use of resource.

ANSWERS AND SOLUTIONS

PRACTICE TEST

I. SOLUTIONS TO MULTIPLE CHOICE QUESTIONS

1. A. A 10% wage increase will decrease the quantity of labor demanded by 0.5% (i.e., 1,000,000 × .005 = 5,000) and will increase the quantity of labor supplied by 1.5% (i.e., 1,000,000 × .015 = 15,000).
2. B. The wage rate is the opportunity cost of not working.
3. D. Both effects will operate to reduce work effort and, at any given wage rate, the labor supply. See p. 460.
4. B. This model is known as the "dual market model." Supply is restricted in Occupation A, forcing the wage higher. Workers suffering discrimination crowd into Occupation B, with a correspondingly lower wage.
5. B. Unemployment benefits increase search time because the costs of remaining out of a job are reduced. See p. 463.
6. A. Although unions have favored strategies designed to increase the demand for labor, the threat of redundancy due to mechanization has caused Option A to be viewed with caution.
7. B. Featherbedding is the preservation of unnecessary jobs. See p. 470.
8. A. An increase in demand will boost the wage and employment levels.
9. A. Reducing the marginal tax rate, it was believed, would increase the opportunity cost of leisure and encourage higher labor-force participation rates. See p. 458.
10. D. A cut in the marginal tax rate would increase the opportunity cost of not working (studying) and would raise Bill's after-tax income following graduation.
11. C. Males have a negative wage elasticity—a wage increase will reduce the quantity of labor supplied. The evidence shows the opposite for females. See p. 460.
12. A. Cutting the marginal tax rate increases the opportunity cost of not working. Labor supply, then, should increase.
13. C. Lower tax rates make leisure more expensive without providing extra income.

14. A. An increase in income maintenance programs reduces the "pain" of not working and leads (some) persons to work less. Reducing such programs has the opposite effect.
15. C. See p. 464.
16. D. Both effects operate in the same direction—to reduce work effort. See p. 460.
17. A. This is an example of countervailing power. See p. 471.
18. B. Income maintenance programs reduce labor supply. Ellwood and Summers calculate the effect to be 4.8%. See p. 462.
19. A. Given the supply of labor, an increase in demand will boost hiring levels and the wage. Recall that MRP is affected by the price of the final output.
20. A. The labor union exerts countervailing power and, while increasing wages and employment, moves the industry toward a more efficient position.

II. SOLUTIONS TO APPLICATION QUESTIONS

1. a. See the diagrams below.

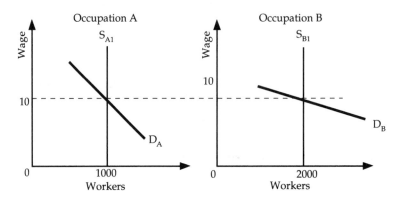

   b. Wages will increase in Occupation A and decrease in Occupation B.
   c. Employment in Occupation A will decrease by 40% to 600 and that in Occupation B will rise by 20% to 2,400. Using the wage elasticity values, a decrease in the quantity of labor available in Occupation A will increase the wage by 100% to 20 opeks, while an increase in the quantity of labor available in Occupation B will decrease the wage by 100% to 5 opeks.
   d. See the diagram below.

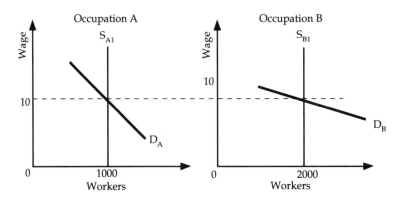

e. See the following diagram. The shaded area in the left-hand diagram represents the value of production lost by removing 400 workers from Occupation A. The shaded area in the right-hand diagram represents the value of production gained by adding 400 workers from Occupation B. The latter area is smaller than the former—production has fallen as a result of discrimination.

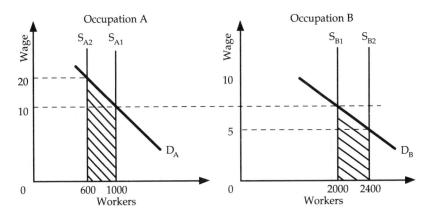

2. a. See the table below.

WAGE PER HOUR	HOURS DEMANDED PER WEEK	NUMBER OF 50-HOUR WORKERS DEMANDED	TOTAL WEEKLY INCOME OF LIFEGUARDS	WEEKLY INCOME PER LIFEGUARD
$5	100,000	2,000	$500,000	$250
$6	80,000	1,600	$480,000	$300

b. Elastic. As wage increases, total income (total revenue) decreases. In fact, elasticity is -1.22. If necessary, see Chapter 5 to review this material.

c. The union could ask for the wage increase and a decrease in the working week to 40 hours. The need for improved quality of vigilance could be used as a reason for the reduced hours. This proposal will maintain the number of lifeguards at 2,000.

3. a. $24 \times 7 = 168$ hours per week.
    b. $168 \times \$5 = 840$.
    c. $40 \times \$5 = \$200$. See the diagram below for the budget constraint AB. Note: This diagram is not drawn to scale.

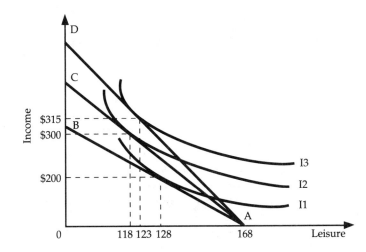

d. $168 \times \$6 = \$1008$.
e. $50 \times \$6 = \$300$. See the diagram above for budget constraint AC.

f. The substitution effect dominates the income effect. An increase in wage rate causes leisure's opportunity cost to increase. Kramer will substitute labor for leisure. The income effect of a wage increase which makes Kramer better off is to encourage him to take more leisure and work less. Because Kramer offers more hours of labor, the substitution effect is dominant.

g. 168 × $7 = $1176.

h. 45 × $7 = $315. See the diagram above for budget constraint AD.

i. The income effect dominates the substitution effect. An increase in wage rate causes leisure's opportunity cost to increase. Kramer will substitute labor for leisure. The income effect of a wage increase which makes Kramer better off is to encourage him to take more leisure and work less. Because Kramer offers fewer hours of labor, the income effect is dominant.

j. See the diagram below.

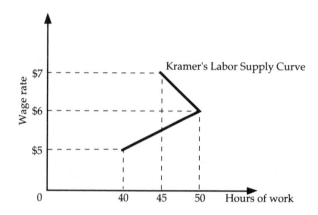

4. a. $1,200; $2,000.
    b. Jack.
    c. Because the expected gains are higher (assuming the costs are equal).
    d. Jack.

5. a. See the completed table below.

# of workers	Total Product	Product Price	MPP	Total Revenue Product	MRP	Wage	MFC
0	0	$2.10	—	0	—	—	—
1	15	$2.00	15	$30.00	$30.00	$2.00	$ 2.00
2	28	$1.90	13	$53.20	$23.20	$3.00	$ 4.00
3	39	$1.80	11	$70.20	$17.00	$4.00	$ 6.00
4	48	$1.70	9	$81.60	$11.40	$5.00	$ 8.00
5	55	$1.60	7	$88.00	$ 6.40	$6.00	$10.00
6	60	$1.50	5	$90.00	$ 2.00	$7.00	$12.00

b. 4 workers will produce 48 units.

c. The firm will hire up to the point where MFC equals MRP (in our case, the best the firm can do is to hire 4 workers, who produce 48 units of output).

d. The equilibrium wage is $5.00 and the selling price of the product is $1.70.

e. imperfectly; imperfectly.

f. Imperfectly competitive product market: To sell more, the firm must reduce price—i.e., a downward sloping demand curve.
    Imperfectly competitive resource market: To hire more workers, the firm must raise the wage—i.e., an upward sloping labor supply curve. Marginal factor cost is not equal to wage, as it would be in perfect competition.

g. See the diagram below. Ideally, the firm would hire the fifth worker for part of a day in order to match MRP and MFC; in our example, discrete units are assumed.

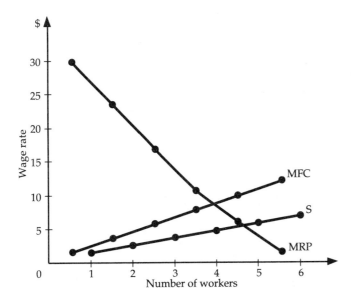

6. a. Price won't change. In perfect competition, the firm can sell as much output as it wants at the going market price.
   b. They're identical.
   c. They're identical.
   d. A marginal factor cost curve would need to be included above the supply curve. Your diagram should now look like Figure 19.6 on p. 471 of the textbook.
   e. MRP; MFC; lower; lower. If you decided that the wage would be higher, it's a fair bet that you went over from the intersection of MRP and MFC to determine the wage. Careful—it's a tempting mistake to make!
   f. MFC lies above the supply curve because, in order to attract an extra worker, the firm must pay him more than the going wage and must pay all other employees at the higher rate too. So the cost of the extra worker is higher than the wage he receives.
   g. increase; more.

CURRENT TOPICS IN APPLIED MICROECONOMICS 20

OBJECTIVES: POINT BY POINT

After completing this chapter, you should be able to accomplish the objectives listed below.

OBJECTIVE 1: Outline the reasons for the concern about health-care reform.

Health-care reform is an important issue because health care costs (which are already high) are spiraling higher, a rising number of citizens lack insurance, and the budgetary involvement of the federal government seems likely to become more pressing. (page 475)

Government involvement may be appropriate—free-market efficiency is flawed by asymmetric information, externalities, imperfect market structures, and fee-for-service payments.

While high costs are due in part to expensive technology, a further substantial portion is attributable to inefficiency and fear of malpractice suits. The aging of the population seems not to be an important factor. On balance, asymmetric information, moral hazard, and inefficient reimbursement methods are the main culprits.

PRACTICE

1. By 1996, the proportion of Americans without health insurance was
   A. 30% and rising.
   B. 30% and falling.
   C. 15% and rising.
   D. 15% and falling.
   Answer: C. See p. 476.

2. The moral hazard issue in health insurance refers to the
   A. possibility that those with pre-existing conditions will lie about them.
   B. likelihood that if patients do not bear the costs of health care they will over-demand services.
   C. likelihood that insurers will deny unnecessary procedures in order to increase profit margins.
   D. physicians risk law suits if there is malpractice.
   Answer: C. See p. 478.

3. Adverse selection is indicated by
   A. physicians ordering unnecessary tests as a defense against law suits.
   B. physicians selecting which information to tell the patient.
   C. insurance clients knowing more about their health that insurers know.
   D. the increasing "knowledge gap" between patients and doctors.
   Answer: C. See p. 477.

4. The largest group without health insurance coverage is
   A. those receiving welfare.
   B. the very rich who choose to pay medical expenses as they develop.
   C. workers who opt out of their firm's health insurance plan.
   D. the near-poor, working poor, and middle-income families who work for businesses that provide no health coverage.
   Answer: D. See p. 479.

5. Defensive medicine which means _____ adds about _____ to the cost of the total health care bill.
   A. requesting costly and perhaps unnecessary tests and procedures to forestall malpractice litigation, 3%.
   B. requesting costly and perhaps unnecessary tests and procedures to forestall malpractice litigation, 30%.
   C. allowing the patient to take responsibility for determining the course and duration of treatment, 3%.
   D. allowing the patient to take responsibility for determining the course and duration of treatment, 30%.
   Answer: A. See p. 480.

6. Adverse health insurance selection is caused by
   A. insurance firms controlling the terms of the health insurance coverage.
   B. insurance buyers having better information about their own health than does the insurer.
   C. the insurer hiking the price of medical treatments and splitting the proceeds with the medical community.
   D. high copayments and deductibles.
   Answer: B. The insurance purchaser may be able to hide health problems. To counteract this, insurance companies may refuse to pay on pre-existing conditions. See p. 477.

7. Proponents of government involvement in health-care provision point to each of the following except
   A. the apparent existence of positive externalities.
   B. reimbursement of providers on a fee-for-service basis, which might lead to an oversupply.
   C. the monopoly power wielded by the American Medical Association.
   D. the monopoly power wielded by the health insurance industry.
   Answer: D. The health insurance industry is fairly competitive with numerous options available.

OBJECTIVE 2: Present the arguments for and against immigration and describe the economic impact of immigration.

The argument for immigration hinges on the benefits derived from letting labor move from regions of low wages and low productivity to regions where higher wages can be earned because productivity is increased. The westward movement by settlers in the nineteenth century is an example of such a movement.   (page 482)

The main argument against immigration is that low-income American workers lose their jobs. Most evidence, however, suggests that this is a minor effect. A recent study, focusing on the nationwide impact of immigration suggests that one third of the decline in the wages of high-school dropouts is attributable to competition from immigrants.

Early generations of immigrants paid their way through earnings and tax contributions. However, more recent immigrants have poorer educational and job skills and a greater proportion receive welfare benefits.

PRACTICE

8. Low-wage Arbocalis emigrate to Arbez. In Arbez, the return on capital will
_____ . Wages will _____ in Arboc.
   A. increase, increase.
   B. increase, decrease.
   C. decrease, increase.
   D. decrease, decrease.

   Answer: A. Higher production in Arbez will increase the productivity of the existing capital stock. With fewer workers, wages in Arboc will increase.

9. Early immigrants were net _____ the public purse; recent immigrants have been net —————— the public purse.
   A. contributors to, contributors to.
   B. contributors to, recipients from.
   C. recipients from, contributors to.
   D. recipients from, recipients from.

   Answer: B. See p. 485.

OBJECTIVE 3: Detail the factors that influence the locational decision of a firm, and outline the arguments concerning the effectiveness of state tax and expenditure programs in affecting that decision.

The firm's location choice depends on the same factors that affect its other decisions—potential revenues and costs. The logic developed in earlier chapters still applies—how can the firm maximize profits? Profits differ at different locations, even for a nationally marketed good, because costs differ. The firm's price may differ from location to location. Proximity to resources may be critical—examples are the fishing industry (obviously), the movie industry (good weather), mining, farming. Cost or availability of land may be the key determinant of a firm's location decision. (page 485)

Public policy actions—tax breaks or ready-made infrastructure—do not significantly affect a firm's location decision. (page 486)

> **Comment:** A study of 43 relocating firms found the most important factor to be encouragement from another producer. Some firms wished to be nearer to markets or to gain access to resources. *No firm specified government policy as a key factor.* Among secondary considerations, transport and other costs were important. Government policy was seldom mentioned.

PRACTICE

10. The location of a firm that is not perfectly competitive will affect
    A. neither the price the firm can charge nor the quantity it can sell.
    B. the price the firm can charge but not the quantity it can sell.
    C. the quantity the firm can sell but not the price that it can charge.
    D. both the price the firm can charge and the quantity it can sell.

    Answer: D. Both price and quantity are affected when the firm is not perfectly competitive. See p. 486.

11. Which of the following is least likely to change significantly depending on the firm's location?
    A. The wage rate.
    B. The cost of capital.
    C. Transportation costs.
    D. The quality of the work force.

    Answer: B. The financial sector is highly integrated. Location is not likely to have much of an effect on the cost of borrowing. See p. 487.

12. State tax and expenditure policies
    A. exert an important influence on the location decisions of most firms.
    B. never involve the construction of new infrastructure.
    C. are likely to be weighted more heavily in the firm's location decision than the availability of a trained labor force.
    D. can influence factors that do affect the firm's decision.
    Answer: D. A good road system and a trained labor force can be fostered by public policy actions.

OBJECTIVE 4: Use a monocentric model to discuss the factors that might influence the locational decision of a household. Describe how racial discrimination affects the housing market and explain what is meant by filtering.

The household's utility-maximizing choice of location depends on preferences, incomes, and relative prices for households. How can the household maximize utility?
(page 487)

> **LEARNING TIP:** Early in life, your location decisions were made for you by your family. Probably, your first important location decision was your choice of college (even if you ultimately decided to stay at home). Try to recall which factors were important in making your decision.

Locational decisions by households are strongly linked to the need to travel to work. Commuting time is a cost, so households tend to cluster around high-employment areas. If employment is in the center of the city, residences further out will be less desirable and so, *monocentric models* predict, land rents and population density will be lower in the suburbs.

> **LEARNING TIP:** Given your choice of college, which factors determined your choice of apartment or dorm? Proximity to campus? Transportation? Proximity to part-time work? Differences in rent? Similarly, when you graduate and enter the labor force, will you limit your job search to a limited area? Will you favor cities over more rural areas? Will you, perhaps, seek a job that will obligate you to live in an urban area?

Discrimination has distorted the distribution of housing by denying equal access to all potential purchasers. Racial covenants (now illegal) are an example of discriminatory practices. *Filtering* refers to the flow of aging housing down the socioeconomic scale.
(page 488)

PRACTICE

13. Which of the following is false? Monocentric models
    A. assume that all employment is at the city center.
    B. predict that land prices will be highest in the city center.
    C. predict that equilibrium occurs where higher land prices are balanced by higher transportation costs.
    D. predict substitution of capital for land in the center.
    Answer: C. Monocentric models predict that equilibrium occurs where higher land prices are balanced by *lower* transportation costs. See p. 487.

14. Which of the following is false?
    A. Monocentric models predict that rent and transportation costs are inversely related.
    B. Racial covenants are illegal.
    C. Ghetto premiums are illegal.
    D. Filtering, a result of which is the allocation of the least desirable housing to the least able to pay, is illegal.
    Answer: C. Although they are in part the product of discrimination, ghetto premiums are not illegal.

15. Gasoline prices increase, substantially affecting commuting costs. The monocentric model would predict that land prices would _____ in the city center and _____ in the periphery.
    A. increase, increase.
    B. increase, decrease.
    C. decrease, increase.
    D. decrease, decrease.
    Answer: B. Center locations (where the jobs are) would become more desirable; location in the periphery would become correspondingly less desirable.

16. Studies of rent controls have found each of the following except that they
    A. may benefit the well-to-do renter most.
    B. reduce incentives for landlords to maintain controlled buildings.
    C. may be set too high in poor areas, given market conditions.
    D. have ensured an improvement in the condition of the housing stock.
    Answer: D. The housing stock deteriorates when rent controls apply.

OBJECTIVE 5: Describe the sources and symptoms of urban decline and the programs that have attempted to cure it.

Urban decline has been a concern since the 1960s. It is characterized by deteriorating private and social capital—boarded-up housing, decaying public facilities—and a flight of business activity to the suburbs. The use of taxes on property values (which vary from district to district) to finance expenditures, and local responsibility for public services, education, and social welfare have both contributed to the problem. Cures have included federal and state aid, and growing private investment. (page 489)

PRACTICE

17. Urban decline is exacerbated by
    A. firms moving to the suburbs.
    B. the decline in the inner-city tax base.
    C. the need to replace declining social capital.
    D. all of the above.
    Answer: D. See p. 489.

18. When there is urban decline, we expect to see all of the following except
    A. the tax base shrinking.
    B. social capital deteriorating.
    C. increased segregation by income.
    D. higher tax rates in the suburbs.
    Answer: D. Higher tax rates may occur but, because of increasing property values, tax rate hikes may not be necessary.

19. Property tax policies have done all of the following except
   A. reduced urban decline.
   B. increased segregation by income.
   C. encouraged the flight of businesses from the cities.
   D. encouraged the flight of affluent households from the cities.
   Answer: A. See p. 491.

OBJECTIVE 6: Describe an economic model that views crime as a rational activity. Use the model to assess proposals intended to reduce crime.

Most crime is urban. Although crimes of passion (murder, for example) are committed irrationally in the heat of the moment, most crimes can be viewed as rational acts which impose external costs on society. Typically, both the benefits (usually financial gain from the criminal's viewpoint) and the costs (injury, loss of liberty) of crime are uncertain. Criminal activity should proceed if the expected benefit exceeds the expected cost. From society's viewpoint, increasing the probable cost (the likelihood of capture and conviction, the strength of the penalty) or decreasing the probable benefit should reduce crime.   (page 491)

> **LEARNING TIP:** This section makes heavy use of the marginal analysis first introduced in Chapter 8. Review that argument now.

Comment: While our legal system often makes allowance for mitigating circumstances that result in irrational criminal activity, in other cases (driving while drunk or drugged, for instance) it does not.

PRACTICE TEST

I. MULTIPLE CHOICE QUESTIONS.

Select the option that provides the single best answer.

_____ 1. Monocentric city models would predict that housing would be least expensive
   A. in the inner-city areas.
   B. immediately adjacent to industrial areas.
   C. at the outer edges of the city.
   D. along major transportation arteries.

_____ 2. Lack of health insurance is mainly a problem for
   A. the unemployed on welfare.
   B. the working poor.
   C. the rich who opt out of the system.
   D. the self-employed.

_____ 3. Firms will tend to locate where
   A. property tax rates are minimized.
   B. profits are expected to be highest.
   C. transportation costs are minimized.
   D. revenues are expected to be maximized.

_____ 4. Which of the following is least likely to be affected by the firm's location?
   A. The cost of financing new capital.
   B. The cost of transportation.
   C. The price that can be charged for output.
   D. Wage costs.

_____ 5. Most evidence shows that immigration leads to _____ lower wages and _____ higher rates of unemployment in the country of destination.
   A. greatly, greatly.
   B. greatly, slightly.
   C. slightly, greatly.
   D. slightly, slightly.

_____ 6. Studies show that a major reason why blacks and whites tend to live in separate neighborhoods is that
   A. blacks live separately by choice.
   B. housing market discrimination exists.
   C. blacks are poorer than whites.
   D. there are cultural differences.

_____ 7. Filtering is most closely associated with
   A. depreciation in the value of housing.
   B. racial covenants.
   C. ghetto premiums.
   D. racial discrimination.

_____ 8. Rent control has been criticized for
   A. causing an excess supply of affordable housing.
   B. reducing the stock of affordable housing.
   C. discriminating against poor families.
   D. transferring ownership from landlords to tenants.

_____ 9. One direct cause of urban decline is
   A. excessive property taxes.
   B. inadequate private and social capital.
   C. a failure to zone effectively.
   D. low rental values.

_____ 10. Financing of local government projects through property taxes has
   A. increased segregation by income.
   B. slowed the flight of firms from the cities.
   C. slowed the flight of residents from the cities.
   D. reduced the problem of urban decay.

_____ 11. Each of the following is likely to play a major role in influencing the firm's location decision except
   A. wage rates.
   B. transport costs.
   C. availability of a trained labor force.
   D. low property tax rates.

_____ 12. The price of a good will probably be higher when it is sold
   A. where there are many competitors.
   B. where few competitors are present.
   C. where the cost of capital is high.
   D. where there is much congestion.

_____ 13. Which of the following statements is true?
   A. Low-income housing tends to be located on the outskirts of cities.
   B. Filtering is inefficient because it fails to account for negative externalities.
   C. The cheaper transportation costs are, the greater the pressure to urbanize.
   D. Rent-control laws impose a ceiling on the rent that can be charged to tenants.

_____ 14. Supporters of rent control contend each of the following except that rent control
A. is an alternative to homelessness.
B. has little effect on the behavior of landlords.
C. transfers benefits from landlords to tenants.
D. improves the quality and quantity of the controlled housing stock.

_____ 15. Jackson, Jefferson, and Johnson (the 3J Corp.) is considering opening a new plant. The factor that is least likely to be critical to 3J's decision is
A. the availability of a trained labor force.
B. cheap transportation facilities.
C. the expected wage rate at each location.
D. state taxes at each location.

_____ 16. In the presence of adverse health insurance selection we would expect to see the insurer
A. charging both healthy and sick clients more than the true cost of their coverage.
B. charging healthy clients less than the true cost of their coverage.
C. charging sick clients more than the true cost of their coverage.
D. charging sick clients less than the true cost of their coverage.

II. APPLICATION QUESTIONS.

1. Describe the economy of the region in which you live. Which sectors employ the most workers? Why is the good or service produced in those sectors produced in your area? Are there any natural advantages that have led those sectors to locate in your area? Have those sectors been expanding or contracting? If so, why?

2. Rent control is present in many urban areas.
   a. Are you in favor of restrictions on rent hikes?
   b. Study the diagram below, which shows the demand for and supply of rental housing in Megropolis.
      There is a rent ceiling (maximum rent) of $300 per month. In this market, what is the immediate effect of the rent control?

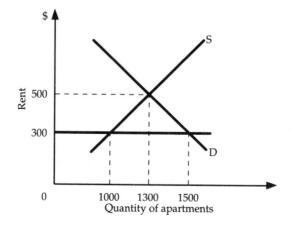

c. What do you think will happen in the longer term?
d. In terms of the diagram, what will be the effect?
e. With declining property values, what will happen to the tax base?
f. To raise enough funds to maintain social capital investment in the area, what must the local government do?
g. What do you think those businesses and household property owners that have the ability to relocate will do?

ANSWERS AND SOLUTIONS

PRACTICE TEST

I. SOLUTIONS TO MULTIPLE CHOICE QUESTIONS

1. C. Housing that is further from the prime locations in the center will be cheaper.
2. B. See p. 479.
3. B. As we've seen throughout the micro course, firms base decisions on profits.
4. A. Sources of capital are national—indeed, international—and operate in a highly integrated market. Location, then, is unlikely to affect the cost of financing capital expenditures. See p. 487.
5. D. See p. 484.
6. B. Preference and income differences may be factors, but the major reason for racial separation is discrimination. See p. 488.
7. A. As housing depreciates in value, it is passed down the socioeconomic scale.
8. B. When the rent is decreased, developers may shelve plans for new construction and allow existing buildings to deteriorate or withdraw the buildings from the market.
9. B. See p. 489.
10. A. The higher property values are, the higher tax collections and government expenditures can be. Indeed, high-value areas can have low tax rates and still generate relatively high revenues that can be plowed back into the community.
11. D. Property tax rates may have an influence, but the other three factors will have a more sizable impact on profits.
12. B. Absence of competitors is a prime circumstance leading to higher prices. The elasticity of demand is reduced because there are fewer substitutes. See p. 486.
13. D. Rent control laws were introduced in order to guarantee low-cost housing. See the Application box on p. 490.
14. D. This has never been a claim. In fact, the quality and quantity of the controlled housing stock has deteriorated.
15. D. Evidence shows that state and local taxes have little impact on business decisions.
16. D. By disguising their true condition, unhealthy clients reduce the premiums they pay, passing on the burden to healthy clients.

II. SOLUTIONS TO APPLICATION QUESTIONS

1. The answer to this one is entirely up to you!
2. a. Most members of the public do favor restrictions on rent increases but this is, of course, an opinion.
   b. There will be a rental housing shortage equal to 500 apartments as quantity demanded expands to 1500 and quantity supplied decreases to 1000.
   c. Because there is a lack of incentives for upkeep, we should expect to see decay, falling property values, and declining tax receipts. There will be a movement of capital away from rental housing towards areas of higher return, including residential housing, storage, demolition, and reallocation of rental land to other uses.
   d. Because the rental housing stock is shrinking, the supply curve will shift to the left, creating greater pressures for rents to rise (and a stronger political argument to *maintain* rent controls!).
   e. The tax base will be declining too.
   f. Increase property tax rates to counteract the shrinking tax base.
   g. Leave the area (perhaps for the suburbs) to avoid the high tax rates.

COMPREHENSIVE REVIEW TEST FOR PART 4

The following questions provide a wide-ranging review of the material covered in Part 4 (Chapters 18–20) of the textbook. Each question deals with a topic or technique important for your understanding of economic principles. If you miss a question you should return to the relevant section of the chapter in the textbook and fine-tune your understanding.

PRACTICE TEST

MULTIPLE CHOICE QUESTIONS.

Select the option that provides the single best answer.

_____ 1. A tax on consumption may be preferable to a tax on income for all of the following reasons except that
   A. one's standard of living depends on consumption, not income.
   B. a consumption tax can raise more revenue than an income tax.
   C. a consumption tax can reduce the double taxation of savings.
   D. a consumption tax can raise the level of economic growth.

_____ 2. Which of the following statements about income taxation is false?
   A. Income tax discourages saving.
   B. Income tax results in double taxation.
   C. Income tax taxes the individual on her/his ability to pay.
   D. Income taxes in the United States are mildly regressive.

_____ 3. Assuming "normally shaped" labor demand and supply curves, which of the following is not true of a payroll tax?
   A. The greater the elasticity of the supply of labor, the greater will be the proportion of the tax borne by firms.
   B. The tax will cause workers' wages to rise.
   C. Some job loss is likely.
   D. The greater the substitutability of capital for labor, the greater the fall in wages.

_____ 4. The retail sales tax is regressive because a rich person pays
   A. more tax than a poor person does.
   B. less tax than a poor person does.
   C. a lower proportion of her/his income in tax than a poor person does.
   D. a higher proportion of her/his income in tax than a poor person does.

_____ 5. Which of the following statements is false?
   A. The marginal tax rate has a greater influence on behavior than the average tax rate has.
   B. Tax shifting occurs when the government moves taxes towards those who have the ability to pay more.
   C. The retail sales tax is more difficult to avoid than the excise tax.
   D. With relatively elastic demand, an excise tax causes a high degree of distortion.

_____ 6. A regressive income tax system takes a greater amount per dollar from a _____ person. The average tax rate is _____ for a richer person.
A. richer, higher
B. richer, lower
C. poorer, higher
D. poorer, lower

_____ 7. Which of the following statements about the effect of the welfare system on the labor supply is false?
A. Evidence suggests that strong nonfinancial rewards from working outweigh the implicit taxes involved in accepting a job.
B. Welfare payments reduce incentives to recipients to work.
C. The availability of welfare benefits significantly encourage out-of-wedlock births.
D. the implicit marginal tax rate on earned income may exceed 100%.

_____ 8. The marginal revenue product of labor is the additional
A. product generated by hiring an additional worker.
B. factor product cost of hiring an additional worker.
C. average product cost of hiring an additional worker.
D. revenue generated by hiring an additional worker.

_____ 9. While male workers have access to either Occupation A or B, female workers are forced into Occupation B. Labor market discrimination should lead to relatively
A. greater use of capital in Occupation A and in Occupation B.
B. greater use of capital in Occupation A and less use in Occupation B.
C. less use of capital in Occupation A and greater use in Occupation B.
D. less use of capital in Occupation A and in Occupation B.

_____ 10. Which of the following statements is false?
A. A monopsonist is the sole purchaser of labor services in the labor market.
B. "Featherbedding" is a way of cushioning the fall in the supply of workers.
C. Income maintenance programs produce income and substitution effects that operate in the same direction.
D. The costs of a continued job search include forgone earnings and time.

_____ 11. Which of the following does not affect the quantity of labor supplied?
A. The wage rate.
B. The marginal tax rate.
C. Workers' preferences for leisure.
D. The marginal physical product of labor.

Use the following information to answer the next four questions. Labor market discrimination crowds women into a limited range of occupations (Range A). Males may work in any occupations.

_____ 12. We would expect to see the marginal productivity of females to _____ and the marginal productivity of males to _____
A. increase, increase.
B. increase, decrease.
C. decrease, increase.
D. decrease, decrease.

_____ 13. We would expect to see the wage of females _____ and the wage of males _____
   A. increase, increase.
   B. increase, decrease.
   C. decrease, increase.
   D. decrease, decrease.

_____ 14. *Ceteris paribus*, following the imposition of discrimination, the job search time for females should _____ - and the job search time for males should _____ .
   A. increase, increase.
   B. increase, decrease.
   C. decrease, increase.
   D. decrease, decrease.

_____ 15. Following the imposition of discrimination, the gain in production by male workers will be _____ than the loss in production by female workers. Ending discrimination should _____ national production.
   A. greater, increase.
   B. greater, decrease.
   C. less, increase.
   D. less, decrease.

_____ 16. Labor supply depends on each of the following factors except
   A. marginal revenue product of labor.
   B. wage rates.
   C. workers' nonlabor income.
   D. workers' wealth.

_____ 17. An increase in the wage rate will provoke a _____ change in the quantity of female labor supplied—the income effect is _____ than the substitution effect.
   A. positive, greater.
   B. positive, less.
   C. negative, greater.
   D. negative, less.

_____ 18. A reduction in the marginal tax rate increases the number of workers seeking jobs. This can be explained by stating that the income effect is _____ than the substitution effect. The opportunity cost of leisure has been _____ .
   A. greater, increased.
   B. greater, decreased.
   C. less, increased.
   D. less, decreased.

_____ 19. One major argument against free immigration is that
   A. immigrants displace low-income domestic workers.
   B. immigrants are "rate-busters" who increase productivity.
   C. profits and prices increase as a result of immigration.
   D. production costs rise because of the special needs of immigrants.

_____ 20. Many poor Arbocalis skimp on health care, become sick, and infect those who do buy health insurance. This represents
   A. a positive externality.
   B. a negative externality.
   C. a public good.
   D. defensive medicine.

APPLICATION QUESTION.

You are an economic advisor at the Clinton White House. The Republican Congress has been arguing vociferously for the scrapping of the progressive income tax system and its replacement with a flat-rate (proportional) tax. The President is considering coming out against the proposal. You have mentioned to him, in passing, that a flat-rate tax will, in effect, increase government tax revenues and reduce the budget deficit (or increase the surplus). The President is puzzled by this. Write a memo detailing the economic theory supporting your opinion.

ANSWERS AND SOLUTIONS

ANSWERS TO REVIEW TEST FOR PART 4

1. B. A consumption tax may or may not raise more revenue—it depends on the tax structure. See p. 434 for a full discussion of this debate.
2. D. Income taxes in the United States are mildly progressive. See p. 441.
3. B. Workers will receive lower wages. Higher taxes increase costs of labor for firms, leading them to cut back hiring. The resultant surplus of workers will drive down the wage rate. See p. 438.
4. C. The mark of a regressive tax is that the average tax rate decreases as income level increases.
5. B. Tax shifting occurs when taxpayers adjust their behavior to avoid a tax.
6. D. See p. 430.
7. C. *Despite* strong financial disincentives to work, the evidence suggests that most single mothers do work. See p. 461.
8. D. See the definition on p. 452.
9. B. As labor becomes more expensive in Occupation A, capital will be substituted. The opposite is true in Occupation B.
10. B. "Featherbedding" is a way of cushioning the fall in the *demand* for workers.
11. D. Marginal physical product affects the demand for labor. See p. 452.
12. C. As more women than before are crowded into Range A jobs, productivity will decrease. The reverse applies for males.
13. C. Labor supply has increased in Range A, pulling down the wage, and decreased in Range B.
14. C. The expected reward for females has fallen while that for males has increased.
15. C. In the presence of discrimination, male productivity has risen less than female productivity has fallen. See p. 464.
16. A. See p. 456.
17. B. See p. 460.
18. C. Workers are giving up leisure time (which has become more expensive as after-tax wages have risen) to work more.
19. A. See p. 484.
20. B. There is a spillover effect that reduces the welfare of the insurance purchasers. See p. 479.

APPLICATION

Mr. President,

A *progressive income tax system* exerts a substitution effect and an income effect on workers. As the tax rate increases, after-tax wage rates decrease, as does the incentive to work. Workers substitute leisure—the substitution effect. The income effect operates in the opposite direction—as tax rates increase, workers lose income, feel poorer, and work harder. If the substitution effect dominates the income effect (and it seems to for the labor force as a whole), hours worked will decrease, the tax base will be reduced, and *tax collections will decrease* with the progressive tax system.

A *flat-rate tax system* has only an income effect. There is no substitution effect because, as income increases, the tax rate does not change so there are no additional disincentives to work. The income effect of a tax is to reduce the worker's income, discouraging him/her from taking leisure time. The income effect may increase work time. Work time certainly won't decrease (there is no substitution effect), therefore the tax base will not shrink and tax revenues will not decrease. In fact, if the income effect is present, *tax collections will increase* with the flat-rate tax system.

Sincerely,

A. Staffer

INTERNATIONAL TRADE, COMPARATIVE ADVANTAGE, AND PROTECTIONISM

21

OBJECTIVES: POINT BY POINT

After completing this chapter, you should be able to accomplish the objectives listed below.

OBJECTIVE 1: Distinguish between an open and a closed economy. Distinguish between a trade surplus and a trade deficit.

In open economies such as the United States, aggregate expenditures are affected by the presence of exports and imports. We have seen international trade steadily increase in importance throughout the last several decades. If exports exceed imports, the country runs a *trade surplus*. In the oil-expensive years of the 1970s and 1980s, the value of imports into the United States increased to over 12% of GDP, and the United States began to experience *trade deficits*—that is, its imports exceeded its exports. (page 498)

> **LEARNING TIP:** Learn the difference between exports and imports. Imports are foreign-produced goods consumed here. Exports are domestically-produced goods sold to customers overseas. Imports and exports are not opposites; they are determined by different factors.

Comment: The two terms, "balance of payments" and "balance of trade", are not synonymous. The balance of trade refers only to exports and imports of goods, while the balance of payments includes all international transactions.

PRACTICE

1. The U.S. trade _____ reached a _____ in the late 1980s.
   A. surplus, peak.
   B. surplus, minimum.
   C. deficit, peak.
   D. deficit, minimum.
   Answer: C. See the table on p. 498.

OBJECTIVE 2: Distinguish between absolute advantage and comparative advantage and explain the logic behind the theory of comparative advantage. Given a particular two-country, two-good situation, calculate which country will trade which good and indicate the feasible range for the terms of trade.

The *theory of comparative advantage* provides the rationale for free trade. Given a two-country, two-good world, and assuming that the countries have advantages in the production of different goods, Ricardo showed that both trading partners could benefit from specialization in the production of the good in which they have the comparative advantage. Each country should specialize in the production of that good in which it has a comparative advantage and trade its surplus. Production and welfare will be maximized. Country A is said to have an *absolute advantage* if it can produce a unit of output with fewer resources than Country B. Comparative advantage, though, is a relative concept. Country A will have a *comparative advantage* in whichever good it can produce comparatively cheaper. Specialization and trade allow a country to consume more of a good than it can produce by itself. (page 498)

> **LEARNING TIP:** If you're like most individuals, you'll need several numerical examples to strengthen your grasp of pure trade theory. The Applications below take you through all the steps included in the text.

> **LEARNING TIP:** Comparative advantage hinges on the concept of *opportunity cost*. (Take a little time to go back and review the material you learned in Chapter and 2, especially Application questions 2, 7 and 10 of this Guide. They will lead you through the opportunity cost concept that underlies the theory of comparative advantage.) The producer (person, firm, or country) with the lower opportunity cost will hold the comparative advantage in that product. Don't be misled-absolute advantage is irrelevant.

> **LEARNING TIP:** Using the production possibility frontier (ppf) diagram, trade will be advantageous if the ppf's have differing slopes. The slope depicts opportunity cost. Differing slopes means that a comparative advantage exists—i.e., that the relative costs of production differ. Even though Country A may be more efficient in producing both goods—an absolute advantage—it is the *comparative* advantage of Country A that will establish the preferred pattern of specialization and trade. The country with the flatter ppf has an advantage in the good on the horizontal axis.

Given that specialization occurs, the *terms of trade* (the "price" of the traded commodities) must be negotiated. For trade to be beneficial, the "price" of the exported good (in terms of the imported good) must be greater than its cost of production. A range of terms of trade will exist. The deal cut within this range will depend on the relative negotiating strengths of the two partners. (page 504)

PRACTICE

Refer to the following table to answer the next four questions. The table shows the possible output levels from one day of labor input.

	Arboc	*Arbez*
Wheat	12 bushels	6 bushels
Cloths	12 yards	12 yards

2. Arbez
    A. has an absolute advantage in the production of cloth.
    B. has an absolute advantage in the production of wheat.
    C. has a comparative advantage in the production of cloth.
    D. should export cloth to Arboc.
    Answer: B. Arbez can produce absolutely more wheat per worker than Arboc can.

3. The opportunity cost of one bushel of wheat in Arboc is
    A. ½ yard of cloth.
    B. 2 yards of cloth.
    C. 6 yards of cloth.
    D. 12 yards of cloth.
    Answer: B. Six bushels take the inputs that could have produced 12 yards of cloth, therefore 1 bushel costs 2 yards of cloth.

4. Which of the following statements is false?
    A. Arboc has an absolute advantage in the production of wheat.
    B. Arbez should export wheat to Arboc and import cloth from Arboc.
    C. The opportunity cost of wheat is twice as high in Arboc as in Arbez.
    D. The opportunity cost of a yard of cloth in Arbez is one bushel of wheat.
    Answer: A. Arboc is half as productive per worker as Arbez in wheat production.

5. Arboc and Arbez decide to specialize according to the law of comparative advantage and trade with one another. We would expect that
    A. the trade agreement will be somewhere between 1 bushel of wheat for 1 yard of cloth and 1 bushel of wheat for 2 yards of cloth.
    B. the trade agreement will be somewhere between ½ a bushel of wheat for 1 yard of cloth and 2 bushels of wheat for 1 yard of cloth.
    C. Arboc will benefit from trading with Arbez, but Arbez will not benefit from trading with Arboc.
    D. Arboc will specialize in the production of wheat and Arbez will specialize in the production of cloth.
    Answer: A. The Arbezani opportunity cost of 1 bushel of wheat is 1 yard of cloth. Arboc's opportunity cost of 1 bushel of wheat is 2 yards of cloth.

6. The ratio at which exports are traded for imports is known as
    A. the exchange rate.
    B. the trade balance.
    C. the balance of exchange.
    D. the terms of trade.
    Answer: D. See p. 504.

Use the following diagrams, which show the production possibility frontiers (ppf's) for Malaysia and Sri Lanka, to answer the next nine questions. Each country has an equal quantity of resources.

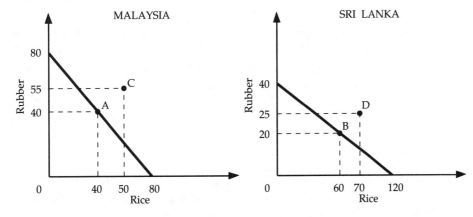

7. Which of the following statements is true?
   A. Malaysia has an absolute advantage in the production of rubber; Sri Lanka has an absolute advantage in the production of rice.
   B. Sri Lanka has an absolute advantage in the production of rubber; Malaysia has an absolute advantage in the production of rice.
   C. Malaysia has an absolute advantage in the production of both goods.
   D. Sri Lanka has an absolute advantage in the production of both goods.
   Answer: A. See p. 499.

8. Which statement is false?
   A. In Malaysia, the opportunity cost of one unit of rubber is one unit of rice.
   B. In Malaysia, the opportunity cost of one unit of rice is one unit of rubber.
   C. In Sri Lanka, the opportunity cost of one unit of rubber is three units of rice.
   D. In Sri Lanka, the opportunity cost of one unit of rice is three units of rubber.
   Answer: D. The Sri Lankan opportunity cost of one unit of rice is a third of a unit of rubber.

9. Which of the following statements is true?
   A. Malaysia has a comparative advantage in the production of rubber; Sri Lanka has a comparative advantage in the production of rice.
   B. Sri Lanka has a comparative advantage in the production of rubber; Malaysia has a comparative advantage in the production of rice.
   C. Malaysia has a comparative advantage in both goods.
   D. Sri Lanka has a comparative advantage in both goods.
   Answer: A. See p. 499.

10. Given that Malaysia and Sri Lanka decide to trade,
    A. Malaysia should specialize in the production of rubber; Sri Lanka should specialize in the production of rice.
    B. Malaysia should specialize in the production of rice; Sri Lanka should specialize in the production of rubber.
    C. Malaysia and Sri Lanka should each devote half their resources to the production of each commodity.
    D. Malaysia should specialize in the production of rubber; Sri Lanka should produce some rice but continue to produce some rubber.
    Answer: A. Malaysia's comparative advantage lies in rubber production; Sri Lanka's lies in rice.

11. Before trade, Malaysia produced at Point A on its ppf and Sri Lanka produced at Point B. Given complete specialization based on comparative advantage, total rubber production has risen by _____ and total rice production has risen by
_____
    A. 80, 120.
    B. 120, 80.
    C. 40, 60.
    D. 20, 20.
    Answer: D. Total rubber production was 60 (40 + 20); now it is 80. Total rice production was 100 (40 + 60); now it is 120.

12. After trade, Malaysia is consuming at Point C and Sri Lanka is consuming at Point D. Malaysia is exporting _____ units of rubber and Sri Lanka is exporting _____ units of rice.
    A. 80, 100.
    B. 55, 70.
    C. 25, 50.
    D. 15, 10.
    Answer: C. Malaysian rubber production is 80, and domestic consumption is 55, leaving 25 for export. Sri Lankan rice production is 120, and domestic consumption is 70, leaving 50 for export.

13. After trade, Malaysia is consuming at Point C and Sri Lanka is consuming at Point D. Malaysia is importing _____ units of rice and Sri Lanka is importing _____ units of rubber.
   A. 80, 100.
   B. 50, 25.
   C. 25, 50.
   D. 15, 10.
   Answer: B. See the answer to the previous question. In a two-country world, Country A's exports are Country B's imports.

14. Which statement is true?
   A. Only Sri Lanka will benefit if the terms of trade are set at 1 : 2, rubber to rice.
   B. Only Malaysia will benefit if the terms of trade are set at 1 : 2, rubber to rice.
   C. Both countries will gain if the terms of trade lie between 3 : 1 and 1 : 1, rubber to rice.
   D. Both countries will gain if the terms of trade lie between 1 : 1 and 1 : 3, rubber to rice.
   Answer: D. Check these values against the opportunity cost values you calculated in question 8. Also note the correct value of the rubber : rice ratio in question 12.

15. Which statement is false? If the terms of trade are set at
   A. 1 : 1, rubber to rice, only Sri Lanka will gain.
   B. 1 : 2, rubber to rice, both countries will gain.
   C. 1 : 3, rubber to rice, only Malaysia will gain.
   D. 1 : 4, rubber to rice, both countries will wish to produce rice.
   Answer: D. If the terms of trade are set at 1 : 4, rubber to rice, rubber is relatively valuable and can cover its opportunity cost in both countries. Both will wish to produce rubber.

OBJECTIVE 3: Calculate the limiting values of the exchange rate in a given example and relate the exchange rate to the notion of comparative advantage. Describe how changes in the exchange rate can affect trade flows.

Trade flows are affected by comparative advantage and by the exchange rate (the "price" of the domestic currency in terms of a foreign currency). There will be some range of exchange rates that will permit mutually beneficial specialization and trade.
(page 504)

The distribution of benefits from trade depends on the exchange rate. To buy foreign goods one must hold foreign currency, which is bought and sold in the foreign exchange market. If the value of the dollar changes, the relative attractiveness of the foreign goods will be affected. A strengthening yen will increase the price tag of a Toyota for a U.S. buyer, but the price tag of the domestically-produced Chrysler will not change—the relative attractiveness of the Toyota will decline. Tourists watch exchange rates keenly—a stronger dollar is good news because each dollar will buy more foreign currency and, therefore, more foreign goods and services (which have, in that sense, become cheaper).

The previous comparative advantage material (in Chapter 2) was based on production capabilities—supply is important; demand is absent. By incorporating prices, the demand side of the market can be represented.

LEARNING TIP: An increase in the value of the dollar means that foreign goods cost U.S. citizens less (imports increase), but U.S. goods cost foreigners more (exports fall). Choose a foreign country and currency and make up your own example.

PRACTICE

16. The exchange rate is one British pound equals $1.75. If the exchange rate changes to one British pound equals $1.50, we can conclude that, for a British buyer, a pair of American-made moccasins have become _____ expensive and, for a U.S. buyer, a British cashmere sweater has become _____ expensive.
    A. more, more.
    B. more, less.
    C. less, more.
    D. less, less.
    Answer: B. Each pound is worth less U.S. currency—British buyers are becoming poorer. The opposite is true for U.S. buyers of British goods.

17. As the exchange rate changes from one British pound equals $1.50 to one British pound equals $2.00, British traders will gain _____ from trade with the United States, and American traders will gain _____ from trade with the United Kingdom.
    A. more, more.
    B. more, less.
    C. less, more.
    D. less, less.
    Answer: B. Each pound is worth more U.S. currency. British producers, selling the same amount of exports, will be able to claim more U.S. goods than before.

Use the following table, which shows the domestic prices per unit of steel and corn in Slovakia and Slovenia, to answer the next three questions.

	Slovakia	*Slovenia*
Steel	20 koruna	48 tolars
Corn	30 koruna	87 tolars

18. If the exchange rate is 1 koruna = 1 tolar, then
    A. Slovakia will import both steel and corn.
    B. Slovenia will import both steel and corn.
    C. Slovakia will import steel and Slovenia will import corn.
    D. Slovakia will import corn and Slovenia will import steel.
    Answer: B. In Slovenia, the domestic prices of steel and corn are 48 tolars and 87 tolars, respectively. The imported prices are 20 tolars and 30 tolars, respectively.

19. If the exchange rate is 1 koruna = 3 tolars, then
    A. Slovakia will import both steel and corn.
    B. Slovenia will import both steel and corn.
    C. Slovakia will import steel and Slovenia will import corn.
    D. Slovakia will import corn and Slovenia will import steel.
    Answer: A. In Slovakia, the domestic prices of steel and corn are 20 koruna and 30 koruna, respectively. The imported prices are 16 koruna and 29 koruna, respectively.

20. Two-way trade will occur only if the price of the koruna is between
    A. 1.0 tolars and 3.0 tolars.
    B. 1.5 tolars and 2.4 tolars.
    C. 2.4 tolars and 2.9 tolars.
    D. 1.5 tolars and 3.0 tolars.
    Answer: C. If the exchange rate is 1 koruna = 2.4 tolars, no trade in steel will occur. If the exchange rate is 1 koruna = 2.9 tolars, no trade in corn will occur. Between these rates, Slovakia will import steel and Slovenia will import corn.

OBJECTIVE 4: Provide an intuitive explanation of the Heckscher-Ohlin theorem.

The *Heckscher-Ohlin theorem* builds on the theory of comparative advantage by focusing on the differing factor endowments of countries. Some countries seem more labor-abundant (India, China) while others are more capital-abundant (United States, Japan). The Heckscher-Ohlin theorem states that a country will specialize in and export that good whose production calls for a relatively intensive use of the input that the country has in abundance: India should export labor-intensive goods and import capital-intensive goods, for example.   (page 507)

The assembly of audiocassettes requires a large stock of semi-skilled cheap labor with little capital. This favors Mexico. Research into the capabilities of fiber optics requires a large stock of expensive capital. This favors the United States. The production of timber requires an abundant stock of forest land—a requirement that Canada meets.

PRACTICE

21. We observe that Arbez produces wooden ornaments (a labor-intensive activity), and that Arboc produces plastic containers (a capital-intensive activity). Which of the following statements is true?
    A. Arbez has more labor than Arboc; Arboc has more capital than Arbez.
    B. Arboc has more labor than Arbez; Arbez has more capital than Arboc.
    C. Labor is relatively abundant in Arbez.
    D. Labor is relatively abundant in Arboc.
    Answer: C. Assuming that the two countries are being rational, Arbez is producing the good in which it has a comparative advantage.

OBJECTIVE 5: Define a tariff, an export subsidy, and a quota. Outline, using a demand and supply analysis, the costs involved in the imposition of a tariff.

Tariffs, export subsidies, and quotas are examples of trade barriers. *Tariffs* are taxes on imports, designed to force up their price; *export subsidies* are government payments to U.S. exporters, intended to make them more competitive overseas; *quotas* are limits on the quantity of imports. *Dumping* is meant to price competitors out of the market; having achieved market domination, the firm can then raise prices.   (page 508)

PRACTICE

Use the following diagram to answer the next three questions. The diagram shows the American demand for and supply of T-shirts. The world price is $4 per shirt.

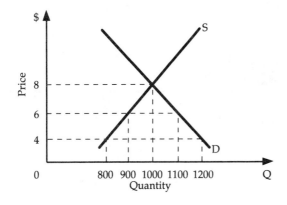

22. In an unrestricted open market, the U.S. will
    A. export 400 T-shirts.
    B. export 200 T-shirts.
    C. import 400 T-shirts.
    D. import 200 T-shirts.
    Answer: C. At a price of $4, there is an excess U.S. demand of 400.

23. The garment industry successfully lobbies Congress to impose a $2 per shirt tax on imports. Now the U.S. will
    A. export 400 T-shirts.
    B. export 200 T-shirts.
    C. import 400 T-shirts.
    D. import 200 T-shirts.
    Answer: D. An excess demand remains that must be met from overseas.

24. The government will collect _____ in tariff revenues.
    A. $100.
    B. $200.
    C. $400.
    D. $800.
    Answer: C. The government collects $2 per shirt on each of the 200 imported shirts.

OBJECTIVE 6: Give the arguments advanced for and against protection. Describe the costs involved in permitting free trade.

The case for free trade is based on the theory of comparative advantage. Trade benefits the participants. Welfare increases if trade flows are allowed to follow their "natural" pattern; obstacles, such as tariffs and quotas, reduce that welfare. Higher-cost production results. (page 512)

The argument in favor of protection is based on the observation that efficient foreign competition will result in job loss for domestic workers and lost production. Individual arguments for protection from foreign competition may include claims that cheap foreign labor is "unfair," that national security must be protected, that trade encourages dependency on foreigners, and that we need to let infant industries develop. Some of these arguments are simply false, and others are misused. (page 513)

PRACTICE

25. Which of the following is not an argument used by protectionists?
    A. Infant industries need support until they are strong enough to compete.
    B. Restricting trade builds up dependency on other counties.
    C. Protection is needed in the light of unfair foreign practices, in order to ensure a level playing field.
    D. Cheap foreign labor makes competition unfair.
    Answer: B. See p. 514.

PRACTICE TEST

I. MULTIPLE CHOICE QUESTIONS.

Select the option that provides the single best answer.

_____ 1. According to the textbook, _____ of all cars and _____ of all consumer electronics bought in the United States are produced abroad.
    A. 50%, 50%.
    B. 50%, 80%.
    C. 80%, 50%.
    D. 80%, 80%.

_____ 2. A country imports less than it exports. It has
   A. an export subsidy.
   B. a tariff quota.
   C. a trade surplus.
   D. a trade deficit.

_____ 3. Relative to Arboc, Arbez has a comparative advantage in the production of goat milk. We can say that Arbez
   A. uses fewer resources to produce goat milk than does Arboc.
   B. must also have an absolute advantage in the production of goat milk.
   C. is the producer with the lower opportunity cost of producing goat milk.
   D. should diversify into other products rather than trade with the high-cost, inefficient Arbocalis.

_____ 4. In Arbez/Arboc trade, an increase in the exchange rate of the Arbezani currency (the bandu) relative to that of the Arbocali currency (the opek) means that
   A. Arbezani goods will appear to be relatively cheaper to the Arbocalis.
   B. Arbocali goods will appear to be relatively cheaper to the Arbezanis.
   C. Arbez will lose any comparative advantage that it had.
   D. Arbez will experience a decreasing trade deficit.

_____ 5. The Heckscher-Ohlin theorem states that Arbez will have a(n) _____ advantage in the production of a good that uses its relatively _____
   A. absolute, scarce input intensively.
   B. absolute, abundant input intensively.
   C. comparative, abundant input intensively.
   D. comparative, scarce input intensively.

_____ 6. Two goods are produced, pins and needles. Jill has a comparative advantage in the production of pins. Relative to Jack, and with the same resources,
   A. Jill is better at producing pins than at producing needles.
   B. Jill is better at producing both pins and needles.
   C. Jill can produce pins more efficiently than Jack.
   D. Jill can produce more pins than Jack.

_____ 7. Jill chooses to trade pins for needles with Jack. It is likely that
   A. Jill's gains equal Jack's losses.
   B. pins are more expensive than needles.
   C. each trader receives goods that he or she values more highly than those he or she gives up.
   D. neither trader can gain more than the other.

For questions 8–10, assume that Arbez and Arboc have the same amount of resources and similar preferences for goat milk and bananas. The table shows the number of labor hours needed to produce 1 liter of goat milk and 1 kilo of bananas.

	Arbez	Arboc
Goat Milk	.3	.6
Bananas	.5	.2

_____ 8. According to the table above,
   A. Arbez has a comparative advantage in the production of both goods.
   B. Arbez has a comparative advantage in the production of bananas, and Arboc has a comparative advantage in the production of goat milk.
   C. Arbez has a comparative advantage in the production of goat milk, and Arboc has a comparative advantage in the production of bananas.
   D. Arboc has a comparative advantage in the production of both goods.

_____ 9. According to the table, one unit of labor hours produces
   A. 3 liters of goat milk in Arbez and 6 liters in Arboc.
   B. 5 kilos of bananas in Arbez and 2 kilos in Arboc.
   C. 2 kilos of bananas in Arbez and 5 kilos in Arboc.
   D. 6 liters of goat milk in Arboc and 2 kilos of bananas in Arboc.

_____ 10. For trade to occur, the terms of trade might be
   A. 2 liters of goat milk for 1 kilo of bananas.
   B. 1 liter of goat milk for 4 kilos of bananas.
   C. 1 liter of goat milk for .7 of a kilo of bananas.
   D. 3 liters of goat milk for 1 kilo of bananas.

_____ 11. Tariffs and quotas are economically inefficient because
   A. the government does not collect any revenues under a tariff.
   B. imports rise and this reduces the welfare of consumers.
   C. producers are saved from the pressure of foreign competition.
   D. domestic prices must be reduced.

_____ 12. Which of the following is an argument in favor of increased protection?
   A. U.S. consumers have become too dependent on foreign countries for their luxury goods.
   B. National defense can be jeopardized if strategic supplies are produced by foreigners.
   C. Running a persistent trade deficit is unhealthy and must be avoided.
   D. Higher tariffs increase the welfare of U.S. consumers.

_____ 13. Each of the following is a trade barrier except a(n)
   A. flexible exchange rate.
   B. quota.
   C. export subsidy.
   D. tariff.

_____ 14. Statement 1: A country with an absolute advantage in the production of a good will also have a comparative advantage.
   Statement 2: A country with a comparative advantage in the production of a good will also have an absolute advantage. Statement 1 is _____ ; Statement 2 is _____
   A. true, true.
   B. true, false.
   C. false, true.
   D. false, false.

_____ 15. A tariff _____ increase the government's tax receipts; a quota _____ increase the government's tax receipts.
   A. does, does.
   B. does, does not.
   C. does not, does.
   D. does not, does not.

_____ 16. In Tokyo, a Big Mac sells for 500 yen. The dollar : yen exchange rate is one dollar per 125 yen. The price of the Big Mac in dollars is
A. 500.
B. .25.
C. 4.
D. 5.

_____ 17. In Tokyo, a Big Mac sells for 500 yen. The exchange rate changes from one dollar for 125 yen, to one dollar for 250 yen. The price of the Big Mac in dollars
A. has increased.
B. has decreased.
C. has not changed.
D. has doubled.

_____ 18. The Heckscher-Ohlin theorem explains the pattern of trade by focusing on
A. comparative advantage.
B. absolute advantage.
C. relative factor endowments.
D. exchange rate variations.

_____ 19. As the exchange rate changes from one British pound equals $1.50 to one British pound equals $1.00, the terms of trade shift _____ the United States. American traders will gain _____ from trade with the United Kingdom.
A. in favor of, more.
B. in favor of, less.
C. against, more.
D. against, less.

_____ 20. We would expect a tariff imposed on an import to _____ the price of the import and to _____ the price of domestic substitutes for the import.
A. increase, increase.
B. increase, not affect.
C. decrease, decrease.
D. decrease, not affect.

II. APPLICATION QUESTIONS.

1. The Arbezani Minister of Trade, a firm believer in the Heckscher-Ohlin theorem, asks your advice regarding some recent changes within the Arbezani economy. In each case, he wishes to know whether or not the Heckscher-Ohlin explanation of trade flows will be strengthened. Arbez has established a free-trade region with its sole trading partner, Arboc.
   a. Arbezani unions in a substantial number of industries lobby successfully for increased restrictions on movement between industries, e.g., longer apprenticeships, work permits, drug testing of new entrants into an industry.
   b. It has been discovered that Arbez and its trading partner, Arboc, have identical endowments of all resources.
   c. Nationalistic Arbezani politicians, concerned about the loss of sovereignty caused by a free-trade area, have successfully passed restrictions on the flow of labor and other inputs between Arbez and Arboc.

2. The nations of Noil and Regit produce loaves and fishes. The labor supply is 12,000 labor units per year in Noil while, in Regit, the labor supply is 72,000 labor units per year. Assume that labor is the only input and that costs are constant within each economy. The costs of producing loaves and fishes, in labor units, are given in the following table.

Units of labor supply needed to produce 1 unit of:	Noil	Regit
Loaves	2	3
Fishes	1	3

a. Calculate the maximum output levels of loaves and fishes for each economy and enter your results in the following table.

Maximum units produced:	Noil	Regit
Loaves	_____	_____
Fishes	_____	_____

b. Draw the production possibility frontiers for each nation.

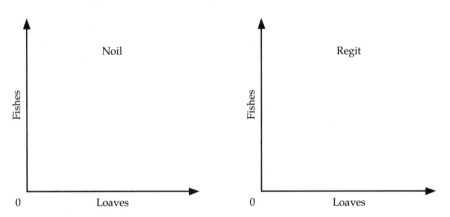

c. When questioned about the possibility of establishing trade between the two nations, the Regitani Minister of Trade states his government's official line—the proposal is ludicrous because Regit has an advantage in the production of each good. Is the Regitani view correct?

In both nations, the custom is to consume two loaves with each fish.

d. Assume that no trade takes place. Calculate the annual production of loaves and fishes that will most satisfactorily meet demand in each country separately. Also determine the total production of loaves and fishes for the two countries without trade.

Maximum units produced:	Noil	Regit	Total
Loaves	_____	_____	_____
Fishes	_____	_____	_____

e. Yielding to pressure, the Regitani government opens its borders to trade with Noil. Based on comparative advantage, which good should Noil specialize in producing? Explain.

f. Assuming that specialization and trade flows are dictated by comparative advantage, determine the quantity of loaves and fishes that can be produced.

g. Suppose that the terms of trade are established at 1 fish = 2 loaves. Determine the consumption of loaves and fishes in each country.

Units consumed:	*Noil*	*Regit*
Loaves	_____	_____
Fishes	_____	_____

h. Has trade been mutually beneficial in this case?

i. Suppose that the terms of trade are established at 1 fish = 1 loaf. Determine the consumption of loaves and fishes in each country.

Units consumed:	*Noil*	*Regit*
Loaves	_____	_____
Fishes	_____	_____

j. Has trade been mutually beneficial in this case?

k. Suppose that the terms of trade are established at 2 fishes = 1 loaf. Determine the consumption of loaves and fishes in each country.

Units consumed:	*Noil*	*Regit*
Loaves	_____	_____
Fishes	_____	_____

l. Has trade been mutually beneficial in this case?

m. Determine the "price" of a loaf (in terms of fish) necessary to have mutually beneficial two-way trade.

3. The domestic price of Arbocali cloth is 4 opeks a yard. The domestic price of Arbezani leather is 12 bandu per hide. Arboc sells cloth to Arbez and Arbez sells hides to Arboc. The opek : bandu exchange rate is 2 opeks per bandu. The exchange rate is flexible.

Ignoring transportation and other such costs, calculate the price in Arbez of a yard of imported Arbocali cloth and the price in Arboc of an imported Arbezani hide.

4. Use the diagrams below to answer this question.

a. What is the opportunity cost of one kilo of bananas in Arboc?
b. What is the opportunity cost of one kilo of bananas in Arbez?
c. Which country has a comparative advantage in the production of bananas?
d. What is the opportunity cost of one liter of goat milk in Arboc?
e. What is the opportunity cost of one liter of goat milk in Arbez?
f. Which country has a comparative advantage in the production of goat milk?
g. If the terms of trade were 1.0 liter of goat milk/kilo of bananas, which country would want to export goat milk?
h. If the terms of trade were 3 liters of goat milk/kilo of bananas, Arboc should produce _____ and Arbez should produce _____ .
i. Suppose that the terms of trade were 1 kilo of bananas/1.5 liters of goat milk. _____ would export bananas and _____ would export goat milk.

5. Arboc and Arbez produce wine and cheese, and each has constant costs of production. The domestic prices for the two goods are given in the table. At the moment 1 Arbocali opek is traded for 1 Arbezani bandu.

	Arboc	Arbez
wine	40 opeks	120 bandu
cheese	20 opeks	30 bandu

a. Which country has a comparative advantage in cheese production?
b. Which country has a comparative advantage in wine production?
c. At the present exchange rate (1 opek = 1 bandu), will two-way trade occur? Explain.
d. Which country will have a balance of trade deficit?
e. What should happen to the value of the opek, relative to the bandu?
f. If the exchange rate is 1 opek = 2 bandu, what would happen to trade?
g. Cheese making is capital-intensive, and wine making is labor-intensive. Which country should have the relatively abundant supplies of labor, if the Heckscher-Ohlin theory is correct?
h. If the exchange rate is 1 opek = 4 bandu, what would happen to trade?

6. Here are the domestic demand and supply schedules for diapers.

Price	Quantity Demanded	Quantity Supplied
$6	800	1,100
$5	1,000	1,000
$4	1,200	900
$3	1,400	800
$2	1,600	700

a. Graph the demand and supply curves.

b. The equilibrium price is $ _____ and quantity is _____ .
c. The world price for diapers is $3. Show this on the diagram as Pw. What will be the levels of domestic consumption and domestic production?

In order to preserve employment, diaper manufacturers contend successfully that theirs is an "infant industry" and should be protected.

d. A tariff is imposed that raises the price of imported diapers to $4. Show this on the diagram as Pt.
e. The tariff causes an increase in price and an increase in domestic production of _____ units. Consumption will fall to _____ units.
f. Imports will be _____ units. The tariff will yield $ _____ in tax revenues.
g. Shade in the areas representing the net welfare loss caused by the tariff.
h. The loss in welfare is $ _____ .

ANSWERS AND SOLUTIONS

PRACTICE TEST

I. SOLUTIONS TO MULTIPLE CHOICE QUESTIONS

1. B. See p. 497.
2. C. See p. 498.

3. C. Arbez might be relatively inefficient in producing both goods but relatively less inefficient in producing goat milk. Because Arbez has a comparative advantage in producing goat milk, its opportunity cost of producing goat milk must be less.

4. B. As the Arbezani currency becomes more powerful, Arbocali goods will become cheaper when calculated in terms of the Arbezani currency.

5. C. See p. 507.

6. A. Remember that comparative advantage is a relative concept. It requires that we compare two producers and two goods.

7. C. In voluntary trade, we expect each trader to gain something more than s/he traded.

8. C. Goat milk is relatively cheap to produce in Arbez and bananas require relatively few resources in Arboc. In a two-good, two-country situation, one party can never have a comparative advantage in both goods.

9. C. .5 labor hour gives 1 kilo of bananas in Arbez—1 hour gives 2 kilos. .2 labor hour gives 1 liter of milk in Arboc—1 hour gives 5 liters.

10. C. The terms of trade must lie in the range from 1 liter of goat milk : ⅗ kilo of bananas to 1 liter of goat milk : 3 kilos of bananas. If Arbez has 6 hours of labor, it could produce 20 liters of goat milk or 12 kilos of bananas—a ratio of 1 : ⅗ . If Arboc has 6 hours of labor, it could produce 10 liters of goat milk or 30 kilos of bananas—a ratio of 1 : 3.

11. C. Tariffs impose welfare losses in two ways. Consumers pay a higher price and, as mentioned in this question, marginal producers are allowed to survive. Option B is incorrect—imports don't increase, they decrease. See p. 512.

12. B. The national security argument is persistent.

13. A. See p. 508 for a discussion of trade barriers.

14. D. A country may have an absolute advantage in the production of Good A and Good B; it may have a comparative advantage in the production of Good A and, therefore, a comparative disadvantage in Good B. Similarly, a country with a comparative advantage in the production of Good A might be less efficient than its partner in producing either good.

15. B. A tariff is a tax that provides revenues; a quota merely restricts the number of units that may be imported.

16. C. 125 yen equal $1. 500 yen equal $4.

17. B. 125 yen equal $1. 500 yen equal $4. 250 yen equal $1. 500 yen equal $2.

18. C. See p. 507.

19. A. Dollars are becoming relatively more valuable.

20. A. A tariff will drive up the price of the import, increasing demand for domestic substitutes whose price will then increase.

II. SOLUTIONS TO APPLICATION QUESTIONS

1. a. Heckscher-Ohlin assumes that inputs are mobile within an economy. Such restrictions will work against Heckscher-Ohlin because, as an economy begins to specialize and trade, it will wish to reallocate inputs.

   b. According to Heckscher-Ohlin, comparative advantage is dependent upon differences in factor endowments. No differences in factor endowments, no comparative advantage: no comparative advantage, no trade. Arbez and Arboc should have no basis for trade.

   c. The new restrictions should not affect the pattern of trade. The Heckscher-Ohlin theorem assumes that inputs are not mobile between countries.

2. a. Maximum units produced:

	Noil	Regit
Loaves	6,000	24,000
Fishes	12,000	24,000

b.   See the following diagrams.

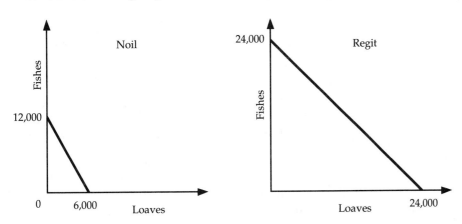

2.   c.   The Regitani view is mainly incorrect. Regit does have an absolute advantage in the production of both loaves and fishes, but it does not have a comparative advantage in both, and it is comparative advantage that determines whether or not trade is advantageous.

 d.   Maximum units produced:

	Noil	Regit	Total
Loaves	4,800	16,000	20,800
Fishes	2,400	8,000	10,400

 e.   Noil should produce fishes. In Noil, the cost of producing 1 loaf is 2 fishes while the cost of producing 1 loaf in Regit is 1 fish. Loaves are less costly in Regit. Regit has a comparative advantage in loaves; Noil has a comparative advantage in fishes.

 f.   Noil can produce 12,000 fishes and Regit can produce 24,000 loaves.

 g.   Units consumed:

	Noil	Regit
Loaves	12,000	12,000
Fishes	6,000	6,000

   Noil can produce 12,000 fishes and export 6,000, earning 12,000 loaves in return. Regit can produce 24,000 loaves and export 12,000, earning 6,000 fishes in return.

 h.   Trade has benefited Noil, but Regit has a lower standard of living than it had before trade!

 i.   Units consumed:

	Noil	Regit
Loaves	8,000	16,000
Fishes	4,000	8,000

   Noil can produce 12,000 fishes and export 8,000, earning 8,000 loaves in return. Regit can produce 24,000 loaves and export 8,000, earning 8,000 fishes in return.

 j.   Trade has benefited Noil, but Regit's standard of living is unchanged.

k. Units consumed:

Units consumed:	*Noil*	*Regit*
Loaves	4,800	16,000
Fishes	2,400	8,000

Noil can produce 12,000 fishes and export 9,600, earning 4,800 loaves in return. Regit can produce 24,000 loaves and export 4,800, earning 9,600 fishes in return.

l. Trade has benefited Regit, but Noil's standard of living is unchanged.

m. The terms of trade need to be between 1 loaf = 1 fish and 1 loaf = 2 fish.

3. A yard of imported Arbocali cloth will cost 2 bandu in Arbez. An imported Arbezani hide will cost 24 opeks in Arboc.

4. a. ⅓ of a liter of goat milk.
    b. 1⅔ liters of goat milk.
    c. Arboc.
    d. 3 kilos of bananas.
    e. ⁶⁄₁₀ of a kilo of bananas.
    f. Arbez.
    g. Arbez, because it can produce a liter of goat milk at a cost of less than one kilo of bananas and, therefore, can gain through this specialization.
    h. bananas, bananas. One kilo of bananas can be sold for 2 liters of goat milk. Both Arboc and Arbez can produce bananas more cheaply than this (⅓ of a liter of goat milk and 1⅔ liters of goat milk, respectively).
    i. Arboc, Arbez. One kilo of bananas can be sold for 1.5 liters of goat milk. Arboc can produce bananas more cheaply than this (⅓ of a liter of goat milk) and so will produce bananas. One liter of goat milk can be sold for ⅔ kilo of bananas. Arbez can produce goat milk more cheaply than this (⁶⁄₁₀ of a kilo of bananas) and so will produce goat milk.

5. a. Arbez. Wine is four times as expensive as cheese in Arbez, but only twice as expensive in Arboc.
    b. Arboc. Each country must have a comparative advantage in one of the goods.
    c. No. Because Arboc can produce both goods more cheaply, the Arbezanis will import both. The Arbocalis will not wish to buy either Arbezani product.
    d. Arbez, because it has some imports and zero exports.
    e. The Arbocali currency (the opek) should be heavily demanded (by Arbezanis seeking to buy Arbocali goods). The demand for the bandu will be low. The opek will rise in value; the bandu will fall in value.
    f. At a price of 30 bandu (15 opeks), Arbezani cheese will now be cheaper than Arbocali cheese (at a price of 20 opeks). Arboc will import cheese. Arbez will continue to import Arbocali wine. At a price of 40 opeks (80 bandu), Arbocali wine is still cheaper than that produced in Arbez (at a price of 120 bandu).
    g. Arboc.
    h. At a price of 30 bandu (7.50 opeks), Arbezani cheese will be cheaper than Arbocali cheese (at a price of 20 opeks). Arboc will import cheese.

    At a price of 40 opeks (160 bandu), Arbocali wine will be more expensive than that produced in Arbez (at a price of 120 bandu). Arboc will import wine.

    Arboc will have a trade deficit and Arbez a surplus.

6. a. See the diagram below.

b. $5, 1000.
c. See the diagram above. 1400, 800.
d. See the diagram above.
e. 100, 1200.
f. 300, $300.
g. See the diagram above.
h. $(50 + 100).

ECONOMIC GROWTH IN DEVELOPING NATIONS 22

OBJECTIVES: POINT BY POINT

After completing this chapter, you should be able to accomplish the objectives listed below.

General Comment

The focus of this chapter is the ways in which developing countries might become developed and the problems that they might encounter along the way. If you study by making lists, be careful in this chapter because three separate topics are covered—a description of the Third World, how development might be promoted, and some Third World problems. Make up lists using each of these headings.

OBJECTIVE 1: Describe the relationship between economic development and economic growth. Distinguish among conditions in the so-called First, Second, Third, and Fourth World countries.

In the past, the nations of the world have been roughly divided into three groups: the First World (western, industrialized), the Second World (ex-Socialist, whose future is now uncertain), and the Third World (poor, largely agricultural). There is some mobility—Taiwan, Korea, and Brazil, for instance, are breaking away from others in the Third World category, while a number of nations are lagging so far behind that they have been called the "Fourth World" group. The main characteristic of a Third World country is that the great majority of its inhabitants are poor. Other dimensions that distinguish the "haves" from the "have nots" are: health care, educational facilities, and the percentage of the population engaged in agriculture. (page 529)

> **Comment:** There's no single unambiguous term that distinguishes the "developing nations" as the textbook deals with them. After all, in one sense, the United States is a developing economy too. "Third World" tends to have some political undertones. Remember that these nations are a pretty varied group, including South American, Asian, and African countries as diverse as Mexico and Mali, Taiwan and Togo. Don't allow yourself to overgeneralize!

PRACTICE

1. The poorest of the developing nations are sometimes known as the
   A. First World.
   B. Second World.
   C. Third World.
   D. Fourth World.
   Answer: D. See p. 529.

2.   Most of the Fourth World nations are to be found in
   A. Latin America.
   B. sub-Saharan Africa.
   C. Southeast Asia.
   D. the former republics of the Soviet Union and its satellites.
   Answer: B. Most of the very poorest nations are found to the south of the Sahara desert in Africa.

3.   Per capita GDP is _____ in developed countries, and infant mortality is _____

   A. higher, higher.
   B. higher, lower.
   C. lower, higher.
   D. lower, lower.
   Answer: B. See Table 22.1 (37.1) of the textbook.

OBJECTIVE 2: List the factors that influence economic development. Explain why capital infrastructure is important for economic development.

No single theory has emerged to explain the development process, but various factors have been identified as potential constraints on development. These include a low rate of accumulation of physical capital, a lack of human capital, a lack of social overhead capital (infrastructure), and a lack of entrepreneurial ability.   (page 532)

LEARNING TIP: Pay attention to what is happening in your own state and locality. Many of the sources and strategies discussed in this chapter are not limited to poor foreign regions. Debates on economic development are frequent at the state and local government level.

Comment: As the textbook notes, economic growth and economic development are not the same phenomenon. Simply because an object is expanding doesn't mean that it is also developing. However, you'll find it helpful to refer back to Chapter 19 (34) and locate the factors that promote growth.

PRACTICE

4.   The brain drain refers to
   A. the movement of talented personnel from a developing country to a developed country.
   B. the absence of skilled entrepreneurs in the developing countries.
   C. declining literacy rates.
   D. the loss of human capital through the ravages of malnutrition.
   Answer: A. See p. 535.

5.   Each of the following has been advanced as a plausible constraint on development except
   A. the quantity of available capital.
   B. the quantity of available labor.
   C. the quantity of infrastructure.
   D. the quantity of entrepreneurial ability.
   Answer: B. The typical developing country has adequate numbers of workers, although specific skills may be limited.

6. Capital shortages are a typical problem for developing countries. Each of the following is a plausible cause of capital shortages except
   A. lack of incentives leading to low saving rates.
   B. the inherent riskiness of investment in a developing nation.
   C. government policies, such as price ceilings and appropriation of private property.
   D. widespread poverty resulting in little surplus after consumption needs are met.
   Answer: D. The vicious-circle-of-poverty hypothesis fails to account for the success of previously poor nations like Japan. See p. 534.

OBJECTIVE 3: Name and describe four strategies for economic development.

Four development strategies have been attempted.

   a. Development used to be equated with industrialization; many Third World nations sought to move away from agriculture and toward industrial production. However, merely trying to replicate the structure of the developed nations does not guarantee development. Opinion now favors a balanced growth in both agricultural and industrial sectors—"walking on two legs."
   b. *Import substitution* calls for the encouragement of home-grown substitutes for imported goods. This strategy has failed in almost every case; it results in high-cost production protected by trade barriers.
   c. *Export promotion* calls for producing goods for the export market and has seen some measure of success, although it depends on the willingness of the developed nations to import Third World production.
   d. Finally, the economy must choose the appropriate balance between free enterprise and central planning. Planning permits coordination of economic activities and the channeling of funds into efficient projects, but may be difficult for a Third World nation to administer.   (page 535)

Following the Second World War, the initial emphasis was largely on rapid growth. The 1970s, however, saw increasing concern about how the benefits of growth were (or were not) being distributed. Despite growth, poverty persisted for a large percentage of those living in the developing countries, and aid was often tied to programs to satisfy basic needs. More recently, income redistribution has lost its prominence to market efficiency.

PRACTICE

7. Experience suggests that, of the following, the development approach most likely to succeed is
   A. rapid industrial mechanization coupled with labor migration to the industrial centers.
   B. intensive training of human capital to occupy technologically advanced positions in import-substitution industries.
   C. a balanced promotion of both the agricultural sector and the manufacturing sector.
   D. slow, careful industrial growth combined with rapid expansion in food provision to improve human capital.
   Answer: C. This is the "walking on two legs" strategy. See p. 536.

8. Noil is a small sub-Saharan nation with few sophisticated resources. However, it constructs an airport and hotel with lavish Western facilities and offers safari trips into its beautiful mountain ranges to groups from the developed countries. Noil is best described as having opted for a(n) _____ _____ development strategy.
   A. import substitution.
   B. export promotion.
   C. rural exploitation.
   D. balanced growth.
   Answer: B. Tourism is an export.

9. Generally, import substitution policies have
   A. failed in almost every case.
   B. succeeded, but only while the cost of imported oil was held down.
   C. not been an unqualified success but have had a better track record than export promotion policies.
   D. succeeded in Latin America but failed in Africa and had mixed results in Asia.
   Answer: A. Import substitution policies reduce exports and foster inefficient, inappropriate (i.e., capital-intensive) production methods.

10. The small Asian nation of Regit chooses to follow an import substitution strategy and builds a fertilizer plant to serve its rice farmers. Based on similar experiments elsewhere, we would expect to see all of the following except
    A. high fertilizer production costs.
    B. the imposition of tariffs to protect domestic fertilizer production.
    C. capital-intensive fertilizer production techniques.
    D. a rise in the international competitiveness of the nation's rice farmers.
    Answer: D. High-cost fertilizer will reduce the ability of the rice farmers to compete with foreign rice.

11. Each of the following is a tactic typical of the export promotion strategy except
    A. reducing the value of the domestic currency relative to other currencies.
    B. increasing the nation's ability to compete domestically with the exports of other nations.
    C. the provision of subsidies to exporters.
    D. the provision of preferential investment tax breaks to exporting firms.
    Answer: B. This is typical of import substitution. See p. 537.

OBJECTIVE 4: Outline the problems caused by rapid population growth and policies that have been instituted to deal with them.

The Third World death rate has tumbled sharply because of better medical treatment, but the birth rate has declined much more slowly. Although large families may provide a cheap labor pool today and support in old age tomorrow, rapid expansion in the population places burdens on public services and may be undesirable from the viewpoint of society. In some nations, economic incentives have been applied successfully to encourage smaller families.   (page 539)

PRACTICE

12. Birth rate minus death rate equals the
    A. fertility rate.
    B. mortality rate.
    C. natural rate of population increase.
    D. development rate.
    Answer: C. See p. 542.

13. Malthus predicted that the world population would grow at a(n) _____ growth rate while the production of food would increase more _____
    A. increasing, rapidly.
    B. increasing, slowly.
    C. constant, rapidly.
    D. constant, slowly.
    Answer: D. See p. 540. Note that a constant rate of growth means rapid absolute growth in the population—10% of 100 is only 10; 10% of 10,000 is 1,000.

14. High fertility rates may cause all of the following except
    A. falling saving rates.
    B. reduced availability of social programs for each individual.
    C. labor shortages.
    D. food shortages.
    Answer: C. As the population expands, there should be no labor constraint.

OBJECTIVE 5: Outline Third World agricultural problems and the policies that have been used to deal with them.

Inadequate food supplies may be caused by policy actions. A nation that chooses to hold down prices for the benefit of consumers may see its farmers cutting back production. The so-called "Green Revolution"—the emergence of high-yield resilient plants—should increase productivity but it has been resisted, partly because it is new and risky, and partly because of the costs involved in change.   (page 543)

PRACTICE

15. Government establishment of low food prices is usually meant to
    A. discourage farming.
    B. make domestic farm production competitive with imports.
    C. please the small, but politically powerful, urban population.
    D. make domestic farm production more efficient.
    Answer: C. Urban dwellers may be more educated and organized—a bigger threat to the longevity of the government in power. See p. 544.

16. Third World food shortages are largely a consequence of
    A. the Green Revolution.
    B. natural limits on production.
    C. policy mistakes.
    D. exporting too much.
    Answer: C. See p. 544.

OBJECTIVE 6: Outline the evolution of the debt crisis and the problems confronting borrowers and lenders in resolving this crisis.

In the 1970s, banks, rich with the deposited "petrodollars" of the OPEC nations, reduced interest rates and embarked on a vigorous program of lending. Capital-starved developing countries chose to borrow—in some cases to pay for the trade deficits caused by high oil prices! In the late 1970s, the world economy faltered and Third World export revenues shrank. Interest on the loans became (and remains) hard to pay. Some nations threatened to default. Many sought to reschedule their debt repayment in exchange for promises of economic austerity designed to cut back on imports and to increase exports.   (page 545)

PRACTICE

17. Under a debt rescheduling agreement, the borrowing country is expected to increase incentives to _____ and to reduce _____
    A. consumers, export spending.
    B. consumers, imports.
    C. exporters, the federal government deficit.
    D. exporters, imports.
    Answer: D. A debt rescheduling agreement will require the country to increase exports and reduce imports. Only by increasing its foreign earnings can a nation hope to reduce its debt burden.

PRACTICE TEST

I. MULTIPLE CHOICE QUESTIONS.

Select the option that provides the single best answer.

_____   1. Which of the following are characteristics of the average developing country?
              A. Large populations and high savings rates.
              B. Low levels of human capital and low per capita GDP.
              C. High infant mortality and high pollution indexes.
              D. Low health standards and high literacy rates.

_____   2. Import substitution occurs when a country
              A. becomes developed.
              B. erects trade barriers.
              C. no longer has sufficient foreign exchange to buy imports.
              D. strives to produce goods that were previously imported.

_____   3. Economic development occurs when there is an increase in the
              A. per capita nominal GDP.
              B. per capita real GDP.
              C. material well-being of the nation's citizens.
              D. labor force.

_____   4. Lack of economic development might be caused by
              A. a low marginal propensity to consume.
              B. an excess supply of private overhead capital.
              C. a high literacy rate.
              D. inadequate amounts of social overhead capital.

_____   5. Which of the following is an example of an improvement in social overhead capital?
              A. A multinational corporation opens a new plant.
              B. The workers at the local textile mill establish a credit union.
              C. There is an increase in the rate of growth of per capita real GDP.
              D. A national adult literacy program is established by the government.

_____ 6. Labor is relatively abundant in Arboc. Arboc might best be able to develop by
   A. using production techniques that are capital-intensive.
   B. using production techniques that employ labor and capital in fixed and equal proportions.
   C. specializing in the production of labor-intensive commodities which should therefore be relatively cheaper to produce.
   D. specializing in the production of capital-intensive commodities, which should therefore be marketable at relatively higher prices.

_____ 7. Local firms in Arboc are unlikely to undertake large investment projects such as highway construction because
   A. the government is unlikely to share the cost.
   B. interest rates are higher for the borrowed funds necessary for such projects.
   C. the "free-rider" problem will result in a low (or zero) rate of return.
   D. international agencies such as the World Bank and the IMF prefer short-term projects.

_____ 8. Adopting the strategy of "walking on two legs" means that
   A. men and women should be treated equally in the workplace.
   B. import substitution and export promotion should be attempted simultaneously.
   C. attention must be paid to developing both the industrial sector and the agricultural sector.
   D. the dependent links with old colonial nations should be severed.

_____ 9. Import substitution might fail to promote economic development if
   A. producers use domestic inputs that are lower in cost than imported inputs.
   B. firms make use of capital-intensive production methods that fail to reduce unemployment.
   C. such goods require labor-intensive methods of production.
   D. after establishment, these industries are subsidized by the state.

_____ 10. The "export promotion" strategy calls for
   A. the running of a balance of trade deficit.
   B. the production of goods that are demanded by consumers in the developed countries.
   C. the production of export goods for domestic consumers.
   D. the domestic production of goods that previously had been imported.

_____ 11. Sending savings from the Third World nation of Arboc to the United States _____ to growth in Arboc's physical capital. New Arbocali import controls will tend to _____ investment in Arboc.
   A. leads, increase
   B. leads, decrease
   C. does not lead, increase
   D. does not lead, decrease

_____ 12. Following the signing of NAFTA, capital flowed into Mexico. Initially this resulted in
   A. increasing external debt and an increase in the value of the peso.
   B. increasing internal debt and a decrease in the value of the peso.
   C. decreasing external debt and an decrease in the value of the peso.
   D. decreasing internal debt and a decrease in the value of the peso.

_____ 13. IMF stabilization policies might call for
   A. cutbacks in government spending and a currency devaluation.
   B. nationalization of foreign investment.
   C. higher subsidies to importers of capital goods.
   D. tax cuts and a currency devaluation.

_____ 14. The poorest 20% of the world's population is estimated to receive _____ of the world's income.
   A. .5%.
   B. 2.0%.
   C. 2.5%.
   D. 5.0%.

_____ 15. Which of the following variables tends to be high in the developing countries?
   A. Life expectancy.
   B. Literacy rates.
   C. Infant mortality.
   D. Proportion of the population in urban areas.

_____ 16. Under a debt rescheduling agreement, the borrowing country may be expected to _____ the value of its currency in order to _____ exports.
   A. increase, increase.
   B. increase, decrease.
   C. decrease, increase.
   D. decrease, decrease.

_____ 17. All of the following discourage Third World development except
   A. the lack of skilled entrepreneurs.
   B. insufficient social overhead capital.
   C. insufficient labor-saving technological innovation.
   D. inadequate amounts of human capital.

_____ 18. _____ is a development strategy that is designed to encourage sales abroad.
   A. Import substitution.
   B. Export promotion.
   C. "Walking on two legs".
   D. Dependency.

_____ 19. Rapid population growth rates may cause all of the following except
   A. an eventual increase in the proportion of working-age adults in the population.
   B. an increase in the number of dependents.
   C. decreases in the rate of capital formation.
   D. decreases in saving rates.

_____ 20. Governments may set food prices low in order to
   A. encourage greater food production.
   B. make domestic producers competitive with foreign producers.
   C. stimulate a willingness to adopt more efficient farming methods.
   D. maintain the political support of urban consumers.

II. APPLICATION QUESTIONS.

1. Compare and contrast the economic conditions in the "First World" and the Third World. Take a "typical" country from each group, for example, France and Peru. Examine such issues as life expectancy, number of doctors per thousand persons, educational level, rate of inflation, unemployment, and so forth. (A good source is the _World Development Report_, published annually by the World Bank—it will be in your library.) Compare the figures for an NIC (newly industrialized country), such as Taiwan or Korea with those of a sub-Saharan African nation. Is there really such a thing as a "typical" Third World nation?

2. Suppose that 10 units of food are required per person per year in the developing nation of Arboc. Due to improved crops and farming techniques, food production will increase by a fixed amount every 10 years—suppose this amount is 1000 units of food so that, in 2000, food production will be 11,000 units. Arboc currently exports its surplus food production. Imports run at a constant 2,000 units. Because of high birth rates and decreasing death rates, Arboc's population increases by 50% every 10 years.
   a. Given the conditions specified, complete the table below.

Year	Food Production	Population	Food Requirements	Food Surplus/Deficit
1990	10,000	400	4,000	+6,000
2000	11,000			
2010				
2020				
2030				

   b. What happens in or about the year 2020?
   c. Other things unchanged, what will happen to Arboc's balance of trade?
   d. Given the situation in 2030, what do you think will happen to Arboc?

3. Choose a typical developing country. Profile your country by doing research (by reading, for example, The World Bank's annual _World Development Report_) into the characteristics listed below.

The characteristics require numbers. The numbers in parentheses are the values for the United States from the 1997 Report.
   a. Life expectancy at birth   _____   (77)
   b. Adult illiteracy rate   _____   (< 5%)
   c. Population with access to safe water (%)   _____   (90%)
   d. GNP per capita   _____   ($26,980)
   e. Agriculture as percentage of output   _____   (<3%)
   f. Infant mortality rate (per 1,000 live births)   _____   (8)
   g. Percentage of population living on less than $1 per day _____ (0%)

ANSWERS AND SOLUTIONS

PRACTICE TEST

I. SOLUTIONS TO MULTIPLE CHOICE QUESTIONS

1. B. See p. 529 for a full discussion of the characteristics of developing nations.
2. D. Import substitution is a strategy that attempts to establish a domestic industry that can provide goods to replace imports. See p. 537.
3. C. Improvements in per capita GDP do not guarantee development. See p. 539.
4. D. To grow, an economy needs an adequate quantity and quality of resources, including socially provided resources.
5. D. Social overhead capital includes projects that cannot be undertaken privately.
6. C. This is an application of the Heckscher-Ohlin theorem from Chapter 20 (35).
7. C. Unless a toll is charged, use of this public good will be free.
8. C. The Chinese phrase "walking on two legs" describes the need to have both agricultural and industrial sectors developing together. See p. 536.
9. B. To be effective, the strategy must play to the strengths of its own economy—typically labor-intensive production. See p. 537.
10. B. See p. 537.
11. D. See the discussion of capital flight on p. 534.
12. A. See p. 545.
13. A. See p. 546.
14. A. See p. 532.
15. C. See Table 22.1 (37.1).
16. C. If the borrowing country reduces the value of its currency, its exports will be cheaper for foreigners to buy.
17. C. The quantity of labor is not a significant constraint in the Third World. Labor-saving technology, then, is not critical to successful development.
18. B. See p. 537.
19. A. As more children are born, even as the population ages, the proportion of adults will decrease.
20. D. See p. 544.

II. SOLUTIONS TO APPLICATION QUESTIONS

1. Although there is no single model for a developing nation, certain common characteristics emerge—high birth rates, improving life expectancy, improvements in literacy rates, better/more nutrition and shelter, and so on.
2. a. See the table below.

Year	Food Production	Population	Food Requirements	Food Surplus/Deficit
1990	10,000	400	4,000	+6,000
2000	11,000	600	6,000	+5,000
2010	12,000	900	9,000	+3,000
2020	13,000	1,350	13,500	− 500
2030	14,000	2,025	20,250	−6,250

    b.   Food requirements outstrip food production.

    c.   As the food surplus decreases, less will be available for export and the balance of trade will become less favorable. Somewhere around 2015, the surplus will become a deficit.

    d.   This is an open question. Arboc will be heavily in debt, and will need to import food to feed its population. Imports of industrial goods would slacken. Reduced health care (per person) might cause famine and disease, reducing the population. Arboc might borrow to finance its overseas spending and might have to receive ongoing foreign aid. Population control policies would have to be considered.

3.   Answers will depend on the country chosen.

ECONOMIES IN TRANSITION AND ALTERNATIVE ECONOMIC SYSTEMS

23

OBJECTIVES: POINT BY POINT

After completing this chapter, you should be able to accomplish the objectives listed below.

General Comment

It is unlikely that you will have had much, if any, face-to-face exposure to other economic systems. The material that Case and Fair present will give you useful information and may clear up some misconceptions that you have built up over time. Be especially careful of value-laden labels when you encounter economic and political discussions in the media. Compare, for example, the sentence "The Arbezani Administration opened negotiations with the Arbocali regime" with "The Arbezani regime opened negotiations with the Arbocali Administration." Clearly, labels can reinforce or upset our perceptions.

OBJECTIVE 1: Distinguish between the capitalist and socialist economic systems and the democratic and communist political systems.

Capitalism and socialism are at the two ends of the economic spectrum; democracy and communism are at the two ends of the political spectrum. Economic systems are classified on the basis of where the ownership of productive resources resides—in capitalism, it's with the private individual; in socialism, it's with the government. (page 552)

No economic system adheres to pure socialism or to pure capitalism—each economy is a blend of the two extremes. China is "socialist" but has (increasing) private ownership; the United States and Japan are "capitalist" but each contains a powerful public sector.

PRACTICE

1. In a _____ economy, most capital is privately owned.
   - A. democratic.
   - B. communist.
   - C. capitalist.
   - D. socialist.

   Answer: C. Note that "democracy" refers to a political system, not an economic one.

2. In a _____ economy, the people own the means of production directly, without state intervention.
   - A. feudal.
   - B. communist.
   - C. capitalist.
   - D. socialist.

   Answer: B. In a communist economy, it was argued, the state would wither away. In fact, the communist economies of the world have really been socialist—e.g., the former Union of Soviet *Socialist* Republics.

3. The Austrian economist Hayek argued that
   A. political freedom is not necessary for economic freedom to exist.
   B. political freedom and economic freedom depend on each other.
   C. economic freedom is not necessary for political freedom to exist.
   D. political freedom and economic freedom, although desirable, are not linked.
   Answer: B. See p. 554.

4. In a socialist economy, economic decisions are made by _____ _____ ; capital is owned by _____ _____
   A. the market, private citizens.
   B. the market, the government.
   C. centralized planning, private citizens.
   D. centralized planning, the government.
   Answer: D. The Soviet Union, for example, made five- and one-year plans through the Gosplan agency. See p. 553.

OBJECTIVE 2: Explain the main aspects of the labor theory of value and why Marx believed that capitalism would perish.

There are two key elements to Marxian analysis: the labor theory of value and the exploitation of workers by capitalists.

The *labor theory of value* states that the relative value of each good and service depends on the quantity of labor used up in its production. Capital is used in production, of course; Marx explained that capital embodies past labor.   (page 555)

Marx considered capitalism to be unfair because profit derived from the ownership of capital is based on the exploitation of labor. The capitalist, who is in a strong bargaining position, expropriates the *surplus value* produced by labor. Progressively, production becomes less labor-intensive—with relatively less labor to exploit, the rate of profit will fall. To compensate, capitalists increase the rate of exploitation and wages are driven to the subsistence level. Marx predicted that capitalism would collapse in the wake of falling profits, worker unrest, and increasingly violent business fluctuations. Capitalism would be replaced by socialism and, ultimately, communism.

> **Comment:** Many students are surprised to learn that Marx undertook economic analysis; he is more often thought of as a political thinker. "Marxian", rather than "Marxist", is the correct term to use when referring to Marx's economic ideas.

> **LEARNING TIP:** You may find Marx's views pretty difficult to swallow, partly because of the new terminology but partly because the bulk of the textbook has been suggesting to you that the economy tends towards an equilibrium. Marx's extensive research made him see the industrialized world of the mid-nineteenth century quite differently.

> **LEARNING TIP:** The labor theory of value tries to explain the long-run pattern of relative prices, although market imperfections and temporary fluctuations in demand and supply can cause actual price levels to deviate from this pattern.

> **Comment:** Where neoclassical economists find harmony in production and distribution, Marx detected antagonism. In Marx's view, the vehicles for growth—the division of labor and new technology—became juggernauts that would crush and alienate the workers and move the economy toward greater concentration of power. Marx's account of capitalist accumulation predicted increasing instability rather than stability.

PRACTICE

5. For Marx, the "means of production" include
   A. only capital.
   B. only capital and labor.
   C. only capital and land.
   D. capital, land, and labor.
   Answer: C. The means of production are not equivalent to the "factors of production" you met in Chapter 3.

6. The Marxian term for profit is _____ and the Marxian term for the wage rate is the _____
   A. surplus value, rate of exploitation.
   B. surplus value, value of labor power.
   C. the value of labor power, surplus value.
   D. the value of labor power, rate of exploitation.
   Answer: B. See p. 556.

7. In Marxian analysis, which of the following statements is true?
   A. The rate of profit tends to fall over time.
   B. Additional capital accumulation increases the rate of profit.
   C. Additional capital accumulation increases surplus value.
   D. As wages fall, production will become more labor-intensive.
   Answer: A. Capital must be paid for but can't be exploited. Profits derive from the ability of the capitalist to exploit workers.

OBJECTIVE 3: Summarize the economic performance of the Soviet economy from 1945 until its collapse. Outline the steps necessary to make Russia economically viable as a market-based system.

The Soviet economy was centrally planned. Early Soviet growth rates were impressive, mainly due to remarkable rates of capital accumulation, but faltered in the 1980s. The Gorbachev proposal—economic *perestroika* (restructuring) coupled with political *glasnost* (openness)—called for decentralization, increased incentives, and the removal of price controls—in other words, a move toward a market system. It was a case of too little, too late. (page 558)

Russian progress towards a market-based economy was initially unsteady, with soaring inflation and plunging production. By 1995, privatization had taken root, but disagreement remains regarding how fast each new measure should be implemented.

Six requirements for a successful transition from socialism to a market-based economy have been identified:

1. macroeconomic stabilization,
2. deregulation of prices and trade liberalization,
3. Privatization of the means of production,
4. the establishment of a "support system" for the market,
5. a social safety net to lessen the distress of unemployment and poverty, and
6. external assistance.

There was much debate whether the reform requirements should be introduced rapidly "shock therapy" or phased in gradually. In fact, due to the crippled state of Russian state-owned enterprises, shock therapy was not a feasible option, even if it had been the preferred alternative.

> **Comment:** The economic reforms within the former Soviet republics and their allies in Eastern Europe remain very much in the news. You should be able to flesh out the material in this chapter by keeping your ears and eyes open to the news reports. Have the economic reforms been identical in each country? How much success/resistance are they experiencing?

Tragedy of Commons: Property owned communally, such as the bison, the dodo, or the grasslands of sub-Saharan Africa, is usually rapidly depleted. Taking the example of common grazing land, there is little incentive for the individual farmer to conserve pasture, and indeed the opposite may be true. Self-interest dictates that one would make the most of the "free" resources, although such thinking by each farmer would lead to a depletion of resources. At this point you might note the old saying that "Good fences make good neighbors." Capitalism, then, relies on the emergence of self-interest and the rewards of private property because the former without the latter would result in the tragedy of commons.

> **LEARNING TIP:** From the mid-90s, Cuba had begun shifting position on economic matters. The Vietnamese (and Vietnamese businesspersons in the United States) had argued successfully for the relaxation of U.S.-imposed commercial barriers. Both of these economies are well worth watching.

PRACTICE

8. Each of the following is seen as a requirement for a successful transition from socialism to a market-based economy except
   A. price regulation.
   B. provision of a commercial infrastructure—i.e., market-supporting institutions.
   C. removal of trade barriers.
   D. a freely operating labor market.
   Answer: A. To ration scarce resources efficiently, prices should be free to adjust.

9. In the face of high inflation in August 1993, Boris Yeltsin announced that "old" (pre-1993) rubles would be worthless and, except for a limited amount, individuals could not convert "old" into "new." Yeltsin's main objective was
   A. to increase interest rates.
   B. to encourage workers to work longer hours.
   C. to stabilize prices.
   D. to attract the hard currency of tourists.
   Answer: C. The Russian economy was threatened by hyperinflation; Yeltsin was trying to drain away some of the money that was chasing too few goods.

10. Stalin's main economic objective was
    A. rapid industrialization.
    B. the establishment of a viable consumer goods sector.
    C. *perestroika.*
    D. a balanced budget.
    Answer: A. See p. 558.

11. Deregulating prices is likely to cause _____ ; removing subsidies will cause _____ in the short term.
    A. higher prices for staple items; unemployment.
    B. higher prices for staple items; increased employment.
    C. lower prices for staple items; unemployment.
    D. lower prices for staple items; increased employment.
    Answer: A. Staple items were underpriced; inefficient firms will be driven out of business without subsidies.

12. The notion that collective ownership of resources may be inefficient because individuals do not bear the full cost of their own decisions is called
    A. exploitation.
    B. the tragedy of commons.
    C. surplus value.
    D. the externality effect.
    Answer: B. See p. 563.

13. Each of the following is an example of the tragedy of commons except
    A. pollution in the Great Lakes.
    B. overgrazing of shared tribal land.
    C. the decimation of the American bison by nineteenth-century settlers.
    D. the slaughtering of his entire herd by a Texan rancher.
    Answer: D. The herd is private property.

OBJECTIVE 4: Explain why the Chinese economy has grown so vigorously since 1978.

The Chinese economic system mirrored the Soviet system until 1958, when the Great Leap Forward signaled a move away from large-scale capital-intensive production toward smaller-scale localized production. Since 1978, ideological constraints have been loosened, personal incentives have been restored and, particularly in agriculture, dramatic improvements in performance achieved. There is private enterprise and foreign investment, and allocation through markets is increasing, but China is still properly classified as a centrally planned economy because, to a significant extent, ownership of resources remains with the government.   (page 565)

Nagging problems for the Chinese include the threat of food shortages, the continued presence of state-owned enterprises, and the future of Hong Kong.

PRACTICE

14. Which of the following statements about China is false?
    A. China has a stock market.
    B. Since 1990, China has actively discouraged investment by Western capitalist corporations.
    C. Since 1990, there have been reports of "capitalist mania" occurring.
    D. The Great Leap Forward featured a shift from large-scale capital-intensive production to small-scale labor-intensive production.
    Answer: B. China is a magnet for Western venture capital.

OBJECTIVE 5: Explain the economic performance of Japanese since 1945.

The Japanese "economic miracle" was based on high rates of saving and investment, the effective use of appropriate technology, an aggressive pro-growth economic stance by the government, and a flexible, well-trained labor force. In the 1990s, though, Japan's export-driven economy faltered, partly because of the global economic slowdown and partly because of the rising value of the yen, both of which reduced the demand for Japanese goods. The economic instability felt in 1997 and 1998 in the Asian markets, and reflected in its stock markets, compounded the problems encountered by Japan.   (page 569)

PRACTICE

15. Which of the following statements about post-1945 Japan is false?
    A. Japan has used quotas, tariffs, and subsidies to protect key industries.
    B. Japanese households have a high rate of saving.
    C. Of the industrialized nations, Japan has the smallest public sector.
    D. Japan has always spent a larger portion of its GDP on research and development than the United States.
    Answer: D. Until the late 1980s, U.S. research and development spending was a higher proportion of GDP. See p. 569.

16. The bases of Japan's "economic miracle" seem to have been all of the following except
   A. high rates of saving and investment.
   B. the development of a highly trained labor force.
   C. the adoption of appropriate technology.
   D. a government committed to a "hands off" position to industry.
   Answer: D. The Japanese government (which from 1955 until 1993 had seen power remain in the hands of one party, the LDP) consistently exercised significant control over the private sector, through MITI.

17. If the Japanese permit their currency to be persistently overvalued in international currency markets, we would expect to see
   A. an increase in Japanese exports and imports.
   B. a decrease in Japanese exports and imports.
   C. an increase in Japanese exports and a decrease in Japanese imports.
   D. a decrease in Japanese exports and an increase in Japanese imports.
   Answer: D. By overpricing the yen, Japanese exports become unattractive overseas, while foreign goods become more attractive in Japan

PRACTICE TEST

I. MULTIPLE CHOICE QUESTIONS.

Select the option that provides the single best answer.

_____ 1. According to Marx, the rate of profit has a tendency to _____ , causing capitalists to _____ the rate of exploitation.
   A. rise, increase.
   B. rise, decrease.
   C. fall, increase.
   D. fall, decrease.

_____ 2. For Marx, the conflicts in capitalism include all of the following except
   A. inflation and an increasing government deficit.
   B. alienation and increasing exploitation.
   C. progressively more violent business cycles.
   D. the emiserization of the workers.

_____ 3. Marx saw society evolving
   A. through imperialism, capitalism, and communism to socialism.
   B. through feudalism, capitalism, and socialism to communism.
   C. through imperialism, and capitalism, and feudalism to communism.
   D. through capitalism, feudalism, and socialism to communism.

_____ 4. Capitalism and socialism are distinguished primarily by
   A. the ownership of labor.
   B. the number of political parties.
   C. the ownership of capital.
   D. the distribution of income throughout society.

_____ 5. According to Marx, the wage is determined by
   A. the surplus value of labor.
   B. the cost of the bare essentials of subsistence.
   C. the marginal revenue product of labor.
   D. the marginal physical product.

6. In Marxian terms, the value of a machine must be dependent upon
   A. the amount of labor embodied within it.
   B. how productive the machine is.
   C. how productive the workers are who use the machine.
   D. the price of the final good produced by the machine.

7. Japan's economic success has been based on all of the following except
   A. very high rates of consumption.
   B. a highly trained labor force.
   C. rapid absorption of technology.
   D. a pro-growth government policy.

8. The "tragedy of commons" exemplifies the problem of _____ _____ in the case of resources that are owned _____ _____
   A. inefficiency, privately.
   B. inequity, privately.
   C. inefficiency, publicly.
   D. inequity, publicly.

9. Each of the following is seen as a requirement for a successful transition from socialism to a market-based economy except
   A. macroeconomic stabilization.
   B. privatization.
   C. price regulation.
   D. a freely operating labor market.

10. The surplus value of labor is
    A. equal to the wage rate paid to the worker.
    B. the difference between the subsistence wage and the actual wage received.
    C. the rate of exploitation.
    D. the difference between the value of production and the actual wage received.

11. In Arboc, the state provides goods such as education, national defense, universal health care, and roads. Other industries, which are privately owned, face government regulations on pollution and worker safety. Minimum wage legislation is present and wage earners are taxed on their income. Arboc is best described as
    A. socialist.
    B. communist.
    C. capitalist.
    D. totalitarian.

12. "Shock therapy" refers to
    A. the sudden change experienced by the Soviet Union following *perestroika* and *glasnost*.
    B. the overthrow of the Soviet Union's economic system.
    C. Stalin's goal of electrification of collective farms.
    D. rapid deregulation of prices, liberalization of trade, and privatization.

13. Each of the following is a major concern for China's future except
    A. food shortages.
    B. unemployment.
    C. bankruptcy and sale to foreigners of state-owned enterprises.
    D. inflation.

_____ 14. Since the 1950s, the greatest part of Japanese domestic investment has been financed by
   A. domestic savings.
   B. government development grants.
   C. external investment.
   D. the Japanese trade surplus.

_____ 15. For Marx, the value of a product depends on
   A. the rate of exploitation.
   B. the interaction of demand and supply.
   C. the amount of labor used to produce it.
   D. the amount of labor and capital used to produce it.

II. APPLICATION QUESTIONS.

1. In the Marxian economy of Arboc, 500 units of value are produced. Production requires current labor and machinery, which embodies 100 units of past labor.
   a. Calculate the value of current labor used in units of value.
   b. If workers are paid 300 units of value, how many units of profit will capitalists derive?
   c. Calculate the rate of exploitation (surplus value/value of labor power).
   d. Calculate the rate of profit (surplus value/value of production).

   Now suppose that output doubles.

   e. Output is _____ units of value.
   f. Calculate the value of current labor used in units of value.
   g. If the wage rate is unchanged, calculate the units of value that workers will receive.
   h. Surplus value is _____ .
   i. Calculate the rate of exploitation (surplus value/value of labor power).
   j. Calculate the rate of profit (surplus value/value of production).

   Relative to the initial situation, output has doubled but, to achieve this, the production technique has become more capital-intensive. Machinery is worth 400 units of past labor.

   k. Calculate the value of current labor used in units of value.
   l. If the wage rate is unchanged, calculate the units of value that workers will receive.
   m. Surplus value is _____ .
   n. Calculate the rate of exploitation (surplus value/value of labor power).
   o. Calculate the rate of profit (surplus value/value of production).

   Suppose that the subsistence wage is 200 units of value, given the current level of output. Machinery is worth 400 units of past labor.

   p. Calculate how many units of surplus value capitalists can expropriate.
   q. Calculate the rate of exploitation (surplus value/value of labor power).
   r. Calculate the rate of profit (surplus value/value of production).

2. List the following countries from most capitalist to most socialist:
   Russia; United States; France; Cuba; Japan; China.

3. The table gives the output of workers.

Workers	Output	Marginal Product	Subsistence Wage	Surplus Value
0	0	—		—
1	10			
2	19			
3	27			
4	34			
5	40			
6	45			
7	49			
8	52			

    a. Use the information in the table to calculate the marginal product.
    b. Suppose that the subsistence wage is 5 units of value. Fill in the fourth column.
    c. A profit-maximizing capitalist can hire as many workers as she wishes at the subsistence wage. How many workers would she hire?
    d. Calculate the surplus value. Enter the values in the fifth column.
    e. Calculate total production and the surplus value.
    f. Calculate the rate of exploitation (surplus value/value of labor power).

4. Russia's economic reform package includes:
    a. price controls: _____ (increased/decreased/removed)
    b. market-supporting institutions: _____ (increased/decreased/removed)
    c. ownership of resources: more _____ (centralized/privatized)
    d. external aid: _____ (increased/decreased/removed)
    e. job security: _____ (increased/decreased/removed)
    f. trade: _____ (restricted/liberalized)
    g. money supply growth: _____ (increased/curtailed)

ANSWERS AND SOLUTIONS

PRACTICE TEST

I. SOLUTIONS TO MULTIPLE CHOICE QUESTIONS

1. C. As additional capital is accumulated, the rate of profit falls. This decline prompts capitalists to increase exploitation of workers. See p. 556.
2. A. Marx did not consider inflation and the government deficit in his writings.
3. B. See p. 557.
4. C. n a capitalist system, ownership of the means of production (capital and land) is in the hands of capitalists and in the hands of the state under a communist system.
5. B. Capitalists, in search of profits, will drive down the wage to the minimum (subsistence) level. See p. 557.

6. A. The value of any type of production (including machines) is determined by the amount of labor involved in its production.

7. A. See p. 569.

8. C. "Commons" are commonly-owned land. Typically, this resource is treated inefficiently.

9. C. To achieve efficiency, prices must be permitted to adjust to changes in demand and supply.

10. D. See p. 566.

11. C. With the exception of the health care, Arboc is quite like the United States.

12. D. See p. 565.

13. B. Despite a burgeoning population, China is in need of skilled workers to meet the new demands of its economy.

14. A. See p. 569.

15. C. The value of capital depends on the value of labor necessary to produce so, ultimately, the amount of all production depends on amount of labor used.

II. SOLUTIONS TO APPLICATION QUESTIONS

1. a. $500 - 100$ units of past labor value = 400 units of labor value.
   b. 400 units of labor value $- 300 = 100$ units of profit.
   c. Rate of exploitation = surplus value/value of labor power = $100/400 = .25$.
   d. The rate of profit = surplus value/value of production = $100/500 = .2$.
   e. $500 \times 2 = 1000$.
   f. $1000 - 100$ units of past labor value = 900 units of labor value.
   g. 300.
   h. Surplus value = $900 - 300 = 600$.
   i. Rate of exploitation = surplus value/value of labor power = $600/900 = .67$.
   j. Rate of profit = surplus value/value of production = $600/1000 = .6$.
   k. $1000 - 400$ units of past labor value = 600 units of labor value.
   l. 300.
   m. Surplus value = $600 - 300 = 300$.
   n. Rate of exploitation = surplus value/value of labor power = $300/600 = .5$.
   o. Rate of profit = surplus value/value of production = $300/1000 = .3$.
   p. Surplus value = $600 - 200 = 400$.
   q. Rate of exploitation = surplus value/value of labor power = $400/600 = .67$.
   r. Rate of profit = surplus value/value of production = $400/1000 = .4$.

2. There can be some dispute here—systems evolve and emphases change—but a plausible ranking would be: Japan; United States; France; Russia; China; Cuba.

3. a. See the following table.

Workers	Output	Marginal Product	Subsistence Wage	Surplus Value
0	0	—	5	—
1	10	10	5	5
2	19	9	5	4
3	27	8	5	3
4	34	7	5	2
5	40	6	5	1
6	45	5	5	0
7	49	4	5	-1
8	52	3	5	-2

    b. See the table above.
    c. 6.
    d. See the table above.
    e. 45; 15.
    f. ⅓.
4. removed; increased; privatized; increased; decreased; liberalized; curtailed.

COMPREHENSIVE REVIEW TEST FOR PART 5

The following questions provide a wide-ranging review of the material covered in Part 5 (9)—Chapters 21–23 (35, 37–38) of the textbook. Each question deals with a topic or technique important for your understanding of economic principles. If you miss a question you should return to the relevant section of the chapter in the textbook and fine-tune your understanding.

PRACTICE TEST

MULTIPLE CHOICE QUESTIONS.

Select the option that provides the single best answer.

_____ 1. A tariff imposed on imported French wine will cause the U.S. price of French wine to _____ and U.S. production of wine to _____
   A. increase, increase.
   B. increase, decrease.
   C. decrease, increase.
   D. decrease, decrease.

_____ 2. Trade barriers _____ welfare. Barriers _____ domestic employment in industries that lack a comparative advantage.
   A. increase, increase
   B. increase, decrease
   C. decrease, increase
   D. decrease, decrease

_____ 3. A U.S. tariff imposed on goods that can be produced more cheaply overseas would tend to
   A. benefit American consumers by making these goods cheaper.
   B. make the goods more expensive in other (overseas) markets.
   C. equalize the costs of production between U.S. producers and foreign producers.
   D. make U.S. producers artificially more competitive relative to foreigners.

Refer to the following table to answer the next nine questions. The table shows the possible output levels from one day of labor input. Costs are constant within each country.

	England	Portugal
Wine	9 bottles	6 bottles
Cloth	18 yards	9 yards

_____ 4. England has an absolute advantage in the production of
A. cloth.
B. wheat.
C. both goods.
D. neither good.

_____ 5. The opportunity cost of one bottle of wine in Portugal is
A. ⅔ of a yard of cloth.
B. 1⅓ yards of cloth.
C. 1½ yards of cloth.
D. 9 yards of cloth.

_____ 6. England and Portugal decide to specialize according to the law of comparative advantage and trade with one another. We would expect that the terms of trade will be somewhere between
A. 1 bottle of wine for 1 yard of cloth and ½ of a bottle of wine for 1 yard of cloth.
B. ⅔ of a bottle of wine for 1 yard of cloth and 1½ bottles of wine for 1 yard of cloth.
C. ½ of a bottle of wine for 1 yard of cloth and 1½ bottles of wine for 1 yard of cloth.
D. ½ of a bottle of wine for 1 yard of cloth and ⅔ of a bottle of wine for 1 yard of cloth.

_____ 7. Which of the following statements is true?
A. England has a comparative advantage in the production of wine; Portugal has a comparative advantage in the production of cloth.
B. England has a comparative advantage in the production of cloth; Portugal has a comparative advantage in the production of wine.
C. England has a comparative advantage in both goods.
D. Portugal has a comparative advantage in both goods.

_____ 8. Suppose the terms of trade are that 1 bottle of wine trades for 1 yard of cloth. England should specialize in _____ production; Portugal should specialize in _____ production.
A. cloth, cloth.
B. cloth, wine.
C. wine, cloth.
D. wine, wine.

_____ 9. Suppose the terms of trade are that 1 bottle of wine trades for 1¾ yards of cloth. England should specialize in _____ production; Portugal should specialize in _____ production.
A. cloth, cloth.
B. cloth, wine.
C. wine, cloth.
D. wine, wine.

_____ 10. According to the theory of comparative advantage, trade between the two partners
A. will equalize their consumption levels.
B. will benefit all industries in each country.
C. will permit each partner to use its resources in the most efficient way.
D. will permit each partner to achieve a consumption mix at some point on its production possibility frontier.

_____ 11. In terms of production possibility frontiers, if England's maximum production of cloth is 1800 yards, its maximum production of wine is _____ bottles. If Portugal's maximum production of wine is 1200 bottles, its maximum production of cloth is _____ yards.
   A. 0, 0.
   B. 900, 900.
   C. 900, 1800.
   D. 1800, 900.

_____ 12. Based on the information in the previous question, we should now conclude that
   A. England has an absolute advantage in the production of both goods.
   B. England has an absolute advantage in the production of cloth only.
   C. Portugal has an absolute advantage in the production of wine.
   D. England has an absolute advantage in the production of neither good.

_____ 13. The United States and the United Kingdom both produce cashmere sweaters and leather vests. In the United States, sweaters sell for $150 and vests sell for $150. In the United Kingdom, sweaters sell for £60 and vests sell for £100. Suppose the pound (£)/$ exchange rate is £1 = $2.
   A. The United States will import both sweaters and vests from the United Kingdom.
   B. The United States will import sweaters from the United Kingdom: the United Kingdom will import vests from the United States.
   C. The United States will import vests from the United Kingdom: the United Kingdom will import sweaters from the United States.
   D. The United Kingdom will import both sweaters and vests from the United States.

_____ 14. Each of the following has been identified as a significant factor in Japan's post-war success except
   A. very high rates of saving and investment.
   B. a highly trained labor force.
   C. the Japanese trade surplus.
   D. a pro-growth government policy.

_____ 15. The economic system of the Soviet Union is best characterized as
   A. market-based socialism.
   B. centrally-planned communism.
   C. centrally-planned socialism.
   D. decentralized communism.

_____ 16. Hayek believed that
   A. the economic system would influence the development of the political system.
   B. economic reform could occur without significant change in the established political system.
   C. economic reform is the road to serfdom.
   D. the market system could flourish even in a totalitarian state.

_____ 17. Marxian labor theory of value states that the value of a product depends on
   A. its price in the open market.
   B. its costs of production before it reaches the market.
   C. the quantity of labor required to produce it.
   D. the wage of workers employed by the enterprise.

_____ 18. The Russian transition to a market economy required all of the following except
   A. deregulation of prices.
   B. privatization of the means of production.
   C. the institution of controls over wages.
   D. the removal of trade barriers.

_____ 19. In the early transitional phase to a free labor market and liberalization of prices in Russia we would most likely see all of the following except
   A. increased risk of unemployment.
   B. increased instability in prices.
   C. increased instability in wages.
   D. reduced incentives to work.

_____ 20. Marx based his prediction that capitalism would collapse on the belief that the capitalist system would
   A. cause workers to unionize.
   B. drive workers' wages to subsistence level.
   C. create a huge bourgeois class which would favor revolution.
   D. reduce the incentives to exploit workers.

APPLICATION QUESTION.

The nations of Arboc and Arbez each produce shirts (S) and potatoes (P). The production possibility frontier for Arboc is described by the equation $S = 60 - 2P$. The production possibility frontier for Arbez is described by the equation $S = 60 - 4P$.

1. Draw a production possibility frontier graph that shows all the points that are feasible for Arboc. Put "shirts" on the vertical axis and "potatoes" on the horizontal axis. Draw a separate ppf diagram for Arbez. Include the values at the end-points of the ppf in each case.

2. Arboc has a constant-cost production possibility frontier. How do you know?

3. Is the product mix, 20 shirts and 20 units of potatoes, on Arboc's ppf? If not, is it a feasible output mix?

4. On the Arbocali ppf, what is the opportunity cost of each shirt?

5. On the Arbezani ppf, what is the opportunity cost of each shirt?

6. Which country has a comparative advantage in the production of shirts? Which country has a comparative advantage in the production of potatoes?

7. If the terms of trade were 1 unit of potatoes traded for 1 shirt, what would be the pattern of trade?

8. If the terms of trade were 1 unit of potatoes traded for 3 shirts, what would be the pattern of trade?

9. Now assume Arboc becomes more efficient and can double its output of both shirts and potatoes. Which good(s) should Arboc now produce and trade? Explain your answer.

10. Explain what will happen to the opportunity cost of shirts in Arbez if a new high-yielding hybrid potato is introduced into Arbez.

ANSWERS AND SOLUTIONS

ANSWERS TO REVIEW TEST FOR PART 5 (9)

1. A. The tax will push up the price of the import. This will increase the demand for substitutes.
2. C. See p. 512 for the statement of the case for free trade.
3. D. Typically, tariffs are for the protection of producers, not for the benefit of consumers.
4. C. England can produce absolutely more cloth and more wine per worker than Portugal can.
5. C. Six bottles take the inputs that could have produced 9 yards of cloth, therefore 1 bottle costs 1½ yards of cloth.
6. D. The English opportunity cost of 1 bottle of wine is 2 yards of cloth. Portugal's opportunity cost of 1 bottle of wine is 1½ yards of cloth.
7. B. The English opportunity cost of 1 bottle of wine is 2 yards of cloth. Portugal's opportunity cost of 1 bottle of wine is 1½ yards of cloth.
8. A. The English opportunity cost of 1 bottle of wine is 2 yards of cloth—it doesn't pay to produce wine. Similarly for Portugal, because 1 bottle of wine costs 1½ yards of cloth.
9. B. The English opportunity cost of 1 bottle of wine is 2 yards of cloth—it pays to produce cloth and trade it for wine. For Portugal, because 1 bottle of wine costs 1½ yards of cloth, it pays to produce wine and trade it for cloth.
10. C. Each country will be able to consume a combination of goods beyond its ppf and use its resources in the least costly (most efficient) manner.
11. C. England can produce twice as many units of cloth as units of wine. Portugal can produce 3 units of cloth for every 2 units of wine.
12. A. The maximum production levels for cloth are equal, and wine production is greater in Portugal, but those considerations do not get to the heart of absolute advantage. England uses fewer resources per yard of cloth and per bottle of wine—just as we concluded in question 4.
13. B. In Britain, imported sweaters cost $120 and vests cost $200—sweaters are cheaper in Britain; vests are cheaper in the United States.
14. C. See p. 569.
15. C. See p. 554.
16. A. See p. 554. Beware Option C! Hayek did not believe that economic reform, *per se*, led to serfdom, rather that reforms combined with political coercion could reduce personal freedoms.
17. C. The wage of workers may not reflect their true contribution. In addition, value depends on the labor (past and present) represented by the product.
18. C. For the market economy to function correctly, both wages and prices must be free to adjust.
19. D. The move from a planned economy to a market economy involves risk.
20. B. Capitalist exploitation of workers would lead to their "emiserization" and growing dissatisfaction.

APPLICATION

1. See the following diagram.

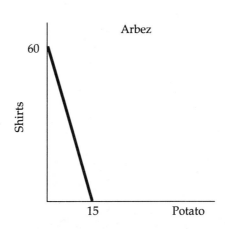

2. Arboc's production possibility frontier graphs as a straight line—the trade-off is constant as resources are switched between goods.

3. The product mix, 20 shirts and 20 units of potatoes, is feasible. If 20 shirts are produced (using one third of Arboc's resources), the other two-thirds can be employed producing potatoes.

4. In Arboc, each shirt costs ½ of a unit of potatoes.

5. In Arbez, each shirt costs ¼ of a unit of potatoes.

6. Arbez has a comparative advantage in the production of shirts while Arboc country has a comparative advantage in the production of potatoes.

7. If the terms of trade were 1 unit of potatoes traded for 1 shirt, both countries would wish to produce and trade shirts.

8. If the terms of trade were 1 unit of potatoes traded for 3 shirts, Arboc would gain by producing potatoes and Arbez would gain by specializing in shirt production.

9. The opportunity cost of shirts and potatoes has not changed in Arboc, therefore Arbez retains its comparative advantage in the production of shirts.

10. The opportunity cost of shirts will increase, possibly to the point that the comparative advantage will switch over from shirt production to potato production.